Books by Ernest J. Simmons

ENGLISH LITERATURE AND CULTURE IN RUSSIA

PUSHKIN

DOSTOEVSKY: THE MAKING OF A NOVELIST

LEO TOLSTOY

RUSSIAN FICTION AND SOVIET IDEOLOGY

CHEKHOV

CHEKHOV

CHEKHOV

A Biography

by Ernest J. Simmons

An Atlantic Monthly Press Book

LITTLE, BROWN AND COMPANY · BOSTON · TORONTO

ATLANTIC-LITTLE, BROWN BOOKS
ARE PUBLISHED BY
LITTLE, BROWN AND COMPANY
IN ASSOCIATION WITH
THE ATLANTIC MONTHLY PRESS

*Published simultaneously in Canada
by Little, Brown & Company (Canada) Limited*

PRINTED IN THE UNITED STATES OF AMERICA

Chekhov is an incomparable artist. An artist of life. And the worth of his creation consists of this — he is understood and accepted not only by every Russian, but by all humanity.

— LEO TOLSTOY

Preface

THERE ARE VARIOUS ways of writing a biography, but one way not to write it is to leave the reader in doubt, at the end, about how the hero would act in any given situation. The image must be a complete one, for to possess the whole man is to know his whole life, his total personality as it develops and takes final shape. In a special sense the enigma of Chekhov's complex personality yields to resolution, if ever, only through an awareness of the myriad of small actions that determined and gave meaning to the significant periods of ebb and flow in his forty-four years. A high degree of selectivity is necessarily involved in what has been set down, but all the accessible data connected with Chekhov's life, including his creative writings, that would contribute to an understanding of the man has been drawn upon, in the effort to achieve a faithful and living portrayal.

To the many previous studies of Chekhov's life and works, I am particularly grateful for all I have learned from them. If a new attempt at biography seemed appropriate, it was because of a mass of fresh material that has appeared in Russia over the last ten years, much of it in connection with the hundredth anniversary of Chekhov's birth in 1960. Scores of new letters have turned up, diaries and memoirs of close friends, and especially the important letters of Chekhov's sister to her famous brother and the reminiscences she wrote before her death in 1957 at the age of ninety-four. Then the vast corpus of material bearing on Chekhov's life and writings has recently been chronologically arranged and excerpted, with an elaborate system of references, by the Russian scholar N. I. Gitovich. This huge volume has proved to be of inestimable value. All this fresh evidence has illuminated many dark corners of Chekhov's life, and particularly the part that women played in it.

Inevitably, extensive use has been made of the more than four thousand letters of Chekhov, one of the treasures of Russian epistolary prose, in which the writer's character fascinatingly unfolds over the years in the course of correspondence with hundreds of people. The main source for these, as well as for Chekhov's creative writings, is the twenty-volume *Complete Works and Letters*, published in Russia in 1944–1951. When letters have been translated from this edition, instead of in footnotes the addressee and the date have been indicated in the text — information which is of help to the reader and also facilitates easy checking of the source. However, footnotes are used in certain places to indicate sources of quoted letters not in this edition or in earlier collections, these sources having been used occasionally when passages in letters in the complete edition have been deleted for ideological or other reasons.

In general, however, footnotes on the Russian sources for the numerous translations I have made have been omitted; and, instead, a comprehensive bibliographical survey has been added at the end, where all these sources are listed.

All dates conform to the Russian practice of using the Julian calendar (Old Style), which is twelve days behind the Gregorian calendar of the West in the nineteenth century, and thirteen days behind in the twentieth century.

For many services in procuring material for the study, I am grateful to Mr. Robert H. Haynes of the Harvard College Library, and to Mr. Harold D. Gordon and Mr. David K. Turpin of the Libraries of Columbia University. And to the administrations of Columbia University and its Russian Institute I am also grateful, for released time and financial aid during the early stages of research for this book.

Not a conventional pat, but a heartful prayer of thanks goes out to my wife for her help and her infinite tolerance during my many months of self-imposed exile in the attic.

E.J.S.

Contents

Part IV

Part V

Part VI

Part I

CHILDHOOD, BOYHOOD, AND YOUTH
1860–1886

CHAPTER I

"Tea, Sugar, Coffee, and Other Groceries"

"I'VE GOT TO GO OFF on business; so you, Antosha, mind the store, and see that all goes well there." The full-bearded face of Pavel Yegorovich Chekhov was stern. He wore his thick winter coat and high leather boots.

Nine-year-old Antosha — the future writer — looked up at his father from a Latin grammar which he had been studying by candlelight. Tears came to his eyes and he began to blink hard.

"It's cold in the store," he murmured, "and I've been shivering ever since I got out of school."

"Never mind. Dress warm and it will be all right."

"But I've got a lot of lessons for tomorrow."

"Study them in the store," ordered his father, a rising note of irritation in his voice. "Get going, and see that you take care of everything. Hurry! Don't dawdle!"

In vexation Antosha threw down his pen, snapped the grammar shut, pulled on his padded school overcoat and tattered boots, and followed his father out into the growing darkness of a bitter winter's evening.

It was only a short distance from the Chekhov house to the grocery store. As the proprietor and son entered, two red-nosed Ukrainian peasant boys, condemned to the wretched servitude of apprenticeship, ceased stamping their feet and swinging their hands, blue with the cold, and came to respectful attention.

"Sit behind the counter," the father directed Antosha. Then crossing himself several times before the ikon, he departed.

Still sniffling, Antosha pulled up a case of Kazan soap for a seat and opened his Latin grammar to continue writing out his exercises. He stuck his pen in the inkwell and the point scraped on ice. There was little difference between the temperature in the unheated store and outdoors. In disgust Antosha gave up all thought of homework. He knew that his father would not return for about three hours. Sticking his hands in the sleeves of his coat, and hunching from the cold, like the two apprentices, he worried over the low mark he would receive in Latin the next day and the reprimand this would provoke from his teacher and father.

"Thus Antosha served his time in the store which he hated," remarks Chekhov's oldest brother Alexander, from whose reminiscences this account is taken.[1] "There he learned his school lessons with difficulty or failed to learn them; and there he endured the winter cold and grew numb like a prisoner shut up in four walls, when he ought to have been spending his golden school days at play."

The wares in father Chekhov's lowly place of business in provincial Taganrog resembled those in an old-fashioned general store in rural New England. Along with groceries, one could buy kerosene, lamps, wicks, sandals, herring, cheap penknives, tobacco, yarn, nails, pomade, and various nostrums for common ills. And if one wished, one could get drunk on vodka there, for spirits were sold in a separate but connected part of the store. Filthy debris on the floor, torn soiled oilcloth on the counters, and in summer swarms of flies settled everywhere. An unpleasant mélange of odors emanated from the exposed goods: the sugar smelled of kerosene, the coffee of herring. Brazen rats prowled about the stock. One drowned in a vat of mineral oil, and the humorless but religious-minded father Chekhov paid a priest to reconsecrate the oil, which somehow failed to convince amused customers that prayer had cleansed the defiled commodity.

Old-timers and hangers-on, attracted more by the liquor than by the groceries, made a kind of club of the store. Warmed by vodka in the cold winter nights, they kept the wearied shopkeeper up till one in the morning while they swapped dirty stories, always leeringly admonishing: "But you, Antosha — Don't listen. You're still too young."

Tending store, which was ordinarily open from five in the morning to eleven at night, was a regular assignment for the three older Chekhov boys. Sometime their mother would gently remonstrate with her husband when she thought that little Antosha was being put upon.

---

[1] Chekhov's sister and brother, Mariya and Mikhail, question the truthfulness in part of Alexander's reminiscences, which are quite critical of their father's behavior, but the evidence of Chekhov himself tends to support their veracity.

"He's got to get used to it," Pavel Yegorovich would answer. "I work. Let him work. Children must help their father."

"But he's been sitting in the store all week. At least let him take Sunday off to rest."

"Instead of resting, he fools around with street urchins. If one of the children isn't in the store, the apprentices will snitch candy, and the next thing will be money. You yourself know that without one of us there the business will go to pieces."

This line of argument usually silenced the mother. Like her husband, she was convinced that the apprentices were little thieves. Certainly provocation was there in abundance. The apprentices, brothers ten and twelve years old, led a miserable existence. They had to work five years without pay and received only the barest essentials in food and clothing. And among the tricks of the trade they learned from their master was how to cheat customers through short weight and measurement. This acceptable form of thievery, so contrary to the precepts of honesty and uprightness which God-fearing father Chekhov lavished on his children, puzzled and hurt the sensitive Antosha. He brought the problem to his mother, but she assured him of his father's probity. As for Pavel Yegorovich, he had no doubt about his honesty. Religion and conscience were one thing, trade was another, and he never mixed them. This familiar kind of compromise with integrity began to bother Antosha and it intensified his dislike of working in the grocery store.

The father's brand of integrity also included a form of tyranny not uncommon in the patriarchal circles of Russian lower-class families in those days. The cuffings and whippings which he dealt out to the apprentices induced a nervous trembling in Antosha, who could barely restrain his tears at the spectacle of any human suffering. Nor did Pavel Yegorovich spare the rod with his own children. To his wife's protests he would answer with complete sincerity: "I was brought up in this manner and, as you can see, I'm none the worse for it." The memory of these whippings haunted Chekhov even as a grown man and he could never forgive his father the humiliation and indignity he endured.

When Antosha had finished his third year at school, fear of his father's anger kept him and his brother Alexander tied down to tending a grocery stand near the railway station. They worked day and night throughout the whole summer vacation at this subsidiary venture, only one of several that failed. In this family, which had to watch every kopeck, the children were schooled to the necessity of being help-ful. But the excessive demands of their father, which were rooted in lack of imaginative comprehension of a child's normal needs and urges, often made their existence a peculiarly joyless one. "You can't run about because you'll wear out your shoes," he would counter An-tosha's complaint at the long hours in the store. "It is bad to fool around with playmates. God knows what they'll teach you. In the shop, at least, you'll be a help to your father." Or when Antosha insisted that he could not get any homework done in the store because of the cold, the customers, and the requirement of entering every sale in the huge ledger, or because of the noisy interruptions of vodka-drinking hangers-on, Pavel Yegorovich attributed all this to his laziness and day-dreaming: "Why, I find time to read over two sections from the Psalter every day and you are unable to learn a single lesson!"

The moment Antosha lived for, during his store-minding, was when his father entered to relieve him. The youngster would respectfully ask if he might go because he had lessons to do. "Have you read the Cate-chism?" "I've read a little of it." "Then go. But watch out, learn your lessons, and don't play around, or . . . " Antosha would slowly exit, walk contemplatively out of sight of the store windows, and then sud-denly fly off in high spirits like a bird just released from a cage.

Memories of these endless hours of servitude in his father's grocery store always remained with Chekhov. They not only imaginatively in-formed the unhappy lives of the children of his tales, but they also helped to inspire his pathetic judgment of those years: "There was no childhood in my childhood."

« 2 »

In his determination to rise above the bondage into which he had been born, Chekhov's father never rid himself of his serf heritage of harshness and acquisitiveness. Very few of Russia's foremost writers emerged from this kind of environment. The familiar pattern was the secure, cultured, and often idyllic gentry background that produced Pushkin, Turgenev, and Tolstoy. Genius, of course, could be distilled from the lowly beginnings and adversities of the Chekhov family, but the struggle left its scars on the developing personality and creative imagination. Squeezing the slave out drop by drop, as Chekhov ex-pressed it, was the endless battle of his life.

Grandfather Yegor Mikhailovich Chekhov, coming from a long line of serfs in the Voronezh Province, began this process of self-emancipation. Shrewd, driving, and thrifty, he was transferred from work in the fields to his master's sugar-beet factory, where he soon became foreman. He learned to read and write and saw to it that his three sons acquired this much education. In 1841, at the age of forty-two, after years of saving, he realized the dream of his life — he bought his freedom and that of his wife and sons for thirty-five hundred roubles, a veritable fortune in the eyes of a peasant in those days, yet this sum was not large enough to include his only daughter in the deal. However, his owner, Count A. D. Chertkov — father of the future disciple and literary executor of Leo Tolstoy — "generously" threw in the girl.

Once free, Grandfather Chekhov lost no time in thrusting his sons out into the world to make good the liberty he had bought for them. Though a stern father to his children, he was determined to get them established in life on a social level higher than that from which they sprang. And he set them an example by his own energy in business affairs, which finally won for him the responsible position of steward of the large estate, near Taganrog, belonging to the son of the famous hero of the 1812 war, Ataman M. I. Platov.

To this southern Russian town of Taganrog on the Azov Sea Grandfather Chekhov, in 1844, sent his nineteen-year-old son Pavel Yegorovich, after he had served an apprenticeship for three years in Rostov, to work in the countinghouse of the merchant I. E. Kobylin. The oldest son, Mikhail Yegorovich, was sent as an apprentice to a bookbinder in Kaluga; and the youngest, Mitrofan Yegorovich, to a merchant in Rostov.

Taganrog first won general notice in 1825 as the place where the colorful Emperor Alexander I mysteriously died; it is now much more celebrated among Russians as the birthplace of Chekhov. When that writer's father went there to live, this thriving port of some thirty thousand inhabitants represented a strange mixture of Russian and European cultures. A large part of the population was foreign — mostly Greeks, some Italians and Germans, and a few English. And they controlled the economic life of Taganrog through their export-import firms, such as Valyano, Skarmang, Kondyanaki, Missuri, and Sfaello. Here too the Greeks predominated, as wealthy grain merchants and shipowners whose shady business operations not infrequently fell afoul of the law. To a considerable extent these foreign millionaires also legislated the cultural life of the town and under their auspices it took on an incongruous European glitter. They were the patrons of the local theater; they supported a fine symphony orchestra to play in the public garden; and they lavished flowers and money on the prima donnas they imported to sing Italian opera. Even their marble tombs were commissioned from the best sculptors of Italy. Thoroughbred horses harnessed to carriages of foreign manufacture carried their wives, dressed in the latest European fashion, to elaborate dinner parties, and in the clubs their husbands gambled for stakes running into thousands of roubles.

This veneer of foreign culture and social finery contrasted sharply with the external appearance of Taganrog and the old-fashioned patriarchal way of life of the bulk of the Russian population, who lived a hand-to-mouth existence as workers, stevedores, petty shopkeepers, and clerks. In spring, mud, almost ankle-deep in places, covered all but the main streets, and in the summer they were a tangled mass of weeds, burdock, and uncut grass. At night people went about with lanterns, for only the two principal thoroughfares were illuminated and these inadequately. Town authorities regarded with insufferable complacency the kidnaping of pretty young girls, who were whisked off the streets into carriages, destined for Turkish harems. Any day one might see stray dogs barbarously clubbed to death at the bazaar, convicts punished on a scaffold in a public square or harnessed like horses to carts, dragging sacks of flour and grits from the warehouse to their prison. Every Saturday an attendant, with a large twig broom on his shoulders, roamed the streets shouting: "To the bath! To the bath! To the public bath-house!"

Among the Russians in Taganrog the initial social status of young Pavel Yegorovich working away in Kobylin's countinghouse was a lowly one. Long hours, fawning servility to anyone a rung higher on the ladder, and occasional blows were his lot in return for a pittance of pay. In the formation of the narrow, unattractive side of his nature, this grim experience completed anything his stern father had left undone. However, if the struggle for security hardened him, an impractical and artistic side, never fully realized, endowed Pavel Yegorovich with softer, more human traits that found expression in a love for art. As a boy he had learned from the village deacon to read music and to sing; another village deacon taught him to play the violin; and he himself cultivated a small talent as a painter. In some respects, his aggravating religiosity was simply a manifestation of his devotion to the beauty of the ritual and of his passion for sacred music — which he later participated in professionally.

Not until Pavel Yegorovich had worked for ten years did he feel that he was sufficiently established to risk matrimony. Through his brother Mitrofan, who had recently come from Rostov to open a small grocery store in Taganrog, he met his friend Ivan Morozov. This led to an introduction to Ivan's family — his widowed mother, and her two daughters, Evgeniya and Fedosiya. The Morozovs, of serf origin, had come from Vladimir Province. The family had prospered until the father, a textile salesman, suddenly died from cholera on one of his business trips. The widow, with her son and two daughters, settled in Taganrog. Pavel Yegorovich courted the nineteen-year-old Evgeniya Yakovlevna Morozova, and married her on October 29, 1854.

Their life together began inauspiciously, for to save money they lived with the Morozovs. Soon the Crimean War stifled the trade of the seaport, and Taganrog itself was bombarded by the Anglo-French fleet. The pregnant Evgeniya Yakovlevna fled the town to a suburb, where she gave birth to her first child, Alexander (Sasha), only ten months after her marriage. After they returned to the town, the young couple moved to a little house which Pavel Yegorovich's father had acquired. As time passed, however, the cherished hope of Pavel Yegorovich — to rid himself of the slavery of Kobylin's and start a business of his own — grew closer to realization. He had been scraping and saving for years; by 1857 he felt that he could wait no longer — he opened his first grocery store.

A new dignity came with the new business. Pavel Yegorovich was at last a proprietor, his own master. A touch of the Micawber in his nature inspired illusions of grandeur and he began to refer to himself as a "merchant" and to his little shop of cheap groceries as a "commercial enterprise." But the meager profits were paced by his rapidly growing family. A second son, Nikolai, appeared a year after Pavel Yegorovich went into business. The couple had to move in 1859, for Pavel's brother Mitrofan had also married and now exercised his claim on their father's little house. On January 17, 1860,[2] a third son, Anton Pavlovich Chekhov (Antosha), was born. A larger house had to be taken the next

[2] Though this is the date entered on Chekhov's birth certificate, he once told I. A. Bunin that the deacon officiating at his baptism had mistakenly dated his birth a day late, and in at least two of his letters he refers to January 16 as his birthday. However this may be, January 17 was accepted by Chekhov, his family, and friends as the day of his birth.

year when the mother gave birth to Ivan. Then the family moved again, for a fifth child, a daughter Mariya (Masha), was born in 1863 and another son, Mikhail (Misha), less than two years later.

If six children in ten years kept father Chekhov in a continual state of worry as the provider, they sorely tried the stamina and fortitude of his young wife (a seventh child, born in 1869, died two years later). But she was a devoted mother and a careful and thrifty housekeeper. Her love for her husband remained despite his overbearing behavior, the traditional serf attitude in marriage that somehow clung to Pavel Yegorovich and which is perhaps best summed up in the peasant proverb: *Beat your wife as you beat your old sheepskin coat.* It was oppressive and horrible to remember, Chekhov wrote his brother Alexander years later, how their father's despotism and lies ruined their mother's youth and spoiled their own childhood. The children never forgot the terrible scenes at the dinner table provoked by some trifle such as oversalted soup, when he would furiously berate their mother and call her a fool. Only too often was she forced by his tyranny or unwise judgments into the position of protector of the children. Then she would softly and tearfully plead with him in their defense. Chekhov recalled with pain how his father would smilingly bow and scrape before customers while selling them cheese the smell of which nauseated him, or the fawning petitions for favors that he would write to wealthy citizens of the town.

Both mother and father, however, shared a consuming ambition to help their children advance in the world and enjoy the better things of life which circumstances had denied to their parents. Their father never wearied of trying to impart to them his own love of music and art, and there is perhaps more truth than cliché in the nice perception of Chekhov's maturity concerning himself and his brothers: "We get our talent from our father and our soul from our mother."

With the passing of years it was not Pavel Yegorovich's success in business but his assumed dignity and sense of social responsibility that won for him the respected position he yearned for in Taganrog. He was finally designated as a merchant in the second guild, held an honorary position connected with the police, and at one time accepted membership in a town trade deputation. An indefatigable reader of newspapers, which he carefully collected, filed, and bound, he studiously prepared himself to discuss all manner of political and civic affairs with his associates. Dressed in a high silk hat and wearing an immaculately starched white linen shirt, he never failed to attend the town official ceremonies and celebrations. Though he began to be regarded as a man of substance, his actual material position was far from that. And now, with the expanding needs of his large family, and with living costs rising, he was faced with the serious problem of educating his children — which he dimly recognized as an essential status-forming necessity.

« 3 »

"Well, here I am," Alexander recalls his father arguing with his mother. "I work in my store from morn to night and, according to my reckoning, the losses mount every year. Is that the way things go with Valyano or Skarmang? A fellow sits warmly and quietly in his office there, writes and clicks away at the abacus, and without straining himself receives a thousand roubles a year in cash. We must send the children to the Greek school."

"But wouldn't it be better to send them to the Taganrog school?" his wife gently inquires.

"The Lord take it — the Taganrog school! What good is it? There's Yefremov's son; he's finished the fifth year and learned Latin, and what does he get out of it? He sits on his father's neck or goes about the town doing nothing. . . ."

Pavel Yegorovich had been listening to the Greek hangers-on in his grocery store, and especially to Vuchina, teacher of the parish school of the local Greek church, who had a personal monetary interest in urging that the Chekhov boys attend his school. The picture was an enticing one. A bright young Russian with a good knowledge of Modern Greek could qualify for an excellent job in the office of one of the Greek export-import firms. And if he were smart enough, there was no telling where he might go from there. Pavel Yegorovich had no experience with foreign languages and was naïve in the matter of educational programs. But his imagination willingly nurtured a vision of his sons earning a salary of a thousand roubles or more through the simple expediency of learning Modern Greek. Only the tuition of twenty-five roubles a year stood in the way. A customer's unexpected payment of a large grocery bill solved this problem. The father's mind was made up. Against the advice of his wife and certain family friends, he selected Antosha and Nikolai to enter the Greek parish school.

Actually, this educational institution was a kind of prison camp for the tough youngsters of Greek sailors, craftsmen, and petty grain brokers who wished to keep their children off the streets and away from the docks, where they raided discharged cargo in search of nuts, grapes, and oranges. The school building consisted of a single room accommodating about seventy boys ranging in ages from six to twenty. Five rows of dirty, variously carved and initialed benches symbolically represented the school's five classes. A sixth bench in front was for beginners. Modern Greek, syntax, some history, and a bit of arithmetic were the only subjects offered. Vuchina, amiable and sadistic by turns, taught all five classes, although he sometimes had the aid of a part-time assistant.

Alexander relates that terror gripped Antosha when he and his brother entered the school for the first time and the tall, bearded teacher directed them to the preparatory bench. Antosha was only seven and Nikolai two years older. When Vuchina disappeared for a moment in his little office at the back of the room, a big boy leaned over, grabbed Antosha by the hair, and pushed his nose painfully into the bench. The teacher reappeared and handed the brothers two little Greek alphabet books, ordering them to obtain twenty-five kopecks for each from their father. He pronounced a few letters from the alphabet, told them to learn the rest, and sauntered back to his office, on the way banging together the heads of two boys he had caught whispering.

The Chekhov brothers were bewildered at hearing Greek all around them and having their questions answered in this language. When they were unable to run through the alphabet the next day, Vuchina scolded and then paid no more attention to them. He instructed each of the five classes in turn, mostly through oral recitation of set pieces which the pupils learned by heart. Punishment was frequent and for the slightest infraction — blows of a ruler on the hand or head, kneeling on rock salt for lengthy periods, or being locked up in the schoolroom till evening without dinner.

From nine in the morning to three in the afternoon Antosha and Nikolai sat with folded hands at their beginners' bench. Apart from occasional shoves and kicks by the older boys, no one took any notice of them. After several weeks the part-time assistant was assigned to help them with Greek, but before any tangible progress was made, he had to leave for his other job. No doubt the brothers, detesting the teachers, the language, and the alien surroundings, quietly sabotaged the meager instruction accorded them. Though they did not dare to complain to their father, they poured their hearts out to their mother about the impossibility of learning Greek. Yet when Pavel Yegorovich visited the school to check up on the progress of his sons, Vuchina genially assured him that the youngsters were doing remarkably well. The elated father contentedly began to reckon how long it would be before Nikolai would be a clerk in the Valyano firm and Antosha in the office of Skarmang. Not until the Christmas vacation did he learn the sad truth. Before some Greek guests he proudly ordered the boys to display their knowledge of the language. Neither could read more than a word or two.

"You've gone to school for an entire half year and have still not begun to read!" exploded Pavel Yegorovich.

"No one in school shows us how to do it," the brothers answered simultaneously.

Since he had already paid the full tuition, and perhaps because he still had hopes, Pavel Yegorovich insisted that the brothers finish out the year. At the conclusion of it, when he ascertained that his sons had made little further progress in solving the mysteries of Greek, he decided to follow his wife's counsel and enter Antosha in the preparatory class of the Taganrog School for Boys.

This institution was one of those typical provincial *gymnasiums*, which were the backbone of the Russian educational system. Their graduates received certain privileges, such as belonging to the beginning rank in the traditional table of fourteen ranks established by Peter the Great, exemption from military service, and the right to apply for admission to a university. Several hundred students attended the Taganrog institution, which offered the usual eight years of instruction concentrated on Greek and Latin, but Church Slavonic and Russian, German, religion, geography, mathematics, and history were also taught.

Antosha entered the preparatory class in August 1868, at the age of eight, and was promoted to the first regular class the following year. Kept back twice for failures in certain subjects in the third and fifth grades, he did not finish until June 1879. Although not a brilliant student — he graduated eleventh, with about a B-minus average, in a class of twenty-three — his performance might easily have risen above this level under more ideal home conditions of study. The official "certificate of matriculation" issued at the time of his graduation suggests worthy character traits rather than intellectual achievement: ". . . in general his behavior was *excellent*, his punctuality in attendance, in the preparation of lessons, and also in the fulfillment of written work was *extremely good*, his diligence *very good*, and his curiosity in all subjects was uniform. . . ."

School experiences often constitute a memorable chapter, either glorious or unfortunate, in the formative years of genius, but Chekhov's eleven years in the Taganrog School for Boys seem to represent merely the accomplishment of an allotted task. He obviously made no profound impression on the school or the school on him. Nor does there appear to have been any particular residue of sentiment in later years, only a passing recollection, in a letter, of the terror he endured at the anticipation of being called upon when he did not know his lessons. The teachers were an undistinguished lot living in an atmosphere of spying and being spied upon, for the director laid down rules to guide their deportment both within the school and outside it. And peepholes in the classroom doors enabled an inspector to keep the pupils' behavior under surveillance. The Russian democratic movement was at its peak at the end of the Sixties, and reactionary government officials regarded students as the very stuff out of which revolutionists were made. The Latin teacher, according to the school's historian, "took upon himself the duty of searching out political suspects among the young people, and since he possessed a talent for understanding a student, he nearly always guessed correctly and pursued the matter mercilessly." In Kovalenko's condemnation of the snooping, pathologically suspicious teacher Belikov in *The Man in a Shell*, Chekhov is perhaps recalling all that he cared to remember of his Taganrog school and instructors: "I don't understand how you can tolerate that informer, that nasty mug. Ugh! How can you live here? The air you breathe is vile and stifling! Are you pedagogues, teachers? No, you are wretched functionaries and your temple of learning is a police station, and it has the smell of one." Only the priest, E. P. Pokrovsky, the teacher of jurisprudence and religious history, won any popularity among the students. They admired his originality and intellectual independence that would lead him to discourse eloquently on Shakespeare, Goethe, or Pushkin in his course on religious history. An occasional visitor to the Chekhov household, he did not hesitate to tell the parents that, apart from Alexander, there was nothing exceptional about the abilities of their children. Toward the end of his schooling Antosha seems to have cultivated the acquaintance of a few of his teachers and of the director, E. P. Reitlinger, who once presented him with a ticket for a violin concert.

Nothing noteworthy happened in Antosha's school life until his seventh year, when L. F. Volkenstein was expelled for slapping the face of another student who had offensively called him a "yid." At Antosha's urging Volkenstein's whole class petitioned the director to remove the expulsion under the threat of their refusing to attend classes, and the administration, awed by this show of unanimity, complied.

In his early years, when little Antosha was plumpish in appearance with a pale, round face, dimpled cheeks, large brown eyes, and close-cropped hair, his demeanor puzzled both his teachers and comrades. An element of shyness and reserve mingled with happy spontaneity and bubbling inventiveness. The unchildlike gravity and posture of "good little boy" which impressed adults blurred the image of an essentially fun-loving nature. He enjoyed telling his schoolmates amusing stories which he had culled from his reading. "In the advanced classes" — runs one of the very few comments on Chekhov from his teachers — "he revealed a definite character trait in the sharp, neat words with which he hit off this or that pedagogue or schoolfellow. Now and again he would come up with some witty undertaking, but he himself always remained apart from it. His comrades, however, would seize upon the idea and it became the source of fun and laughter."

Many household chores and interminable hours in the grocery store no doubt played their part in Chekhov's undistinguished scholarly record and perhaps also in his meager participation in school activities and friendships (for a brief period he wrote for the school magazine). Schoolwork was heavy and there was little time available in which to do it well. In addition, his father, apparently still dubious about the earning power of a liberal arts education, insisted that the thirteen-year-old boy supplement it by enrolling in the tailoring class of the district industrial school. For in the record books of this institution are several relevant entries, such as: "To the student Chekhov (Anton) materials for pants to be made by him." The pants, it appears, were duly finished and destined for brother Nikolai who, in the fashion of the day, had insisted that the legs be made as narrow as possible. The young tailor complied so well that Nikolai had great difficulty getting into these "macaroni pants," as Antosha nicknamed them.

Apart from tending shop, however, the chores that cut most heavily into Antosha's time during his school years were churchgoing and the choir which his father organized. This enterprise of Pavel Yegorovich's was an outgrowth of both his religious zeal and his love for music, and he was prepared, if need be, to whip his sons into the happiness which he so much enjoyed. He never missed vespers or early and late mass on Sundays, and on religious holidays he spent almost the whole day in church and compelled the family to follow his example. After losing a position as assistant director in a church choir because he insisted on prolonging the musical part of the service, he decided to form his own choir. He gathered together a group of singing enthusiasts, mostly blacksmiths, and rehearsed frequently and doggedly from ten to midnight in a large room adjoining his grocery store. Pavel Yegorovich soon realized that his blacksmiths' deep voices, which sounded like the clanging of the anvils they worked on in the daytime, required an infusion of fresher and lighter tones. Children were the obvious answer. Alexander and Nikolai were assigned first and second soprano parts, and, for some odd reason, little Antosha became the alto. They all sat on soapboxes around a table. Pavel Yegorovich would take out his violin and the rehearsal would begin. Though the sheet music lay before them, this was a mere formality, for not a single one of the blacksmiths could read a note. They sang "by ear" and memorized the words.

Through his ecclesiastical connections Pavel Yegorovich obtained church jobs for this strange choir of brawny blacksmiths and reluctant children, and they sang together for several years for nothing or a few roubles. To labor on behalf of the Lord is never harmful, he told the miserable youngsters, and in this good work he sincerely believed that he was earning a place in paradise for himself. All the same the brothers, and especially Antosha, dreaded every Sunday and holy day. Their father was stern, correct, and demanding in this labor of love. If they were to sing in the early morning, he aroused them at two or three o'clock and out they would go, no matter what the weather. After their return from mass they drank tea and then Pavel Yegorovich would simulate a church service at home. Swinging a lighted censer, he first perfumed the room, then gathered the family before the ikon for prayers, and finally directed religious singing by all present. Soon the bells for the late mass would sound and again they would all set out for church.

On rare occasions, their sister Masha recalls, the brothers would endeavor to derive a modicum of fun from these onerous religious duties. Once Father had already left for early mass, expecting the others to follow immediately. Antosha, however, refused to get out of bed, despite his mother's pleas and the threat of his father's anger. Fearful that they would be late, she finally hustled off with the rest of the family. On the way to church they met Antosha coming from the opposite direction. He had been in bed fully dressed all the time, and had dashed off the moment she was out of sight, contriving by short cuts to seem to be coming from church. On this same occasion Nikolai, who had been assigned to the tower to ring the church bells, greeted his mother's approach with that deafening crescendo which was properly reserved solely for the priest's approach. For this prank he caught it from his father.

Homework, play, and sleep were all sacrificed to choir rehearsals, performances, and incessant church attendance. Recollecting these trials in later years, Chekhov wrote with some bitterness: "I was brought up in religion and received a religious education; I sang in the choir, read from the Apostles and the Psalms in church, attended regularly at matins, and was compelled to assist at the altar and ring the bells. And what is the result? I remember my childhood as a pretty gloomy affair, and I'm not a bit religious now. When my two brothers and I, standing in the middle of the church, sang the trio 'May My Prayer Be Exalted,' or 'The Archangel's Voice,' everyone looked at us with emotion and envied our parents — but at that moment we felt like little convicts." (*March 9, 1892.*)

CHAPTER II

"Before Men You Must Be Aware of Your Own Worth"

TIME TENDS TO SOFTEN the hardships of the past, especially when they are recollected in the warm glow of success in life. When Chekhov recalled his early years, however, it was usually with a sense of pain and regret over his lost childhood. Here time seems to have distorted the image somewhat. Although the record is often gloomy, existence in the family circle at Taganrog was by no means an entirely bleak one. Oddly enough, the two main sources of detailed information about this period — the reminiscences of Chekhov's oldest brother Alexander and of his youngest, Mikhail — present strikingly contrasting pictures, which may well have been influenced by the unstable temperament and wayward life of the first and by the pleasanter personality and successful career of the second. Ordinary discretion would suggest that the truth probably lies somewhere in between these two accounts.

Certainly, in a family only one generation removed from serfdom, it was little short of a miracle that all six children should have received a higher education. Through the chain reaction of social progress begun by Grandfather Chekhov's liberating roubles, his son's children were able to exploit freely the natural abilities that sprouted within them: Alexander became a journalist and successful writer; Nikolai a talented artist and illustrator; Anton one of Russia's greatest authors; Ivan an able pedagogue; Mikhail a well-known jurist and writer; and Mariya a capable teacher and artist. And within his limited means the stern, quixotic father strove to foster these abilities in his children by providing them with some elements of culture which would have puzzled and perhaps disgusted their serf grandfather. He taught them to read music, to sing, and to play the violin, and for a time he employed a piano teacher and an instructor in French. His readiness with the rod, outbursts of temper, and narrow religious piety did not prevent the development of a warm, affectionate feeling in the family circle. In some measure his despotic behavior helped to inspire the unusual devotion to each other that existed among the children. But the care and gentleness of the mother was the cement that bound them all together. When they were little she held them enthralled by her accounts of traveling about Russia with her father, tales of peasant hardships under the old days of serfdom, and stories of the bombardment of Taganrog in the Crimean War. Often their old nurse would spell her with more fantastic yarns drawn from the rich treasury of Russian folklore. Pleasant evenings of song were organized at home when singing was not a chore, or the father and Nikolai would play duets on the violin or be accompanied on the piano by Masha.

The reserve Antosha often displayed to outsiders vanished in the family circle. He was the liveliest and most original of the children, always ready for a joke or a humorous enterprise, characteristics that remained with him throughout his life. Misha recalls going to the bazaar with him one summer day on an errand for his mother, to buy a duck. All the way home Antosha kept plaguing the fowl so it would quack: "Let everyone know that we're going to dine on duck," he declared. Antosha, an enthusiastic pigeon fancier with his own dovecote at home, liked to roam around the bazaar inspecting the caged songbirds; he himself sometimes trapped and sold songbirds for a few kopecks.

During the long summer vacations from school, there were occasions, despite the household tasks, when the children were allowed to escape into the joyous realm of youthful play and sports. Summers in Taganrog were extremely hot. The boys went around barefoot and at night slept in the small garden in shelters of their own making — Antosha's was under an arbor of wild grapes. There he scribbled verses and for some whimsical reason imagined himself as "Job under the banyan tree." A little girl, the daughter of a widow who lived in a tiny cottage in the Chekhov yard, shyly courted him through touching verses written in chalk on the garden wall. In the uncavalier fashion of a thirteen-year-old boy, he countered her tenderness with mocking couplets in which he advised: "It is better for girls to play with dolls / Than to be writing verses on garden walls." And when she poutingly called him "peasant" one day as he was stoking the samovar in the garden, he conclusively ended the romance by banging her over the head with the dusty charcoal bag.

Fishing, swimming at the seashore, and walks in the public garden occupied the free summertime of the Chekhov children. In diving one day Antosha received a severe cut on his forehead which left a permanent scar. Unlike many townsfolk, however, the family could not afford a summer place away from the heat of Taganrog, but they took trips into the countryside, especially to Grandfather's village about sixty miles away on the Donets steppe. Years later Chekhov vividly recalled a vacation at Grandfather's, as a boy of twelve, and how he was ordered to keep tally on the output of a steam threshing machine. The hissing, whistling machine, with "its cunning, playful expression," seemed alive, and it was the perspiring men who appeared to be machines. And Misha describes a trip which the children took the next summer (1873) to Grandfather's, spending two days at a charming village on the way. Accompanied only by their mother — apparently the father had to remain behind to take care of the grocery store — the children considered the journey a prolonged lark. They drove out into the steppe in a hired peasant cart. Alexander wore a broad-brimmed paper hat which he had made for the outing, and the barefoot Nikolai an old collapsible opera hat which he had procured somewhere. There were stops on the road, picnics, romps in the meadows and orchard raiding. Antosha played a leading role in the endless practical jokes, most of which were concentrated on separating Nikolai from his battered stovepipe. Success came when they were in swimming; Antosha knocked it off from behind and the hat, sadly enough, filled with water and sank in the pond.

Twenty-five years later Chekhov remembered this outing in a letter to a Taganrog friend, and regretted that writers did not take advantage of the wild beauty and rich historical material associated with the Donets steppe.

On Sundays the family would sometimes have dinner with Uncle Mitrofan, who was more successful in the grocery business than his brother. Also deeply religious, he became an elder of the parish church and was given to interlarding his speech with Biblical language. But Antosha liked this uncle, who really practiced the Christian virtues he preached; he forbade corporal punishment, always behaved kindly to his wife and children, and treated his niece and nephews with gentle consideration. Antosha also visited the homes of a few of his classmates, especially that of Andrei Drossi, whose father was a well-to-do wheat broker. In this pleasant household, which provided some cultural entertainment, conversation, and musicales, the youngster was a general favorite with the grownups as well as with the children and servants.

A favorite pastime of the Chekhov children was to escape into the make-believe world of domestic play-acting, in which they often dramatized and ridiculed the cant and vulgarity of Taganrog life. Here, too, Antosha's superior qualities of imagination and inventiveness and his droll sense of the comic won him unquestioned leadership. After his first visit to the theater at the age of thirteen he became fascinated by it. He went as often as he could, seeing such plays as *Hamlet*, Gogol's *The Inspector-General*, Griboedov's *Woe from Wit*, and a dramatization of *Uncle Tom's Cabin*. To attend the theater a schoolboy had to have permission from the school head and be accompanied by a parent. Antosha and some of his young friends found a way around these obstacles by making themselves up in dark glasses and their father's coats and sitting in the gallery. The power and mystery of disguise intrigued Antosha and he acquired considerable skill in it and in mimicry. He liked nothing better than to imitate at home the characters he saw on the stage. Once, disguised as a beggar, he completely took in his kind and gentle Uncle Mitrofan, who, moved to compassion by his plea, readily gave him alms.

Such skill showed off to good advantage in the domestic theatricals which the Chekhov children contrived. Antosha would be the dentist in *Dental Surgery*, and after a scene of many torments he would extract, with the coal tongs, a bottle-cork of a tooth from the "patient" Alexander and proudly display it to a roaring audience. Or — when his father was not present — he would transform himself into a decrepit ecclesiastic who was being examined for the post of village deacon by Alexander as the bishop. Antosha's face changed, his voice grew tremulous, and all the faltering of a panic-stricken old man was perfectly simulated. He concocted other scenes drawn from the school and social life of Taganrog — such as an old professor delivering a lecture, or his favorite, which he acted many times and always with new and amusing variations — the town mayor at a ceremonial function in church. In his school uniform, with an antique sword over his shoulder, he strutted through the pompous paces of the mayor and concluded the scene with a ludicrous inspection of the Cossack guard.

Real plays inevitably entered into the repertory of these domestic performances. Parents, relatives, and neighbors particularly enjoyed the children's staging of Gogol's *The Inspector-General* and laughed heartily when Masha, as the mayor's daughter, ran off the improvised stage in confusion when Nikolai as Khlestakov attempted to embrace her before the spectators. But Antosha, as the mayor, grotesquely made up, padded with pillows, and adorned with medals he had cut out, captivated all by his acting.

Antosha's adolescent abilities as an actor and writer of dramatic scenes spread beyond the family circle. At the age of fifteen he was invited to participate, during the vacation period, in more formal amateur theatricals which were organized, in the interests of charity, by the Drossis. He performed a number of comic parts, but his outstanding hit was in the role of an old crone in Grigoriev's piece, *The Coachmen, or the Prank of a Hussar*, which on popular demand was repeated again and again. "It is impossible to imagine," Andrei Drossi recalled, "the Homeric laughter of the audience upon the appearance on the stage of Anton Pavlovich; and, to do him justice, he acted the role in a masterly fashion." Here too were staged scenes on Taganrog life, which Antosha wrote and in which the spectators were sometimes able to identify themselves.

The sap of literary talent had already started to run. Though none of these early dramatic efforts has survived, they were clearly concentrated on the foibles, oddities, and incongruities of people. Themes and details of several of his later works can be traced to these lost boyish skits, if we may judge from contemporary accounts of them. And the schoolboy verse that he scribbled at this time also dealt with humorous subjects. If Chekhov's passion for the theater and dramatic writing began in his boyhood, so did his special literary tendency to discover the comic in the banality and absurdity of life.

Unhappily theatricals at the Chekhov household came to an end in 1875 when Antosha had to part with his two older brothers, indispensable co-workers in this domestic fun. The despotism of their father probably played a major part in the rebellion and subsequent instability of Alexander and Nikolai. Whereas Antosha quietly struggled within the family circle against parental severity, it tended to turn his older brothers into lonely, alienated youths. As early as his last year in school, the brilliant nineteen-year-old Alexander broke away from the family. He accepted a position as tutor to the children of the school's director and lived in his house. The degree of estrangement of father and son is reflected in a letter of Pavel Yegorovich to Alexander at this time: "Sasha, I gather that you don't need us, that the freedom we've given you guides your youthful years. . . . I'm only sorry that you've begun so early to forget your father and mother, who are devoted to you with all their hearts and have not spared means or health in bringing you up. From now on I ask you only one thing: Alter your character and be good to us and to yourself. . . ."

Having graduated in the spring of 1875, Alexander, who had won the school's silver medal for outstanding ability in his studies, decided to enter Moscow University. And Nikolai left with him, although he had not yet finished his schooling. For he, too, was in revolt against his father. Besides, he had already revealed exceptional artistic talent and wished to study at the Moscow School of Sculpture, Painting, and Architecture. To Antosha it seemed as though they had gone out into a world of light leaving him to struggle, alone, with the tyranny of their father and the tedium of Taganrog. He keenly missed his two older brothers, for they were closest to him in the family in spirit and intellect. All three had reached a common understanding of what was false and dishonest in the life around them, and they shared each other's pleasure in making fun of it. Partly to keep in touch in a sphere which he knew would amuse them, Antosha began the *Stammerer*, a humorous manuscript magazine, in which he wrote up funny scenes of Taganrog life. Since he valued Alexander's literary judgment highly, the youthful author eventually abandoned the project after his parents received a letter from their son in Moscow, in which he commented: "Tell the editor of the *Stammerer* that his sheet is not as interesting as formerly. There's not enough salt in it."

« 2 »

Pavel Yegorovich had himself to blame for the financial misfortune that overtook his family toward the end of 1875. The year before he had built a house on a plot of land in Taganrog given to him by his father. The construction, in which he was badly cheated, consumed all his available capital and he had to borrow five hundred roubles from a local mutual credit association. A friend and worker in the association, a certain Kostenko, agreed to endorse the note.

In the ensuing year trade in the grocery store went from bad to worse. Alexander received a sad letter from his father: "Day by day my business falls off terribly. I'm in the dumps, am losing heart, and I don't know what Mama and I will do. Ah, money, money! How difficult it is to obtain it without patronage and in an honest way." Actually the laying of a railway to Vladikavkaz had for some time diminished the significance of Taganrog as a port and trading center, and Pavel Yegorovich had neither the foresight nor business acumen to anticipate changing conditions or to meet ordinary competition. At best, he was a petty trader dealing in goods that yielded an absurdly low profit. As Chekhov once explained to his brother Alexander, their father's whole fault was a narrow outlook and a determination to pursue every kopeck while he let the roubles get past him. And as his yearning for social status increased with the years, he tended to neglect his business. One reason his children had to spend so many hours in the grocery store was because their father was so frequently off on civic duties, religious ceremonies, and choir directing.

The family soon began to feel the pinch of sharply falling income. Things got so bad that little Misha and Ivan were sent to their grandfather's home for periods of time in order to save on food. The mother wrote her two elder sons in Moscow in her quaint ungrammatical and unpunctuated style which is not duplicated here: "Antosha and Vanka [Ivan] have now sat home [from school] for a whole week. They demand payment and we have no money. Yesterday, October 9, Pavel Yegorovich went to plead with the director. They have excused Vanka from payment, but Antosha is still at home and for him and Masha we must pay forty-two roubles. What grief!"

The letter was a cry for help, but the two older sons needed help themselves. Hoping to obtain a doctorate in mathematical sciences at the university, Alexander supported himself and his brother by copying out lecture notes for others. The artist Nikolai did nothing beyond his painting. God would provide, he believed, and, often half-starved, he went about dirty and unkempt. When Alexander could afford the price of a stamp, he sent pleading letters to his hard-pressed family, asking for assistance, especially for Nikolai, whose clothes were in rags, but he received only religious counsel from his father. "When you're sick at heart," Alexander angrily wrote him, "and are filled with gloomy thoughts, you hope for at least friendly comfort and a sympathetic word, but instead you get advice to go to church."

In the course of 1876 catastrophe overwhelmed the Chekhov family. By the middle of April the father, unable to pay the five hundred roubles which he had borrowed to help build his house, or even the interest on this sum, was forced to declare himself bankrupt. Kostenko, who had to make good his surety to the mutual credit association, promptly sued Pavel Yegorovich for the money. Facing the certainty of a debtor's prison, he stealthily slipped into a railroad car on a little siding near Taganrog and, with a ticket apparently paid for by his father, escaped to Moscow. After more than thirty years of striving, this humiliating exit from the scene of his small triumphs brought an end to youthful dreams of material and social success. Worse still, this fifty-year-old father had become a failure in the eyes of his six children.

The distracted mother, in an effort to save something from the debacle, ordered Antosha to query a moneylender about the possibility of his buying the house, but he showed no interest. Nor did any of the family's relatives come to the rescue — kindly disposed Mitrofan protested his own poor financial situation at that time. At this juncture, G. P. Selivanov, a clever gambler and a professed friend of the family, offered to help. In their need for money, the Chekhovs had taken in him and his niece, Alexandra, as lodgers, and Antosha tutored the niece to prepare her to enter the Taganrog School for Girls. Since Selivanov was an official in the civil court where the suit against Pavel Yegorovich was pending, the mother's hopes were raised. Through legal trickery, however, Selivanov managed to have the house deeded over to him by paying a mere five hundred roubles, the sum of the original loan; then by decision of the court the movable furnishings of the house were ordered auctioned, the proceeds going to Kostenko to reimburse him for the interest he had paid on the loan.

Left without a home or furniture after twenty-two years of married life, the weeping mother set out for Moscow, in July 1876, to join her

took in people, a new capacity to form friendships, and a growing awareness of the charms of schoolgirls. Part of the attraction of the Drossi household was the young daughter Manya. They took walks together in the town park, he submitted to her demands for candy in order to be admitted to her room, and on one occasion anxiously waited for her in a blizzard to walk her home from school.

Late in life Chekhov replied to a friend's request for a biographical note with a brief sketch in which, among other things, he declared: "I was initiated into the secrets of love at the age of thirteen." So ironic and spoofing is the whole account that this singular bit of information perhaps should not be taken too seriously. As an example of love at first sight, however, he once told his friend A. S. Suvorin of an incident that could have occurred only when he was a boy and perhaps on a visit to his grandfather. While he was looking in a well one day a girl of fifteen stepped up to draw water. So captivated was he by her beauty that he immediately began to embrace and kiss her. The girl offered no protest, forgot entirely about her pail of water, and for a long time they remained silent, pressing close together and staring at their reflections in the well. More positive, perhaps, was the confidence to Misha of the many "happy and gay" love affairs he enjoyed during the last two years at school, and the pose of the surfeited swain which he adopted in a lost letter to Alexander, in which he had apparently avowed his intentions of giving up this frivolous business. For the older brother, now deep in the frivolity of Moscow, sagely replied that there was both sense and nonsense in his decision, and he advised: "You don't have to be a worshiper of the wenches, but neither is it necessary to run after them."

Now, as an amusing and lively young man without a family, Anton received invitations from kind friends during the summer vacation periods. His landlord's well-to-do-brother, I. P. Selivanov, had him out to his country house as a guest and took him on business trips in the steppe region. The family of jovial fat "Makar," his schoolmate Vasily Zembulatov, invited him to their summer place. But he particularly enjoyed his stay at the Don steppe farmhouse of his pupil Peter Kravtsov, who was not much younger than his teacher. Here a semiprimitive life prevailed. Everything seemed half-wild — nature, the savage, unfed dogs, and even the barnyard fowls which were shot down by the trigger-happy Kravtsovs when required for food. Anton entered into this frontier existence with zest and learned to shoot, to hunt, and to ride restive horses. He loved the immensity of these plains stretching to the hori-

zon, their profusion of varicolored wildflowers, and the mysterious loneliness of the steppe at night, under the stars, when quiet moments of
self-communion seemed filled with an eternity of time and space.

Letters between Anton and members of his family were frequent, although very few of his survived the enforced moves of the family in
Moscow during these three years of separation. His parents' letters
never failed to contain recitals of poverty, sickness, and discouragement;
Alexander drew a grim picture of continual domestic bickering which
included a carping defense of his insistence on living apart from the
family. In his own letters Anton tried to comfort and amuse them with
tidbits about the doings of their old friends at Taganrog, and often he
accompanied them with little gifts from his small earnings. At times
he would draw a moral from the youthful wisdom he was acquiring and
it would glow with the precocity of talent and a dawning sense of his
own worth. "Why do you refer to yourself as an 'insignificant and inconspicuous little brother'?" he asks in a reply, already quoted from, to
one of Mikhail's letters. "So you consider yourself insignificant? . . .
Do you know before whom you ought to be conscious of your insignificance? Before God, perhaps, the human intellect, beauty, and nature,
but not before men. Before men you must be aware of your own worth.
You're an honest person, aren't you, not a rogue? Well, then, respect
yourself as an honest fellow and remember that no honest fellow can be
insignificant. Do not confuse 'humbling yourself' with a 'consciousness
of your own insignificance.' "

With money for a one-way ticket from Alexander and his rash assurance that somehow the return fare would be forthcoming, Anton
undertook the trip of eight hundred miles to Moscow to visit the family
during the Easter vacation of 1877. Though amply prepared for it, he
must have been shocked by their poverty-stricken existence, so different
from their way of life at Taganrog — the sleazy neighborhood, the
crowded single-room apartment with its drab, hand-me-down furnishings and lack of the most commonplace necessities. All slept on the
floor, for there were no beds. On occasions Nikolai and an artist friend
stole wood from carts to heat the stove. The mother earned a bit by
sewing, and the father had just obtained a laboring job on a construction.

Failure in life seemed to increase both Pavel Yegorovich's sternness
and humorlessness in his relations with the children. Was it misplaced
facetiousness or merciless intent that dictated the family regimen which

he tacked on the wall under the solemn title: "Work Schedule and Domestic Duties To Be Observed in the Household of Pavel Chekhov in Moscow"? To each of the children — Nikolai, Ivan, Misha, and Masha — was assigned a time to get up in the morning and a time to go to bed at night; they were told when to eat and to go to church, and what they should do in their free time. At the end of the listing he wrote: "Failure to fulfill these duties will result first in a stern reprimand, then in punishment during which it is forbidden to cry. *Father of the family*, PAVEL CHEKHOV." Eleven-year-old Misha complained that he had been punished for oversleeping eight minutes, because the time on the schedule had been changed after he went to bed, to which Pavel Yegorovich illogically replied: "Get up and look at the regulation, and if it is too early for you to rise, then go back to sleep." Sixteen-year-old Ivan yelled so loudly during a savage beating for an infraction of the rules that the neighbors protested.

Neither household schedules of work nor threats of paternal punishment existed any longer for Anton. His air of independence and self-assurance commanded respect. The months of separation and a demonstrated ability to take care of himself somehow seemed already to set him apart from the other members of the family, who rejoiced over his visit. He had reached a point in his development, as he said later, when the difference between the time when he had been punished and the time when he ceased to be punished was immense. His steadiness and practical sense contrasted with the growing waywardness of his two older brothers, and his parents now began to look upon Anton, despite his youth, as their only hope.

However, young Misha's eager offer to show him the city soon dissipated Anton's initial gloomy impressions of the household. Unlike most members of the family, who longed for Taganrog, he gloried in the sights and sounds of Moscow on this first visit: the noisy, crowded streets with their fine carriages and important-looking people, picturesquely ragged *izvozchiki* in their tiny conveyances loudly bargaining over fares, Guards officers in their resplendent uniforms, and the fashionable shops with their richly decorated windows. But most of all he was delighted with the center of Moscow, whose famous views and buildings he had so often seen in picture books — the crenelated walls of the Kremlin with its many copper-green and gold-topped bell and church towers, Red Square and the fairytale-dream of St. Basil's cathedral, and the imposing façade of the Bolshoi Theater and its neighbor, the Maly Theater. And great was his joy when his cousin, Mikhail Mikhailovich Chekhov, invited him to meet some friends and attend the theater.

Anton had wanted very much to meet his cousin Mikhail, who was nine years older, for he had already begun a correspondence with him back in Taganrog. The son of Uncle Mikhail Chekhov, now a successful bookbinder at Kaluga, Mikhail had come up to Moscow as a young man to take a position in the trade division of the wealthy cloth merchant, I. E. Gavrilov, and he had done well. From his mother's letters Anton had learned of Cousin Mikhail's kindness to his stricken family. Though he clearly admired his cousin, Anton's cultivation of his friendship was not entirely divorced from the hope that he would continue to be a benefactor to his parents. In fact, a few months after Anton's visit, his father, through the aid of Cousin Mikhail, obtained a good position in the office of the merchant Gavrilov, which paid him thirty roubles a month and allowed him free room and board at his place of work, an extra which he accepted. He came home to his family on weekends.

Back in Taganrog — a return trip which, despite Alexander's assurances, was delayed because of lack of money to pay Anton's fare — Anton hastened to renew his correspondence with his Cousin Mikhail. These letters, among the earliest extant of Chekhov, are an interesting mixture of the deferential attitude of a poor relation with more than a suggestion of the chatty, witty style and often intellectually penetrating substance which, when fully developed later, made his correspondence absorbing reading. He stresses their bond of friendship as that of an older brother for a younger, and in every letter he conveys his warm regards for Cousin Mikhail's brother and sister (whom he hardly knows) and his parents (whom he had not met), and also for his Moscow friends (to whom he had been merely introduced). His cousin's advice on smoking is solicited and his sister's marriage becomes a subject for mutual family self-congratulations. In a more familiar vein Anton thanks his cousin for all he had done for him on his visit. Since Moscow, he writes, his head has been in a whirl. He regrets that he was not at the wedding: "I didn't drink with you as I drank at Moscow. Yet I love all kinds of festivities, Russian merrymaking with waltzes and dances and drinking." There is nothing new in Taganrog, he complains. "Mortal boredom! Recently I went to the Taganrog theater and compared it with the Moscow theater. An enormous difference! And between Moscow and Taganrog there is a great difference. If only I can finish school then I'll fly to Moscow on wings. I rejoice over it!" In fact, only one reason prevents him from planning another visit soon, and "The minister of finance," he writes, "will explain the reason to you." (*May 6, June 8 and July 29, 1877.*)

But running through the letters as a kind of counterpoint to their friendship are references to Anton's parents and their straitened circumstances. As though to make doubly sure that his cousin will continue to visit them, Anton surprisingly asks him to carry letters to his mother intended for her eye alone, For there are things in life, he explains, which one can confide only to a person one trusts. And he touchingly adds: "Please go on comforting my mother who is physically and spiritually broken. She has found in you not only a nephew, but something much more and better than a nephew. Her character is such that the moral support of others has a powerful and salutary effect on her. It is a most stupid request, isn't it? But you will understand it, especially as I have described it as 'moral,' that is, spiritual support. In this unhappy world there is no one dearer to us than our mother, and you will greatly oblige your humble servant by comforting his mother who is more dead than alive." (*May 10, 1877.*)

Indeed, before long Cousin Mikhail finds himself transformed into an ally in Anton's concern over his parents. "Tell Mother," Anton writes him familiarly, "that I've sent her two money letters and that I'm surprised she has not yet received them." Or, "If you see my papa, tell him that I got his kind letter and am very grateful for it." And he goes on to add: "In the whole world the only people about whom I have nothing to regret are my mother and father. Should I ever achieve great things, then it will be because of them. They are wonderful people, and their endless love for their children is beyond any praise and outweighs their failings, which are the result of a difficult life. . . ." (*July 29, 1877.*)

Perhaps fearing that he might discourage his businesslike cousin with this heavy emphasis on the plight of his family, in one of his letters Anton looks forward to a brighter future for all when he will take up life as a merchant. "I think that we shall have to endure a bit longer. I will make a fortune, and that I will do so is as certain as twice two equals four (and also that I will reach the top). Then I will feed you only rolls and honey and regale you with the best wine for the brotherly attachment with which you now respond to our esteem and attachment for you. You're a glorious fellow in many ways, and I tell you this without flattery, in a brotherly spirit." (*June 9, 1877.*)

« 4 »

Whatever youthful illusions Anton may have had about making a fortune, one could be certain that he would not attempt to achieve success in trade. His wretched memories of that form of endeavor and the people connected with it had forever put a business career out of his mind. When queried by schoolmates about his future plans, he would solemnly reply that he intended to become a priest. However, the first hint that medicine might be his career dates from 1875. That summer, on the way to visiting the estate of I. P. Selivanov, he fell seriously ill from peritonitis after going in swimming and had to put up for the night at the wayside tavern of a Jew. The landlord and his wife and brother — who years later inspired memorable portraits in Chekhov's famous story, *The Steppe* — tended him all through the night. The next day he was brought home and cared for by his mother and the school physician, Dr. Schrempf. Chekhov recovered with difficulty, and always attributed to this attack the hemorrhoidal condition which never ceased to trouble him for the remainder of his life. His illness and the friendship that sprang up between him and Dr. Schrempf, who told Anton of his own youthful experiences as a medical student at the University of Dorpat, first suggested to Chekhov the idea of becoming a physician. And two years later, in a letter from Alexander, we learn that Anton had already mentioned the possibility, after he finished school, of going to the University of Zürich to study medicine — a notion which his brother opposed as impractical in his circumstances. But his mother had made up her mind. In February 1879, she wrote him: ". . . Hurry and finish your Taganrog schooling and, please, come to us soon; I'm impatiently waiting. And as you respect me, mind that you enter the Medical School; it is the best career. . . . And I want to tell you, Antosha, if you are industrious you will always be able to find something to do in Moscow to earn money. . . . I can't help thinking that it will be better for me when you come."

Four months later Anton passed his final examinations quite well and graduated from the Taganrog school. The official permit which he had to obtain from the town administration for residence elsewhere in Russia included the following vital statistics: "*Age:* 19; *Height:* 5 feet 11 and three-quarter inches; *Hair and Eyebrows:* blond; *Eyes:* brown;

Nose, Mouth, Chin: regular; *Face:* elongated, clear; *Special Marks:* a scar on the forehead under the hair."

Anton must have experienced a feeling of exhilaration at the thought of impending change, the familiar sense of joy which later some of the characters of his tales expressed in bidding farewell to their former lives. He always retained mixed feelings about Taganrog, but he was not sorry to leave it now. He had acquired a contempt for the smallness and meanness of people there, had learned to be independent, and he was prepared to guard this independence against the encroachments of all. Though the struggle to finish school while supporting himself and helping his family had toughened him and intensified his quiet ambition to get ahead in the world, it had not in the least sucked him dry. That is, if circumstances and experience had taught him to regard life with perhaps excessive seriousness for his age, he was filled with an irrepressible desire to enjoy it.

Though humanitarian urgings had no doubt played their part in Anton's selection of a medical career, the material security and the dignity attaching to the profession must have been overriding reasons for his choice. Even in these youthful years at Taganrog, however, he was conscious of the spark of literary talent that smoldered within him. Though there is no evidence this early that he had been dreaming of a literary career, some inner compulsion kept driving him on to write. In 1877 he sent a number of "little trifles" to Alexander, who had already begun to submit pieces to Moscow magazines. Two of Anton's brief tales Alexander tried out on *Alarm Clock.* "The rest," he wrote, "are weak. Send shorter and sharper ones." Whether the two submitted were ever published is not definitely known.

The next year Anton sent Alexander a full-length drama, *Without Fathers,* a comedy, *Diamond Cut Diamond,* and a vaudeville skit, *Why the Hen Clucks,* a quantity of manuscript which suggests that the eighteen-year-old youth did not regard his literary efforts as an idle pastime. As usual, Alexander's criticism was merciless and to the point. Although he granted that in *Without Fathers* "two scenes had been fashioned with talent, on the whole it is an inexcusable though innocent fabrication." *Diamond Cut Diamond* he read to a group of friends, which included a popular dramatist, and their reaction, which Alexander passed on to his brother, must have encouraged the youthful author back in Taganrog: "The style is excellent, it has intelligence, but there is little keenness of observation and no sense of experience. In time, *qui sait?* A clever writer may emerge."[1]

But the realization of this dream would have to wait. Now the stern realities of medical studies faced him. After graduation Anton waited around Taganrog for part of the summer in order to collect a small scholarship of twenty-five roubles a month, awarded him by the town to aid his further study. Finally, on August 6, 1879, he set out for Moscow. Always practical, he had with him two classmates, D. T. Saveliev and V. I. Zembulatov, who also intended to study medicine, and he had persuaded them of the wisdom of renting rooms from his mother, — who by now, with her husband working, could afford a larger apartment.

The family were eagerly awaiting him. On a warm summer's day an *izvozchik* drove up to the Chekhov door. From the little carriage jumped a tall handsome young man, dressed in plain clothes. Smiling at a boy waiting at the gate, he greeted him in a deep voice: "How are you, Mikhail Pavlovich?" For a moment young Misha did not recognize his brother. Then he dashed into the house shouting: "Anton is here!"

CHAPTER III

"Father Antosha"

YOUNG MISHA's noisy excitement ran through the family like a current of electricity. They flung themselves upon Anton, hugged and kissed him. Tears of joy were in their eyes. His mother exclaimed that she had thought he would never arrive. Misha was at once despatched to send a telegram to Father across the river, where he worked at Gavrilov's warehouse — it cost only a kopeck a word for local telegrams. And that evening, when Father appeared, all the Chekhov clan had gathered. There, too, was Mother's widowed sister — dear, sweet Auntie Fedosiya, who lived with the family, loved her niece and nephews, was constantly afraid of fire and hence slept with her galoshes on. And after the two new lodgers had discreetly allowed Anton time to visit with his folks, they also arrived — short, chubby Zembulatov, more interested in making an advantageous marriage than in studying medicine, and the quiet,

---

[1] The manuscripts of these youthful dramatic works have been lost.

studious, and attractive Saveliev. They made merry over wine and vodka — fortunately Anton had in his pocket the first installment of his scholarship — and then all sat down to a bountiful meal of the proud mother's best cooking. Misha could not remember when it had been so jolly in the Chekhov household.

The morning after tempered the joy of reunion when Anton found leisure to take stock of his new surroundings. This was the twelfth apartment the impoverished family had been forced to move to in the three years since they had left Taganrog. Their basement dwelling in one of the houses owned by St. Nicholas's Church in the Grachevka district oozed dampness and the smell of drying laundry. Through the cellar windows could be seen only the hurrying feet of passers-by. Nor was the neighborhood any more palatable. St. Nicholas's was situated in a notorious Moscow region of licensed brothels. Rundown apartment houses and their inhabitants and shabby shops and their keepers exuded the indigence and sleaziness which are the usual accompaniment of cheap immorality and corruption.

Nine people now crowded into this four-room basement. The next day a tenth was miraculously added: N. I. Korobov, a youth from Vyatka, "as tender as a girl," also destined for the School of Medicine. Somehow his father imagined that living with the Chekhovs would have a good moral influence on him during his studies. The family bartered space for material gain. The only sure source of income was what their father Pavel Chekhov could spare from his meager pay of thirty roubles a month. Occasionally Nikolai, who rarely got up before noon, would sell a painting or pick up a bit of money giving lessons in drawing. Alexander, living elsewhere, could barely support himself as a university student. The younger children — Ivan, who was studying for his teacher's diploma, Masha, and Misha — needed help to continue their schooling. So the combined income of sixty roubles a month from the three lodgers now made the difference between mere subsistence and a table the like of which the family had not enjoyed for a long time. Even at that, every morning at five o'clock young Misha had to trudge the long distance to the Sukharev market, where the peasants from the countryside sold their meats and vegetables cheaply.

The thought of five years of grueling medical studies in these drab surroundings and unpromising conditions of existence did not discourage Anton. It might have been easier to follow the example of Brother Alexander and hole up in a single room somewhere, free from the cares and expense of a large family. His scholarship assured him of three hundred roubles annually and he was prepared to earn whatever additional money he required. His experiences during the last three years at Taganrog had convinced him of his ability to fend for himself and keep up his studies at the same time.

Young as he was, however, Anton at once sensed the lack of direction in the family affairs, now that Pavel Yegorovich lived apart at his work and visited only on Sundays. The mild mother was used to taking and not giving orders, and she eagerly turned to Anton for the advice and guidance which her two older sons were unable or too unconcerned to offer. The younger children also accepted him as their authority in everything ("Father Antosha," Alexander jokingly dubbed him). With that deep feeling of loyalty and duty which was a part of his developing personality, Chekhov seriously undertook these new responsibilities. Practically, as well as morally, he now became the head of the family.

Soon a brief inner struggle took place between Chekhov and his father when the latter paid his weekly visits. For some time Pavel Yegorovich's iron control over his children had been crumbling. His separation from them, the fact that they were growing older, and his failure in business, all contributed to this loss of parental prestige. Now he felt the challenge in Anton's assumption of family leadership — and he resented it. His son's quiet but firm demeanor was not devoid of filial respect, but Pavel Yegorovich sensed that it was more formal than real, and entirely lacking in any of the old fear. Nor did the ironic attitude which of late Pavel Yegorovich had been adopting toward the excesses of Nikolai and Alexander impress the third son. The father clearly understood that no more lists of "Work Schedules and Duties" were to be tacked on the wall and no more beatings were to be administered. As time wore on, Pavel, like the rest of the family, submitted to Anton's authority; and eventually, under his son's enlightening influence, he actually began to regret his parental harshness of the Taganrog days.

"What does Anton say?" "What does Anton think?" was now heard in the household before any member made an important decision. His will became the dominant one, Misha recalls. "Remarks hitherto unknown to me were the order of the day in our family: 'That's not true,' 'We must be fair,' 'Don't tell lies,' and so forth." Lies and injustice, Chekhov tried to convey, were incompatible with any affirmation of human worth. He demanded that all contribute, however little it might be, to the material well-being of the family, and he set them an example by his willingness to accept the major financial burdens of the house-hold. "His first thought was to pay for everything himself, to earn enough for all," his mother told a friend while reminiscing about her son's early days in Moscow.

Clearly, in starting out upon his career, there arose in Chekhov an irresistible urge to identify his family with himself in his struggle to grow out of the poverty, tawdriness, and unrefinement of the milieu into which he had been born. As "head of the family" he had taken over the old vision of Pavel Yegorovich, but he instinctively realized that success achieved on his father's scale of values would not be worth the effort. His own scale, however, was still imperfect, but then he realized that everything in nature has its price — that gentleness, humane feel-ings, and a kind disposition are attained only by means of sacrifice. These qualities he himself had to acquire before he could impress them on the members of his family. And toward the end of his life he admitted that as a young man there were elements of harshness and hot temper in his disposition and that he had learned to control these defects only by rigorous self-discipline.

The struggle, no doubt, was a difficult one, for it began at the point where this nineteen-year-old youth took upon himself the support of his family, which he never entirely relinquished for the remainder of his life. Further, as he prepared to enter the university, he had on his mind the need to help pay for the education of his younger brothers and sister, the secret wish to make Alexander and Nikolai realize the true dignity of their talent, and the hope that he would eventually be able to release his father from humiliating employment and improve the sorry material circumstances of his mother's existence.

« 2 »

On a sunny morning in August 1879 Misha showed his older brother the way to Moscow University on Mokhavaya. Chekhov entered the battered gates of the old building, passed the drowsy caretaker, and sought the registration place for first-year medical students. The small, dirty room with its low ceiling and bare grimy walls, packed with noisy, pushing students and filled with tobacco smoke, made a disagreeable impression on him. He had imagined the university as an elegant temple of learning, and found it a collection of dilapidated, gloomy, and unattractive buildings.

He quickly discovered, however, that the courses of the School of Medicine were regarded as the most difficult ones to pass in the university, and that its staff included many distinguished teachers and scientists. Lectures and laboratory work occupied the first-year students from early morning till three in the afternoon. Chekhov took his new studies very seriously, attended lectures regularly, and faithfully performed all required tasks. But after a few months of application he began to wonder about his chances of success. The status and security which he associated with the profession of medicine now seemed a long way off and obviously could be achieved only by the hardest kind of effort.

A good deal of collaborative medical study and social fraternizing went on between Chekhov and the three student lodgers. The unpleasantness of their cramped, dingy basement, as well as the improved material situation of the family, soon brought about a move, in September, to a slightly larger second-floor apartment in the same Grachevka district. Zembulatov and Korobov now occupied one room and Saveliev another, but Anton, Nikolai and Misha had to crowd into a third. Though their lodgers stayed on only for the remainder of the university term, Chekhov's friendship with them continued years after they had all become physicians. While they were still students, we find Chekhov writing to Saveliev to thank him for the "ravishing frock coat" he had borrowed to attend the marriage of another medical student. On the other hand, with that endless, self-sacrificing generosity which became one of Chekhov's most lovable traits, he responded to Saveliev's request for a small loan, money which he had to scrape together himself: "Don't think you are embarrassing me. That is not a comradely thought. And I'm literally *in no sense* making a sacrifice in lending you the money." (*February* 6, *1884.*)

Apart from his lodgers, two of them former Taganrog classmates, Chekhov made no other close friends among the numerous medical students. This is all the more surprising in that the majority of them had in common with him not only the same professional studies, but also the same problems of existence — the everlasting search for odd jobs to pay their rent, to replace a threadbare coat, or to mend a pair of boots so they would not have to go to class wearing only leaky galoshes.

Nor did Chekhov participate in the organized social and political activities of his fellow students. The assassination of Tsar Alexander II on March 1, 1881, brought to an end hopes of further reform which the emancipation of the serfs had encouraged at the beginning of his reign. A period of dark reaction set in under his successor Alexander III. The universities fulfilled their traditional role as centers of opposition to all forms of legal coercion and the suppression of public opinion. In vigorous demonstrations students protested the government's repressive actions. If Chekhov attended any of the various student assemblies during these stormy times, and there is some evidence that he did, it was only as a passive spectator, for he appears to have remained indifferent to the revolutionary ferment seething in Moscow University after the Tsar's assassination.

The reasons for this apparent unconcern were complex. That Chekhov preferred to seek friendships outside the university and was too absorbed in other matters to take part in student activities are inadequate explanations. His old Taganrog schoolboy trait of avoiding participation in the rough-and-tumble of his classmates seems to have carried over into his university years. Nor had the bankruptcy of his family and their subsequent lowly position driven him into sympathy with the radical-minded boys who secretly read illegal revolutionary literature in the upper classes of his Taganrog school. However, if he now failed to make common cause with his university comrades, who were deeply agitated over oppressive Tsarist acts, it does not argue a critical unawareness of economic, social, and political abuses. His singular attitude was rooted in an inherent dislike for intellectual herd-mindedness. And even this early in his development, the representatives of progressive ideas left him quite unimpressed. He saw something false and rhetorical in the student movement and guessed that these youths were infected by the very ills which they wished to eradicate and would lose their radicalism as soon as they left the university and started to build careers as doctors. In his own hard school of experience Chekhov had already learned that the views a man has on the important issues of society should have some relation to the life he lives. When he found the two incompatible, he suspected deceit. Organized efforts to improve man's material condition, as well as the state of the soul, he had already begun to distrust. He avoided submitting the freedom of his own personality to the authority of any group, just as he refused to abandon his spiritual independence by accepting the faiths of others. So now he regarded the university as a place where he was studying to become a physician, not a revolutionist.

« 3 »

On the way home from university classes that first winter, Chekhov would stop once a week at a newstand to buy the latest issues of the humorous magazine, *Alarm Clock* and *Dragonfly*. He could ill afford the few kopecks, for most of his scholarship money went to his mother for household expenses. With cold, trembling fingers he turned the pages to the fine print of their "Letter Box" sections and ran his eye expectantly over comments to would-be authors. At last, in the November 12 *Alarm Clock*, his eye caught a familiar title; with vexation he read that his sketch, *Boring Philanthropists*, would not be published.

In what was a highly competitive business, most of the humorous magazines led a hand-to-mouth existence, paid their contributors starvation wages, and often treated them like poor petitioners. Since length was ordinarily associated with serious reading, all manuscripts had to be brief. Editors required writers to shape their contributions to the seasons of the year and to holiday periods such as Easter or Christmas. The multitude of genres included parody, anecdotes, jokes, aphorisms, satiric sketches, short stories, and dramatic scenes. Pieces on all forms of popular entertainment were favored, and stock situations and types that would appeal to many levels of the population were pushed hard, such as the cuckolded husband, overeager damsels, young fops getting married, bribe-taking officials, temperamental artists and actors, bungling doctors, peculating shopkeepers, prankish students, and frustrated old maids.

Shortly after his arrival in Moscow, writing for those humorous magazines over which he used to pore with delight in the Taganrog library had occurred to Chekhov as the most promising way of adding to his slender resources. Alexander, who two years ago had attempted to place Anton's schoolboy efforts in *Alarm Clock*, had now achieved some success as a writer for these magazines; he continued to encourage his brother to try.

Then, on January 13, 1880, Chekhov read in "Letter Box" section of the St. Petersburg weekly *Dragonfly* laconic but exciting news, addressed to him: "Not at all bad. Will print what was sent. Our blessings on your further efforts." Shortly thereafter, a letter arrived from the editor to inform him that he would receive an honorarium of five kopecks a line (about a quarter of a cent a word). Impatiently, Chekhov ran through every succeeding weekly copy of *Dragonfly*, but not until

March 9, in issue Number 10, did he find his tale: A *Letter from the Don Landowner Stepan Vladimorovich N., to His Learned Neighbor Dr. Friederick*. It was signed simply ". . . v." His family rejoiced over this first printed work. The twenty-year-old Chekhov's literary career had begun.

A *Letter* is a slight thing of several pages, an amusing parody on popular scientific knowledge as reflected in the "profound observations" of a limited Don landowner on such questions as man's descent from monkeys and the possibility of living on the moon. Perhaps some of the learned nonsense which the schoolboy Chekhov had spewed forth in his lecture as the old professor in the Taganrog domestic skits entered into the substance of A *Letter*, and the laughably archaic turns of speech of the Don landowner may well have been suggested by Grandfather Chekhov's old-fashioned letters to his son. In the same issue of *Dragonfly* appeared another still briefer composition in which Chekhov merely listed, by way of ridicule, the stereotyped devices and characters of writers of fashionable romances.

Chekhov lost no time in following up the advantage he had won with the editor of *Dragonfly*. Since tales and sketches had to be brief, the payment on each was necessarily small, but if he could publish many of them he had visions of a substantial income to add to the family purse. Now every moment he could steal from his medical studies he spent on writing. He plied *Dragonfly* with manuscripts, and in the course of the remaining months of 1880 nine more of them were printed. They vary from a few pages of parody on Victor Hugo's novels to sharply satirical and ironic miniature short stories or ancedotes on how a father tries to bribe a schoolteacher to raise his son's mark (*Daddy*); how a loathsome landowner forces a betrothed peasant couple, whom he has caught stealing his apples, to beat each other as a penalty (*For Apples*); and the picture of a bride-to-be thoughtlessly subjected to the cynical views on marriage of her mother, father, and finally her future husband (*Before the Wedding*). Most of these contributions were signed by the pseudonym ANTOSHA CHEKHONTE, or some variant of it — the nickname which that waggish and much admired Taganrog teacher of religion, Father F. P. Pokrovsky, had used when calling upon Chekhov to recite in his classroom.

One of these pieces, *My Jubilee* (signed PROSAIC POET) portrays a character who whimsically offers to celebrate the termination of his writing career on having just received his second thousandth rejection.

This may well have been a wry hint to I. F. Vasilevsky, the sarcastic editor of *Dragonfly*, for failures had been accumulating in discouraging numbers. To make matters worse, *Dragonfly's* "Letter Box" rubbed salt in the wounds of authors who had failed. This department of the magazine was a cruel device that spared no would-be contributor's feelings. "You'll receive castor oil instead of an honorarium," it had warned one hopeful author. Now it was hardly less offensive to Chekhov. It rejected one of his manuscripts with: "A few witticisms don't wipe out hopelessly vapid verbiage." "*The Portrait*," it acidly declared, "will not be printed; it doesn't suit us. You've obviously written it for another magazine." And one tale was turned back as "Very long and colorless, like the white paper ribbon a Chinaman pulls out of his mouth." When, at the end of 1880, the "Letter Box" commented on Chekhov's latest contribution: "You don't bloom — you are fading. Very sad. In fact, it's impossible to write without some critical relation to the matter," he lost all patience and decided to break off relations with *Dragonfly*.

Since the manuscripts of the rejected pieces have not survived, it is impossible to evaluate the fairness of the biting criticism of *Dragonfly's* editorial office. In the case of one of these contributions, at any rate, an associate of the magazine is quoted as saying: ". . . the stupid editorship of *Dragonfly* rejected a tale of a certain Antosha Chekhonte . . . and nothing more talented has as yet appeared in *Dragonfly*." However, if one may judge from Chekhov's manuscripts that were printed at this time, the editors were probably more right than wrong in their rejection of the others. For some of these published stories are feeble and despite their brevity betray the crudeness and wordiness of a novice.

Discouraged, Chekhov ceased writing for several months. Nor were his hopes of adding substantially to his income much encouraged by the payment he received for the last six pieces he published in *Dragonfly* — the sum of thirty-two roubles, or about sixteen dollars.[1]

« 4 »

After passing his final examination at the end of the first year in the School of Medicine — he did well in all subjects except anatomy — Chekhov left Moscow for Taganrog in July. Repeated difficulties over

---

[1] At that time in Russia a rouble was worth approximately fifty cents, but its purchasing power, like that of the dollar in the 1880's, was at least four to five times greater than today.

his scholarship remittance compelled him to go there to straighten the matter out with the municipal authorities. Fortunately he was able to combine the trip with an extended stay at the nearby summer home of the Zembulatovs. The two medical students enjoyed impressing the local provincials with their mystery. In his room Chekhov mounted a human skull on a heap of books, and the "scientists" prevailed upon Zembulatov's young brother to collect a quantity of frogs and rats which they dissected in the garden while the peasants looked on in awe and fear. As usual, however, Chekhov was the life of the household. In a huge straw hat and flaming red shirt, he went fishing, made friends with the village priest, sang in the choir, and with his jokes and pranks kept everyone around him in a jolly, playful mood.

Over the fall and winter of his second year at the university, Chekhov turned his attention to dramatic writing. Brother Misha remembers being asked to make a clean copy of a very long four-act play the contents of which concerned "horse thieves, shooting, and a woman who throws herself under a train, etc." Chekhov took the manuscript to the actress Mariya Yermolova in the hope that she would use her influence to get it accepted for performance at the Maly Theater. The play was rejected, and apparently in disgust Chekhov destroyed the manuscript. However, a rough copy turned up some years after Chekhov's death. It is referred to in Russian as "A play without a title" and has been translated into English under several titles.[2]

The published draft reveals that Misha's memory of the play was somewhat faulty. Though there are melodramatic effects, this unusual effort of the young Chekhov contains an amazing mixture of comedy and tragedy. The various love affairs of the weak-willed hero Platonov are developed in a frame of reference that involves an appraisal of the social forces that dominated contemporary Russian life. Here Chekhov is the dramatist of action and of social criticism, and though the results are sometimes marred by theatrical clichés of the times, excessive details, and awkward structure, they do reveal a surprising degree of dramatic mastery for a youth of twenty-one, as well as a feel for dialogue and a striking use of stage possibilities. More significant, perhaps, is

[2] Such as *That Worthless Fellow Platonov*, *Don Juan in the Russian Manner*, *A Country Scandal*, and *Platonov*. In recent years it has also been performed in France and Germany, as well as in England and the United States, although usually in a shortened form with various adaptations to suit the modern stage. It was also produced in Russia in 1959 and 1960 under the title, *Platonov*.

that some of the characterizations, themes, and devices of this play were carried over to the later famous plays.[3]

To obtain a medical education, however, Chekhov had to earn money. In the summer of 1881 he took a brief vacation, again to Taganrog, but this time with Nikolai in order to attend the merry wedding of his uncle Ivan Morozov, an event that later provided the brothers with material for an amusingly illustrated caricature which offended his Taganrog relatives and friends. Upon his return to Moscow he once again tried his hand at short pieces for the humorous magazines. This time, *Alarm Clock* printed his offering, *Saint Peter's Day*, a kind of Pickwickian account of the zany behavior of a hunting party more bent on liquid spirits than on sport. And toward the end of the summer the Chekhov brothers had the good fortune to get in on the ground floor of a new illustrated literary and humorous magazine, *Spectator*, established by V. V. Davydov, a maverick entrepreneur filled with grandiose notions about publishing. Besides his occasional contributions, Alexander for a time worked as secretary to the editorial board; Nikolai illustrated whole issues with brilliant drawings; and in the course of the last four months of 1881, Chekhov placed eight pieces in *Spectator*.

As his activities with the humorous magazines increased, so did Chekhov's circle of friends drawn from the contributors to this lowly and ephemeral press. They were an odd lot of cross-grained reporters and writers, hardly noted for their abstemiousness, but occasionally quite talented. The lonely, stooped, pockmarked, unkempt poet of *Alarm Clock*, L. I. Palmin, was one of the oddest and most talented. A protector of abused animals, he was usually followed by a pack of lame and blind dogs when he went calling. He lived in poverty in a tiny hole with an old housekeeper who drank beer with him in the evening until they were both stupefied. Yet Palmin was a kind and generous friend and a man of principles whose libertarian views were regarded suspiciously by the authorities. He endeared himself to Chekhov, whose talent he was one of the first to recognize. They saw each other frequently during this period of Chekhov's literary apprenticeship, and he learned much from Palmin's precise sense of language. Writing to

---

[3] Misha also reports that at about this time (1880–1883) Chekhov wrote another play, *The Nobleman*, which was forbidden by the censor, and a one-act play or vaudeville, *The Clean-shaven Secretary with the Pistol*. The manuscripts have never turned up, although a poem, *Forgive Me, My Snow-white Angel*, incorporated in the one-act play, has survived.

a friend about him, Chekhov observed: "Conversation with him never wearies one. To be sure, while the talk is going on you must drink a lot, but in this way you can be assured of three to four hours of talk. And you do not hear a single lie, a single vulgar phrase, even though this is at the cost of one's sobriety." (*February 1, 1886.*)

One day Chekhov returned home from *Alarm Clock's* editorial office, a kind of club where writers and hangers-on lounged and gossiped, and said to his mother: "Tomorrow a certain Gilyarovsky will call. It would be a help if you were most hospitable to him." The day was Sunday and Mother Chekhov prepared an elaborate dinner. V. A. Gilyarovsky took the family by storm. A vital energy seemed to emanate from his stocky, powerful frame and he talked in a forceful, authoritative manner. At once he became "Uncle Gilya" to the young people, did card tricks, had them feel his muscles, and told absorbing stories about his wanderings and many jobs as barge hauler on the Volga, stevedore, factory worker, circus acrobat, horse trainer on the Kalmuck steppes, and scout in the Russo-Turkish war. To the grownups he gave snuff and shocked them with off-color anecdotes. Gilyarovsky was the "king of reporters" in Moscow, contributing accounts of local events, sketches, tales, and poetry. He knew everybody in the city and was as much at home in the drawing rooms of aristocrats as with thieves and cutthroats in the dank flophouses of Moscow's Khitrov Market. Fantastically muscular, he delighted to show off his feats of strength — such as breaking chairs, uprooting trees, and holding back a team of horses. Gilyarovsky became a steady visitor at the Chekhovs and an unfailing source of information and amusing copy when Anton was hard-pressed for material for his own journalistic efforts.

Other friends from the cheap press were added to the circle. The sweet-natured, prematurely aging F. F. Popudoglo, an accomplished stylist, helped Chekhov in the craft of writing. But he was already afflicted with alcoholism and a fatal disease, and he would sadden the vibrant Chekhov with his constant preaching of how time was passing them by. There was also the queer, volatile P. A. Sergeenko, a former student in the Taganrog school, who wrote for a living and vigorously advocated Tolstoyism. Then brother Nikolai brought home his bohemian band of young artists who drank and argued far into the night on modernism versus conservatism in art. One of the painters Nikolai introduced to Chekhov at the end of 1880 was the future great landscape artist Isaak Levitan, whose brilliant canvases seemed so often to catch the spiritual qualities of Chekhov's remarkable word-pictures of nature. And the still younger school friends of Misha and Masha added to the noise and confusion, to the talk, music, singing, and game-playing. Indeed, the family, which in the winter of 1880 had moved again to a larger place in the pleasanter district off Sretenka Street, now began the custom of maintaining a kind of perpetual "open house" — in which Chekhov, with his love of life and people and movement, took obvious delight, despite occasional complaints about too many visitors. Whatever the strain on the family's pocketbook, no visitor was ever turned away.

The association of the three elder brothers in literary endeavors was frequent and intimate at the beginning of Chekhov's career. Though Alexander and Nikolai uncomplainingly accepted Anton's leadership in family affairs, they did not always take kindly to the exercise of his superior moral qualities. Chekhov admired the talents of both and, over the years, tried to save them from the excesses of their vices, but he never overestimated his powers as a reformer. Alexander was unusually well read, even learned on some subjects, an exceptional linguist, and at his best a gifted writer; when not in his cups he could be a gay, charming, and witty companion. But a drink too much turned him into a vulgar, foul-mouthed, thoroughly objectionable person. And liquor had already become a habit with Alexander by the time Chekhov came to Moscow; he was running into debt, developing shiftless ways, and boring everyone with tales of his misfortunes. One evening, after a drunken, scandalous performance in the family circle, when Alexander had used vile language in the presence of his mother and sister and threatened to punch Chekhov in the jaw, the twenty-one-year-old "head of the family" sat down and wrote him a stern letter, recounting his offenses and declaring that he would no longer tolerate such behavior. The word "Brother," he wrote, "with which you tried to frighten me when I left the battlefield, I'm ready to throw out of my own lexicon at any time, not because I have no heart, but because one must be prepared for anything in this world. I do not fear anything and I give the same advice to my own brothers." (*March, 1881.*)

Though Nikolai's talent was greater than Alexander's, his way of life was even less defensible. Nevertheless, perhaps more than kinship, their mutual recognition of the artist's soul in each drew Nikolai and Anton very close together during these first few years in Moscow. Both loved laughter, music, and nature. Together they bargained with editors, wandered the Moscow streets for material, sat in cheap taverns, and visited the friends they held in common. More important — they worked together, Nikolai illustrating Anton's tales. Though rather original in his larger canvases in oils, Nikolai's real artistic brilliance emerged in wonderfully humorous drawings of typical city scenes and the oddities of the human beings who peopled them. But he was completely undependable, and no urging of Anton would persuade him to fulfill a commission on time or accept one that he was not in the mood to undertake. He would prefer to talk with his brother about his love affairs — he had already acquired a mistress — and his naïve notion that any girl he cared for ought to be willing to sacrifice her hopes of marriage and a family for the sake of his art. Or he would disappear for several days on a prolonged drunk, returning home finally, late at night, to vomit all over the house; and, fully clothed, he would fall on the divan and pull a covering over his head, his feet sticking out grotesquely in filthy socks filled with holes.

Kinsfolk from Taganrog and Kaluga, and the two Chekhov cousins, Mikhail and his brother Grigory in Moscow, not infrequently took advantage of the "open house." In September 1881 Mother Chekhov's relatives from Shuya, Ivan Ivanych Lyadov and his brother-in-law Gundobin, whom Anton promptly nicknamed "Mukhtar," paid a visit. After making merry at home, Anton and Nikolai took their guests to the *Salon des Variétés*, Moscow's popular cancan and eating and drinking establishment, and ended a long evening of wassailing in the vicinity of the Grachevka district's licensed houses. The budding author saw in this experience good copy for a *Spectator* sketch. Frowzy funmakers of the *Salon des Variétés* are sharply etched in their drunken postures, and characterizing remarks at the tables are caught in flight — Fräulein Luisa, "tall, fat, sweaty, and as slow as a snail; the contour of her corset is clearly visible on her vast back"; " 'Man!' pleads the girl with the sharp chin and rabbit eyes, 'treat me to a meal.' " And into the middle of the account Chekhov unashamedly slips Nikolai (Kolya) and the guests:

" 'A g-glass of vodka! D'ya hear! Vodka!'

" 'Shall we have a drop, Kolya? Drink, Mukhtar!'

"A man with a shaven head stupidly stares at the glass, hunches his shoulders, and with a shudder gulps the vodka.

" 'I can't, Ivan Ivanych! I've a bad heart!'

" 'I don't give a tinker's damn! Nothing can happen to your heart if you drink.'

"The youth with the bad heart drinks."

Places of entertainment, art, and culture in Moscow were the reporter's beat, and Chekhov took full advantage of them in his spare time in search for copy. A horsecar, in the spring, took him to Sokolniki Park on the outskirts of the town. There he drove around the gardens, listened to the military band whose musicians munched salted cucumbers between their numbers. Or he watched the fine carriages trot by with their society ladies and dandies indifferently staring at the strollers and hawkers. Most of all he liked the smell of burning charcoal and the sight of smoke curling up from the samovars of picnickers in the pine groves.

In 1881 he frequented the All-Russian Exhibition which opened in Moscow. There he and Nikolai heard P. A. Shostakovsky, founder and director of the Philharmonic Orchestra, play a rhapsody of Liszt by way of advertising the virtues of a piano of one of the exhibiting manufacturers, and so taken were they by the performance that for weeks afterwards the rhapsody, played by Nikolai, resounded in the family circle. Chekhov became acquainted with Shostakovsky and used him as the model for the director in his tale *Two Scandals*. One day at the Exhibition the newspapers announced a terrible train wreck in which many lives were lost. After reading the account Chekhov grew agitated and said loudly to a friend: "Such catastrophes can happen only in our swinish Russia." A passing general overheard the remark and turned fiercely on Chekhov. "What did you say, young man? Repeat it exactly — 'in our swinish Russia'? What's your name? Who are you?" Chekhov was quite bewildered and tried to explain, but the general interrupted: "Good enough, sir. You will answer for this," and swept on. Fear of arrest — quite possible on the strength of a denunciation by a general — worried Chekhov, for it would mean the end of his university studies. But nothing happened.

Chekhov also regularly visited the Fantastic Theater of the daring and imaginative manager, M. V. Lentovsky, situated in a simulated ancient ruin in the Hermitage Park. This was good for an article, in which Chekhov mingled faint praise with reproof over the incongruity of staging cheap modern vaudeville in an atmosphere of pseudo-medievalism.

The visit of the great Sarah Bernhardt at the end of 1881 capti-vated the city and kept Chekhov on the run attending her afternoon and evening plays at the Grand Theater. The two articles that he de-voted to the event are cast in the light, humorous vein demanded by *Spectator*. "More than anything else in the world she loves *réclame*," he writes in his half-joking account of her career. On her trip to America she visited "a professor of black magic, the enchanter Edison, who showed her all his telephones and phone-phones. According to the testimony of a French artist . . . , the Americans drank up the whole of Lake Ontario in which Sarah bathed." Yet he could not resist the temptation to intersperse among his quips serious criticism of Bernhardt and the playing of the French actors in her company. His Taganrog schoolboy interest in the theater had been intensified by access to the much richer theatrical world of Moscow, which had already become a favorite subject for his pen. Critical insights into nearly everything about the theater show — even this early — a surprising degree of perception, and in matters of staging and acting he clearly anticipated the advanced ideas of the famous director Stanislavsky. "Every sigh of Sarah Bern-hardt," he writes — "her tears, her death agonies, all her acting — is nothing other than a lesson cleverly and faultlessly learned by heart. . . . She turns every one of her heroines into women as unusual as herself. . . . In all her acting there glows not talent, but an enormous amount of hard work." And he concludes: "There were moments in her acting which touched us almost to tears. But the tears did not flow because all the charm was effaced by artificiality."

Chekhov could be just as severe on Russian acting. In a serious criticism of a performance of *Hamlet* at the Pushkin Theater at this time, he keenly analyzed several aspects of the production and damned the lead role of the popular actor Ivanov-Kozelsky: "It is not enough to feel and be able to transmit this feeling correctly on the stage; it is not enough to be an artist. An actor must also have a great fund of knowledge. To play Hamlet one must take pains to be educated."

In his hunt for subjects to write about, Chekhov also turned his critical eye on literature. In particular, he found the craze for the popular foreign romances a fit subject for amusing satire. To the editor of *Alarm Clock*, A. D. Kurepin, he spoke disparagingly of the mel-odramatic romances of the Hungarian writer Moricz Jokai, which were widely read in translation in Russia. Kurepin responded with the usual retort — it is one thing to criticize, but could he do as well? To the editor's horror, Chekhov at once offered to wager that, though he knew nothing about Hungary save what he had read in Jokai's novels, he would produce a romance which the readers would think was a translation of Jokai. The result was the short novel, *The Unnecessary Victory*, which appeared serially in *Alarm Clock* in 1882, signed A. CHEKHONTE. Soon Kurepin was receiving enthusiastic letters from readers, one of which declared: "Ah, how interesting! Can't we have something else by the same author? And why not give the author's real name? Truly, is it not Moricz Jokai?"

CHAPTER IV

Aesculapius versus Apollo

DURING THE SUMMER of 1882, after he had finished his third year of medical study, Chekhov spent some time in the little town of Voskresensk, a few miles from Moscow. There, two years before, the stolid, uncommunicative Ivan, the forgotten brother of the family, had been appointed to teach in a small parochial school. Its patron, a wealthy cloth merchant, placed a sizable house at the disposal of bachelor Ivan. The family seized upon this happy circumstance to escape the heat and dust of Moscow and settle in Ivan's house over the summer months.

Many of the townsfolk of Voskresensk soon got to know Ivan's brother Anton, a tall, thin, graceful young man with longish hair and broad-brimmed black hat. They were attracted by his friendly smile and the tender look on his Christlike face that now bore the faint outlines of a mustache and beard. Chekhov popped up everywhere, at the post office, at the tavern with the gold samovar on its blue sign, and at the office of the local justice of the peace. With quiet curiosity he talked with everyone, and before long not a few of these people appeared in disguised form in a Voskresensk cycle of tales. Ivan also introduced him to some of the officers of a battery stationed in the town, and Chekhov, as a medical student, was particularly happy to make the acquaintance of the distinguished physician P. A. Arkhangelsky, who directed the rural hospital at Chikino about two miles from Voskresensk.

Back in Moscow in the fall Chekhov resumed his studies. Though he now spent a good deal of time, as an advanced student, in the clinic for children's diseases, he evinced no particular interest in medical specialization. If he had any specialty, it seemed to be trying to earn money, and the effort it entailed made application to medicine increasingly difficult. His classmate Korobov remarked at this time: "Chekhov wrote an unusual amount and with his earnings served as the chief support of his impecunious family." On the whole, however, his teachers and fellow students were quite unaware of his literary endeavors. They did not connect the tales appearing under the pseudonym A. CHEKHONTE with the medical student whom they knew as Chekhov.

He sought subjects everywhere, in his own daily experiences, in the newspapers, among reporters, and even in the letters he received. Chekhov announced at home that he would pay ten kopecks for an idea for a story and twenty for a complete outline, awards which young Misha occasionally won. More serious drawbacks were the hit-and-miss nature of writing for the cheap Moscow press, its niggardly rate of remuneration, and its vacillation in paying authors. He desired more stable publishing connections and a higher return for his efforts. In 1882 an accidental meeting took place that removed these anxieties and proved to be highly significant for Chekhov's future literary development.

On a cold day toward the end of October, Chekhov's friend, the poet Palmin, and the stubby, corpulent, bushy-bearded N. A. Leikin, editor and owner of the well-known Petersburg humorous weekly, *Fragments,* drove in a carriage along a Moscow street. Leikin was visiting the city in connection with the sale of his books. He was also in search of writing talent, and sought the aid of Palmin, one of his contributors. Suddenly the poet pointed: "There go two talented brothers; one is a writer, the other an artist. They collaborate in our humorous magazines."[1]

The businesslike Leikin at once stopped the carriage and was introduced to Chekhov and his brother Nikolai. Chekhov felt flattered. He remembered laughing over Leikin's tales in the humorous magazines he had read in the Taganrog library, and he could actually recall characters and incidents from the stories of this man who was now esteemed as an editor of a highly successful journal. Since it was too cold to talk on the street, Leikin invited them all to a nearby tavern. His mustache,

[1] Palmin, in a letter to Chekhov at the end of October 1882, gives a somewhat different account of how Chekhov first began to contribute to *Fragments.* See N. I. Gitovich, "Iz dnevnika N. A. Leikina" ("From the Diary of N. A. Leikin"), in *Literaturnoe Nasledstvo* (*Literary Heritage*), Moscow, 1960, LXVIII, 499.

beard, and even his ears moved rhythmically to chewing on a piece of sausage which he washed down with beer. Leikin quickly came to the point. Would Chekhov care to send him his stories? They must be short, lively, and amusing. He would pay eight kopecks a line, considerably more than Chekhov had been receiving. And he would also be interested to see some of Nikolai's illustrations.

Chekhov secretly rejoiced. Here was an outlet at once for the best of the rejected tales he had at home. Then there was the increased remuneration and the thought that so solid a magazine would pay on time. Nikolai, and perhaps even Alexander, could be brought in! He immediately assured Leikin that he would send him manuscripts, and he expressed the hope that he would become a regular contributor to *Fragments*.

Chekhov lost no time. A little more than a week after his meeting with Leikin, he found a letter addressed to him in *Fragments*. The tale he had submitted was too long. "The form is excellent. Your collaboration has long been desired by us. Write more briefly and we will pay you more generously." Another parcel of manuscript promptly went off, and eight days later (November 14) Chekhov received a personal letter from Leikin informing him that of the five stories sent, three would be published and two returned. And Chekhov's first tale in *Fragments* appeared on November 20, which marks the beginning of his extensive association with that journal.

Stories followed each other rapidly. Leikin urged him on and praised his efforts. Payments began to arrive and the delighted Chekhov wrote the editor that he would contribute to *Fragments* with special eagerness. In fact, his unexpected success seems to have gone a bit to his head, for at the turn of the year we find him writing to his medical classmate Saveliev, who had recently married: "Darling mine, dear boy! The fact is I put my head in a noose. . . . I cantered about all evening yesterday and achieved a drunken condition on five roubles of rum, nor did I catch . . . I'm off right now to roam. Alas! Do forgive me, but what devil possessed me not to marry the daughter of a rich merchant!" (*January, 1883.*)

The few such admissions in Chekhov's letters at this time exist as tantalizing reminders that neither his absorption in medical studies, writing, and family responsibilities, nor his everlasting lack of money prevented him from somehow indulging in the customary gaiety and lovemaking of youth. Cryptic references to intimacies with a ballerina and a French actress in Lentovsky's theater, to his expert knowledge of prostitutes, and to drunken parties with Palmin, army officers, and girls of dubious morality suggest a not inconsiderable devotion to the "science of the tender passions." But Chekhov was persistently evasive in conversation or correspondence about affairs of the heart, preferring always to treat them in a joking tone. To prying friends who wondered about the latest candidate for his affections or whether he was going to marry soon, he would reply with humor or even sarcasm, as in a note at this time to Saveliev's young wife: "I shall come to Taganrog at the end of June in the full hope that I'll find the bride you promised me. My conditions: beauty, gracefulness, and, alas, a little matter of twenty thousand! Nowadays our youth has become horribly mercenary." (*February 24, 1884.*) In general, Chekhov was extremely secretive about the personal and intimate concerns of his life. His deepest thoughts and feelings he expressed more readily not in letters, but to the readers of his tales. Even those closest to him did not know what went on in his soul. He could be good and kind without loving, helpful and flattering without belonging. Restraint was a characteristic of his personality as well as of his art.

« 2 »

There was little such restraint in brother Alexander, who had fallen in love with a married woman whose husband refused to give her a divorce. He took her, as his common law wife, and her son to Taganrog, where, having lost his job on *Spectator*, he had accepted a position in the customs service. Chekhov excitedly wrote him there that he would soon receive *Fragments*, the best of the humorous magazines, to which he now contributed. And he generously offered to help his brother place his stories in this publication, an opportunity which Alexander badly flubbed by submitting tales entirely unsuited to *Fragments*. The younger brother, who as a schoolboy had deferred to Alexander's literary ability and advice to restrict the length of his "trifles," now in turn urged Alexander to make his tales "shorter and sharper."

However, his brother's letters from Taganrog over the end of 1882 and the first months of the next year chilled Chekhov's enthusiasm. Alexander always managed to turn good fortune into adversity; human weaknesses undermined the one and an inclination to make himself miserable led him to prefer the other. The post of a customs officer at Taganrog seemed demeaning to him, and life in this provincial town intolerable after Moscow. He was full of complaints on these scores, as well as about the cool treatment Uncle Mitrofan and other Taganrog relatives accorded the married woman with whom he was living. And nearly every letter concluded with some small commission to be performed by his brother.

One of Alexander's letters from Taganrog, in this case addressed to Nikolai, brought forth a lengthy rebuke from Chekhov. After a light beginning, in which he admitted to having read the letter, he took Alexander to task for his weepy complaints about Nikolai not writing him when Alexander knew full well that his brother would not even bother to answer business letters which offered attractive artistic commissions, and with not realizing that Nikolai was in the process of "destroying a fine, powerful Russian talent" by his loose living. Instead of "supporting and encouraging a talented and good-natured man with strong words which would be of inestimable use to him, you write him sad, dull words. . . . If, instead of being teary, you had written about his work, then he would have sat down at once to his painting and would no doubt have answered you."

Though Alexander was an artist himself, well-educated and clever, Chekhov pointed out that he tended to concentrate on unimportant feelings, subjectively experienced, instead of on sincere human emotions. In reality, he declared, this had been the main trouble in his comments to Nikolai. "In your writings you underscore trifles. Yet you are not a subjective writer by nature. It is not an innate but an acquired trait. To get rid of this acquired subjectivity is as easy as to take a drink. You need only to be more honest, to throw yourself overboard, not make yourself into the hero of your own novel, to renounce yourself if only for half an hour. You have a story in which a young wedded couple kiss all through dinner, slobber, weep oceans of tears. There is not a single sensible word in it, one thing only — *complacency!* But you did not write for the reader. You wrote because *you* like that kind of chatter. However, suppose you were to describe the dinner, how and what they eat, what the cook is like, how insipid your hero is, how content with his lazy happiness, how stupid your heroine is and how ridiculous is her love for this napkin-bound, sated, overfed goose. We all like to see happy, contented people, that is true; but to describe them, what *they* said and how many times they kissed, is not enough. You need something else — to free yourself from the personal impression that a calm, honeymoon happiness produces on anyone who is not embittered. Subjectivity is a terrible thing. It is bad in that it exposes the poor author completely. I'll wager that all wives of priests and clerks who read your works are in love with you, and if you were a German you would get free drinks in all the beer halls where German barmaids serve. If it were not for this subjectivity, you would be the best of artists. You well know how to laugh, to sting, to ridicule, and you have such a rounded style, have experienced much, have seen too much. Alas! the material is all wasted."

Further, Chekhov sharply criticized Alexander's attitude toward his parents, especially his father, who deplored his son's affair with a married woman. It was Alexander's defensive posture in the whole matter that irritated Chekhov, and the notion that he could persuade his obdurate father to change his own set of morals to suit his son's. "Everyone has the right to live with whom he wishes and how he wishes — it is the right of a mature man; yet you, it seems, do not believe in this right if you find it necessary to send advocates. . . . What is your cohabitation, then, from this point of view? It is your nest, your warmth, your grief and joy, your poetry — yet you bear yourself toward this poetry as though it were a stolen watermelon; you regard everyone with suspicion (what a person says or thinks about this), you fuss with everybody, you whimper, you groan." (*February 20, 1883.*)

« 3 »

The demands of Chekhov's medical training intensified just at the time when the market for his journalistic and literary efforts expanded considerably. "I'm becoming popular and have already been reading critics on myself," he wrote Alexander at the beginning of February, 1883. Nearly every letter of Leikin now had a word of praise for his stories and sketches and four or five other magazines were happy to print his pieces. But Chekhov had no illusions about either the nature of his success or the artistic quality of these "amusing trifles" which he would dash off at a sitting. With excessive humility, he dubbed them "literary excrement." And he told Alexander, "I'm a newspaperman because I write much, but this is temporary. I'll not die as one." (*May 13, 1883.*) His real career, he believed, was that of medicine, and about this he was deeply serious. "I'm steeped in medicine," he wrote Alexander in the same letter, "although I still do not have faith in myself as a physician. . . ."

Chekhov's letters reveal the difficulties and anxieties he experienced during this fourth year of medical study. Frequent attendance at operations, long histories of patients to write up for his professors — who admired the clarity and literary skill with which he performed this task — and often calls for medical assistance from indigent writing friends, such as Palmin and Popudoglo, kept him frantically busy. He was proud of the fact that of the various physicians who had at one time or another treated Popudoglo, he, still a student, was the only one to diagnose correctly the disease which finally carried him off. In tribute to their friendship, Popudoglo left him his extensive collection of books, which became the basis for Chekhov's substantial library. Though Chekhov discarded many of them as worthless, he insisted on reimbursing his friend's widow from his own scanty means for this gift from her husband.

Throughout his schooling Chekhov always dreaded examinations, and now the bizarre conditions under which he had to prepare for them increased his fears. Alexander, in a short story that is actually a realistic account of the home conditions his brother had to contend with in studying, describes Chekhov deep in his lecture notes, when Auntie Fedosiya wanders in:

"Korbunka, Korbunka, Korbo, come and eat. You poor thing, Korbunka, you have not eaten today."

Chekhov, silent, looks under the table and chairs and quietly says:

"Auntie, the dog isn't here. Hunt for it somewhere else, and don't disturb me, I'm busy."

Before she withdraws Aunt Fedosiya must expatiate on Korbo's virtues. Chekhov returns to his studies. Soon there is a knock on the door and young Misha enters looking for a pencil. Chekhov orders him out and Auntie is quickly back again scolding him for having made Misha cry. After a long argument on this subject, he finally gets rid of her and settles down once again. But soon Masha comes in and wants to know "what is the meaning of 'psychic substance?'"

"Darling, I'm busy, and anyway I don't know what it means!"

"What, and you in the Medical School!"

"But what's that got to do with it?"

"How, 'what'? You should know everything."

"Mother of God, be off!"

"To hear this from you! You're a boor. I'm going, I'm going. You're a boor."

For a short time the hard-pressed student enjoys some peace. But he has hardly resumed his lecture notes when from the next room comes the incessant noise of his mother's rickety sewing machine. She is running it slowly so it will not disturb him, but the very deliberateness of the motion makes the sound much more nerve-racking. Then Auntie appears to ask him if the noise of the sewing machine bothers him. Next the front door-bell rings, and in comes Alexander very much in his cups. With desperate eagerness Chekhov accepts his invitation to go over to his place and have a drink. He knows that Alexander will soon be sound asleep and that in the quiet of his single room he can sit up all night, undisturbed, preparing for his examinations.

Even as early as his student days Chekhov manifested more interest in the scientific theory of medicine than in the practice of it. He contemplated at this time a scientific work, "A History of Sexual Authority," and in a letter to Alexander he drew up an extensive outline of the project. Applying the evolutionary method of Darwin, he wished to analyze the question of the mutual relations of the sexes among various samples of the animal world, beginning with the simplest organisms and ending with man. But nothing came of this proposal, in which he hoped to prove that the male superiority over the female was related to the length of her period of childbearing, and that the degree of superiority would be lessened if the term of pregnancy could be reduced.

In the summer before he graduated from Medical School, however, Chekhov received some experience in the practice of medicine when Dr. Arkangelsky invited him to assist in the reception of patients and in going the rounds in his rural hospital at Chikino. Chekhov spent many hours in the hospital, and though he displayed an expected uncertainty in his activities at this stage, Dr. Arkhangelsky observed that he labored with concentrated attention and obvious love for the work and for the sick who passed through his hands. However long-winded and irrelevant they might be in telling of their illnesses, he listened patiently and never raised his voice.

There were compensations for the hours of hospital duties in the pleasant gatherings frequently held in the evenings at Dr. Arkangelsky's home. Here his young medical disciples, some of whom later became well-known physicians, and the Chekhov brothers staying at Voskresensk discussed contemporary political questions, the recent works of M. E. Saltykov-Shchedrin and I. S. Turgenev, declaimed the verse of N. A. Nekrasov, and sang popular folk songs.

The three lively children of Colonel B. I. Maevsky, who commanded the local battery at Voskresensk, were often Chekhov's companions on walks and mushroom-hunting expeditions. These youngsters inspired the charming story *Children*, and years later the Maevsky family and the artillery officers grouped around it were no doubt in Chekhov's mind when he created the characters of *The Three Sisters*. One of these officers, Lieutenant E. P. Yegorov, suddenly proposed to Masha — who was taken completely by surprise, for she had never had a single serious conversation with him. Marriage had not yet entered her head and the bewildered Masha asked Chekhov for advice. He told her to forget about it, and he would take care of the matter. And he apparently did, for they all continued to meet on very friendly terms at the Maevskys' and Lieutenant Yegorov never once broached the subject again.

So pleasantly did the time speed by during these summer months that Chekhov neglected his writing and apologized to Leikin for not sending him more items. "The summer is not the time to do anything," he asserted. "Only poets can unite their scribbling with moonlight nights and love. They can be in love and at the same time write verse. With us prose writers, it is a different business." (*August 1 or 2, 1883.*)

Once back in Moscow, however, Chekhov again applied himself zealously to his writing. Reluctantly he accepted Leikin's proposal that, in addition to his numerous fictional efforts, he contribute a regular column to be called "Fragments of Moscow Life." He disliked the gossipy reportage and the tiring and time-consuming running around the city for copy which such a column would require. But he had to earn still more money, for the financial demands being made upon him by the family were increasing all the time. Earlier in 1883, in responding to Alexander's request from Taganrog for medical advice on the illness of the daughter who had recently been born to him, he voiced one of his rare complaints about the burdens he had assumed in his struggle to help the family: "Do not envy me, brother! Writing, apart from the 'twitches' [a nervous affliction, perhaps due to strain from overwork, which began at this time and long troubled Chekhov] brings me nothing. The hundred roubles a month which I receive vanish in the belly and I haven't the means to change my graying, indecent coat for something less shabby. I pay bills in all directions and nothing remains. The family itself gobbles up more than fifty roubles. . . . If I were living alone, I would live like a rich man. . . ." (*May 13, 1883.*)

And the conditions under which he did his writing now began to try his patience and shred his nerves. A victim of his own unfailing hospitality, as well as of that of members of his family, he sometimes found it necessary to give up his bed for a night and seek one in the house of a friend. Late in August, when Alexander arrived for a visit with his wife and two children, Chekhov explained to Leikin why the column he was sending was "pale" and the story "a sick trifle": "I write under the most wretched conditions. Before me my nonliterary work mercilessly whips my conscience. In a neighboring room howls the child of a relative who has just arrived. In another room Father reads aloud to Mother. . . . Someone has wound up the music-box and plays *La Belle Hélène*. I want to scamper off to the country, but it is already one o'clock in the morning. For a writing man it would be hard to imagine a more wretched situation. My bed is occupied by a relative who conducts a conversation with me about medicine: 'My daughter must have a pain in her stomach and that is why she cries.' I have the misfortune to be a medical man and everyone thinks it necessary to 'have a chat' with me about medicine. And when they are bored talking about medicine, they take up the subject of literature." (*August 20 or 21, 1883.*)

« 4 »

There were times, it appears, when the desperate need for money compelled the hard-working medical student to piece out his small earnings from the magazines with other work. For about 1884 Chekhov was engaged to teach Russian to a senator's two young sons who were preparing to enter a lyceum. One of them, A. S. Yakovlev, whom Chekhov later aided in his efforts to become a writer of fiction, left an interesting account of the youthful teacher in his shabby clothes who immediately charmed them with his genial smile, kind eyes, and a method of instruction devoid of any form of punishment. And when by chance they overheard their father telling a visitor that their tutor was a promising author, their prankish behavior was transformed into reverential awe. When Chekhov commented on their unusual restraint, the boys explained that they regarded writers and artists as superior beings. "My friends," Chekhov declared with an air of indifference, "your father exaggerates. I don't have any talent, and I write because I have to, otherwise your good teacher would have nothing to eat and he needs to eat every day. Isn't that so? I'm just thankful that there are kind editors who print Antosha Chekhonte." Within a few months the job ended, for the boys passed their examinations.

At about the same time the young teacher was writing brother Alexander that his own examinations would soon be upon him, and if he managed to prove his right to enter the fifth and last year of the Medical School that would be "*finita la commedia*." But clinics in nervous diseases, surgery, obstetrics, and skin diseases competed with the humorous magazines for his time as he found it necessary to increase the number of his contributions. "I was badly corrupted," he wrote several years later, looking back on this period, "by the fact that I was born, grew up, went to school and began to write in an atmosphere in which money played a shockingly major role." (*August 29, 1888.*) Every minute he was not studying he was running about the city, seeking fresh copy for his column on Moscow life — to theaters, court trials, inquests, park entertainments, and social gatherings. And when deadlines loomed with nothing written, he would visit Palmin, Gilyarovsky, Levitan, and other friends to pump them for the latest gossip. It is little wonder that toward the end of the year he wrote Leikin: "I'm extremely weary, spiteful, and ill. . . . The devil knows where I get the time to work — that is why I didn't send you a tale for the last number. . . . And to the fatigue, add hemorrhoids." (*December 10, 1883.*)

Despite his incredible load, Chekhov found time to read the manuscripts of aspiring authors, to entertain many old friends, and to make new ones. Leikin, on a visit to Moscow, brought with him the famous author N. S. Leskov who was Chekhov's favorite Russian writer at this time. With his characteristic sense of emphasis, Chekhov wrote Alexander of their meeting, at which Leskov presented him inscribed copies of his best-known works:

"Half drunk, he turned to me and asked: 'Do you know who I am?'
" 'Yes, I know.'
" 'No you don't know. I'm a mystic.'
" 'I know this.'
"Staring at me with his old eyes he prophesized: 'You will die before your brother.'
" 'Perhaps.'
" 'I'll anoint you with oil, as Samuel anointed David. Write.'
"We parted friends." (*Between October 15–20, 1883.*)

In the second half of 1883 Chekhov decided that popular interest in his writing warranted a collected volume of his tales. He selected twelve stories, gave them the title of *At Leisure,* coaxed Nikolai into illustrating them, and persuaded a printer to undertake the job. Before the printer had produced half the copy in galleys, his money ran out and Chekhov had no means of his own to support the completion of the book, which had to be abandoned. A second attempt, however, in the middle of the next year, resulted in the publication of his first book: *Tales of Melpomene.*

At last, on June 25, 1884, Chekhov enthusiastically announced to Leikin: "I've finished my medical studies," and he gleefully signed his letter: "Doctor and District Physician A. CHEKHOV." He was at Voskresensk with his family, luxuriating in the thought that he had taken his last examination and indulging himself in a delirium of laziness. In the mornings, he put on his rubber boots, and with an old local grandad went off to fish for pike or tench. Or he visited with his friend the postmaster, who gave him an idea for a story, collected his newspapers and letters, and rummaged about the heap of mail on the open shelf reading the addresses "with the zeal of a curious idler." And in the evenings he promenaded around the neighborhood in the company of friends, married couples and their children. "It is possible to live like this," he declared. "Only one thing is bad: I'm lazy and earn little."

Chekhov's escape into a life of idleness was very brief. He soon associated himself with the Chikino hospital as a practicing physician. His first earnings seemed miraculous — five roubles from a young lady with a bad tooth which he failed to cure; one rouble from a monk whose case of dysentery he treated successfully; and three roubles from a Moscow actress, summering at Voskresensk, whose upset stomach he cured. "This success in my new career," he jokingly wrote Leikin, "threw me into such rapture that I gathered all those roubles together and at an inn . . . bought vodka and beer for my table, and certain medicines." (*August 23, 1884.*)

Having expressed a wish to assist at an autopsy in the murder of a worker near Voskresensk, Chekhov received permission to attend. However, the medical instinct in him was subordinated to the literary, for he at once wrote to Leikin a full account of the whole proceedings which could almost stand as a brilliantly realistic short story. In fact, he eventually used the substance for his tale *A Dead Body,* in which with his customary artistic sense he concentrated not on the murder, but on the two peasants who guarded the corpse in the woods throughout the night.

In July, when the head of the little rural hospital at Zvenigorod took a two weeks' vacation, Chekhov agreed to substitute for him. To assume such responsibility with his limited experience seemed foolhardy, but he regarded the opportunity as a challenge. To be sure, he had the help of an experienced *feldsher*, a medical assistant. However, his first operation, a minor affair on a little boy, stumped him. He was unnerved by the child's screaming and kicking and the mother's sobbing. In distress he summoned Dr. P. G. Rozanov at Chikino, who came at once and performed the operation most efficiently.

After two weeks at Zvenigorod it seemed to Chekhov that he had been there ten years. He began to suspect that Russian novelists had idealized the life of the rural doctor — which he could see was filled with the daily care of festering sores, diarrhea, tapeworm, the dirt and ignorance of peasants, and the dull escape to the cheap village pub with its bad beer. Chekhov was bored at Zvenigorod. He took refuge in contemplating an extensive project, "A Medical History of Russia," designed as a dissertation to be offered for a higher degree in medicine. Whenever he could afford the time in Moscow, he had attended the university lectures of the eminent historian V. O. Klyuchevsky, and they had revealed to him the richness and significance of the Russian past and its importance for any understanding of the present. This experience led him to plan a work on the inception and historical development of medicine in Russia. He had already compiled an extensive bibliography and had begun reading in ancient historical annals and folk literature. Though he soon dropped the project, it remained lodged in the back of his mind for years. If nothing else, however, it represents his tendency to prefer the theory and peripheral aspects of medicine over its practice. It is curious that one of his first undertakings, as a physician, was to conduct, with the aid of two young colleagues, a purely theoretical medical-sociological study in a Moscow brothel.

As a beginning physician, the practice of medicine seemed to Chekhov a surer way of supporting himself and the family than the practice of literature. He was happy to leave the rural hospital of Zvenigorod and return to Moscow, where he hung on his door the sign DOCTOR A. P. CHEKHOV.

Very little money came in. The literary friends or social acquaintances he treated either did not have any money or considered it undignified to offer him payment for his services. After attending the sick children of one of his few well-to-do friends, the parents gratefully offered him a kind of family souvenir, a purse with an ancient Turkish gold coin in it. It was good for ten roubles at the pawnshop whenever Chekhov was hard-pressed.

Indeed, toward the end of October of 1884, after several months of practice, Chekhov felt compelled to write an unhappy letter to his brother Ivan at Voskresensk: "I'd like it if you could get a position in Moscow. Your income and mine would enable us to live like gods. I earn more than any of your lieutenants, yet I have no money, no decent food, nor a corner where I can sit and work. . . . I'll get sixty roubles and it will immediately vanish."

However, a dark cloud shadowed his efforts, the tragic import of which Chekhov, a twenty-four-year-old doctor on the threshold of a great literary career, quite characteristically refused to admit. For on December 10, 1884, after two exhausting weeks of reporting a sensational trial for *Petersburg Gazette*, he wrote to Leikin: "Over the last three days blood has been coming from my throat. This flow prevents me from writing or going to Petersburg. I must say I hadn't expected this to happen to me. I haven't seen any white sputum for three days, and whether the medicaments with which my colleagues stuff me will do any good, I cannot say. My general situation is satisfactory. No doubt, the cause is some broken blood vessel." His only concern were the patients he was unable to treat. "It is sad to turn them over to another physician — well, there go my profits!"

CHAPTER V

Chekhov and the Humorous Magazines

CHEKHOV ENTERED literature through the back door, and his progress from the kitchen to the front parlor was not easily achieved. When his first "trifles" appeared in 1880, Dostoevsky, Turgenev, and Tolstoy were still living, and their greatest novels had already been published. During that year the last installments of *The Brothers Karamazov* came out, yet there is no evidence that the harried young medical student was particularly aware of this significant literary event. Nor were distinguished authors of the day likely to pick up *Dragonfly, Alarm Clock,* or *Fragments* and wonder about an Antosha Chekhonte who contributed pithy stories that occasionally had the ring of genuine art. Such cheap publications did not find their way into the libraries of the landed gentry or the studies of highborn city-dwellers. In short, at the outset of his writing career Chekhov was little concerned with the lofty traditions of contemporary Russian literature and lacked any inspiring personal associations with its finest representatives.

Though Chekhov knew most of the masterpieces of Russian nineteenth-century fiction and the works of certain foreign novelists, his own literary beginnings were singularly uninfluenced by his reading. The initial efforts of no artist of Chekhov's future eminence ever so completely and directly emerged from the very stuff of life. Dostoevsky's shrill morbidity and involved psychological analysis were distasteful to Chekhov, who was not above poking gentle fun at the devious mental and emotional divagations of Dostoevsky's saints and sinners. It is possible, however, that Chekhov may have learned something from the quality of Gogol's humor, the satirical example of Saltykov-Shchedrin, and the stylistic polish and thematic compactness of a few of the best short stories of Turgenev. In actuality, the great preceding age of realism had run its course: Dostoevsky died in 1881, Turgenev two years later, and Tolstoy, though he lived on to 1910, had already turned his back on art. Chekhov was much less an imitator of anything that had gone before than a brilliant innovator, in form and content initiating a new development in Russian literature.

When he started to contribute to humorous magazines, Chekhov moved into a literary atmosphere and social milieu quite different from those which had nurtured the creative talents of his great predecessors. "The reign of mediocrity has started," Turgenev wrote in a letter in 1874; and by the beginning of the Eighties a period of extreme social and political stagnation had set in which became deeply reactionary after the assassination of Alexander II. Under the blighting influence of Konstantin Pobedonostsev, Procurator of the Holy Synod and principal adviser of Alexander III — a man who could "stop further decay like frost but could never help a living thing to grow" — all the vital intellectual and artistic forces of the country were plunged into apathetic gloom. At his urging progressive public opinion was either severely limited or brutally suppressed. Under these conditions the growing urban middle class, divorced from the leadership of the intellectuals, developed readers for whom the literature of the landed gentry, with its concern for the great questions of the day, had become irrelevant. A new kind of reading matter which would reflect the values, interests, and way of life of the "little people" of the city was needed, and the humorous magazines sprang up in abundance as one of the responses to this demand.

These cheap, showy little publications were run by clever and sometimes unscrupulous men whose main endeavor was to entertain and amuse the varied strata among the city's inhabitants. "Whenever I think of the editor of *Daily News*," declared Chekhov, "I have the feeling that I've swallowed a woodlouse." Since the rigid censorship could and did put magazines out of business overnight, most editors tried to avoid dangerous themes. In general their political and social approach, if they could be said to have had any, emphasized a form of Russian nationalism that garishly reflected the official patriotism of government pronouncements. Fun was poked at all foreign types and there was frequently a patent anti-Semitism. Every effort was made to reflect the tastes of the city's petty-bourgeoisie; but during the period of their thriving, the humorous magazines quite clearly helped to form the tastes of their readers.

« 2 »

Unlike many great literary artists at the beginning of their careers, Chekhov did not experience any compelling inner urge to express himself. He had no new word to say to a disturbed and expectant world, nor did moral and social problems agitate his mind and cry out for solution in artistic form. Chekhov began quite simply because he had to earn money. The humorous magazines offered an obvious market for the vein of fun in him which he had begun to exploit as a schoolboy. There was no question of making literature his profession. But deep within him lodged an inherent artistic sense, which would insistently demand fulfillment in any exposure to writing.

"I attempted everything except novels, poetry, and denunciations" Chekhov said of his start in the humorous magazines. (*September 14, 1889.*) Apart from miniature tales, he contributed dramatic sketches, amusing notes for calendars, articles on various themes, reviews, imaginary letters and telegrams, aphorisms and anecdotes, captions for caricatures, and he often supplied verbal suggestions for illustrations. He searched nearly every corner of Moscow life, every profession for the incidents and heroes and heroines of his stories — clerks, lower government officials and their wives and daughters, the clergy, army officers, writers, actors, musicians, doctors, lawyers, merchants, artisans, coachmen, janitors, apothecaries, and schoolboys. And to these he added landowners and peasants. At the outset it was "humor, nothing more," that he stressed in all these genres and characters, the primary ingredient demanded by his medium.

During the first and most of the second year Chekhov probably wrote many more tales than were accepted. Inexperience, a lack of contacts, and the fact that he was unknown to the editors stood in his way. Apart from his favorite pseudonym, Antosha Chekhonte, he used others, such as THE QUICK-TEMPERED MAN, BROTHER OF MY BROTHER, A PHYSICIAN WITHOUT PATIENTS, A MAN WITHOUT SPLEEN. They were a kind of wardrobe from which he selected the attire that best suited the circumstances of his appearances before the public.

Jokingly Chekhov called his miniature tales "smelts," for the cost of a meal of the tiny fish would just about equal what he was paid for a story at the rate of a quarter of a cent a word. And at the beginning the difficulties he experienced in collecting his pittance wore out his patience. Sometimes he was paid with the copper coins just turned in from sales of an issue on the street. Or, after hours of waiting in the magazine's office, he would be told that the editor had gone out. In his dual role of medical student and author, Chekhov could ill afford to waste so much time, and he prevailed upon young Misha to go the rounds of the editorial offices and collect his money — ultimately he "formalized" this connection by providing his brother with a half-serious, half-farcial "Medical Certificate," in which Misha was solemnly "empowered to receive from editorial offices for which I work as much money as he deems necessary." Misha recalls his tours of duty on this degrading assignment, and the endless waiting. When he had finally cornered an editor, he would be brusquely asked: "What are you hanging around for?"

"For the three roubles, of course."

"Well, I don't have them. Perhaps you'd like a ticket for the theater, or perhaps a new pair of pants. Then go to my tailor Arontrikher and order a pair of pants on my account."

Even as a novice, however, Chekhov's pride and firmness saved him from being exploited by editors of the more vulgar and salacious sheets. Because of its reprehensible practices, he turned against the *Daily News*

— Chekhov nicknamed it "Filth of the Day" — and, though he was in financial need at the time, he rejected the attractive offer of *Moscow Leaflet's* editor because he disapproved of the pornographical emphasis in that publication.

Necessity dictated quantity, and anyway the Moscow humorous magazines were not especially interested in quality. Chekhov had to learn to write swiftly in the cramped setting of an "open house." There he would perch at the edge of a table or on a window sill at his work, while the room often resounded to the conversation, songs, piano playing, and card games of the family and their guests. The din and jollity, curiously enough, seemed to stimulate him, though when protracted — and if his writing went badly — the noise might get on his nerves. He would quickly cross out a story that failed to come easily and immediately start another on a different theme on the back of the same sheet. So lightly and impersonally did he regard these early contributions that on one occasion, at least, he allowed a fellow writer the use of his pseudonym, Antosha Chekhonte, to help him place his pieces, and agreed to turn over the payments to him.

In fact, the average reader of the humorous magazines would have detected little difference between the earliest miniature tales of Chekhov and those of many other contributors. In both cases the stories were slightly elaborated anecdotes with the same situations and characters and with pretty much the same type of humor. Chekhov, no less than his rivals, aimed at a standard form of entertainment. Yet an innovating artistic power is evident in a few of his contributions during these first two years — a poetic touch of nature description; sharp, realistic dialogue; a groping for the human being beneath the stereotyped surface features of the drunken merchant or the forlorn damsel desperately anxious for marriage.

These artistic gropings developed with surprising rapidity once Chekhov found a secure market for his writing in Leikin's *Fragments* and received the friendly encouragement, however misdirected, of its editor. He had published only thirty-two pieces in 1882, at the end of which year he met Leikin. The very next year his total soared to the phenomenal figure of more than a hundred and twenty pieces, most of them appearing in *Fragments*. With a sense of gratitude for the part Leikin played in his literary career, Chekhov wrote him later: "*Fragments* is my baptismal font and you are my godfather." (*December 27, 1887.*)

« 3 »

Leikin, as the first writer of consequence he had met, impressed the youthful Chekhov. A forerunner in developing the miniature humorous tale, his published collections sold well. In company he could be counted upon to let drop the fact that Alexander III had read a volume of his stories to members of his family. Besides, Leikin owned and edited the most successful and the cleanest humorous magazine.

A self-made man, coming from a family of petty traders, Leikin had known poverty in his youth before making his mark as a writer in the Sixties. He had a small gift for realistic description and the precise use of words, but his success as a humorist had killed his taste for any other kind of literature. In turning his writing entirely into an article of trade, the tight-fisted Leikin had not lost his soul, but he had lost any capacity he may have had for discriminating between the appearance and substance of art. "He is a good, harmless man but bourgeois to the marrow," Chekhov described Leikin once he had learned to know him better. (*November 3, 1888.*)

At the beginning of their association, Leikin made it clear to Chekhov that contributions to *Fragments* must follow a few simple rules: without exception, they must be humorous, no longer than a thousand words, concerned with topical themes, and avoid the risqué. Above all, serious subjects were taboo. The censor's awful blue pencil could ruthlessly ruin a whole issue. Even a harmless word such as "cockade" would be stricken because it might insult the honor of the Imperial Army, and "baldheaded" was expunged because of possible reflections on the bald head of Alexander III. Leikin acted as a kind of preliminary censor and often cut out what he thought would be offensive words, passages, or ideas. Despite this treatment, not a few of Chekhov's contributions to *Fragments* fell afoul of the official censor.

In the early stages of their extensive correspondence, Chekhov obviously tried to please and even to flatter Leikin. He praised the handling and intelligence of *Fragments*; soon they were on familiar enough terms for Chekhov to feel free to ask small favors and to recommend other writers. On his part, Leikin quickly recognized that he had an invaluable and most versatile contributor in Chekhov.

The editor's immediate concern was to bind the writer securely to *Fragments* and, particularly, to pump copy out of him at the rate of at least one piece for each weekly issue, a rate that Chekhov maintained and even increased at times. With editorial insight and not a little exaggeration — since Chekhov was then only twenty-three — Leikin declared: "You write me about some timidity or other, that you are sometimes afraid to send a tale. . . . What are you afraid of? You are an experienced author and you have already adequately shown what you can do. Further, you have a literary nose, you feel when and precisely what is needed, and this is the important thing." But the main demand was for copy, swiftly and on time, and all considerations of art were sacrificed to this newspaper mentality. "You must write more," he urged. When Chekhov, with a new feeling of pride in his work, began to take pains, Leikin wrote: "Here, for example, is what occupies much of your time: Why do you rework your tales? Who does this today?" Yet whenever Chekhov deviated from what Leikin considered the unalterable humor pattern of *Fragments*, the manuscript would be firmly rejected. However, in technical matters of style and emphasis, where Leikin's extensive experience as a writer could be helpful, Chekhov paid attention to his advice and comments.

A combination of need and Leikin's persistent pressure prodded Chekhov to make superhuman efforts in feeding the hungry maw of *Fragments*. In addition to the various genres he performed in, he undertook, at Leikin's insistence and against his own better judgment, the purely journalistic task of the column "Fragments of Moscow Life." This appeared twice a month and in all he contributed about fifty columns before he gave it up in spite of Leikin's plea that he continue. At first Chekhov used the pseudonym RUVER, but when Moscow friends discovered his authorship, he adopted the signature ULYSSES, since it was essential to preserve anonymity in a kind of writing that could involve him in personal difficulties. Chekhov's letters register his complaints about the onerous obligation he had assumed and his conviction that he had no real capacity as a columnist. After wandering about the city all day searching for material, he would return home weary and with ragged nerves to sit up late and write his column. Then, in order to meet the deadline, he had to take the copy to the Nikolaevsky Station to catch the early morning train to St. Petersburg.

The whole city was his preserve — the manners and morals of Muscovites, their theater, music, literature, and the press, court trials and civic events. The material was rich enough, but in handling it he had to subscribe to the light, humorous, satiric demands of *Fragments*. Attack and not praise was the order of the day: "Shoot both to the left and right and wound all unmercifully," ordered Leikin. Serious subjects could never be treated seriously, and pressing problems had to give way to those of illiteracy of advertisements, cockroaches in the bread, the shameless behavior of undertakers, and the filthy toilets of the Maly Theater. Much as Chekhov disliked this task, his experience in writing "Fragments of Moscow Life" unquestionably broadened and deepened his relation to reality and tremendously sharpened his powers of observation. The extraordinary thematic scope and unexampled richness in situations and characters in the total volume of Chekhov's stories certainly reflect the influence of this early experience as a columnist.

As time passed and Chekhov's relations to *Fragments* became secure, he began to question its practices and Leikin's editorial attitude. Though these criticisms arose partly out of his sincere interest in the success of the magazine, they were also prompted by an emerging artistic sense that led him to revolt against some of the crudities of the fiction genre of humorous magazines. He complained of being forced to write to a prescribed limit of a thousand words a story. He measured this out, he told Leikin, by the four sides of the small notepaper he wrote on, and if he had to run over he was assailed by doubts. Promising not to take advantage of the liberty, he pleaded for more space. ". . . I bless you to twelve hundred, fourteen hundred, or even fifteen hundred words," Leikin replied, "if only you'll unfailingly send me something for every issue."

Chekhov's frequent mention of money difficulties in his letters to Leikin were palpable hints that the rate of about a kopeck a word, though better than the rates of the Moscow magazines, was now inadequate, and particularly in the light of his success in *Fragments*, of which the editor constantly assured him. But Leikin never took the hint. At the end of 1884 Chekhov pointedly informed him that he had sent a story to *Diversion*. "But I hope you are not angry with this desertion of *Fragments*. I'm a family man and needy. Money is essential and *Diversion* pays me more than a kopeck a word. I cannot afford to earn less than a hundred and fifty to a hundred and eighty roubles a month, otherwise I'd go bankrupt." (*November 16, 1884.*)

In fact, Leikin deeply resented and feared Chekhov's publishing tales in other humorous magazines, an opportunity that increased as he became better known. Some of these were pieces Leikin had rejected, others, Chekhov would soothingly explain, were too long or not up to Leikin's standards. At times, in order to avoid hard feelings, Chekhov would send a story and inform Leikin that it was not worthy of *Frag-

ments, although he was convinced that he could easily place it elsewhere. Worried over his rivals, however, Leikin would relent on his editorial scruples. "Never mind," he would condescendingly write Chekhov, "the oven also bakes various kinds of bread." And he would print the story. The situation eventually led to angry words. It was by no means solely a question of higher payment — other magazines now seeking Chekhov's contributions could rarely afford to outbid even the relatively low rates of *Fragments.* Chekhov had reached a point in his literary development where Leikin's dictated form and content had become irksome and he claimed the privilege of a literary artist to write as he pleased and to publish wherever he desired. Eventually Leikin had to accept the fact that, however important money might be to Chekhov, he would not sell his freedom as an author.

Indeed, before long Chekhov found the courage to tell Leikin that occasionally his magazine was "dry." Life was not always funny, he pointed out. Misery and sadness were also real and a part of life and could be artistically embodied in fiction. And these elements Chekhov boldly incorporated into a number of miniature tales he submitted to Leikin during 1883–1884. Outwardly they resembled the anecdotal pattern of the typical humorous magazine piece. But behind the humor appeared the terrible sadness of the lonely man's existence. Suddenly the low comedy of the customary shallow story of *Fragments* was ennobled by the higher human perception of art. The serious note annoyed Leikin and he would object, although sometimes he missed it altogether and accepted the tale. What he disliked, however, manifestly pleased the readers of his magazine, who began to pay closer attention to the contributions of Antosha Chekhonte. Yet Leikin remained quite oblivious to the fact that he was witnessing the miracle of the artistic maturing of an innovator working within the simple pattern of the lowly miniature tale of the humorous magazines. In a few years he would be proud to claim the undeserved honor of "discovering" the great writer Chekhov.

« 4 »

Tales of Melpomene neither established Chekhov as a writer nor earned him much money. Though the six stories on theatrical themes, in this little collection of ninety-six pages selling at sixty kopecks, had appeared separately shortly before, he had carefully revised them for the purpose of the book, which he published on credit, agreeing to pay the printer's cost within four months. Over the summer of 1884, Alexander, who had quit his job in the customs service at Taganrog and returned to Moscow while Chekhov was at Voskresensk, agreed to play the part of a business agent in placing copies of *Tales of Melpomene* for sale in the various city bookshops. Jokingly but with unconscious prophecy, he wrote his brother: "Russia will hear about you, Antosha! Die soon so you can witness the tears of the North, West, and from across the seas! Your glory will grow, but people very unwillingly buy your book."

One obstacle in the way of the book's reception was the title. The word *Skazki* in Russian carries the implication of "fairy tales" or "nursery tales," and the tragic muse Melpomene, however descriptive of the contents of the collection, was hardly a familiar name in the vocabulary of the average reader. Confused by the title, booksellers placed their copies in the children's section. A general reprimanded one of the bookstores for selling such an immoral work to youngsters. Alexander hastened to inform Chekhov that the printer was receiving letters such as one from the provinces which stated: "I have been unable to find in literature any other fairy tales to read to my five children except those of Andersen and others, therefore I ask you to send me the fairy tales of Melpomene." And Alexander teasingly offered to suggest to education and religious officials that the book be used in the schools and by preachers.

From 1880 through 1884, while Chekhov studied at the university as a full-time medical student, he published close to three hundred pieces in the humorous magazines, most of them short stories, although at least two run to short novel length.[1] They occupy three thick volumes in the latest edition of his works. The vast amount of hackwork in this amazing total might almost have stifled the budding artist in him, and with his rigorous standards Chekhov included only a few of these early tales in the first collected edition of his works which he supervised from 1899–1901. Among them are at least a dozen little masterpieces, which would find an honored place in any extensive anthology of his best tales — tales such as *Autumn*, *A Daughter of Albion*, *Death of a Government Clerk*, *Fat and Thin*, *The Decoration*, *Surgery*, *A Chameleon*, *A Civil Service Examination*, and *Proper Measures*.

Although the editors and the conditions under which he worked were

[1] Apart from *The Unnecessary Victory*, Chekhov wrote *Drama at a Hunting Party*, serialized in the *Daily News* of 1884. It is a short crime novel which to some extent parodies this genre, so popular at the time.

inimical to the serious, sad, and lyrical moods that from the beginning were an inseparable part of his creative nature, Chekhov learned a few things of importance for his future development in this tawdry school of the humorous magazines. Before him the short story in Russian literature had been only an incidental art form, and Turgenev alone practiced it with an evocative brevity. Though at times the pressure to confine what he had to say within the rigid limits of the miniature tale annoyed him, Chekhov quickly realized the artistic virtue of this form in which he ultimately became one of the world's great masters. He made it his own special genre and contrived to compress the whole life of a man within its tiny compass. To write with talent, he finally decided, meant to write with brevity, to talk briefly about big things. Casting a backward glance over this early period of literary apprenticeship, he once told Bunin: "It is fine for you writers nowadays. They praise you for the little tale, but they used to scold me for it. And how they scolded. If you wished to be a writer then, you wrote novels, otherwise they wouldn't speak or listen to you and would keep you out of the important magazines. For the sake of the miniature story, I broke my head against a wall on your behalf."

Many of the motifs, situations, and characters which Chekhov drew from the teeming life of the city were not unlike those in the miniature tales of other contributors to the humorous magazine. Indeed, many of these same features appear in an elaborated form in the longer stories which he wrote at the height of his artistic powers. In the best of the early tales, however, his method of handling this material was quite different from that of his rivals. For one thing he refused to accept the popular insensitivity to abuses of power by people of rank, parents, clergy, and government officials with their unwarranted pretensions to blind obedience. A social conscience, utterly alien to the tone of the humorous magazines, compelled him to mingle humor with the ugly sides of life. "A little story," he insisted in a letter to Leikin, "which contains a good plot and an effective protest, will be read with pleasure, so far as I am able to observe — that is, if it is not dull." (*After April 17, 1883.*) And one may plainly observe this artistic transition as Chekhov moved from the external humor of an anecdotal situation, in the very first tales, to an accusatory humor in certain of the stories written after the second half of 1883. Here, the humor is not jolly or farcical; it is ironic or satiric. It is the dull laughter of the amusing situation in *A Chameleon* which exposes the slavish psychology of people who debase their human worth before the pomp of rank and the power of constituted authority. Or it is the sad laughter of the wry situation in *The Death of a Government Clerk,* where the general fails to understand the compulsion to apologize of the sneezing subordinate who was born to be obsequious; or of the amusing meeting of old friends in *Fat and Thin,* where the equality born of hallowed childhood memories vanishes before the symbol of rank. In such tales we have a psychological treatment of humor, which, in more subtle forms, became a characteristic of Chekhov's later works. Another early example of an artistic device which Chekhov used so effectively later may be found in *Autumn* (1883). In this mandatory "seasonal" piece of the humorous magazine there is more than a suggestion of the lyrical landscape in which nature, never independent of man, is intimately identified with his psyche.

Any careful study of Chekhov's total literary development dispels the common notion that the apparently striking contrast in tone and emphasis between his early and later tales can be explained only by a kind of creative dualism. For critics point out the difference between hundreds of humorous and often farcical tales of his early period, written in an optimistic spirit of fun, and the bulk of his mature stories depicting the cruelty, greed, hypocrisy and stupidity of a life sad without end. To be sure, there is a rollicking, laughing quality in most of Chekhov's early tales; the humorous magazines demanded it. Nor was his own happy, life-loving temperament inconsistent with this approach. Even as a youth, however, Chekhov gives every evidence of being an acute observer of life's serious moments and deeply responsive to its tragedies. And this quality is also apparent in some of his early tales in which he reveals the dismal lives of his fellow men wasted in the murk of commonplace vulgarity. In short, both approaches may be observed from the beginning. Like Gogol and Maupassant, humor and satire were his defense against the sadness of life and the "flabby, sour, and dull time" in which he lived.

When he finished his university studies, however, and began his career as a doctor, it never occurred to the modest twenty-four-year-old Chekhov to attribute any special significance to the considerable body of writing he had done. A few comments scattered through his letters suggest that an artistic conscience was alive — such as his expressions of regret at spoiling a fine theme because of the hurried conditions under which he worked; and that conscience dictated his eventual determination to write as he pleased rather than as his editors required. But apart from a little popularity he had won in the humorous magazines as Antosha Chekhonte, no single author or critic of distinction had as yet given him the kind of encouragement that would have sent his spirits soaring and might have prompted him to identify his future hopes with the high seriousness of art. If he had any hope after these five years of unremitting toil, it was the modest one that he might conduct his life ahead with talent — which for Chekhov meant to work, to search, and to suffer, but always so that the working and searching and suffering would lead to experiencing a great and real joy in life.

CHAPTER VI

"All My Hopes Lie Entirely in the Future"

ON HIS TWENTY-FIFTH BIRTHDAY (January 17, 1885) Chekhov received a letter from Alexander, who commemorated the event in a jesting jingle:

> But you in your talent stand before all,
> A dandy in dress coat, handsome and tall;
> You glow in your glory for all to see,
> While I stand in the rear unimportantly.

Chekhov did not allow the first shock of a handkerchief flecked with blood to get in the way of the customary birthday celebration. However, his own expert medical knowledge belied the pious explanation which he had used to assuage the fears of family and friends over his recent illness. Besides, the telltale racking cough periodically returned and he was also aware of the history of tuberculosis on his mother's side of the family. But ugly truth fades before youth's enchantment with life. He imagined himself an Arcadian prince, he wrote the worried wife of Saveliev, because so many sympathetic friends had called on him during his illness. This same imagination transformed the fear of premature death into a young man's mirage of limitless time in which to achieve the ends of destiny. Whatever delusions Chekhov indulged in, there is incontrovertible evidence, even this early, that he recognized the stubborn fact of the potential seriousness of his illness. Passing references in his letters, written 1885–1886, to his coughing again, or comments that if he failed to move from a cold and musty flat his "cough-ing and blood-spitting" would return, were now accompanied by no disarming rationalizations. And in a letter to Taganrog to Uncle Mitro-fan, at the beginning of 1885, he wrote frankly of his recent illness and of his notion of borrowing money to go abroad for a cure or to the Crimea or the Caucasus, well-recognized localities for the treatment of victims of tuberculosis.

In this same letter, however, Chekhov made a point of assuring his uncle Mitrofan of his present good health and well-being. His medical practice improved bit by bit, and every day he spent more than a rouble on cabbies in visiting the sick. "I have many acquaintances," he writes, "and quite a few of them fall ill. I treat half of them gratis and the other half pays me three to five roubles a visit." Gently he rejected his uncle's suggestion that he settle in Taganrog. Though it might be quieter, healthier, and jollier there, he was interested not only in the practice but also in the science of medicine, and for this, as well as for his writing, Moscow was the logical place to be. "I have not yet ac-cumulated any capital and will hardly get rich quick," he admits. "But I live well enough and do not want for anything. If only I remain alive and in good health, the family's situation will be *secure*. I've bought new furniture, hired a fine piano, keep two servants, and give small musical evenings at which people sing and play. I'm not in debt and don't intend to get into it. Formerly we bought our provisions (meat and groceries) on credit. I've stopped that now and we pay cash for everything." (*January 31, 1885.*)

Chekhov exaggerated his record of success for Uncle Mitrofan's bene-fit, for it was a point of personal pride with him to assure this pious and well-doing relative, who often received begging letters from his brother Pavel Yegorovich, that the family responsibilities which his nephew had assumed were in capable hands. Indeed, the family had mounted an-other rung or two in its slow climb up the ladder since Chekhov began his medical practice. Ivan had left Voskresensk to take a more remu-nerative position in Moscow as head of an elementary school. Sister Masha had finished the Higher Course for Women and soon began to take instruction in painting and to teach history and geography in a private Moscow school for girls. And young Misha had just begun his studies in the School of Jurisprudence in the university. The unhappy artist Nikolai, whose bohemian ways and chronic drinking had become intolerable, had left the family and was living around the city with any friend who would take him in. He had completely surrendered to his weaknesses, which were aggravated, in his case also, by the dread signs of tuberculosis. Yet Chekhov's concern for this wayward brother never faltered. He continued to seek out artistic commissions for Nikolai and would bring him home to nurse him in his periods of illness.

Nikolai never demanded anything of his brother Anton, but Alexander's importunings went on ceaselessly. After leaving his position in Taganrog, he had worked for only a short time in St. Petersburg in the customs service before being transferred to Southern Russia to the post of secretary in the Novorossiisk customs office. Wherever he was or whatever he did, he moved in a self-created atmosphere of frustration and discontent; he complained constantly of living conditions, of his superiors on the job, or the people he worked with. The birth of another child added to his family burden, but he hopefully christened him "Anton." He accepted the honor, Chekhov wrote, and would give the baby a copy of his book and free medical service. More practically, Chekhov continued his efforts to increase his brother's income by giving him literary advice, arranging editorial contacts, and helping to place his manuscripts. Alexander had not been long in Novorossiisk when he wrote: "You haven't got married; well don't. Let life be an example to you. . . . I'm always in debt." He had eight persons to feed, he explained, himself and his wife, three children, and three servants. Chekhov found it hard to understand why his brother could not live in the provinces on 120–150 roubles a month when, a couple of years back, he himself had supported the whole Chekhov family in expensive Moscow on 100–120 roubles a month. Soon Alexander was pleading with him to borrow enough money to pay his debts and transport him and his family to Moscow or Petersburg from Novorossiisk, which he could no longer tolerate.

A touch of Alexander's improvidence existed in Chekhov's nature, and one form in which it manifested itself was his compulsive tendency to give rather than to receive. If he were unlikely to get rich soon in medicine, as he remarked to Uncle Mitrofan, one reason was his philanthropic attitude toward the practice of it. At first he worked hard, receiving patients from ten in the morning to two in the afternoon, and thereafter making calls. The calls often took him long distances and transportation expenses sometimes canceled the small fees he received.

On one occasion the inexperienced young physician, upon returning home from seeing a patient on the other side of the city, suddenly realized that the dosage of one of the ingredients he had prescribed would turn the remedy into a poison. He rushed back to his patient and arrived in time to prevent a catastrophe, but the cabby and not the doctor got the fee. Patients were numerous enough, but not paying ones. "My signature," he wrote to Leikin, "begins to take on a definite and fixed character which I attribute to the enormous number of prescriptions I write — of course, nearly all of them gratis." (*November 17, 1885.*) He became the favorite doctor of the indigent fraternity of newspaper and magazine writers, who constantly took advantage of his kindness. As a gesture of good will to the merchant Gavrilov, who employed his father, Chekhov readily agreed to provide free medical service to the firm's workers. And free advice to numerous friends of the family and to his own friends, in letters or in personal visits, made him wonder why had he not become a lawyer instead of a doctor. After many such visits to the home of his friend, the budding artist A. S. Yanov, where he treated Yanov's mother and three sisters for typhus, Chekhov left with the disturbing feeling that it might be wiser to drop his medical career. For their illness took a bad turn: the mother died, and then one of the daughters passed away while Chekhov, overwhelmed with a sense of futility, sat at the bedside holding her cold hand.

Nor did Chekhov's assurance to Uncle Mitrofan — that he lived well enough and wanted for nothing — bear much relation to his actual material situation. The main treat for his guests was still the cheap jellied-fish dish which his mother prepared so well. Knives and forks and a large teapot often had to be borrowed, and the dress coat in Alexander's jingle really belonged to a kind friend who loaned it to Chekhov when he attended the marriage of his colleague Dr. Rozanov. Pitifully small sums of money had to be borrowed. On February 17, 1886, he applied to the economics teacher, M. M. Dyukovsky, a close friend of the family: "I write so that you'll have still another manuscript of a great author. In ten to twenty years this letter may sell for 500–1000 roubles. I envy you." And then he asked for a loan of twenty-five roubles — "for I now have nothing but inspiration and an author's glory, but without firewood it gets cold." Hardly a week passed when he had to turn to him again for ten roubles more: "There's not a shadow of money in my pocket," he wrote. "Expenses are terrible." A summons to court by a creditor to discharge a hundred-and-five-rouble debt of Alexander and Nikolai reduced him almost to despair. In the face of Leikin's repeated urging to visit Petersburg, he finally answered with unaccustomed sharpness: "Owing to the fact that I live with a numerous family, I never have a spare two roubles in my pocket, and a minimum of fifty roubles would be required to make this trip even in the most uncomfortable and cheapest manner. And where am I to get the money? I find it impossible to squeeze this out of family expenses. To cut their dishes down from two to one would cause me twinges of remorse and conscience. . . . To write more than I do now is out of the question, for medicine is not like the law profession: if you do not work, you fall behind. Hence, my literary earnings are a fixed quantity. They may become less, but not more." (*October 12, 1885.*)

Actually Chekhov combined practicality in money matters with a wastefulness that resulted from an expansive nature which compelled him to seek the happiness of all around him whatever the cost. To meet him meant to receive an invitation to his house, and these invitations were made with such charm, humor, and persuasiveness that they were well-nigh irresistible. "I hope, now that we are almost neighbors," he wrote to his cousin Mikhail at this time, "you will not be an infrequent guest, at least every week. Except for Tuesday, Thursday, and sometimes on Saturdays, I'm always at home in the evenings. Come early so you can stay longer. *P.S.:* On Tuesdays I'm home after nine, on Thursday only until nine, so that there is not a single day when you risk not seeing me." (*October 12, 1885.*) And guests came in numbers and often, attracted by his magnetic charm; but such hospitality added considerably to the family expenses.

Indeed, Chekhov's world of personal contacts began to expand rapidly as soon as he embarked on his medical career. Heedless of the cost, he believed it essential to provide a more appropriate setting for his work and for the family and their many friends. To expunge the memory of the philistine drabness of their old Taganrog milieu and the impoverished haunts of the early Moscow years seemed progress of sorts. He rented a house in a residential section across the Moscow River but soon left it for one nearby the first but larger and pleasanter to live in. Here they could all lead a fuller life, with adequate room to entertain in style. For the first time he had a study to himself, which also served as a medical office. Tuesday evenings were devoted to music. Guests from the conservatory performed, and his own literary and artistic friends came as well as those of Misha and Masha, who was being courted at the time. Without compunction Chekhov would drop his work for any gay gathering. He loved to attend the regimental balls at the Alexandrovsky barracks. A week of carousing as best man at the wedding of Dr. Rozanov and celebrating both Saint Tatyana's Day — the annual student festival at the university — as well as his own twenty-sixth birthday, left him with "a heavy head, spots in the eyes, and despairing pessimism." Apropos of this he wrote a friend, "The holidays cost me about three hundred roubles. Now, isn't that insane?" (*January 18, 1886.*)

And Chekhov's world of practical activities also began to increase in scope. His reading in belles lettres was now supplemented by scientific journals and books. Darwin's works he found at this time a positive pleasure. "I like him terribly," he declared. And he continued to busy himself with the preparation of his "History of Russian Medicine" and to talk over with Dr. Rozanov the possibility of editing a new medical periodical.

Not infrequently Chekhov visited the studio of a group of young artists, many of whom were to become famous. They were providing the décor and scenic painting of an exciting new opera project in Moscow. When the spirit moved him he would entertain them with stories, most of them sheer improvisations, full of infectious humor and saturated with striking observations and unusual images. Not only the contents, but Chekhov's skill as an actor — his deep and finely modulated voice, mimetic ability, and effective gesturing — kept the company of artists in gales of laughter. The more unrestrained Levitan, recalls one of them, rolled on the floor and kicked his feet in delight.

In that spirit of levity which characterized much of the correspondence between the brothers, Chekhov wrote Alexander, on January 4, 1886: "I'm still unmarried and have no children." Nevertheless, the question of marriage seemed to be very much on his mind during this year. He envied his young friends such as Dr. Rozanov who had entered into matrimony, and his letters at this time were dotted with curious, often unconnected references to the need for a wife. When the niggardly Leïkin questioned him on how he spent his money, Chekhov forcefully declared: "On women! ! ! !" And in another letter he told the editor: "I ought not to be writing stories but falling in love." (*February 16, 1886.*) At one point it appears he was thinking of asking for the hand of Gavrilov's daughter, a step that would have delighted Chekhov's mother, who always hoped he would marry into the family of a rich merchant.[1]

There was also the "bouquet of pretty girl friends" his sister Masha brought home. And one of them — possibly a young lady by the name of Dunya Efros — became the object of his ardent pursuit, at least for a time. He confided in V. V. Bilibin, secretary of *Fragments* and a writer of ability with whom Chekhov had already struck up a friendly and frank correspondence: "Yesterday, while accompanying a certain young lady home, I proposed to her. I want to jump from the frying pan into the fire." (*January 18, 1886.*) Perhaps he turned to him because Bilibin had just become engaged and both he and his bride-to-be professed a warm interest in Chekhov's matrimonial intentions. "When I speak about women I like," he replied to one of their queries, "then I usually restrain my words . . . a trait remaining with me since my school days. Thank your fiancée for her regards and concern and tell her that my marriage is probably — alack and alas! The censor does not permit it . . . My *she* is a Jewess. Courage is necessary for a wealthy Jewess to accept orthodoxy with its consequences — well, it is not necessary and not needed. And we have already quarreled over this. Tomorrow we'll make it up and in a week we'll fall out again. Vexed that religion is a problem, she has broken pencils and a photograph on my table — this is characteristic of her. She is a terrible spitfire. I shall undoubtedly part from her within one or two years after marriage."[2]

How serious were Chekhov's intentions is unknown, as in the case of other women who entered his life. In subsequent letters to Bilibin over the early months of 1886, his "passion" for the spitfire seemed to dwindle into a kind of joke. There is no news about his marriage, he writes, and then mentions his recent acquaintance with a charming French girl. And in his next letter: "I'm still not married. I've *finally* parted with my fiancée. She broke off with me. But I've not bought a revolver and don't keep a diary. Everything in this world is changing, mutable, approximate, and relative." Then, on March 11, he informed Bilibin that he would write no more about his spitfire. "Perhaps you

[1] Chekhov mentioned the possibility of his marrying Gavrilov's daughter in a letter to his brother Alexander, March 24, 1888.

[2] February 1, 1886. The passages in Chekhov's letters to Bilibin referring to this mysterious affair are, for the most part, deleted in the Soviet *Polnoe sobranie sochinenii i pisem* (*Complete Works and Letters*). However, they have been restored in the publication of these letters in *Literaturnoe Nasledstvo* (*Literary Heritage*), Moscow, 1960, LXVIII, 162-173.

are right in saying that it is too soon for me to marry. I'm a bit giddy, even though I'm only a year younger than you. I still sometimes dream that I'm in school, terrified that the teacher will call on me when my lesson is unprepared. Obviously, I'm still a lad."[3]

« 2 »

"I terribly love anything that is called an estate in Russia. This word has still not lost its poetic sound," Chekhov wrote Leikin on October 12 after the latter informed him, in 1885, that he had just bought an estate. Perhaps Anton was thinking of the charming idyls in Turgenev's tales or the lyric atmosphere of love and gracious living on country estates in Tolstoy's writings. This traditional pattern of existence of the landed gentry not only aroused in Chekhov a yearning to experience its pleasures, but also was identified with his striving to move outside the confining circle of a petty shopkeeper's son. Though purchasing an estate was unthinkable, he did begin to dream, with his customary unconcern in such circumstance for his limited income, of renting a summer house.

With brother Ivan's move to Moscow, his Voskrensensk house was no longer available for the summer. Chekhov at first explored the possibility of renting a house near Zvenigorod, but it turned out to be unavailable. Then he learned that the Kiselevs, who owned an estate at Babkino, less than four miles from Voskresensk, were willing to rent a house — Ivan, who had been a tutor in the family, had introduced them to the Chekhovs during one of their visits to Voskresensk. With the aid of an advance of a hundred roubles from *Alarm Clock* and a conviction that he could earn the remainder of the expenses over the summer months, Chekhov hired his first *dacha*.

Loaded down with books, papers, a samovar, pots and pans, and jars of preserves, the Chekhov family arrived at Babkino at one in the morning in early May 1885. They quietly drove past the Kiselev mansion to their smaller hired house at the other end of the park. The door was open. They lit the lamps and discovered to their delight that the accommodations surpassed all their expectations — large, comfortable rooms, spotlessly clean, and well furnished. Their kind hostess had supplied washstands with water and placed cigarette boxes, ashtrays, and matches on the table. After emptying their suitcases, they sat down

[3] Dunya Efros, very likely the "fiancée" Chekhov mentions in the letter, eventually married E. Z. Konovitser, and they both remained close friends of the Chekhov family.

to vodka, wine, and a bite to eat. Before he turned in Chekhov looked out the window at the darkened trees and the river. The song of a nightingale suddenly burst upon the country stillness of the night. He could not believe his ears.

The next morning Chekhov, like an excited child on his first visit to the country, explored every corner of the Kiselev estate. The manor house, situated on the high bank of the Istra River, was surrounded by a huge English park, and beyond the stream unfolded a vista of forest broken by meadows and several ponds. Formal gardens brightened the approach to the buildings and near his own *dacha* were flower beds and a conservatory. The muffled sound of church bells coming from the edge of nearby Daraganovsky Forest seemed to accentuate the peacefulness of the scene.

Chekhov had barely arrived at Babkino when he received a letter from Alexander who congratulated him on his good fortune in being a friend of "Count" Kiselev and living on his estate, and he wondered what their grandfather, who had been one of the hired help on the estate of Count Platov, would have thought of all this. Actually A. S. Kiselev, the owner of Babkino, was only the nephew of a count, a distinguished diplomat during the reign of Nicholas I. He had married Mariya Vladimirovna, daughter of V. P. Begichev, the cultured and worldly director of the Imperial Theaters of Moscow. She was a beautiful, vivacious, strong-minded woman, and a successful writer of children's stories. The Kiselevs had two attractive youngsters, Alexandra (Sasha) and Seryozha. This typical "nest of gentlefolk" enjoyed all the refinements of the landed gentry — servants, tutors, governesses, the country pleasures of hunting and fishing, rich food, numerous visitors, and long evenings of card-playing or serious conversation on politics, literature, and the arts, readings from the leading reviews, and improvised musical concerts. However, an element of decay had already set in at Babkino as the generous and genteel owners thoughtlessly wasted their substance, and eventually it became the prototype for that other bankrupt estate in *The Cherry Orchard*.

Chekhov at once fell in love with Babkino and its happy family, and all the Kiselevs loved him. He had always felt conscious of the need to maintain his self-esteem among Taganrog and Moscow associates, who often forgot their own worth in bowing and scraping before every symbol of authority. Though he had no desire to elevate himself above others, he could not tolerate the condescension of rank or superior social status. With the circle at Babkino, however, he at once felt at his ease. The world he had grown up in vanished in their company. A mutual recognition of human worth was the basis of their friendly intercourse. And how could they fail to accept him? With his gifts for sociability, he was in no time on the most intimate terms with the Kiselevs, their children, and visitors. He evinced an intense interest in everything that concerned them, and with his love of fun and practical jokes, he quickly became the center of hilarity in this circle.

There was work to do, however, if he were to pay for all this summer pleasure. Chekhov arose at seven and sat writing all morning on a discarded sewing-machine table, looking out of the huge square window of his room at the warm landscape of river and the woods beyond. The fresh impressions and new experiences at Babkino provided him with material for a number of tales. He also used as themes anecdotes that Mariya Kiseleva translated for him from French periodicals. Nor did he neglect his medicine. For several days he substituted for Dr. Arkhangelsky at the Chikino rural hospital, and as soon as the peasants around Babkino learned that he was a physician, they came with their ills. "The sick swarm here and plague me," he wrote Leikin. "In the course of the summer several hundred have come and I've earned the total of one rouble." (*September 14, 1885*.) His sister and Mariya Kiseleva assisted him in this work, for the mistress of an estate in a remote country district often treated peasants for minor ills. Masha recalls how terrified they became after lancing an abscess, because they mistakenly believed they had employed a scalpel which Chekhov had used in an autopsy, and she also worried about feeding a peasant camphor instead of castor oil, although the patient returned the next day cheerfully looking for more of the remedy.

The afternoons Chekhov devoted to varied relaxation. Though he went hunting once and brought down a hare, his favorite sport was fishing. Often Mariya Kiseleva would accompany him and they sat for hours, dividing their time between fishing and talking about literature. Or little Seryozha and Sasha, who adored Chekhov for his fun-making, would persuade him to go picking mushrooms in the woods or to play croquet. To amuse them he wrote a spoofing tale, "Soft-boiled Boots," which he illustrated with pictures he cut out of old newspapers and magazines.

Returning from his afternoon excursions, Chekhov applied himself again to writing and medicine until supper at eight. After the meal, all gathered in the drawing room of the Kiselevs. Many eminent figures in the musical, literary, and theatrical world were well known to the host and hostess or to Begichev, and the conversation frequently dwelt upon their artistic accomplishments or private lives. Mariya Kiseleva told of her acquaintance with Dargomyzhsky and Tschaikovsky, who at one time had been in love with her. Indeed, Chekhov's first critical contact with music began in this household, where it was a cult. In the evenings the well-known tenor of the Grand Theater, M. P. Vladislavlev, sang to the accompaniment of the governess, an accomplished pianist; the hostess, who had a fine voice, also sang. The songs and piano selections, especially Chopin's Nocturnes, deeply moved Chekhov. When the moon was up, these concerts were often concluded by the governess's playing Beethoven's Moonlight Sonata, which she did to perfection. The lights were extinguished, and Chekhov usually sat alone on the stoop by the open door. At the conclusion of the performance all the company silently departed.

Chekhov introduced the Babkino circle to a different form of entertainment. His friend Levitan dropped in at the estate and Chekhov promptly invited him to stay at his *dacha* so that they could go hunting together, a sport to which the artist was devoted. The following summer at Babkino, Chekhov learned that Levitan was hiding out at a village a short distance away and had fallen into one of his habitual periods of melancholia. With his brothers Misha and Ivan, Chekhov organized a surprise visit at night in a downpour of rain. They finally found the hut and, like a trio of bandits in their outlandish garb, they dashed in and thrust a lantern into the face of the sleeping artist. "The devil knows what this is!" he exclaimed, and he jumped from his bed and seized a revolver. Soon they were all roaring with laughter and Levitan's melancholy vanished.

Within a few days the painter was invited to stay at Babkino, for the Kiselevs were well acquainted with his work. Though excessively temperamental and a demonstrative and incorrigible flirt, he and Chekhov were kindred spirits in their extravagant sense of fun. Chekhov put a sign up over his guest's door, "Pawnshop of the Merchant Levitan," and read humorous verses about his visit to Babkino. Once the two friends, dressed as Bedouins, their faces blackened with soot, went out into the open field; while Levitan prayed to the East on a rug, Chekhov shot a blank cartridge at him from the bushes and carted the "corpse" away. On another occasion Chekhov staged an elaborate trial, with Levitan as the defendant, Kiselev as judge, and himself, dressed in a gold-embroidered outfit which he borrowed from his host, as the prosecuting attorney. In a speech he brought indictments against Levitan for evading military service, maintaining an illegal distillery from which Nikolai Chekhov obtained his liquor, and running a private pawnshop. Misha testifies that Chekhov's amazing histrionic ability "made us all die of laughter."

The married sister of the hostess, Nadezhda Golubeva, tells of her introduction to these high jinks on her visit to Babkino from Petersburg during Chekhov's last summer there. A large number of guests had come, for a dance had been planned. As a newcomer to these things, she grew frightened when during one game of charades four howling Ethiopians entered into the room, carrying a stretcher on which sat a terrible Turk. They went straight to her, and the Turk brandished a scimitar over her head. The maskers were no less bewildered than she was by her cries of terror. Finally the Turk jumped down and gallantly presented himself: "The artist Levitan!" The Ethiopians, upon removing their masks, turned out to be the four Chekhov brothers. In the confusion the whole point of the charade had been lost. Chekhov, in directing the dance that followed, invented so many amusing and exhausting figures that the laughing guests, out of breath, pleaded with him to cease. Nadezhda Golubeva recalled her sister's words about Chekhov: "He is amazingly talented and has a refined understanding of people. Although he is still so young and has only just finished medical school, he possesses an enormous fund of humor, an extraordinary poetic sadness, and a profound comprehension of the human soul."

Often the two men roamed about the picturesque countryside, Chekhov with a fishpole and Levitan with a shotgun for which he sometimes substituted an easel and brushes. Though both were nature enthusiasts, Chekhov brought to his admiration a spontaneous quality of enchantment with all of God's wonders. Like a lad with his first sweetheart, he seemed to find in nature ever new and delightful surprises, and he returned home from a contemplation of its beauties with the exhilaration — as he aptly put it — of a lover returning from a rendezvous. In his wanderings through the fields and woods about Babkino, alone or in the company of Levitan, Chekhov learned to observe nature closely and to possess it in his imagination. Soon these impressions were transformed into sentient, descriptive passages variously mirroring the moods of his characters and serving as a contrapuntal effect in the action of his tales. And Levitan, Russia's greatest landscape painter, wrote him: "I do not speak about the mass of very interesting thoughts, but the landscapes in these tales are the height of perfection. . . ."

Though the languid-eyed Levitan, with his shock of black hair and nervous manner, was always a favorite visitor at Babkino during Chekhov's stays there, his volatile nature, changing swiftly from melancholy to mirth caused as much misery as merriment. For him to see an attractive woman was to make love to her. And once, meeting Masha on a wooded path at Babkino, he dropped on his knees and declared his passion: "Sweet Mafa [he pronounced the Russian *sh* sound as *f*], every feature of your face is precious to me." The shocked Masha could think of nothing better to do than run to her room and cry. When she failed to appear at dinner Chekhov investigated and Masha told him through her tears what had happened. She reports him as replying: "Of course, if you want to, marry him, but bear in mind that he needs a woman of the Balzac type and not one such as you." Masha did not quite know what he meant, but she sensed that he was warning her. She kept clear of Levitan for a week, giving him no answer, and he went about gloomy and morose. Eventually they resumed their old, friendly relations and Levitan aided her in her first efforts to paint, professing to see a real talent in Masha. Chekhov, whose central position in Masha's life had already begun to manifest itself, must have breathed easier — he had kept a beloved sister and also a friend who was near and dear to him. With the tenacious memory of a woman for whom the self-justification of old-maidhood became a necessity, Masha commented many years later about this "romance" with Levitan: "In truth, he more than once told me, and repeated not long before his death when he was seriously ill and I visited him: 'If I had ever married, Mafa, then it would only have been you.'"

As Chekhov's first happy summer at Babkino drew to a close, inevitable financial difficulties began to plague him. Even money to transport the family and their effects back to Moscow was lacking. Twice he wrote Leikin for funds, threatening that if two hundred roubles were not forthcoming he would have to remain in Babkino for the winter. His worries were further aggravated, his friend Dr. Rozanov reported, by the fact that he had once again begun to cough and spit blood. By the end of September, however, the money arrived and he returned to Moscow. In his bread-and-butter letter to Mariya Kiseleva, he complained that Moscow was "hellishly boring," that he saw Sasha and Seryozha in his dreams, and that he could think of nothing except "fishing poles, perch, creels, and the worms in the expanse of green lawn." (*October 1 or 2, 1885.*)

« 3 »

In the spring of 1885 Chekhov enjoyed a piece of good fortune: Leikin offered to persuade the editor of the big daily newspaper, *Petersburg Gazette*, to accept him as a regular contributor of a weekly story. He grasped the opportunity, for this publication would allow him more freedom than *Fragments* in the selection of themes and in the length of his tales. *The Last of the Mohicans*, his first story in *Petersburg Gazette*, appeared on May 6, and he continued to write regularly for this newspaper to the end of 1888.

Leikin's good offices in this instance were a calculated risk. It was clearly to his advantage to aid the career of his brilliant young contributor, whose discovery as "another Saltykov-Shchedrin" he had been proudly taking credit for in Petersburg literary circles. Yet he also hoped that this gesture of good will would bind Chekhov closer to him with the glue of gratitude. And since the newspaper's space rates were less than those of his own publication, he did not fear its financial competition for Chekhov's services.

In a further effort to ingratiate himself, Leikin undertook to publish, under *Fragments* imprint, Chekhov's next collection of tales. In agreeing to his terms — the initial profits to be used to retire publication costs, and subsequent income to be divided equally between them — Chekhov wrote with perhaps more sarcasm than intentional self-depreciation: "As you've probably observed, I'm in general impractical, trusting, and a milksop." (*January 28, 1886.*) He requested only that his friend, the architect F. O. Shekhtel, be allowed to draw the vignette for the book — he was a patient and would do it free. Actually the thrifty Leikin took no unusual risk in this venture and anticipated a substantial profit, as well as added prestige, for his imprint. For he had been deliberately concealing from his protégé Chekhov's growing popularity among Petersburg readers, who were beginning to ask about Antosha Chekhonte: "Who is this person? Where does he live? What's the point of this strange pseudonym?"

Leikin's attempts, however, to turn Chekhov into a submissive and model contributor to his magazine failed to overcome the mounting asperity in their relations. Chekhov's decision in 1885 to abandon his column, "Fragments of Moscow Life," particularly annoyed the editor. But Leikin became thoroughly angry over the repeated appearance of an assortment of tales in Moscow humorous magazines under the pseudonym Chekhonte. Chekhov tried to explain that the Moscow editors were using his pseudonym against his wishes, and that he would try in the future to restrict it to *Fragments*. "I would be happy to drop all work for *Alarm Clock* [one of the offending magazines]," he wrote, "but I don't think you would want this. The odd thirty, forty and sometimes fifty roubles a month, thank God, are of help to a proletarian like myself. . . . However much I write and however often I send you my prose, my remuneration does not cease to fluctuate between forty-five and sixty-five roubles a month." (*November 23, 1885.*) The comparison was pointed, and so was his hint that *Fragments* paid him inadequately.

Chekhov's changing opinion on Leikin and his policies is reflected in correspondence with Bilibin about the details of the preparation of his book. He went into the matter with some care, as though convinced that this second effort would be of much more consequence to him than *Tales of Melpomene*. Bilibin tried unsuccessfully to persuade Leikin to raise his payments to Chekhov. If Leikin had agreed, Chekhov commented after Bilibin's failure, the editor would have felt it necessary to contribute twice as much of his own writing to *Fragments* in order to offset the increase in the magazine's budget. "Heaven forbid! Pity the man." (*March 11, 1886.*)

At the end of 1885, however, Leikin, while on a business trip to Moscow, made a generous gesture: at his own expense, he invited his protégé to accompany him back to Petersburg for his first trip to that city. Chekhov stayed with Leikin from December 10–24. He had long been dreaming of this trip. Petersburg had become the literary center of Russia; it was the home of M. E. Saltykov-Shchedrin, D. V. Grigorovich, N. S. Leskov, V. M. Garshin, Gleb Uspensky, and A. N. Pleshcheev; and in the writings of the city's great dead — Pushkin, Dostoevsky, Nekrasov — the image of Petersburg lived forever. As he drove from the railway station to Leikin's house and gazed at the broad thoroughfares and beautiful buildings, there was now nothing about him of the provincial youth who only eight years before had arrived in Moscow for his first visit and gaped in unsophisticated wonder at the city's manifold attractions. Now he felt socially secure, was the "head" of a family, a practicing physician, and nearly every week his short stories were appearing in two of the important publications of this city.

Nevertheless, his reception in Petersburg took him completely by surprise. He had expected the editorial staffs of *Fragments* and *Petersburg Gazette* to evince some interest in him, and he found Bilibin the friendly, refined, and discriminating writer and critic that he had imagined him to be from his letters. (The staff of *Petersburg Gazette*, he observed, greeted him "like a Persian shah.") But he was amazed to discover that well-known publicists and authors such as A. S. Suvorin, the wealthy owner of the most powerful daily *New Times* and a writer and dramatist of some note, and V. P. Burenin, one of that newspaper's celebrated contributors, and the old and distinguished novelist Grigorovich, and others, were not only glad to meet him but had been critically reading and appreciating his stories! Leikin, though associated with these circles, had given him no inkling of this.

After Chekhov's return to Moscow, he hurried to write Alexander in a tone of excited exaggeration: "You must remember that all Petersburg follows the work of the Chekhov brothers. I was struck by the reception which the Petersburgers accorded me. . . . All invited me and sang my praises. If I had known that they were reading me, I would never have written things to order. So remember, they read you." (*January 4, 1886.*) And he told Bilibin two weeks later: "Formerly, when I didn't know that they read my tales and passed judgment on them, I wrote serenely, just the way I eat pancakes; now, I'm afraid when I write."

And to kind Uncle Mitrofan in Taganrog, who had visited the Chekhov family several months before, he euphorically wrote that his head was dizzy from the praise showered on him in Petersburg; that he had superb accommodations there, a pair of horses, splendid meals, and tickets gratis to all the theaters. Never had life been so sweet to him, he concluded.

In still another letter to Alexander about his visit, Chekhov significantly declared: "Leikin, for whom my presence in Petersburg was in many respects disadvantageous . . . is a liar, a liar." (*February 3, 1886.*) He had learned that Leikin had concealed the success of his literary efforts in Petersburg from him and, in his own interests, had been trying to discourage the idea of his availability to other publications in the city. Chekhov could hardly afford to break with Leikin at this stage; besides, he felt grateful to him for giving him his first real chance to publish regularly in a respected magazine; but he was determined now not to allow *Fragments* to interfere any longer with the type of story he wrote or where he published.

« 4 »

For a few influential people in Petersburg's journalistic and literary circles, Chekhov's visit had attached a name and a vital personality to a pseudonym about which they had been curious for some time. Soon those forces behind the scene which could help to shape a literary career were set in motion. Thus: The eminent novelist Grigorovich drew Suvorin's attention to Chekhov's exceptionally fine tale, *The Hunter*, which had appeared in *Petersburg Gazette*. Impressed both by the story and by his meeting with Chekhov, Suvorin, at the beginning of January 1886, sent him an invitation to contribute to *New Times*, an offer that would have gone to the head of any young Russian author. "I'm happy over it . . . and envy you," wrote Bilibin when he learned the news, and in the same letter he reported that Leikin had said sourly: "Let him publish his longer pieces there."

In February, *The Requiem*, Chekhov's first tale in *New Times*, appeared, and his long association with this newspaper and its distinguished editor began. Suvorin paid him twelve kopecks a line, the highest rate he had ever received. Chekhov jubilantly informed the sympathetic Bilibin that his second story in *New Times* "brought me seventy-five roubles, somewhat more than a month's income from *Fragments*." (*March 11, 1886.*) He might have added that neither did Suvorin, unlike Leikin, place any limitations on the length of his tales or fix deadlines for their delivery. These were valued concessions, for, as he explained to Leikin, before he had finished the first page of a story, a patient would enter his study for medical aid, and by the time the second page was written, an urgent message would summon him to the sickbed of a friend. Then dinner would interfere with the third page . . . and so on.

So pleased was Chekhov with these new conditions of work that he warmly thanked Suvorin in a letter that initiated one of his most extensive correspondences with a single individual. "I write comparatively little," he declared in an incredible understatement, "not more than two or three short stories a week. But the hours for *New Times* will be found," he assured him, "and I rejoice over the conditions of my collaboration." And with ingratiating but understandable humility before this powerful mogul of the publishing world, he added: "Thank you for the flattering things you say about my work and for having printed my story so soon. You may judge for yourself how refreshing, even inspiring, has been the kind attention of an experienced and gifted person like you in the matter of my writing. I agree about the end of my story which you have deleted and I'm grateful for your helpful advice. I've been writing for the last six years, but you are the first person who has taken the trouble to advise and explain." (*February 21, 1886.*) At Suvorin's request, Chekhov allowed *New Times* to publish his stories under his own name.

For the first time, Chekhov glimpsed a literary career that might go beyond the limitations and banalities of the humorous magazines. To Bilibin he confided a fresh hope: "I will write a big thing, but on the condition that you'll find a place for it among the offerings of the thick journals [the great quality periodicals that printed the belles lettres of famous authors]. After my debut in *New Times,* is it possible to suppose that they will now accept me in some one of the thick periodicals? What do you think? Or am I mistaken?" (*February 28, 1886.*)

Chekhov's hopes were perhaps stimulated by what he felt was greater freedom in the selection and treatment of themes. Though he continued to specialize in humor, he was handling serious subjects more and more over 1885 and the early months of 1886, and with an independence that bore the hallmark of the emancipated artist. Boldly he informed Leikin, about the manuscript of *Anyuta* sent to *Fragments:* "There is nothing illiberal in it. Indeed, it is time to get rid of hedging." (*February 3, 1886.*) Sure enough, the censor objected; not so much because Anyuta was the mistress of the student in the story as because she had served several other men in this capacity.

The frequency with which this dread dragon either banned outright or demanded changes in Chekhov's stories eloquently testifies to the author's persistence in writing as he pleased. "How oppressive and shocking," he wrote Leikin when the latter fulminated against the severity of the censorship. "How unreliable is the bit of bread literature gives us . . ." (*October 12, 1885.*) Chekhov could ill afford to lose his fee for each banned story, and at times he would agree to deletions if they seemed of little consequence. So arbitrarily did the censorship function that it was often possible to outwit it by the simple device of changing the title of a tale and sending it to another magazine. This was the procedure used in the case of Chekhov's famous story *Sergeant*

Prishibeyev. He had submitted it first to Leikin under the title A *Super-fluous Guardian.* With his usual obtuseness to artistic merit, Leikin found it too long and dull in parts, and cut it in order to "lessen the dullness." But the story failed to get through the Censorship Committee, which declared: "This piece belongs to those in which ugly social faults are described, revealing the consequences of increased police surveillance. Because of the exaggeration of the harm of such surveillance, the piece cannot be accepted." Chekhov changed the title to *Sergeant Prishibeyev* and sent it to *Petersburg Gazette,* where it was published, with the approval of the censor, pretty much in the form in which he had originally written it.

The range of observation, emotion, and satire had noticeably broadened and deepened in the best tales of 1885–1886, and Chekhov's accuracy in the language of description and dialogue was rapidly approaching the perfection of his later masterpieces. His experiences at Babkino increased his interest in and knowledge of the peasant type appearing in the rambling old woman of A *Tedious Business.* She so confused the village deacon in listing her relatives for prayers for the dead that both the living and the dead become inextricably mingled in his head in a cynical catalogue of sameness that does blasphemous violence to a holy rite. And the peasant hero of *The Hunter,* an exquisite fusion of nature's sultry moods and the emotional frustration of unrequited love, is brilliantly characterized through the effective use of dialogue that poses the hopeless opposition of a peasant girl's longing and the hunter's love of open fields and cool forests with gun on shoulder. The same device of skillful dialogue reveals perfectly the peasant mentality of Denis Grigoriev in *The Malefactor,* who stubbornly argues with the magistrate his right to unscrew nuts from the bolts of the railroad tracks — after all, there are so many of them, and they make ideal sinkers for fishing lines!

In other tales of this period, biting and realistic satire is employed to expose the vulgarity of the spoiled rich — for example, that of the wife in *An Upheaval.* When a brooch disappears (her weak-willed husband, whose fortune she has appropriated, had stolen it) she has the room of the shy young governess Mashenka searched — "I for one don't trust these learned paupers too far." And Mashenka, for the first time in her life, experiences the feeling "that is so familiar to persons in dependent positions who eat the bread of the rich and powerful and cannot speak their minds." In A *Calamity,* however, the youth Chekhov displays surprisingly mature psychological insight in probing the complex emotional struggle that goes on in the mind of a notary public's pretty wife who is passionately pursued by her husband's lawyer friend. When the lover compels her to admit insincerity in denying him, he then cynically reassures her by declaring that "only savages and animals are sincere. Once civilization has ushered in the need for such comforts as, for example, feminine virtue, sincerity is out of place." When she finally recognizes the danger of succumbing to her lover's pleas, and begs her obtuse husband to take her away on a trip, he offers instead a silly, sententious homily on husbandly prerogatives, on which Chekhov comments: "There are a great many opinions in this world, and a good half of them are professed by people who have never been in trouble."

This rich fare Chekhov could vary with the simple and beautifully written story, *Grief*, of the old Petersburg cabby who had no one to talk to about the death of his son. Attempts to confide his sorrow to passengers on this snowy night, the description of which is so perfectly attuned to his sad, gently litany, are unfeelingly blocked by a wall of human indifference. Yet he must tell someone of the sorrow that burdens his soul. So after he has stabled his little mare, he begins: "Supposing, now, you had a foal, and you were own mother to that foal. . . . And supposing suddenly that little foal were to die. . . . You'd be sorry, wouldn't you?" The horse chews as its master feeds it, breathes on his hand, and listens.

Such enduring tales, however, amount to only a small fraction of the more than a hundred stories Chekhov produced in 1885 and the first few months of the following year. In the welter of average pieces, not infrequently cluttered with low comedy and tasteless witticisms, these few perfectly chiseled works of art, such as *The Hunter*, *Grief*, and *Sergeant Prishibeyev*, seem almost like accidental fruits of his genius. The continued haste with which he wrote and the uncomplaining way in which he at times accepted the inept editorializing of Leikin on some of his masterpieces suggest that he did not really understand or value his gifts. To be sure, with his inborn modesty about everything connected with his creative art, no writer ever undervalued his artistic powers more grossly than Chekhov, and especially in the early years of his career. He constantly referred to his tales as "rubbish," "junk," "a chewed rag," and if he nurtured any artistic ambitions, he never wore them on his sleeve. When he agreed to Suvorin's request to sign his own name to his stories, he admitted that he had always thought of restricting his signature to learned medical articles that he wished to write. "My family name and crest I've given to medicine, which I shall not desert for the rest of my life," he declared to Bilibin. "Sooner or later I shall part with literature."[4] Nor were the Moscow authors with whom he associated likely to encourage in him a sense of the importance of his art and the necessity of valuing his readers. For to these literary hacks and journalists of the humorous magazines, whose sole concern with writing was a commercial one, with few exceptions he was, at best, a talented entertainer. Artistically he had become a lonely figure among them. Up to this point Chekhov lacked the advice and encouragement of older authors of distinction, who might have taught him to adopt a serious attitude toward his art and to develop a sense of self-criticism.

« 5 »

Chekhov's visit to Petersburg jolted him out of his accustomed attitude that writing was solely a means of adding to his income. The knowledge that at least a few people of literary merit read his fiction with an eye to something other than mere entertainment awakened in him a fresh understanding of that lofty spiritual worth which obligated the artist to all. Three months after this visit he received his first letter from a nationally famous author, the venerable Grigorovich, whom he had met briefly in Petersburg. Gripped by the dawning awareness of a newly discovered destiny, Chekhov was moved almost to tears by the contents:

"DEAR SIR, ANTON PAVLOVICH:

"About a year ago I read by chance a story of yours in *Petersburg Gazette*; I do not recall its title. I remember only that I was struck by its qualities of outstanding originality and chiefly its remarkable accuracy and truthfulness in its descriptions of people and nature.

"Since then I have read everything that bore the signature of Chekhonte, although I was inwardly vexed at a man who held so poor an opinion of himself as to consider the use of a pseudonym necessary. While reading you, I continually advised Suvorin and Burenin to follow my example. They listened to me and now, like me, they do not doubt

[4] February 14, 1886 — *Literaturnoe Nasledstvo* (*Literary Heritage*), Moscow, 1960, LXVIII, 165.

that you have *real* talent — a talent which places you in the front rank among writers in the new generation.

"I am not a journalist nor a publisher. I can be useful to you only as one of your readers. If I speak of your talent, I speak out of conviction. I am almost sixty-five, but I still feel so much love for literature and follow its success with so much ardor and rejoice when I find in it something living and gifted, that I cannot refrain — as you see — from holding out both hands to you.

"But this is by no means all. Here is what I wish to add. By virtue of the varied attributes of your undoubted talent — the precise truth of your internal analysis, your mastery of description (the snowstorm, the night, the background in *Agafya* etc.), the plasticity of your feelings which in a few lines projects a complete picture (the clouds above the setting sun 'like ashes over dying coals,' etc.) — I am convinced that you are destined to create some admirable and truly artistic works. And you will be guilty of a great moral sin if you do not live up to these hopes. All that is needed is esteem for the talent which so rarely falls to one's lot. Cease to write hurriedly. I do not know what your financial situation is. If it is poor, it would be better for you to go hungry, as we did in our day, and save your impressions for a mature, finished work, written not in one sitting, but during the happy hours of inspiration. One such work will be valued a hundred times higher than a hundred fine stories scattered among the newspapers at various times. In one leap you will reach the goal and will gain the notice of cultivated people and then all the reading public.

"Why is it that you often have motifs with pornographical nuances at the basis of your tales? Truthfulness and realism not only do not exclude refinement but even gain from it. You have such a powerful sense of form and a feeling for the plastic, that you have no special need, for example, to speak about dirty feet with turned-in toenails or a clerk's navel. These details add exactly nothing to the artistic beauty of a description and only spoil the impression among readers of taste. Have the generosity to forgive such observations, for I resolved to make them only because I sincerely believe in your talent and with all my soul desire its fullest development.

"Several days ago I was told that you are publishing a book of tales. If it is to appear under the pseudonym of CHE-KHON-TE, I beg you earnestly to telegraph the publishers to print it under your real name. After your recent stories in *New Times* and the success of *The Hunter*, the book will also have great success. It would be agreeable to have some assurance that you are not angry over my remarks, but that you accept them in the spirit that I write — not as an authority but out of the simplicity of an old heart."

Grigorovich's letter caused an emotional explosion in Chekhov. There, staring him in the face, was at last the recognition — and from an authority he could respect — which his whole being cried out for. Buried in his subconscious, perhaps ever since the days of his schoolboy scribbling, had been an image of himself as a literary artist. All the timidity, reticence, and modesty of his nature had prevented him from positively identifying himself with such a lofty ambition. And now Grigorovich, the celebrated author of two minor classics, *The Village* and *Anton Goremyka*, had told him, a former shopkeeper's son, that he had "real talent" and was destined to create "admirable and truly artistic works." It was like the longed-for answer to a prayer which he had never had the courage to utter. Three days later (*March 28, 1886*) Chekhov replied in perhaps the most emotional and outspoken letter of the several thousands that he wrote during his lifetime:

"Your letter, my kind, warmly beloved herald of glad tidings, struck me like a thunderbolt. I nearly wept, I was profoundly moved, and even now I feel that it has left a deep imprint on my soul. As you have smiled on my youth, so may God give you peace in your old age. I, indeed, can find neither words nor actions to show my gratitude. You know with what eyes ordinary people look upon such outstanding people like yourself, hence you may realize what your letter means for my self-esteem. It is worth more than any diploma, and for a beginning author it is an honorarium now and for the future. I am as in a daze. I lack the ability to judge whether or not I merit this great reward. I only repeat that it has overwhelmed me.

"If I have a gift which must be respected, then before the purity of your heart I confess that I have not respected it up to now. I felt that I had such a gift, but I had grown accustomed to regarding it as insignificant. Reasons of a purely external nature suffice to render one excessively mistrustful and suspicious toward oneself. Such reasons, as I now recall, I had in abundance. My whole family have always referred condescendingly to my work as a writer and have never ceased offering me friendly advice not to give up a real profession for scribbling. I have hundreds of friends in Moscow and among them a score of writers, yet I cannot recall a single one who would read me or recognize me as an artist. In Moscow there is a so-called 'Literary Circle.' Talented and mediocre people of all kinds and ages meet there once a week to gossip in the private room of a restaurant. If I were to go there and read even a bit of your letter, they would laugh in my face. During the five years of my roaming from newspaper to newspaper, I became infected with their own common views on the triviality of literature and soon grew accustomed to regarding my own work slightingly — so I simply sat down and wrote! That is the first reason. The second is that I am a physician and up to my neck in medicine. No one has lost more sleep than I have over the fable of hunting two hares at one time.

"I write all this to justify to you, in some small degree, my grievous sin. Hitherto I have treated my own literary work frivolously, carelessly, without thinking. I do not recall *a single* tale of mine over which I have worked more than a day, and *The Hunter*, which pleased you, I wrote in the bathhouse! I have written my stories the way reporters write up their notes about fires — mechanically, half-consciously, caring nothing about either the reader or myself. I wrote and tried in every way not to waste on my tales images and pictures which were clear to me and which, God knows why, I kept to myself and carefully concealed.

"What first drove me to take a critical view of my writing was a very charming and, as far as I can judge, a sincere letter from Suvorin.[5] I began to think of writing some purposeful piece, but nevertheless I did not have faith in my own literary direction.

"And now, all of a sudden, your letter arrived. You must forgive the comparison, but it had the same effect on me as a government order 'to get out of the city in twenty-four hours'! That is, I suddenly felt the absolute necessity for haste, to get out of this rut, where I am stuck, as quickly as possible.

"I agree with you in everything. The cynical effects which you attribute to me I myself felt when I saw *The Witch* in print. They would not have been there if this tale had been written in three or four days instead of one.

"I will free myself from hurried work, but not just yet. It is not possible to get out of the rut into which I have fallen. I do not refuse

[5] After Chekhov's death, Suvorin suggested to Masha, who intended to prepare an edition of her brother's letters, that he give her all of Chekhov's letters to him in return for his to Chekhov. This was done; subsequently, Suvorin's letters disappeared. It is possible that he feared the publication of intimate matters and expressions of liberal political opinions in his many letters to Chekhov.

to suffer hunger, for I have already gone hungry, but it is not a question of myself alone. I devote my leisure to writing, two to three hours a day and a little at night — that is, only time enough for small undertakings. In the summer, when I shall have more leisure and fewer expenses, I'll settle to work in earnest.

"I cannot place my own name on my book because it is too late; the cover design is ready and the book is printed. Many Petersburgers apart from yourself advised me not to spoil the volume by using a pseudonym, but I did not listen to them, probably out of vanity. I do not like the book at all. It is a hotch-potch, an untidy accumulation of student pieces marred by the censorship and the editors of humorous magazines. I believe that many, in reading it, will be disappointed. If I had known that I was being read and that you were watching me, I would not have let the book be published.

"All my hopes lie entirely in the future. I am only twenty-six. Perhaps I shall manage to do something, although time passes quickly.

"Please excuse this long letter and do not blame a man who, for the first time in his life, has dared to pamper himself with the great pleasure of a letter to Grigorovich.

"Send me, if possible, your photograph. I have been so encouraged and stirred up by you that I ought to write you not a mere sixteen pages but a whole ream. May God give you happiness and health, and please believe in the sincerity of a profoundly respectful and grateful A. CHEKHOV."

Part II

FIRST FAME AS A WRITER
1886–1889

CHAPTER VII

"Schiller Shakespearovich Goethe"

PRAISE IS A DEVIOUS DESTROYER of modesty, and at the age of twenty-six Chekhov's innate humility of common sense succumbed for a time to old Grigorovich's "discovery" of his talent. Letters went flying in all directions. With that determination of the ex-shop boy to impress his Taganrog shop-owning uncle, Mitrofan, Chekhov began by telling him of his literary earnings from *New Times*: "Yesterday I received from this newspaper 232 roubles for three average-sized tales, printed in three issues. It's a miracle! I simply do not believe my own eyes. And the small *Petersburg Gazette* gives me 100 roubles a month for four stories." (Only a week before he had pleaded with Bilibin, secretary of *Fragments*, to send him money, for he had only four roubles in his pocket.) "But this is not so important as the following," he continued. Then he related the story of Grigorovich's long letter, emphasizing this author's importance as a "great writer." The sample he quoted includes the praise ". . . You have a *real* talent — a talent which places you in the front rank among writers in the new generation." And after quoting from his reply, Chekhov added: "My answer delighted the old man. I received from him another and a still longer letter and his photograph." Then Chekhov, who years later modestly refused to contribute a biographical introduction to an edition of his works, declared to his uncle: "If, God grant, I describe my life in print in the course of the next ten to fifteen years, I will indicate my gratitude to you before all the reading public; but now I can only press your hand." Perhaps a bit ashamed of this degree of self-glorification, he cautiously mentioned at the end of his letter that it should be shown only to members of his uncle's family. (*April 11, 1886.*)

The glorious story had already been told for Bilibin's benefit. Since he was corresponding with an accomplished writer, however, Chekhov tempered Grigorovich's eulogy with a grain of self-depreciation: "He points out that I have *real* talent (and he underlines this), and as evidence of my artistic ability, he cites passages from my tales. He writes warmly and sincerely. Of course, I'm happy, although I feel that Grigorovich has gone a bit too far." (*April 4, 1886.*)

To Brother Alexander, still sadly stewing in his hated post as a customs official in Novorossiisk, Chekhov now in turn played the part of a kind of heavy-handed Grigorovich. The batch of stories which Alexander had sent him were all roundly condemned, with one exception. "Did you write them in a single day?" he asks. "For Christ's sake, esteem yourself. Do not set your hand to anything when your brain is lazy! Don't write more than two tales a week, cut and polish them carefully so that your work will bear the aspect of work. Do not invent sufferings that you've never experienced, and do not paint pictures you never saw, for a lie in a tale is even more boring than in a conversation. . . . I conclude this sermon with a quotation from a letter which I recently received from Grigorovich: 'All that is needed is esteem for the talent which so rarely falls to one's lot . . . save your impressions for a mature, finished work, written not in one sitting. . . . In one leap you will reach the goal and will gain the notice of cultivated people and then all the reading public.'" And with a swagger he concludes: "Leikin has gone out of fashion. I have taken his place. For in Petersburg now I'm in the height of fashion and I would not want to see you left behind." (*April 6, 1886.*)

In this letter to Alexander, Chekhov mentioned that he would soon go to Petersburg to meet Grigorovich, who had a government sinecure, knew many ministers, and hence might help his brother obtain a position in the capital. The literary luminaries there now attracted him like a magnet. (He perhaps wondered if they regarded him in the way Grigorovich did.) There was the usual difficulty of scraping the money together for the trip. He was spitting blood again and the subsequent physical weakness cut down his output of tales. Yet he was afraid to submit himself to an examination by one of his medical colleagues. Though he confessed that he ought to go south, he went north and arrived at Petersburg on April 24 for a stay of two weeks.

After renting a room on the fashionable Nevsky Prospekt and buying new shoes, pants, and an overcoat, Chekhov was off to the editorial office of *Fragments*. There the receptionist greeted him like a bridegroom and praised him as the magazine's best contributor. Bilibin introduced him to his wife, took him for a walk along the Neva, then for a boat trip on the river, and then to Dominique's for drinks and a snack. Next, to the *Petersburg Gazette* editorial office and from there to *New Times*, in whose Saturday Supplement had already appeared his three long tales *Requiem*, *The Witch*, and *Agafya*, which were being excitedly discussed in literary circles. Here he had his first intimate chat with the great editor. " 'Keep trying, young man!' Chekhov quoted Suvorin in a letter to his younger brother Misha. 'I'm satisfied with you, but go to church more often and don't drink vodka. Breathe!' I exhaled. Suvorin, not noticing any smell, turned and shouted: 'Boy!' A youngster appeared to bring me tea with little lumps of sugar and without a saucer. After this the esteemed Mr. Suvorin gave me money and said: 'You must take care of your money. . . . Pull up your trousers!' " On the way out Chekhov ardently squeezed the hand of the attractive young lady who sent him payments for his stories in *New Times*. "Oh miracle of miracles!" he exclaimed to Misha. "Who would have thought that such a genius would emerge from a privy?" (*April 25, 1886*.)

As the hours sped by, other members of the family were also kept informed of the fuss these Petersburgers were making over him. "Today," he wrote brother Ivan, "there will be an evening at Suvorin's where 'everyone' will be present, with Grigorovich at the head." (*April 27–May 2, 1886*.) And to Alexander: "I couldn't be closer to Suvorin and Grigorovich." (*May 10, 1886*.)

Though the relationship was brashly exaggerated at this time, his "closeness" to Suvorin soon became real and highly significant in Chekhov's literary life. Like Leikin a self-made man of peasant background, tall Suvorin dwarfed the pudgy editor of *Fragments* physically, intellectually, culturally, and in the business of publishing. Again like Leikin, he had been something of a liberal in his youth, but in the course of working his way up in the ranks as a journalist and writer of tales and plays he had lost much of his liberalism. In the meantime he had become a very wealthy man. Under his direction, *New Times* had achieved the largest circulation of any newspaper in Russia. He also owned a publishing firm, a magazine, a string of bookshops, and he had a monopoly of the sale of books on railroads. Suvorin liked to think of *New Times* as a "parliament of opinion," and he did make an effort to attract the best writers no matter what their political views were. But the newspaper supported various reactionary causes, such as anti-Semitism, and in the 1880's and 1890's *New Times* was generally regarded by the intelligentsia as a mouthpiece of the government and an organ whose influence could be bought by the highest bidder. The nickname "What-Can-I-Do-for-You?" — which the eminent satirist Saltykov-Shchedrin had applied to *New Times* — stuck to it in the public mind.

At first, Suvorin obviously impressed Chekhov. Hitherto the young writer had known only piddling editors in Moscow who were afraid of critics, of the censors, and of other more important editors. Suvorin seemed afraid of nothing. He exuded power and authority, and talked most interestingly about literature and art. Though at this time Chekhov was dimly aware of Suvorin's reputation and that of his newspaper, he preferred to separate his friendship for an attractive personality from what people were saying about the reactionary views of his newspaper. And he appreciated the expansiveness with which Suvorin, so unlike the cautious Leikin, had handed him a large advance with no conditions attached to it. What he did not immediately grasp was that this was the expansiveness of a man who was accustomed to buying people without haggling. Suvorin had quickly recognized Chekhov's superb art, and wanted him as a regular contributor to *New Times*.

The excitement of Grigorovich's letter and the Petersburg reception subsided once Chekhov had settled down to the pleasant summer routine of Babkino. He had gone there directly from the northern capital. His modesty reasserted itself, and as though annoyed with his former behavior he wrote to Leikin that all the praise must have turned his head. The delightful society of the Kiselevs and their visitors helped to bring him back to a kind of reality he loved. Levitan — whose talent was growing not by the day but by the hour, Chekhov remarked — arrived to add his special flavor to the company. So, for a brief time, did Alexander — who had finally managed to obtain the means to leave Novorossiisk. Even the mysteriously vanishing Nikolai turned up for a few days. In honor of the occasion, Chekhov organized one of his uproariously funny mock trials, in which the erring Nikolai was the defendant — charged, characteristically enough, with infractions of the rules of a public house.

The main topic of conversation during the summer of 1886, however, was the appearance of Chekhov's second book, *Motley Tales*. Despite his assurance to Grigorovich that it was too late to sign the book with his own name, Chekhov, no doubt prompted by his newly aroused artistic ambitions, persuaded Leikin in time to place his real signature on the title page, in parentheses, beside his pseudonym. The sale of *Motley Tales* claimed his serious attention. He urged more advertising and, like any aspiring author, naïvely complained that no bookshop could sell his or anybody else's works if the public did not hear about them.

As the reviews of *Motley Tales* came in over the summer, Chekhov's hopes rose and fell. Though he affected a humorous indifference in his letters, the persistence with which he drew the attention of friends to the reviews, and particularly to the unfavorable ones, suggests how much he suffered. In reality, he had suddenly become very sensitive to criticism now that the Grigoroviches, Suvorins, and his other Petersburg literary devotees were watching his progress. On the whole, the reviews were favorable, but one by A. M. Skabichevsky, the well-known critic of the *Northern Herald*, amounted to a vicious personal diatribe. After a general attack of the book, in which, among other things, he damned Chekhov for making an unseemly noise with his stories and with writing the first thing that came into his head, the critic portrayed newspaper-men — obviously including Chekhov among them — as writers who end like squeezed lemons and "die completely forgotten in a ditch." Chekhov never forgot this review. Toward the end of his life he remarked to Maxim Gorky: "For twenty-five years I've read criticisms of my stories, and I don't recall a single remark of any value nor have I heard a single piece of good advice. Once, however, Skabichevsky produced an impression on me — he wrote that I would die in a ditch, drunk."

Toothache and hemorrhoids during the latter part of the summer added to his misery over the reviews. He had little strength for attending to the sick peasants who came to him from miles around Babkino for free treatment. And the foul weather interfered with his favorite relaxations, fishing and mushroom gathering. Even the impending return to Moscow had its problems — for the family had given up their apartment on Yakimanka Street when they left for Babkino; they could no longer tolerate the noise in the rooms upstairs, which were frequently rented out for dance parties and wedding receptions. Masha, who had gone to the city at the beginning of August to search for a quiet place, soon wrote her brother that she had discovered a most desirable one, in fact a whole house, but that the rent was six hundred and fifty roubles annually and the owner demanded an advance payment of two months. This was more than Chekhov had ever paid for living quarters. Besides, he had written little that summer and was very short of ready cash. Putting aside his differences with Leikin, he now wrote him of his need: that he could get fifty roubles in Moscow, even more, "but I don't want to ask more, to hell with them; it is unpleasant to be obligated to them." Would Leikin add seventy to this and he would pay him back promptly? (*August 20, 1886.*)

Leikin had become used to such requests. With his own sense of thrift and a large income, he could never understand what Chekhov did with his relatively small income. "I don't dissipate, I'm not a dandy," Chekhov told him once. "I have no debts, and not even any kept women: *Fragments* and love I receive gratis." (*April 13, 1886.*) As on nearly every other such occasion, Leikin obliged on this one, and promptly. He had every confidence that Chekhov would work out these advances in stories. With this assistance, Chekhov returned to Moscow at the end of August.

« 2 »

Two weeks after renting this expensive house on fashionable Sadovaya-Kudrinskaya Street, near the center of the city, Chekhov had to pawn his watch and keepsake Turkish gold coin to raise money in a hurry. But the increase in his earnings and his constant effort to improve the material conditions of himself and family seemed to him to justify the move. The two-story house with bay windows looking out on the greenery of the street reminded Chekhov of a "chest of drawers." His combination study and medical office was on the ground floor, and also his bedroom, Misha's, quarters for the maid and the cook, and the kitchen. A fine wolfskin adorned the platform of the ornamented cast-iron spiral staircase that joined the two floors. Chekhov's sister and mother had their rooms on the top floor. Here, too, were the dining room and a living room furnished with a rented piano (the regular payments on it plagued Chekhov), an aquarium, and odds and ends of furniture, some of which had come from the editors of *Alarm Clock* as "honorariums" for contributions by the Chekhov brothers. On the wall hung a large unfinished canvas of a seamstress falling asleep over her work in the early light of dawn, a memento of both the artistic ability and shiftlessness of Nikolai.

In Chekhov's study and along the wall to his bedroom were open bookcases from floor to ceiling. On the foundation of the volumes he had inherited from his dead friend Popudoglo, he had begun to build a substantial library. He haunted the secondhand bookshops and his purchases were extremely varied — mostly Russian belles lettres, but also some foreign works, sets of magazines, and quantities of travel books, memoirs, collections of letters, and reference works. For the most part it was a working library, and the well-thumbed appearance of some of the volumes testified to their frequent use by Chekhov in his writing.[1]

Chekhov's growing reputation had begun to work its magic on members of the family. They now realized that his incessant scribbling, which they had formerly regarded solely as an important factor in the family budget, concealed also a precious talent whose possession involved serious duties as well as pleasant privileges. Even his half-literate mother, becoming hypersensitive with advancing years and prone to burst into tears for no apparent reason, observed the strange "gleam of glory" in her son's face. "Yes," she told a visitor, "it seems that Antosha is no longer mine." But this sense of loss did not lessen her nagging him on his failure to marry the daughter of a rich merchant. Chekhov was not only the center of their world; he was their world. All appreciated the labor and determination that had brought them, in seven years, from the dank, crowded basement in the brothel-infested Grachevka district to the clean, spacious two-story house on fashionable Sadovaya-Kudrinskaya. Old Pavel Yegorovich, now more gentle and kind, had completely capitulated to his son's authority in the household. Though he admired Chekhov's achievements, he secretly despaired of his irreligious attitude. With his old-fashioned values and Taganrog passion for official uniforms, he took more parental pride in Ivan, who, as head of a public school, wore a cockade in his hat and a teacher's dress coat with shiny brass buttons. Ivan kept a room for his father whenever he cared to stay with him in the government apartment, with its free heat and light, which had been allotted to him. Misha, who was finishing his studies in the School of Jurisprudence, came in for a good deal of teasing from Chekhov as a "philosopher" and lovelorn swain. But with a furtive desire, himself, to write, he worshiped his brother and was ever ready to perform endless tasks for him, however menial. Sister Masha fully shared this reverence. In fact, she already sensed the implications of Chekhov's future career and was prepared to devote her life to it.

The brilliant Alexander with his trained critical insight was better equipped than the others to discern not only the superior talent but the

[1] In 1954 his house on Sadovaya-Kudrinskaya Street, where the family lived four years, was designated as a museum in honor of Chekhov.

literary genius of his younger brother. Enthusiastic admiration and genuine affection struggled with envy and regret over his own waning hopes. But he too eventually placed himself entirely at the service of Chekhov, who, at the end of 1886, helped to obtain a position for him as a reporter and copy reader on *New Times*. And soon this older brother — who could write letters "devilishly, infernally, monstrously artistic," as Chekhov once declared, and an occasional jewel of a short story among a spate of conventional ones — willingly became a kind of literary errand boy for Chekhov in Petersburg, dunning the newspapers and magazines for his brother's fees, taking care of all the details of publishing his books, and carrying messages to editors and authors. Yet Chekhov avoided any expression of condescension to Alexander, and his efforts to assist him never flagged. If he often criticized him sharply, it was always with a desire to jolt him out of his lethargy and bad habits and bring him to an active respect for and realization of his indubitable talents.

The rigorous self-discipline which Chekhov had exercised over himself since his youthful days had established a pattern of behavior which he somehow felt was communicable to others. Moderation in all things was one of his precepts, and he kept telling himself that he must not drink or smoke too much, and he willingly submitted to a milk diet to keep down his weight. Above all, indefatigable work he regarded as the sovereign antidote for all the foolish excesses of mankind. The instinct of the teacher lay deep within him and he possessed almost a naïve faith in the power of education to form and guide the moral nature of men and women.

This tendency to instruct was rarely absent from Chekhov's letters to his two older and erring brothers. With a fine pedagogical flair, however, he sugarcoated his instruction, reprimands, and moral aphorisms with jokes and witty language. Alexander was enjoined to teach his little daughter the aesthetics of the stomach by not giving her any old food, and not to soil her eardrums and corrupt the maid by his swearing. More directly he was admonished not to pile up debts. "When a husband and wife have no money, they do not keep servants — this is a commonplace rule." (*April 6, 1886.*)

Unlike Alexander, however, Nikolai could not easily tolerate advice in any form. By now he had become very much of a dipsomaniac. His tramplike existence, pursuit of loose women, and his reckless squandering of talent pained and grieved Chekhov, who repeatedly brought him home from his hideouts, seriously ill, and nursed him back to health, only to have him vanish once again. These flights Nikolai blamed on the criticism of his way of life by Chekhov or other members of the family. On one such occasion Chekhov wrote his well-known letter of moral instruction to Nikolai. Except for the beginning, he made no attempt to use the familiar bantering style in which he so often wrote to his wayward brothers. Nikolai's case now seemed too desperate. The result was a series of moral judgments which, though they are keyed directly to the various lapses of Nikolai, reflect at the same time some of the principles that guided Chekhov's own behavior.

Chekhov wrote in part: "You are angry and insulted, but not because of my gibes. . . . The fact of the matter is that you, as a decent person, feel that you are living a lie; and he who has a guilty feeling always seeks justification outside himself. The drunkard attributes it to some grief in life. . . . Were I to cast my family on the mercy of fate, I would try to justify myself by my mother's character, my blood-spitting, and so forth. This is natural and pardonable. Such is human nature. But that you feel the falsity of your position is also true, for otherwise I would not have called you a decent person."

Chekhov insists that he fully understands his brother, and by way of proving it, he lists his virtues. Nikolai has only one failing and that is an utter lack of culture. All his unfortunate behavior derives from this fault.

"In my opinion," Chekhov writes, "people of culture must fulfill the following conditions:

"1. They respect the human personality and are therefore forbearing, gentle, courteous, and compliant. They don't rise up in arms over a misplaced hammer or a lost rubber band. They do not consider it a favor to a person if they live with him, and when they leave, they do not say: 'It is impossible to live with you!' They will overlook noise, cold, overdone meat, witticisms, and the presence of strangers in their homes.

"2. They are sympathetic not only to beggars and cats. Their heart aches for things they don't see with the naked eye. . . .

"3. They respect the property of others and therefore pay their debts.

"4. They are pure of heart and fear lying like fire. They do not lie even in small matters. A lie is offensive to one who hears it and cheapens the speaker in his eyes. They don't pose, they conduct themselves on the street as they do at home, and they don't bluster in front of their lesser brethren. They are not garrulous and don't inflict their confidences where they are not sought. Out of respect for the ears of others, they are more often silent than not.

"5. They do not humble themselves in order to arouse sympathy in others. They do not play upon the heartstrings in order to excite pity and have a fuss made over them. They don't say: 'I'm misunderstood!' Or: 'I've wasted my efforts!' . . . because all this is striving after cheap effect, and is vulgar, stale, and false.

"6. They are not vain. They don't occupy themselves with such imitation diamonds as acquaintances with celebrities . . . with the rapture of the casual spectator at a salon, or the notoriety of public taverns. . . . If they earn a kopeck, they don't make a hundred roubles' worth of fuss over it, and they don't boast that they can enter places which are closed to others. Sincere talent always remains in obscurity among the crowd; it does not care for exhibition. . . .

"7. If they have talent, they respect it. They will sacrifice their repose for it, and women, wine, and vanity. They are proud of their talent. . . .

"8. They develop an aesthetic taste. They cannot bring themselves to fall asleep in their clothes, look with unconcern at a crack in the wall with bedbugs in it, breathe foul air, walk across a floor that has been spat on, or feed themselves off a kerosene stove. They try as far as possible to restrain and ennoble the sexual instinct. . . . In these relations truly cultured people don't debase themselves. What they require of a woman is not just physical relief, nor horse sweat . . . nor the kind of cleverness that reveals itself in pretended pregnancy and endless lying. What they, and especially artists, need in women is freshness, charm, human feeling, and that capacity to be not a . . . [whore] but a mother. They don't swill vodka or sniff at cupboards, because they realize that they are not swine. They drink only when they are free, on special occasions. For they need to have *mens sana in corpore sano*.

"And so on. Such are cultured people. It is not enough to have read only *Pickwick Papers* and to have memorized a monologue from *Faust* in order to appear well bred and not fall below the circle in which you move. . . .

"What you need is constant work, day and night, incessant reading, study, and will power. Every hour is precious. . . .

"Have the courage to send it all to hell and make a decisive break for good. Come to us, smash the vodka bottle, and lie down with a book, even if it is only Turgenev, whom you haven't read.

". . . Get rid of your vanity, for you are no longer a child. You'll be thirty soon! It is time!"

"I'm expecting you. So are we all." (*March* [?], *1886.*)

However much Nikolai may have been impressed by the mature wisdom of these moral preachments from his twenty-six-year-old brother, they do not appear to have had the slightest effect on his deportment. Chekhov's belief in this kind of instruction grew out of his own prolonged struggle to educate himself, and the spiritual beauty he eventually achieved he hoped to instill in those around him. Yet, with his immense love of life and all its pleasures, it was no easy task, as he later admitted, to squelch the philistine aspects of his nature. In the light of his own behavior over his first literary success, he had every reason to feel self-conscious in admonishing Nikolai to eschew celebrities, not to exaggerate his earnings from art, and to hide his talent from the crowd. Indeed, I. L. Leontiev-Shcheglov, a young writer who soon became acquainted with Chekhov, declared: "In that first period of joyous youth and success, Chekhov revealed, at times, vexatious features — a studentlike thoughtless arrogance and even rudeness."

Such reactions were rare among the authors attracted to the tall, graceful Chekhov over 1886–1887. All were captivated by his appearance and manner. With his capacity to make friends, many, upon meeting him for the first time, felt that they had known him for years. As he talked his face grew animated, and he occasionally brushed back his shock of thick hair or toyed lightly with his youthful beard. To the fastidious Petersburger I. L. Leontiev-Shcheglov, Chekhov's careful dress had a touch of the provincial Muscovite. Simplicity dominated his movements and gestures. All were struck by his expressive eyes set in a long, open face with well-defined nose and mouth. His eyes seemed to reflect the wisdom and jollity so often found in his stories. A. S. Lazarev-Gruzinsky, another able young writer who began a long friendship with Chekhov at this time, thought him uncommonly good-looking. To test his opinion he asked a mutual friend, a beautiful woman, and she replied: "He is very handsome." V. G. Korolenko, a political exile recently returned from Siberia and a distinguished literary rival for whom Chekhov had the profoundest respect, visited him for the first time in 1887. He seemed "like a young oak," wrote

Korolenko, "thrusting its branches in various directions, still awkward and unformed, but in which one already divined the strength and total beauty of a great future growth." All found freshness, originality, and humor in his sparkling conversation as he talked in his deep baritone about art, literature, public figures, or just trifles. Sometimes he would improvise tales for their amusement, and when excited about a good theme that had popped into his head he would at once suggest to a literary friend that they collaborate on it.

There were few quiet evenings in the new house on Sadovaya-Kudrinskaya. At least one guest was usually present at dinner. Korolenko noted the friendly atmosphere as they sat around the samovar, the sympathetic smiles of Misha and Masha, and how Chekhov, always the center of attention, was "fascinating, talented, and with such an obviously happy outlook on life." Chekhov continued to set the family pace for warm, generous hospitality. His new friends now mingled with the old ones, such as Palmin, Gilyarovsky, and Shekhtel, and all got on well with the younger visitors of Masha and Misha. As Chekhov sat writing downstairs in his study, their thumping on the piano, singing, and noisy, youthful laughter overhead did not bother him. Rather, the sounds seemed to inspire his work. He loved music, and when his writing stuck and the house was quiet, he would ask Misha to play the piano, for the music seemed to lubricate his thoughts and imagination. "I positively cannot live without guests," he told Suvorin. "When I'm alone, for some reason I become terrified, just as though I were alone in a frail little boat on a great ocean." (*June 9, 1889.*) For he loved life more than the meaning of life, and in his lonely vigils its meaning and futility filled his thoughts with the unutterable pathos of human existence. More often than not he preferred to join the company upstairs, where he at once took over with his jovial antics. He might bring with him the latest price list of an apothecary shop and, striking a histrionic pose, offer rollicking comments, flecked with the risqué, on all the items mentioned. Or he would flirt with Masha's girl friends and join in the singing and merrymaking. The ancient Grigorovich, tall, handsome, and immaculately dressed, attended one of these evenings. He quickly entered into the youthful spirit of the affair. Like some old sinner he outrageously courted the young ladies, stayed till the end of the party, and then gallantly offered to escort one of the prettiest girls home. According to Misha, Grigorovich reported on the event to Suvorin's wife: "Anna Ivanovna, my dear, if you only knew what takes place at the Chekhovs'!" And raising both hands to heaven, he exclaimed: "A bacchanalia, my dear, a real bacchanalia!"

« 3 »

By the end of September, 1886, it had become clear that the income necessary to maintain the new house and this kind of hospitality would make a mockery of Grigorovich's stern injunction to Chekhov to write less. He must write more and more. Being a prominent author, he informed his good friend Mariya Kiseleva, was hardly a delight. "To begin with, it's a gloomy life. Work, from morning to night; and not much sense in it." Money was as scarce as hens' teeth, he informed her, he had cigarettes only on holidays, and yet he was writing terribly hard for at least five different publications. Though he had not set up his shingle on the new house, he found that he must still continue his medical practice. Then turning more cheerful, he admits that "the writing business has its good points too." His book was not doing too badly, money would arrive in October, and he was already beginning to reap some laurels: "People point me out in restaurants, pursue me just a wee bit, and treat me to sandwiches. . . . When medical colleagues meet me they sigh, bring the conversation around to literature, and assure me that medicine disgusts them." And to the question she had put to his sister about his marrying: "The reply is no, and I'm proud of it, for I'm above marriage!" And he concludes with the fillip of a man for whom money is as scarce as hens' teeth: "A few days ago I was at the Hermitage and ate oysters for the first time in my life. Not very good. If the Chablis and lemon had been omitted, they'd be absolutely revolting." (*September 21, 1886.*)

Mariya Kiseleva, who now wished to combine fiction for adults with her children's stories, was making heavy use of Chekhov as a literary adviser. He had already begun the practice of assisting aspiring authors and the effort increased in volume as his fame grew. Rarely was his study table free of the manuscripts of novices. He undertook this self-imposed obligation with care and assiduity. At times it almost seemed as though he were running a professional literary agency, with several trained assistants at his command. Long letters of detailed criticism would go back to the authors with their manuscripts which were sometimes meticulously edited or even rewritten. A promising author might be urged to send him still more stories to read. Or he would try to place the manuscripts himself or personally talk to a publisher in an effort to interest him in putting out a book for a beginner. And frequently he attempted to use his influence on editors of magazines to publish notices or reviews of the work of some young writer. Chekhov simply could not remain indifferent to an appeal for aid of any kind. If one could not give everything that was asked, he insisted, one must at least give something. In responding to requests for help, he never worried about being deceived by impostors. It was better to be deceived by them, he argued, than fail to answer an appeal for assistance.

Toward the end of November Chekhov took his sister for a visit to Petersburg not very long after he had written the architect Shekhtel (he had drawn in the letter a picture of himself hanging by the neck from a hook): "The fact is that the firm of A. P. Chekhov and Co. now experiences a financial crisis. If you don't lend me twenty-five to fifty roubles to the first of the month, then you are a heartless crocodile." (*November 19, 1886*.) And he offered brother Nikolai, who already owed hundreds of roubles, mostly to Shekhtel, as surety. In Petersburg Chekhov and his sister were the guests of Leikin, who by now was deeply worried about losing his most popular author as a regular contributor to *Fragments*. The trip seems to have been largely a brotherly gesture — to introduce Masha to the capital. Chekhov expressed his delight over her raptures and the fact that gay lieutenants pursued her. His only comments on his own activities are in a letter to Mariya Kiseleva. He rushed about town paying calls and listening to compliments "which my soul abhors. Alas and alack! In Petersburg I'm becoming fashionable, like Nana. While Korolenko, who is serious, is hardly known to the editors, all Petersburg is reading my twaddle. Even Senator Golubev [her brother-in-law] reads me. This is flattering, but my literary sensitivity is outraged. I feel ashamed of the public, which runs after literary lapdogs simply because it fails to notice elephants, and I'm deeply convinced that not a single dog will know me when I begin to work in earnest." (*December 13, 1886*.)

Chekhov, of course, liked success, but as these observations suggest, he had not lost his critical integrity in the face of sudden popular recognition. However, he had hardly returned to Moscow when he began receiving letters from Alexander, who had just taken up his position on *New Times*, which might easily have convinced him that he was an elephant and not a lapdog. "Your last piece, *On the Road*, has caused a furor in Petersburg," Alexander wrote. "Everywhere the only recommendation I hear is: 'The person I have the honor to present is the brother of that Chekhov who writes for *New Times*.' May the devil take you!" Coming out of Suvorin's office, Grigorovich bumped into Alexander and almost kissed him, thinking he was Anton. And when the confusion was straightened out, the old man went into ecstasies over *On the Road*. Alexander told of attending a meeting of a literary society and hearing a paper read on Chekhov's art. An Article by the established critic L. E. Obolensky, entitled *Chekhov and Korolenko*, had already appeared in the serious and well-known periodical *Russian Wealth*, in which Chekhov was praised as a greater literary artist than his eminent rival. In my presence, wrote Alexander, people talk as though they were convinced that there is "a divine spark in you, and as though they were expecting something from you — just what they do not know." The press, in its customary recapitulations of literary accomplishments at the conclusion of the year, devoted considerable space to the youthful writer Chekhov as a coming new force in Russian literature. And on February 2, 1887, Chekhov was informed that he had been elected a member of the Literary Fund, an old organization to aid needy authors and scholars. It was a distinguished honor, accorded to prominent men of letters.

The snowball of praise that old Grigorovich had started rolling had now become an avalanche, or so it seemed to Chekhov. The situation began to depress him. He complained of the numerous requests to contribute to publications, of his many social invitations, and of the exhaustion he experienced in writing at high pressure under these circumstances. "My work," he wrote Uncle Mitrofan, "is nerve-racking, disturbing, and involves strain. It is public and responsible, which makes it doubly hard. Every newspaper report about me agitates both me and my family. . . . My tales are read at evening public recitations, and wherever I go people point at me . . ." (*January 18, 1887*.)

Perhaps with old Grigorovich's advice in mind, Chekhov now began to think of dropping the humorous magazines, although at this time he could not pay his first month's dues to the Literary Fund. He had already begun to cut sharply his contributions to *Fragments*, and with some exasperation he wrote Alexander about an intended visit of its editor: "I await Leikin with a sinking heart. He is once again wearing me down. There is real discord between me and this Quasimodo. I've rejected extra and deadline writing and he sends me tearful letters, blaming me for a falling-off of subscribers, for betrayal, duplicity, and so forth. He asserts that he receives letters from subscribers with the question: 'Why doesn't Chekhonte write?' . . . I would be happy not to work for *Fragments*, for the trifle has now become repulsive to me. I desire to work on a larger scale or not at all." And in despair he demanded: "My soul, please, tell me: when will I be able to live like a human being — that is, when will I be able to work and not be in want?" (*January* 17, 1887.)

The strains that had been building up in Chekhov during the past year, since receiving Grigorovich's letter, found their expression in a feeling of frustration in his life and in his writing. Though many kept telling him that he should write less, he saw no other way of earning the money that he and his family needed. Many wealthy admirers received him with respect, he rather cynically told Shekhtel, but it had never occurred to anyone to make him a present of a thousand or two thousand roubles. Yet he knew as well as Grigorovich that he could not preserve the integrity of his art and regularly dash off three to four stories a week. Though he enjoyed the praise he had been receiving on the basis of a few first-rate tales in *Motley Stories* and *New Times*, he had no illusions about either the exaggerated nature of this *réclame* or its ephemeralness if longer works of a deeper, more artistic and enduring quality were not forthcoming. Readers were already seeking for "tendencies" in his writing, for some indication of his position on the moral, social, and political problems that beset the country. They were expecting something "big," and the expectation tormented him.

Chekhov's understandable reaction to this crisis in his affairs was to flee, to get away so that he could think calmly about his future and his art undistracted by family, fame, and pressures. The idea for his first long story, *The Steppe*, which he designed for publication in one of the monthly literary periodicals, may also have entered into his decision, for upon first announcing it to Suvorin, he wrote: "So that I won't dry up, at the end of March I'm going to travel South, to the Don region, in Voronezh Province, and so forth, where I'll greet the spring and refresh my memory on things that have already begun to grow dim. It seems to me that by doing this my work will get along in a more lively manner." (*February* 10, 1887.)

A telegram from Alexander on March 8 that he was seriously ill brought Chekhov to Petersburg in a hurry. It was a wretched trip and his only distraction on the train was reading "dear sweet Anna" (*Anna Karenina*). He found Alexander's wife much more ill than her husband. A typhus epidemic had struck and to Chekhov Petersburg seemed like a city of the dead, with funerals and people in mourning everywhere. He visited Grigorovich, who was also seriously ill. The old man embraced and wept over him. Chekhov feared he would die, which "will be an irreplaceable loss to me," he wrote Mariya Kiseleva. (*March* 17, 1887.) The only pleasant result of this dreary business was a talk with Suvorin which lasted from nine in the evening till one in the morning, "a conversation interesting in the highest degree," he told his brother Misha. In its course Suvorin offered to publish a volume of his tales, and gave him an advance of three hundred roubles on future stories. (*March* 13, 1887.)

Chekhov was delighted with this unexpected piece of good fortune. The money made possible his projected trip to the South. Now nothing would keep him from going. Nearly every letter he wrote at this time affirmed his determination to set out, as though he were afraid that something would turn up to prevent the journey. He hurried off a list of his tales to Suvorin for the proposed book and appointed Alexander to take care of all the publishing details. "For such a job," he jokingly wrote, "I'll permit you to put on your visiting card: 'Brother of the Distinguished Author.'" (*March* 19, 1887.) And he asked him for letters of introduction to people in Taganrog. Yet, as the time of his departure grew near, a strange feeling of loneliness came over Chekhov at the thought of separating from his family and friends. Letters to Alexander, Leikin, Shekhtel, Mariya Kiseleva, and others invariably conclude with the most pressing requests to be sure to write him frequently while he was away. He'd need their letters. He left Moscow on April 2, 1887.

« 4 »

Easter was approaching. Just ten years ago at this time young Chekhov had set out from Taganrog on his first trip to Moscow. Now he was returning to his native town which he expected to use as a base for trips into the Don steppe. The train poked along nearer to Taganrog and his excitement mounted as with eager eyes he picked up familiar landmarks. Soon the broad expanse of the sunlit sea hove in sight, the Rostov line twisting beautifully, the jail, the poorhouse, St. Mikhail's Church with its clumsy architecture, and then the station. Uncle Mitrofan's seventeen-year-old-son, Yegorushka, dressed to kill in hat, gloves, and cane, was there to meet him. A carriage conveyed them in state to Uncle Mitrofan's.

"Why it's — it's Antoshichka!" exclaimed his aunt. "Da-ar-ling!"

Chekhov wrote accounts of his trip in lengthy and fascinating diary-letters to his sister, who read them to the family and then carefully preserved them as source material for future stories. Grateful though he was for the hospitality of his uncle's overheated house, much about it annoyed him — the "blah-blah-blah" of his finicky aunt; the fat slob of a servant; stinking water in the washbasin; cheap prints on the walls; gray napkins, and the undersized couch on which he slept, with its stiff and stuffy pink quilt. The change of diet induced a severe case of diarrhea, and, running to the toilet at night, "miles off, beside a fence," near which rascally pranksters lurked, was "more dangerous to life and limb than taking poison." Only two persons in Taganrog, he observed, permit themselves the luxury of a chamber pot: the mayor and one of the wealthy Greeks. "All the rest must either pee in bed or take a trip to God's outdoors."

Pious Uncle Mitrofan, however, Chekhov found as delightful and hospitable as ever. A revered elder of the church, he arrayed himself in his uniform, put on his big medal, and assisted at the Easter services. The Taganrog cathedral, reeking of incense, the procession of ikon bearers, and the music of the choir must have brought back to Chekhov unhappy memories of his childhood when he was compelled to attend these interminable religious ceremonies and, under the stern eye of his father, sing in the choir with his brothers.

Equally poignant memories lurked around every corner as he strolled the streets of his native town. The old family house, empty and deserted — Selivanov the landlord had vanished — depressed him. "How could we have lived in it?" he reflected. His feelings about Taganrog were strangely mixed. A nostalgia for remembered sights and scenes and people was countered by the shuttered houses with their peeling plaster, dirty, drab, and often deserted streets, misspelled signs over shops, dumb faces of dock-workers, dandies with their long overcoats and caps, and the "universal laziness and satisfaction with a futile present and an uncertain future . . ."

The presumption of some of the inhabitants whom Chekhov had hardly known in the past annoyed him. One of them cantered up: "By God, how about coming over to my place! I always read your weekly articles. My old man is quite a type! Come and see for yourself. Say there, I'll bet you forgot that I'm married! My God, I have a little girl now. And how you've changed!" Chekhov thought his old and favorite teacher, Father Pokrovsky, who had become an archdeacon, acted like a cock of the roost on his own dungheap. The old police official, Anisim Vasilich, whom Chekhov had been trying to avoid, finally cornered him: "Wa-al, for the Lord's sake! I've been telling that Yegorushka of yours where I live, so why ain'tcha dropped in?" Not a few old friends of the family, however, dined and wined him royally, and the young ladies present, curious to find out "What kind of bird this Chekhov was," pushed him hard with their attentions. He thought most of them not bad-looking or stupid — "But I am indifferent," he wrote, "for I have diarrhea, which stifles all tender emotions." (April 7–19, 1887.)

Apart from diarrhea, Chekhov was also afflicted by bronchitis, phlebitis of the shin, and his old hemorrhoids. "My infirmities are endless!" he complained to Masha, and they contributed to low moments on the trip which sometimes made him wonder why he had ever left Moscow. However, as soon as he departed from the house of his religious-minded uncle for Novocherkassk, his obstinate diarrhea vanished. "Evidently," he quipped, "the odor of sanctity has a weakening effect on my insides." At Novocherkassk, in a borrowed frock coat, he played the part of best man at the wedding of a friend — a regular Cossack affair, with music, old women bleating like goats, and scandalous carousing. "I was so drunk all the time," he wrote Masha, "that I took bottles for girls, and girls for bottles." His wit and gallant behavior attracted the pretty but shy provincial misses, who struck him as being absolute sheep; one of the boldest, in an effort to show him that she was well-versed in the niceties of Moscow young ladies, kept tapping him on the arm with her fan and saying: "You bad boy, you!" He taught her to reply to cavaliers, in the Ukrainian accent of the district: "How naïve you are!" The frequent and resounding kisses of the bridal couple induced a taste of oversweet raisins in his mouth. "My phlebitis in the left leg got worse, what with all the kissing." (April 25, 1887.)

Chekhov pushed on from Novocherkassk to Ragozina Ravine. He stepped out into the night when the train stopped at a siding. "Veritable marvels" loomed before him — the moon and the limitless steppe, with its barrows and strange emptiness and deathlike stillness. These were among the memories of his youth that he wished to recapture. At Ragozina Ravine he stayed for about ten days on the Don steppe at the home of the Kravtsovs, which he had visited years before as the tutor of their son Peter. Little had changed in the half-primitive existence of this Cossack family — the walls were covered with rifles, pistols, sabers, and whips; cartridges, instruments for mending guns, tins of powder and bags of shot littered the premises. Shooting of all species of wild and domestic birds and animals went on incessantly. To leave the house at night one had to call a Cossack guard for fear the savage dogs of the host would tear a stranger to bits. The food was rough but palatable, except the soup, which reminded Chekhov of the slops left when "a group of fat marketwomen" had a bath. He was amused at the "rational" system of farming that had been introduced by a young Cossack who had bought himself five roubles' worth of recent treatises on agriculture. The most important part of this system, writes Chekhov, is "the wholesale slaughter which does not cease for a single moment. They kill sparrows, swallows, hornets, ants, magpies and crows to prevent them from eating the bees; then they kill the bees to keep them from spoiling the blossoms of the fruit trees; finally they cut down the fruit trees so they will not exhaust the soil. In this way," Chekhov soberly concludes, "they set up a regular cycle which, though somewhat original, is based on the latest scientific data." (*April* 30, 1887.) As in his youth, he enjoyed a limited exposure to this kind of raw country existence, despite the discomforts, and he left the Kravtsovs with a mind well stocked with vivid impressions of the steppe and its inhabitants.

A room with a bed and mattress, a washstand, and a chamber pot, all for seventy-five kopecks, in the small provincial town of Slavyansk, to which he journeyed after leaving Ragozina Ravine, seemed like sheer luxury after the wooden sofas and washtubs he had been sleeping on. He stayed there only overnight and set out the next morning, in a carriage, for Holy Mountains Monastery where he expected to spend a couple of days. On the long drive the weather was lovely, birds sang, and native peasants on the road doffed their caps to him, "taking me probably for Turgenev," he commented jokingly to Masha.

Holy Mountains Monastery, on the bank of the Donets River, at the foot of a huge white rock covered with gardens, oaks, and ancient pines, was a celebrated spot for religious pilgrimages. The pleasant monks gave Chekhov an unpleasant room with a pancake-like mattress.[2] Since it was the feast day of Saint Nicholas, Chekhov estimated that some fifteen thousand pilgrims, most of them old women, had gathered at the monastery. Before each of the many services, there could be heard the

---

[2] Chekhov's story, *The Rolling Stone* (*New Times*, 1887), was based on his stay in the monastery. His roommate there, who figures in the story, Chekhov later described to a friend as a police spy.

wailing of a bell and a monk crying out in the voice of a creditor who implores his debtor to pay him at least five kopecks on the rouble: "Lord Jesus Christ have mercy upon us! Please, come to Mass!" Although Chekhov took part in a Procession of the Cross on the river, for the most part he avoided the religious services and spent his time at a favorite spot on the bank of the Donets observing the hordes of pilgrims. In return for the excellent cabbage soup, dried fish and porridge which the monks provided free to all, he offered free medical service to a few of the monks and old women.

On the return route to Moscow, Chekhov stopped off again at Taganrog. Though he liked walking in the city gardens of his youth and flirting with "the millions of girls," he still had to put up with the endless chatter of his aunt and the stinking water in the washbasin. Hence he was happy to leave for home on May 17. The trip of some six weeks had served its purpose — it had given him a badly needed rest and change of scene, and it had stored his mind with much fresh material for writing. The only disgusting thing about it, he wrote Leikin, was an everlasting shortage of money which had prevented him from doing many things he wanted to do. He had had to live like a pimp, he complained, and in the end began to feel like a Nizhni-Novgorod swindler who retains his sleekness while sponging on others.

« 5 »

Chekhov's southern ramblings, however, failed to dispel his dissatisfaction with himself and his writings. The day after his return to Moscow he left for Babkino, though this summer retreat had now begun to pall on him. He contemplated renting a *dacha* on the Sea of Azov, and then decided that the railroad would have to provide free tickets if he were to transport all his family that distance. Neither the familiar pleasures of Babkino nor the appearance, in August, of his third book, *In the Twilight*, could mitigate the boredom and spiritual unease which he complained of frequently to friends in the course of the summer. By the beginning of September he seemed anxious to return to Moscow.

A mysterious hint that something of a serious nature troubled Chekhov is suggested by his correspondence at this time with his trusted friend Shekhtel. On May 17, he had cheerfully congratulated the architect on his intention to marry and had added: "I encourage it and would willingly imitate you if only a suitable bride could be found." A few weeks later he wrote him again. The letter contains a baffling passage, made more cryptic by several erasures: "Our last frank conversation produced a refreshing impression on me, for in the first place, it increased my fellow feeling for you, and in the second place, I've learned from this a most precious bit of information, namely, that I'm not the only martyr nor, as it seemed to me, a person without backbone in certain cases; these occasions always caused me excessive agitation and fears and I became a martyr to the core, although I had not assessed my own spiritual condition; [a line and a half erased] each time my spiritual sensitivity reached a point where every trifle agitated it, I became more spineless, and I could not look on things simply. . . ." (*June 4-5, 1887.*)

In letters to another dear friend at this time, Mariya Kiseleva, Chekhov complains of the grayness and boredom of life, that he has no new thoughts and the old ones are all mixed up in his head like worms in a green fishing box, that his existence is empty, and that he "writes little, drinks vodka in the evenings, and suffers from nervous spasms." And he adds that Mlle. Syrout, whose beauty he describes but about whom nothing else is known, "I have not seen again, but her image never leaves me for a moment. . . . Permit me to remain silent about the remainder of my breakable dolls. . . . Depressing boredom. Get married, but why?" (*September 13, 1887.*) At the same time he informed Leikin: "Though it is long since I've written, this does not mean that the fountain has dried up. Alas, the fountain does not want to flow! Over the last three weeks I've abandoned myself in cowardly fashion to melancholy. I've avoided the bright lights, I cannot hold a pen; in short, 'nerves' — which you do not recognize. I was in such a psychic state that I absolutely could not work." (*September 11, 1887.*)

Chekhov rarely mentioned any reasons for his disturbed state of mind, and when he did he usually ascribed it to family difficulties, lack of money, or even bad weather. With his unfailing secretiveness about intimate matters, he was unable to make the real reasons clear even to his brother Alexander, with whom he was ordinarily quite confidential. Early in September he started a letter to him with the statement: "I'm beginning to get back to normal." This remark referred to his letter to Alexander on September 5, but one, unfortunately, which has not survived. From Alexander's reply to this lost letter, we get some indication of the seriousness of Chekhov's condition, if not any clearer notion of the actual causes. "You say," declares Alexander, "that you are all alone, that you do not speak or write to anyone. . . . I don't understand one thing in your letter: your weeping over the fact that you hear and read lie after lie, petty but incessant. Nor do I understand precisely what it is that offends you and causes moral vomiting from an excess of vulgarity. . . . But that you are not in condition to work, this I believe. . . . I would regard myself as the most villainous of pessimists if I agreed with your phrase: 'My youth has vanished.' "

Chekhov's spiritual illness over 1886 and 1887 is not traceable to any single cause. Fundamentally it was a consequence of a struggle to identify his artistic mission which in one form or another troubled him for the rest of his life. The simplicity of existence had suddenly become complicated by compelling responsibilities, real or imaginary, to society, which he felt he must assume if he were to justify himself as a serious artist. Writing was not just a means to a material end, it was an end in itself and one that involved a debt of duty and conscience to humanity. The adjustment was a painful one.

Over this period, however, other factors no doubt aggravated Chekhov's spiritual turmoil. Brother Nikolai's swift descent on the downward path deeply worried him. During one of Nikolai's sieges of illness following a prolonged drinking bout, Chekhov wrote in morbid tones to Mariya Kiseleva: "Life is a nasty business for everyone. When I'm serious it seems to me that people who nourish an aversion to death are illogical. So far as I understand the order of things, life consists of nothing but horrors, squabbles, and trivialities that mingle and alternate one with the other." (*September 29, 1886.*) And the comment to Alexander about his vanishing youth, viewed in conjunction with other evidence, suggests that once again Chekhov had grown concerned about his unmarried state and the inexorable passing of time. Perhaps he was thinking of himself when he has Ognev, in the fine story *Verochka* (1887), wonder why he cannot respond to the heroine's love. Was the cause too much mental preoccupation, Ognev sadly asks, or "merely that irresistible devotion to objectivity which so often prevents people from actually living" and hence leads them to regard ecstasy and passion "as affected and unreal"? Had his "grim struggle for bread, his friendless, bachelor life" brought him to this? And the lies which caused Chekhov moral vomiting may well have been cheap gossip that connected his name with some young lady, or they could refer to harsh things said about him in the reviews of his book where, as he put it, he was recognized as either a genius or a psychopath.

In his dawning sense of artistic responsibility, what probably worried

Chekhov much more was the gossip and criticism about his connections with Suvorin and the reactionary *New Times*. His initial hope that he could separate friendship for Suvorin from the newspaper he published soon ran into severe testing. At this time Chekhov regarded the prose writers Korolenko and Garshin, and the extremely popular civic poet, S. Ya. Nadson, whose verse concentrated on the evils of despotism and on social injustice, as the foremost Russian authors of his generation, although his opinion about Nadson's poetry soon changed. As the young Nadson lay dying at the end of 1886, one of the principal writers of *New Times*, the vitriolic V. P. Burenin, published a series of articles on him in that newspaper, in which he jeered at the poet as a parasite who deliberately played at being ill in order to live off private charity. Chekhov shared the popular reaction of outrage and the conviction that the article hastened Nadson's death. At about the same time popular indignation was directed against Suvorin when he was sued and compelled to make restitution for "lifting" some hitherto unprinted poems from an edition of Pushkin in order to piece out the imperfections of his own edition.

Various remarks in Chekhov's letters indicate that these events jolted his complacency about Suvorin's publishing ventures. "I can hardly avoid having contempt poured upon me for my collaboration with *New Times*," he declared to Alexander. And his tone of awe toward the "great man" changed markedly. He was not afraid of the generals, he told his brother in another letter, and he now boldly advised Alexander, who was timid about expressing his views on the staff of the newspaper: "*New Times* needs you. You will be even more essential if you refuse to conceal from Suvorin that there is much about *New Times* that you don't like. An opposition party is necessary, a young party, fresh and independent. . . ." (*September 7 or 8, 1887.*)

Such circumstances, as well as the demands of his critics and readers, had begun to compel Chekhov to face the problems of the relation of art to society. He was aware that in the endless struggle between revolutionary-minded intellectuals and a reactionary government many had grown disgusted with questions of politics and social reform. Not a few of the intelligentsia, however, found spiritual consolation and moral direction in the new, electrifying doctrine of Leo Tolstoy — his search for truth, the urge to self-perfection, opposition to violence in any form, and man's duty to live by the moral law.

In the Chekhov home on Sadovaya-Kudrinskaya at this time much discussion went on about Tolstoyism. Lazarev-Gruzinsky recalls Chekhov's arguing on one such evening that "it is necessary to be thoroughly discriminating about the Tolstoyan theory of nonresistance to evil, although it is impossible to speak honestly either for or against it." And he clearly sought in the teachings of Tolstoy for elements of moral and social conviction which might serve to satisfy those who were presently puzzled over the absence of any core of belief in his tales. For a time Tolstoy powerfully influenced Chekhov's writing. Written during 1886–1887, such stories as *Excellent People*, *A Misfortune*, *Sister*, *The Meeting*, *Cossack*, *The Beggar*, and *The Letter* are pure Tolstoyan creations. Critics quickly recognized the influence and with some chagrin Chekhov admitted that one of his admirers, a Tolstoyan, had praised several of his tales in a review in the belief that he also was a Tolstoyan, whereas the critic had found fault with Korolenko because he was not an adherent. More annoying was an anonymous lampoon in *Diversion*, pointedly entitled "Tendentious Anton," in which he was ridiculed as a veterinary doctor who had neglected his profession in the interests of writing moralizing stories. He wryly dismissed it in a letter to Alexander in which he explained that he had been called a veterinary in a lampoon, "though I have never had the honor of treating its author." (*October 21, 1887.*)

Though the position of the great Russian writers Dostoevsky, Turgenev, and Tolstoy had been in the best sense of the word that of the teacher who influences the minds of people, Chekhov's artistic metabolism could not function properly in this manner. To obtrude personal views in literature ran counter to his rooted conviction that art must remain purely objective; yet the current demands for moral and social significance in literature did sway him. He was acutely sensitive to the paltriness, the moral obtuseness, and mediocrity of the society in which he lived. His natural artistic response was to write about these failings with profound pity, but without any crusading anger or disgust. However, in this period of painful change and spiritual perplexity, he earnestly sought to define his position toward the moving purpose and future direction of his art.

« 6 »

Was earning a living as a writer compatible with an artistic conscience, with having a purpose and an aim in art? It pleased Chekhov to hear his praises sung by Petersburg friends and to have the celebrated composer Tschaikovsky write of his "joy in discovering such a fresh and original talent." And it flattered him to receive, at long last, invitations to contribute to the sophisticated monthly magazines, to be asked by the well-known Burenin for permission to base a comedy on one of his tales, and to achieve that final tribute to fame — the plagiarism of a story by a young writer. However, he and his family had to live. He might be willing to starve in fulfilling his duty to art, but he could not permit the members of his family to do so. With some misgivings he now began to restrict his output to fewer and more artistically significant stories, and the drop from 116 pieces in 1886 to 69 the following year was some measure of his success in this effort. To maintain his income he insisted that other publications meet the remuneration of twelve kopecks a line of *New Times*. It was offensive, he wrote Leikin, that *Petersburg Gazette* should continue to pay him only seven kopecks a line; and by the beginning of 1887 this newspaper equaled its rival's rate. But the stingy Leikin, though fearful of losing Chekhov, raised him from eight to only eleven kopecks. Chekhov pointed out to Alexander how much more others earned in the "fat" monthly magazines and that Suvorin could do worse than raise him to fifteen kopecks a line: "I rob myself in working for the newspaper." (*Between October 10–12, 1887.*)[3]

Suvorin, scenting an opportunity to monopolize Chekhov in this situation, offered him an assured income of 200 roubles a month and suggested he take up residence in Petersburg. Chekhov refused both propositions, for now he did not wish to be under the thumb of any editor or be a slave to the special requirements of a particular publication. In warning Leikin about a diminution of his contributions, he urged him to take on new young talent to write to the prescriptions of *Fragments*, for if he and older contributors continued for long in the same vein, they would become repugnant to themselves. If they were displaced by others, then we, he wrote, "would gain much; we would win the right to write as we wish, in a way that would be more suitable to literature than that of the present day-laborer, and we would be more satisfied with ourselves than now." (*September 2, 1887.*)

In this transition period Chekhov began to devote some thought to the artistic problems of the short story, but his critical criteria were be-

[3] Tolstoy, who described the newspaper and magazine business in Russia as an intellectual brothel, was paid for *Anna Karenina* at a rate five times greater than Chekhov was receiving at this time.

deviled by the necessity to practice the form on several levels — the purely anecdotal miniatures for the humorous magazines such as *Fragments* and, at the other extreme, his best efforts for *New Times*, largely unrestricted in length or theme, and then the stories for *Petersburg Gazette*, which often included a mingling of the special qualities of those in the other two publications.

When Alexander informed him that he was planning a long descriptive piece, Chekhov at once set down the conditions that would determine its artistic success: no undue emphasis on political, social and economic factors; persistent objectivity; veracity in the description of active figures and objects; absolute brevity; boldness and originality; no triteness; sincerity. "In my opinion," he wrote, "a true description of nature must be very brief and possess the character of relevance. Commonplaces such as 'the sinking sun, bathing in the waves of the darkening sea, sheds a light of purple gold,' and so forth, or 'the swallows, flying over the surface of the water, twittered merrily' — such commonplaces must be excluded. In descriptions of nature one ought to seize upon the little particulars, grouping them in such a way that when you close your eyes after reading you see a picture. For example, you will get the effect of a moonlit night if you write that a glow like a light from a star flashed from a broken bottle on the milldam, and the round, black shadow of a dog or wolf appeared, etc.[4] Nature becomes animated if you are not squeamish about employing comparisons of its phenomena with human activities, etc.

"Details are also the thing in the sphere of psychology. God preserve us from generalizations. Best of all, avoid depicting the hero's state of mind; you ought to try to make it clear from the hero's actions. It is not necessary to portray many active figures. The center of gravity should be two persons — he and she." (*May 10, 1886*.)

A few months later, however, when the serious-minded Korolenko visited him, Chekhov surprisingly said: "Do you know how I write my little tales? Well, here you are." He looked around the table, took up the first thing his eye fell on — an ashtray — and placed it before him. "Tomorrow, if you wish, there will be a story. The title: *The Ashtray*. Nevertheless, about a year later, he insisted to his young friend N. D. Teleshov, a beginning author, that one cannot write out of one's head,

---

[4] Chekhov employed this very image of a moonlight night in his story, *The Wolf* (*Petersburg Gazette*, March 17, 1886); and in Act IV of *The Sea Gull* Treplev also comments on it.

that one must not invent. In a cheap tavern where they sat at dawn after attending a wedding, Chekhov pointed to a greasy spot on the wall, made by the heads of numerous cabbies resting against it: "Here you complain that there are few subjects. Indeed, is this not a subject? . . . There, look at that wall. It would seem that there is nothing interesting about it. But if you look closely at it, you'll find something in it, something all *its own* which no one else has found or described."

At this point in his career Chekhov was plainly more concerned with the technique of the short story than with the purpose of art. The sheer cleverness of the devices by which he achieved his brilliant effects seemed at times to give him more satisfaction than the moral awakening of a character or the revelation of human evil. In answer to Alexander's failure to discover a theme in *Happiness*, a highly successful story based on his impressions of the Don steppe which he had gathered on his recent trip, Chekhov rather cockily explains: "My steppe story appeals to me precisely because of its theme which boobies like you don't find in it. It is a product of inspiration. A quasi-symphony. In essence it is a piece of nonsense. It pleases the reader because of an optical illusion. The whole trick rests in the additional ornaments like the sheep and in the finish of the separate lines. I could write about coffee grounds and astonish the reader by means of such tricks." (*June 21, 1887*.)

With his natural dislike for systems of thought of any kind, Chekhov instinctively resisted the pressure of literary friends to declare himself on the great problems of life and death. In fact, he was not sure that art should have any purpose or that writers should endeavor to offer solutions of the problems that troubled the minds of men. To formulate these problems correctly in the spirit of objective realism was the most the writer should attempt and then let the reader make up his own mind about the solutions. When Mariya Kiseleva questioned the objectivity of his realism, he responded in a remarkable letter which offers a more comprehensive view of his artistic practice in this respect.

She had read Chekhov's *Mire*, a very frank story of how an alluring Jewish woman had seduced a Russian officer and his cousin, and tricked them out of a sum of money. Chekhov's correspondent had reproachfully questioned his taste and wondered about the reality of this kind of "filth," and why, as an artist, he did not concentrate upon the "pearls" of life in his fiction. Chekhov began his answer by admitting that he had no fondness for this kind of literature but that the question of its right to exist was still a moot one. "Everything in this world," he continued, "is relative and approximate. There are people who can be corrupted even by children's literature, or with particular pleasure skim through the Psalms and the Proverbs of Solomon for piquant passages; there are also some who, the more they acquaint themselves with the sordidness of life, the purer they become. Publicists, jurists, and physicians, absorbed in all the secrets of human sin, are not known for their immorality, and very often realistic writers are more moral than archimandrites. And finally, you cannot make a man who has already gone through a whole barrel drunk on one glassful."

Then turning directly to Mariya Kiseleva's charge, Chekhov wrote: "Indeed, to think that literature bears the responsibility of digging up the 'pearl' from the muck heap would amount to rejecting literature itself. Literature is called artistic because it depicts life as it actually is. Its aim is truth, unconditional and honest. To narrow its function to such a specialty as digging for 'pearls' would be as fatal for it as if you were to require Levitan to paint a tree and omit the dirty bark and the withered leaves. I agree that the 'pearl' idea is a fine thing, but surely a man of letters is not a confectioner, nor a dealer in cosmetics; not an entertainer; he is a responsible person bound by the realization of his duty and conscience; since he is in it for a penny he has to be in for a pound, and no matter how painful it is, he is compelled to struggle with his fastidiousness and soil his imagination with the dirt of life. . . . A man of letters must be as objective as a chemist; he has to abandon worldly subjectivity and realize that dung heaps play a very respectable role in a landscape and that evil passions are as inherent in life as good ones."

Chekhov concludes this section of his letter by asserting that because of "the triviality" of his own tales, he does not commune with his conscience when writing them. But he firmly disagrees with Mariya Kiseleva that editors ought to reject a contribution if it does not suit their own objective ideas about morality: "Sad would be the fate of literature (whether it be important or trivial) if it were left to the mercy of personal views. That's the first thing. In the second place, there is no police force which could consider itself competent in literary matters. I agree that it is impossible to get along without restraints and the big stick, for knaves will find their way even into literature, but no matter how you try, you cannot devise a better police for literature than criticism and the conscience of the authors themselves. People have been trying to discover some such thing since the creation of the world, but nothing better has been found." (*January 14, 1887.*)

Mire is in no sense typical of the rich variety of tales that Chekhov wrote during 1886–1887. An objective revelation of "truth, unconditional and honest" would characterize the most successful of them. Many, though not all, appeared in *Motley Tales* and *In the Twilight*, which he significantly dedicated to Grigorovich. In 1887 he also published a fourth book, *Innocent Speeches*, an unimportant collection which he described as "a dozen of my youthful sins," a volume he sold to a shyster publisher when he was desperately short of money. That feeling of beauty in men — he wrote his uncle Mitrofan — which cannot endure what is commonplace and trivial, ennobles the heroes of *Volodya* and *On the Road*. Many other tales embody the sentiments which he expressed in the same letter: "One must not humiliate people — that is the chief thing. It is better to say to man 'My angel' than hurl 'Fool' at his head, although men are more like fools than angels." (*January 18, 1887.*)

On the whole, there are more fools than angels in the best of the tales written during this period of change, such as *Agafya, The Enemies, The Nightmare, Volodya, Polinka, An Encounter, The Kiss,* and *On the Road,* but Chekhov never loses a sly, wistful affection for them despite their helpless efforts to struggle against the order of things. He had now fully learned that humor and tragedy, like love and hate, are often only the separate sides of the same coin, that life's misfortunes may be intensified by humor or softened by its wise, gentle smile — as in *A Letter,* when the drunken priest persuades the irate father that to forgive his erring son is more efficacious than to reprimand him. This subtle mingling of pathos and humor, which leaves the reader with the feeling of not knowing whether to laugh or cry, Chekhov deftly introduced into a vein of fiction new at this time — his stories of children, such as *Vanka* and *The Runaway,* or his famous story about the performing dog, *Kashtanka,* written for both children and grownups.

More deeply than ever before Chekhov perceived in life's ironic pattern the pervasive disharmony between people's hopes and the reality of things. The tearful effort of the dressmaker's daughter, in *Polinka,* to obtain sympathy and understanding from the young salesman who loves her is hopelessly frustrated in a conversation in which their mutual unhappiness is muted in the descriptions and prices of the dress goods which she must purchase for her mother. *The Enemies* is more than a story of human grief insulted by vulgarity — Dr. Kirilov had been called away from his wife's suffering at the deathbed of their son by Abogin, whose "sick" wife had taken advantage of his hunt for a physician to run off with her lover. It is also the tragedy of two men completely unattuned to each other because of their desperate circumstances and social position.

Chekhov had also learned to distill from the intricacies of life a unique sense of mood which seemed to be compounded of an abiding but pleasant sorrow and a profound feeling among his characters that something of vital importance had been lost and would never be found again. It was a creative essence that more and more readers were beginning to identify with his finest tales. The mood is poetically fused with the whole substance of the story and often echoed by the carefully constructed background of nature. *Verochka* is essentially a story of mood poignantly struck by the young scholar's realization of love irretrievably lost. And in *The Kiss*, the haunting memory of the embrace of an unknown woman in a dark room fills the life of the pathetically comic and unattractive artillery officer with vague longings and hopes until he sadly comes to the conclusion that he has been indulging in daydreams, and the reader too shares his mood of vanished dreams. A mood is also created in *On the Road*, the brilliant tale which had sent Grigorovich and others into ecstasies. Here, however, the profound, almost Dostoevskian, psychological analysis of the failure Likharov, the restless seeker after some rewarding faith, struck a deeper, more original and purposeful vein in Chekhov's developing art. *Happiness*, which Chekhov regarded as his finest effort up to this point, is a wonderful prose poem dedicated to the theme that there is happiness enough in the world if we only know how to find it. The conversation of the shepherds in the enchanted spaciousness of the steppe is a sad allegory of man's eternal search for meaning, for happiness, in a world of frustrating shadows. It was also the allegory of Chekhov's own life.

« 7 »

In 1887 several factors influenced Chekhov to attempt a large work — the advice in Grigorovich's letters of ardent encouragement, the expectation of enthusiastic admirers that something "big" would come from his pen, his own aroused ambitions, and no doubt the hope of greater financial gain which such a successful effort would assure him. Further, he realized that the short story did not provide scope for either the correct formulation of serious moral and social problems or the "new word" which some of his critics were demanding. The novel in Russia had been the traditional medium for ambitious authors who aspired to impressive artistic achievement and also believed they had something important to say. Apparently Chekhov thought he was ready to make the attempt. In October he wrote Alexander that he had a novel under way which involved "the head and the members of a military tribunal, that is, conservative people." However, he made only one other reference to it and then destroyed the manuscript. With an artistic technique formed through extensive practice of the short story and finely attuned to its single incident, few characters, and its quickly realized denouement, Chekhov obviously found it extremely difficult to master the long and complicated narrative form of the novel. Yet it remained the dream of his life to write one.

On the other hand, the dramatic emphasis in Chekhov's short-story technique and the quality of his dialogue lent themselves naturally to the form of drama. His adolescent attempts at playwriting no doubt grew out of an instinctive recognition of this special talent, nor had he lost his interest despite the rejections of "Platonov" and the censor's condemnation of a one-act play, On the Highway (1884) as "gloomy and sordid." This one-act play had been based on his short story In the Autumn. In fact, not a few of Chekhov's tales of incident, with their sharp dramatic dialogue, required little adaptation for the stage in the traditional one-act "vaudeville" form which he greatly admired in the theater. In addition to his love of fun and sense of the incongruous in farcical situations, he was able to endow the old-fashioned lifeless vaudeville with living characters. "In one hour and five minutes," he told Mariya Kiseleva on January 14, 1887, he wrote his first published vaudeville Kalkhas (later entitled Swan Song). "I began another but I didn't have time to finish it." This one-act play, a dramatization of his tale Kalkhas (1886), is an amusing study of the contemporary actor and the conditions of the Russian stage.

In the days of his youthful journalism for the humorous magazines, Chekhov had mercilessly criticized the condition of the Moscow theaters — the shoddy contributions of local playwrights, the abysmally low level of the productions, and the sloppy, untalented performances of uncultured and often drunken actors. This contempt, inspired really by his long love and keen understanding of the lofty possibilities of the theater as an art medium, is reflected in another letter to Mariya Kiseleva (*September* 13, 1887): "I was twice at the Korsh Theater" — two years before he had described it as bearing a striking resemblance to a mixed salad — "and on both occasions Korsh tried to persuade me to write a play for him. I answered: With pleasure. The actors assured me that I would write a good play because I'm able to play on people's nerves. I responded: *Merci*. And, of course, I will not write a play. . . . I don't want to have anything to do with theaters nor with the public. To hell with them!" Despite this tart rejoinder, three weeks later we find him informing his friend, the novelist N. M. Yezhov, "My play is ready." In the light of his present desire to do something large and striking, F. A. Korsh's request for a full-length, four-act play proved to be irresistible.

The play was *Ivanov*. "I went to bed, thought of a theme, and wrote it," Chekhov told Alexander in a letter dated October 10–12. It took him ten days, he declared, and though he could not judge of its worth, all liked it. "Korsh hasn't found a single mistake or fault in it so far as stage technique is concerned — evidence of how good and sensitive my judges are. . . . The plot is complicated but not stupid. I end each act like a short story: all the acts I contrive peacefully and quietly but at the end I give the spectator a punch in the nose. My entire energy is expended on a few really powerful and striking scenes; however, the bridges joining them are insignificant, limp, and trite. Nevertheless I'm pleased, for however bad the play may be, I've created a type of literary significance. . . ." By October 21 he knew that Korsh would produce the play. The terms had glittering prospects — 8 per cent of the gross receipts — a sure income of 600–1000 roubles, he calculated — and then who could tell how many times *Ivanov* might be performed? With perhaps more business zeal than authorial modesty, he asked his brother to have inserted in the "Theatrical Chronicle" of *New Times* the following note, which he drafted: "*Ivanov*, a comedy in four acts, has been written by A. P. Chekhov. After a reading in one of the Moscow literary circles (or something of that sort), it produced a most powerful impression. The subject is new, the characters are sharply etched, and so' forth." (*Between October 6–8, 1887.*)

Over the next two months *Ivanov* dominated Chekhov's correspondence as well as his thoughts and activities. Even the devoted Alexander grew annoyed: "I've just received your letter and I must confess that I've never read anything more silly. You carry on about your play like a man who everlastingly fusses about something." No doubt

Chekhov's unusual excitement was largely caused by the fact that *Ivanov* was the first of his dramatic writings to be staged. The frenetic measure of self-praise he indulged in, however, could come only from a man who was uncertain about the success of his artistic creation; this was reflected in his clear insights into the play's deficiencies. He sat up to three in the morning discussing *Ivanov* with the able actor V. N. Davydov, who was to take the lead and whom Chekhov described as being "in raptures over the play." He informed Yezhov: "If I am to believe such judges as Davydov, then I know how to write plays. It seems that instinctively, because of some kind of flair, and without being aware of myself, I have written an entirely finished piece and not made a *single* stage error." (*October 27, 1887.*)

As soon as Chekhov began to attend the rehearsals, his hopes for the success of *Ivanov* received a sharp setback. The actors talked nonsense and did not appear to understand the import of their roles. Even Davydov as Ivanov now seemed a bit inadequate. So discouraged did he become that at one point, as he told Leikin, he actually proposed to Korsh — "a merchant," he now dubbed him, "who seeks the success not of his artists and plays, but only of a full house" — to withdraw *Ivanov* (he thought of moving it over to the Maly Theater). The producer, however, would not dream of releasing the play. When Leikin wrote Chekhov that an author ought to keep away from rehearsals because he only confused and cramped the style of the actors and frequently offered stupid suggestions, Chekhov acrimoniously replied: "The author is the proprietor of the play and not the actors; everywhere the casting is the obligation of the author if he is not absent; *all* my instructions up to this point have been helpful and have been carried out as I indicated; the actors themselves ask for instruction. . . . If the author's participation is to be eliminated entirely, then the devil knows what will happen." (*November 15, 1887.*) That is, at the outset of his career as a playwright Chekhov was firmly convinced the author must insist that his play be produced as he had written it. To this end, he believed that an expert knowledge of the theater was essential to the playwright, who should be prepared to adapt the characters, dialogue, action, and spirit of his play to the productive means available in a given theater.

Of the ten rehearsals promised only four took place and Chekhov attended all of them. They amounted to only two, he complained, for in the others the actors behaved as though they were in a tournament, engaging in arguments and foul language, and most of them stumbled through their lines only with the aid of the prompter or through inner conviction. One of the actors testified that Chekhov behaved well at the rehearsals and did not interfere with them; other evidence indicates that he worked hard with the actors. Meanwhile a tryout performance of *Ivanov* took place at a provincial theater in Saratov on November 10, from which, Chekhov lamented, he realized not a kopeck, for he lacked the necessary fifteen roubles for membership in the Dramatic Society which would have guaranteed him an honorarium.

The Moscow opening night finally arrived — November 19. After the performance Chekhov entertained all the actors at his house and then got off to Alexander a characteristically amusing account of the opening. The family, filled with anxiety, sat in a box while Chekhov remained behind the scenes in what he described as a kind of prisoner's cage. Contrary to his expectations, he felt cool and collected, but the actors were excited, tense and crossed themselves as they went on the stage. The first act, he thought, was a great success despite the producer's blunders and the tendency of Ivan Kiselevsky, who played the important role of Count Shabelsky, to speak his own lines instead of Chekhov's. When the guests came on in the second act, however, they did not know their parts, mixed everything up, and spoke nonsense. But this act, as well as the third, wrote Chekhov, were enormous successes. There were many curtain calls. Chekhov himself was summoned three times, "and as I'm bowing, Davydov takes my hand, and Glama, in the style of Manilov, presses my other hand to her heart. Triumph of talent and virtue." The last act, however, was spoiled for him by the clowning of the best man at the wedding and because Kiselevsky, who was now "drunk as a cobbler," fumbled his lines and turned a "poetic dialogue into something odious and boring." (*November 20, 1887.*) Yet at the end bedlam reigned in the audience. Loud hissing was drowned out by applause and stamping of feet. In the refreshment bar people came to blows. In the gallery students wanted to throw somebody out and the police escorted two obstreperous individuals to the street. The place was in an uproar and Chekhov's sister almost fainted. His friend Dyukovsky, "who got palpitations of the heart, ran out of the theater," while Aleksei Kiselev for no good reason clutched his head in his hands and cried out in all sincerity, "Now what am I going to do?"

At the moment Chekhov seemed more impressed by the turmoil caused by his play than by anything else. The prompter had told him, he wrote Alexander in a letter which he jubilantly signed, "Schiller Shakespearovich Goethe," that in all his thirty-two years of service he had never witnessed such excitement in the audience and behind the scenes. And, Chekhov proudly asserted, "there has been no other occasion at Korsh's when the author was called before the curtain after the second act." (*November 24, 1887.*) This immediate stirring effect somehow made inconsequential the reactions of the Moscow reviewers, which were both favorable and unfavorable. One described the play as "brashly cynical, immoral, and repulsive."

Chekhov's unusual interest in the excitement of the audience at the opening of *Ivanov* was anchored in the fact that he had written a tendentious full-length play designed as a kind of answer to those critics who now expected from him something large and significant, a work that would confront squarely one of the strident social issues of the day. In the character of Ivanov he attempted to expose a type that had been much written about but inadequately understood — from Chekhov's point of view — by contemporary novelists and dramatists. Ivanov was intended to symbolize those people among the educated class who, dissillusioned by the repressive political and social conditions that followed the assassination of Alexander II, had fallen into dejection and despair. Chekhov wished to debunk this type, to unmask the futility of the intellectual who dreams pleasantly about his past accomplishments but quails before the abuses of the present, then experiences a vague sense of guilt over them, and ends with unstrung nerves among the "shattered" and "misunderstood" people of society.

After the second performance, which he felt was acted better, Chekhov began to wonder, on the basis of comments he heard, whether the audience really understood the point of *Ivanov*. He was irritated and weary, he wrote Alexander, and had acted like a psychopath over all of November. With a sense of relief he tried to get back to his short-story writing and busied himself about a one-act vaudeville, *Hamlet, Prince of Denmark*, on which he had agreed to collaborate with his friend Lazarev-Gruzinsky. Though he wrote the beginning of this spoof on the acting of *Hamlet*, he found so many faults in Lazarev-Gruzinsky's continuation that he let the project drop.

Soon news from Petersburg that *Ivanov* was being talked about there — Chekhov had sent a copy to *New Times* for reading — aroused his interest in the play all over again. Alexander had suggested that it ought to be produced in the capital. Despite the success of *Motley Tales* and *In the Twilight*, their sale had been relatively small. A large success with *Ivanov* in Petersburg would bring him badly needed roubles. At the end of November he was off to the northern capital.

To save money, and at Alexander's pleading, Chekhov stayed with his brother. This was a bad mistake. He found the flat dirty, foul-smelling, and suffocating, Alexander despondent, and his wife ill. But *Ivanov!* All his literary friends were talking about it — he had taken care now to provide them with copies. Suvorin, a dramatist himself, discussed it with him by the hour. In a letter to Davydov, Chekhov carefully summarized all the comments and criticisms he had heard. Apart from a weak ending, in which Ivanov dies from a heart attack, his Petersburg friends found nothing of real importance to criticize. Quite the contrary, he wrote his brother Misha: "All are positively in raptures over my play, although they scold me for my carelessness." (*December 3, 1887.*) They laugh at the Moscow reviewers, he reported, regret that he ever allowed Korsh to put it on, and cannot wait until it is produced in Petersburg.

It is little wonder that Chekhov burst out in this letter to Misha: "Petersburg is glorious. I feel as though I'm in a seventh heaven. . . . How I regret that I cannot always live here!" He had dinner and spent the night at Leikin's, glad to get away from the dirt and wailing of Alexander's household. He gave a well-received reading at a literary society, and the important *Northern Herald* had just appeared with a long and appreciative article on him. And information had already reached him that the literary section of the Academy of Sciences was considering him for the distinguished Pushkin Prize in literature, a possibility which he could hardly take seriously; he told Alexander that he would not accept it unless the prize (a thousand roubles) were divided between him and Korolenko.

Unknown society ladies invited him to call and the famous painter I. E. Repin received him at his studio. Suvorin and other eminent figures in the publishing and literary world entertained him. He dined with the young writer I. L. Leontiev-Shcheglov and through him met the old distinguished and amiable poet A. N. Pleshcheev, who, thirty-eight years before, as a member of the revolutionary-minded Petrashevsky Circle, had stood on a platform next to Dostoevsky in Petersburg's Semenov Square, waiting for execution, a sentence which, in "his infinite mercy," Nicholas I commuted at the very last minute to exile to Siberia at hard labor. Pleshcheev and Chekhov became fast friends.

There also in Petersburg Chekhov renewed his acquaintance with Korolenko, to whom he had written less than two months before: ". . . I was extremely happy to meet you. I say it sincerely and with all my heart. In the first place, I deeply value and love your talent; it is precious to me for many reasons. In the second, it seems to me that if you and I live in this world another ten to twenty years, we shall assuredly find points of contact. Of all the Russians now successfully writing, I am the most light-minded and the least serious; I'm regarded with doubt. If I may express myself in the language of the poets, I have loved my pure Muse but I have not respected her; I've been unfaithful to her and often taken her places not fit for her to go." And he sent with this letter the first chapter of Thoreau's *Walden*, which had been appearing, in translation, in *New Times*. "There is thought, freshness, and originality in it," he remarked, "but it is difficult to read. The architecture and construction are impossible." (*October 17, 1877.*)

In his first meeting with him Korolenko had observed Chekhov's light-mindedness, but he also discovered a serious aspect which he felt was expressed fully for the first time in *Ivanov*, a work devoid of the carefree objectivity of Chekhov's early tales. Sensing a change in Chekhov's social outlook, Korolenko now invited him to meet the celebrated writer of peasant fiction, Gleb Uspensky, and the *Northern Herald's* famous populist leader and stern expounder of social significance in literature, N. K. Mikhailovsky. The four spent the better part of a day dining and talking together. Chekhov mentioned to Misha that they "chattered in friendly fashion," but Korolenko thought the meeting was not a particularly pleasant one as Chekhov argued at cross-purposes with Uspensky and Mikhailovsky. Perhaps these rather grim reformers reminded him too much of certain aspects of his Ivanov.

Chekhov returned to Moscow in an elated frame of mind, contemplating some changes he wished to make in *Ivanov* before submitting it for performance in Petersburg. One of his final letters of 1887 was to Leikin, who had asked for a Christmas story. He had tried, he wrote, but the tale turned out so badly that in all conscience he could not send it. "You say," Chekhov continued, "that it is all the same to you how the story turns out, but I do not share this view." (*December 27, 1887.*) Fame now could never justify artistic failure. On December 5 he had published his last story in *Fragments* as a regular contributor. It was like a symbolic gesture of farewell to the literary past represented by A. CHEKHONTE.

CHAPTER VIII

"My Holy of Holies . . . Is Absolute Freedom"

SHORTLY AFTER Chekhov returned to Moscow, another project drove the revision of *Ivanov* out of his mind. On January 1, 1888, as though he had taken a sudden New Year's Eve resolution, he seriously tackled his lengthy story, *The Steppe*, which he had no doubt started somewhat earlier. Certainly the idea had long been fermenting in his mind, and his trip to the Don region the previous spring had provided him with abundant material. The ancient Pleshcheev, who headed the literary department of the "thick" magazine *Northern Herald*, had been after him for some time to contribute a long tale, and now old Grigorovich, in a letter from Nice, also waved him on. Though there was something annoyingly paternal in the unsolicited concern of these venerable writers, their encouragement grew out of a solid belief in Chekhov's sprouting genius. Give up the trifles and the newspapers, Grigorovich urged all over again. What about a novel, he asked, and he suggested a theme involving problems of the day — a lad of seventeen whose dire poverty drives him to suicide? A good subject, Chekhov warily replied, but more suited to a Grigorovich or writers of his generation who, besides talent, had erudition, whereas contemporary writers did not have the ability to handle such serious problems. Anyway, he countered, he had already undertaken a long piece on the steppe — baggage trains, sheepherders, inns, night storms, birds, and the lilac distance. There were places in it where he could almost smell the steppe grass.

But in this new kind of fiction he had his worries, he told Grigorovich. Since he was not in the habit of writing at length, he continually feared to write superfluously. The pages were crowded. Instead of an artistic impression of the steppe, there was danger of a dry, detailed inventory of impressions, a kind of steppe encyclopedia. Yet "You must spoil before you spin," concluded Chekhov. "And I don't quail." He was sure that his story would open the eyes of his rivals and reveal to them the wealth of motifs and poetry in the Russian steppe.

As though fearful of displeasing this persistent advocate of large canvases in fiction, Chekhov hastened to inform Grigorovich that he also had in mind a full-length novel. It would involve a whole district, he explained, "domestic life, several families . . . common people, intellectuals, women, love, marriage, children . . ." (*January 12, 1888.*) Once again, Chekhov was indulging in his dream of creating a comprehensive picture of Russian life which in effect would amount to a synthesis of the innumerable genre pictures of his short stories. He now had a tentative title for it: *Tales from the Life of My Friends.* Pleshcheev, too, was told of this vast plan and he promptly wrote back: "I await your novel like manna from heaven . . . for I now regard you as the greatest artistic force in Russian literature." And Chekhov worked away at this projected novel over parts of 1888, but the ultimate synthesis still evaded him.

In striving to rise above the level of his newspaper stories, Chekhov appreciated the friendship and encouragement of older literary artists. Apart from his contacts with young authors, such as Leontiev-Shcheglov, Lazarev-Gruzinsky, Yezhov, Barantsevich, all of whom regarded him as a teacher rather than an equal, Chekhov lacked serious and mature literary confidants among his large circle of Moscow friends. To Korolenko, who had likewise urged him to do something formidable for *Northern Herald,* he wrote: ". . . there are no people around me who either value my sincerity or have a claim on it." (*January 9, 1888.*) And with obvious eagerness he told him of his hopes and worries about *The Steppe,* in which he could not seem to convey a picture where all the details would merge into one whole, like stars in the heavens.

Except for a few days' visit to Babkino, Chekhov slaved over *The Steppe* all through January. Though he promised himself a drunken diversion on Saint Tatyana's Day, this festive Moscow University occasion turned out to be boring and wretched, for no friends visited to get drunk with him — which was perhaps fortunate, for he had no money to entertain them.

The Steppe was his first experience with a prolonged effort on a lengthy story (his youthful romance, *An Unnecessary Victory,* and his early crime novel, *Drama at a Hunting Party,* he had dashed off piecemeal). But *The Steppe* he valued as art: ". . . it is my *chef d'œuvre,* I'm unable to do better," he wrote Lazarev-Gruzinsky, who, like nearly all his friends, was regularly kept posted on this work in progress. (*February 4, 1888.*) Despite his natural tendency to compress scenes and situations, such as the brilliant description of the storm which cost him a week of effort, the story grew longer and to his surprise he eventually found that he had written what amounted to some eighty printed pages. If he was conscious of its merits as he worked away, he had many moments of depression over real or fancied failures. Often he declared to friends that it was dull; that the subject was too limited and of little significance; that there was no romance in it — "a tale without a woman is like a steam engine without steam," he told Leontiev-Shcheglov. (*January 22, 1888.*) Yet he wrote *The Steppe*, he declared, the way a gourmet eats woodcock — not in haste, and with thought and feeling.

Chekhov's first experience at preparing a story for one of the highbrow magazines alternately flattered and vexed him. He complained to Pleshcheev that these fashionable journals, ruled by literary cliques, were steeped in a kind of party boredom and were oppressive. It was only a snobbish prejudice, he decided, that drove authors to contribute to them. "Is it not all the same," he asked the poet Ya. P. Polonsky, who wrote for both the cheap press and the thick magazines, "whether the nightingale sings in a huge tree or in a bush?" (*January 18, 1888.*) The truth of the matter was that his time-consuming concentration on *The Steppe* deprived him of the quick financial returns of writing for the newspapers, and he was finally forced to steal away for several hours to dash off a story for the *Petersburg Gazette* — one of his little masterpieces, *Sleepy*. He had bills to meet, he justified himself to Pleshcheev. Indeed, he still only half believed in his talent and wondered about the sacrifices necessary to test his ability to soar. "In our talent there is much phosphorus but no iron," he wrote Leontiev-Shcheglov, who had sent him a review of the works of young writers, in which Chekhov had been favorably mentioned. "We, if you will, are beautiful birds and we sing well, but we are not eagles." (*January 22, 1888.*)

By February 3 Chekhov had made the last correction in the manuscript of *The Steppe* and sent it off to Pleshcheev. It was his initial bid, in the great world of letters, for the serious attention of those who read Tolstoy, Leskov, and Saltykov-Shchedrin. In his accompanying note he anxiously demanded: "For God's sake, my friend, don't stand on ceremony but write me that my tale is rather bad and dull if that is actually the case. I terribly want to know the real truth."

Within five days Chekhov had Pleshcheev's rapturous reaction: "I read it with eagerness. Having begun it, I couldn't tear myself away. Korolenko also. . . . It is so charming, so endlessly poetical. . . . It is a gripping thing and I prophesy for you a great, great future." Pleshcheev went on at length to praise the "inimitable descriptions of na‑ture," and he urged him to continue such character creations as Dymov and little Yegorushka. "I'm profoundly convinced that an enormous suc‑cess awaits this tale. . . . Poets, and artists with a poetic flair, ought simply to go mad over it." And Pleshcheev concluded by saying that the whole editorial board talked of nothing but Chekhov. Indeed, that Great Cham of social thought and its significance in literature, N. K. Mi‑khailovsky, was another member of the editorial board who read the manuscript of *The Steppe* and wrote Chekhov to praise his talent, which he had previously underestimated; but at the same time he grimly ad‑vised him to break off all connection with such a reactionary newspaper as *New Times*. Chekhov is reported to have answered him firmly that when he was weak and unknown and eagerly trying to get ahead, Suvorin was the only one to extend him a helping hand.

Nevertheless, such pre‑publication recognition from these literary moguls on his first effort at breaking into the fashionable magazines was clearly valued by Chekhov more highly than his earlier successes in the cheap press. He conveyed his delight to various friends. Even lowly cousin Yegorushka in Taganrog quickly learned the news. "The story is not yet printed," wrote Chekhov, "but it has already created quite a stir in Petersburg. There will be much talk about it in the capital." (*February 9, 1889.*) Quite characteristically it was the re‑muneration which he mentioned most frequently in his correspondence. A thousand roubles for a single story which had taken only a month to write!

His response to Pleshcheev exuded the highest spirits. To receive more such letters, he declared, he would give up smoking and drinking for the rest of his life. Pleshcheev and Korolenko must accompany him on a Volga trip in the spring. There would be plenty of wine and music. Al‑ready the itch was upon him, he added, to undertake something big again. There was the novel: "What marvelous women! What funerals and what weddings!" (*February 9, 1888.*) And to Alexander he jubi‑lantly announced: "I'll probably not return to the newspapers! Farewell, past! I'll occasionally write for Suvorin, but the remainder I'll prob‑ably drop." (*February 15–17, 1888.*)

Early in March *The Steppe* appeared in the *Northern Herald*. Reac‑tions quickly followed. "I hear so much praise of *The Steppe*," wrote Pleshcheev. "Garshin is out of his mind over it. He read it through twice at a sitting." This must have deeply impressed Chekhov, for along with

Korolenko he placed at the very top of the list of contemporary young prose writers the brilliant, pessimistically sensitive V. M. Garshin, whom he had met on his last visit to Petersburg. Indeed, a mutual friend reported Garshin as saying during a call: "I've come to tell you some remarkable news. A new, first-class writer has appeared in Russia . . . it is as though an abscess has broken and I now feel so fine, better than I have felt for a long time." And the various published reviews that soon appeared in the periodical press lauded Chekhov's latest effort as a highly talented and original work, although some of the critics had reservations about one aspect or another. Suvorin forgot his tea while reading the tale, wrote Alexander from Petersburg, and he reported Burenin as saying that all of Korolenko and Garshin paled before it. Only in Gogol and Tolstoy could you find such writing, declared this feared pundit of *New Times*.

As Chekhov himself sensed, in *The Steppe* he had contributed something fresh and new to Russian literature, and this novelty no doubt accounted for some of the extravagant praise. For the tale is a kind of lyrical hymn to the endless expanse of the Russian steppe, a theme only Gogol before him had treated, in *Taras Bulba*, but with a different artistic purpose and less effectively. The story is the simple account of a boy of nine, Yegorushka, whose uncle, bent on trading, takes him along in a cart across the steppe to deliver him to a family friend in a distant town where he is to go to school. A series of adventures occur which break up into several short stories, an obvious concession to Chekhov's difficulty in writing a lengthy, sustained, sequential narrative. The steppe and the boy provide the essential unity, but what color and life and characters Chekhov packs into these pages! The whole is a tone poem of nature, in which the sights and sounds and smells of all living things of the steppe are caught in their ebb and flow from the dewy fresh dawn through the merciless heat of the day to sunset and the cooling darkness of night. Then the gathering forces of the storm, transformed like so much else in the narrative by the wondering imagination of a child, assume strange and striking shapes and colors and meaning: "To the left someone seemed to strike a match in the sky — a pale phosphorescent streak gleamed and went out. There was a distant sound as though someone were walking barefoot over a metal roof which gave off a hollow rumble."

Brief encounters, incidents, and snatches of conversation define and perfectly etch the peasants, traders, and drivers who people the broad steppe road steeped in the mystery of ancient legends, fearsome bandits, and deeds of violence. There are the brilliant characterizations of the innkeeper Moses and his brother Solomon, inspired by figures from Chekhov's youth, as are many other features of the tale; the wonderfully human priest who accompanies Yegorushka and his uncle; the harsh, whip-wielding steppe entrepeneur Varlamov; and the fascinatingly evil and dominating peasant Dymov, whose further adventures, Pleshcheev thought, would make excellent material for a play. Chekhov surprisingly answered: "You wrote that you liked Dymov as a subject. Such natures as that of the insolent Dymov are created by life not for heresy, hoboing, or for leading asinine lives, but for out-and-out revolution. But there will never be a revolution in Russia, and Dymov will end by drinking himself to death or landing in prison." (*February 9, 1888*.)

However, the character who worms his way into the hearts of readers is little Yegorushka, the quiet, reflective, and rather sad child. His experiences during this journey across the steppe, so thrilling for him, seem to mature and develop his personality. One part of his life is over, and Chekhov characteristically ends his tale with a picture of little Yegorushka sitting on a bench, alone, far from home, and weeping. Anxiously he anticipates the new, strange fate that awaits him in school, and he wonders: "What sort of life will it be?" . . . The question was an invitation to continue the story, and Chekhov affirmed his intention of making Yegorushka the central figure of a novel. But like all his plans in this respect, it was never fulfilled.

« 2 »

Chekhov felt lazy and sucked dry after finishing *The Steppe*. He wanted simply "to lie in bed and spit at the ceiling." Would he ever do any serious writing again? he asked. Meanwhile, the fifteen hundred roubles which he had so far earned that year had already been "scattered" — household expenses, debts, entertainment. Creditors were an importunate breed, he said, worse than mosquitoes. There was not even enough money left to pay Kiselev the hundred roubles owed him — Chekhov ought to have married wealth, he plaintively told his friend. Nor did the spare time he now devoted to medicine help much. He received only three roubles for healing the servant of a countess, he ironically explained, but at least he had the pleasure of talking with his patient's mistress. Though he was proud to point out that *Ivanov* was being performed at various provincial theaters, he received no further income from it. And his one-act play, *Swan Song*, which was finally staged at the Korsh Theater on February 19, 1888, brought in very little.

Three days later, he informed Leontiev-Shcheglov: "For lack of something to do, I sat down and wrote a vaudeville entitled *The Bear*." The idea had occurred to him after seeing his friend, N. N. Solovtsov, play the part of a swashbuckling sailor tamed by a society woman in a Russian version of Pierre Berton's vaudeville, *Les Jirons de Cadillac*. This giant actor with his roaring voice suggested to Chekhov the behavior of a "Russian bear" in a similar situation. Lazarev-Gruzinsky tells of visiting Chekhov at this time and hearing him read the manuscript with all the perfection of a practiced actor — Chekhov rarely agreed to read any of his writings in public because he thought it undignified, but he thoroughly enjoyed such home performances. The sophisticated *Northern Herald*, he conjectured in mock seriousness, would now anathematize him for writing such trivial things, but *The Bear*, when it was produced six months later (October 28), turned out to be the most successful of his one-act plays. Over the years it became a constant source of income — a milch cow, he said, instead of a bear. "A gypsy," he later wrote Suvorin, "would not have got so much from a real bear as I got from an imaginary one." (*March* 6, 1889.) Curiously enough, it was the only dramatic work of Chekhov that Tolstoy admitted liking; he roared with laughter when he saw it on the stage.

A letter from the long-silent Leikin, whom Chekhov had quite forgotten in his excitement over *The Steppe*, informed him of a projected visit to Moscow. When he arrived early in March, the visit became a welcome excuse for festive gatherings of old friends, Gilyarovsky and Palmin, along with Lazarev-Gruzinsky, the young and hopeful aspirant to Chekhov's forfeited place in the pages of *Fragments*. Chekhov accompanied Leikin back to Petersburg. He had some business there, but also he could not resist the temptation, as on the occasion of previous successes, to sample the climate of opinion about *The Steppe* in this discriminating literary center. If he had expected any discriminating criticism from Leikin, he was disappointed. For this "discoverer" of Chekhov, now very much on the defensive with him, made the long train trip miserable by shamelessly boasting about his own literary prowess and by pestering him for critical judgments on his writings.

Chekhov spent most of his week's stay at Petersburg as a house guest of the Suvorins. And this wealthy son of a former serf, who had long since squeezed the slave out of himself, handsomely entertained another former serf's son who was still struggling with the slave in him. Dazzled, Chekhov wrote Lazarev-Gruzinsky that his cup ran over and that Suvorin was one of "the *remarkable* men of our time." (*March 22, 1888.*) His separate suite of two rooms, tastefully furnished with a grand piano, harmonium, a bed, fireplace, and an elegant desk, had its own entrance and a special toilet which seemed a miraculous luxury to Chekhov. The valet assigned to him had a well-bred physiognomy and Chekhov thought him better dressed than himself. Nor could he get used to this servant walking reverentially around him on tiptoe, trying to anticipate his every wish. In addition a carriage was placed at his disposal. "In general," he wrote Mariya Kiseleva, "I felt like a scoundrel." (*March 25, 1888.*)

Staying with the Suvorins, however, had its drawbacks, not the least of which was the impropriety of coming home half-drunk or accompanied by a lady friend. And whenever he was at home they monopolized him. Before dinner Madame Suvorina would regale him with her detestation of the human race or with how she had just bought herself a jacket for 120 roubles. And after dinner the conversation would switch to migraine headaches, while the youngsters of the family would stare at him goggle-eyed waiting for him to say something clever; for after all, was he not the famous author of *Kashtanka?* From dinner to teatime there were philosophical monologues by Suvorin in his study, with the hostess occasionally entering into the conversation, "but inappropriately," Chekhov wrote to Misha, "speaking in a bass voice, or imitating a yapping dog." (*March 15, 1888.*)

Was it Suvorin's good business sense, or a conviction that Chekhov had a great literary future ahead of him, or just the expansiveness of friendship, that prompted him, in a most serious manner, to propose that Anton marry his little daughter, who at that moment — Chekhov later wrote to Alexander — was crawling under the table at his feet? "Wait five or six years, my friend, and get married," Chekhov quoted him. "What the devil more do you need? I would not wish for anything better." (*March 24, 1888.*) Chekhov jokingly asked him, as a dowry, for the *Historical Herald,* a well-known periodical which Suvorin controlled, and suggested that he might throw in the editor for good measure. But Suvorin solemnly replied that he could have half the total income of *New Times* for a dowry.

At the moment, however, Chekhov wanted nothing more intimate with Suvorin than a book contract. He had no difficulty in coming to an agreement with him for the publishing of another volume of his tales, as well as a second edition of *In the Twilight*, although there were still a number of unsold copies on hand. And a further project was talked about — a volume of his tales especially designed for children. Alexander, whose sobriety at this point Chekhov marveled at, was commissioned to take care of the details of these projects.

Business, however, was not the only interest of Chekhov during this stay in Petersburg. There were gay parties with Pleshcheev and Leontiev-Shcheglov. He was introduced to the owner and editor of *Northern Herald*, Anna Yevreinova, "a very sweet and clever old maid," whose face reminded him of a roasted starling, and he spent an evening with the poet Polonsky who had dedicated verses to him; in return, Chekhov graciously requested that he be allowed to dedicate to Polonsky one of his best stories, *Happiness*, in his proposed new collection. Wherever he went, he wrote Misha, they talked about *The Steppe*. In the editorial office of *New Times*, according to Alexander, the famous Leskov had told him that his brother was a genius, and Chekhov heard that the great Saltykov-Shchedrin was in raptures over the story. Everywhere in Petersburg, he informed Mariya Kiseleva, he bathed in glory and sniffed incense. They nicknamed him "Potemkin," he said, although he had no Catherine, but they regarded him as a favorite of the Muse. Perhaps he also heard at that time how Garshin had read *The Steppe* aloud to a distinguished gathering, including the eminent painter Repin. Several present, still devoted to Turgenev's literary manner, criticized what they thought was a lack of purpose and ideas in the story. But Garshin, with tears in his voice, defended the "pearls of language," the poetry, and the inimitable technique of Chekhov, whom he regarded as a bright new sun in Russian literature. Chekhov made a point of calling on this sympathetic admirer, one of the most popular writers of the day, but he was not at home. To his horror he learned a couple of weeks later that the emotionally unstable Garshin had committed suicide by throwing himself down his stairway. Chekhov willingly agreed to contribute a story to a memorial volume in his honor. And to Suvorin he wrote: "An unendurable life! But a stairway, that is terrible. I saw it: dark, dirty." (*April* 3, 1888.)

Less than a month after Chekhov's departure, two young Petersburg literary rivals, V. A. Tikhonov and Leontiev-Shcheglov, were discussing him. That night Tikhonov entered in his diary: "I won't say anything here about Chekhov's talent, which in any case is the freshest, most brilliant, and finest among all our contemporary writers. But Leontiev-Shcheglov characterized him for me as a human being, and without knowing him personally, I fell in love with Chekhov. In him there is everything (according to Leontiev-Shcheglov) that I most admire in a man."

« 3 »

Though it was still March and the weather foul when Chekhov returned to Moscow, he smelled spring in the air. For he had already begun to think of a spring trip and to conjure with the family's summer vacation plans. Such impatient anticipation sometimes had its source in the turbulent and often oppressive existence in the family home on Sadovaya-Kudrinskaya. In April Alexander, whose wife was dying, asked him to take in his two children for a time. Chekhov felt compelled to counter that it would be better for Alexander to pay Auntie Fedosiya and her son enough to hire a small apartment and take care of the children. His house was crowded, Chekhov explained. There were eight people, including Nikolai, who had turned up again and went around drunk and half-dressed. Then their brother Ivan usually "visited" from three in the afternoon until late at night, and on all holidays, and his father every evening. "They are all nice people," Chekhov wrote, "jolly — but egotistic, pretentious, excessively talkative, accustomed to stamping their feet, and impecunious." (*April 26, 1888.*) He was more forthright to Leontiev-Shcheglov. His family bound him hand and foot, he said. "You have a *wife* who forgives you if you have no money, but I have a *household* that comes crashing down on me if I don't earn a certain number of roubles every month, crashes and weighs on me like a millstone about my neck." (*April 18, 1888.*)

Lack of funds, as well as a lack of desire on the part of Korolenko and Pleshcheev to make the trip, ended Chekhov's hope of going down the Volga in early spring. If possible, however, he was determined to get out of Moscow to a summer place at the beginning of May. With a twinge of conscience, he informed his old friend Kiselev that the family wanted to go to the South and not to Babkino. His father wished to see his native haunts before he died. The old couple required peace and comfort and a church nearby; all he himself needed was to be near a post office, and peasants he could treat medically. He had already written his childhood friend, Alexandra Selivanova, with whom he maintained contact, to look for a summer house in Slavyansk, and also to his cousin Yegorushka at Taganrog to hunt for one on the Sea of Azov.

Meanwhile, his close friend, A. I. Ivanenko, a Moscow Conservatory flutist with misdirected literary ambitions, enthusiastically urged on Chekhov the beauties of his native Ukraine. He knew just the place — a house on the estate of the Lintvarevs in the village of Luka on the Psyol River near his birthplace Sumy. Chekhov asked him to inquire, and upon receiving a favorable answer, impetuously rented the house for a hundred roubles.

Chekhov's imagination, no doubt stimulated by the chauvinistic Ivanenko, at once took fire over this *dacha* which he had never seen, and he described it in glowing terms to friends and invited them to visit him in the summer. "I assure you the place is ravishing," he wrote Pleshcheev in one of his characteristically irresistible invitations. "The Psyol, a broad and deep stream, is filled with fish; there is a pond and a rustic mill. The *dacha* is situated at the foot of a hill, covered with orchards. The place is surrounded with woods. There is an abundance of young ladies." And, Chekhov added: "I give you my word of honor that we shall do *nothing*, we shall cultivate indolence, which is so good for you. We shall eat, drink, get up early, and go to bed early, catch fish, visit the fairs, enjoy music, and nothing more." So pack your suitcase, he concludes, take only enough money for the train ride, "bring some cigars, which are unobtainable in the South," and say farewell to your Melancholy Mandolin[1] for a whole month, and

"Forward! Without fear and doubt."[2] (*March 31, 1888.*)

And for good measure, he adds, bring along your son Nikolai, and Leontiev-Shcheglov.

Taking advantage of a trip which his brother Misha was making to Taganrog in late April, Chekhov asked him to visit the *dacha* on the way and report back to him. The report was disillusioning in the extreme: the house in decay, a mudhole in the yard with pigs wallowing in it, the garden run down, and to make matters worse the liberal-minded Lintvarevs — one of whose sons had been expelled from the university for radical activities — behaved coldly to Misha, who was dressed in his student uniform.

Since Pleshcheev had already accepted his invitation, Chekhov felt it

[1] The *Northern Herald*.
[2] The first line of a well-known poem by Pleshcheev.

necessary to write him, on the basis of the adverse report, that though the Psyol was truly a broad and deep river, the *dacha* was an unpoetic ruin with no comforts, vile furniture, and only two emancipated young ladies in the neighborhood. There was no question of giving him the best room in the house since they were all equally bad. Nevertheless, however unattractive the place was, it was healthier and more spacious than Pleshcheev's Petersburg tundra, and he still hoped he would come. He regretted only that Pleshcheev did not like to fish — "To catch a perch is loftier and sweeter than love!" (*April 25, 1888.*)

« 4 »

When Chekhov and his family arrived at the Ukrainian *dacha* in early May, he discovered to his relief that Misha, who all along had been partial to Babkino as a summering place, had much exaggerated its unfavorable aspects. Babkino, he declared, could not hold a candle to it. The rooms were large, clean, and comfortable, but ordinary conveniences were lacking — retreating to a ditch or the bushes did not irk him in fine weather, but when it rained or when he had diarrhea he objected. However, he told Suvorin, there were compensations in the spaciousness of the surroundings, which at once aroused his enthusiasm and titillated his imagination — the beautiful green banks of the Pysol, the romance of a watermill with its miller and his daughter who sat at the window obviously waiting for something to happen, the song of nightingales, the distant barking of dogs, and "the tightly boarded, very sad and poetic country places, where dwell the souls of beautiful women, aged, doddering feudal retainers, and young girls longing for the most conventional type of love." (*May 30, 1888.*) Everything about the place reminded him of the ancient fairy tales he had known for so long.

With his gregarious nature Chekhov was soon on the most familiar footing with his hosts, the cultured Lintvarevs. They were more serious and more numerous than the Kiselevs of Babkino: the widowed mother, who read Schopenhauer and every issue of the *Northern Herald*, was noticeably pleased to have a young man of letters in her house; the oldest daughter Zinaida, a saintlike physician rendered blind by a brain tumor, astounded Chekhov by her calm expectancy of death while she laughed and joked on the terrace as she listened to someone reading his tales; the shy, tender second daughter, Elena, also a doctor, with whom he could never agree medically when he assisted with her patients, a woman dearly loving family happiness but condemned, he thought, never to enjoy it, never to be happy; and the homely youngest daughter, Natalya (Natasha), a strong, tanned, muscular girl, bony as a shad, who liked to sing, roared with laughter at the slightest provocation, read Marx, and taught a school which she had set up in the village. At times Chekhov attended her class to observe how she taught Ukrainian to the children. Natalya, who was not indifferent to Chekhov's charm, eventually became a close friend of the family. Of the two sons, Pavel, the oldest, expelled from the university, was modest, quiet, hardworking, and seemingly content with his lot, whereas the youngest, Yegor, aspired to a Tolstoyan way of life and was fanatically determined to be a great pianist. With equal ease Chekhov also got to know the local landowners and peasants whose companionship he sought on fishing expeditions. These Ukrainian peasants, he decided, were superb types. He enjoyed their jolly disposition, cleverness, and amusing conversation.

With that ability he had to adapt himself to new and strange places, Chekhov plunged at once into the summertime pleasures of his new surroundings — bathing, fishing, flirting, attending the local fairs, and arranging musical and literary evenings, very much as at Babkino, in the manor house of the Lintvarevs. Their friends quickly became his friends. Yet he found time also for some medical practice and writing. He finished a long story, *The Lights*, for the *Northern Herald*; he did a short piece, *A Trifle from Life*, for *New Times*; and he saw through the press his new collection, *Tales*, which appeared in early June.

Impatiently Chekhov kept urging his laggard friends to visit, tirelessly extolling the charms of his Ukrainian paradise. Toward the end of May Pleshcheev arrived, along with Ivanenko. The venerable poet, whose verses — full of faith, progress, and love for the masses — were still popular, at once became the idol of the Luka inhabitants. The young girls brought him flowers, took him boating, and sang romantic ballads to him. He ate to exhaustion, smoked endless cigars which half-suffocated his youthful worshipers, and composed poetry by reading each line aloud so that people in the house thought he was talking to himself. Though Chekhov compared him to an ikon that was revered because it was old and had once hung in the company of miracle-working ikons, he sincerely liked Pleshcheev and, after his departure, wrote him an affectionate letter to tell the poet how the whole neighborhood missed him.

Among his guests was the stolid, balding Kazimir Barantsevich, who, in Chekhov's eyes, compensated for his dullness as a person and fiction writer by being a mighty fisherman. Brother Alexander, whose wife had died, also arrived at Luka with his children, after some urging and financial help from Chekhov. Inclined to drown his grief in vodka, Alexander overreached himself when he insisted on participating in the performance of a conjuror at Sumy Park. Although the audience was much amused by the spectacle, Chekhov felt obliged to withdraw with his embarrassed sister and the Lintvarev ladies out of earshot of his drunken brother's language. Apparently ashamed of his behavior, Alexander left hurriedly for Petersburg. However, he had remained long enough at Luka to conceive a passion for Elena Lintvareva and wanted to marry her, although his own wife had been dead but a short time. Chekhov, whom Alexander tried to use as something of an intermediary in the affair, gently argued with him, insisting that any happy marriage must be based on love and that he could see, as yet, no evidence of this on either side. If Alexander were really serious, Chekhov said, he should spend some time with the Lintvarevs and ascertain whether Elena did or could love him. No doubt the suggestion was also designed to protect as good and fine a woman as Elena, for he was aware of the kind of impression Alexander would make on the Lintvarevs, a family of teetotalers, after a prolonged visit. Apparently Alexander also realized it and soon dropped the matter. Besides, he was already drifting into a liaison with Natalya Alexandrovna Golden — whose married sister lived with his brother Nikolai — which eventually ended in marriage.

Luka was not far from the Ukrainian countryside which Gogol had made famous in his *Sorochinsky Fair* and *Mirgorod* tales, a fact that had originally attracted Chekhov to this region. So with the greatest anticipation he snapped up an invitation from the Lintvarevs to visit relatives of theirs with whom he had already become acquainted — Alexander and Sergei Smagin, who lived in a village in the Mirgorod District, not far from Sorochinsky in Poltava Province. In leisurely country fashion Chekhov, his sister, Natalya Lintvareva, and her cousin drove almost three hundred miles over the course of a week in a comfortable four-in-hand carriage. The handsome Alexander Smagin had already evinced an interest in Masha. On the road there was no end of laughter, adventures, and comic misunderstandings among this gay company. They took part in weddings in the villages where they stopped, heard lovely music in the evening stillness, and went to sleep in an atmosphere heavy with the sweet smell of new-mown hay. Against the background of this bewitched Gogolian landscape, even the crumbling and decrepit estate of the Smagins, where they stayed for five days, seemed to Chekhov poetical, sad, and beautiful in the extreme. "What places! I'm positively charmed," he wrote Leikin. And in his unrestrained delight he impulsively thought of giving up literature, settling in some village on the bank of the Psyol, and devoting himself entirely to the practice of medicine. In conveying his rapture over the Ukrainian countryside to Lazarev-Gruzinsky, he curiously took this occasion to congratulate him on his marriage, which he described, along with that of Yezhov, as a demonstration against his own bachelor state. He would willingly assume the bonds of Hymen, he wrote, but he was prevented by circumstances. Were these family circumstances or those of his precarious health? He does not say. But he frankly told Lazarev-Gruzinsky that he envied him. "I regret that I'm not married, or at least that I have no children." (*June 26, 1888.*)

In the midst of his dithyrambs about the wonders of the Ukraine, the restless Chekhov suddenly abandoned it all, on July 10, and set out for Feodosiya in the Crimea to visit the Suvorins, who had a summer place there. Some inner urge or presentiment kept driving him on, drawing him always elsewhere, as though he wished to embrace and include everything accessible to man in what he divined would be a short life. Much of this month's trip, like that of the previous year to the Don steppe, he vividly described in letters to his sister as material which he might wish to use later for stories. The journey from Sumy to Simferopol by way of Kharkov bored him, but thereafter his first view of the mountains bathed in moonlight stirred his imagination. He reached Sevastopol at night and the sudden glimpse of the sea delighted him, but in the morning the sight of the stevedores on the docks loading cement — clothed in tatters, their sweaty faces baked red-brick by the sun — filled him with a feeling of dull depression. He next made his way to Yalta, the resort city where he was destined to spend the last few years of his life. At this time the boxlike hotels in which unhappy consumptives were pining, the idle rich longing for cheap adventure, and the young ladies and gentlemen prattling about the beauties of nature, of which they had no understanding, all struck him as shoddy and disgusting. He hastened to leave Yalta for Feodosiya.

The Suvorins, in whose attractive summer home he spent twelve days, greeted him warmly. They were zealous in entertaining him and introduced him to their friends in the neighborhood, including the old and famous marine painter, I. K. Aivazovsky, at whose home he dined sumptuously. Chekhov admired the artist's beautiful young wife, but her ancient husband — who had been personally acquainted with Pushkin — struck him as a combination of general, bishop, artist, Armenian, naïve old peasant, and Othello. Aivazovsky was proud of the fact that he had never read a book in his life — because, he explained, he had opinions of his own. Formal social gatherings, however, palled on Chekhov. He preferred to spend his time on the beach at Feodosiya — where, he said, he could live for a thousand years without being bored, and enjoy sea bathing in water that was as soft as the hair of an innocent girl.

The real friendship that had begun between Chekhov and the Suvorins during his stay with them in Petersburg developed into intimacy at Feodosiya. It was impossible to be with Suvorin and be silent, Chekhov remarked; they discussed all possible subjects day and night. Despite her constant chatter, Suvorin's wife now won his admiration for her originality and cleverness. And her husband, he wrote Leontiev-Shcheglov, "is a great man. In art he is like a setter hunting a snipe — that is, he works with a devilish flair and always burns with passion. He is a poor theoretician, has no taste for science; there is much he doesn't know and he is self-taught in everything, but from this comes his sheer doglike soundness and wholeness, and hence his independence of mind." (*July 18, 1888.*) There is some reason to believe that, during this stay at Feodosiya, Chekhov discussed and outlined his play *The Wood Demon*, which he offered to do in collaboration with Suvorin.

Though Suvorin vowed he would keep his guest there until September, Chekhov soon felt he must get away. He liked these lazy, luxurious days: arising at eleven, coffee on the beach, bathing under the hot sun, games, excursions, meals with rich food, jolly evenings, stimulating conversation, and getting to bed at three in the morning. But his conscience had begun to trouble him. No writing was getting done and news from Masha warned him of the low state of finances at Luka. He seized the occasion to leave with Suvorin's son, Aleksei, on his trip to the Caucasus. They left Feodosiya by steamer for Batum, making brief stops at the New Athos Monastery in Abkhazia, and at Sukhum.

No description, Chekhov felt, could do justice to the setting of the monastery — eucalyptus and olive trees, cypresses, tea plants, and the magnificent background of sea and mountain. If he stayed there a month, he remarked, he could write fifty fascinating tales; a thousand subjects peered out of every bush, the shadows and half-shadows on the mountains, and the sky and sea. His narration, in a letter to Misha, of his trip from Sukhum to Poti in a wretched little cargo steamer, the *Dir*, is related with all the detail and finish of a short story. In the night the boat narrowly avoided being wrecked in a collision with another steamer, a fate that actually overtook the *Dir* the following autumn. From Poti they proceeded to Batum, which seemed to Chekhov to have nothing special about it except its great number of brothels. Though he found the road to Tiflis original and poetical, that to Baku he pronounced an abomination of desolation. And Baku itself, with its extreme heat, the smell of kerosene, and naptha-soaked mud squelching under one's feet, disgusted him. Though the two travelers intended to push on to Samarkand, Aleksei Suvorin received a telegram at Baku informing him of the sudden death of his younger brother Valerian, and he hurried back to Feodosiya. With some regret over not continuing the journey, Chekhov also decided to return home to Luka and arrived at Sumy on August 7.

He had hardly got resettled in his *dacha* when he began to busy himself with an idea that had occurred to him on his visit to the Smagins. How wonderful it would be to buy a farm in the lush Mirgorod area! He would build a wing on the property and offer it to friends and authors. Yes, he would set up a colony of writers! Like him, they would surely enjoy a retreat from the noisy cities to the quiet of this lovely countryside. The purchase could easily be financed by a mortgage, and he hoped that Suvorin, to whom he broached the idea, would help. Chekhov made another visit to the Smagins in August to search out an ideal spot. And he found a farm in "a remote, poetic place," situated between two large villages which had no physician, a fact that increased his interest in the location. The only trouble was that the owner demanded more than he thought the farm was worth. He wrote Suvorin that if he should decide to buy, then he might avail himself of his offer of fifteen hundred roubles, but only on the strict condition that it was to be regarded as a loan. With considerable firmness Chekhov pressed home this point, as though his very integrity were at stake. "I tell you frankly and confidentially," he wrote, "that when I first began to work for *New Times* . . . I promised myself to write as often as possible in order to earn more. There was nothing bad in that. But when I got to know you better and you became a friend, my anxiety grew acute and work for the paper for the sake of money lost its real value for me, and I began to speak and promise more than I could do; I began to fear that our relations would be clouded by the thought that I needed you as a publisher and not as a man . . . All this is silly and offensive and merely indicates that I attach too great importance to money, but there is nothing I can do about it." (*August 29, 1888.*)

Chekhov's dream of buying a farm in the Ukraine and starting a writers' colony continued to obsess him for some time until he reluctantly abandoned the idea.

"Ah, how I hate to leave here!" Chekhov wrote to Pleshcheev. ". . . Every day it grows more beautiful . . . Moscow with its cold, its rotten plays, restaurants, and Russian thoughts terrifies my imagination. I would willingly live the winter as far as possible from it." (*August 13, 1888.*) Nevertheless, at the beginning of September he had to return to Moscow.

« 5 »

Ten days of hard work after his return (he had accumulated a debt of five hundred roubles over the summer) left Chekhov yearning for spring again and the idle pleasures of the Ukraine. But Suvorin's advice at this point — that he give up medicine and devote himself entirely to literature — rubbed him the wrong way: ". . . I feel more contented and more satisfied with myself when I realize that I have two professions and not one. Medicine is my lawful wife and literature my mistress. When I grow weary of one, I spend the night with the other. Although this may seem disorderly, it is not so dull, and besides neither of them loses anything at all from my infidelity. If I did not have my medical work, I could hardly give my leisure and my spare thoughts to literature.[3] There is no discipline in me." (*September 11, 1888.*) With some pleasure he later pointed out to Suvorin that the ladies were singing his praises over "The Name-Day Party," a story he wrote that

[3] In Chekhov's correspondence there are variants of this well-known statement of his dual devotion to medicine and literature. A curious one, in a lost letter of 1897 to his Czech translator B. Prusík, is quoted in an article by Prusík about Chekhov: " 'You ask what I'm interested in apart from literature. I'm occupied with medicine. I regard medicine as my lawful wife and literature as my mistress, who is dearer to me than a wife.' " See *Literaturnoe Nasledstvo* (*Literary Heritage*), Moscow, 1960, LXVIII, 212.

year. "It really isn't bad to be a doctor and to understand what you are writing about. The ladies say the description of the confinement is *true*." (*November 15, 1888.*)

As usual, family difficulties interfered with Chekhov's concentration on work and taxed his nervous energy. In the autumn he agreed to take into the house the young son of his friends at Babkino, Seryozha Kiselev, who planned to enter a Moscow *gymnasium*. Apart from helping out the Kiselevs, Chekhov thought that the presence of the youngster would freshen up the household. However, the responsibility he assumed for Seryozha's conduct and illnesses imposed a further strain on him. And brother Nikolai's behavior had reached a point of scandal where all members of the family, except Chekhov, wished him elsewhere. Nikolai had deeply offended his most faithful friend, the architect Shekhtel. And now the police were on his trail. Since he had never finished school or had a regular position, and hence lacked a passport, the authorities were attempting to compel him to fulfill his military service. Though this may have been exactly what the incorrigibly wayward artist most needed, the thought filled Chekhov with horror and he sought the influence of highly placed friends to save Nikolai from this fate.

To add to his worries, Suvorin, who had stopped off at Chekhov's house on his way back to Petersburg from Feodosiya, sheepishly confessed that in a moment of anger he had written an offensive letter to Alexander over one of his tales which he had published in *New Times* and signed AL. CHEKHOV. It is possible to write bad stories, Suvorin had declared, but one ought not to usurp the name of another. This public confusion of names was by now an old matter which the brothers had amicably settled between themselves. But aware of the extreme instability of Alexander, Chekhov hastened to write him to patch up the affair: "We cannot escape the hour of death and we have not long to live, and hence I do not attribute serious significance to my own writing, to my name, or to my literary mistakes. I advise you to do the same. The more simply we regard these delicate questions such as Suvorin touches upon the more equable will we be in our lives and relations." And he wearily concluded: "An. Chekhov or Al. Chekhov — is it not all the same?" (*September 24, 1888.*) Shortly after this incident Suvorin wrote Chekhov that Alexander had got into a drunken brawl and offended members of the staff of *New Times*. This might mean the end of Alexander's job on the newspaper. Chekhov worried. He at once dispatched a diplomatic letter to Suvorin, in which he frankly admitted that his brother was a chronic drunkard and tried to explain the reasons for his behavior. He would send Alexander, he promised, a politic-scolding-tender letter — which usually had an effect on him.

Such cares and worries, as well as dogged work and the cold and dampness of Moscow, contributed to worsening Chekhov's already poor health. On several occasions during 1888 he experienced warning hemorrhages. Although as a physician he must have been aware of the nature of his disease, he still refused to admit it to friends. When Elena Lintvareva, a doctor herself, began to suspect his symptoms over the summer and later recommended that he take measures, he jokingly asked her what measures — cease work or go to Nice — and then he requested her not to speak any more about measures. On the other hand, when Suvorin, at this time, confronted him with the same suspicion, he willingly gave him a detailed account of the history of his hemorrhages. But he argued, as he had done earlier, that a flow of blood from the lungs should not necessarily be regarded as a sign of tuberculosis, unless it were accompanied by other telltale symptoms which he had never observed in himself. If the first hemorrhage several years ago had been a genuine sign of tuberculosis, he concluded, he would already be dead. Though he now admitted that he had been having hemorrhages at the rate of one or two a year since the first flow, Chekhov, so wise in many things, refused to draw the obvious conclusion. Was it inertia, fear of the truth, a sense of fatalism, or a conviction of destiny beyond the interference of any human agency?

The anxieties of the autumn, however, were mitigated by a joyous event. On October 7 four members of the Division of Russian Language and Letters of the Academy of Sciences, of which Grigorovich was one, having heard a report by the eminent Academician and Director of the Petersburg Public Library, A. F. Bychkov, unanimously voted to award the Pushkin Prize, "for the best literary production distinguished by high artistic worth," to *In the Twilight*, by Anton Pavlovich Chekhov. The next day Grigorovich sent Chekhov his congratulations, but the old man did not forget to add that the committee also unanimously expressed its sincere regret that Chekhov failed to esteem his talent, wrote for the cheap press, and often hurried his work. One may suppose that Grigorovich himself had pointed out these favorite faults to the committee, and the action probably contributed to the fact that Chekhov received only five hundred roubles, half the regular prize. At a public meeting of the Academy of Sciences on October 19, an official announcement was made of the award.

Although Chekhov had been nurturing hopes on this score since the end of the previous year, the news filled him and his family with exultation. Telegrams and letters of congratulation arrived. He wandered about like a man in love, he told Suvorin. In their inexpressible joy his mother and father babbled nonsense, and his sister, faithful custodian of his reputation, made the rounds of his friends to explain the significance of the prize. Modestly he wrote Grigorovich of his joy and gratitude, and that without his help and that of Polonsky and Suvorin he would never have won the award which other young writers, such as Korolenko, were more entitled to than he. Over the last year, he asserted, he had given up the cheap press except *New Times*, which he did not place in this category, and besides, he was obligated to Suvorin. Further, he had a novel in mind which he outlined, but he planned to take a long time over it for, he significantly declared: "I still do not have a firm political, religious, and philosophical outlook; I change it monthly and therefore I'm compelled to limit myself to the description of how my heroes love, marry, produce children, die, and how they speak." (*October 9, 1888.*)

To Suvorin he more realistically interpreted what he believed should be the significance of the award precisely to him: "I repeat once more: second- and third-class newspaper writers ought to erect a monument to me or at least present me a silver cigarette case; I have showed them the road to the thick magazines, to laurels, and to the hearts of decent people. Although this has been my unique service, that which I've written, and for which they gave me the prize, will not live in the memory of people ten years." (*October 10, 1888.*)

Invitations to parties, dinners, and social events multiplied, the usual tribute to the winner of a national prize. In November a special invitation compelled his presence at the opening evening of the Society of Arts and Literature. There he met for the first time Konstantin Stanislavsky, the man who in a few years would help to make the most celebrated playwright in Russia. Although even at this time Stanislavsky was known in Moscow theatrical circles, Chekhov did not bother to mention him in his account of this event to Suvorin. The aim of the Society, he sarcastically remarked, was unity, and all around him he saw only deadly boredom and shocking taste. A young lady sang and the well-known actor, Lensky, read one of Chekhov's tales. A listener within earshot of Chekhov declared: "A rather weak story!" at which a mischievous mutual friend insisted upon introducing Chekhov to the embarrassed critic. The reason people invited him everywhere and regaled him with food and drink, he declared to Suvorin, was simply because they liked what was not ordinary in him. Yet he was also an ordinary mortal and if tomorrow he should appear so in the eyes of his friends, they would cease to love and pity him.

Chekhov experienced something of the same reaction in a visit he made to Petersburg for ten days in early December. Again he stayed with the Suvorins. Well-wishers tore him apart, he said, and rode him like a post-horse. There he met the great Tschaikovsky, who had admired his tales for some time and whose music delighted Chekhov. At the Russian Literary Society, *An Attack of Nerves*, a tale he had recently completed for the volume in honor of the late Garshin, was read by the actor Davydov. A lively discussion followed, in which Chekhov answered questions from the audience.

A visit to Alexander induced a cold fury which he later poured out to his brother in a letter. The sight of Alexander parading before the chambermaid in his underwear shocked him, and his shouting and use of vile language in the presence of his children and his nasty insults to the cook and Natalya Alexandrovna Golden, who was then living with him, invoked dismal memories in Anton of his father's behavior when they were children. At the very least, he angrily wrote Alexander, he should have some regard for his offspring. "You must not use obscene language in their presence with impunity, insult the servants, or shout furiously at Natalya Alexandrovna: 'Get the hell out of here; I'm not supporting you!' " (*January 2, 1889.*)

Another unpleasant occurrence during this visit was that, in the hurly-burly of being entertained, he neglected to make formal farewell calls on close friends, notably Leontiev-Shcheglov and Grigorovich. Chekhov promptly heard that this slight deeply offended Grigorovich, and to make amends he sent him a long letter of apology, actually the last letter he ever wrote this man, who was once reported to have said of a critic of his favorite young author: "Why, he's not fit to kiss the foot of a flea that bites Chekhov." Though Chekhov owed much to Grigorovich's initial encouragement and influence, his failure to honor the old man with a visit may well have been subconsciously prompted by his friend's annoying possessiveness and persistent criticism of his connection with the humorous magazine and newspapers. Chekhov tended to regard his work for the cheap press as an invaluable training ground for a young writer. And by now his own higher artistic standards must have convinced him that he had quite exaggerated Grigorovich's authority in the literary world and had overpraised his merits as a writer of fiction. However, as the sentiments of his letter of apology indicate, Chekhov, so sensitive himself in these matters, must have experienced a feeling of guilt over his slight to a friend who had meant so much to him at the outset of his career. It is little wonder that he left Petersburg "bored and sad."

Misfortunes pursued him back in Moscow. He frankly wrote Suvorin that certain people were gossiping that his trips to Petersburg and his aid in the production of Suvorin's play *Tatyana Repina*[4] at the Maly Theater were to be explained by the fact that he was courting his daughter. To make matters worse, Pleshcheev wrote him on December 31 of a rumor that he intended to move to Petersburg and take a position on *New Times*. The editor of the liberal *Northern Herald* made it clear that any close connection with the "shameless trash and fellows" who wrote for this newspaper would associate him with their reactionary views, and besides such work would have a destructive influence on his talent. In reply Chekhov explained that Suvorin had jokingly offered him a position on *New Times* at six thousand roubles a year, and that he himself, because he considered the matter as of no consequence, had probably been responsible for its circulation. But now that Pleshcheev had made an issue of it in such terms, Chekhov, with his obstinate independence challenged, asserted that he saw no harm in accepting a position on *New Times*. If they paid him a thousand roubles a year he would agree to read manuscripts for the paper, and if they were willing to offer him a thousand roubles a month, he would give his whole attention to the work and — he pointedly informed Pleshcheev — "I would conduct an unrelenting struggle for my own independence and for those views which I hold in journalism." (*January 2, 1889.*)

In fact, as 1888 drew to a close an accumulation of disagreeable happenings soured Chekhov's endless good-nature and undermined his spirit. He informed Suvorin that he contemplated moving to Petersburg

[4] Chekhov gave Suvorin a good deal of advice about the structure of this play and its production. And in March 1889 he sent Suvorin a manuscript, entitled *Tatyana Repina. A Drama in One Act.* It was a half-serious effort, written in one sitting, Chekhov said, to provide a kind of epilogue to Suvorin's serious play, in which the further fate of some of the characters is worked out. Suvorin liked it so much that he had two copies printed, one for himself and one for Chekhov.

with his mother so that he could engage in serious work, for his writing was suffering in Moscow. After being called away late one night from work on a stubborn story in order to heal the lacerated head of his drunken friend, the poet Palmin, he wrote Suvorin: "In general, I lead a tedious life and from time to time I begin to feel hatred, something that has never happened to me before. Long, stupid conversations, guests, petitioners, the two-or-three-rouble payments from patients which are spent on cabs, leaving me nothing — in fact, everything is in such a muddle that I feel like running away from home. People obtain loans from me and don't repay them, they take away my books, and have no regard for my time. All I lack is an unhappy love-affair." (*December 23, 1888.*)

And three days later he continued in the same vein to Suvorin: "All week I've been as mean as a son of a bitch. . . . On the first evening of the holiday I hovered over a sick man who died before my eyes. On the whole, there have been many unhappy motifs. Spitefulness is a kind of pusillanimity. I acknowledge it and scold myself."

‹ 6 ›

Over 1888 one may observe an intellectual as well as an artistic flowering in Chekhov. Perhaps the success of *The Steppe*, his first deliberate effort to claim a place among Russia's leading writers, helped to jar him loose from an inherent timidity and encouraged him to assert himself in sharp and often memorable language on social and artistic questions. Ideas flowed easily and his frame of reference expanded. Although at times he evinced a daring reaching out to identify himself with contemporary issues, especially in the area of literature and criticism, his self-assertiveness was conditioned by the doubts and anxieties of a young man.

In conversations and letters Chekhov now began to lay about him with surprising directness in contemporary literature and criticism. With few exceptions he disapproved of most of the young writers and tended to attribute their failings to the defeatism and social sickness of the times. They were uninterested in the lives of simple people; they were too timid, too subjective, and too narrow in their outlook. When Pleshcheev informed him of the envy of certain young writers over his winning the Pushkin Prize, Chekhov lashed out: "These sons of bitches ought to rejoice and not envy. They have neither patriotism nor love for literature but only their own ambition." (*October 25, 1888.*) What particularly distressed him was the clannishness of these young writers, their eagerness to form groups to protect their own material interests or to support literary platforms. When one of them invited him to join a Petersburg group that proposed to carry announcements of one another's works in their books, Chekhov wrote to one of them, Leontiev-Shcheglov, that he could understand "solidarity and such stuff" on the stock exchange, in politics, and in religious affairs, but not among literary men. "To lend a helping hand to one's colleague, to esteem his personality and work, not to gossip about him or envy him, not to lie or play the hypocrite with him — for this you've got to be not so much the young literary figure as just a plain human being. Let us be ordinary people, let us adopt the same attitude *toward all*, then an artificially-wrought solidarity will not be needed." (*May 3, 1888*.)

It may have been Chekhov's apprenticeship to the humorous journals and cheap press that made him so hostile to the thick periodicals that catered to the literary elite. Although he had been happy enough to be taken up by the *Northern Herald*, he suspected that some of these publications looked down their noses at him. Snobbish well-wishers were glad that he had deserted *New Times*, he informed Suvorin, so now he would hasten to publish a tale in his newspaper before their joy evaporated. His suspicion that several of the thick periodicals secretly took their orders from government officials had some basis in fact. Writing to Pleshcheev about the liberal *Russian Thought*, a magazine in which Chekhov later played a prominent part, he declared: "Under the banner of science, art, and oppressed free-thinking among us in Russia, such toads and crocodiles will rule in ways not known even at the time of the Inquisition in Spain. You will see! Narrowness, great pretensions, extreme ambition, and the complete absence of any literary and social conscience will do their work." (*August 27, 1888*.) The fact that most literary critics in this and other thick periodicals had acclaimed his best contributions up to this point did not prevent him from dubbing them all as "flatterers and cowards," afraid either to praise or blame and, in particular, not believing in themselves. When the important critic, A. I. Vvedensky, who had attacked him, expressed surprise that Chekhov had failed to visit him, he scornfully retorted: "I could not call upon him because I don't know him. In the second place, "I'm not accustomed to associate with people to whom I'm indifferent, just as I don't dine at the jubilees of writers I don't read. In the third place, the time has not yet come for me to go to Mecca on a duty call." (*April 9, 1888*.)

Chekhov paid more serious attention to a long and rather favorable article on his writing in *Northern Herald* by the young Dmitri Merezhkovsky, who later became quite celebrated as a poet, novelist and leader of one wing of the Symbolist Movement. The article lacked simplicity and definition, Chekhov thought, but he particularly objected to Merezhkovsky's attempt to apply an essentially scientific approach in an analysis of creative art.

The absence of a vigorous, effective professional criticism disturbed Chekhov. Because of this lack, he complained, a mass of lives and works of art were vanishing before the eyes of his generation. Though all praised to the skies *An Attack of Nerves*, he pointed out, only the old novelist Grigorovich had singled out for comment the description of the virgin snow falling on the street lined with brothels. Chekhov wrote to Suvorin: "If we had any criticism, I would know that I provide material — good or bad, it doesn't matter — and that to people who devote themselves to the study of life, I am as necessary as a star to an astronomer. Then I would work hard and would know for what I worked." (*December 23, 1888.*)

However severe he was on his rivals, Chekhov was more severe with himself. On the whole, he had lived up to his resolution to shun hasty writing; he published only nine stories in 1888, although four of these, and by far the most notable artistically (*The Steppe, The Lights, The Name-Day Party, An Attack of Nerves*), are long short stories — he sometimes referred to them as "little novels." Yet he did not abide by his decision to abandon the cheap press; lack of funds, perhaps force of habit, and a desire not to forsake entirely Suvorin's newspaper, led him to publish three short stories in *New Times* and also two in the *Petersburg Gazette*. As he confessed, he did not yet know his own strengths and weaknesses in the longer type of tale and he struggled mightily with these works, cutting, polishing, juggling the parts, sometimes abandoning what he had written and starting anew. Again and again in his letters he stigmatized the results as "boring," "dull," "monotonous"; he had intended *The Lights* to be philosophical, but it ended in a "vinegary taste." In his infinite concern to avoid the superfluous in his lengthier stores, he achieved by artistic measure and economy of means a refinement of expression that was truly classical, and an illusion of reality — based on his favorite touchstones of objectivity, truthfulness, originality, boldness, brevity, and simplicity — that seemed quite complete.

Concentration on the longer tale complicated the debate that had been going on in Chekhov's mind concerning the relation between art and life. The moral suasion of Tolstoyism, with its strong element of reformed Christianity, had already begun to lose some of its charm for Chekhov, who, if not an atheist at this stage of his development, could properly be described as a confirmed agnostic. In fact, a brief sketch in 1888, *A Story without a Title*, concerning a group of monks who desert their monastery for a town after hearing their abbot's seductive description of its sinning population, may well be regarded as a satire on the unreality of Tolstoy's moral preachments. However, such stories as *The Lights* and *An Attack of Nerves* have a distinct Tolstoyan flavor. They are powerful problem pieces in which the connection between ethical and social values is implicit if not actively argued. With a courage that he had formerly lacked, Chekhov now declared bluntly that "Russian life beats down the Russian man." In greeting Grigorovich at Christmas he sadly observed: "It is a poetic holiday. I'm only sorry that people are poor and hungry in Russia. . . ." And he asked Suvorin why he did not publish an article about the way Tatars were left uneducated and were pushed around by their Russian overlords. Or why not do an article on the slavery of prostitution in Moscow, a shocking revelation which he himself had provided in his *An Attack of Nerves*, which is a profound study of a typical Garshin theme: society's personal guilt in relation to the victims of its social order.

Chekhov appears to have entered the lists himself in a planned series of articles for *New Times*. One of them, *Moscow Hypocrites*, defended shop clerks whose employers had prevailed upon the City Council to alter the Sunday closing law. Another, *On Pauperism*, takes as its text the current drive against street beggars. Everybody in Russia, Chekhov demonstrates, is trying to get something for nothing, and he concludes his article: "When all layers of society, from the highest to the lowest, learn to esteem the labor and the kopecks of others, street beggary, domestic, and every other kind, will vanish."

The debate, however, foundered at the edge of politics, although Chekhov lived in a country where social problems were defined in terms of one's political allegiance. Pleshcheev professed to see nothing of the "direction" which Chekhov had mentioned, nothing against either liberalism or conservatism, in *The Name-Day Party*, whose central character, a rank conservative, rails against the evils of liberalism. And generalizing on this point, Pleshcheev repeated a type of criticism which now positively angered Chekhov — namely, that readers found in his tales neither sympathy nor convictions, a lack which they attributed to Chekhov's indifference or to his desire to be entirely objective. "But indeed," he ambiguously answered, "do I not protest against lying in the story from beginning to end? And in truth, is this not direction?" (*October 7–8, 1888.*) In a subsequent letter he returned to Pleshcheev's charge: "It seems to me that I could sooner be accused of gluttony, drunkenness, light-mindedness, coldness, anything you wish, rather than a desire to put myself in a certain attitude. I have never concealed my position. . . . It is true that the suspicious thing in my story is the attempt to balance the pluses and the minuses. But I do not balance conservatism against liberalism, which for me are not the chief things at all, but the lying against the truthfulness of characters. . . . When I present such types or speak about them, I do not think of conservatism or liberalism, but of their stupidity and pretensions." (*October 9, 1888.*) In the same vein he commented upon Elena Lintvareva's warning to him not to associate with such a reactionary as Suvorin. These young ladies and their politically-minded cavaliers are pure souls, he wrote Suvorin, but nine tenths of their political purity is not worth a straw. It was all based on misty and naïve antipathies and sympathies for people and labels but not for facts. "It is easy to be pure when you are able to hate a devil you do not know and love a God whom it never occurs to you to doubt." (*September 11, 1888.*) Freedom, he thought, could be menaced just as much by the Left as by the Right.

This was Chekhov's dilemma: his firm conviction that the artist must remain a free individual beyond the restraining bonds of political parties, creeds, prejudices, and labels. With passionate sincerity, he summarized this conviction in a letter to Pleshcheev: "I fear those who look for tendencies between the lines and want to regard me precisely as a liberal or a conservative. I am not a liberal, a conservative, an evolutionist, a monk, or indifferent to the world. I should like to be a free artist — and that is all — and I regret that God has not given me the strength to be one. I hate lies and violence in all their aspects. . . . Pharisaism, stupidity, and idle whims reign not only in the homes of merchants and in prison; I see them in science, in literature, and among young people. Therefore I cannot nurture any special feeling for policemen, butchers, learned men, writers, or youth. I regard tradesmarks or labels as prejudices. My holy of holies are the human body, health, intelligence, talent, inspiration, love, and the most absolute freedom — freedom from violence and falsehood in whatever form these may be expressed. This is the program I would hold to if I were a great artist." (*October 4, 1888.*)

At this time Chekhov did not seem to realize that his "holy of holies" was uncompatible with his belief that as an artist he must objectively depict society in a spirit of noninvolvement in its great moral problems. If art has any definitive answers to the eternal disharmony of life, they must be the purely subjective responses of the artist himself.

Suvorin had protested that Chekhov failed to solve the problem of pessimism in *The Lights,* a story that insists upon the decisive relationship between man's philosophy and his actions. And Leontiev-Shcheglov had criticized him for ending the story with the sentence: "You cannot make head or tail of anything in this world." The artist-psychologist must analyze especially the soul of his hero, the critic maintained.

The writer's task, Chekhov answered Suvorin, is not to solve such questions as God or pessimism, "but to depict only who, how, and in what circumstances people have spoken or thought about God or pessimism. The artist must not be a judge of his characters or of what they say, but only an objective observer." The reader must make his own evaluation of what is said, Chekhov insisted; the author's task was to throw some light on his characters and to speak their language. (*May 30, 1888.*) And to Leontiev-Shcheglov, he replied: "It is not the psychologist's business to pretend that he understands what no one understands. Then we will not be charlatans and will frankly declare that you can't make head or tail of anything in this world. Only fools and charlatans know and understand everything." (*June 9, 1888.*)

Chekhov's emphasis on objectivity in the process of literary creation may well have been influenced by his scientific training. He believed that outside matter there was no experience, no knowledge, no absolute truths. And he appears to have looked upon social phenomena very much as the natural scientist rather than as the artist-sociologist, for he was an enemy of everything romantic, metaphysical, and sentimental. In his tales he diagnosed life as a physician diagnosed disease, but as an artist he refused to offer prescriptions for the moral and social ills of mankind.

Chekhov seemed to believe at this time that all the artist could do was to draw life as it is, for there was nothing he could decide about it. To be sure, creation was a premeditated act in which the artist consciously posed definite questions, but he was not obliged to resolve these questions. Even in the selection of his themes, Chekhov maintained, the artist must remain objective and he must handle them truthfully, that is, in relation to life as it is. Any tendentiousness or emphasis on particulars must be eschewed.

Toward the end of 1888, however, Chekhov obviously began to have serious doubts about objectivity in art. "I sometimes preach heresies," he wrote Suvorin on October 27, "but I have never once gone so far as an absolute negation of problems in art. . . . The artist, however, must pass judgment only on what he understands; his circle is as limited as that of any other specialist. . . . If one denies problems and purpose in creative work, then one must recognize that the artist creates without design, without purpose, under the influence of some aberration. . . ." It was important in art, he pointed out, not to confuse the solution of a problem with its correct presentation.

The debate which Chekhov carried on within himself and with his correspondents about art and its purpose reflected in reality an acute dissatisfaction with his own writing. In this same letter he informed Suvorin ". . . I haven't yet begun my literary career" — Plots for five big stories and two novels swarmed in his head, while what he had already published was trash. There were subjects that sat in his mind like discarded books in a storehouse. He loved them. "If my love is mistaken, then I am not right, but it is possible that it is not mistaken! I'm either a fool and a presumptuous person, or I'm actually an organism capable of being a fine writer; all that I now write displeases and bores me, all that sits in my head interests me, touches and agitates me." In moments of frustration he preferred the doers, the activists, to the bookish scholars or to literary artists who only wrote about life. In an obituary notice at this time on the famous traveler N. M. Przhevalsky, whose exciting career as an explorer he enthusiastically admired, Chekhov significantly asserted: "Such personalities are living documents demonstrating to society that in addition to the men and women who spend their lives discussing optimism and pessimism, writing mediocre stories to kill time, and drawing up unnecessary schemes and cheap dissertations . . . there are people of another sort, capable of heroic feats, possessing faith, and thoroughly conscious of their aim. If the positive types created by literature provide valuable educational material, those created by life itself are beyond price."

« 7 »

Not until the beginning of October did Chekhov return to the task which, at the end of the previous year, he had promised himself to complete — a revision of his play *Ivanov* for a performance in Petersburg. He radically altered the second and fourth acts, wrote a new monologue for the hero, and retouched the characterization of Sasha. "If they don't understand my *Ivanov* now," he told Suvorin, "I'll throw it into the stove and write a novel — 'Enough'!"[5] This effort and perhaps the huge success of *The Bear*, which was being performed in several cities at this time, intensified his interest once again in everything connected with the theater. He busied himself in getting his one-act play *Swan Song* through the censor for production in Petersburg, and wrote another one-act farce, *The Proposal*, which concerns the hilarious unreasonableness and stupidity of two people who wish to marry. These one-act plays, where his spirit of fun had full scope, came easily to him. When he had written himself out on fiction, he jokingly declared, he would make his living by composing one-acters. "I believe I could write a hundred a year," he boasted to Suvorin. "Subjects for one-act plays sprout out of me like oil from the soil of Baku." (*December 23, 1888.*) Chekhov also occupied himself now with *The Wood Demon*, the play that he had sketched the past summer at Feodosiya and in which Suvorin, who had written a number of dramas, agreed to collaborate. When Suvorin sent his draft of the first act, however, Chekhov, obviously dissatisfied with it, drew up a series of brilliant descriptions of the characters of the proposed play as guides for Suvorin, and in some of them are discernible the clear lineaments of characters in the later *Uncle Vanya*, which was based on *The Wood Demon*. Suvorin quickly begged off and the project was dropped for the time being, although Chekhov continued to urge him to collaborate on some other subject — a tragedy, he suggested, on Holofernes and Judith, or Napoleon at Elba — he was aware by now of his friend's preferences and limitations as a dramatist.

Caught up in his new interest, Chekhov missed few performances at the Maly theater and the Korsh, and even acted as Suvorin's agent when the latter contemplated buying the Korsh playhouse, although nothing came of the matter. He improved his knowledge of staging and

[5] A reference to Turgenev's tale with this title, which is a kind of swan song to his literary efforts. (*Between October 4–6, 1888.*)

acting and cultivated further his acquaintance with the actors and actresses, some of whom, such as Davydov and A. P. Lensky, became his close friends. At times he seemed to play the part of a booking agent, soliciting the manuscript plays of his friends, criticizing them very skilfully, then submitting them to Korsh and the actors, who had a great deal to say about the approval of a play. And in some cases, if selected, he would choose the cast and see the play through rehearsal. He performed all these functions, for example, on behalf of Suvorin's play *Tatyana Repina* which was produced at the Maly Theater.

Curiously enough, Chekhov's intimacy with the theater — which he had achieved as an habitué, a reporter and critic of the stage, and a dramatist — seemed to intensify his contempt for many of its practices. Repeatedly he lashed out against the theater; it had fallen into the hands of scoundrels, ignoramuses, and drunks. Most of the plays he saw he regarded as slanders on life. "We must strive with all our power to see to it that the stage passes out of the hands of grocers and into literary hands, otherwise the theater is doomed," he told Suvorin in full anticipation of the conviction held by Stanislavsky and Nemirovich-Danchenko when they set out to reform the Russian stage a few years later. (*November 3, 1888.*) "I do not have any love for the stage," he wrote Leontiev-Shcheglov. "The contemporary theater — it is an eruption, a nasty disease of the cities. One must clean up the disease, but to like it — that is unhealthy. You will begin to quarrel with me, and to use the old phrase: The theater is a school, it educates — and so forth. But I'll tell you how I see it: The theater at present is not higher than the crowd; on the contrary, the life of the crowd is higher and more intelligent than the theater. This means that it is not a school but something quite different." (*November 7, 1888.*)

Rather cynically Chekhov explained to Suvorin that it was possible to hate the theater and at the same time write for it with satisfaction. You go to the manager's office to pick up your royalties with the same element of expectation and surprise with which the fisherman goes to his net to see what the catch is. "An agreeable amusement," he concluded. (*November 18, 1888.*)

Whatever Chekhov may have felt about the execrable conditions of the Russian theater, it did not prevent him from working away on the revision of *Ivanov* over the last three months of 1888. Despite the mixed success of its Moscow performance, he had decided, and with considerable reason, that the point of this realistic play, which attempted to portray life as it is, had been badly or entirely misunderstood by the audience and even by friends who had read copies of it. The principal reason for his drastic changes in the last act was to clarify the characterization of the hero. He wished to make it clear that Ivanov did not die because of the slanders and public insults heaped upon him, but because he had reached the end of the road; that even the love of Sasha, who had unsuccessfully endeavored to reform him, had only lowered him in his own eyes.

With a deep feeling of relief, Chekhov finished the revision on December 19 and sent a clear copy to Suvorin. "Now my Mr. Ivanov is much more intelligible," he wrote. "The finale does not entirely satisfy me (except for the shot, everything is flabby), but I comfort myself with the thought that its form is not yet final. . . . I give you my word that I shall never again write such intellectual and rotten plays as *Ivanov*." (*December 19, 1888.*) And he asked Suvorin to see that the play was brought to the attention of the Petersburg Alexandrinsky Theater, whose producer had requested it for his benefit night. He even listed the actors and actresses who, he thought, should play the principal roles.

Much to Chekhov's chagrin, the reactions from Petersburg, which were not long in coming, indicated that even the revised version had not always conveyed the meaning he had struggled so hard to put into the play. The producer imagined Ivanov to be a superfluous man in the Turgenev tradition, and a leading actress of the company wanted to know why the hero seemed to be such a scoundrel. Suvorin advised that Ivanov be endowed with some quality that would make it apparent why women were attracted to him, and he asked why Doctor Lvov was a great man. Chekhov replied that if three people had misunderstood him in this fashion, then he had not put down what he wished to write and the play ought not to be produced. Patiently he wrote out for Suvorin a detailed description of just how he understood each of the main characters. And he concluded: "If the audience leaves the theater with the conviction that Ivanovs are scoundrels and Doctor Lvovs are great men, then I'll have to give up the theater and send my pen to hell. . . . In my imagination Ivanov and Lvov appear as living people. In all conscience I tell you sincerely that these people were born in my head, not out of ocean spray or preconceived ideas, not of 'intellectuality,' and not by chance. They are the result of observation and the study of life. . . . If they have emerged on paper lifeless and indistinct, it is not their fault but my lack of ability to convey my own ideas. It seems as though I took up playwriting too early." (*December 30, 1888.*)

News from the Alexandrinsky Theater that the play would be performed gladdened him. Yet he was still worried about its inadequacies, and on the last day of the year he wrote Leontiev-Shcheglov that if certain conditions which he had posed for the production of *Ivanov* were not accepted he would withdraw the play.

CHAPTER IX

"There Is a Sort of Stagnation in My Soul"

JANUARY 31, 1889 — the opening night of the Petersburg performance of *Ivanov* — seemed so close! Much work still had to be done on the play. Chekhov had come to stay with the Suvorins in order to see *Ivanov* through rehearsal. He could not overcome a feeling of inadequacy in playwriting, for which, he decided, one must have a special talent. Parodying an earlier observation, he remarked to Pleshcheev that fiction was his legal wife but the dramatic form "a showy, noisy, impertinent and tiresome mistress." (*January 15, 1889.*) Worse still, he said, to make over what he considered a bad play was as difficult as trying to turn the old trousers of a soldier into a dress coat.

However, much more than money, which Chekhov had by no means lost sight of in this venture, was now at stake. Though he had realized that the hurriedly written *Ivanov*, which he had served up in Moscow two years ago, would not do for the more sophisticated Petersburg theater patrons and critics, his thoroughly revised version had now run into additional complications which called for further changes. Since the opening was designed as a benefit performance for F. A. Yurkovsky, this eminent director of the Alexandrinsky Theater had taken the precaution to assign the roles to his foremost players. The great actress Mariya Savina would play the part of Sasha — one that Chekhov had deliberately reduced in importance in the revision — and he now felt it necessary to build up that portrayal and even add lines doing justice to the special qualities of her art. All this involved additional corrections, interpolations, and again some radical changes in the fourth act, which he never resolved to his own satisfaction. The early rehearsals discouraged him and he ominously wrote brother Misha that nothing good would come of it. And not long before the opening Davydov declared that he must drop the lead, which he had played so well in Moscow, because he simply could not understand Chekhov's altered characterization of Ivanov. In despair, Chekhov visited him in the evenings and patiently coached him on the spiritual and intellectual content of the role, yet at the rehearsals, he complained, he continued to quarrel and become reconciled with "the tedious Davydov" ten times a day.

Though Chekhov had grown to hate *Ivanov* long before the Petersburg opening night, something told him that his extensive revisions had improved the play, that he had portrayed people who were not contrived, and that in his protagonist he had succeeded, where other Russian novelists and playwrights had failed, in creating a believable image of the educated, disillusioned man of the eighties obsessed by the inner emptiness of his life. Where he had gone wrong, he guessed, was in the shading of the characterization and in the manner of his presentation of Ivanov. More than talent and freshness were needed here, and especially a feeling of personal freedom which, as a self-made intellectual, he had only just begun to acquire. Rather poignantly he wrote to Suvorin: "What gently born writers have been endowed with by nature, self-made intellectuals buy at the price of their youth. Write me a story about a young man, the son of a serf, a former shopkeeper, a choir boy, high school and university student, brought up on respect for rank, kissing the hands of priests, belonging to a generation alien to thought, offering thanks for every mouthful of bread, often whipped, going to school without shoes, quarreling, tormenting animals, fond of dining with rich relatives, playing the hypocrite before God and people without any cause, except out of a recognition of his own insignificance — then tell how that young man presses the slave out of him drop by drop and how he wakes up one fine morning and feels that in his veins flows not the blood of a slave, but real human blood." (*January 7, 1889.*)

Preoccupied with the business of his play, Chekhov saw few Petersburg friends apart from Pleshcheev and Leontiev-Shcheglov. He had dinner with Barantsevich. He sought a brief meeting with old Grigorovich, no doubt to ease his conscience for his failure to call on him on his previous visit. Though he still loved the old man, he remarked to Suvorin, he had begun to detect a virtuoso-like insincerity in Grigorovich. One evening he accepted an invitation to a party at the home of

S. N. Khudekov, editor and publisher of the *Petersburg Gazette*. There he met Lidiya Avilova, a tall attractive lady of twenty-four, with rosy cheeks and luxurious hair which she wore in two long thick braids. She was the sister-in-law of Khudekov, married to a young man working in the Ministry of Education, to whom she had recently borne a son. As a mere girl Lidiya Avilova had nourished ambitions to be a writer and had passionately admired Chekhov's tales, some of which she knew by heart. His starched collar that hung around his neck like a horse collar and his plain tie were forgotten when they were introduced and he held her hand in his and smiled at her tenderly. He told her of his worry about *Ivanov*, and at supper they talked of writing. "Living images create thought," he said, "but thought does not create images." And he went on to explain that the life which he depicted in his stories was that "which you have not seen or never noticed before: its divergence from the norm, its contradictions." Before they parted, he said that he would send her a ticket for *Ivanov*, and he urged her to let him see her manuscripts: he would read them attentively. In her memoirs, Lidiya Avilova wrote of this first meeting: "Something exploded in my soul. . . . I scarcely doubt that something the same happened to Chekhov. We looked at one another with surprise and joy. 'I'll come again,' said Chekhov. 'Shall we meet?' " Subsequent events suggest that her feminine intuition, about her own feelings, at least, was correct.

Though to Madame Suvorina he pretended indifference on the opening night, Chekhov later confessed that he was terribly agitated about the play. His fears quickly vanished. Its originality, and the brilliant acting, captivated the audience, and at the concluding scene between Ivanov and Sarah at the end of the third act, the audience acclaimed the author and director in a tremendous ovation. The theater-going public — surfeited with virtuous, self-sacrificing heroes prating about human dignity and the happiness of people — were agreeably surprised by Chekhov's effort to tell them the truth about themselves. On every hand the play was hailed. With minor exceptions, the many reviews were highly favorable, reflecting pretty generally the opinion of the *Petersburg Gazette*, which wrote that *Ivanov* represented "the triumph of a truly powerful talent. . . . Its success was colossal, the kind of success which rarely happens on our stage." In general, opposition to the play centered in the "left" writers such as Mikhailovsky, Korolenko, and Gleb Uspensky. For them its tendentiousness lacked a meaningful social message. The still greater and much more conservative author

Leskov thought otherwise. He jotted down in his diary that there were, unfortunately, too many weak, will-less Ivanovs in Russia who evaded the significant problems of society. "A wise play," he concluded. "A great dramatic talent."

A wealthy admirer, N. M. Sokovnin, arranged a banquet in Chekhov's honor the night after the opening performance. All the toasts embarrassed the author, but when the host drank to *Ivanov*, which he compared to Griboedov's immortal masterpiece *Woe from Wit*, the unhappy Chekhov blushed. "Not even Shakespeare had to listen to the speeches that I heard," he ironically wrote later to Leontiev-Shcheglov, who was present at the occasion. (*February 18, 1889*.) The next day he hurriedly left for Moscow. He felt suffocated, exhausted, like a hunted hare. When lucky, he was a coward and always felt a desire to crawl under a table — this was the excuse he offered Barantsevich for his hasty departure. "There are two heroes at present in Petersburg," he wrote to Mariya Kiseleva after his return home: "the naked Phryne by Semiradsky,[1] and myself fully clothed. Both have created a stir." (*February 17, 1889*.) The news from his brother Alexander that he had collected from the Alexandrinsky Theater 994 roubles in payment for five performances of *Ivanov* and two of *The Bear* placed a happy period to Chekhov's first dramatic efforts in Petersburg.

« 2 »

Back at Sadovaya-Kudrinskaya after his Petersburg triumph, Chekhov felt somewhat bored and let down. He now could not tolerate people talking about *Ivanov*. Though he already contemplated another play, he urged Leontiev-Shcheglov, a fiction writer with a passion for drama, that since they were not generals in this genre, they ought not to demean themselves by contending with subalterns. To regard writing plays as a kind of sport was all right, but one must not take it seriously. As for himself, he experienced a strong desire to return to humble stories. To write plays was not in his character, he told Leikin in the course of explaining why he had left Petersburg without calling on him — he had been so pushed by people. Although he asked Leikin, who knew them well, to give his regards to the Khudekovs, whose "wife is a very sympathetic woman," he did not mention her sister, Lidiya Avi-

[1] A canvas of the artist G. I. Semiradsky, depicting "Phryne at the Feast of Poseidon in Eleusis," which at that time was on exhibition at the Petersburg Academy of Arts.

lova, who believed that she had made a deep impression on Chekhov.[2]

However, he did not hesitate to encourage Alexander, who, a bit envious of his brother's success, asked his advice on whether he should attempt a play. Try to be as original and clever as possible, Chekhov advised, and don't be afraid to write foolish things. Brevity is the sister of talent. Declarations of love, he added, the infidelity of husbands and wives, and the tears of widows and orphans have long since been written about. Though the subject should be new, a "fable" was unnecessary. And he concluded with the cautionary point that morals do not purify plays any more than flies purify the air.

In fact, Alexander, whose second marriage would soon take place, had strangely begun to worry about his financial future and queried his brother on buying a farm in the Ukraine. Chekhov discouraged such a venture because of Alexander's small income, but the request rekindled his old desire to set up a writers' colony in the Ukraine. For the first time in his life he now felt in affluent circumstances, a feeling, alas, that was of short duration. He had almost fifteen hundred roubles locked away in his drawer, and with some assurance he believed that he could count on an annual income of from three to four thousand, for his tales were selling well enough to go into repeated editions and regularly brought in small sums, as did his one-act plays. Another collection of stories, *Children*, appeared in March 1889. And at this time a lottery ticket for seventy-five thousand roubles cast its magic spell over him to the inevitable period of disillusionment. Convinced that his assured income was adequate to risk a mortgage of ten thousand roubles, he went to Kharkov in March on a dual mission — to look for an estate for Suvorin, who was interested in such a purchase, and to find a farm for himself which, he told Alexander, would be a refuge against possible poverty and a place where all the Chekhovs could gather. But he could not find a place sufficiently quiet and remote. Shortly thereafter he complained to Alexander: "I spent three hundred roubles a month, I'm a mild person, but I seem unable to do anything that is agreeable either to myself or to the others." (*April 11, 1889.*)

These remarks, of course, apply to the family. Though they expected much, they gave in return a great deal of the devotion and loyalty which his exacting nature required. Years of living together, during which he had played the part of father of the family, had developed

[2] This letter to Leikin (February 21, 1889) is to be found in *Literaturnoe Nasledstvo* (*Literary Heritage*), Moscow, 1960, LXVIII, 180.

deep ties of affection which none of them would dream of severing. His aging mother sometimes annoyed him with her old insistence that he marry a rich woman, like the widow A. M. Siberyakova, a millionairess and a target of Chekhov's jokes. Indeed, this notion became a rumor, especially in Petersburg. "I'm not thinking of marrying for millions," he wrote Leontiev-Shcheglov in an effort to spike the gossip, "and whenever and if I marry, it will not be for money . . ." (*March 11, 1889.*) Though the nagging of his mother vexed him at times, he was very tender with her and wrote her when he was away. He liked to tease her over her religiosity: "Mother," he would ask, "what do the monks wear for drawers?" And in her soft, low voice she would declare to those present: "That again! Antosha everlastingly asks this."

Misha, now twenty-five, finished his law studies at the university in 1889 and sought both a position and a wife. When he sacrificed family obligations in his persistent wooing of eligible girls, Chekhov grew irritated, but he always protected and aided this younger brother and now pestered his influential friends to help Misha in finding a suitable position. The twenty-six-year old Masha, who combined teaching in a private girls' school with painting, still evinced no desire to escape from the family nest by marriage. With something of Chekhov's sense of duty, she ably supported his authority in the household. An outward constraint concealed spiritual depths and even a typical Chekhovian humor in her quiet nature. Chekhov had full confidence in Masha. Her devotion to her brother and dedication to the cause of his growing fame became generally known and often made her an intermediary for those who wished to meet him. He behaved with extra charm to the girl friends she introduced into the house, and expecially to Lidiya Stakhievna Mizinova, also a young schoolteacher, who remained one of his close favorites for years — Misha asserted that "brother Anton was interested in her as a woman." The "beautiful Lika," as Chekhov promptly nicknamed her, captivated all by her appearance and manner — curly, ash-blond hair, lovely gray eyes, the fresh coloring of her fine features, and a complete absence of affectation in her exquisitely feminine grace and shyness. When Masha first brought her to the house, she left Lika in the hallway while she went upstairs to get something. Misha descended and stared at the bashful Lika, who pressed close to the wall, dropped her gaze, and tried to hide her face in the fur collar of her coat. He went into Chekhov's study: "Say, Anton, Masha has just come in with a beauty! She's in the hallway." Chekhov promptly emerged, stared, and went upstairs. So did Misha, and the two of them, to the consternation of Lika, repeated their busy trips up and down the stairway several times. Lika told Masha, when she rejoined her, that there seemed to be a terrible lot of menfolk in her family.

Young friends enjoyed visiting the Chekhov household, for they could always be sure of interesting conversation, entertainment, or of encountering some visiting celebrity. They might hear the critic P. N. Ostrovsky, brother of the famous dramatist, discussing literature or politics with Chekhov; or listen enraptured to a recitation by the great actor Lensky; or be vastly amused by a fascinating imitation of a ballerina by the stout but nimble actor Davydov.

Chekhov had become a favorite with the Moscow actors. Lent began badly with him this year, he wrote Suvorin, for after a night of revelry he returned home at ten-thirty in the morning, slept till five, and then went to a supper with the actors and actresses of the Korsh Theater. "The actresses are sweet; I loved them yesterday and was so touched that I even kissed several of them at parting." (*February 20, 1889.*) Indeed, Chekhov's frail health did not seem to diminish his capacity for carousing. The fact that his revered moral preceptor Leo Tolstoy had this year published a letter in the press to deplore the shameless student intemperance on Saint Tatyana's Day did not prevent Chekhov, as an "old grad," from attending this university festivity as usual. "My hands still tremble," he wrote a friend on the morning after. The asceticism Tolstoy preached never deeply influenced Chekhov's natural but by no means abnormal love for the pleasures of the flesh.

After indulging in such pleasures, however, Chekhov was prone to accuse himself of laziness, despite the prodigies of labor he accomplished. His need for companionship was often a need for material, for the characters of his stories were not infrequently drawn from his direct experience with life. For example, at this time he often attended the weekly gatherings of artists and writers at the Kuvshinnikovs'. They were gay parties. The husband was a self-effacing physician, but his wife — about forty and no beauty — was a dilettante painter and liked to surround herself with artists. When the hour came for supper, the husband would suddenly appear, knife and fork in hand, and announce that a repast was ready. With something of the wonder of a discoverer, his wife at this point would hail him: "Kuvshinnikov! Let me press your hand! Gentlemen, see what a kind face he has." And all the company would push past him to the table loaded with food. Levitan, that brilliant painter and connoisseur of women, rarely missed the parties of the Kuvshinnikovs. He became the teacher of his hostess and decided that long trips with her down the Volga in the summer were necessary for his purpose. People began to talk. Chekhov silently observed, and three years later his wonderful story *The Grasshopper* immortalized the situation.

The Moscow circle of young writers also welcomed Chekhov to their literary and social gatherings. Less distinguished than the Petersburg group, they were passionate liberals — which may account for their slowness in recognizing Chekhov's great talent. Their ideological hero was Mikhailovsky, and they also worshiped the writings of Saltykov-Shchedrin with his emphasis upon social satire. Nemirovich-Danchenko recalls Chekhov at one of these gatherings — tall, handsome, modest, and restrained in his gestures. In such groups he preferred to listen and observe rather than talk. When he did speak, pushing his long hair back in a characteristic gesture and his face illuminated by a charming smile, he spoke always to the point, with quiet independence and no trace of artificiality. Like most present, he knew by heart the speeches of V. A. Goltsev, who often addressed the group. He was the editor of the well-known Moscow progressive magazine *Russian Thought*, and his forensic efforts in the liberal cause were as boring as they were well-intentioned. Chekhov, as previously indicated, disliked this magazine and cared less for its editor, and not till a few years later did he learn to appreciate the virtues and political courage of Goltsev. Once a cab in which Chekhov and Nemirovich-Danchenko were riding collided with a horsecar. Nemirovich-Danchenko remarked that they could easily have been killed. "Dying would be bad enough," replied Chekhov, "but Goltsev's funeral speech would be worse."

Chekhov's prestige among the Moscow writers helped to bring about his election, in 1889, to the select Society of Lovers of Russian Literature. Membership this same year in the Society of Russian Dramatic Writers and Opera Composers probably pleased him more, for one of its functions was to protect the royalty rights of members no matter where their plays might be performed throughout Russia. He even agreed to serve on an executive committee of this society, which must have been something of a chore — he notes that one of the meetings lasted from seven in the evening till three in the morning. His willingness to serve, despite his instinctive dislike for organizations, was no doubt connected with the practical purpose of the society. Yet his comic sense prevailed at the meetings. It was impossible to describe them, he wrote Suvorin: they ought to be performed. In fact, he published in *New Times*, anonymously, an amusing dramatic spoof of the meetings: *Obligatory Declaration.*

« 3 »

After putting *Ivanov* behind him, Chekhov turned once again to that frustrating challenge of his creative life — his attempts to write a novel. Many hours during 1889 were dedicated to this agonizing effort. By way of preparation he plunged into the reading of fiction. "If I could live another forty years," he wrote Suvorin, "and read, read, read, and learn to write with talent, that is, concisely, at the end of that time I would fire at you with so great a cannon that the heavens would shake. But now, like the rest, I'm only a Lilliputian." (*April 8, 1889.*) And Chekhov sincerely believed this as he contemplated the great Russian writers of the past. When at this time his friend Tikhonov wrote that the eminent zoologist N. P. Wagner regarded him as the greatest Russian author, "an elephant among all of us" (Turgenev's phrase about Tolstoy), Chekhov promptly replied he had been so little caressed as a child that endearments still struck him as something unfamiliar, a new experience. Though he would now like to be kind to others, he refused to believe that either he or any of his generation of writers would be esteemed by posterity as an elephant. At best, he said, they would be known collectively as "the Eighties" — that is, a "sort of team." (*March 7, 1889.*)

However, he did not always spare the reputation of the older writers. He declared to Suvorin that Dostoevsky, whom he was then reading, was ". . . pretty good but too long-winded and too indelicate. There is much that is pretentious." (*March 5, 1889.*) And like Tolstoy, Chekhov now wondered why he had ever considered Goncharov a first-class writer. "His *Oblomov* is in no sense an important thing," he wrote Suvorin at the beginning of May. "The hero himself is a far-fetched character, not nearly big enough to make it worth while writing a whole book about him. He is a flabby sluggard like so many, a commonplace nature, average, petty; to rank him as a social type is to make too much of such a person. I ask myself: If Oblomov were not such a sluggard, what would he be? And I answer: Nothing." Nor do the rest of the leading characters in this celebrated novel come off much better. Saltykov-Shchedrin, Chekhov admired; but with reservations. Shortly after that famous satirist's death, in 1889, he wrote Pleshcheev: "I'm sorry about Saltykov. His was a firm, strong mind, the mean spirit that inhabits the petty, average, spiritually distorted Russian intellectual has lost in him its most implacable and troublesome enemy . . . only Saltykov could condemn openly. Two thirds of his readers did not like him, but all believed him. No one doubted the sincerity of his contempt." (*May 14, 1889.*)

Curiously enough, Chekhov did not undertake to re-read any of Tolstoy this year, but the gray seer of Yasnaya Polyana had for the first time begun to read Chekhov, and cryptic entries in his diary record both praise and criticism. On the whole, it was Gogol, an artist so close to him in certain respects, who aroused Chekhov's positive enthusiasm. He had been reading his tales again and seeing his plays. "But how direct and how powerful is Gogol," he wrote to Suvorin, "and what a great artist he is! . . . He is the greatest Russian writer."

Certainly Gogol's *Dead Souls* and its hero Chichikov appear to have been very much in his mind when he resumed work on his novel, according to a comment in an article by Suvorin after Chekhov's death. "On several occasions," Suvorin wrote, "he described to me the broad theme of the novel with its half-fantastic hero who lives on forever and takes part in all the events of the nineteenth century."

Chekhov continued to think of the novel in terms of the title he had mentioned to Grigorovich the previous year: *Tales from the Life of My Friends.* Whenever he sat down to it, he felt as he did after eating a good meal. To Pleshcheev he wrote that he would dedicate the novel to him, and he lightly mentioned to Suvorin that he would soon be coming up to Petersburg to auction off the manuscript to the highest bidder. He had just finished one of the tales, he wrote Anna Yevreinova, editor of the *Northern Herald* (he had planned the novel as a series of separate but thematically connected short stories). For the first time, he explained, circumstances were ideal for his concentrating on a lengthy major work — he had enough money ahead and had given promises to no one for any other writing. Now he didn't leave the house, he informed her; he wrote and wrote. "Ah, what a novel! If it were not for the thrice-accursed conditions of censorship, then I would promise it to you in November. There is nothing in the novel inciting to revolution, yet the censor will spoil it. Half of the active characters say: 'I do not believe in God,' there is a father whose son has been condemned to prison for armed resistance, a district police officer who is ashamed of his uniform, a marshal of the nobility whom all hate, etc. It is rich material for a censor's blue pencil." (*March 10, 1889.*)

The very next day Chekhov also announced the glad tidings to Suvorin: "What do you know? I'm writing a novel!! I write and write and there seems to be no end to my writing. I have begun doing it, i.e., the novel, all over again, correcting and abridging considerably what has already been written. By now I've already sketched nine individuals. And what a plot!" Though each chapter would consist of a separate story, he assured Suvorin that the whole would be securely tied together through a common basis of plot, ideas, and characters. However, technical problems bothered him, he admitted. "I'm still weak in this quarter and feel that I'm making many mistakes. There will be excessively lengthy passages and inanities. Although in places I do stray into conventional types, I shall try to avoid faithless wives, suicides, kulaks, virtuous peasants, devoted slaves, moralizing old ladies, kind old nurses, rustic wits, red-nosed captains, and the 'new' people."

Before many weeks had passed, however, Chekhov's enthusiasm began to fade. Pleshcheev, to whom he had sent the beginning of the work, wrote to Korolenko on August 24: "I regret that he does not continue his novel, the first three chapters of which I have read. I liked them very much."[3] Though material factors arose which interfered with the work, a more serious difficulty was the usual one with him in attempting to write a novel — a lack of focus which would enable him to synthesize the varied experiences he described and thus give his novel a cohesive artistic direction and social aim. Some suggestion of his mounting uncertainty and the reason behind it may be observed in a letter to Pleshcheev (*April 9, 1889*): "My novel had made considerable headway and then ran aground while waiting for a tide. . . . I have based this novel on the life of good people, on their characters, deeds, words, thoughts, and hopes; my purpose is to kill two birds with one stone: to draw life faithfully and at the same time to show how far this life diverges from the norm. The norm is unknown to me, as it is to any of us. We all know what a dishonorable act is, but what honor is we do not know. I shall cling to the frame nearest my heart, one which has already been tried by men stronger and wiser than I. This frame

[3] These three chapters and any further manuscript material of the novel were apparently destroyed by Chekhov.

is the absolute freedom of man, freedom from violence, prejudices, ignorance, the devil, freedom from passions, etc."

Within another month his statements of intention grew less frequent, his zeal for the novel muted. Then he began to respond to questions of correspondents about when the novel would be published with the information that it was too early to think of this; that it would take two to three years to finish it: "I write a bit on my novel but I delete more than I write," he informed Pleshcheev on June 26. Finally, he grew silent about the novel for the remainder of 1889.

Obviously the paralyzing difficulty was Chekhov's inability to encompass his twofold objective — to depict life's norm and at the same time to show how certain of his characters diverge from the norm. But if he could not envisage the norm, clearly he could not be sure of the deviations from it. Chekhov was no doubt correct in assuming that to cope successfully with the complex structure of the novel the artist, in order to perceive the vital connection of the parts to the whole, must have a unified vision of the norm of life. It was just this perception that he lacked at this time. As a dispassionate witness of life as it is, with a negative conviction that we are all slaves to unconscious instincts, he had as yet failed to develop a focus in life, a social symbol of faith, which he could apply artistically as the unifying principle in the vast canvas of a novel.

« 4 »

Nikolai's serious illness at the end of March 1889 was one reason why Chekhov interrupted his work on the novel. The artist brother, on a periodic turn of duty with his common law wife, had come down with typhoid fever. Though the traveling consumed several hours each way, Chekhov regularly made two daily visits over more than a week to tend Nikolai. To have a sick brother is a sorrow, he remarked, but to be a physician and have a sick brother was a double sorrow. Indeed, Dr. Chekhov quickly ascertained that typhoid fever, from which Nikolai was soon cured, was the least of his worries; tuberculosis had also made deep inroads. Consultations with medical colleagues confirmed the fact.

Chekhov realized that the ailing Nikolai should be removed to the dry and warmer climate of the Crimea, but there was no money for this; and besides, his lack of a passport would have made such a long journey difficult if not impossible to arrange. Though Chekhov himself had planned a trip to the Caucasus in the early spring, he now decided to give this up and take Nikolai at once to the *dacha* on the Lintvarev estate — which he had again rented for the summer — in the hope that the pleasanter Ukrainian weather at this time of year would benefit his brother. The whole situation filled him with gloom. He wanted his mother and younger brother to precede him and prepare the house for the sick man, but Misha begged off — he did not wish to desert his current light-o'-love in Moscow. "What a commission for a creator to be entrusted with!" the vexed Chekhov wrote Suvorin. "One is ill, the other in love, a third talks too much — and so forth. What trouble I have with all of them." (*April 22, 1889.*) He arrived at Luka with Nikolai on April 25, feeling that his horizon was now circumscribed by very dark clouds.

Though the novelty of this charming spot in the Ukraine had somewhat worn off, Chekhov gloried in the burgeoning spring with its freshness and emergent colors and its symphony of mingled song and sound of nightingales, bitterns, cuckoos, and frogs. Blossoming fruit trees — like brides in their wedding gowns, he observed — bore a look of innocence, as though they were ashamed to have people stare at them. Then there was the broad Psyol River, with its lovely banks already adorning themselves in dress of varied green. Nature he regarded as a sedative that pacifies man, makes him carefree and thus able to see things clearly, to be just, and to work properly.

As the days wore on, however, Chekhov's spirits drooped while he watched Nikolai wasting away before his eyes like the wax of a brightly burning candle. His deep compassion must have been mingled with a terrifying premonition as he recognized in himself the dangerous symptoms of his brother's disease — earlier that year he had had another slight hemorrhage. He grieved at times that he was a physician and hence morbidly aware of the significance of Nikolai's constant racking cough, which impressed upon him the sad indefiniteness of his own future. As a patient Nikolai could be exacting, irascible; he behaved like a veritable general, Chekhov wrote his brother Ivan. Nikolai had no thought of death and dreamed only of the time when he would again begin to practice his art. But as he grew weaker he became milder, more affectionate, and dozed in a chair most of the day.

In contrast to the previous summer, life had become insufferably dull for Chekhov — who loved gaiety, he declared, more than an honorarium. Since his friends had been informed of Nikolai's serious illness, they naturally hesitated to visit, despite Chekhov's rather quixotic pleas that they come and help share his boredom. A few, like Suvorin, who understood his special need, came. And he and Chekhov fished for hours at the picturesque old mill on the bank of the Psyol and talked endlessly about literature and the theater. P. M. Svobodin, who had brilliantly acted the role of Shabelsky in *Ivanov*, arrived for a stay and at once endeared himself to the family and Chekhov, with whom he shared a love for humor and practical jokes. He amused all by his clowning and grimacing, and positively dumbfounded the peasants by fishing in a dress coat, top hat, and white gloves. Or, as a lark, he and Chekhov set aflutter the patrons of a hotel in a neighboring town, Svobodin perfectly acting the part of a distinguished count and Chekhov that of his valet.

Such pleasures, however, were few that summer and the prolonged agony of attending Nikolai at times filled Chekhov with an almost irrational urge to escape, to go anywhere rather than remain at the *dacha*. He dreamed constantly of Odessa, the Caucasus, Paris; he studied French and German; and at moments he seemed guilty of wishing for his brother's death so that he could get away to Europe. "I would be happy to scamper off to Paris," he wrote Tikhonov, "and from the top of the Eiffel Tower survey the world, but — alas! — I'm bound hand and foot and do not have the right to move a step from here." (*May 31, 1889.*) And, learning that Suvorin planned to go abroad, Chekhov pathetically wrote him at the beginning of May: "What pleasure it would give me to go to Biarritz, where there is music and lots of women! If it were not for the artist I would really go with you. I'd find the money." In fact, most of his closely guarded savings had already vanished. He replied to Alexander, who was much concerned over Nikolai's illness and offered any help he could give: "The very best help would be money. If there had been no money, Nikolai would now be in a charity hospital. Consequently, the chief thing is money. Even five to ten roubles would not go amiss." (*May 8, 1889.*)

It was this overwhelming need to breathe air other than that of the sickroom which led Chekhov, in the middle of June, after some ten weeks of ceaseless care of Nikolai, to encourage Alexander to come and take his place for a few days while he went to Poltava Province to visit his friends the Smagins, where he had had such a pleasant time the year before. He left with Svobodin and several members of the Lintvarev family. On the way a cold wind blew up and it began to rain, which Chekhov regarded as a punishment for his having deserted Nikolai. They arrived at the village of the Smagins at night, wet and chilled, and got into cold beds. The next morning, June 17, the foul weather continued. Chekhov commented later that he would never forget the gray skies, muddy roads, and the tears on the trees. That morning a peasant from the town brought him a soggy telegram: KOLYA IS DEAD. He at once went by horse to the nearest railway station. The return trip became a nightmare of delays — he had to wait hours for connections. In one town he wandered about the streets, then sat by a wall in the public park, feeling cold and terribly depressed. Behind the wall he could hear the voices of actors rehearsing a melodrama. Finally he arrived at Luka to enter a house in deep mourning. Nikolai had passed away in Alexander's arms, the first of his family to die.

Chekhov wrote M. M. Dyukovsky, one of his brother's closest friends, that Nikolai had been buried in the Ukrainian manner. The brothers and friends carried the coffin into the church to the accompaniment of tolling bells. Then, after the service, they bore it to the village cemetery, remote and peaceful, where birds sang constantly and the grass smelled sweet. Shortly after the funeral, a cross was erected which could be seen from the distant fields. "If there were any faults in his past," Chekhov sadly concluded, "he has expiated them by his sufferings." (*June 24, 1889.*)

« 5 »

After writing Suvorin that there was not a kopeck's worth of poetry left in life, that all his desires were dormant, "In short, to hell with everything," Chekhov cleared out of his *dacha* on July 2. It bothered his conscience to leave the family behind in the same unhappy mood, but after the trying experiences of the past months and the death of Nikolai, he could not stand the sight of the house any longer. Where he went seemed of no consequence. He thought of joining Suvorin, then in Vienna, but then a telegram from Lensky inviting him to Odessa, where he and the actors of the Maly Theater were on tour, settled the issue. He would leave for abroad from Odessa.

The noisy, carefree actors and actresses of the Maly Theater were an antidote for any depressed state of mind, and besides they were extremely fond of Chekhov. For ten days he basked in their jolly company, staying with them at the Northern Hotel, where they were quartered. In the morning he went for a swim with one of them, then for coffee in a café by the famous stone steps of Odessa. At noon he would accompany the actress Glafira Panova on a shopping tour and have ice cream with her at sixty kopecks a portion — it was so hot, Chekhov complained, that he spent almost half of the small sum he had gathered for this trip on ice cream.

The well-known dramatic actress Cleopatra Karatygina was rather shocked when Chekhov was first introduced to her at a fashionable bathing pavilion. For he strolled up, elegantly dressed in a gray suit and soft hat, eating sunflower seeds out of a large paper bag like any peasant. But they became fast friends and he inscribed two of his books to her and his photograph. She recalls how he and his constant Odessa companion, his old Taganrog schoolmate Sergeenko, appeared once at her room for tea, Sergeenko shouldering like a rifle a long loaf of French bread. Chekhov regularly attended the theater, where he saw performances of such plays as *Hamlet* and *Don Juan*, and was sometimes called backstage to treat a coughing actress. After supper and drinks, all the company would gather at Cleopatra Karatygina's room for tea, a visit which lasted until two in the morning in a babble of conversation about the theater and actresses and actors. He might then accompany the dark-eyed Glafira to her room and on the way to his own be cornered by the fat actor Grekhov, and they would go off to a café to drink and talk till dawn.

This frivolous regimen was varied by excursions to the environs of Odessa. On one of these trips Sergeenko introduced Chekhov to a friend, I. N. Potapenko, a young Odessa journalist and writer. The admiring Potapenko, with whom Chekhov became very friendly several years later, acutely observed that as usual he was reticent on this first meeting, for he disliked lending himself to any of those who anticipated that he would say brilliant things. Chekhov did not like to stand out in a group.

Since he had failed to hear from Suvorin concerning his whereabouts at this time, Chekhov abandoned his intention of going abroad. On the other hand, he had already grown weary of feminine company, he remarked, and of listening to the gossip of these actresses whose jealousy of each other, in which the assignment of roles played a major part, irritated him. Though his money was running out, he rather indifferently decided to push on to Yalta, a place for which he had no particular affection. The Maly Theater company gave him a merry send-off to the boat and presented him with two neckties.

Life at Yalta, however, turned out to be varied and lively and no doubt helped to jolt Chekhov out of his depressed mood. In fact, his spirits improved so much that he again turned to writing — a long story for the *Northern Herald*. And soon he met several old friends and made new ones, went swimming frequently, and once almost lost his life in the water when a peasant narrowly missed his head with a heavy boathook.

One of the new friends he made and to whom he eventually became quite attached was young Elena Shavrova, one of three talented sisters of a Kharkov landowner. He saw a good deal of her at Yalta and encouraged her literary efforts, correcting and sending one of her stories to *New Times*. Indeed, his fame seems to have preceded him at Yalta, for soon he was being pressed by a number of would-be authors to read their manuscripts. With one of these, A. Gurlyand, he discussed the theater and made the well-known observation, which he was to repeat later: "If in the first act you hang a pistol on the wall, then in the last act it must be shot off. Otherwise you do not hang it there." And Gurlyand also reports him as saying: "One ought not to be afraid of the farcical in a play, but moralizing in it is abominable."

Though Chekhov thought living was cheap at Yalta, his entertaining and numerous trips to tourist sights, one of them as far as Bakhchisarai, compelled him at the end of a couple of weeks to write to Alexander to say that he had not a kopeck in his pocket to leave, and he asked his brother to send him at once the latest accumulation from the sale of his books. When Chekhov received the money, he left Yalta on August 9 and arrived at his *dacha* three days later. Apparently the shade of Nikolai still haunted the house and he and the family were happy to leave for Moscow at the beginning of September. On the train home, however, he seems to have recovered a bit of his old esprit. Professor N. I. Storozhenko, the celebrated Shakespearian scholar and Masha's former teacher, whom she held in reverent awe, sat near them in the coach. Chekhov quickly observed that his sister, afraid that he and the cellist Semashko, who accompanied the family, might say or do something that was undignified, pretended not to be associated with them. To punish her he ostentatiously played the part of a cook of Countess Keller and Semashko became a valet. Bowing low in peasant fashion to his mother, he declared in a loud voice that he hoped she would find a good servant's position in Moscow.

« 6 »

A *Dreary Story: from the Notebook of an Old Man*, the lengthy piece of fiction which Chekhov had been working on at Yalta, continued to absorb him after he returned to Moscow. The long and disappointing effort on his novel, as well as Nikolai's illness and death, had limited any concentration on the short story, for up to this point in 1889 he had published only one tale, *The Princess*, an almost morbid revelation of the parasitism of a wealthy lady who excuses her incredible self-indulgence by false piety and hypocritical almsgiving. One may detect in it a note of social protest against the flagrant abuses of rank and riches.

Excellent as is the characterization of the central figure in *The Princess*, the tale leaves one with the impression of an incomplete sketch which Chekhov perhaps thought was adequate for *New Times*, the newspaper in which it appeared. But the much longer A *Dreary Story*, intended for the magazine *Northern Herald*, he regarded as another major effort. He frankly admitted to the editor that the story was a reflection of "that abominable frame of mind from which I could not separate myself all summer." This "frame of mind," however, had been with him for some time. It was a complex of anxieties, aggravated by his critics and growing out of his noninvolvement — in either his art or personal life — in the great questions of the day. His belief that art had no mandate to answer such questions had been shaken recently by the thought that his noninvolvement was perhaps connected with a lack of philosophical convictions. The situation suggested a story about a thinking man who discovers at a critical moment in his life that he has no philosophy, no ruling idea to aid him in resolving his dilemma. No doubt Nikolai's death pointed up this conception, which now became the theme of a thinking man who finds himself a spiritual bankrupt when confronted with the ultimate question — death.

The subject was new, Chekhov confided, the characters different, the situations unique, and he was convinced that the tale would cause a stir and be abused by the enemy camp, an outcome which he thought all to the good. One may also see in it an answer to his friend, the critic P. N. Ostrovsky, who insisted that a writer, if he could not depict contemporary society with its beliefs and ideals, must at least depict it in its search for beliefs, in its anguish over the absence of an ideal. It is man's "anguish over the absence of an ideal" that Chekhov embodied in the main character of A Dreary Story, an anguish which he himself plainly experienced.

As he worked away, frequent artistic doubts about his writing assailed him. He refused to send the story in at the time he promised; he had to recast whole pages, to polish; he worried over his inexperience with this new theme, and above all he feared to appear stupid. Perhaps the features that troubled him most were the long speeches from the notebook of the old professor in the tale. They could not be dispensed with, he assured Pleshcheev, for "they characterize the hero, as well as his frame of mind and his shuffling before himself." (September 24, 1889.) Perhaps one ought to be old, he ruminated, if one were to write in so much detail about the observations of an old man, but it was not his fault that he was young. Disappointed over his progress at one stage, he wrote Leontiev-Shcheglov: "This is not a story but a dissertation. It will suit the taste only of lovers of boring and heavy reading, and I'll make a mistake if I don't send it to the Artillery Journal." (September 18, 1889.)

Chekhov finally dispatched the manuscript to the Northern Herald toward the end of September. Pleshcheev's favorable reaction must have banished some if not all of his worries over the piece. "You have done nothing so powerful and profound as this," wrote the editor, and he praised the characterizations of the old professor and his ward Katya. In parrying one of Pleshcheev's strictures, that not enough was known about the secondary characters, Chekhov made the interesting point that this was the professor's fault since all information depended upon his notebook, and one of his chief traits was his complete unconcern for the inner life of those around him. If his nature had been different, said Chekhov, then the lives of Katya and his daughter Liza might have been less negative. Nor would Chekhov accept Pleshcheev's advice that, for obvious reasons, he change the title of A Dreary Story: he did not fear the scamps who indulged in poor jokes about a title, and if by chance some good ones were struck off, he would be happy to have given them the opportunity.

Chekhov had some reason to be concerned with sustaining reader interest in A Dreary Story. In conception and treatment the piece represented a new departure for him, and as an outgrowth of accumulated feelings stirred by his recent thinking on the relation of art to life and on the death of his brother Nikolai, the story is more subjective than he had allowed himself to be in any serious work up to this point. The distinguished old scientist, Professor Nikolai Stepanovich, knows that he will soon die, and as he reviews his past and present existence he comes to the terrible conclusion that the total success of his life — his passion for science; his behavior to his wife, daughter, and ward Katya; his views on theater, literature, colleagues, students; even the very picture which his fertile imagination has painted of himself and his achievements — has all been entirely devoid of what might be called a "general idea" which would serve as a god for a living man. His life has suddenly come to have no meaning, and on the threshhold of the grave he feels himself a spiritual bankrupt. His favorite Katya, who adored the old scientist and might have brought him solace, has ruined her life because she too lacked "a ruling idea." Though he fully understands the tragedy of her hopeless drifting, he is utterly unable to advise her when she pleads for his aid, thus symbolizing the futility of his own life as well as that of his ward. Some readers imagined that Katya's disillusion was caused by a hopeless love for her guardian. Chekhov regarded this as an "impure suspicion" and wrote Pleshcheev: "If people lose belief in the friendship, respect, and boundless love which exist outside the sphere of sex, at least they should not attribute bad taste to me. If Katya were in love with an old man barely alive, it would be, you must agree, sexual perversity, a freak which could interest only a psychiatrist, and then merely as an unimportant and untrustworthy anecdote. If there had been in it only this sexual perversity, would it have been worth while to write the story?" (*October 21, 1889.*)

The old professor's lengthy analyses of himself and his social milieu reflect Chekhov's own state of mind, which to some extent was shared by those democratic intellectuals who eschewed organized political effort or revolution as answers to the "accursed questions" that confronted their backward country. And this lack of a "ruling idea" with which to approach broad social and political problems poisoned the wellsprings of inspiration in a personal life. As the professor puts it: his attempts to know himself, all his thoughts, sensations, and conceptions, had nothing in common with one another, nothing which might weave them into a single whole. Even contemporary Russian authors, he declares — in a passage that plainly echoes Chekhov's thinking — lack the chief element of artistic freedom, for "they have neither the independence nor the manliness to write as they like, and therefore there is no creativeness."

With the pride that he then took in his artistic objectivity, however, Chekhov protested the charge, and perhaps unjustifiably, that the professor's views were his. "In the whole story," he replied to Suvorin on this matter, "there is only one thought which I share and that one lodges in the head of the professor's son-in-law, the rogue Gnekker, and it is: 'The old fellow has gone crazy!'" But all the rest, he asserts, is imagined or contrived. "For me, as an author," he declared, "in their essence all these opinions have no value at all. Their substance is not the point; that is changeable and not new. The whole essence is in the nature of these opinions, in their dependence upon external influences, and so forth. They should be examined like things, like symptoms, entirely objectively, without attempting to agree or dispute with them. If I describe St. Vitus' dance, surely you would not regard it from the point of view of a choreographer? Would you? The same holds true of these opinions. I had no intention to stun you with my views on the theater, literature, and so forth. I merely wished to make use of my own knowledge to depict that vicious circle into which a good and wise man fell with all his desire to accept from God life as it is and to think about everybody in a Christian way, yet willy-nilly grumbling and muttering like a slave, and abusing people even in those moments when he is forcing himself to express a fine opinion of them." (*October 17, 1889.*)

Tolstoy's moral influence may once again be observed in the emotional, intellectual, and artistic groping of Chekhov in *A Dreary Story*, which forces comparison with *The Death of Ivan Ilyich*. For the hero of Tolstoy's famous tale, like the old professor, suddenly finding himself face to face with death, looks back over his past life and perceives its tragic emptiness. But unlike the professor, who can discover no hope for himself at the end of life's "dreary story," Ivan Ilyich beholds the inner light of Faith, Renunciation, and Love. In a deeper sense, the two works also suggest a comparison between the two authors: between the detached and skeptical Chekhov, and Tolstoy the believer; between the calm incredulity of a Chekhov endlessly searching for something not to be found on earth and fearing always to surrender himself completely to either joy or sorrow, and a Tolstoy passionately seeking faith and, after draining the cup of life with all its joys and sorrows, declaring that man must desire nothing if he is to find his own soul.

Perhaps not unexpectedly for Chekhov, many of the reviews of *A Dreary Story* were highly critical and several compared it unfavorably to *The Death of Ivan Ilyich*. Of the few good reviews, Chekhov probably took least satisfaction in that of the eminent Mikhailovsky, who had previously been so begrudging in his praise. He asserted that the tale was "the best and most significant of all that Chekhov had written up to this time," and he concluded his article: "From time to time talent ought to feel with horror the anguish and dullness of 'reality,' it ought to erase such anguish by 'what is called a general idea or the god of a living man.' *A Dreary Story* is the begetter of such anguish. That is why this tale is so fine and lifelike, for the author has put into it his own pain." Mikhailovsky was right.

« 7 »

The paucity of Chekhov's fictional output during 1889 also bears some relation to his preoccupation with writing plays. Despite his frequent and harsh criticism of the theater and dramatists, the Petersburg success of *Ivanov* and the widespread popularity of his "vaudevilles" or one-act plays drew him irresistibly to the stage. "I'm expecting the Order of Stanislav and appointment as a member of the State Council" he joked when he heard that Alexander III had complimented a brilliant performance of *The Proposal* at the summer palace. Svobodin, who played the lead, said the Tsar laughed loudest of all, and when the actors, at his request, told him what other plays Chekhov had written, His Majesty exclaimed: "Ah, yes, *Ivanov, The Bear!* I regret that I've not seen them!" If he were alone in the world, Chekhov remarked, he could live for two or three years solely on the income from his published collections of tales and performances of his plays. Besides, the theater was in his blood and its challenge lost nothing from the fact that he now considered writing for it as something of a sport.

With little effort Chekhov dashed off two more one-act plays in 1889. *A Tragedian in Spite of Himself* was based on his short story *One of Many* (1887), an account of a much harrassed husband who every morning is charged with the numerous errands of his wife and her friends when he leaves his summer cottage for his office in town. *The Wedding*, a miniature light comedy with a large cast of characters, is one of Chekhov's most celebrated one-act plays. In this instance he drew upon several of his previous works — a humorous sketch *The Marriage Season* (1881) and two short stories, written in 1884, *A*

Marriage of Convenience and *A Wedding with a General*. To this material must be added his firsthand observations in 1885 of the garish weddings in the Moscow flat over his, which was hired out for such purposes. On these occasions the Chekhov family would sometimes hold mock weddings and match the noise above their heads with raucous toasts and frantic dancing to the music upstairs. The play is a hilarious satire on the vulgar shopkeepers' conception of a wedding which was never complete without a hired general, although in this case it is a naval officer of lower rank whose voluntary attendance as an "invited" guest introduces a poignant note of outraged human dignity when the shabby deception is exposed.

However, Chekhov's major dramatic undertaking was the full-length *Wood Demon*, which he worked on intermittently over much of 1889. This was the play he had initially sketched at Feodosiya in collaboration with Suvorin When he returned to it at the beginning of 1889, Suvorin having already bowed out, it is likely that Chekhov conceived of it as a conventional comedy very much as *Ivanov* had been a conventional drama of action. By spring, however, when he had drafted two acts, his comments to Suvorin suggest that he was attempting to do something different. For one thing, he felt a much greater sense of power than when he wrote *Ivanov*. And he added, "The play is terribly queer and I'm surprised that such peculiar things can come from my pen." (*May 4, 1889.*) A week later he informed Suvorin that all the characters were positively new. "In general, I tried to avoid the superfluous and I think I've managed. In a word, there's no gainsaying that I'm a clever fellow." To Pleshcheev he described *The Wood Demon* as "a big comedy-novel," filled with nice healthy people, a happy ending, and a lyrical tone. Above all, he explained, it was "literary significance" that he wished to achieve in this play. (*September 30, 1889.*)

In short, it appears that Chekhov was experimenting with *The Wood Demon* and vaguely moving in the direction of the "inner action" plays of the great period of his dramatic writing. He now wished to present on the stage life as it is, avoiding the theatrical effects of which he himself had been somewhat guilty in *Ivanov*. However, with the further desire to transcend the artistic position of a mere observer of life, he again succumbed to the influence of Tolstoy by introducing a moral purpose and aim. For the play is essentially a struggle between good and evil, in which characters representing virtue ultimately convert those who are evil-minded. Old Serebryakov, a retired professor, and his virtuous second wife, the young and beautiful Elena, typify this moral struggle. The portrayal of Serebryakov has in it something of the flavor of Chekhov's generalization, in another connection, to Suvorin: "I have my knife out for professors, although I know that they are excellent people. Like authors, they have no daring and much self-importance." (*November* 27, 1889.) Mikhail Khrushchev, the wood demon and the prototype of Mikhail Astrov in *Uncle Vanya*, symbolizes, in his passionate and poetic love of trees, the force for good in human affairs that resides in nature. The involved love triangles and Serebryakov's cunning plan to sell the estate which does not belong to him complicate the action and at the same time provide previews of motifs which Chekhov made better use of later in his more famous plays.

Work on *The Wood Demon* went forward by fits and starts. Not only the events of his personal life and the efforts on his novel and on *A Dreary Story* interrupted its progress, but also the apparent difficulties he experienced in coping with a new dramatic approach. In periods of discouragement he dropped the play more than once, although he jubilantly anticipated the six to seven thousand roubles he thought it would bring him — and he had already promised *The Wood Demon* for a benefit performance for Svobodin in Petersburg and for Lensky in Moscow. In September, however, he returned to it with a will, rejected what he had written up to that point, and started out afresh. Later he wrote Suvorin that he worked on it "with great satisfaction and even with enjoyment. . . ." (*October* 17, 1889.)

At the beginning of October Chekhov gave copies of *The Wood Demon* to Svobodin and Lensky, although he regarded the play, and especially the fourth act, as requiring more revision. Shortly thereafter he heard from Svobodin, who had read the play to the Committee of the Alexandrinsky Theater on which Grigorovich sat (it was regarded as an unofficial committee since some of its regular members were still on vacation). The committee, wrote Svobodin, had rejected *The Wood Demon* for performance primarily because of "the absence of action and its tedious dialogue." Perhaps more important, the director also indicated that the Grand Duke, a patron of the theater, would clearly not like the play.

Some two weeks later, Chekhov received a letter from Lensky. "I will say only one thing: Write tales. You refer too scornfully to the stage and to dramatic form. You esteem them too little to write a play.

This form is more difficult than that of fiction, and — forgive me — you are too spoiled by success in order, so to speak, to start fundamentally to study dramatic form from the beginning and to love it." To add to the rout, this letter was followed by one from Nemirovich-Danchenko, who had also read the play: "Lensky is right, you ignore too many of the demands of the stage, but I've not observed scorn for them, rather simply a lack of knowledge of them."

In his chagrin Chekhov could not have known that Svobodin, a most experienced and talented actor, had written a friend, V. M. Lavrov, to deplore the action of the committee in banning the play from the Alexandrinsky Theater, which was inundated, he said, with stupid, untalented trivialities. *The Wood Demon*, he wrote, "is not a conventional comedy, but life-like figures, living speech, and characters which are beyond the whole Alexandrinsky trash that does not deserve even a part of a play of Chekhov."

On the surface Chekhov seemed to take his failure philosophically. He thanked Lensky for his letter and humbly agreed that his talent was apparently not that of a playwright. He also willingly accepted the advice of Nemirovich-Danchenko on revising *The Wood Demon*. And he could appreciate the humor of a caricature of himself as a playwright which appeared in *Fragments* at this time. The drawing depicted him driving a troika. One horse was labeled "Ivanov," the second, "The Bear," and the third, "The Wood Demon." The troika is halted at a crossroad, one of which bears a sign: ROAD TO FICTION and the other: ROAD TO DRAMA. Chekhov good-naturedly replied to Leikin that when he published his own humorous journal, he would insert in it a caricature of this prolific author — an Eiffel Tower made up of his books.

Beneath the surface, however, Chekhov was deeply hurt, especially over the attitude of the Petersburg Theatrical Committee, a few of whose members, such as Grigorovich, had formerly professed their devotion to him and had offered him advice on how to write successful plays. He referred to their rejection as a "field court-martial," and in regard to an inspired piece in the *Petersburg Gazette* saying that the committee had condemned *The Wood Demon* because it was merely a dramatized story, he wrote Pleshcheev: "It follows that either I am a bad playwright, to which I readily put my signature, or all these gentlemen who love me as a son and implore me for the love of God to be myself in my plays, to avoid clichés, and to provide complicated conceptions, are hypocrites." (*October 21, 1889.*)

But what angered Chekhov more than anything else in the whole matter was the rumor in Petersburg that he had designed old Professor Serebryakov as a satire on Suvorin. He tended to hold Grigorovich responsible for this rumor, as also did Pleshcheev. Chekhov implored Suvorin not to believe a word of this and offered an analysis of the old professor to support his point. "Ah, how happy is this Grigorovich!" he declared. "And how they would all rejoice if I had added some arsenic to your tea or exposed you as a spy serving the secret police." This kind of gossip is not a trifle, he went on to say. "The other day I met at the theater a Petersburg writer. We talked. Learning from me that at various times in the summer Pleshcheev, Barantsevich, you, Svobodin, and others visited me, he sighed sympathetically and said: 'You are wrong if you think this is a good advertisement. You are much mistaken if you count on them.' That is, I invited you so that I should have someone to write about me, and Svobodin in order that I should push my play on him! After my conversation with this writer, I had a feeling in my mouth as though I had swallowed, instead of vodka, a glass of ink with flies in it. All this is a trifle, nonsense, but if it were not for these trifles, all human life would be made up of delights, whereas now it is half disgusting." (*October 17, 1889.*)

Although everything about *The Wood Demon* had grown distasteful to him — for a time he would not let Suvorin see a copy of it and he refused offers to publish it — he nevertheless obviously continued to nurture the hope of seeing it performed. In November, his friend, the actor N. N. Solovtsov, read the play and, declaring himself to be in raptures over it, urgently requested it for the new Moscow Abramov Theater with which he was connected. Accordingly Chekhov promptly set about revising *The Wood Demon* for performance, especially the fourth act, and he continued to make changes during the period of rehearsals. Nevertheless, its opening performance on December 27 was almost unanimously condemned in the reviews. The articles accused him of ignorance of the conditions of stage representation, a mechanical reproduction of life, and with blindly copying the trivial aspects of reality.

On the whole, his critics can hardly be blamed for failing to discern the reasons behind his selection of content or the new principles of dramatic structure that he had fumblingly attempted to work out.

For again and again Chekhov employs the old conventions of the theater in *The Wood Demon*, using melodramatic effects which he had criticized in contemporary plays; and in his attempt to depict life as it is he failed to create it in his play. Obviously he had not yet fully understood the direction in which he was moving — by concentrating on the inner substance of people, he wished to reveal them as they really exist and not as they appear to be in real life. And just as this kind of concentration would require a realism that stressed not the events of life but a character's inner reaction to them, so must it be articulated by a dialogue that would reflect inner rather than outer action. Chekhov seemed finally to recognize that his attempts at innovation in *The Wood Demon* were crude, for he would never permit the play, despite much pressure on him, to be published. However, after he had perfected his innovating approach to drama, he transformed *The Wood Demon* into one of his greatest plays, *Uncle Vanya*.[4]

« 8 »

The years 1885 to 1889 were among the happiest in Chekhov's relatively short life. By the end of this brief period he had emerged from obscurity to become one of the most appreciated and discussed writers of the day. The hardships and harsh memories of his early youth were behind him, and he had brought his family from indigence to a position of material security and social acceptance. If he still had to worry somewhat financially, he could count on a reasonably steady income and the knowledge that many publishers were bidding for the products of his pen. Although not yet thirty, he had made swarms of friends, and many of the nation's foremost writers and artists sought his acquaintance. It was in 1889 that the great Tschaikovsky, whose music, particularly his opera *Eugene Onegin*, Chekhov loved, visited at Sadovaya-Kudrinskaya Street. They exchanged inscribed photographs, and Tschaikovsky invited Chekhov to do the libretto of an opera based on Lermontov's story *Bela* (although the composer died before anything could come of this project), and Chekhov received permission to dedicate to

---

[4] It is generally supposed that Chekhov wrote *Uncle Vanya* in 1896 and considered it a new play, although it is plainly a reworking of *The Wood Demon*. However, there is some evidence, though not conclusive, that he actually completed this task between March and April of 1890. A summary of the facts supporting the early date of *Uncle Vanya* may be found in N. I. Gitovich, *Letopis zhizni i tvorchestva A. P. Chekhova* (*Chronicle of the Life and Works of A. P. Chekhov*), Moscow, 1955, pp. 282-83.

Tschaikovsky his forthcoming collection of tales, *Gloomy People*. Upon sending him his photograph Chekhov rapturously added, "and I would send you the sun if it belonged to me." Masha described her famous brother at this time as wonderfully high-spirited, always jolly, always working, incessantly joking, and absolutely unable to do without company.

Over this whole period of glorious success and carefree existence, however, various elements of discontent — a number of which have already been pointed out — seriously disturbed Chekhov's satisfaction with his accomplishments. Like the overseer in his beautiful story *Happiness* (1887), Chekhov no doubt believed that there was happiness enough for all in this world if only we knew how to look for it, a significant motif that runs through so much of his writing. But, as the wood demon put it in Chekhov's play, most people wandered in the dark forest of life, groping their way, with only enough intelligence, knowledge, and feeling to ruin their own lives and those of others.

Chekhov's customary reticence in all the inner circumstances of his life leaves one very much in the dark as to why his moments of discontent over this happy period culminated, at the end of 1889, in a decision of striking importance for himself and his career. No doubt Nikolai's death and the self-image which his brother's illness suggested — besides the frustrated efforts on his novel, the critical misunderstanding of what he had attempted to do in *A Dreary Story*, and the utter failure of *The Wood Demon* — had all contributed something to his mounting spiritual malaise.

His sense of disillusionment was also undoubtedly influenced by the still unresolved social and artistic problems which had begun to trouble him at the very outset of his success as an author. To a certain extent his anxieties mirrored those of all thinking people of the Eighties, this "epoch of social stagnation." But the charge of the liberal critics that his writings lacked a social outlook tended only to confirm the natural independence of a mind that held in some contempt the programs of both the liberals and conservatives. Nor could he easily tolerate the kind of criticism that held him culpable for remaining a friend of the reactionary Suvorin and for continuing to publish in his newspaper. By now he perhaps understood the curious political ambivalence of Suvorin's mind, whatever may have been the policy of *New Times*, better than most of his critics. It was noticeable, however, that Chekhov had lately grown extremely touchy about any favors from Suvorin that could be

interpreted as aiding Chekhov's career. In the face of a veiled suggestion that Suvorin might use his immense influence to have *The Wood
Demon* produced in Petersburg, Chekhov deftly counteracted the possibility by warning him that "every word of mine is understood in Petersburg as a request and every one of yours as a protection." (*November 1,
1889.*)

If Chekhov's artistic convictions prevented any direct preaching about
the unhappiness, suffering, and vulgarity of Russian life which he revealed in his tales, his critics were wrong in assuming that he accepted
"life as it is." His turning to the moral principles of Tolstoy during this
period, a philosophy essentially uncongenial to him, was some measure
of his concern, and his seemingly unlimited willingness to help a constant stream of petitioners betokened a degree of involvement in human
misfortune that demanded more personal sacrifice than wordy preachments did. And occasionally he lashed out at inequities, as when he
wrote Suvorin to condemn an article in *New Times* for applauding the
fact that diligent German housemaids worked like navvies for a mere
two or three roubles a month. "In the first place" he declared, "it is
revolting to talk about servants as though they were convicts; in the
second place, servants are equal members of society and are made of
the same flesh and blood as Bismarck; they are not slaves but free
workers." (*March 11, 1889.*)

An inability, like that of the old professor in *A Dreary Story*, to
formulate a "ruling idea" with which to confront the problems of his
own life and those of society no doubt aggravated Chekhov's disturbed
state of mind at the end of 1889. Nor did he find much help in the
conflicting and often partisan views of the intelligentsia. Rather pointedly he wrote Suvorin on October 28: "You say that it is impossible to
imagine anything more contemptible than our liberal opposition. Well,
what about those who do not form the opposition? They are hardly any
better. The mother of all Russian evil is gross ignorance, and this is
present in the same degree in all parties and movements."

Two months later Chekhov returned to this theme by way of an
exchange he had been having with Suvorin over the recent novel of the
popular French author Paul Bourget, *Le Disciple*, which Suvorin
praised highly when it appeared in translation in *New Times*. Chekhov
sharply criticized the work because of its indictment of determinism and
its insistence that the scientific approach led to evil. To compel man to
turn his back on a materialistic approach to life, Chekhov asserted,

amounted to forbidding him to seek the truth. He found still more reprehensible Bourget's belief that those things which in the age-long struggle
with nature restrain the brute in men and distinguish them from dogs can
be lightly discredited by psychological experiments involving infinite talk
about conscience, freedom, love, honor, and morality. Chekhov questioned whether such authors help us to seek for the better and to admit
that the bad is truly bad. Rather, he declared, they contribute to degen-
eration, as they do in Russia, where they "help the devil to beget the
wood lice and mollusks we call the intelligentsia. The drowsy, apathetic,
lazy, philosophizing, cold intelligentsia, who cannot even invent for
themselves a decent design for paper money; who are not patriotic; who,
sad and colorless, get drunk on one glass and visit brothels at fifty
kopecks; who grumble and blithely negate *everything*, since it is easier for
a lazy brain to deny than to assert; who refuse to marry and raise children, and so on." (*December 27, 1889.*)

Chekhov himself was a member of this intelligentsia, and more than
once he had wondered whether his own literary efforts were of any use at
all in the atmosphere of social defeatism with which he was surrounded.
Not only had the quantity of his writing fallen off sharply in 1889, but
at times he seemed deliberately to avoid creative work. He convinced
Suvorin to send him the rejected manuscripts of the literary division of
New Times and he would revise those that he deemed worth saving for
publication. Although he minimized the effort because of the rapidity
with which he functioned as an editor, yet he obviously spent much time
on this thankless task, sometimes going so far as to rework entire stories.
"In *The Singer*," he wrote of one of these to Suvorin, "I've made the
middle the beginning, the beginning the middle, and the end I've transformed into somthing quite new. The young lady, when she reads it, will
be quite horrified." (*November 20, 1889.*)

In short, Chekhov had reached a spiritual breaking point, which had
been building up in him over this whole period of his first success; it
compelled him for a time to turn his back on art and seek relief in some
other activity, very much as Gogol and Tolstoy had done in similar crises
in their lives. "I don't have much passion," he had written Suvorin on
May 4. "Add to this the following psychopathic symptom: over the past
two years, and for no earthly reason, I've grown sick of seeing my works in
print, have become indifferent to reviews, to talks on literature, to slanders, successes, failures, big fees — in fact, I've turned into an utter fool.
There is a sort of stagnation in my soul. I explain it by the stagnation in

my personal life." In the middle of December, he again wrote Suvorin that not a single line of his writings had any serious value in his eyes. And with some perturbation, he added: "I want passionately to hide myself somewhere for five years and engage in serious, painstaking work. I must teach myself, learn everything from the beginning, because as a writer I'm a complete ignoramus; I must write with a good conscience, with feeling, with meaning, write not eighty pages a month but sixteen. I must leave my home and live on seven to nine hundred roubles a year and not, as now, on three to four thousand. I must spit on a great many things. . . ."

Chekhov's mind was made up. At the end of 1889 brother Misha rather naïvely explains the reason behind the kind of activity Chekhov had decided upon. While reading Misha's classroom notes on criminal law, Chekhov remarked: "All our attention is centered on the criminal up to the moment when sentence is pronounced, but as soon as he is sent to prison, we forget about him entirely. But what happens in prison? I can imagine!" Then, Misha added, he suddenly began to plan a journey to Sakhalin Island, thousands of miles away on the Pacific, to study life in the penal colony there. It was difficult to know, concluded Misha, whether he spoke seriously or jokingly.

A deeper, more poignant reason may be read in Chekhov's cryptic comment to Suvorin on December 7: "In January I'll be thirty. Hail the old bachelor; useless life, burn to the end!"

Part III

FRUSTRATION, TRAVEL, LITERARY MATURITY

1889 – 1892

CHAPTER X

"Mania sachalinosa"

THIS EXPLANATION of the complex factors compelling Chekhov to seek a radical change might be more convincing if it were not for his selection of the God-forsaken Island of Sakhalin as the instrument of his spiritual regeneration. Some friends regarded the trip as little short of madness, and the reasons he gave for going were contradictory and not always serious. With his penchant for secrecy in personal matters, he created the impression of running away from some undisclosed emotional experience. One supposition is that he was in love with Lidiya Avilova and, realizing the hopelessness of this situation, had fled to the other side of the world to try to forget her and his unhappiness. All the evidence for this rests upon the assertion which she made in her memoirs years later (A. P. *Chekhov in My Life*, 1947). There she quotes him as declaring that he fell deeply in love with her at their first meeting in January 1889. His precipitate departure from Petersburg on that occasion, after the performance of *Ivanov*, and the fact that he avoided returning to the city, are offered in confirmation of the notion that he did not dare trust himself because of his powerful feeling for Lidiya. The assumption is that his Tolstoyan moral principles forbade breaking up the married life of others, and that anyway his sense of duty and financial commitments to his family made it impossible for him to support, in addition, a married woman and her child.

Whatever may have been Lidiya Avilova's feeling for Chekhov, there is no tangible evidence on his part that he was in love with her. His hasty departure from Petersburg he explained repeatedly in letters to friends and in a manner consistent with his nature — he became surfeited with the praise showered upon him on the occasion of the success of *Ivanov*.[1] Nor did he avoid Petersburg thereafter. He had every intention of visiting in the second half of 1889 for the opening of *The Wood Demon*, but when that play was rejected he understandably dropped the trip. On the other hand, he went to Petersburg at the beginning of 1890 on the business of his Sakhalin venture, and though he remained there a whole month, he appears to have made no effort to see Lidiya. He ate a lot of dinners and suppers, he later wrote Pleshcheev, "but did not captivate a *single* lady. . . ." Nor should one take too seriously Tolstoyan influence on Chekhov's private morals; the evidence clearly indicates that he paid frequent active tribute to the proverbial trilogy of wine, women, and song. And without in any sense being a philanderer, his personal credo of absolute freedom in human relations would justify love for another man's wife if it were genuine, although he pointed out in his fiction the misery that can ensue from such a situation. "Everyone has the right to live with whom he wishes and how he wishes," he had told Alexander in defense of his brother's passion for a married woman who also had a child. That Chekhov's exaggerated sense of duty to his family at that time could have prevented him from affirming a love once conceived is probably true, but it can be just as logically argued that it would have kept him from falling in love at all. He was surrounded by attractive girls and was very likely a bit in love with more than one, especially with Mizinova, "the beautiful Lika," who was obviously deeply attached to him. In March he wrote Suvorin that if he could only bring together in a summer *dacha* all his recent girl acquaintances, then it would make for a jolly kind of eventful confusion, a prospect that hardly suggests that he was spending his time mooning over Lidiya Avilova.

The truth of the matter is that she appears to have made no particular impression on him at all when they first met, to say nothing of the notion that a passionate love, growing out of this meeting, provoked his sudden decision to run away to Sakhalin. For she wrote him shortly after this meeting. He never answered. And he explains why in a letter to her three years later, after they had met again: "I have only one fault. Here it is. Once I received a letter from you, in which you queried me on the score of an idea in one of my current stories. Since I was barely

[1] In a letter to Suvorin's wife (*October 19, 1896*), in which Chekhov explains why he hurriedly left Petersburg after the performance of *The Sea Gull*, he wrote: "On this score I had previously decided that I would leave the next day, whether or not the play was a success. The clamor of glorification stuns me and, as after the performance of *Ivanov*, I did leave the next day."

acquainted with you at that time and had forgotten your married name, Avilova, I threw your letter away and pocketed the return stamp — so I generally behave with all queries, especially those of women. Then, in Petersburg again, you referred to this letter and I recalled your signature and felt at fault." (*March 19, 1892.*) Of course, if he had been interested, Chekhov could easily have ascertained the name of Lidiya Avilova.

On the other hand, one can easily point to additional evidence in the early months of 1890 which seem to support the belief that Chekhov's initial reason for going to Sakhalin grew out of a feeling of acute dissatisfaction with his life and art. Though he was something of a fatalist and believed that circumstances commanded and possessed men, he never renounced the struggle to improve himself and those around him morally and artistically. When Leontiev-Shcheglov, the ex-staff captain with waxed mustaches, tragic laugh, atrocious handwriting, and misplaced ambition to be a great dramatist, darkly hinted in a letter that he wished to pick a quarrel on matters of morality and artistry, Chekhov promptly responded that his was a normal morality. He did not covet anything of his neighbors, not even his neighbor's wife, he wrote, and though he had wasted his substance, laughed madly, overate, drank to excess, and fornicated, he could not imagine that in these respects he deviated up or down from the norm. As for what is artistic or inartistic, Chekhov declared, he divided all productions into two categories: those he liked and those he didn't like. "I have no other criteria, and if you ask me why I like Shakespeare and do not like Zlatovratsky [a popular author], I cannot tell you. Perhaps in time, when I get smarter, I will acquire a criterion, but meanwhile all talk about 'artistry' only wearies me and seems like a continuation of those scholastic polemics with which people wore themselves out in the Middle Ages." If criticism possessed truth and immutable laws, he added, why has it not revealed them to us? "Then we wouldn't find existence as boring and tedious as it is now. You wouldn't be lured into the theater and I to Sakhalin." And he ended by warning his friend not to build literary hopes over his Sakhalin expedition. "I'm going not for observations or impressions, but simply to be able to live for a half year as I have not lived hitherto." (*March 22, 1890.*)

To this confidant Chekhov came as close as he ever did to conveying the inchoate feeling that initially determined him to go to Sakhalin. It is obvious that he identified his spiritual pain with the complaints of his critics about the purpose of his art and life. In this respect, it is interesting to observe him, shortly before beginning his journey, rising angrily to defend himself against a charge of unprincipled writing made by V. M. Lavrov, one of the editors of the liberal *Russian Thought*. "As a matter of fact," he wrote, "I would not even reply to slander, except that in a few days I shall be leaving Russia for a long period, perhaps never to return, and I lack the will power to refrain from an answer." After insisting upon his probity as an author and the fact that he had not contributed a single line of which he need be ashamed, he turned to what he no doubt rightly considered to be the basis of Lavrov's charge: "If I were to assume the proposition that by 'unprincipled' you have in mind the melancholy circumstance that I, an educated author and one frequently published, have nothing for those whom I love, that my literary activity has left no trace, for example, on our agricultural governing boards, the new court procedure, freedom of the press, on freedom in general, and so on, then in this respect *Russian Thought* should in all fairness look upon me as its comrade and not blame me, since up to date it has not done any more than I have in this field, and neither you nor I am to blame for this." (*April 10, 1890.*)

In making his debater's point, Chekhov's conscience must have bothered him, for he fully realized, whatever may have been his artistic justification, that he deliberately had not waged a battle for social change in his writings. Like Tolstoy, he perhaps wondered whether it was not wiser to turn his back on art and strive for moral perfection, or still better, like his hero, the traveler Przhevalsky, give it all up and go trudging across the whole of Siberia to the Pacific to perform real deeds rather than write about imaginary ones in fiction.

« 2 »

In satisfying a strongly felt need to escape, however, the choice of Sakhalin may well have been just as haphazard as his brother Misha suggests. The existence of this forbidding island seems never to have occurred to Chekhov previously, but it is possible that a visit to a penal colony now appealed to his aroused social conscience. Discussions about the island had begun to appear in the press at this time, and perhaps he thought that such a trip might serve as an answer to those who criticized his lack of interest in contemporary problems. Further, with his immense curiosity about places and people in his vast country, a journey of these proportions must have captured his imagination. To be sure, there may have been other considerations. Did he think of the glory that had customarily surrounded Russian writers returning from ordeals in Siberia? But these had been exiles, like Dostoevsky and Korolenko. Or perhaps he had in mind the transformation which critics had observed in the art and outlook of writers after their contact with wild nature and the rough people of primeval Siberia. In his reminiscences, Koronenko tells of discussing this very point with Chekhov in the case of the mentally sick Garshin. Korolenko argued that if Garshin could for a time tear himself away from the Russian reality that tormented him and steep himself in the quiet remoteness of a primitive Siberian existence, it would have a salutary effect. "No," answered Chekhov, "his is not a situation that can be changed; the molecular particles of the brain have been scrambled, and they cannot be brought together again by anything."

Whatever dictated the choice of Sakhalin, once having made the decision Chekhov felt impelled to justify it both to himself and to mystified friends. No doubt their positive objections to what seemed to them a senseless, arduous, and even dangerous undertaking were partly responsible for forcing Chekhov, in his own defense, into formulating a plan for a well-rounded scientific investigation of the convict population on Sakhalin. As he plunged into the necessary reading and preparation, the developing scope and purpose of the plan gripped him. He had returned to his first love, that of science — this elaborate investigation seemed like a compensation for the aborted dissertation on the history of medicine of six years ago.[2] Now he had a practical objective and he was happy over it. Disturbed thoughts and vague inner urges had coalesced into a concrete plan of action and one with a useful purpose.

By early March Chekhov, with evident satisfaction, felt able to answer the protesting Suvorin with a firm defense of his reasons for going to Sakhalin. Modestly he began by saying that he did not believe his expedition would yield anything valuable in the way of either literature or science. "I want to write one to two hundred pages and in this way repay in some small part the debt I owe to medicine which, as you know, I've treated in swinish fashion." Already the research he had done had taught him a great deal, he wrote. "Moreover, I suppose the trip will be an uninterrupted six months of labor, physical and mental,

[2] Years later Chekhov stated this as a fact. In complying with the request of S. P. Diaghilev to list his works chronologically, he noted in the letter (*December* 20, 1901): "*The Island of Sakhalin* was written in 1893 — this was in place of a dissertation I had planned to write after finishing Medical School in 1884."

and for me this is also essential, for I'm a Ukrainian and have begun to grow lazy. I must become my own animal trainer. Though the trip may be nonsense — stubbornness, a whim — consider the matter and tell me what I have to lose by going? . . . For example, you write that Sakhalin is of no use or interest to anybody. Is that really so? Sakhalin is useless and uninteresting only to a society that does not exile thousands of people to it and spend millions to maintain it. . . . Sakhalin is the only place where one can study the colonization of convicts; all Europe is interested in it; then is it of no interest to us? . . . From the books I've read and am reading, it is clear that we have sent *millions* of people to rot in prison, we have let them rot casually, barbarously, without giving it a thought; we have driven people in chains, through the cold, thousands of miles, have infected them with syphilis, made them depraved, multiplied criminals, and we have thrust the blame for all this on red-nosed prison officials. Now, all educated Europe knows that the officials are not to blame, but rather all of us; yet this has nothing to do with us, it is not interesting? . . . No, I assure you, Sakhalin is of use, and is interesting; and I regret only that it is I who am going there and not someone else who knows more about the business and would be more capable of arousing public interest." (*March 9, 1890.*)

Suvorin, with his carefully nurtured government contacts, must have blinked when he read this tirade. However, that apostle of social change, Mikhailovsky, would have cheered and announced that Chekhov had at last come of age. Both the concern of one and the expectation of the other would have been quite misdirected.

« 3 »

Once having decided upon a scientific study of Sakhalin Island's penal colonies, Chekhov spared no efforts to prepare himself for the task. He journeyed to Petersburg to collect a bibliography, do some reading, and, hopefully, to make government contacts that might facilitate the work of an unofficial investigator. The most important of these was Mikhail Galkin-Vrasky, head of the national prison administration. This official and the others he appealed to listened politely to Chekhov's explanation of the scientific and literary purpose of his proposed trip, but no helpful advice or letters of recommendation were forthcoming. In fact, it was discovered, years later when the Soviet government opened the archives of the prison administration, that Galkin-Vrasky had sent a secret memorandum to instruct the head of the

Sakhalin prisons to prevent Chekhov from interviewing certain categories of political prisoners and exiles.

Though as usual Chekhov stayed with the Suvorins in Petersburg, he shunned excessive hospitality, keeping pretty much to his room, conning various issues of *The Maritime Miscellany*, and compiling a preliminary bibliography on Sakhalin of sixty-five titles. His only relaxation was seeing a few plays, attending a dog show, visiting Repin's studio, and forgathering occasionally with intimate friends such as Leontiev-Shcheglov and Pleshcheev. He returned to Moscow highly pleased with his labors and strangely unconcerned over the annoyance of the many friends he had failed to see. Let them be angry, he wrote Suvorin. In a month in Petersburg, he declared, he had done more than these friends could accomplish in a year.

Chekhov had timed his departure for Sakhalin in the early spring when the ice in the Siberian rivers would be melted. He had calculated that this ought to get him there in the summer, which would allow several months of work on the island so that he could ship out before the winter set in. However, he soon began to feel that such a schedule left precious little time for all the reading he must still do to prepare himself. He set sister Masha and her girl friends to work in the Rumyantsev Library, copying out passages from books, and brother Alexander in Petersburg was pestered for material from old newspaper files. Suvorin's office he turned into a kind of lending library to procure books and magazines. "In my Sakhalin work," Chekhov enthusiastically wrote him in the middle of February, "I shall prove myself such a scholarly son of a bitch that you'll throw up your hands. I've already stolen much thought and knowledge from the books of others which I shall pass off as my own. It is impossible to do otherwise in our practical age."

He had to turn himself into a geologist, a meteorologist, and an ethnographer, Chekhov complained, and he had to learn about the price of coal per ton in Sakhalin in 1862 and all about the soil, the subsoil, sandy loam and loamy sand. He read books on criminal law, prisons and exile in Russia, colonization on Sakhalin, and he piled through official reports of the head of the administration of prisons and numerous books and articles on travel in Siberia.

Though he had nothing in his head except Sakhalin — "*Mania sachalinosa*," he wrote Pleshcheev — and had even drafted an introductory five pages of the beginning of a book on the island, financial needs compelled him to squeeze out some time for fiction. His seventh book,

Gloomy People, dedicated to Tschaikovsky, a collection of ten published tales, all carefully reworked and including such masterpieces as *An Attack of Nerves* and *A Dreary Story*, appeared at the end of March. Since he had heard that the *Northern Herald* was going out of business (actually it only changed ownership), he sent in to *New Times* a longish story, *The Devils*.[3] It is an account of how two horse thieves, strikingly portrayed, victimize a pompous braggart of a medical assistant. The tale's effectiveness is heightened by Chekhov's characteristic impartiality which not only quite realistically permits crime to triumph, but also allows the cozened medical assistant to imagine how wonderful his life might be if he could only pursue the dashing, carefree existence of his cozeners.

Although Suvorin published *The Devils*, he was plainly troubled, as other critics had been in the past, by Chekhov's detached approach to his characters and their human problems. This was the old artistic quarrel, but it is interesting to observe that in restating his position now Chekhov for the first time makes a slight concession by agreeing that under different circumstances art might be combined with a subjective element. "You scold me for objectivity," he wrote, "calling it indifference to good and evil, the absence of ideas and ideals, and so forth. When I depict horse thieves you would like me to say: the stealing of horses is bad. But surely this has long since been known without my saying it. Let the jury pass judgment on them, but my business is to show them as they are. I write: You are dealing with horse thieves — then you should know that they are not beggars but well-fed people, that they belong to a cult, and that horse stealing with them is not just theft but a passion. Of course, it would be pleasant to combine art with preaching, but for me personally this is extremely difficult, and almost impossible because of technical considerations. Clearly, in order to portray horse thieves in seven hundred lines, I must all the time speak and think as they would, and feel with their feelings; otherwise, if I introduce subjective notes, the characters will become indistinct and the story not as compact as all short stories ought to be. When I write I count entirely upon my reader, for I assume that he himself will add the subjective elements that are lacking in the tale." (*April 1, 1890.*)

To Suvorin's criticism Leontiev-Shcheglov added a further pinprick.

[3] In Chekhov's *Collected Works*, the title of *The Devils* was changed to *The Thieves*, and it has been translated into English as *The Horse Stealers*.

Leo Tolstoy, whom Chekhov placed at the very top of Russian art, with Tschaikovsky and Repin in second and third place, and himself "in the ninety-eighth spot," had discovered, according to Leontiev-Shcheglov, a false note in his *An Attack of Nerves*. The great master pointed out that the hero of the tale ought first to have slept with one of the prostitutes and only then experience the anguish of a tormented conscience. Obviously Tolstoy had not quite grasped the point of the characterization.

Interestingly enough, in these early months of 1890, Tolstoy's celebrated *Kreutzer Sonata*, an outstanding attempt to preach a moral ideal through the medium of artistic narrative, was going the rounds in hectograph copies and causing the greatest excitement among readers (its publication was not permitted by the government until the following year, when it appeared in the thirteenth volume of Tolstoy's collected works). According to a contemporary, instead of the greeting "How do you do?" upon meeting, people asked, "Have you read *The Kreutzer Sonata?*" Chekhov also read it, despite the mountain of Sakhalin material before him. He was deeply impressed, and his praise of so subjective a work was perhaps some indication of growing uncertainty in his own artistic method. "You really didn't like *The Kreutzer Sonata?*" he replied to Pleshcheev's letter on the book. "I don't say that it is a work of genius, eternal — I'm no judge in such matters — but in my opinion, in the mass of those things being written here and abroad you will hardly find anything of equal power in the seriousness of its conception and the beauty of its execution. While not mentioning the story's artistic merits, which in places are striking, one ought to be thankful for just one of its features, that it is extremely thought-provoking. As I read it, I could scarcely keep from shouting: 'That's true!' or 'That's ridiculous!' "

Chekhov's appreciation, however, is alloyed with strictures that not only reveal his scientific training, but also suggest the considerations which ultimately led him to repudiate Tolstoyanism as inimical to human progress. For he pointed out to Pleshcheev that he could not easily forgive "Tolstoy's boldness in treating of things he does not know about and which in his stubbornness he does not wish to understand. Thus, his pronouncements on syphilis, foundling homes, the repugnance of women to sexual intercourse, and so forth are not only debatable but even expose him as an ignorant man who in the course of his long life has not taken the trouble to read two or three books written by specialists.

However, these defects vanish like feathers before the wind; in the light of the story's worth, you simply don't notice them, and if you do, it is only because you are vexed that the story did not avoid the fate of all human efforts which are never perfect or free from error." (*February 15, 1890.*)

Though engrossed in the preparations for his journey, Chekhov also took a lively interest in widespread student disturbances that broke out in March. Riots began when the authorities banned the admission of young ladies into student quarters because they suspected them not only of prostitution, but also of political activities. However, the demands of the students, who were outraged by Cossack beatings, went far beyond this incident, amounting to an academic bill of rights which they presented to a government bent on rigid control of the universities. It is curious that Chekhov's reactions were rather unsympathetic to the students. His adverse opinion on organized efforts for human betterment had not changed much since the similar disturbances in his own student days. On the other hand, he not only applauded the individual protest of youth as an essential of character building, but he complained more than once that this form of rebellion was too little in evidence among the youth of the time.

But April, the month of his departure on a journey of some ten thousand miles, was fast approaching; and Chekhov complained that he had still a year's work to do in reading and note-taking. Actually, he had done a very extensive amount of preparation and he soon began to clear his study of the many books and magazines that he had borrowed. Since the Transiberian Railroad did not exist then, most of the trip would have to be made by river boats and horses. In the popular imagination, the Siberian *taiga* swarmed with bandits and the journey was regarded as a perilous one. Chekhov could not take these warnings very seriously. The only dangers before him, he commented, were the toothaches from which he suffered, and he added that the long knife he had bought was for cutting sausage and hunting tigers. However, along with a sheepskin coat, an army officer's waterproof leather coat, and a pair of topboots, he also procured a revolver. And he took the precaution to inform Suvorin: "In case I'm drowned or anything of that sort, you might keep it in mind that all I have or may have in the future belongs to my sister; she will pay my debts." (*April 15, 1890.*) Though he imagined that he had equipped himself very well, as things turned out he lacked a number of essential items for such a journey.

The most worrisome factor was the question of finances; besides the considerable expenses for the trip, he had to assure the family of an adequate monthly income. And because he felt that his sister would be bored without him over the many weeks he would be away, he wished to send her on a vacation in the Crimea. Chekhov pooled all his resources. Fortunately at this juncture 600 roubles came in from the latest performances of *Ivanov*, and he received 782 roubles for *The Devils* and also royalties from the collections of his stories that Suvorin had published. Yet he had to plead with Leikin to send him any accumulation on the sales of his early *Motley Tales*. In addition Suvorin willingly advanced 1500 roubles against articles Chekhov would write on the trip for *New Times*, and also provided him with a correspondent's credentials, a hopeful substitute for the official letters of recommendation which Chekhov had failed to obtain, for he was quite uncertain that the authorities at Sakhalin would permit him to conduct his scientific investigation.

Then there were the many last-minute farewell visits and letters to friends and the unfinished business of a number of his petitioners to clear up. An impeccable conscience would not permit Chekhov to leave such matters undone. Only a short time before departure, his young protégé, the writer Yezhov, visited Chekhov, bringing his wife who was desperately ill with tuberculosis — he had to take her to the warm climate of the south of Russia. Chekhov at once hurried off a request to Suvorin to send him a hundred roubles. He explained that he would present the money to Yezhov on the eve of his journey as an advance against a story, with the delicate suggestion that he procure a first-class ticket for his very sick wife. The effort succeeded. Even three days before his own departure, bedeviled with a multitude of fussy details, Chekhov found time to write Suvorin again to urge him to publish in *New Times* the piece of his old friend Gilyarovsky.

Finally the twenty-first of April arrived. That evening at eight o'clock the family, the Kuvshinnikovs, Lika, Semashko, Ivanenko, and Levitan accompanied Chekhov to the Yaroslavl Station. In the midst of the gay, nervous small talk of leave-taking there was an undercurrent of sadness. Dr. Kuvshinnikov hung over Chekhov's shoulder a flask of cognac in a leather sheathing, and elicited from him the promise that he would drink the contents only on the shores of the Pacific Ocean. The train pulled out and the journey into the unknown began.

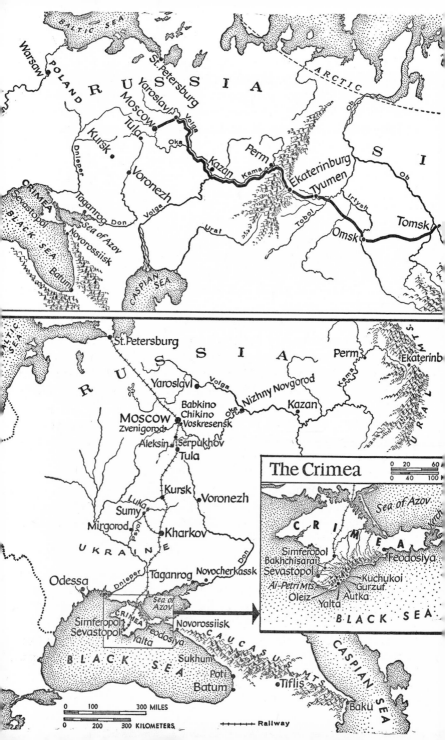

Top Map

BALTIC SEA

Warsaw

POLAND

St.Petersburg

R U S S I A

ARCTIC

Yaroslavl

Moscow

Volga

Tula

Kursk

Oka

Perm

Kazan

Kama

Ekaterinburg

Ob

S I

Voronezh

Tyumen

Dnieper

Taganrog

Don

Sea of Azov

Volga

Ural

Tobol

Irtysh

Ob

Tomsk

CRIMEA

Sevastopol

Novorossiisk

Batum

BLACK SEA

CASPIAN SEA

Omsk

Bottom Map

BALTIC SEA

St.Petersburg

R U S S I A

Perm

Ekaterinb

URAL MTS

Yaroslavl

Volga

Nizhny Novgorod

Kazan

Kama

Babkino

Chikino

Oka

Moscow

Zvenigorod

Voskresensk

Aleksin

Serpukhov

Tula

Kursk

Voronezh

Luka

Sumy

Psyol

Mirgorod

Kharkov

U K R A I N E

Odessa

Dnieper

Taganrog

Don

Novocherkassk

Sea of Azov

CRIMEA

Simferopol

Sevastopol

Yalta

Feodosiya

Novorossiisk

CAUCASUS MTS

BLACK SEA

Sukhum

Poti

Batum

Tiflis

Baku

CASPIAN SEA

The Crimea (inset)

0 20 60

0 40 100

C R I M E A

Sea of Azov

Simferopol

Bakhchisarai

Sevastopol

Feodosiya

Ai-Petri Mts

Kuchukoi

Gurzuf

Oleiz

Autka

Yalta

BLACK SEA

0 100 300 MILES

0 200 300 KILOMETERS

+++++ Railway

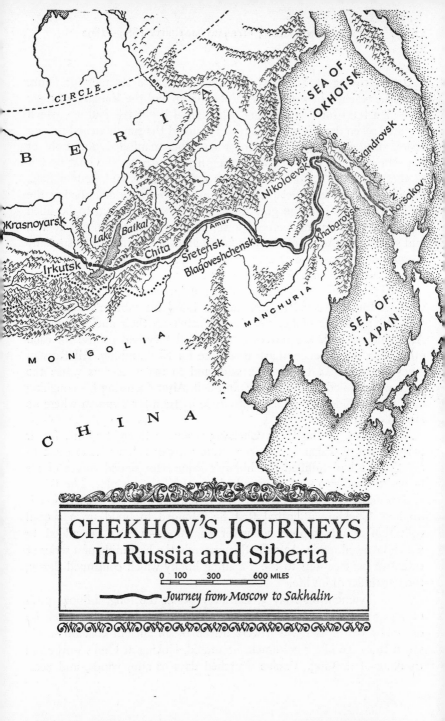

CIRCLE

S I B E R I A

Lena

SEA OF
OKHOTSK

S A K H A L I N

Alexandrovk

Korsakov

Nikolaevsk

Krasnoyarsk

Lake Baikal

Amur

Chita

Irkutsk

Sretensk

Blagoveshchensk

Khabarovsk

MANCHURIA

SEA OF
JAPAN

M O N G O L I A

C H I N A

CHEKHOV'S JOURNEYS
In Russia and Siberia

0   100   300   600 MILES

Journey from Moscow to Sakhalin

« 4 »

Upon arriving at Yaroslavl, Chekhov boarded a steamer for Perm, which he reached by way of the Volga River, and the Kama, and there he took a train for Ekaterinburg. This initial leg of the journey, which required seven days, was uneventful. He noted the sun-drenched monasteries on the banks of the Volga and they reminded him only of pleasant places to sit and fish. During his first day on the boat he felt neither sad nor gay and sat motionless and silent. His soul, he remarked, seemed to be made of gelatin. The Kama, however, he described as the dullest of rivers, and the gray towns on its banks seemed to be filled with people who manufactured lowering clouds, boredom, wet fences, and street filth. A few of the passengers aroused his curiosity, especially a group of lawyers, one of whom was reading *In the Twilight* and talking with his colleagues about the author.

At Ekaterinburg Chekhov stayed at the American Hotel for a couple of days, for he wished to rest and to fulfill his mother's request to seek out a relative of her sister's and patch up their ancient quarrel. After one try with the relatives, he decided they had no use for each other. Nor did Chekhov have much use for Ekaterinburg. All Russian cities seemed alike to him, he said, and to make matters worse the place was assailed by rain, snow, and hail. After doctoring his coughing and hemorrhoids, he was happy to leave by train for Tyumen where he arrived on May 3.

At Tyumen in the Urals Chekhov strangely thought of his far-off native town of Taganrog. For he wrote a letter to an official there to say that he had fulfilled the library's request for signed copies of his books and had also sent an inscribed copy of Tolstoy's play, *The Power of Darkness*. Obviously pleased by the request and the recognition it implied, Chekhov indicated that he intended to build up a special collection of autographed books for Taganrog — a town, he added, to which he owed much. Actually this was only the beginning of a series of extensive benefactions to the Taganrog library which continued during the remainder of his life.

From Tyumen, on May 3, Chekhov began the long, arduous push of about a thousand miles to Tomsk in a hired basketwork chaise drawn by two horses which were driven by an ancient coachman. He sat in this cage like a goldfinch, he mused, looking at God's world and thinking of nothing. Twelve wretched days of rain, winds, and occasional snow flurries . . . for though it was May, there was as yet no sign of approaching summer in this part of Siberia. Dressed in two pairs of trousers, wrapped in his new sheepskin coat, his freezing feet under the leather overcoat, Chekhov drove on fearfully exhausted by the cold, by the bumping of the chaise over extremely rough roads, and by the constant jingle of bells. His cheap new boots soon pained him so much that he had to stop and take them off to relieve his chafed heels. Finally, he had to buy felt boots. After three days of such travel his collarbone, shoulders, and vertebrae ached from the ceaseless jolting so that he could neither stand, sit, nor lie in comfort. As the days passed, however, his body grew used to the lurching and bumping, grinding and creaking, and his headaches, hemorrhoids, coughing and slight bloodspitting mysteriously vanished in this rugged existence in the open air.

Soon Chekhov began to observe with interest life along the Siberian road and in the villages and stations where he stopped for refreshments and changes of horses. He passed a group of thirty or more convicts, worn out from hundreds of miles of plodding in clanking leg irons, escorted by weary soldiers with rifles. The chaise overtook occasional tramps with pots on their backs. They would murder a poor old woman to take her petticoat for their leg-wrappers, Chekhov explained in a letter, or knock out the eyes of some brother exile, but he learned from his driver that they never harmed regular travelers. In fact, he commented, there was no basis for the popular notion back home of the dangers of the road. Even stealing in these regions was almost unheard of, he wrote.

The mixture of peoples in the villages intrigued him — emigrant Russians, Ukrainians, Tatars, exiled Poles and Jews. And he marveled at how well they got along together. "My God," he wrote his sister, "how rich Russia is in good people! If it were not for the officials who corrupt the peasants and exiles, then Siberia would be the richest and the happiest of lands." (*May 14–17, 1890.*)

Food became a problem on the road and Chekhvov soon realized that he had made a mistake in not taking along a quantity of provisions, especially tea, for he loathed the local substitute which he described as a concoction of sage and beetles. For days he went without a regular dinner, preferring to fill up on the fine Siberian bread, pies, and pancakes rather than submit to traditional dishes of vile roasted salt meat, fish cooked with scales, and "duck broth," a perfectly disgusting dish, he said, composed of a muddy-looking liquid with bits of wild duck and uncooked onions floating in it.

Very late one night, on the fourth day out, Chekhov drowsily watched serpentine tongues of flame on both sides of the road fitfully illuminating the darkness as they sprang up and swiftly died down — the peasants were burning last year's grass. Suddenly a heavy, three-horse mail coach thundered down on the chaise. His driver quickly pulled over to the right to let it pass. But a second mail coach, racing immediately behind the first, plunged into Chekhov's vehicle. He was thrown to the ground with all his baggage tumbling on top of him. A third careening coach fortunately was stopped by the wreckage of the second. Chekhov picked himself up. The light chaise was badly damaged, the horses hurt, and soon a violent altercation, almost ending in a fight, took place between the coachmen as they blamed each other. In the cold dawn of this open alien country, the air rent by the savage swearing of the crew, a feeling of terrible isolation came over Chekhov. Eventually the broken shaft of the carriage was mended, with the help of the straps of Chekhov's luggage, and they crept along gingerly to the next station.

Meanwhile, the heavy Siberian rains had set in and as he approached the Irtysh River natives tried to persuade him, because of news of floods, to wait at the tiny station he had reached. But Chekhov had decided that two of his faults on this journey, which had already cost him extra expense, trouble, and inconvenience, were his tendency to listen to persuaders and his readiness to give in. Stubbornly he disregarded the advice. Soon there loomed up before him what seemed like an immense lake, from which patches of earth appeared and bushes stuck up. However, he refused to turn back. At times he and his driver had to get out and lead the horses through the water over broken bridges on the road while the wind and rain whipped about them. When he finally reached the ferry station of the Irysh, after heroic efforts, the boatmen refused to budge because of the high winds. Disconsolate, he had to remain there for the night, watching the white waves splash on the clay bank and imagining that the river gave forth a strange sound as though someone were nailing up coffins under the water.

The same vile weather continued to bedevil him during the remainder of the way to Tomsk. The River Ob had also overflowed its banks and he got across with difficulty; and on the River Tom a violent wind blew up which threatened to swamp the rowboat. The boatman advised waiting in the willow bushes nearby, but the passengers urged him to go on lest they have to spend the night there. The river became more sinister as a gale-driven rain lashed sideways. His heart was heavy, Chekhov wrote, and he kept thinking that if the boat capsized, he would first throw off his sheepskin coat, then his jacket. As the opposite bank drew nearer, the rowers pulled at the oars more cheerfully. Little by little his heart grew light, and when the bank was only twenty feet away, he was suddenly filled with joy. "It's good to be a coward," he reflected. "You don't need much to feel very happy all of a sudden!"

So bad were the roads that in the last two days of his trip to Tomsk, Chekhov had not been able to travel much more than a total of forty miles. He arrived in the city on the evening of May 15, and he regarded it as no compensation for his laborious journey to be told at the hotel that there had not been as cold and rainy a spring as this one since 1842. Chekhov decided to remain in Tomsk till the rains were over.

« 5 »

He found Tomsk a dull and intemperate town, devoid of attractive women, and with an Asiatic disregard for justice. The few intellectuals Chekhov met were also dull, including the editor of the local newspaper who drank him out of six roubles' worth of vodka. The Assistant Chief of Police paid a call, not to make any charges but with the manuscript of a play which he wished to promote. They had drinks together and he invited Chekhov downtown to inspect the brothels. "I have just returned from these houses," he wrote Suvorin. "Revolting. Two o'clock in the morning." (*May 20, 1890.*)

Much of the five days he spent at Tomsk was devoted to letter writing and to the first of the articles on his trip which he had undertaken to do for *New Times*. They are chatty, informative sketches, nine in number, containing perfect little genre pictures of situations and vivid portrayals of people he encountered on the road, as well as passages of sharp criticism of bureaucratic officials and of the hopeless lives of Siberian exiles. Chekhov also used the stay at Tomsk to replenish his travel equipment. The trunk he had carted all the way from Moscow was dispensed with in favor of a large folding leather sack that would not stick in his ribs. And for a hundred and thirty roubles he also bought a small carriage, in the belief that he would save money if only he could sell it at the end of his journey.

In his new carriage Chekhov left Tomsk on May 21 for his next major stopping place, Irkutsk, another thousand miles away. Accompanying him in their own vehicle were two lieutenants and an army doctor. Bad as the roads had been so far, they were as paved highways compared to the ferocious ruts and liquid mud on the way to Irkutsk. His carriage repeatedly broke down and the heavy repair costs set him to wondering whether his money would hold out. "I pay more than I need to," he wrote his sister in a mood of self-criticism. "I do the wrong thing, and I say the wrong thing, and I'm always expecting what does not happen." (*May 28, 1890.*) As he emerged from the interminable forest before Krasnoyarsk to glimpse a mountain range in the distance, his spirits rose. The sun shone on budding birch trees and there were no more cold driving winds and rains. Summer had at last come to Siberia. When he arrived at Irkutsk on June 4 he decided, in this cheerful mood, that it was the best of all Siberian towns.

The bliss of a steam bath, profound sleep in a comfortable bed in a decent hotel, a change to clean clothes from his messed and dirty outfit of the road, and then a stroll around remote Irkutsk with its theater, museum, and a park that sported a band concert — all these ordinary pleasures somehow minimized the physical hardships and the dangers through flood and field which Chekhov had undergone. He now looked back on it all with the satisfied wonder of accomplishment. In a letter to Alexander, he thanked God that he had been given the strength and opportunity to make this journey, for he had experienced a great deal, he said, that was new, important, and interesting. He could now dwell in his letters and articles on the mysteriousness of the illimitable forest, the *taiga,* that he had passed through, the misty and dreamy mountains beyond, which had reminded him of the Caucasus, and the wild beauty of the Yenisei, that "fierce and mighty warrior" of rivers which he had crossed to get to Irkutsk. If man began boldly on the banks of the Russian Volga — Chekhov wrote in his last sketch for *New Times* — he may end with a moan that is called song, his bright golden hopes replaced by what goes under the name of "Russian pessimism." However, if life began with a moan on the banks of the Siberian Yenesei, it may end, he prophetically predicted, with an audacity which we Russians have never dreamed of.

In a moment of homesickness during this pause from travel, Chekhov had wired the family to pool its resources and send him a long telegram. (Shortly after his departure they had given up the house on

Sadovaya Kudrinskaya as too expensive to maintain during his long absence, and had moved to the summer *dacha* on the Lintvarev estate.) The response informed him that his mother and Misha were off on a trip south to Holy Mountains; his sister, accompanied by Natalya Lintvareva, was in the Crimea; and his father at Ivan's in Moscow, where they were presumably following the stages of his journey on the large wall map he had procured for them. Chekhov wrote his mother from Irkutsk a long and interesting letter about his trip, gave her directions about money matters, and pleaded for details about the family. Was she taking good care of her bad leg? What had happened to Auntie Fedosiya and her son? How was Misha's love-life going? He himself, he declared, must be in love with the beautiful Lika, for he dreamed of her the other night. She was a queen, he insisted, compared to the Siberian women and girls, who were like frozen fish — "You'd have to be a walrus or a seal to have an affair with them." And in an expansive mood he urged upon her the wisdom of searching for a farm which he could buy. "When I return to Russia I'm going to rest for five years — that is, I'm going to stay in one place and twiddle my thumbs. A farm would be most appropriate. I think the money can be found, for my affairs are not in a bad way. If I work off the advance (half of it is worked off already), next spring I shall certainly obtain another advance of two or three thousand to be paid off in installments over a five-year period. This won't trouble my conscience, since the bookstores of *New Times* have already earned on my books more than two or three thousand, and I shall earn still more for them. I don't think I shall undertake anything serious until I'm thirty-five; I want a taste of personal life which I once had but did not pay enough attention to because of various circumstances." (*June 7, 1890.*)

The anodyne of travel, of new interests and experiences, was already beginning to work its cure of the mental turmoil and spiritual ache.

« 6 »

Chekhov left Irkutsk on June 11 for the last leg of his journey to the Pacific. The distance to Lake Baikal was relatively short and he traveled it with the three army officers, for he had sold his carriage at Irkutsk, taking a very considerable loss. As long as he lived, Chekhov wrote his mother, he would never forget the trip across the vast mirror-like surface of the lake in brilliant sunny weather. It sent a shiver over him to peer two thirds of a mile down into the crystal-clear turquoise-blue water and see the rock formations at the bottom. And the long road across Transbaikalia (present Buryat Mongolia) to Sretensk, with its varied scenery of forest, plains, and mountains, delighted him. Here he boarded the steamer *Yermak* on the Shilka River which flows into the Amur. The extensive part of his trip, close to three thousand miles by horses, had ended. It seemed strange not to hear the jingling of bells and to be able to go to bed and stretch his legs out at full length and not wake up with his face covered with dust. However, as he now looked back on this Golgotha of gruesome Siberian roads and gullies which he had traversed, he wrote his mother on June 20: "My journey has been as happy as God may grant to anyone. I have not once been ill, and of the mass of things I had with me I have lost nothing but a penknife, a strap off my suitcase, and a little jar of carbolic ointment." His spirits were high, he declared, as though he had passed an examination.

On the *Yermak* Chekhov had treated himself to a first-class passage, for he wished to be alone. He had grown weary of the company of his army officers, one of whom chattered incessantly, and besides he feared they would want to borrow more money from him — they had failed to repay a loan of a hundred and fifty roubles which he had unwisely given them.

Chekhov once neatly summed up Siberian scenic attractions by saying that before Lake Baikal one saw mere prose; after it sheer poetry. "I've already come seven hundred miles down the Amur," he exulted in a letter to his sister, "and have seen a million gorgeous landscapes; I feel giddy with ecstasy!" The riverbanks were original and luxuriant, and wild life was visible everywhere. Here was an ideal place for a *dacha*, he imagined. Near the Cossack village of Pokrovskaya the *Yermak* ran aground on a sandbank. While the boat was being repaired, another from the opposite direction was forced to halt. A military band on it played, passengers danced, and no one noticed the passage of time in this holiday atmosphere.

The people of the Amur region on the boat and in the towns and villages which he visited, on both the Russian and Chinese sides of the river, fascinated Chekhov. Their conversation largely concerned gold mines, for nearly everybody seemed to be involved in this occupation, even priests and exiles. They grew rich, he observed, as quickly as they grew poor, and never drank anything but champagne. He treated a miner's pregnant wife; the grateful husband thrust a whole handful of bills on him, and though Chekhov protested that he also was rich, he somehow found himself coming away with fifteen roubles.

What particularly delighted him was the air of freedom these pioneer people exuded. No one bothered to observe religious fast days and both girls and peasants smoked cigarettes. "The air on the steamer is red-hot with the talk that goes on," he wrote Masha. "Here no one is afraid to speak his mind. For there is no one to arrest him and no place to exile him, so one can be as liberal as one likes. All the people are independent, self-reliant, and logical." (*June 23–26, 1890.*) They were indifferent to what went on in Russia. A captain of one of these riverboats would never dream of surrendering an escaped convict who traveled with him. In fact, Chekhov told Suvorin, "The lowest convict breathes more freely on the Amur than the highest general in Russia." (*June 27, 1890.*)

At Blagoveshchensk Chekhov transferred to another riverboat, the *Muravyov*, and continued down the Amur to Nikolaevsk, one of the easternmost towns of Russia, only about eighteen miles from where the river flows into the Pacific. There he boarded the liner *Baikal*, along with a few other civilians, a large party of soldiers, and some convicts. The passage across the Gulf of Tatary began. It seemed to him that he had come to the end of the world. However, as the coastline of Sakhalin loomed in the distance, he remarked that "the delight which I experienced was increased by the proud consciousness that at last I was seeing this shore." The *Baikal* dropped anchor and on July 11 a cutter, towing two barges full of convicts, took Chekhov to the landing at Alexandrovsk, the principal town and prison center of Sakhalin.

« 7 »

The justifiable fears of Chekhov that the authorities of Sakhalin would obstruct or even reject his plan to study the inhabitants of the island were quickly dissipated. General V. O. Kononovich, the experienced and intelligent administrative head at Alexandrovsk, gave him a friendly reception and promised every assistance, even to throwing open the central archives of the prison system and providing him with statistical data. These promises were confirmed a few days later by A. N. Korf, the Governor-General of the whole area, who was on a tour of inspection. He informed Chekhov that he could go wherever he wished and inspect official documents, although he was not to have relations with political exiles. At a large reception in honor of the

Governor-General, given by the administration, Chekhov met most of the officials of Sakhalin.

Quartered at first in the house of the local physician on the main street of Alexandrovsk, a town of about three thousand people, Chekhov was immediately struck by the fact that the typical street noise was the clanking of leg irons as the convicts marched back and forth to work. There were five principal penal settlements on Sakhalin to which criminals, often of the worst type, were sent and employed at hard labor on various projects. Upon release they were confined to the island as colonists, a practise that brought about frequent disorders. For the region was afflicted with a wretched, foggy climate, heavy rainfall in summer, and bitter cold and severe storms in winter, with snow falling from October to May. Fishing, coal mining, and agriculture were the chief occupations, although the poor soil and very short growing season made successful farming almost impossible. Apart from administrative personnel and several thousand prisoners, the rest of the population consisted largely of colonists from among the former convicts. Women, naturally, were considerably in the minority, although many had voluntarily followed their convict husbands into exile.

Shortly after arriving Chekhov began his investigation with a well-formed plan in mind and some idea of the kind of book he wished to write. Basically his intention was to conduct a census of the island. To facilitate this purpose he persuaded the prison printshop to produce quantities of a questionnaire which he devised, with blank spaces for his own annotations. As he later explained, the intention of this census was to give him an opportunity to meet and talk with people rather than to obtain population statistics.

He began by visiting the prisons, interviewing convicts, and taking down formal statistics and copying out relevant passages from official documents. According to the testimony of one observer, Chekhov was unusually successful in gaining the confidence of even the most hardened criminals. Though they were ordinarily taciturn, suspicious, and deceitful, they conversed with him simply and truthfully.

Next he traveled in all kinds of weather over much of central Sakhalin to interview individual penal colonists and fill out a census card for each. The dimensions of this incredible task for a single investigator may be imagined, for he estimated that he completed close to ten thousand cards, all of which may be found today in the archives of the

Lenin Library.[4] He trudged from hut to hut, often alone, but sometimes accompanied by a prison aid and a guard with a revolver. It was necessary for him to arise at five in the morning and work till late at night in order to complete this task in time. Soon he was writing his mother that a strange blinking had developed in his eyes, followed by severe headaches. The material piled up and he informed Suvorin that he had enough of it for three dissertations. However, these innumerable interviews form the basis for the rich sociological data that contributed much to making the book he eventually wrote, *The Island of Sakhalin*, the valuable and intensely human document it is.

With his acute sensitivity to human suffering, it was not always easy for Chekhov to remain the detached scientific investigator and refrain from voicing a protest against the cruelty, hunger, and desperate conditions of life that he observed everywhere on this island of the damned. If one may judge from the contents of grateful letters which he later received, on more than one occasion he stealthily provided moral and material assistance to some of these unhappy exiles.[5] But he fully realized that his "good behavior" would be regarded as a kind of hostage for the official sanctions he needed to be allowed to finish his study. The wretched fate of the women and children in particular deeply pained him. Prostitution had long since become an accepted way of life, even for the "free women" who had come to await the release of their husbands. They often had no other means of existence. And the sale of young daughters by their mothers had become a commonplace. Indeed, women were regarded as mere chattels. Chekhov quotes a sample petition of a colonist to the prison director: "We humbly beg your honor to allow us a cow for milk in the above-mentioned place and a person of the female sex to take care of household matters."

[4] The census cards had thirteen entries, such as the settlement where the respondent lived, the number of his house, his name, age, etc. Some of the queries could be answered by underlining, such as "literate, illiterate," "married, widowed, single." Despite the simplicity of the card, it is difficult to imagine that in only three months on Sakhalin, Chekhov could have completed 10,000 of these cards without considerable assistance, and he certainly could not have conducted personally ten thousand interviews in this period of time.

[5] Chekhov's letters to convicts and officials on Sakhalin after he left the island have been lost, but a number of their letters to him exist in the manuscript collection in the Moscow Lenin Library. They reveal the extent of his kindness to them and the high regard in which these people held him. An interesting selection of these letters has recently been published: M. V. Teplinskii, "Novye materialy o sakhalinskom puteshestvii A. P. Chekhova" ("New Material on A. P. Chekhov's Sakhalin Journey") in *Anton Pavlovich Chekhov*, Sakhalin, 1959, pp. 180-225.

Children were the principal victims of these horrible circumstances. Churches and schools were totally inadequate (he wrote his pedagogue brother Ivan to send him a quantity of textbook materials). Children were largely educated by their convict environment. Shackled prisoners were such a commonplace that these undernourished youngsters had built up their games around them and their guards, and around lashings and executions. Girls of thirteen lived as prostitutes and were often pregnant at fifteen; Chekhov interviewed one who had been sold into prostitution at nine. Among completely amoral colonists these children were uncertain of their filial ties. Chekhov tells of visiting one hut and finding in it only a boy of ten, barefoot, with a freckled face, and shoulders hunched as though warding off a blow. He asked the boy what his father's name was.

"I don't know," he answered.

"What do you mean? You live with your father and don't know his name? You ought to be ashamed."

"He's not my real father."

"So, he's not your real father?"

"He lives with my mother."

"Is your mother married or a widow?"

"A widow. She came here because of her husband."

"What does that mean — she came because of her husband?"

"She killed him."

"Do you remember your father?"

"I don't. I'm a bastard."

In his talks with General Kononovich, as well as with Governor-General Korf, Chekhov found them filled with enlightened views on penal practice, yet convicts at hard labor on the island were regularly chained to their wheelbarrows and corporal punishment was by no means infrequent. In *The Island of Sakhalin* he described a flogging that he witnessed: the physician's examination to determine if it was safe to give the prisoner the ninety lashes of his punishment; the slow, deliberate preparation; the binding of the victim to a bench; the sadistic executioner and the equally sadistic spectators who always asked permission to watch; the prison official's methodical counting of each blow, and the cries and pleading of the victim as his quivering naked body was quickly transformed into a bloody mass of raw flesh. Well before the ninety blows had been administered Chekhov had to flee to the street, where, in his imagination, he could still hear the

official mechanically droning away — "Twenty-four . . . Twenty-five . . ."
It was long before he could forget this experience. With grief in his
voice and nervously wringing his hands, he told a prison doctor: "Indeed, I remember with horror that, when the lash whistled and struck
the condemned man's body, something in me was torn to pieces and
groaned in a thousand voices."

One outlet for Chekhov's feeling of protest was satire. When the
spirit moved him he would gather a few trusted families among his
friends and read humorous tales he had written which poked fun at
Sakhalin officials. But these manuscripts he immediately destroyed after
they had served their purpose. There is also some evidence to the effect
that he read to a selected group a three-act comedy he had written. It
was called *General Flirt* and pilloried a well-known Sakhalin official
nicknamed "The Flirt." Subsequent information several years later
indicated that Chekhov intended to rework this play for publication,
but it never appeared in print and he apparently destroyed the manuscript.[6]

Having finished his study of central Sakhalin on September 11,
Chekhov journeyed to the southern part of the island (before the
Russo-Japanese War, the whole of Sakhalin belonged to Russia) where
there were a few more prisons and penal colonies. He centered at
Korsakov and continued his investigation, which covered a substantial
amount of territory in this southern area.

As Chekhov emerged from a settler's hut after his last interview and
filled out the last questionnaire, his feelings about the success of this
long, hard task were distinctly mixed. He wrote Suvorin, perhaps with
some slight exaggeration, that he had seen everything at Sakhalin
and that there was not a single convict or settler who had not talked
with him. With his future book in mind, however, he was wise enough
to realize that it was not what he had seen but how he had seen it
that really mattered.

Only when his task had been completed did Chekhov really sense
how intense was his dislike for everything connected with this accursed
island. "I'm homesick and weary of Sakhalin," he wrote his mother on
October 6. "For three months now I've seen no one but convicts or

6 The evidence that Chekhov wrote this play is summed up by N. I. Gitovich in
"A. S. Feldman. Chekhov na Sakhaline," in *Literaturnoe Nasledstvo* ("A. S. Feldman.
Chekhov on Sakhalin," in *Literary Heritage*), Moscow, 1960, LXVIII, pp. 594-
596.

people who can talk of nothing but penal servitude, the lash, or jail-birds. It is a depressing existence."

Winter in this region would soon arrive. Chekhov had to hurry, for there was always the possibility that the Gulf of Tatary would freeze over and so delay his return trip by sea. On October 13 natives rowed him out from the Korsakov landing to the *Petersburg*, anchored in the gulf and bound for Odessa.

Chekhov's long and difficult journey and his experiences on Sakhalin had quite clearly brought about a catharsis of the incessant and agitating inner promptings that had sent him off on this implausible adventure. He never regretted the effort, and the extensive practical endeavor proved to be an important factor in a transition period of his life, as well as a significant influence on his social outlook.

« 8 »

The homeward voyage took almost two months but it was a tourist lark compared to his overland trip to Sakhalin. Suvorin had tried to persuade him to return by way of the United States, a plan which Chekhov had originally entertained, but he now dismissed this as both dull and too expensive. For after he left Vladivostok — the Russian Far East seacoast, he declared, depressed one by its poverty and ignorance — his ports of call were famous cities of the storied East. Japan had to be bypassed because of cholera, but Hong Kong, with its exquisite bay, impressed him as it does all foreigners. In the city he was moved to indignation by Russian fellow-travelers who abused the English for exploiting the natives. "I thought to myself," he commented on this fact to Suvorin, "Yes, the English exploit the Chinese, the Sepoys, and the Hindus, but they do give them roads, aqueducts, museums, and Christianity; you exploit them too, but what do you give them?"[7]

A typhoon overtook the *Petersburg* in the China Sea and the ship heeled over as far as thirty-eight degrees during the heaviest gusts. Disaster seemed imminent and the captain advised Chekhov to keep his revolver by him to hasten the end in case they went down, but the ship rode out the storm. The burial of two passengers at sea unnerved

---

[7] This condemnation of the Russians and praise of the British is deleted — with the usual dots indicating an omission — from the Soviet edition of the letters: *Polnoe sobranie sochineni i pisem A. P. Chekhova* (*Complete Works and Letters of A. P. Chekhov*), 1949, XV, 130. The full text of the letter, dated December 9, 1890, may be found in *Pisma A. P. Chekhova* (*Letters of A. P. Chekhov*), edited by M. P. Chekhova, vols. I-VI, Moscow, 1912–1916.

him. To watch a corpse, wrapped in sailcloth, somersaulted into the water and to remember that it was several miles to the bottom filled him with horror at the thought that such a fate might await him. The incident stirred his imagination and resulted in the fine short story *Gusev*, written during the course of the trip and published later that year in *New Times*. It is a grim tale of two discharged and hopelessly ill soldiers on shipboard on their way home. The fiery, independent Pavel Ivanich rails against the fate that has overtaken their lives in the service, but old Gusev faces death with Christian humility and complete resignation. The serenity of the burial service at sea is rendered gruesome as the dark form of a shark stealthily approaches the sinking canvas shroud that contains the remains of Gusev.

Somehow Singapore left a sad impression on Chekhov, but this was more than compensated by his next stop, Colombo, a heavenly place, he declared. And into this paradise of Ceylon, he wrote Suvorin, he traveled on a sight-seeing trip by rail "and had my fill of palm trees and bronze-skinned women. . . ."[8] On the stopover in India, as he later wrote Uncle Mitrofan by way of impressing the old man, he saw wild elephants and cobras and remarkable Indian conjurors "who literally perform miracles." And on a sudden impulse he acquired here three mongooses which he brought back to Russia with him.

The remainder of the long voyage appears to have been a rather dull affair, made especially boring by his anxiety now to get home. Once, while suffering from the hot, humid weather encountered in the Indian Ocean, he brashly jumped into the water from the bow of the ship while it was in motion, getting back after his swim by climbing up a rope flung to him from the stern. The route took him to Port Said, through the Suez and past Mount Sinai, the sight of which moved him; to Constantinople, with which he fell in love; and then to Odessa, where he entrained for Moscow.

Apprised of his coming by telegraph, Chekhov's mother and Misha had gone forward to Tula to intercept him. They found him at the station restaurant with a Sakhalin priest and a naval officer whom he had picked up on the way, and with one of the mongooses sitting up

---

[8] (*December 9, 1890.*) Chekhov apparently boasted too much about this incident. Leontiev-Shcheglov records in his diary after meeting him: "A bronze-skinned woman under a palm tree . . ." And brother Alexander wrote him jokingly sometime after Chekhov's return from Sakhalin: "Greetings to your anonymous wife and the children produced by you in your trip around the world. I hope they are not few in number. . . . Suddenly somewhere in Ceylon there is a Chekhov. . . ."

on the table and eating with them, much to the delight of a crowd that had gathered. The meeting of mother and son was a touching one. They resumed the rest of the short trip to Moscow together, where they took him to the new house on Malaya Dmitrovka Street which the family had moved into that fall. It was December 8. Chekhov had been away almost eight months. His great adventure had ended.

« 9 »

The first day after his arrival Chekhov wrote a long letter to Suvorin. His head was in a whirl, he declared, and his baggage filled with manuscript notes and census cards. In retrospect now, Sakhalin seemed like a regular hell. He recapitulated what had happened since his last letter. And then, out of the fullness of a wave of moral indignation, he expostulated: "God's world is good. It is only we who are bad. . . . One must work, and to hell with everything else. The important thing is that we must be just, and all the rest will come as a matter of course. I want terribly to talk with you. My soul is in an upheaval." (*December 9, 1890.*)

Chekhov certainly wanted to get to work at once on the mass of material he had brought back, and he half-seriously threatened to marry any intelligent girl who would classify it for him. Conditions, however, were less than ideal for undertaking the additional research he now saw was necessary and for writing the kind of book he planned — a picture of Sakhalin that would be at once scientific and artistic. For one thing the new house, a small two-story structure, seemed uncongenial. It would take getting-used-to. Then, in the first days after his return, hordes of visitors and reporters turned up. And the house was kept in a continual bedlam by the mongooses. Though excessively friendly with people, these engaging little animals, lacking cobras to attack, made for dogs and cats. They got into everything — clothes, shoes, food supplies, the inkwell. The gloves of visitors left on the hall table were torn to shreds and top hats invited messes. The family gave away two of them in the hope that they could cope with one. What troubled Chekhov most, however, was illness. Though he had enjoyed excellent health throughout most of his long journey — the constant outdoor life may well have lengthened his span of years — as soon as he got back to Moscow he was afflicted with severe coughing, headaches, a general feeling of lassitude, and what he described as "palpitations of the heart."

Though the will to work was strong, Chekhov had to struggle against a feeling of debility. He feared also that the vivid impressions he had of Sakhalin would soon fade. The urge within him was not merely a matter of paying his delayed debt to science. He had a purpose now, a message to offer to his country — the senselessness of the suffering which one group of people inflicts upon another. Somehow he felt that what he had endured on this long journey and the promise of the book to come had purged his soul of that agonizing sense of purposelessness which had troubled him so long. If the critics had regarded his tales as unprincipled writings, he would now reveal principles such as the editors of *Russian Thought* had not dared to embody in their liberal pages.

The consciousness of change in his outlook is clearly reflected in his comments to Suvorin at the end of 1890: "How wrong you were when you advised me not to go to Sakhalin! I have . . . myriads of midges in my head, a devilish lot of plans, and all sorts of things, so what a sour creature I would be now if I had sat at home. Before my journey *The Kreutzer Sonata* seemed to me to be an event, but now it seems to me absurd and ridiculous. Either I've grown up because of my journey or I have gone crazy — the devil knows which." (*December 17, 1890.*)

CHAPTER XI

"Landowner A. Chekhov"

WELL, CHEKHOV HAD NOT GONE CRAZY; but the mysterious pulse of life now throbbed with quickened beat. Sakhalin had taught him that one must not only know all about life, but must also do something about it. The way he lived in the city seemed so petty, so bourgeois and dull that he felt ready to bite. To make matters worse, he had to put aside the Sakhalin material and concentrate on a story, for the months spent on the journey had cut heavily into his earnings. At the same time, however, he began a systematic canvass of Moscow friends to persuade them to contribute textbooks for Sakhalin schoolchildren.

The early weeks of January, 1891, found Chekhov in Petersburg. He not only had much to talk over with Suvorin, with whom he stayed, but he wished to push the collection of textbooks in the capital. And he also thought that, away from the hubbub of Moscow, he might make some progress on the short story he had begun which had already taken

on the proportions of a novella. This latter hope was a vain one, for he
was deluged with invitations from people who wanted to hear all the
details about the grim existence of convicts on the Island of Sakhalin.
He soon grew bored with these "conversations and imbecilities," and
as tired "as a ballet dancer after five acts and eight tableaux" from
running around to endless dinners where, besides trying to interest his
hosts in textbooks for Sakhalin, he had to answer many foolish questions on his recent travels. In reality, he had little faith, as he told
A. F. Koni, the distinguished lawyer and lover of literature whom he
met at this time, in the private philanthropy of such socialites to
remedy the ugly conditions among the children of the penal colonists
on Sakhalin. He would prefer to see an effort made by the government
itself. Koni proposed that they call on his friend, Elizaveta Naryshkina,
a lady high in court circles, to persuade her to arrange for a meeting
with the Empress in order to interest her in supporting the establishment of an orphanage for Sakhalin children. Although nothing came of
this plan, Chekhov's vigorous campaign to collect textbooks and also
reading material for school libraries met with success — more than
2200 volumes were eventually shipped to Sakhalin. However weary he
grew of the parade of visitors, a few of them government officials,
Chekhov no doubt took some satisfaction in writing his brother Ivan
from Petersburg: "They attribute a significance to my trip to Sakhalin
which I could hardly have expected. . . . All look forward to my book
and foresee a real success for it, but I have no time to write!" (*January
27, 1891.*)

The pressing business of Sakhalin was not allowed to interfere with
convivial gatherings with close Petersburg friends whom he had not
seen or heard from for months, and on his birthday, January 17, they
tendered him a sumptuous dinner at the stylish Malo-Yaroslavets
Restaurant. Strangely enough, there were other "friends," largely journalists and young rival authors, whose antagonism at this time Chekhov
felt deeply. "I'm surrounded by a thick atmosphere of ill-feeling," he
wrote his sister, "extremely vague and incomprehensible to me. They
feed me dinners and sing vulgar praises in my honor, but at the
same time they are ready to devour me. What for? The devil only
knows. If I were to shoot myself I would give nine tenths of my
friends and admirers the greatest satisfaction. And how pettily they express their petty feelings!" (*January 14, 1891.*) Some of this chagrin
may be traceable to an article in *New Times* by the sharp-tongued

Burenin, who listed Chekhov, along with Korolenko and Uspensky, as new writers who had already begun to fade instead of to flower. Earlier Alexander had reported to his brother a squib which the sarcastic Burenin had been reciting to his colleagues in the newspaper office:

> A talented writer named Chekhov
> To Sakhalin Island did set off,
>   To search for inspiration
>   Amidst abomination.
> And when he didn't find it
> Returned and didn't mind it.
>
> The moral of my creation:
> Don't strain so for inspiration.

Chekhov's early rise to fame had naturally provoked a good deal of envy and ill-will among his contemporaries in literature. In this connection, an entry in V. A. Tikhonov's diary is relevant. After expressing his admiration of Chekhov's difficult journey to Sakhalin, he adds: "What a powerful, purely elemental force is Anton Chekhov. . . . But how many enviers he has acquired among our writers. Albov, Sheller, Golitsyn are not the least! Certain of them — for example, my own brother — have become hateful to me because of this envy and eternal disparagement of the name of Chekhov."[1] Some of this ill-will had undoubtedly been inspired by Chekhov's friendship with Suvorin. Without the aid of this powerful publisher, these rivals sneered, Chekhov would never have achieved or maintained his success. Leontiev-Shcheglov, a bit envious himself, sets down in his diary the opinion of several young Petersburg literary rivals: "Chekhov is a 'Suvorin kept woman'!" And he comments: "But all this scandalmongering, no doubt, is from envy of his unbelievable success. Phui — what . . . swine they are!" What many did not understand, however, was the genuineness of the friendship and Chekhov's refusal to exploit it for his personal gain. If anything, his book contracts with Suvorin lost him money, for with repeated editions that resulted from his growing popularity, he could quite justifiably have demanded a higher rate of return. Nor did he take advantage of an offer by the *Petersburg Gazette* of forty kopecks a line to force an increase in Suvorin's rate in *New Times*, which was then only twenty-five kopecks. In many respects, he employed his friendship

[1] This brother, A. A. Tikhonov, a writer and editor, remained unfriendly to Chekhov. Of the other authors mentioned, only M. N. Albov, editor of the monthly *Northern Herald*, achieved any measure of success.

more in the interests of others than in his own. Scores of people sought his aid in influencing Suvorin on their behalf, and he rarely refused. Sometimes they were these same literary rivals and not only his protégés such as Lazarev-Gruzinsky or Yezhov. He tirelessly entertained such requests from budding authors. A new one at this time was Elena Shavrova, the girl he had met at Yalta three years ago. Now in Moscow, she asked his assistance in placing her stories in *New Times*. After going over fifteen of her tales, he willingly agreed, scolded her for writing so little, and urged: "Write twenty more tales and send them to me. I'll read them all with satisfaction, for you need drill." (*November 19, 1891.*) In 1891 Ivan Bunin, who later became a close friend of Chekhov, also asked him to go over the manuscripts of his stories.

Suvorin, who was twenty-six years older, held more confidences of Chekhov at this time than perhaps any other friend or member of his family. Unlike Suvorin's many enemies among the liberals, Chekhov had some awareness of the dual nature of his political and social views, which were publicly revealed in his letters and diary only after his death — he could be a harsh critic, in private, of the reactionary measures of the Tsar's government.

While staying with Suvorin in Petersburg, the two friends discussed the possibility of sharing an estate for the summer, or at least of renting adjoining *dachas*. The older man, aware of Chekhov's extreme restlessness since his return from Sakhalin, also suggested that they tour western Europe together — a trip Chekhov had long desired to make. This attractive prospect obsessed him when he got back to Moscow, which now seemed more unlovely than ever. Another trip so shortly after being away for eight months! Would the family understand? He knew they would oppose it. Then there was the question of money. He applied himself to his story, but it grew still longer and the end was nowhere in sight. He could borrow from Suvorin and also get an advance from *New Times* — sheer self-indulgence! He must put the idea out of his head, he decided. A few days with the Kiselevs at Babkino, however, proved no antidote for his wanderlust, and he next planned a visit to brother Ivan in Vladimir Province, where he had gone to teach school. Then suddenly, on March 5, he dashed off a note to Suvorin: "We are going!!! I agree to go wherever you like and when you like. My soul is leaping with delight. It would be stupid on my part not to go, for when would such an opportunity come again?" With chagrin Masha accused: "Antosha, you are a fidgety person!"

He hurried to Petersburg, took in an exhibition of Levitan's paintings there with the ancient Grigorovich as his officious guide, saw the great Duse in a performance of Shakespeare's *Antony and Cleopatra* — "I have never seen anything like it before," he wrote his sister — and on March 17 he left, with Suvorin and his eldest son Aleksei, for Vienna.

« 2 »

Only a few months before Chekhov had traveled in a broken-down carriage over thousands of miles of rutted and then quagmire roads, past wretchedly primitive Siberian villages. Now he was traveling to the polished centers of Europe "like a railway Nana" in a luxurious compartment, with beds, looking glasses, huge windows and rugs. The opulence distorted his judgment. The superpatriot Dostoevsky had seemed bent on inspecting the drains of Europe on his first trip abroad, and had returned home to tell his countrymen of the filth he had observed. The aristocratic Tolstoy, used to the good things of life, had accepted the luxuries of Europe on his initial visit as a matter of course, but regarded with a critical eye its social inequities. Chekhov experienced something of the childlike wonder of his favorite Gogol, who, when he discovered the ancient beauties of Rome, claimed Italy as his second fatherland.

At first Chekhov's letters to the family were ecstatic. Everything about Vienna appeared diabolically elegant. Its shops were a perfect delirium, a dream, and architecture, he discovered, could really be an art. The cabmen, like dandies in their top hats, amazed him as they sat in their boxes, reading newspapers; he could not get over their politeness and readiness to oblige a customer. And like most Russians on their first contact with the West, he found it strange that here one was free to read anything and say what one liked.

When he reached Venice, that enchanted dream upon the water, all discrimination fled. There he met Merezhkovsky steeped in a similar state of euphoria. Rather pathetically Chekhov wrote brother Ivan: "It is easy for a poor and oppressed Russian to go out of his mind in this world of beauty, wealth, and freedom. One wants to remain forever, and when one stands in the churches and listens to the organ, then one longs to become a Catholic." (*March 24, 1891.*) Nevertheless, his rapture did not prevent him from observing that a spirit of conservatism in Venice had resulted in the preservation of many worthless paintings along with indubitably great works of art.

During the remainder of his tour through Italy — Bologna, Florence, Rome, Naples — Chekhov viewed all the usual tourist attractions. Perhaps aching feet, physical exhaustion, poor weather, and a surfeit of Baedeker had something to do with the recovery of both his critical sense and his sense of humor. Florence's Venus di Medici, if dressed in modern clothes, he imagined, would be hideous, especially about the waist. In Rome, despite the rich Italian food, he longed for a bowl of Russian cabbage soup and some buckwheat porridge. Rome reminded him of Kharkov, and Naples he described as a filthy city. Even the European trains he now found less comfortable than those in Russia. As he prepared to leave Italy, however, he confessed to his sister: "If I were an artist and alone and had money, then I would live here in the winter. For Italy, apart from its natural scenery and warmth, is the only country in which one feels convinced that art is really supreme over everything, and that conviction gives one courage." (*April 1, 1891.*)

The expenses of the trip constantly worried Chekhov. The Suvorins, he complained, lived like Doges and Cardinals in the most luxurious hotels, and he felt it necessary to maintain the same style. If he had been alone, he wrote home, he could have done the whole tour on three hundred roubles, whereas he estimated that he would be in Suvorin's debt to the extent of a thousand. The situation troubled his conscience, for he knew that the family, which had been hostile to this trip anyway, coming so soon after his Sakhalin journey, would have to pinch themselves until he returned. Yet no sooner had he got to Nice than he set off for Monte Carlo and lost a considerable sum of money at roulette. With manifest satisfaction he wrote all about it to his brother Misha. "You will say, of course," he joked, " 'What villany! We are so poor, and there he goes playing roulette!' Entirely just, and I give you permission to slay me. But I'm personally very pleased with myself."

The realization of an experience he had long dreamed of, however, did not blind him to the meretricious allure of the Casino and the luxurious restaurants in the neighborhood, or to the shoddy values of the rich who patronized them. "I love wealth and luxury," he added in this same letter to Misha, "but the roulette here leaves me with the impression of a kind of luxurious watercloset. You feel there is something in the atmosphere that offends your sense of decency and vulgarizes nature, the moon, and the sound of the sea." (*April 15, 1891.*)

Chekhov was rather happy to move on to Paris, where he found the people magnificent and the city enchanting. But he arrived on May Day,[2] and was caught up in a police charge against demonstrating workers and somewhat roughly treated. There were many Russians in Paris, some of whom entertained him — among them old Pleshcheev, who, after Chekhov had left for Sakhalin, had inherited a huge fortune. At a dinner this former editor of the *Northern Herald*, who had driven sharp bargains with Chekhov for his contributions to the magazines, now tried to force a loan of a thousand roubles on him in an effort to persuade him to remain longer in Paris. Chekhov firmly refused. But months later, with that delicacy that was so characteristic of him, he felt obliged to write Pleshcheev to apologize for rejecting the loan and to assure him that if he had needed the money he would have borrowed it from him as readily as from Suvorin. With his almost morbid fear of offending a friend, Chekhov was ready to ask Pleshcheev to forgive him for not borrowing money from him!

In truth, Chekhov had at last become bored with the trip, and Suvorin's insistence on the completion of his portrait by a Paris painter, which prevented them from getting back to Moscow in time for Easter, particularly annoyed him. It was the first Easter that he had missed with his family since coming to Moscow, and he regretted it. In Paris he thought of the Moscow church bells on Easter Eve, pealing forth the joy of Resurrection, a performance which he loved to hear. There, after going from church to church, he would return home in the early hours of the morning and the family would sing: "Christ Is Risen." He wrote his sister: "Men who tie boa-constrictors around their bodies, ladies who kick to the ceiling, flying people, lions, *cafés chantants*, dinners and luncheons — all begin to sicken me. It is time I was home. I want to work." (*April 24, 1891.*) He arrived in Moscow on May 2 after some six weeks abroad.

« 3 »

The day after he returned from Paris — from Sodom and Gomorrah, where he had seen naked women, he told his friend A. I. Urusov — Chekhov left Moscow for the *dacha* at Aleksin which Misha had rented for the family. Since the plan to share a summer house with the Suvorins had not materialized, Chekhov, while abroad, had instructed his brother to find a house, and Misha, then a tax assessor in Aleksin,

[2] Chekhov arrived in Paris on April 19 Old Style by the Russian calendar, which would be May 1 in Europe.

a town in the province of Tula, an overnight trip from Moscow, had taken the easy way out by selecting this *dacha*, not far from the town and near the Oka River. The little four-room house, from which one could see a railroad bridge across the river, disappointed Chekhov. After traveling abroad, life in this crowded "villa" seemed a bit vapid; he felt like a prisoner in a fortress.

Chekhov's main concern now was to get back to his writing. The trip had thrown him heavily into debt and this fact depressed him. He assured Suvorin that the eight hundred roubles he owed him personally would receive first claim and the thousand advance which he had taken from *New Times* would have to wait a bit. His financial responsibilities for his sister, for Misha, and for Ivan had ended, for all three were earning adequate salaries. In fact, he was proud of Ivan, whose stubborn efforts had been rewarded by a government medal for excellence in teaching and a new and advanced position in Moscow. The usual precarious situation of the unstable Alexander in Petersburg, however, became critical this summer because of the birth of another child.[3] In his need for funds in this emergency, Alexander had not scrupled to use his brother's name and "borrow" money from Anton's earnings at Suvorin's publishing house. He confessed the transaction later and eventually repaid the sum. Instead of being angry, Chekhov gave him permission to make use of this account if at any time he urgently needed money. Though Chekhov feared being in debt himself, he lent money with thoughtless abandon. Nor did he hesitate at this time, when circumstances had released him from some of his old family obligations, to assume still another one, for he agreed with his aging father that he should quit his job at Gavrilov's and live permanently at home. As a regular member of the family again, Father Chekhov added an old but familiar increment of unpleasantness to the dinner table conversation.

On Mondays, Tuesdays, and Wednesdays Chekhov worked away on his Sakhalin book. He intended to direct his attack against life sentences of exiles, he informed Suvorin, asking him to send additional source material — for his observations had taught him that the convict, deprived of all hope of ever returning to his native land and to his relatives and friends, loses his moral sense and his grip on reality. The other days of the week he devoted to *The Duel*, except Sundays when

[3] This was Mikhail Chekhov, the future distinguished actor of the Moscow Art Theater.

he wrote short stories. He worked with zest in this crowded country household where he felt like a crayfish in a net with a lot of other crayfish. What he missed most was an opportunity to read serious literature, the balm for his soul. He envied Misha who had plenty of time to read foreign authors in the original and occasionally to do professional translations. Chekhov always regretted his ignorance of foreign languages, for every time he read a translation, he kept altering and transposing the words in his brain. If he could only have done the translation himself, he once remarked, he was sure it would have turned out light and ethereal, like lacework.

In the middle of May the arrival of Lidiya Mizinova and Levitan interrupted Chekhov's rigorous work schedule. Much merriment ensued over the problem of where to sleep the guests in the tiny, crowded *dacha*. As usual, Chekhov was in his element in the company of the beautiful Lika, who unfailingly stimulated his sense of fun. Over the last two years this captivating girl had become an intimate with the family. Though she was only ten years younger than Chekhov, the brother-sister relationship that had initially developed between them involved nuances which went much deeper with the passage of time. These stronger emotions were especially evident on Lika's side. The "brother" pose took the form of frequent advice on her health, on eating starchy foods, her social deportment, and the details of her career. The "lover" aspect was a curious combination of seriousness and elaborate raillery, as though he wished to discourage an affection which he suspected but yet was afraid did not exist. In his many letters to her he utters mock imprecations against her wooers, real or imaginary, or he pleads with her to visit: "Come to smell the flowers, to walk, to fish, and to blubber. Ah, lovely Lika! When you wet my right shoulder with your tears (I have taken out the spots with benzine) . . ." Or he pretends to be one of her lovers sending her his photograph (that of some unknown youth): "I'm sending you my ugly face. We'll be seeing each other tomorrow. Don't forget your Petka. A thousand kisses!!! I've bought Chekhov's stories. How delightful they are! You buy them, too. My regards to Masha Chekhova. What a sweetheart you are!" Or, under a transparently assumed name, he writes: "I love you passionately, like a tiger, and offer you my hand." (*May* 17, *June–July,* 1891.)

Though in all this make-believe Chekhov may have been indulging vicariously in experiences he had missed as a youth, the condescension it implies seems eventually to have had the desired effect of chilling the warm hopes of the charming Lika. His behavior compelled her to recognize, however unwillingly, that he had probably already resigned himself to bachelordom. In fact, Chekhov now began to refer to himself as a confirmed bachelor, and in a letter at this time to Suvorin, who had recently become quite solicitous about his friend's unmarried state, Chekhov replied: "I don't intend to get married. I should like to be a little, bald old man sitting at a big table in a fine study." (*May 10, 1891.*)

The guests had hardly settled in when two empty carriages drove up with an invitation to visit Bogimovo about eight miles away. Levitan and Lika explained to the baffled host that on the boat to Aleksin they had become acquainted with a certain E. D. Bylim-Kolosovsky, the proprietor of Bogimovo, and learning that they were friends of Chekhov, he had warmly invited them all to visit his estate. Chekhov at once decided that they must go. The first view of Bogimovo entranced him — the huge brick house in which Catherine the Great had slept on the way to meet her lover Potemkin; the spacious park and lime tree alleys; the lovely garden with lilacs and apple trees in bloom; the pond with a poetic mill and the river in the distance. (Misha asserts that this estate later became the setting for the well-known story, *The House with the Attic*.) When Chekhov discovered that the whole upper floor with its enormous rooms, including a drawing room with ornate columns, was vacant, he realized how acutely dissatisfied he had been with his plain little *dacha*. Though it meant more roubles, the upper floor of Bogimovo was rented and the family soon moved in.

Within a few days life at Bogimovo resembled the carefree routine of the family's summer stays with the Kiselevs at Babkino and with the Lintvarevs at Luka. Chekhov quickly established pleasant relations with the owners and two other families that had rented bungalows on the estate. The Bylim-Kolosovskys were cultured and kind people, although the wife bored Chekhov by her gentle persistence in introducing into any discussion what she considered the evil of the age — pessimism. He was more interested in V. A. Wagner and his family and that of the painter, A. A. Kiselev (another Kiselev). The zoologist, Wagner, an enthusiastic admirer of Chekhov's fiction, was at that time engaged on a study of spiders. Chekhov admired the scientific precision of his mind, and in the evenings, when the company gathered, exciting discussions developed on such subjects as natural selection, will power, and inherited characteristics. Wagner stoutly opposed Chekhov's conviction that will power and wisely directed education could overcome inherited evil traits. He insisted that nature did not joke with its victims. Clear echoes of these debates can be heard in the theories of the scientist Von Koren in *The Duel*, which Chekhov was writing at this time.

Occasionally dramatic sketches took the place of evening debates. The Kiselev children, drawing on Chekhov's early humorous tales for themes, staged and acted them to the delight of all. The children were fascinated by Chekhov's favorite mongoose. Once when they were sitting in the garden, a large snake appeared and terrified the youngsters. Chekhov shouted to Misha to bring the mongoose from the house. The little animal, seeing the snake, at once coiled itself into a ball, sprang and seized the snake's head in its teeth, crushed it, and dragged the body off into the tall grass. Unfortunately, the destructive instincts of the mongoose, to which Chekhov was so much attached, could not be so readily restricted to slaughtering snakes, and not long after this episode the animal had to be sent to the Moscow Zoo, where Masha regularly visited it.

With his customary enthusiasm for sharing his pleasures, Chekhov sent urgent invitations to friends to come to Bogimovo to walk, fish, and gather mushrooms with him. Suvorin paid two short visits and Natalya Lintvareva a much longer one. Chekhov rejoiced in her loud laughter that filled the house from morning to night. "The enchanting, amazing Lika," however, refused to come a second time, despite repeated pleas cast in the special "kidding" form he reserved for her. One letter accused her of being "captivated by the Circassian Levitan," and was signed with a heart pierced by an arrow. These communications she usually answered in a lingo of similar exaggeration mingled with sarcastic jokes.

But debts were weighing heavily on Chekhov's conscience, and with few exceptions he did not allow the joys of country living to interfere with his writing schedule. He ordinarily arose at four or five in the morning when all was quiet in the house and made his own coffee — one of those bachelor habits, he remarked, to which he had now become resigned. Sitting on the broad window bench in his spacious room, from which he had a fine view of the park, he wrote until eleven, when he would go for a walk to pick mushrooms or to fish. After dinner at one and a brief nap, he would resume his writing until evening.

The book on Sakhalin was both a torment and a comfort to him. He would dig for hours to obtain the facts for a single sentence, a kind of effort that exasperated the creative artist in him. Then he would happily read over a passage in which he had described the fierce weather on the island, convinced that it would chill the reader to the marrow. Recent government decrees, one on building a Siberian railroad and another to allow exiles to return to their native towns or villages once their sentences expired, pleased him and supported his conviction that he was dealing with an important current subject. Suvorin, however, assured him he was wasting his time, and, half-believing him, Chekhov protested that he would finish the book by fall. Then, aware of this self-deception, he burst forth to Suvorin: "I'm writing my Sakhalin and I'm bored, bored. I'm utterly sick of life." (*August 28, 1891.*) In his next letter, however, he felt it necessary to set the record straight for the benefit of his tormentor: "Sakhalin moves forward. There are times when I long to sit over it for three to five years and work at it furiously; but at other times, I'm overcome by moments of doubt and then I could spit on it. It would be a fine thing, by God, if I could devote three years to it! I shall write much rubbish, because I'm not a specialist, but really I shall also write something worth while. The theme of Sakhalin is so splendid that it might live a hundred years after me, for it could be the literary source and aid for all who studied and were interested in prison organization." (*August, 30, 1891.*)

What clearly deprived Chekhov of the total concentration he needed was the nagging realization that this time-consuming work took him away from writing the fiction on which his livelihood depended. Before the summer ended, he had to give up any idea of finishing the Sakhalin book by the fall and shift his major attention to *The Duel* and other stories. He finished *The Duel* in the middle of August and with some trepidation sent it off to Suvorin who was then at Feodosiya. He also finished a shorter tale, *Peasant Wives*, for *New Times*, and there is some evidence that during the summer he sketched out one if not two other stories.

Contributing to the pressures that built up around him at Bogimovo were the "mass of sick people and the smell of iodoform," as he expressed it in a letter to Mariya Kiseleva. For, as usual in his summer vacations, he insisted on offering his medical services to the peasants in the locality. When Suvorin complained to him of the callousness of a physician at Feodosiya who had treated one of his household, Chekhov sprang to the defense of his profession. The doctor, he explained, must be forgiven a great deal because of the loathsome hours and days that make up so much of his life. For, in the face of the incurable, he is forced to preserve his external tranquillity while so often being ashamed of himself and his science. Chekhov had his own fill of such loathsome hours that summer, and grew weary of peasant women and their babies and the endless tedious weighing-out of powders. Yet the strong qualities of these peasant patients would often renew his courage and elevate the humanity in him which was the lodestone of his art. "A peasant woman was carting rye," he wrote Suvorin of one of his patients, "and she fell off the wagon head first. She was terribly injured. . . . They brought her to me. She was moaning and groaning and praying God for death, and yet she looked at the peasant who carried her in and murmured: 'Let the lentils go, Kirila, you can thresh them later, but thresh the oats now.' I told her to forget the oats, that now there was something more serious to talk about, and she said to me: 'But his oats are ever so good!' A bustling peasant woman, one to be envied. Death comes easy to such people." (*August 18, 1891*.)

As he smelled the autumn in the air, Chekhov yearned to take off with the cranes. In fact, flight had by now become a psychic need of his nature. No matter how busy or how seemingly content he was, the desire for change, to be somewhere else, obsessed him. In the very thick of his summer activities, he wrote friends that he would like to go to the Crimea, to Norway, to America. When Suvorin stopped over on his way to Feodosiya, Chekhov accompanied him on part of the journey. He even made plans to visit him in August, for he thirsted for the sea, the sands, and nocturnal conversations, and he gave up his proposed trip only because he did not wish to incur more debt.

Part of his difficulty was overwork and the conviction that his efforts were getting him nowhere. Suvorin, worried over these occasional fits of despondency, advised him to leave his family, but Chekhov replied that this was not in his power, that the family was his law of necessity. He told Alexander that he sometimes dreamed of winning forty thousand roubles in a lottery and cutting himself off completely from writing, which he was sick of, and buying a piece of land where he could live in idle seclusion. In truth, he had begun to taste the good things of life and wanted more of them. He wrote Suvorin that he envied him. "I should now like carpets, an open fireplace, bronzes, and learned conversation. Alas! I shall never be a Tolstoyan! In women I love beauty above all things, and in the history of mankind, culture, expressed in carpets, carriages with springs, and keenness of wit!" (*August 30, 1894.*) Instead, as he left Bogimovo for Moscow at the beginning of September, he had to be content with the knowledge that he had done a good deal of writing that summer and that with his earnings he had paid off a thousand roubles of debt.

« 4 »

If Chekhov's experience in the hell of Sakhalin had aroused him to the need of doing something practical about the ills of the country, they had also increased his impatience with the feckless philosophizing of the do-nothing intelligentsia. Rather unfairly, he vented this annoyance on the most celebrated of all the contemporary theorists, Tolstoy, who had actually attempted to do a great deal that was practical in aiding the underprivileged. Having just read the "Afterword" to *The Kreutzer Sonata*, Chekhov wrote Suvorin: "To hell with the philosophy of the mighty of this world! All the eminent sages are as despotic as generals, and as discourteous and lacking in delicacy as generals, because they know they won't be punished. Diogenes spat in people's beards, knowing that nothing would happen to him; Tolstoy abuses doctors as scoundrels and is ignorant in important questions, because he is like a Diogenes whom you can't lock up or scold in the newspapers. And so, to hell with the philosophy of the great of this world! All of it . . . isn't worth a single filly in his story *Kholstomer*."[4] (*September 8, 1891.*)

The "Moscow Hamlets" he saw around him in the city, the superfluous intellectual types — eternally bored, utterly self-centered, poseurs in all things cultural, and incapable of improving the lot of others because they were totally unaware of their own failings — Chekhov bitingly satirized in an article, *In Moscow*, which appeared under a pseudonym in *New Times* in December, 1891. The "Hamlet" in the article naïvely keeps wondering about the advice of a certain gentleman whom he had confronted with the ever-present problem of his boredom: "Oh, take a piece of telephone wire and hang yourself to the first telephone pole!"

Chekhov himself tried to do something practical by exposing one of these charlatans among the intelligentsia who had perpetrated a scientific fraud. A brochure of the distinguished scientist K. A. Timiryazev was brought to his attention, in which he revealed the extensive waste

[4] Tolstoy's famous short story about the horse Strider.

of public funds on an animal experimental laboratory in the Moscow Zoological Garden. Professor A. P. Bogdanov, who ran the laboratory, or rather completely neglected it and yet made false claims about the scientific value of his experiments, had so far been able to keep the truth of the situation out of the press. Chekhov made a serious investigation of the facts, in which he availed himself of the assistance of his Bogimovo friend, the zoologist Wagner. The result was a scathing article, *Conjurors* (October, 1891), published anonymously in *New Times,* for he feared to harm the career of Wagner whose friendship with him was known among scientists. With a deft combination of scientific skill, satire, and humor, Chekhov exposed the deception of the animal experimental laboratory and heaped ridicule on the spurious claims of Professor Bogdanov. The article caused a considerable stir in scientific circles.

In the stories that Chekhov wrote over 1891, this concern with the problems of the intelligentsia takes a more imaginative and psychological direction. An exception is *The Peasant Women,* which he wrote in a hurry, tearing himself away from his work on the Sakhalin book, "for I'm sitting here literally without a two-kopeck piece in my pocket," he told Suvorin. "It is dull," he added as an afterthought, "to write about the peasantry." (*June 16, 1891.*) The story was published in *New Times* (*June, 1891*). The evil-begetting power of evil, much as in Tolstoy's drama of peasant life, *The Power of Darkness* — a play that fascinated Chekhov when he saw it and which may well have influenced his central theme — penetrated the atmosphere of the tale. For there is something horrifying at the end, when the two young peasant wives are in bed together, after having heard Matvei's gruesome tale of the seduction of his friend's wife and the husband's murder. The wanton Varvara whispers to Sofya that all their troubles would be over if they did away with her drunkard of a husband and their common father-in-law. And we somehow know that they will commit this terrible crime. It is interesting that I. Gorbunov-Posadov, agent for *The Intermediary,* Tolstoy's series of inexpensive booklets designed to entertain and offer moral instruction to the mass reader, asked and received Chekhov's permission to reprint *The Peasant Women,* because it "excellently depicted the type of a people's Tartuffe, a debauchee, a hypocrite, and an atheist."

If *A Dreary Story* marks the beginning of a more mature, psychologically denser period in Chekhov's writing, then *The Duel* may be regarded as a continuation of this kind of probing in depth into the life forces which bring about a state of mutual isolation among his characters. He worked hard over this lengthy effort, which, he said, cost him a pound of nerves. It disappointed him to have to publish this novella in *New Times*, a daily newspaper, for it had to appear piecemeal over eleven issues during October and November, 1891. Some of the staff members, whose regular contributions had to be sidetracked, expressed their annoyance over what they described as Chekhov's "monopoly" of *New Times*.

Laevsky in *The Duel* is a "Moscow Hamlet" and the scientist Von Koren mercilessly exposes him as one who blames his defeatism, his fake culture, and his hypocrisy on the age in which he lives. A university graduate, Laevsky wants his friends to believe, says Von Koren, that he had once been devoted to civilization but that it had disillusioned him and turned him into a second Tolstoy. The hard-working, practical-minded scientist declares that such drones as Laevsky represent a danger in society and ought to be destroyed, for they tend to reverse the law of natural selection — the weak prevail over the strong. Laevsky, he is convinced, will only go on repeating such base actions as running off with another man's wife, ruining her life, and then deserting her.

Though Chekhov would agree with Von Koren that the problems of the day required fresh solutions, he was not prepared to abandon Laevsky to the customary intelligentsia escape from failure. For the mutual isolation in the relations of Laevsky and Nadezhda Fyodorovna is resolved by the jealousy he experiences when he learns of her succumbing to another. It is almost as though Chekhov were rejecting Tolstoy's theory in *The Kreutzer Sonata* on the devastating effects of jealousy on the physical foundation of love. Laevsky realizes that his harsh treatment had been responsible for the weakness that had led her into temptation, and this knowledge arouses in him the determination to try to begin their life anew. "In the search for truth," he speculates at the end, "men make two steps forward and one step back. Suffering, mistakes, and weariness of life thrust them back, but the thirst for truth and a stubborn will drive them on and on. And who knows? Perhaps in the end they will arrive at the real truth."

In response to the eager requests of two young literary friends who had recently become editors of magazines, Chekhov, in 1891, sent *The Wife* to M. N. Albov for the *Northern Herald* and *The Grasshopper* to V. A. Tikhonov for *The North*. Neither tale appeared, however, until January of the next year. Though much shorter and more compact, *The Wife* bears certain thematic resemblances to *The Duel*. There is the alienation, the same isolation of two human beings from each other, and the partial resolution that comes from a kind of spiritual experience. The tale is drenched in that typical Chekhovian emotional atmosphere, as gentle, penetrating, unifying, and poetic as the lyrical atmosphere of a Chopin nocturne. For years Pavel Andreevich and his pretty young wife had been drawing apart until their feeling for each other had become one of positive hatred. As a retired engineer and an intellectual, he had lost contact with reality in his complete self-absorption. His reaction to a famine situation among the peasantry in his region is one of annoyance. It is this inhumanity and insensitivity to people that poisoned the love of his wife, who actively organizes relief for the peasants. A chance evening spent with the sloppy, talkative but very human district physician, Dr. Sobol, opens up new avenues of thought and action for Pavel Andreevich. For one thing, he learns that the rigidly righteous philanthropy of almshouses and orphan asylums is no substitute for the kind of personal giving that come from the heart.

It is the philistinism of one level of the Moscow artistic world that Chekhov depicts in *The Grasshopper*, whose theme, as already indicated, was suggested by the parties at the Kuvshinnikovs which Chekhov attended, and by the affair of the hostess with Levitan. Olga Ivanovna, the pretty "grasshopper" of the story, is an elegant amateur painter who devotes her life to the search for a great man without ever realizing, until it is too late, that the simple, kind, and uncomplaining man who is her husband, Dr. Dymov, is potentially at least just such a great man. The essential vulgarity of her esthetic sense renders her incapable of distinguishing between true and false beauty. The true beauty of her husband's self-sacrificing death on behalf of science evades her, whereas the man she thinks is extraordinary, the painter Ryabovsky, can turn his poetic description of a lovely July night on the Volga into a cheap overture to seduction. But what of her husband, she asks herself before submitting? " 'The happiness he has had is quite enough for an ordinary man like him,' she thought, covering her face with her hands." The grasshopper's remorse over the tawdry end of her illicit romance is no less effusive than that over the tragic death of her husband, but Chekhov makes it quite clear that neither loss will alter in the slightest the trivial, superficial, and philistine nature of this passionate "lover of the arts."

The Grasshopper caused a commotion among Moscow intellectuals and rumor quickly established the living models — the Kuvshinnikovs and Levitan — of the three principal characters. Even Chekhov's good friend Lensky, who frequently visited the gay parties of the Kuvshinnikovs, spotted his image in the "fat actor" of the story and indignantly broke off relations with the author. In fact, the reworked manuscript of *The Grasshopper* betrays Chekhov's obvious efforts to eliminate patent resemblances between his characters and the real people who inspired them. He always firmly denied the correspondences and pointed out the differences between the ages, appearances, and qualities of his characters and those of the so-called prototypes. But he seems to have protested too much. At any rate, Levitan thought so, and at one point it seemed as though a challenge to a duel might be forthcoming. These two old friends, despite the efforts of intermediaries, ceased to speak to each other for several years.

Chekhov's admiration for doctors and scientists stands out in these stories of 1891. In a letter to his protégé, Elena Shavrova, on one of her manuscript tales which she sent him for criticism, he delivered a stern rebuke for what he considered reprehensibly slanted characterizations of a gynecologist and a professor. "I don't venture to ask you to love the gynecologist and the professor," he wrote, "but I venture to remind you of the justice which for an objective writer is more precious than the air he breathes." (*September 16, 1891.*) He had himself portrayed a number of doctors in his previous tales, favorably and unfavorably. But the bumbling, infinitely kind Dr. Samoilenko and the forthright zoologist Von Koren in *The Duel*, the practical-minded, indefatigable Dr. Sobol in *The Wife*, and the heroic Dr. Dymov in *The Grasshopper* provide striking contrasts to the bored defeatists and frustrated intellectuals in these stories. They are hard-working, practical men and in varying degrees concerned with the problems of society. If this comparison argues a prejudice on behalf of the scientifically trained mind, it must be remembered that Chekhov's objectivity compelled him also to show up the fraud of a real scientist at this time — Professor A. P. Bogdanov.

« 5 »

In a letter to Suvorin from Bogimovo on August 28, Chekhov had mentioned, in passing: "There is a famine year coming. There will probably be every sort of illness and even uprisings on a small scale." Before winter set in his forebodings were realized. Millions of peasants in central and southeastern Russia faced starvation because of crop failures. At first the government treated the matter as though it were a state secret. The censorship discouraged the press from printing articles about the famine and the Minister of Internal Affairs, I. N. Durnovo, forbade the private raising of funds to help the sufferers, insisting that this was the prerogative solely of the Red Cross and the Church.

Chekhov, like many public-spirited citizens, wanted to help, but it was not easy to do so in this atmosphere of governmental obfuscation. One had to have the courage and authority of a Tolstoy, Chekhov remarked, to act in opposition to all the prohibitions and follow the dictates of one's conscience. When this "philosopher," whose theories he had so recently flouted, wrote an article on the famine for a collection published on behalf of the hunger victims by the *Moscow Gazette*, a volume to which Chekhov contributed a chapter from his Sakhalin book, he exclaimed to Suvorin: "Tolstoy — ah, that Tolstoy! In these days he is not a man but a superman, a Jupiter." (*December 11, 1891.*) Indeed, Tolstoy's tremendous, self-sacrificing efforts on behalf of the famine-stricken no doubt had something to do with inspiring Chekhov's own zeal in the cause. In a sharp article earlier in 1891 Tolstoy had forced the issue on the attention of the public, and he had published abroad still another and more sensational article, which the Russian censors had forbidden, so that the world soon became aware of the extent of the catastrophe and poured into the country various forms of aid. Tolstoy himself organized on a huge scale several hundred food kitchens that fed thousands of peasants, and he carried on this work and raised large sums of money for the cause despite government opposition.

The path of individual initiative along Tolstoy's lines naturally appealed to Chekhov. He knew that educated and wealthy groups in Moscow, disturbed over rumors of malfeasance in the local Red Cross office and the waste and shameless theft of funds, had vainly requested permission from the government to send their own agents into the famine-ridden provinces, to investigate on the spot and to open food kitchens if necessary. With the example in mind of his successful circumvention of top government officials in conducting his Sakhalin investigation, Chekhov saw no reason why he should not go directly to one of the stricken areas and by his own efforts, or in co-operation with a local agency, organize aid for the peasants. He recalled his old friend of Voskresensk days, the artillery officer E. P. Yegorov, who was now head of a Zemstvo, or County Council, in Nizhny Novgorod, a province that had been badly hit by the famine, and he wrote him early in October to request an interview.

Shortly thereafter Chekhov was laid up for weeks with a severe attack of influenza, involving lung complications. The days of convalescence dragged on wearily, saddened by an unusual series of deaths — his beloved Aunt Fedosiya; such close friends as the poet Palmin and A. D. Kurepin, prominent Moscow journalist; V. P. Begichev, the distinguished father of Mariya Kiseleva; and Dr. Zinaida Lintvareva, for whom he wrote a moving obituary. Visits from Korolenko and old Grigorovich cheered him a bit, and he was pleased to receive a letter from Tschaikovsky with rather belated thanks for the dedication to him of *Gloomy People,* in which he wrote about how difficult it was for a musician to explain in words his feelings concerning art "and precisely how those attributes of your talent act so fascinatingly and captivatingly on me." And it was during this time, often while lying in bed, that Chekhov corrected the proofs for a separate edition of *The Duel* in book form, and put the finishing touches on *The Grasshopper* and *The Wife,* which concerned the theme of the famine and his conviction that the inspiration for human aid should come from the heart as well as from the head. In December, about the time he had fully recovered, Chekhov wrote another one-act play, *The Jubilee,* based partly on his short story, *A Helpless Creature* (1887). He revised it the next year, and though the comic elements in it are quite hilarious, there is a dark undercurrent of savage satire against some of the practices of private banks.

His old fear of facing the truth about his health probably had something to do with the slowness of Chekhov's recovery. "Medical treatment and anxiety about one's physical existence," he wrote Suvorin, "arouse in me something close to revulsion. I will not be doctored. I'll take water and quinine, but I'll not permit myself to be sounded." (*November 18, 1891.*) It was the family disease of tuberculosis that only a month before this letter had carried off Aunt Fedosiya.

As he regained strength Chekhov returned to his hope of participating in famine relief. He had warmly praised a piece on the subject by Suvorin in *New Times* that objected to the tendency of officials to blame the crop failure on the laziness and drunkenness of the peasants. "There is always a certain element of insolence," Chekhov wrote, "in being well-fed, as in every aspect of power, and that element expresses itself chiefly in the well-fed preaching to the hungry. If consolation is revolting at a time of real grief, what must be the effect of preaching morality, and how stupid and offensive such moralizing must seem." (*October 19, 1891.*) He wrote again to Yegorov, who had answered Chekhov's earlier letter by conveying a plan to buy up the cattle and the horses of the peasants in his Nizhny Novgorod district. For the peasants, unable to feed themselves or their stock, had to slaughter or sell it. This situation would virtually guarantee a repetition of the famine condition the following year since the peasants would be unable to run their farming operations effectively without their animals. Yegorov's intention was to buy the animals, feed them through the winter, and redistribute them to the peasants in the early spring.

Chekhov enthusiastically embraced this plan and he at once set to work to raise money to purchase the animals. With some practicality he decided that the best device would be an appeal in the press aimed at the rouble or half-rouble of the middle-class man, for rich donors, he reasoned, had already made their contributions to famine relief and would be unlikely to give more. Begging letters to friends also went out; personal visits were made. He had turned into one of the "philanthropic ladies," he wrote the architect Shekhtel, in asking him to make a plea for funds at any dinner or meeting he attended. And in making the same request of his Ukrainian friend A. I. Smagin, he informed him that he was out to raise 100,000 roubles. Ivanenko was asked to give a concert on behalf of the fund and Natalya Lintvareva for grain if there were any surplus on the family estate. And he interviewed the rich Varvara Morozova (not related to his mother's family) to persuade her to interest her favorite charity, the Committee on Literacy, to make a donation — he was unwilling to ask the millionairess herself for money, since he was her guest. Small sums began to dribble in. He kept a record of all who gave and the amounts, so he could publish the list in the press. Soon he was sending money to Yegorov, rather pitiful sums — now 116 roubles, then 17, next 11. To make matters worse, he kept sending this money to the wrong address in Nizhny Novgorod and valuable time was lost before he and Yegorov straightened the matter out.

« 6 »

Disappointed but not discouraged, Chekhov went to Petersburg toward the end of December to try his luck at raising money among his friends there. He also wanted to talk to Suvorin, with whom he stayed, about a joint project on famine relief. The festivities at the beginning of the new year, however, seemed to have driven the hungry peasants out of his mind. At the Khudekovs' on New Year's Day, to celebrate the twenty-fifth anniversary of the *Petersburg Gazette*, Chekhov saw Lidiya Avilova again. In the three years since their first meeting, she had acquired two more children. Their conversation, as she recalls it in her memoirs, took a fanciful turn on an old-fashioned romantic theme that Chekhov would have ordinarily detested — that they had known each other in some life long forgotten. Lidiya represented herself as having "waited" for him in Moscow even before her marriage. " 'Why did you wait?' Anton Pavlovich asked in surprise," she quotes him as saying. " 'Because I wanted to know you so badly, and my brother's friend Popov told me that he often saw you and that you were a fine fellow and would not refuse his request to visit us. But you did not come.' " And she has Chekhov replying to this: " 'Tell that Popov of yours, whom I don't recall at all, that he is my worst enemy.' " Though she appears to attribute a serious significance to this reply, it could also be entirely in keeping with the flirtatious manner he had adopted in this resumption of an acquaintance with a woman whose marriage name he had failed to take the trouble to ascertain three years before and therefore had not answered her letter. At this party she introduced him to her husband, and according to her both men behaved to each other with frigid politeness.

On this occasion, Chekhov again asked her to send him her tales in manuscript, a gesture, as already pointed out, he often made to beginning authors. She did, and he replied in two letters of sharp criticism, good advice, and qualified praise of her ability. There is nothing in the letters to differentiate them from similar ones which Chekhov wrote to budding authors. In her memoirs, however, she quotes from his third extant letter to her, erroneously representing it as "the beginning of my correspondence with Anton Pavlovich" — probably because it was the first to contain a personal note. It appears that her indignant husband had told her of a rumor which had come to his attention. After the party celebrating the twenty-fifth anniversary of the *Petersburg Gazette*, Chekhov and some of the other guests had gone to a restaurant — actually it was to Leikin's house. There, according to her husband, who apparently had heard the story from Leikin, Chekhov had got drunk and boasted to the enthusiastic guests that he would take Lidiya from her husband, make her get a divorce, and marry her. Though she, and ultimately her husband, became convinced that the story had been made up out of whole cloth by Leikin, she alluded to it in a letter to Chekhov. In quoting his answer in her memoirs, she judiciously omits a large section of criticism of one of her tales, and even in the personal part she deletes sentences, without the usual indication of dots, that either reflect on her judgment or do not contribute to the picture of his deep but restrained love for her which she is intent on presenting in A. P. Chekhov in My Life. In the relevant part of the letter, with Avilova's omissions indicated by brackets, Chekhov actually wrote: "Your letter distressed and bewildered me. [You write about certain 'strange things' which I'm supposed to have said at Leikin's, then you beg me in the name of esteem for women not to speak of you 'in that spirit,' and finally you even say 'for having been truthful just this once I can find my name dragged into the mud.'] What is the meaning of this dreaming of yours? [Mud and me.] My self-esteem will not permit me to justify myself; further, your accusations are too unclear to allow me to decide on what grounds I can defend myself. As far as I can determine, it is a question of gossip. Isn't it so? I earnestly implore you (if you trust me no less than the gossipers), don't believe all the nasty things people say in your Petersburg. Or, if you find it impossible not to believe, then [don't] accept them wholesale but with reservations: either concerning my marriage to someone with [five] million and affairs with the wives of my best friends, etc. For God's sake, calm yourself. [If I don't sound convincing enough, have a talk with Yasinsky, who was with me at Leikin's after the anniversary. I recall that both of us, he and I, talked at some length of what fine people you and your sister are. We were both somewhat high after the jubilee, but if I had been as drunk as a cobbler, or had lost my mind, I would not have lowered myself to 'that spirit' and 'mud' (didn't your arm wither over that little word!), for I would be restrained by my usual decency and devotion as to my mother, sister, and to women in general. To speak badly about you, and in Leikin's presence!] However, God be with you. To defend myself from gossip is like begging a loan from a Jew;[5] it is useless. Think as you wish about me." (March 19, 1892.)

[5] The word "Jew" is omitted in the text of the Soviet edition of Chekhov's letters.

This fuller quotation from Chekhov's letter places the incident in its proper perspective. It does not reflect well on the wisdom of the way that Lidiya Avilova took to reveal her dawning love to Chekhov, nor does it suggest that his feeling for her ran any deeper than that which he exhibited to various other feminine correspondents.

It is difficult to ascertain precisely when Avilova, who died in 1943, wrote *A. P. Chekhov in My Life*, which first appeared, in 1947, in a volume of reminiscences about Chekhov by various figures.[6] Since a small section of her work was published in a Soviet periodical as early as 1940,[7] it may be assumed that the whole manuscript was prepared about this time, that is, some fifty years after the earliest events described. Since she appears to have kept no diary at the time, she had to depend entirely on her memory, after a lapse of many years, in reproducing the substantial amount of dialogue between herself and Chekhov. When Chekhov's sister planned an edition of his letters, Avilova surrendered only copies of his letters to her; the originals were subsequently stolen and have never been recovered. However, she apparently did not turn over copies of all his letters. One is definitely known to have been retained by her, and two others, contradicting some of the facts of her memoirs, she asked Chekhov's sister not to publish.[8] When she wrote her memoirs, she no doubt depended upon the six-volume edition of Chekhov's letters, edited by his sister, which appeared from 1912–1916. Her own letters to Chekhov she demanded back after his death, and these also have disappeared — which makes it impossible to verify certain of the data in her memoirs.[9]

To complicate the situation, a recent Soviet publication now makes it clear that the editor of Avilova's memoirs took liberties with the language of the manuscript and even omitted some of the material.[10]

[6] *A. P. Chekhov v vospominaniyakh sovremennikov* (*A. P. Chekhov in the Remembrances of Contemporaries*), ed. by A. K. Kotov, Moscow, 1947, pp. 323-395.

[7] "Poslednee svidanie," in *Literaturnaya gazeta* ("Last Meeting" in *Literary Gazette*), No. 42, August 4, 1940.

[8] Chekhov's sister honored this request, but these two letters (*February 14, 1895 and October 21, 1898*) appeared after Avilova's death in the Soviet edition of Chekhov's letters.

[9] By chance, however, three of Avilova's letters to Chekhov from 1904 have survived and are in the Chekhov archives in the Moscow Lenin Library.

[10] The first complete version of Avilova's memoirs is to be found only in the 4th edition of *A. P. Chekhov v vospominaniyakh sovremennikov* (*A. P. Chekhov in the Remembrances of Contemporaries*), Moscow, 1960, pp. 200-293. There are important omissions and some tampering with the wording of the text in the previous

In her Foreword to *A. P. Chekhov in My Life*, which was never printed with the original work and has only lately turned up in the Chekhov archives in Moscow,[11] Avilova explains why, in her old age, she decided to write her recollections of Chekhov. "This is a love affair," she declares, "which no one has ever known, although it consumed a whole ten years. It was 'our love affair.' . . . Not one word is invented in my romance. I have written much about myself, my thoughts and feelings. . . .

"All the time I was writing I worried about being carried away by my fantasy, dreams, suppositions, guesses, and thus altering the truth. But I could not permit a single inaccuracy in my recollections of him, so sacred in Anton Pavlovich's memory to me. Because of this fear, I'm afraid that my romance resembles the minutes of a meeting.

"It distresses me that Chekhov, the hero of my account, rarely speaks. Hence it may seem that I did not value in him the great man that he was, and that I have referred to him as to any other person with whom I might have been in love.

"However, this is not so. Anton Pavlovich had an enormous influence on me, although I never took down his words. It was impossible to do this. He did not like to talk and spoke little. Somehow his attitude to life and people did not come out in conversation, for he often conveyed his thoughts in a few words or even by the expression on his face. . . .[12]

"In short, I have written about my romance as well as I could, as it in fact happened, and as it has remained in my memory. It has been my lot to hear investigators of his life say: 'How amazing! No women, no love . . .'

"They have concluded: 'He was cold, dry, hard. He could not love.'

"And they will probably write this in biographies of him. It is possible that my romance will help to close this gap and will appear to be significant and interesting despite the lack of clever conversation.

"While affirming nothing, I leave it to those who read this to decide themselves whether Anton Pavlovich was dry and cold — whether there was really no love in his life."

---

three editions of this work. The 4th edition is used for quotations here and for the purposes of the present discussion.

[11] The Foreword was published for the first time in *Literaturnoe Nasledstvo* (*Literary Heritage*), Moscow, 1960, LXVIII, 260-261.

[12] This may have been the experience of Avilova in her conversations with Chekhov. However, Chekhov himself, and many of his contemporaries, have left the impression that he thoroughly enjoyed conversation with people who interested him.

Lidiya Avilova's memoirs contain important biographical material about Chekhov. When the writer Ivan Bunin, who got to know Chekhov well in the last few years of his life, read the published memoirs, though not a complete version, he said that the contents came as a revelation to him. And without making any close study of all the facts in the case, he categorically accepted Avilova's contention that she was the great love of Chekhov's life.[13] Bunin even implies that this was one of the reasons why Chekhov had no room left in his heart for Lika Mizinova.[14] Bunin was acquainted with Avilova, and they corresponded when both were living abroad. So significant a part did he attribute to her in Chekhov's life that he reproduced most of her memoirs in his last work on Chekhov, as well as her letters to himself and his wife. Yet it is a curious fact that though he and Lidiya Avilova were devoted admirers of the dead Chekhov, not one word about him appears in these letters.[15]

What was fact and what may have been fiction in Lidiya Avilova's assertion that Chekhov was in love with her may best be considered in terms of the events as they chronologically occur in her memoirs. It should be said, however, that *A. P. Chekhov in My Life* is written with the flair of an able author who had had the benefit of Chekhov's criticism in achieving a literary career for herself. Indeed, it seems at times that an element of fiction encroaches upon the rigid prescription of veracity in memoir writing. So thought the editor of the volume in which her memoirs appear, for he declares: "Avilova, as it were, writes a novella about herself in the course of commenting on her quite extensive correspondence with Chekhov. . . . In all of this it is impossible not to note the author's immoderate subjectivity and one-sidedness in her treatment of the material connected with Chekhov."[16]

Chekhov made no effort to see Lidiya Avilova again during the remainder of his stay in Petersburg at the beginning of 1892. In fact, he had already become involved with "the Ukrainian queen," as he dubbed her: the lovely actress Mariya Zankovetskaya, whom he had met at the Suvorins'. He drank champagne with her till four in the morning, took

[13] See I. A. Bunin, *O Chekhove* (*Concerning Chekhov*), New York, 1955.

[14] Compare with the above, pp. 66-67.

[15] See Bunin (note 13), pp. 134-206.

[16] A. K. Kotov's "Predislovie," in *A. P. Chekhov v vospominaniyakh sovremennikov* ("Foreword," in *A. P. Chekhov in the Remembrances of Contemporaries*), Moscow, 1960, p. 15.

« 7 »

her tobogganing two days later, swore he would write a play for her to star in, and almost allowed her to persuade him to buy a farm near hers in the Chernigov Province.

But what of the hungry peasants? Chekhov had obtained almost no money in Petersburg. He returned to Moscow on January 11, made an unsuccessful effort to find his "Ukrainian Queen" at home, and three days later left for Nizhny Novgorod to see Yegorov and talk about aiding the famine-stricken. After discussions with Yegorov and dinner with the governor, he traveled around the villages in the bitter cold and almost lost his way in a fierce snowstorm. The situation struck him as very bad, and he observed that local officials in no sense obstructed private initiative. But, he complained, private philanthropy had done almost nothing for these vigorous Novgorodian peasants whom he admired. Petersburg donors, he sarcastically commented, expected 1800 pounds of sugar to take care of the needs of 20,000 people, on the principle of the Biblical miracle of feeding 5000 with five loaves. "There wouldn't be any famine in Nizhny Novgorod," he wrote Suvorin, "if people in Moscow and Petersburg did as much about the famine as they talk about it." (*January 22, 1892.*)

After a week of hard work a severe cold, accompanied by sharp pains in the back, forced Chekhov to return to Moscow. He continued to raise funds for Yegorov, but as soon as he recovered from his illness, he set out, on February 2, with Suvorin to help in relief work in Voronezh, an expedition they had agreed upon when Chekhov was in Petersburg. Various factors contrived to turn this effort into a very unsatisfactory performance from Chekhov's point of view. For one thing, Suvorin played the combined role of a kind of government inspector and a wealthy entrepreneur bent upon offering worldly wisdom rather than practical endeavor. This approach involved them in various ceremonial dinners with the governor of Voronezh, other officials, and local celebrities, a degree of sociability entirely irksome to Chekhov. He was even asked to be present at the rehearsals of an amateur performance of his play *The Wedding* for the benefit of the famine-stricken. To be sure, relief was much better organized there than in Nizhny Novgorod and at most they had business to do with food kitchens in only two villages. "In anything that concerns food kitchens and so forth," he wrote his sister, "we indulge in nonsense and are as naïve as youngsters — of course, these remarks refer not to me but to that bronze statue that stands on the table in my study" — a reference to Suvorin. (*February 9, 1892*.) At the end of ten days of what he regarded as rather wasted activity, Chekhov returned to Moscow. In his sincere but not very effective attempts to aid in the famine, he must have secretly envied the practical idealism, the commanding national authority, and the tremendous capacity to get things done that made for the huge success of another writer engaged in famine relief — Leo Tolstoy.

« 8 »

Ever since his first visit to the idyllic country seat of the Kiselevs at Babkino, Chekhov had dreamed of possessing such an estate. He had not exactly become status-minded, for he never forgot his lowly origin and he could discover virtues in it as well as deplore the deprivations it had thrust upon him. Much success had come to him early, and success is a stairway constantly inviting one to mount higher. Though he had no illusions about taking a place among the Turgenevs and Tolstoys, fortunate inheritors of landed wealth, his sampling of this form of country life had served to increase his desire to possess it permanently.

There were also practical reasons why Chekhov indulged in this dream. Of late, he had curiously become uncertain about his future as a writer. Where was it all leading to? At times, he even felt vaguely torn between medicine and literature and chafed over the conviction that he lacked the ideal conditions to profess either of them successfully. "Ah, my friends, how bored I am!" he had exploded to the Suvorins on October 19, 1891. "If I'm a doctor, I ought to have patients and a hospital; if I'm a literary man, then I ought to live among people instead of on Malaya Dmitrovka with a mongoose. I need a bit of social and political life, even though it be a small bit, but this life within four walls, without nature and people, without a country, without health or appetite — this is not life. . . ."

In fact, Chekhov's existence in Moscow had been growing increasingly distasteful to him. He rarely saw genuine literary people at his home, he declared, and city life, whether that of Moscow or Petersburg, had recently become his target for frequent satiric jibes or expressions of acute dislike.

However, the basis of the compulsion that drove Chekhov on to the realization of his dream was an intense weariness with the financial limitations that cabined and confined the pattern of life which he now wished to pursue. This meant continued dependence, the last remaining element of slavery for a man whose goal in life was absolute freedom. To continue to live in the city with his constantly mounting expenses would force him into a ceaseless struggle to make both ends meet. Now he felt the need of much free time, unencumbered by money worries, to think, to read, to plan, and to write lengthy pieces, even novels, that would not be dependent upon the exigencies of the market. Chekhov reasoned that if he owned a place in the country he would be relieved of the city's high rents and living expenses and the extra costs of hiring a *dacha* every summer. The income from his books and plays, he estimated, would take care of the fixed expenses of himself and his family in the country, where it was much cheaper to live, thus enabling him to forgo "pot-boiler" writing and do what he wished with all this released time. And he optimistically calculated how he would spend it. Apart from reading and what writing he cared to do, he would practice medicine in the country for nine months of the year. The other three, the winter months, he would come to the city, preferably to Petersburg, to see his friends, enjoy the theater and music, and devote himself intensively to writing. From hints in his letters it is also clear that he believed his health would improve if he could live in the country.

Expressions of this hope and even several ineffectual attempts to realize it since Chekhov's first literary success have already been chronicled. During all of 1891 and the early months of 1892 he pursued the hope, and its fulfillment became an essential condition of his peace of mind. At the end of October, 1891, he wrote Suvorin that he was reading *War and Peace* with the same interest and naïve wonder that he had experienced on first reading it. He disliked only the portrayal of Napoleon, in which forced explanations and tricks of all sorts made him appear stupider than he was. And he continued: "When I live in the provinces (about which I dream now day and night) I shall practice medicine and read novels." He had taken Suvorin entirely into his confidence about all the details of his plan of buying a place in the country, one aspect of which was the desire that his friend would purchase a house nearby.

Chekhov's interest still centered on the Ukraine, and in November he definitely commissioned his old friend there, A. I. Smagin, to search out a suitable place in the area of the Psyol. At first he had in mind a small farm which would be easily within reach of his slender means.

Toward the end of that month a letter from Smagin electrified him; his friend had turned up a house that would cost only five thousand roubles! The overjoyed Chekhov at once wrote for details and sent his sister, who relished the opportunity to see Alexander Smagin, to look over the farm. "Ah, if it should only come off! he added. "My soul yearns to escape from Moscow. . . . Every night spring smiles on me in my sleep." (*November 21, 1891*.) And the next day he hurried off a letter to Suvorin to tell him the good news and the wonderful plans he was building on it. "Ah, freedom, freedom!" he exclaimed. "If I can live on no more than two thousand a year, which is only possible in the country, I shall be absolutely free from all anxieties about the amount of money coming in and going out. Then I shall work and read, read. In a word, it will be marmalade and not just life."

As the days passed and the slow-moving Smagin failed to answer his several letters for information about the details of the house, the rooms and land, and a sketch of the place, Chekhov's fears mounted about the reality of this possible purchase. To hurry Smagin he warned him that he had already begun to collect furniture for the farm. Finally, before he left for Petersburg in late December on the business of raising money for the famine, he impatiently wrote Smagin: "If I don't move into the country this year, and if the purchase of the farm fails to go through for some reason, I shall be in the position of playing the part of a great villain in relation to my health. It seems to me that I'm dried up like an old cupboard, and that if I go on living in Moscow next season, and give myself up to scribbling excesses, Gilyarovsky will read an excellent poem to welcome my entrance into that farmstead where there is neither sitting nor standing nor sneezing, but only lying down and nothing more. It is *absolutely essential* for me to leave Moscow." (*December 16, 1891*.)

Chekhov's fears about the availability of the farm turned out to be well-founded. He learned first from Masha and then from Smagin, at the beginning of January, 1892, that the owner of the place had decided not to sell it. And several other prospects which Smagin proposed in the same area were found, upon inquiry, to be unsuitable. "How sad this is!" he wrote his friend. "If you only knew what an unhappy disillusionment it is! Well, where am I to spend the summer? What am I to do? Where am I to search?" (*January 4, 1892*.)

Shortly after this disappointment, and no doubt prompted now by a feeling of urgency, Chekhov asked his sister to inquire about an estate advertised for sale in the newspaper. Since it was in the Moscow province, far from the preferred Ukraine in the sunny south, Masha and also Misha demurred at what seemed like sheer foolhardiness. Besides, it was winter, the worst possible time to inspect the attractions or failings of an estate in the country. But Chekhov insisted, and his threat to go abroad in the spring if he did not buy a house settled the matter. Misha and his sister went to look over the place, and though they could not form a very clear idea of it, since it was buried under snow, their first tentative impression was favorable.

On the day Chekhov left for Voronezh to aid victims of the famine — February 2, 1892 — he wrote Lazarev-Gruzinsky to inform him that he had started negotiations to buy an estate which could be reached by third-class trains from Moscow for only one rouble and one kopeck. The purpose of the letter was to ask his friend to sound out a wealthy acquaintance on the possibility of a loan of fifteen hundred roubles, a request which was eventually turned down.

Chekhov actually committed himself to buying the estate, Melikhovo, before seeing it. He did not visit it until shortly after he returned from Voronezh on February 12. Melikhovo, truly an estate and not a mere farm, was two and one half hours by train from Moscow, near a little village of the same name, six miles from the Lopasnya station, and about fifteen from Serpukhov. There were 675 acres, about half of it poor woodland, an orchard, a "mangy stream," two ponds, and fruit trees. The house, like the auxiliary buildings on the estate, had been recently built, but its relative smallness disappointed him and it had no toilet. The room selected for his study pleased him because of its view and its three huge French windows. With a touch of humor he listed the effects that came with the estate: a piano, three horses, a cow, four geese, two dogs, ten wornout hens, a carriage, carts, sleighs, and seed beds. All this could be bought for thirteen thousand roubles, much more than he had ever intended to spend on a farmstead. Though he had no firm intention of farming the land, he eagerly listened to an account that he might obtain an income from produce that would run annually from one to two thousand roubles. In any event, his first view of Melikhovo that winter satisfied him, and the prospect of fishing from the window of his room — one of the ponds was only a few paces away from the house — delighted him.

The next few days, in which he became absorbed with notaries, banks, insurance companies, and "similar parasitical establishments," threw him into a frenzy. Everywhere he turned he had to pay for this or that service he had never anticipated. He wrote V. A. Tikhonov:

"I'm like a person who has entered an inn with the sole purpose of eating chopped beef and onions, but, having met some fine pals, has gone to work on the bottle, got as drunk as a pig, and then has to settle an account for 142 roubles and 75 kopecks." (*February 22, 1892.*) Actually, before the purchase was completed, he estimated that he had spent close to a thousand roubles for these extra expenses. And the owner of Melikhovo, a shaved-headed artist, N. P. Sorokhtin, infuriated Chekhov by his repeated lies about various details connected with land boundaries and the condition of the buildings.

At the end of February the weary Chekhov announced to Suvorin, whose offer of a loan won his deep gratitude, that the sale had been all but completed. The settlement was a three-way affair. He paid four thousand roubles down to Sorokhtin and obtained a mortage from him of five thousand which Chekhov agreed to pay within five years at 5 per cent. The remaining four thousand he secured from the Land Bank in another mortgage. The total interest on the mortgages amounted to considerably less than he would have to pay for his Moscow rent and that of a summer *dacha*. The mortgage to the artist, he told Suvorin. he hoped to pay off within three years at the most, for he would apply to it all the money he received from his books. As for his personal loan, half of this ought to be liquidated by August, for he had not taken any money recently from the sale of his books. His only wish now, he asserted, was to find a suitable estate for him not far from Melikhovo. "How glad I am that I will no longer have an apartment in Moscow!" he wrote Suvorin a few days later. "This is a solace that I never dreamed of." (*March 3, 1892.*)

On March 5 Chekhov took possession of Melikhovo. Among the many things he brought with him was a cartload of medical supplies; he regretted only that he had not also bought a microscope, for he wished to do some research. His first letter from Melikhovo, to brother Ivan, asked for more prosaic items — a curry comb and brush for cleaning horses, twenty pounds of nails, twenty of rye bread, and five loaves of French bread. "My impression and state of mind," he added, "are splendid, such as they have not been in a long time." (*March 5, 1892.*)

Chekhov's fondest dream had come true. The son of a serf, only thirty-two years of age, had become the owner of an estate! He had squeezed out of himself the last drop of the slave. In a lyrical letter to his brother Alexander about the acquisition of Melikhovo, he signed himself with characteristic humor, but perhaps in this case not unmixed with a feeling of pride: LANDOWNER A. CHEKHOV.

Part IV

THE MELIKHOVO PERIOD
1892 – 1898

CHAPTER XII

"Drive the Poets and Fiction Writers into the Country"

As THE SNOW MELTED that first spring on Chekhov's "ducal estate," as he jestingly called it, one unsuspected blemish after another stood out discouragingly. Some of the sheds were dilapidated, the fence enclosing the yard needed repairing, and the pond in front of the house was so tiny that he referred to it as an aquarium. The woodland he had bought he described as "switch wood," and the bare fields struck him as plain, flat, naïve, stupid, and without beauty. Worse still, he now discovered that the one-story, ten-room house had no charm and needed to be completely done over inside. It swarmed with bedbugs, beetles, and cockroaches, so that one would have to burn it down, he remarked, in order to get rid of them. Every day he trapped a number of mice alive and then carefully released them in a little copse some distance from the house. In his chagrin he recalled the spacious estates of friends where he had spent his summers. Everything at Melikhovo seemed in miniature — the house, the tiny pond, the stunted trees, the small garden and orchard. Like his miniature tales, however, where a few pages may convey a depth of thought and philosophy and a broad picture of Russian life, he sensed that Melikhovo, if treated creatively, could expand to the horizon in the beauty with which he would endow it.

The peasant in Chekhov, of which he often spoke, arose to the challenge to conquer this land, to make things grow, and to turn his house into a snug domicile. Laborers, carpenters, painters, and masons were hired. The sheds and fence were repaired, a new well was dug and a large iron wheel mounted to draw up the bucket, and a watercloset was installed. The whole house was redecorated, papered, painted; partitions were erected, and the inefficient tile stoves were torn down and rebuilt.

Chekhov wrote that he began to see the charms of capitalism when he discovered how cheap it was to hire workmen in the country. It cost only thirty kopecks a day for two laborers to fill the ice cellar. And a young peasant who worked in the fields, cleaned boots, and tended the flower garden earned only five roubles a month.

All in the Chekhov household labored harder than the hired help during this spring of reconstruction. A strict regimen was established. They arose with the sun, had their main meal at noon, and retired early. Each had assigned tasks. The mother did household chores, the father weeded the paths in the neglected garden and made new ones, sister Masha took charge of the large vegetable garden, Misha was responsible for the extensive field work, and Chekhov pruned and cared for the orchard and planted bulbs. Often they were so tired at evening that they could hardly drag themselves off to bed. And they slept so soundly that the commotion and ringing of the fire bell in the village failed to awaken them one night when a neighbor's house burned down.

Despite his misgivings, Chekhov was irresistibly drawn to attempting to farm a part of the many acres of land on the estate in an effort to realize some income. Though he admitted that he knew nothing about agriculture save that the earth was black, he tried to obtain knowledge by reading books on various aspects of the subject and by seeking advice from friends such as Leikin, Yegorov, Smagin, and Kiselev, who farmed their estates. Three more horses were bought to supplement the three sorry jades that had come with the property, and also chickens, geese, and a few sheep, pigs, cows, and a heifer that sang from morn to night in a thick baritone. Though the high price of seed discouraged him, he planted over thirty acres each of oats and clover, some rye, and buckwheat, and quantities of lentils, potatoes, cabbages and peas. During every day he could steal from his post at Aleksin, Misha tirelessly worked at and supervised this farming with the aid of two hired peasants, Frol and Ivan.

Chekhov concentrated on the orchard and flower garden. He added eighty apple and sixty cherry trees that first spring, and in the course of time set out hundreds of pine, elm, oak, and also lilac and rose bushes, and a variety of flowers. If he had little strength for hard, physical labor in the fields and clumsily could not hammer a nail without drawing blood, he willingly spent hours in the orchard and garden. Chekhov loved trees and flowers and imparted the same love to such characters as Mikhail Khrushchev in *The Wood Demon* and to Mi--

khail's reincarnation in *Uncle Vanya* as Dr. Astrov, who felt that he had contributed to man's happiness when he heard the murmuring of the young forest he had planted with his own hands. The unkindest thing Chekhov could say about Laevsky, that intellectual parasite in *The Duel*, was that he had not planted a single tree or grown a single blade of grass in his own garden. Each tree and flower Chekhov planted aroused in him a special feeling of well-being. He spoke of the enchantment of the pines in the setting sun which reddened their trunks, and of the oaks which took on a mysterious aspect at twilight. When his roses and tulips bloomed, he proudly showed them to his guests, and when he was away he worried about his plants as about deserted children, and would write his sister to see that they got proper care. The artist in Chekhov incessantly drove him to beautify Melikhovo. He planned the landscaping, built hothouses, a barn, a bathhouse, and had a much larger pond dug and stocked with so many species of fish that Misha jokingly asserted it could have been used as an experimental station by a learned ichthyologist.

As spring progressed into summer with all its glory of growing things, Chekhov jubilantly wrote Suvorin: "Every day there are surprises, one better than the other. The starlings have returned; everywhere there is the gurgling of water. . . . One's mood is calm, contemplative, and animal, in the sense that one does not regret yesterday or look forward to tomorrow. From here, far away, people seem very good; and that is natural, for in going away into the country we are not hiding from people but from our own vanity, which in the city, among people, is unjust and active beyond measure. Looking at the spring, I have a dreadful longing that there should be a paradise in the other world. In fact, at moments I am so happy that I superstitiously pull myself up and remind myself of my creditors. . . ." (*March 17, 1892.*)

« 2 »

By summer, life at Melikhovo had settled down to a pleasant and comfortable routine. Besides the two hired hands, a cook and a chambermaid served the family. Masha, Ivan, and Misha lived at Melikhovo during their summer vacations, but even before their vacation periods Masha, and often Ivan — both were teaching in Moscow less than fifty miles away — regularly made the trip on Fridays for the weekend. Chekhov frequently used these occasions to ask them to bring necessary supplies from the city — five pounds of coffee he ordered in one letter, a plain copper coffeepot, onions and horseradish, and a pound of Epsom salts. Everything about the estate deeply concerned Masha — the porridge would not boil without her, said Chekhov. With her heavy peasant boots on and a white kerchief over her head, she spent whole days in the fields or on the threshing floor, always anxious to spare her famous brother any physical labor. Ivan, with his Christlike head and with something of his sister's quiet and serious mien, contributed more advice than work. The younger, clever, and talented Misha, however, was a tower of strength in solving the problems of estate management and became quite indispensable to Chekhov. He soon arranged a transfer from his tax job at Aleksin to one at Serpukhov, which allowed him to live permanently at Melikhovo.

Though the low-slung, comfortable house, now completely renovated, had no architectural attractions, it was furnished with taste and kept spotlessly clean. Chekhov showed guests around the rooms, jokingly repeating the visits to each room to create the notion of a huge house. The place had already taken on the semblance of having been lived in by the Chekhov family all their lives. The room of each resembled its possessor — the monastic, cell-like room of Father, with its ikon and lamp, its great religious tomes, and a smell of herbs (he was preparing mysterious liqueurs so that Melikhovo would have something no other estate had); the bright, airy room of Mother, with its immaculate starched curtains, sewing machine, huge hampers filled with household linen, and a comfortable armchair in which this indefatigable old lady rarely had time to rest; the dazzlingly white virginal room of Masha with its narrow white bed, vases of flowers, and an enormous portrait of Chekhov occupying the principal wall space as well as the chief place in her heart; and the large study of Chekhov ablaze with light from its huge window, with a stove and a spacious divan, several well-filled bookcases, a writing table covered with manuscript pages, and walls adorned with paintings of Levitan and drawings by the dead Nikolai. The living room, looking out on the terrace leading into the garden, was modestly furnished with piano, easy chairs, and tables, without frills or superfluous articles.

It was nice to be lord of the manor, Chekhov commented. People were not continually pulling at the doorbell, and he did not mind at times divesting himself of his lordship's status to become a porter. But when he recalled the bills he had run up to renovate the estate, he worried over dying and leaving his family encumbered with debt. The owls hooting at night seemed to him to prophesy that Melikhovo would be sold at auction. He comforted himself, however, by the assurance that to be rich did not mean to have money, but simply to have the means to live in a place like Melikhovo. To be sure, there were minor annoyances. The cook got drunk a bit too often and the chambermaid could not resist stealing small sums from guests — he had a vague notion that some two hundred roubles of his own had vanished. Rabbits nibbled away at the vegetable garden, the cattle strayed into the cabbage patch, and he could not keep trespassers and hunters off his land. Then there was the "miracle of the horse," as he described it — one morning he discovered that his fine mare had been transformed into a broken-down stallion on the point of collapse.

A burgeoning harvest banished these concerns. There were so many cherries he did not know what to do with them, and it pleased him to eat his fill off the trees without anyone's driving him away or whipping him. The earth poured forth produce. "Our farming efforts have been crowned with complete success," he wrote Suvorin. "The harvest is a solid one, and when we sell our grain it will net us more than a thousand roubles. The vegetable garden turned out brilliantly. We have a veritable mountain of cucumbers and wonderful cabbages." (*August 1, 1892.*) Because of famine conditions in the area, however, he ordered not a little of the harvest to be sold at very reduced prices to the peasants, who thought him simple-minded.

Indeed, at the end of this first summer at Melikhovo, Chekhov could triumphantly inform Suvorin that, despite the hard work, he had never in his life spent a summer so well. "I have liked the life and wanted to live. How many trees I have planted! Thanks to our system of cultivation, Melokhovo has become unrecognizable, and it seems now extraordinarily snug and beautiful, though very likely it is good for nothing. Great is the power of habit and the sense of property. And it is marvelous how pleasant it is not to have to pay rent." (*October 10, 1892.*)

Winter, however, was the real test of living in the country, and as it approached Chekhov's spirits quailed. The snow got so deep that hares, standing on their hind legs, peered in at his study window. He told himself that his serf grandfather had put up with such conditions and they ought not to be any punishment for the grandson. Strangely enough, he informed Alexander, it was not dull and he now had plenty of time to write. However, the bare fields and trees and the chickens huddling in the cold filled him with melancholy. Not even sleeping to excess or eating his fill of the traditional country dishes of roast duck and salted mushrooms rejoiced him. Through October and November he found various reasons for going to Moscow on literary business and to see friends. Then he remembered that his original plan for living in the country had called for a visit to Petersburg over the winter months, and he left for that city on December 19.

Chekhov spent five weeks in Petersburg. One of his purposess was to write, but he squandered most of his time in infinite talk and smoking with Suvorin and in social gatherings with friends. While he complained, in one letter, of leading a dull life, yet he made plans to stay longer on his next visit, and in another letter boasted that at Suvorin's he ate, slept, and made merry like a rich beggar and hardly wrote a line. Mariya Kiseleva's married sister, Nadezhda Golubeva, who had not seen Chekhov for six years, coaxed him to dinner — she had been assisted by him in her literary endeavors. "Ah, how delighted I am!" he declared when he discovered that her rather stuffy, socially prominent spouse would not be at home. "You know, I don't have the fine manners of your husband. My papa and mama sold herring." And all through the meal, much to the discomfort of his hostess, he kept jumping up, pacing the room, and returning to the table for a bite — a nervous habit he had always had at meals. After dinner they talked of writing, and he rather unfeelingly criticized women who turned out stories just to pass the time. His offended hostess told him how much he had changed since those jolly Babkino days when they first met, and, after he left, she commented in her account: "Such weariness was apparent in his whole figure! I thought: The spring of his life had passed, there had been no summer, and he is now in his autumn."

Spring came very late at Melikhovo in 1893, with snow on the ground until well into April. The bad weather, as always, made him irritable, and he assured Alexander that he would turn into a drunkard if the sun did not shine. The house had settled in the winter so that the doors were out of line, the snow prevented the farm animals from grazing which meant extra expense for feed, and for weeks the roads were impassable.

At the beginning of May the weather improved and so did Chekhov's disposition. Again his mind seethed with projects — an apiary, a little house in the woods to get away from the guests, the planting of more trees and flowers, a road through the fields so visitors would not have to approach the house by way of the unsightly village. And again the farming got under way, and once more the harvest turned out to be a bountiful one. Happily he wrote Suvorin: "My family costs me nothing now, since lodgings, bread, vegetables, milk, butter, and the horses are all my own and don't have to be bought. And there is so much work, time does not suffice. Of the entire Chekhov family it is only I who may lie down or sit at a table, all the rest toil from morning until night. Drive the poets and fiction writers into the country! Why should they exist as beggars and live on the verge of starvation? Surely city life, in the sense of poetry and art, cannot offer rich material to the poor man." (*April 21, 1893.*)

Chekhov had come to believe this by the end of his second summer at Melikhovo. A dream had been realized and a pattern of existence established that might have satisfied him for the rest of his life if fate had not intervened. He had turned this rather rundown estate into a charming oasis, and he came to love it as something he had created. Friends noticed that at Melikhovo he seemed like a different man, free of the distracted look that often came over his fine features among friends in the city. In the country he was never a spectator but always the active person. Close to nature he seemed to be more himself. When he sat on his favorite mound before the gates of Melikhovo and looked directly into the fields, his eyes lost their sadness and were clear and calm. There were the usual periods of restlessness and dissatisfaction, but on the whole his life at Melikhovo was intense and full. He had his trees and flowers to care for. Guests were endless. The practice of medicine occupied him. And soon he became involved in various community problems. Above all, Melikhovo provided him with rich artistic material and helped to inspire perhaps his greatest creative period.

« 3 »

"Well, now, let us all gather at the muddy spring, for on its edge grow splendid salted and peppered mushrooms," Chekhov would announce, and with laughter at this sally the family and guests at Melikhovo would sit down to dinner. This was a family joke at the expense of his father, who had told of a sermon he had heard at the village church: A thirsty traveler came upon two springs in a forest, a pure one and a muddy one, and he drank from the muddy spring — that is, vodka at the village tavern, instead of faith at the pure fount of the church. If anything, Father had grown more religious in his old age. He never missed church, went through the house swinging a smoking censer pot on holy days, and when not working in the garden, spent much of this time in his cell-like room poring over thick folios of the lives of the saints. At night, when all had gone to bed, he could be heard praying before the ikon in his room and softly chanting the psalms and church ritual. The first Easter at Melikhovo he came into his own when asked to direct an improvised choir at the local church. A priest had to be hired from the nearby Davydov Monastery by taking up a collection of eleven roubles from the village parish, since the church did not have its own priest. The family and their guests composed the choir. Chekhov's harmonious baritone rang out loud and clear. The local peasants were immensely pleased with the service and with the musical efforts of this new family in their midst. And the old father, too, was delighted. Later he told one of the guests what a wonderful voice Chekhov had had as a child when he sang in his choir and how angelic all thought him.

It was a subject that Chekhov preferred to forget, as well as the compulsory church attendance and beatings that had darkened his childhood. Even now he could not treat his father with the affection that he showed his mother. In general, all the children respected their father, but it was a respect mingled with a kind of jocularity that evidenced their freedom from the parental authority which had once been so stern. When guests came he always deferred to Chekhov as the head of the household. Sometimes the father annoyed his son by his severity to the peasants, and by his naïve philosophizing. He would pose such questions as: "What is the snow doing here?" Or "Why is that tree here and not there?" He could be stubborn in his ignorance, as when he insisted on referring to "Adulteration of Milk," which he had read about in a newspaper article, as "Classification of Milk."[1] His preoccupation with recondite religious matters sometimes bored visitors, for he was capable of tiresomely arguing the point of why the Anna Award, First Degree, had been given to a Kostroma church official when an older church official of the same rank at Mozhaisk had received nothing. Chekhov rather unfairly complained to Alexander that the old man, like all Taganrog natives, was incapable of any work around the house except lighting the lamps. Mischievously he parodied his father's humorlessly bare entries of arrivals and departures in the diary which he kept at Melikhovo by inserting such lines as: "*May 18, No. 1:* It is

[1] The father confused the Russian word *falsifikatsiya* with *klassifikatsiya*.

snowing. Thank God, all have gone, and only we two, I and Madame Chekhova, remain."

Although his gentle mother could also be exasperating in her provincial habits and uncomprehending mind, she blossomed as mistress of the manor at Melikhovo, delighted that now, unlike the old Tanganrog days, she did not have to pinch in planning meals. She doted on feeding the family and guests well. Arising before all and going to bed late, her hands were never idle. And at night, for one of Chekhov's favorite woman friends she would slip quietly into the guest's room and place a snack at the bedside: "In case, child, you should suddenly become hungry." Often in her simple manner she would reminisce about Chekhov's childhood and youth, for she reverenced this son who had provided his mother and father with such a "cosy corner" in their old age. She anticipated his desires and every change in his mood was reflected on her face. He had only to emerge from his study and glance at the wall clock for her to jump up from her sewing and bustle off to the kitchen, exclaiming: "Oh dear! Antosha wants his dinner!"

The old hope that Chekhov had often expressed, of obtaining a place in the country which all members of the family could think of as home, was now realized — in the summers, at least. Even Alexander from Petersburg took his vacations with his children at Melikhovo. He had decided to become a vegetarian, and for the thousandth time had sworn off liquor, probably as usual after he got involved in one of his periodic quarrels at *New Times*. Of late, however, his stories, a few of which Chekhov praised highly, had been getting into the major magazines. He had also written a small technical book and found himself in demand as an editor on periodicals. With the slight improvement of his financial situation, he hinted broadly that he would like to buy a piece of land near his brother and build a *dacha*, a proposal that Chekhov parried. But their cordial relations, as well as their sparkling correspondence, continued, and Alexander as always was at his brother's call to perform services for him in Petersburg.

News soon spread in the area that the well-known writer Chekhov had settled at Melikhovo and neighbors, members of the local County Council, doctors and officials of the district came to call. They were met with the greatest affability and pressed to come again. They did, and often. Chekhov grew particularly fond of his neighbor Prince S. I. Shakhovskoi, an agreeable young man and head of the district County Council. Making friends with the peasants was another matter. They were naturally suspicious of newcomers and also a bit contemptuous of the family's ideas of farming. Chekhov even confessed to being a bit afraid in approaching them. But once they learned that he was a physician willing to help them in their illnesses, the ice was broken. And before long he could write Suvorin: "The peasants and shopkeepers are in my hands; I've won out. One had a hemorrhage from the throat, another had his arm crushed by a tree, a third, a sick daughter. It seems that they would be in a desperate situation without me. They now bow respectfully to me as Germans do to their pastor, and I am friends with them and all goes well." (*May 15, 1892.*)

Although Chekhov had mentioned that one of the reasons why he wanted to leave Moscow was to get away from numerous visitors, he had barely completed the initial reconstruction of Melikhovo when nearly every one of scores of letters to his friends contained pressing and repeated invitations to visit him. Now, apart from his natural need to have people around him, he wanted to show off his new estate, in which he took a genuine pride, despite his modest assertion to Suvorin that "very likely it is good for nothing." One strongly suspects that this need arose in part from the boredom he experienced in being alone in the company of his parents.

Barantsevich, a heavy eater, was offered eight meals a day if he would come; to Lazarev-Gruzinsky Chekhov would make a present of five bunches of radishes from his own garden, but he must come to Melikhovo to eat them, and other such whimsical twists were given to his invitations. His friends hardly required any pressure. They came in all seasons of the year, even in the winter. By the summer of 1893 Melikhovo was crowded with visitors, and not only his friends, but people whose acquaintance he had neither sought nor desired — young ladies, authors, local doctors, and distant relatives with their children. Improvised beds had to be set up; they slept four to a room and some even slept in the hallways. One girl — with a head shaped like the top of a bass viol, Chekhov said — with whom the family was barely acquainted, stayed a week and then was tactfully queried by a servant as to when she was leaving. "I'm a guest of Anton Pavlovich and not you," she pouted — and it is very possible that in his vague way Chekhov had invited her and forgotten it. Misha suspected, and with some reason, that one of the guests, a young man recommended to Chekhov, was probably a police inspector in disguise seeking out political subversion in this strangely popular household in the country. The musician

Ivanenko, ailing and out of a job, arrived and stayed for months, making Melikhovo his home while he worked in the nearby office of the County Council, a position that the sympathetic Chekhov had obtained for him. Many of these casual visitors were infatuated worshippers who hung on Chekhov's every word. Yet they consumed quantities of food and drink, and wore out his mother and sister who attended them. At times it became too much even for Chekhov's immense social appetite. He wrote Suvorin: "Ah, if you only knew how weary I am! I'm weary to the point of a breakdown. Guests, guests, guests . . . every passing intellectual regards it as a duty and a necessity to drop in on me and warm himself, and sometimes they even remain and spend the night. There is a whole legion of doctors! It is pleasant, of course, to be hospitable, but the soul must have some measure." (*December 8, 1892.*)

Old friends, however, who had grown close to the family over the years, were always welcome at Melikhovo. Most of them came from Moscow, such as Semashka, Ivanenko, the beautiful Lika, his cousin A. Dolzhenko, Shekhtel, and Gilyarovsky, who wore out Chekhov's horses with his feats of strength, clambered up trees, smashed huge beams, and terrified the dogs. Others willingly came long distances to visit, like A. I. Smagin, Natalya Lintvareva, Suvorin, and Svobodin. Suvorin had visited earlier, before Melikhovo was fully renovated and the water-closet put in; and this wealthy son of a serf had turned his nose up and soon left, much to Chekhov's distress. The amusing, affectionate actor Svobodin spent many days at Melikhovo during the summer of 1892. Chekhov remarked that he had the aged's thirst for peace and quiet, and he had a premonition about Svobodin that came true — that autumn he died in the course of a performance in Petersburg.

The artist Levitan, who had not yet caught up with the publication of *The Grasshopper*, which had only recently appeared, had already visited Melikhovo by April 1892. He insisted that Chekhov accompany him hunting, a sport that Anton did not favor. The artist shot a woodcock and Chekhov picked it up. The bird with its long beak and beautiful plumage was still living, and its black eyes stared at him. Levitan pleaded with Chekhov to kill it. He refused at first, but the artist, in a highly nervous state, continued his pleading. "I had to obey Levitan and kill it," Chekhov reported to Suvorin. "One lovely amorous creature less in the world, and two fools returned home and sat down to supper." (*April 18, 1892.*)

As soon as favorite guests arrived Chekhov dropped whatever he was doing and became the gay host. Although there was a certain Russian charm about the view from Melikhovo, there were very few pleasing places for walks, fishing, and picnic expeditions. One of them was the Davydov Monastery, about two miles away, with an attractive mill on one of the neighborhood ponds which swarmed with fish. Chekhov would organize the family and guests and order the chaise, cart, and racing *droshky* to be harnessed. Dressed in his white tunic with a strap buckled around his waist, he would mount the *droshky*, designating a pretty lady to sit sideways behind him, holding on to the strap. In this regalia he called himself a Hussar. The racing *droshky* would jauntily lead the way to the Davydov Monastery, followed by the chaise and the cart with provisions for a picnic and tackle for fishing. Or he would take a guest with him to sit on the dam of the large pond he had constructed on the estate, the banks of which he had planted with trees and flowering bushes. There they would sit and talk while Chekhov watched with boyish delight the shoals of little fish coming suddenly to the surface and then hiding in the depths.

Hilarity and interesting conversation, which Chekhov dominated, ruled at mealtime. Mother Chekhov loaded the table with her best dishes and Father would dispense his mysterious Melikhovo liqueurs. Chekhov liked to tease his guests and play practical jokes on them. Taking advantage of the naïveté of nineteen-year-old Tatyana Shchepkina-Kupernik, a poetess and short-story writer whom Masha had introduced into the family, he solemnly convinced her that his dove with coffee-colored feathers was a cross between a dove and a cat that lived in his yard (the cat had fur of the same color). Though she thought the explanation a bit odd, how could she doubt the authority of Chekhov? When she told the story of Chekhov's remarkable dove bred from a cat in a Moscow literary circle they greeted it with rapture, and it was long before she could live it down.

After dinner Chekhov would give the men cigars — he had been introduced to these in his trip to Petersburg in 1892 and had become a devoted cigar smoker — and sparkling conversation would ensue. Sometimes he would play with the dogs. Although he had inherited two with the estate, Muir and Merilees (named after a famous Moscow store), Leikin had also presented him with male and female dachshunds, Brom Isaich and Khina Markovna (literally "Bromine" and "Quinine"). Khina grew so fat that her belly almost dragged on the ground. Chekhov pretended that she suffered from this, and when Khina put her paw on his knee and gazed sadly into his eyes, he would change the expression on his face and in a pitying voice carry on a long monologue with the dog, beginning "Khina Markovna! Sufferer that you are! You ought to be in the hospital!" And the guests would roar over this simulated doctor's advice to his canine patient.

In July 1893, the writer I. P. Potapenko, whom Chekhov had met casually four years previously at Odessa and who by this time had become a popular author, visited Melikhovo. At first Chekhov described him as "the god of dullness," but after repeated visits he got to like Potapenko and they became firm friends. Though somewhat weak-willed, Potapenko was simple, sincere, extremely sociable, and always breathing optimism. He sang and played the violin well, had a good wit, squandered money, and was a general favorite with the ladies. Through Chekhov he became acquainted with Lika Mizinova and when the two of them arrived at Melikhovo from Moscow it was a cause for general jubilation, for it meant a day of music. Lika, who was studying opera singing in her spare time, had an excellent voice. The whole family would join in at singing around the piano, calling for their favorite pieces. Chekhov's was a Wallachian love ballad, very popular in Russia then, which Lika would sing, accompanying herself on the piano, with Potapenko playing the violin parts, while through the open windows came the song of birds and the fragrance of flowers in the garden right outside the living room. In the midst of such activities Chekhov would sometimes vanish, though never for long, and would exclaim with a smile on his return from his study: "I've just written sixty kopecks' worth!" These music fests would often last past midnight, but long after all had gone to bed the lamp in Chekhov's study still burned.

These Moscow friends generously repaid his hospitality when he appeared in the city and stayed at the Grand Hotel in his favorite room, Number 5, which was soon known as "Chekhov's Room." As Tatyana Shchepkina-Kupernik recalled, she would find on the notepaper at her apartment a scrawl such as: "At last, the waves have washed a madman on the shore . . . and he stretches out his hands to two white gulls." This was a reference to her and her friend, the attractive young actress Lidiya Yavorskaya, who thought Chekhov charming and pleaded with Lika Mizinova to help her catch him for a husband. With the swiftness of a telegram the news would get around that he was in town and friends would descend on Number 5. He would be regaled with luncheons, dinners, the theater, literary gatherings, concerts, exhibitions, and jolly nights of talk and drink that ran into the morning hours. This gay company was his "squadron" and he was "Avelan," a nickname suggested by the popularity of Admiral F. K. Avelan, who had commanded the Russian squadron that went to Toulon in 1893 to conclude the Franco-Russian alliance, and at this time was being endlessly honored in France and Russia for his successful services. Chekhov had his picture taken with Tatyana Shchepkina-Kupernik and Lidiya Yavorskaya, and the girls roared at the stony face he put on when the photographer said: "Look at the birdie." He entitled the picture: "The Temptation of Saint Anthony." After one such period of being "honored" by his "Moscow Squadron," in November 1893, he wrote Suvorin: "Never before have I felt so free . . . girls, girls, girls!" Yet Tatyana Shchepkina-Kupernik, who came to know Chekhov well, observed that in these gala gatherings he never seemed "to be with us," that he was like an older person playing with children although some in the group were much older than he. Behind his laughter and jokes, one sensed a sadness and a strange aloofness.

« 4 »

Love bloomed with the flowers during these first two summers at Melikhovo. A petite and not unattractive brunette, Countess Klara Ivanovna Mamuna, visited the estate as a friend of Masha's and Lika's, with whom she worked at City Hall. Soon the countess's visits grew frequent, for brother Misha had begun to court her. There was a strong smell in the air, Chekhov darkly hinted, which meant in his brother's language that he was trying to advance his career. Chekhov did not particularly like the little countess. But after some weeks she and Misha became engaged. They had hardly got accustomed to their new status when the countess went on a lengthy visit to her aunt's. Upon her return to Moscow, the languishing Misha hastened to greet his bride-to-be. He saw people hanging about at the windows and the gates of her house. What was happening? asked Chekhov, in telling the story to Suvorin. Nothing less than a wedding — the countess was marrying a rich gold-mine owner. Chekhov must have relished the situation; it was so much like those that he had treated in his early humorous tales. When in his despair the jilted Misha returned to Melikhovo, he pushed the countess's love letters under his brother's nose and begged him to solve this psychological problem. "A woman will deceive someone five times over before she has worn out a pair of shoes," Chekhov rather cynically commented. "However, I think Shakespeare has already spoken adequately on the subject." (*April 26, 1893.*) As for Misha, he threatened for a time to throw up his position and immure himself in a distant province.

The much more serious-minded Ivan, who had received another promotion in the teaching profession, also began to bring a young lady to Melikhovo, Sofya Vladimirovna Andreeva — a Kostroma gentlewoman, a very sweet girl with a long nose, Chekhov described her. He liked Sofya very much and was happy when Ivan told him of his engagement to her. The marriage took place at Melikhovo, July 9, 1893 — a quiet, decorous affair in keeping with the bridegroom's rather solemn nature. Of all the brothers, the able Ivan left nothing to chance in life; he was willing to forgo its thrills for the sake of propriety and hard-earned security.

Love also caressed sister Masha at this time, but only to cause her trouble and pain. The lively and attractive Ukrainian, Alexander Smagin, had visited the Chekhovs in Moscow and then at Melikhovo, and Masha had also seen him on visits to his relatives, the Lintvarevs. So she was not surprised now to receive a proposal. After much heart-searching she went to her brother's study and said softly: "Well, Anton, I've decided to get married." Recalling the scene in her old age, Masha wrote: "Brother, of course, understood who the man was, but he said nothing. Then I realized that this news was unpleasant for him, since he continued to remain silent. But what, in fact, could he say? I understood he could not confess that it would be hard for him if I left for the home of another, for a family of my own. Yet he never pronounced the word 'No.'" Masha left, went to her room, and wept long and bitterly, unable to make up her mind.

For several days, she waited for her brother to speak on the subject. "I thought much," Masha remembered. "Love for my brother, my ties to him, decided the matter. I could not do anything that would cause unpleasantness to my brother, upset the customary course of his life, and deprive him of the conditions for creative work which I had always tried to provide. I informed Smagin of my refusal, which caused him suffering. He sent me a sharp letter filled with reproaches."

Chekhov's terse and unilluminating comment on the matter to Suvorin, on October 18, 1892, reads: "My sister's marriage did not take place, but the romance, it seems, continues through correspondence.

I understand nothing about it. There are guesses that she refused, at least at this time. She is an unusual girl who sincerely does not wish to marry."

There is something almost gratuitous about Chekhov's assumption of his sister's rejection of any personal life of her own at the age of twenty-nine. The bond between brother and sister was mysteriously close and her sense of dedication to him was absolute. She never did marry. To what extent Masha's love for Chekhov was an inhibiting factor in her search for the happiness that marriage brings to a woman is difficult to say with certainty. Her love must have been very great, if we may judge from a curious outburst in one of Alexander's letters to his brother (about June 15, 1893) after a visit to Melikhovo: "Of one thing I'm convinced. Your relations with Sister are false. A single tender word from you with a cordial note in it — and she is all yours. She is afraid of you and she sees in you only what is most praiseworthy and noble."

Whether this unusual devotion between brother and sister played a part in Chekhov's determination to remain single is equally hard to ascertain. Masha seemed confident that he would never marry. In the same letter to Suvorin in which he so emphatically told of her rejection of marriage, Chekhov immediately and equally emphatically added what could almost be construed as confirmation of a pact between them: "Now about myself. I don't want to marry, nor is there the woman. But the deuce with that. It would bore me to fuss about with a wife. However, it would not be a bad idea to fall in love. Without real love, life is dull." Intimate friends, and especially his brother Alexander, were concerned. "You live like an archimandrite," Alexander wrote him. "The golden moments pass and leave no trace, and all that will be left for you will be to go to the Zoological Garden and converse with your mongoose about the joys of bachelordom."

Certainly Chekhov did not find real love with Lidiya Avilova. After their second meeting in January 1892, he wrote her only four letters in the course of that year. These were all answers to ones from her, and, save for one already noted in the previous chapter, they are concerned largely with advice on her literary career and with criticism of her tales, in which he quite forgetfully repeats his stricture that she must remain cold and not interject her own sympathies when she is depicting sad and unhappy people. In 1893 he wrote her only once, as far as we know, and again in answer to a letter of hers. This letter, however, has an interesting bearing on the fourth chapter of her memoirs. She tells there of a third meeting with Chekhov, although she strangely enough does not date it, as she had done precisely in the case of the first two meetings. It is assumed by some Chekhov scholars that this meeting could have taken place only during Chekhov's long visits to Petersburg at the end of 1892 and the beginning of 1893.[2] Lidiya now introduces an aura of mystery into her account. She claims that she received Chekhov's letters in secret, at the post office, *poste restante*, although she tells her husband of the correspondence, and she clearly implies that her sister, Nadezhda Alekseevna, wife of Khudekov, editor of the *Petersburg Gazette*, has entered into a little conspiracy all her own to bring Lidiya and Chekhov together. The sister sees to it, according to Lidiya's story, that the pair meet in her house, but Lidiya insists that she informed her husband in advance of the meeting. The rest of this chapter is mostly Lidiya's report of her conversation with Chekhov. He begins by asking about her children and expresses the opinion that it is fine to have one's own family.

" 'You ought to marry,' " she said.

" 'I ought to get married,' " she quotes him as replying. " 'But I am still not free. Though I'm not married, yet I have a family: a mother, sister, a younger brother. I have obligations.' "

Then he asks her if she is happy. In response she explains that she loves her family, but that she feels as though she is caught in a trap, that she is ceasing to exist because she cannot imagine harming her family in her desire for a better or happier life.

In answer to this obvious hint, Lidiya represents Chekhov as warmly urging her not to surrender her right to express her own personality, not to become reconciled to her present position and allow her family to dominate her existence. " 'If I had married,' Chekhov said thoughtfully, 'I would have proposed to my wife . . . imagine it. . . . I would have proposed to her that we should not live together. In order that there should be none of those dressing gowns, nor that . . . Russian

2 In the invaluable work of N. I. Gitovich, *Letopis zhizni i tvorchestva A. P. Chekhova* (*Chronicle of the Life and Works of A. P. Chekhov*), Moscow, 1955, p. 334, she apparently assumes that this meeting took place at the beginning of January, 1893. The evidence set forth here is that this assumption is erroneous. Chekhov was also in Petersburg between October 31 and November 6, 1892, where he had been summoned because of Suvorin's illness. Again, there is no evidence that he saw Lidiya Avilova during this brief visit, when all his time appears to have been devoted to treating Suvorin and to seeing a few friends.

dissoluteness . . . and that shocking unceremoniousness.' " This is something that Chekhov might have had a character in one of his stories declare.

At that promising point Lidiya is summoned home because of a sick child. It appears, however, that this was just a ruse of her jealous husband. She concludes this chapter of her memoirs by declaring: " 'But I knew now. For the first time, without any doubt, definitely, clearly, I knew that I was in love with Anton Pavlovich.' "

In the extremely rich documentary material on Chekhov's life, there is no record of such a meeting. And his only extant letter to her in 1893 (March 1) makes it clear that he did not see her during his stay in Petersburg at the beginning of that year, almost the only logical time when such a meeting could have taken place. Further, the contents of the letter once again fail to suggest any serious feeling on Chekhov's part for Lidiya Avilova. The letter obviously is an answer to one from her in which she scolded him precisely for not making the effort to see her at her sister's house when he was in Petersburg in January, for continuing to forget her name, and for not keeping his promise to write. "I will not try to justify myself," he replied, "because it is not in my power. . . . However, I will only say that the reason I didn't go to Nadezhda Alekseevna's was not because I feared to meet there my most wicked enemy,[3] but simply because, to my shame, I'm a dissolute, undisciplined man. Twenty times I resolved to go to her on the date of her evening-at-home, and twenty times dinners, suppers, guests, and every kind of unexpected event destroyed my resolution." After this quite unromantic excuse, he tries to cheer her up by saying that he would have liked to see her at her sister's, that her stories are being praised, and — once again — that she should write more coldly. He concludes with remarks that reveal perhaps Avilova's suspicion of the unreality of her futile pursuit as well as Chekhov's realization of the unhappy weakness in this woman. "You're foolish to call your letters 'psychopathic.' You've not yet arrived at the point of writing such letters. Wait, when you become a famous author and begin to publish fat novels in the *Herald of Europe*, then your turn will come: the mania of greatness will seize you and you will then look down on our brotherhood from the heights and will write in your letters such sentences as: 'Only the thought, the one thought that I serve the holy,

[3] The "most wicked enemy" no doubt was a reference to Leikin, and in this context it is another example of Lidiya Avilova's overworked imagination.

the eternal, the immovable, has kept me from suicide!' However, I seem to be writing nonsense. Forgive me."

Indeed, this letter suggests that Chekhov had discerned the irrational passion of Lidiya Avilova and was trying with some gentleness to discourage her. However irrational or purely imaginary the account of her meeting with him in the fourth chapter in her memoirs may be, her pursuit of Chekhov continued.

His efforts to discourage Lika Mizinova, however, very likely sprang from a real fear of the strength of his feeling for her. If he had made a sacrifice of the beautiful Lika to his constant need for tenderness, the protracted period of disengagement brought her unhappiness and reflected no credit on Chekhov. As a close friend of the whole family, Lika was always a most welcome guest over the first two years at Melikhovo. But the frequency of her visits must be attributed in some part to urgent invitations he made to her in letter after letter. Nor did he fail to see her on most of his trips to Moscow, and he pressed her to come to Petersburg when he visited there — actually the time when it has been assumed that he might have been seeing Lidiya Avilova! In the summer of 1892 Chekhov and Lika appear to have planned a trip to the Caucasus together — which, however, did not materialize. His letters to her over this period invariably contained some such endearment or plea as: "Indeed, my angel, you have so turned my head that I'm ready to believe twice two equals five;" "My all to you . . . do you understand? All"; "I'm dull without you and would give five roubles for the possibility of talking with you even if that lasted only five minutes"; "I don't need to write, only to sit close to you and talk"; "Write me, do you hear? I beg you on my knees"; "I await you and dream of your coming as a Bedouin in the desert dreams of water"; "Be sure to come. You know how I need you. Don't deceive me, Likusya, for heaven's sake, come!"

Such language and sentiments no doubt led Lika on, but the mixture of levity and seriousness in his letters, and perhaps in his conversation, confused and irritated her. He encouraged his "rivals" and then pretended jealousy of them. Or he would send her a letter he had addressed to Trofim, the imaginary lover he had invented: "Trofim! You son of a bitch. If you don't stop pursuing Lika, I'll shove a corkscrew into you, you cheap riffraff, in the place that rhymes with lass. Ah, you turd! Really, don't you know that Lika belongs to me and that we already have two children? You pig's snout! You toadstool! Go out into the yard and refresh yourself in a mud puddle, for you've gone nuts, you son of a bitch! Feed your mother and respect her, but let the girls alone. You beast! ! ! LIKA'S LOVER."[4]

The correspondence indicates that Lika's bafflement over this treatment led to frequent quarrels. In her letters she charged him with egoism, with always wanting his own way, and with doing things solely for his own satisfaction. And he accused her of distorting his words, with acting like a shrewish governess, and with worrying too much about being an old maid. Then, like lovers, they would write of the sweet joys of making up. "Ah, how I would like it (if I could) to tighten the lasso more firmly," she wrote after one of these reconciliations. For a long time Masha was convinced that her brother was very much in love with Lika.

Chekhov was obviously fully aware of Lika's love for him, but his efforts to counteract it were in conflict with a powerful inner desire not to break off relations with her. Apart from his serio-comic behavior and his occasional treatment of her as a naughty little girl, he tried to discourage Lika by harping upon the fact that he was growing old and was good for nothing. In a rare moment of self-examination that sheds some light on the confused feelings that allowed him to tamper with the affections of this charming girl, he wrote her in a serious vein from Melikhovo on March 27, 1892: "Lika, when will it be spring? Regard this question literally and do not seek in it any hidden meaning. Alas, I'm already an old young man, my love is not the sun and does not create spring either for me or for that bird which I love! Lika, I do not love you so ardently. I love in you my past sufferings and my lost youth." In short, it was already too late. Although he was only thirty-two, the golden period of youth when love bloomed in the spring had vanished.

Toward the end of her visits to Melikhovo in 1893, Lika had apparently come to the same conclusion — that Chekhov had no intention of marrying her or anybody else. She wrote him a frank letter: "You know quite well *how* I feel about you, and hence I'm not at all ashamed to write about it. I know also that your behavior toward me is condescending and indifferent. My strongest wish is to cure myself of the hopeless condition in which I am now, but it is very difficult to do it by

[4] These expressions are drawn from Chekhov's letters to Lika Mizinova, dated April 22, August 13, and November 1892; also July 16, July 27–30, and December 19, 1893.

myself. I beg you to help me. Please don't ask me to come to see you, and don't try to see me. This may mean nothing to you, but it may help me to forget you. . . ."

Perhaps it was Lika's frustration over her love for Chekhov and the emotional disturbance it caused that led her to pay attention to Potapenko, whom she met at Melikhovo during the second half of 1893. With feminine instinct, she may have had the ancient device of jealousy in mind — a hopeless motif where Chekhov was concerned. Soon Lika and Potapenko were making the trip together from Moscow to Melikhovo. They had music in common, and Chekhov seemed deliberately to further their affinity in this respect by pleading with them to play and sing together on every possible occasion. The fact that he had a wife and two children did not lessen Potapenko's zeal for philandering. On October 7, 1893, Lika wrote Chekhov a frightened letter, in which she pleaded: "I must, you understand, I must know whether you are coming [to Moscow] and when, or not at all. It is all the same, only I have to know. In fact, only two to three months remain to me in which to see you, and after that, perhaps, never." Apparently, this was a last effort on Lika's part before she submitted to Potapenko. Chekhov, however, had no resources to cope with such a situation. The springtime of youth had died; marriage had passed him by.

CHAPTER XIII

"For the Lonely Man, the Desert Is Everywhere"

THE CARTLOAD OF MEDICAL SUPPLIES Chekhov had brought with him to Melikhovo was no idle gesture. His practice in Moscow had been dwindling, restricted to a few friends who regarded it as a free personal service. Such a situation was unsatisfactory in terms of both his professions — medicine and writing. For Chekhov made no secret of the fact that his medical practice, which in many respects was distasteful to him, opened a door to interesting literary situations and characters. His ideal image of the doctor was that of the scientist advancing the horizons of medicine. Perhaps, if he had had his way, he would have specialized in psychiatry, a new branch of medicine in Russia which had not been taught at Moscow University when he was a student there. In a conversation with Tatyana Shchepkina-Kupernik, he remarked: "If you want to become a real writer, study medicine. Especially psychiatry. It has helped me and saved me from errors." He made a serious effort to keep up on the latest medical literature. And since his Sakhalin study, social medicine, which was somewhat looked down upon by city practitioners but was advocated by progressive County Councils, had taken on a new importance in his eyes, particularly for country doctors. Chekhov had always connected owning an estate in the country with greater medical activity on his part. He thought of it as an enriching social and human experience, one that would enable him to know the peasantry better and would also provide him with fresh material for his literary labors.

Doctors in the Serpukhov district were few and Chekhov quickly found himself very much in demand by peasants and workers within a radius of fifteen miles of Melikhovo. Hardly a day passed without peasants, usually women with children, arriving at his house for treatment. He went about the business methodically, registering the patients and keeping records. Soon the house took on the aspect of a dispensary. His reception hours were in the morning; at the very break of day a line of peasants would form in the yard. Emergency cases were not infrequent; Misha recalls a field worker being brought into the study with a pitchfork wound in his stomach. Calls at all hours of the day and night and in every kind of weather took him long distances from home. Yet he never refused aid. If he had just returned from a case, weary and ready for tea, only to be called out again, his mother would then protest. "Dysentery, Mother, will not wait!" he replied on one such occasion. In the summers his sister aided him, especially in maintaining the "apothecary shop" — for he prescribed drugs and medicines at his own expense. He rarely received fees from these poor people — occasionally a rouble or two, or a grateful peasant might turn over to him a suckling pig.

Chekhov's reputation as a doctor became so well established that the local County Council, when cholera threatened the area in July 1892, asked him to serve on the Serpukhov Sanitary Council to organize measures against the spread of the epidemic. He agreed, and without salary. Here was a need for social medicine. Chekhov went about the assignment energetically. He read up on cholera and the latest treatment, and on preventive measures in epidemics of this sort. His first task was to arrange for the building of barracks to serve as immunizing wards in the twenty-five villages, four factories, and a monastery that constituted his district. Since the County Council had almost no funds for this kind of activity and at first could not even afford him an assistant (later one was assigned to him), he had to set out himself to raise the money for the barracks. This was often a distasteful job, for some of the rich manufacturers and estate owners in the district treated him as a hired hand. Even the head of the monastery refused aid, and when Chekhov asked him what he would do with those who fell ill in his hostel, he piously replied that they were people of substance and would pay all charges themselves. Chekhov's neighbor, Count Orlov-Davydov, had given five hundred roubles to his doctor for the cholera campaign and then fled to Biarritz to escape the epidemic. To Suvorin, who was also abroad at this time, at St. Moritz, Chekhov wrote: "Before Count Orlov-Davydov's departure, I met his wife. Complete with enormous diamonds in her ears, a bustle, and not knowing how to comport herself properly. A millionairess. With such persons you experience a stupid schoolboy feeling of wanting to be rude." (*August 16, 1892*.) In the end, by virtue of his "beggar-like eloquence," he obtained the funds to provide two excellent barracks completely equipped, and five rather poor ones. And in addition, he begged "lime, vitriol, and assorted stinking junk from manufacturers" for all his twenty-five villages.

Chekhov's task, however, had hardly begun. For weeks he was continually on the go, in a horse and buggy, over roads that he did not know, visiting his villages, lecturing ignorant and mistrustful peasants on the epidemic, and collecting data for meetings of the Sanitary Council which he had to attend. As the cholera wave moved closer to the district, curiously enough many cases of typhus, diphtheria, and scarlet fever appeared in the villages. Chekhov was run off his feet attending the sick. In the short space of a few weeks he reckoned that he had treated about a thousand patients. "My soul is weary," he wrote in this same letter to Suvorin. "I'm bored. Not to belong to oneself, to think only of diarrhea, to start up at night from the dog's barking and a knock at the gate (haven't they come for me?), to drive jades along unknown roads, to read about and expect nothing but cholera, and at the same time to be entirely indifferent to this illness and the people you serve — that, my dear sir, is a mess that might do in anyone."

With the approach of cold weather the danger of the epidemic lessened. Actually, the nearest that cholera got to his district was a village twenty miles away where sixteen people were infected and four died. Chekhov asked to be relieved of his duties by the middle of October, and shortly thereafter he attended a dinner of the Serpukhov Sanitary Council, to whose executive committee he had been appointed, and official thanks were tended him for his efforts.

During the following summer, 1893, a milder cholera scare arose in the neighborhood, and once again Chekhov agreed to serve. Although no cases turned up, he fulfilled all his duties. But this time he felt particularly irked at being confined to the area when he very much wished to travel abroad. For the Sanitary Council he wrote two detailed reports, covering the years 1892–1893, on the temporary dispensary he had set up at Melikhovo to service cholera victims and other illnesses.

Although initially Chekhov had felt a certain elation over his participation in this program of social medicine, in the end he grew impatient and then finally revolted against the hard work. It was a temporary reaction which he had experienced several times before, probably because his complete preoccupation with his "legal wife" had utterly banished all thought of his "mistress" — writing had to be put aside entirely during the cholera epidemics. He felt harried by the demands on his time. No money was coming in. He threatened to throw up medicine entirely. "It is not good to be a physician," he concluded a letter to Suvorin on August 2. "It is terrible and dull and repulsive. . . . A girl with worms in her ear; diarrhea; vomiting; syphilis — *phui!!* Sweet sounds of poesy, where are you?"

Nevertheless, Chekhov's activity as a country doctor at a time of epidemic not only intensified his aroused social sense, but for the first time in his life gave him the exhilarating feeling of belonging to a definite social entity typical of Russian existence at that time — the rural community dominated by the County Council. Though he had been instinctively opposed to organized effort for human betterment and had refused a salary as a County Council physician in order to preserve his freedom of action, he now enthusiastically praised the organized efforts of his rural colleagues to stem the tide of spreading disease. Tolstoy, with his scorn for doctors, Chekhov asserted, ought now to adopt a more respectful attitude toward medicine and the participation of educated people in welfare activities. In contrast to the ignorance and chaos that used to prevail in the past in the face of epidemics in the countryside, Chekhov declared, the intelligent endeavors of this rural educated class had performed wonders in holding down the mortality rate. It gave him a choked feeling, he told Suvorin, to observe how city critics like Burenin in *New Times* poured forth their venom on this class. And he wrathfully condemned a socialistically-minded writer[1] charged with taking advantage of the epidemic to promote riots among the masses. "If our socialists actually exploit cholera for their own ends," he wrote, "then I shall despise them. Employing vile means to attain good ends makes the ends themselves vile. Let them ride on the backs of doctors and medical assistants, but why lie to the people? Why assure the people that they are right in their ignorance and that their crude prejudices are holy truth? Can any splendid future possibly justify this base lie? If I were a politician, I would never resolve to hold up the present to shame for the sake of the future, even though they promised me tons of bliss for a grain of foul lying." (*August 1, 1892.*)

« 2 »

Suvorin's disdain for Melikhovo saddened Chekhov, who had fondly hoped he would be a frequent visitor and might even buy an estate in the neighborhood. He wrote his friend that the place had lost half of its value because of his unwillingness to visit. A slight coldness developed in their relations. When Suvorin invited him abroad in the summer of 1892, there was more acrimony than envy in Chekhov's refusal; he seemed to resent his rich friend's swanking it in Europe while he was tied down to Melikhovo by the cholera epidemic. However, when Suvorin fell ill in October, Chekhov at once responded to his telegram and went to Petersburg to tend him. And he wrote Leontiev-Shcheglov of the illness, which turned out not to be serious: "I don't know what to tell you. . . . For me this would be such a loss that I think I would age by ten years." (*October 30, 1892.*)

Suvorin himself must have worried about his young friend when he learned, at the end of 1892, that Chekhov had taken up with the liberal magazine *Russian Thought*. Before his death the actor Svobodin had interceded with Lavrov, who wrote a gracious apology for the offensive remarks he had printed about Chekhov two years previously. Soon Chekhov was having luncheons and dinners in Moscow with Lavrov and Goltsev, that other editorial pundit of *Russian Thought*, whose fussy professorish ways and academic liberalism had at one time amused him.

[1] Here Chekhov refers to the ethnographer and writer, N. M. Astryev, who at this time was accused by the government of causing cholera riots. It is possible, however, that economic factors also played their part in the riots.

Over cigars and wine Chekhov discovered admirable qualities in these men whose liberal views he had been somewhat contemptuous of, and for their part they enjoyed his wit and occasional pranks, and eagerly looked forward to his contributions to their monthly.

This new alliance with a liberal magazine was in keeping with Chekhov's developing views. Yet when he informed Suvorin that he intended to contribute to *Russian Thought*, he quickly softened the blow by promising to send a story to *New Times*. His feeling of gratitude to his old friend was still proof against his growing detestation of the reactionary writers of his newspaper. The two of them even projected at this time a new periodical, which, like the several collaborations they planned, never materialized.

However, Chekhov's connection with *Russian Thought* soon threatened his intimate friendship with Suvorin. A chance occurrence was the immediate cause of hard feelings. In the scandalous bankruptcy of the company which Ferdinand de Lesseps had formed in France to finance the building of the Panama Canal, it was freely rumored that a Paris collaborator of *New Times* had accepted a bribe of five hundred thousand francs to influence public opinion in the lawsuit that followed. Suvorin's eldest son, Aleksei, who by now played a large role in directing his father's newspaper, went to Paris to investigate the charge and to rehabilitate *New Times* in public esteem. In his efforts, unfortunately, he represented himself as a champion of the whole Russian press which, he claimed, had been calumniated abroad by the accusation leveled against *New Times*. At this, *Russian Thought* ran an article ridiculing his pretensions. To make matters worse, Zhitel, a regular columnist of *New Times*, wrote a piece, with clear anti-Semitic overtones, damning an exhibition of the eminent Jewish sculptor, M. M. Antokolsky.

In answer to a letter from Suvorin, who harshly belabored *Russian Thought* for attacking his son, Chekhov in effect called a plague on both publications. He held no brief for the article in *Russian Thought*, he explained, but nevertheless he deplored the maliciousness with which regular contributors to *New Times*, Suvorin's son and Zhitel and Burenin among them, had been vilifying personalities and causes. And he pleaded with Suvorin not to attempt to answer the attack in *Russian Thought*.

For some time now the mud-slinging type of criticism, a commonplace in the Russian press, had been positively revolting to Chekhov.

Shortly before this incident he had written Suvorin about D. I. Pisarev, a celebrated critic of the 1860's. Commenting on his well-known article on the poet Pushkin, he declared: "Pisarev is the grandfather and father of all the critics of today, including Burenin: the same pettiness in disparagement, the same cold and conceited wit, the same coarseness and indelicacy in their attitude to people." (*March 11, 1892.*)

Chekhov's own criticism, though often sharp, was free of envy, meanness, or petty personalities. Turgenev, whom he was rereading at this time, he found charming but not nearly as good as Tolstoy, who would "never grow old. His language will age, but he will always be young." However, Turgenev's *Fathers and Sons* he found "magnificent" and "a work of genius." But he had little praise for the other major novels. Except for his secondary female types, which he felt were remarkably drawn, Chekhov condemned as "trash" Turgenev's heroines, nearly always regarded by other critics as his finest creations. He described them as insufferably artificial, crystal-ball gazers crammed with high-flown notions out of harmony with their place in society. "When you recall Tolstoy's Anna Karenina," he wrote Suvorin, "all these Turgenev ladies with their seductive shoulders are not worth a damn." (*February 24, 1893.*)

Whatever discretion Suvorin may have practiced in the incident, his son called on Lavrov in the office of *Russian Thought* and slapped his face. Chekhov was outraged. "It means," he told his sister, "that all is ended between me and Suvorin, although he writes me sniveling letters. A son of a bitch who insults people daily and is noted for this strikes a man because they have scolded him. This is fine justice. It is vile." (*March 11, 1893.*) From Petersburg Brother Alexander wrote that both sons of Suvorin, Aleksei and Boris, were making life extremely difficult for him in his work on *New Times*. In the editorial office, he said, his colleagues were quoting the sons as charging Chekhov "with the blackest ingratitude. You, from beginning to end, are obligated to their old man for everything from money to glory. Without him you would be a nonentity. And as a token of thanks, you poke your nose into their family affairs and stir him up against his children."

Chekhov calmly replied that it was a matter of complete indifference to him what the sons of Suvorin thought, and as for the editorial office of *New Times*, he held most of its leading contributors in contempt. If he were worried over Suvorin's reactions to this quarrel with his sons, he gave no sign of it. Indeed, he waited for his old friend to take the first step. A penitent letter came, and Chekhov wrote Alexander: "This means that again all is as before." (*April 30, 1893*.) As yet the ties of self-interest and mutual devotion were too solid to be broken by such an incident, although Chekhov had once again gone on record in very positive terms against some of the journalistic practices of Suvorin's newspaper. A few months after this threat to their friendship, their correspondence became as warm and intimate as ever. When, in the summer of 1893, Suvorin announced his intention of going abroad again, Chekhov regretted that he could not travel with him because of his cholera duties at Melikhovo, and added: "In times of stress and dullness, where shall I go? To whom shall I turn? I fall into devilish moods when I long to speak and write, and except for you, I've no one with whom to correspond and to talk to at length. This does not mean you are better than all the people I know, but it does mean that I'm accustomed to you and that I feel myself free only with you." (*August 7, 1893*.) By the end of 1893 Suvorin's eldest son came to Moscow to make his peace with Chekhov.

« 3 »

Despite the many claims on his time during these first two Melikhovo years, Chekhov managed to keep writing at the center of his daily existence. It is surprising how much he published and how much more he planned over this busy period. The new sights, sounds, landscapes, people, and activities of Melikhovo and its surroundings spurred his imagination and filled his mind with subjects for his pen. The notebooks which he began to keep at this time contain, in addition to non-literary material, observations, character sketches, bits of dialogue, and descriptive passages that have a bearing not only on tales he was writing, but also on pieces designed for the future.

Though creation had long since become a positive need, Chekhov now had to write to meet his debts — in buying Melikhovo he had not anticipated heavy expenditures for improving the place. There were no rich authors in this world, he told Yezhov, and if he were in debt, that was the order of things. True, among Chekhov's literary contemporaries, very few achieved substantial earnings. Printings were small, for books rarely sold in large numbers, and contracts disproportionately favored publishers. After 1905, with the removal of censorship, the publishing business improved greatly and successful authors then earned much money. Comparatively speaking, however, Chekhov's income by this time was better by far than most of his writing contemporaries. By 1893 *In the Twilight* had had seven printings, *Motley Tales*, five, *Tales*, eight, *Gloomy People*, four, *The Duel*, four, and special editions of single stories and of his other collections had gone into more than one printing. So chaotically did he keep accounts that at one point he thought he owed Suvorin's publishing firm for advances when they actually owed him money. In addition, he had begun to receive small sums regularly for the reprint rights of a number of his stories published by *Intermediary*, and at the end of 1893 he was paid twenty-three hundred roubles by the publisher I. D. Sytin for the reprint rights of a series of his early tales. In fact, by 1893 he had reimbursed Suvorin for most of his loan toward the purchase price of Melikhovo, and had liquidated the mortgage held on the property by the former owner, who willingly reduced the sum upon Chekhov's offer to pay in full. He now owed only the bank mortgage. Though his output, talents, and the position he held in the literary world undoubtedly justified a much larger income, with judicious management of his affairs his earnings were adequate to support him and his family comfortably.

Chekhov's literary position was now generally recognized as the foremost one among contemporary writers of prose fiction. Critics praised him not only as an artist, but as a thinker; Brother Alexander wrote him that his Petersburg readers were interested in his social ideas. His stories had already begun to appear in English, French, German, and Czech; and various magazines were not only pressing him for contributions but also offering him attractive positions as editor. Modestly he scolded one publisher who advertised his name in huge letters as the author of a forthcoming story; he had been treated, he said, as though he were a dentist or a masseur. More than ever distinguished writers sought him out. It was conveyed to him at this time that Leo Tolstoy wished to meet him and had actually called at his old Moscow address. Although A. I. Ertel, author of the brilliant novel *The Gardenins*, received a refusal when he asked Chekhov to do a public reading, this initial meeting began a firm friendship between them. On Chekhov's initiative, eighteen of the leading writers and artists of Petersburg gathered for a convivial dinner, on January 12, 1893, at the Malo-Yaroslavets restaurant, a gesture of rare comradeship in Russian letters which he urged should be repeated at regular intervals.

Chekhov now usually wrote more slowly and with much care. He no longer turned out tales at the behest of editors and he told one who pushed him hard to regard him as a contributor who would send in pieces only when he could, even if that meant once in three years. And he tried to avoid taking any advance except for a tale he already had under way. In the light of the extraordinary rapidity with which he had written his early stories, it is interesting to find him now marveling at the speed with which Potapenko produced. "He can write about six-teen printed pages in a day and without a single correction," Chekhov informed Suvorin. "Once, in five days, he wrote eleven hundred roubles' worth. In my opinion this express-train writing is not at all a drawback, as Grigorovich thinks, but a peculiarity of talent. One village wench will thrash around like a sturgeon for two days before she gives birth; for another, to give birth is just like running into a lavatory." (*November 28, 1893.*) At times Chekhov sought relief from intense concentration on his writing in more or less mechanical work, such as copy-editing tales for *New Times*, which he still occasionally did, or even abbreviating Dumas's *Count of Monte Cristo*, a procedure he suggested to Suvorin when he spoke of his intention of publishing a translation of this novel. Chekhov bled it so drastically, he told Suvorin, that the novel looked like a person who had suffered from ty-phoid. Svobodin, observing this task at Melikhovo, drew an amusing caricature, in which he portrayed Dumas weeping copious tears as he stood behind Chekhov's chair and watched him slashing away at *The Count of Monte Cristo*.

In general, Suvorin's passion for French fiction was not shared by Chekhov. For example, he admitted that Zola's novel *Le Docteur Pascal* had some merit, but he disagreed with Suvorin that Pascal was the best character. He was invented and had something bad inside him, said Chekhov, whereas Clotilde was a human being, a personality, and had a waist and breasts that he could feel. And he strenuously objected to Zola's conception of the relations between the ancient Dr. Pascal and the young and attractive Clotilde. When he had diarrhea at night, Chekhov explained to Suvorin, he usually placed a cat on his stomach and it kept him warm like a hot compress. But one has to be a French-man, he continued, to make of Clotilde "a hot-water bottle for a gray-haired cupid with the spindly legs of a cock. It is offensive to me that someone younger and more vigorous did not make use of Clotilde; an old King David, worn out in the embraces of a young girl, is like a melon which, touched by the frost of an autumn morning, still hopes to ripen, for every vegetable has its day. . . . I'm not preaching morality, and no doubt my own old age will not be free from attempts 'to draw my bow,' as Apuleius says in the *Golden Ass*. Judged from a human point of view, there is nothing wrong in Pascal's sleeping with a young girl — that is his own personal affair; what is wrong is that Zola should praise Clotilde for sleeping with Pascal, and it is wrong that he should have called this perversion love." (*November 11, 1893.*)

Including *The Wife* and *The Grasshopper*, which have already been mentioned, Chekhov published twenty-one long and short stories, articles, and notes over 1892–1893, which appeared in no less than seven newspapers and magazines. He also did most of the writing on two other tales and completed his book, *The Island of Sakhalin*. An urge to return to the miniature tales of his early years, persistently nurtured by Leikin and perhaps furthered by his gift of the dachshunds, Quinine and Bromine, led Chekhov to submit four "trifles" in 1892, signed by pseudonyms, the last he ever published in *Fragments*. The short story, *In Exile* (*World Illustration*, 1892), drawn from Chekhov's experience in Siberia, is a poignant account of psychological erosion among those condemned by the law to live in this inhospitable land. Simeon, the ferryman, takes refuge in vodka and the illusory conviction that he wants absolutely nothing from life, a belief opposed by the unhappy Tartar exile who yearns for a sight of his mother and wife, because God made man for happiness, sorrow, and grief.

The Neighbors (*Books of the Week*, 1892) and *Big Volodya and Little Volodya* (*Russian News*, 1893) are two curiously contrasting short stories of human weakness in the relations of the sexes. In the first the naïvely "progressive" ideas of an unhappily married landowner and the daughter of his neighbor bring them together. Unlike the girl's compassionate brother, who senses the somber future of the affair, they are unable to perceive the futility of their eagerness to flout social conventions for the sake of their love. The second tale is a rather cynical revelation of the commonplace frailty of a pretty woman who marries Big Volodya, more than twice her age, for the creature comforts he can provide her, while she is passionately in love with his young friend, Little Volodya, who eventually seduces and then deserts her. Though her husband and seducer continue their genial companionship, the conscience-stricken wife seeks an escape in frenzied dissipation and in an orgy of self-pity.[2]

[2] In 1892, Chekhov also published his charming sketch, *After the Theater*, of a young girl's dreams of love (*Petersburg Gazette*), and another short story, *Fear*,

In the monthly *Russian Thought* appeared the two most notable productions of Chekhov during this period, *Ward No. 6* (1892) and *The Tale of an Unknown Man* (1893), both of them long stories. *Ward No. 6*, perhaps the darkest and most brutal of all his tales, created a tremendous impression and greatly enhanced his reputation. The social awareness that condemned a government for allowing human beings to rot in the prisons of Sakhalin is now turned upon the mental ward of a hospital in a remote provincial town. The good, kind, gentle Dr. Ragin, head of the hospital, has long since surrendered his reforming zeal in the face of local sloth and indifference and taken refuge in philosophy and history, and in vodka and salted cucumbers. In his retreat from reality he develops convictions which enable him to turn his back on the evils that surround him. Thought which leads to a profound striving for a full comprehension of life is all that man needs to be happy. Men must seek peace and satisfaction not in the world outside them, he declares, but in themselves. This belief allows him to over-look or to rationalize away all the filth, inefficiency, and corruption in the hospital he directs, for he has even come to the conclusion that the very existence of such hospitals is an evil. Meanwhile, the brutish watchman, Nikita, becomes the guardian of law and order in the institution, and with his huge fists he unmercifully beats the mentally unsound patients in Ward No. 6 for any real or imaginary infractions of the rules. One of these patients, Gromov, also a philosopher of sorts and with whom the gentle Dr. Ragin loves to argue in Ward No. 6, exposes the inhumanity of the hospital head's beliefs and argues the necessity for action and protest against any form of oppression and violence. Eventually a scheming assistant, eager to supplant Dr. Ragin, exploits the oddities of his behavior and has him declared insane and locked up in Ward No. 6. There the terrible fists of Nikita beat out of Dr. Ragin's head every last vestige of his quietist philosophy, and before he dies of a stroke his tormented conscience illuminates for him the horrible years of physical pain and moral suffering which his way of life had inflicted on many defenseless people.

In writing *Ward No. 6* Chekhov had worried over the absence of any love element, but he was very conscious of "the liberal direction" he had given the story. And liberal-minded critics acclaimed it as the greatest thing he had done and placed it at the top of current fiction.

which, along with several brief unsigned notes on a variety of themes in 1893, were the last of his pieces to appear in *New Times*.

The vaguely suggestive symbolism, however, not uncommon in Chekhov's best tales, puzzled them. Did Ward No. 6 symbolize "the mental prison" Russia, and its ferocious warden Nikita, the Tsar? And, in the humane, educated Dr. Ragin was Chekhov satirizing well-intentioned intellectuals who abstained from the cruel struggle of Russian life? Although Tolstoy was reported to have praised the story highly, did it represent Chekhov's final break with the Tolstoyan doctrine of nonresistance to evil? This uncertainty is part of the ineffable art of the story. The critic A. Skabichevsky pointed out that it was supremely difficult to say who were the healthy and who the spiritually ill people in the stupid society of this remote town, or where Ward No. 6 ended and the region of sane thinking began.

Though Chekhov received some extravagantly laudatory letters on Ward No. 6, curiously enough Suvorin wrote him that the story lacked an "alcoholic kick." Chekhov's reply contains an interesting statement on Russian literature and culture at that time, in which he modestly and quite characteristically underestimates his own contribution. In addition, he clearly indicates at last his rejection of complete objectivity in art and its corollary of portraying life just as it is, a development which no doubt his social experiences and thinking over the last few years had encouraged. Putting aside Ward No. 6, he writes: "Tell me, in all conscience, who of my contemporaries — that is, people from thirty to forty-five — have given the world even one drop of alcohol? Are not Korolenko, Nadson, and all the playwrights of today lemonade? Have Repin's or Shishkin's paintings turned your head? Charming, talented. You are delighted, but at the same time you cannot forget that you'd like a smoke. Science and technical knowledge are now passing through a great period, but for our sort the times are flabby, stale, and dull. . . . The causes for this are not to be found in our stupidity, our lack of talent, or in our insolence, as Burenin thinks, but in a disease which, for the artist, is worse than syphilis or sexual impotence. We lack 'something,' that is true, and it means that when you lift the robe of our muse you will behold there an empty void. Let me remind you that the writers whom we dub immortal or just simply good and who intoxicate us have one very important trait in common: they are going somewhere and summon you to go with them, and you feel, not with your mind but with your whole being, that they have a purpose, like the ghost of Hamlet's father, who did not come and disturb the imagination for nothing. Looking at some of them in terms of their caliber, they have immediate aims — the abolition of serfdom, the liberation of their country, politics, beauty, or simply vodka, like Denis Davydov; others have remote aims — God, life beyond the grave, the happiness of humanity, and so on. The best of them are realistic and paint life as it is, but since every line is saturated with a consciousness of purpose, as though it were a juice, you feel, in addition to life as it is, life as it should be, and you are captivated. And we? We! We paint life as it is, but beyond that — nothing at all. Flog us but we can do no more. We have neither immediate nor distant aims and in our souls there is a great empty space. We have no politics, we don't believe in revolution, we have no God, we are not afraid of ghosts, and personally I don't even fear death or blindness. He who wants nothing, hopes for nothing, and fears nothing, cannot be an artist. . . . You and Grigorovich think that I am clever. Yes, I'm clever enough not to conceal my illness from myself, not to lie to myself, and not to cover up my own emptiness with the rags of others, such as the ideas of the Sixties and so on. I won't throw myself down a flight of stairs, like Garshin; but neither will I flatter myself with hopes of a better future. I'm not to blame for my disease, and it is not for me to cure myself, for this disease, I must assume, has good purposes hidden from us and was not sent in vain." (*November 25, 1892.*)

This attack on a world that Suvorin had had a proud part in making displeased him. He believed that Chekhov's position was insincere and sent his letter to one of his favorite female contributors to *New Times*, Madame Sazonova, for the kind of reaction which he fully anticipated, and then conveyed her written comments to him. Chekhov promptly expressed his annoyance over Suvorin's indiscretion in showing his letter to a third person, and also over Madame Sazonova's views. His remarks are significant, for once again, and now more directly, they underscore the disavowal of his earlier belief that a writer must be concerned solely with life as it is and must not allow his own purpose to obtrude on a work of art. Madame Sazonova argues that the purpose of life is life itself; that the artist must value that which is, and that all his misfortunes come from persistently seeking lofty and remote aims. Here is real insincerity, Chekhov scolded. "She believes in 'life,' and that means that she does not believe in anything if she's intelligent. . . . I write that aims are lacking, and you realize that I consider aims necessary, and that I would willingly go in search of them; but Sazonova writes that man must not be lured by delights he can never attain. . . . If this is not a hag's logic, then surely it is a philosophy of despair. If someone sincerely thinks that high and remote aims are as little necessary to man as to a cow, that in those aims 'are all our misfortunes,' then nothing remains for him but to eat, drink, and sleep, and when he is weary of this, he may rush and dash his brains out against a corner of a box." (*December 3, 1892.*)

Chekhov had actually begun *The Tale of an Unknown Man* some five years earlier and had put it aside for fear that it would never get by the censor. There was some point in his fears, for one of the leading characters, the Unknown Man himself, is a revolutionary terrorist who takes a position as a butler with a government official, Orlov, in order to effect the assassination of his employer's father, an eminent statesman. His zeal for the cause, however, is undermined by his dawning love for Zina, Orlov's beautiful mistress, who has suddenly deserted her husband and descended upon her lover's bachelor quarters.

There are several palpable weaknesses in the story, especially in the unconvincing characterization of the Unknown Man — possibly caused by Chekhov's efforts to avoid the strictures of censorship — in the excessive intellectual attitudinizing, and in the rather limping conclusion. Orlov, on the other hand, is a brilliant portrayal of the cynical Petersburg man-about-town, for whom nothing is sacred, sincere, or honest. He quickly wearies of his mistress, regards her idealizing, self-sacrificing love for him as a transient infatuation, and shamelessly deceives her. Zina is one of Chekhov's most charming feminine portraits. Endowed with something of Anna Karenina's passionate integrity of the heart, she willingly risks society's harsh condemnation in the cause of illicit love. And like Anna, the realization that her idol has feet of clay inflicts a mortal wound to her self-esteem. Participation in the revolutionary activities of the Unknown Man, with whom she goes to Europe, offers Zina the possibility of revenging herself on the miseries of her past. But this last hope also vanishes when she finally learns that he had lost his revolutionary faith and dreams solely of making her his mistress. Like Anna, again, the only way out of the impasse is death; she poisons herself.

Of his literary friends, only I. Gorbunov-Posadov wrote Chekhov a highly favorable reaction to *The Tale of an Unknown Man:* "When we finished reading, along with the tears in my eyes at the end, a joyous feeling arose in my soul, a feeling of joy for our literature." Most of the reviewers, especially the liberal ones, wrote unfavorably of the work.

They could hardly fail to observe that the backsliding terrorist, the Unknown Man, no less than the Petersburg rake Orlov, lacked integrity. But in this respect Chekhov, like Tolstoy, had no use for the violence of revolution.

In reply to the skeptical Suvorin about whether he would ever finish and publish his book on Sakhalin, Chekhov wrote him on August 16, 1892: "No, I cannot abandon my baby. When boredom with fiction overcomes me, it is pleasant to take up with nonfiction. The question of when I shall finish Sakhalin and where I shall publish it seems to me unimportant." In fact, despite his absorption in other things at Melikhovo, Chekhov found time to work away at this project, especially over the summer of 1893. The suspicion that the head of prisons, Galkin-Vrasky, would use his influence with the censorship to prevent the publication of the book apparently entered into Chekhov's reasons for delaying it — until he had some evidence that this official would soon leave his post.[3]

Chekhov's need for money, however, as well as the enterprise of the editors of *Russian Thought*, brought the whole matter to a head. In June, 1893, they pressed Chekhov to publish the work serially in their magazine. He was reluctant to accept serial publication, but the financial terms were advantageous. He now began to concentrate on finishing. All that he had written, he informed Suvorin at the end of July, seemed false, not sufficiently forthright, and weighed down by a heavy pedagogical element. But now that he had begun to describe what a queer fish he had been on Sakhalin and what swine the officials were, the writing went easily and speedily and in spots even humorously.

The Island of Sakhalin began to appear in the last three issues of *Russian Thought*, 1893, and continued through five more issues of this monthly in the first half of the next year. Because of delays by the censor, it was not published in book form until 1895, when it appeared with some changes and with the additions of several chapters at the end. The study of over three hundred pages is a model of the scientific approach, bristling with facts, statistics, citations from authorities, and footnotes. But throughout the book Chekhov never loses sight of his primary purpose — a calm and factual demonstration of the senselessness and often brutal nature of the government's policy of penal servi-

---

[3] Actually, Galkin-Vrasky did offer objections to the appearance of *The Island of Sakhalin* in print, but he was overruled.

tude on Sakhalin. If he had not had the censorship to contend with, the book would probably have been more outspoken.

Many of Chekhov's admirers, apparently expecting a highly subjective work or perhaps a dramatic and artistic one, such as Dostoevsky's brilliant account of prison life in Siberia in *The House of the Dead*, showed their disappointment. Nor did *The Island of Sakhalin*, considering the fact that it came from Chekhov's pen, achieve any great *réclame*, a fact which has perhaps influenced critics and students of Chekhov to underestimate the significance of the book and to overlook its genuine artistic qualities. For a work of this kind, however, it received a substantial number of reviews and notices in the press, a few of which praised it highly, one of them extravagantly asserting that if Chekhov had written nothing else, his name would still receive an honorable place in the role of Russian literature. The book was widely read, was commented upon most favorably by prison experts in Russia and abroad, and markedly influenced other investigations of Sakhalin. Further, the Russian government, prodded by the study, sent its own officials to survey conditions on Sakhalin, and eventually certain reforms were ordered in the administration of the island and in the conditions under which the convicts lived.

Perhaps the fact that *The Island of Sakhalin* is so little read nowadays has also contributed to the notion that it is entirely devoid of artistic merit. The high art of selectivity in the mass of material Chekhov was dealing with is everywhere in evidence; the facts, scenes, and incidents are those calculated to impress and to move the readers. It is even possible to catch him at turning a dull but necessary passage from one of his learned sources into a thing of beauty. Any sensitive reader must conclude that though the book is essentially a scientific study, it could have been written only by the literary artist Chekhov. Once the work had begun to appear in print, he wrote the critical Suvorin: "I'm glad that this rough convict's garment hangs in my literary wardrobe. Let it hang there!" (*January 2, 1894.*)

« 4 »

Only a man of powerful will could have done all this writing and fulfilled his various other self-imposed duties during these first two years at Melikhovo, when for weeks on end Chekhov was also unwell. His illnesses were subjected to the same inexorable will that precluded any self-pity or surcease to his labors. He had always despised laziness, weaknesses and sluggishness of the emotions. In a moment of annoyance, he might burst out to a correspondent like Suvorin about a vile, despicable malady — not syphilis, but his old enemy, hemorrhoids, "with pain, itching, tension, no sitting, no walking, and such irritation throughout the entire body that one feels like lying down and dying." (*April 26, 1893.*) He knew that he ought to have an operation, but again he gritted his teeth and rode out the storm till the next time.

Chekhov continued to adopt somewhat the same attitude to his cough, which all noticed was becoming worse. He airily dismissed it as "bronchitis," or would jokingly use the word "consumption." He displayed a kind of false manliness about his illnesses, as though he were ashamed to pay attention to such matters which concerned only people of little spirit. But the hateful word was on his mind now, and it gave him no rest. It had begun to occur not infrequently in his correspondence. A number of his peasants at Melikhovo suffered from tuberculosis and one died under his care. Potapenko relates how he and Chekhov were on a train from Moscow to Melikhovo. A passenger near them coughed continually. This fact led Chekhov to make his acquaintance — he was an estate owner from Vologda — and to inquire about his health. The man told of his symptoms — dizziness, trouble with his heart, hemorrhoids, and occasional blood-spitting — and that he had been to several doctors and was taking treatment. These were Chekhov's symptoms. " 'All this is nonsense,' Chekhov said. 'You must get out of Vologda Province. Go somewhere in the tropics and live there for two or three years.' " And when the man objected that he was saddled with an estate and a large family, Chekhov earnestly replied: " 'Leave your family, sell the estate, and go! Otherwise it will turn out badly for you.' "

This was advice that Chekhov himself could not take, for, like the man from Vologda, he too shrank from selling an estate and deserting his family. It was a tragedy that he was a doctor and had this dread disease, for otherwise he might have sought the diagnosis of a physician, which he refused to do. He believed his own diagnosis was logical, but it was the logic of self-deception — his naïve assumption that because he had lived several years since he had first experienced a hemorrhage, he would not die of tuberculosis. To be sure, as a doctor, he fully realized how inadequate was the treatment of the disease in those days, but he was aware, at least, of the therapeutic value of a warm, dry climate. The only concession he appears to have made was to give up for a time or cut down on cigars and liquor. He coughed, he said, because he was accustomed to cough, and he went to considerable lengths to conceal his affliction from friends and family, especially his mother and sister. Misha tells that at Melikhovo once, when he was a chance witness of Chekhov's coughing up blood, his brother sternly cautioned him: " 'This is only a trifle. You must not say anything to Masha or Mother.' "

Despite his evasions, news of Chekhov's rather frequent spells of illness at Melikhovo at this time spread. Alexander reported from Petersburg that Leikin was going around weeping and telling any who would listen that his dear friend Chekhov was dangerously ill with tuberculosis and would soon die. Chekhov replied with a quip: "Thank Leikin for his sympathy. When apoplexy gets him, I'll send a telegram." (*October 29, 1893.*) And he added that he did have a cough, but that he was far from tuberculosis.

On the other hand, with a kind of prophetic clairvoyance, he wrote Suvorin (*August 24, 1893*) that his heart bothered him and at times he found it hard to breathe. But he was not worried, he said, and continued: "The enemy that kills the body usually comes imperceptibly, wearing a mask, as for example when you are ill from consumption and it seems to you it is not consumption but merely a trifle. It follows, then, that that is terrible which you do not fear, but that which arouses your apprehension is not terrible. . . . I know that I shall die of a disease which I do not fear. Hence, if I'm afraid, then it means that I shall not die. However, this is nonsense."

« 5 »

But it was not really nonsense. Chekhov had obviously torn away the mask: he did fear. In the long sleepless nights of coughing, which worried his mother as she listened in her bedroom, he saw before him the stark and grim image of his fate. In these moments of truth no deception or wishful thinking could conceal from his medically trained mind the inevitable consequences of his steadily deteriorating health. The wasting form of his poor brother Nikolai must have haunted his memory. The villain was Time. How much of it was left to him?

This race with Time intensified the restlessness so characteristic of his nature. Chekhov had now realized his dreams of owning an estate. He was surrounded by the trees and flowers that he loved to nurture, and the numerous friends whose company he enjoyed, and he had climbed to the foremost place among contemporary writers. However, there were many moments of acute discontent at Melikhovo over these

two years when he passionately yearned to abandon it all. He was growing old, he declared, not only in body but in spirit. His interest in life
had dried up; he experienced a kind of spiritual revulsion to it. "Life is
short," he wrote Suvorin on May 28, 1892, "and Chekhov, from whom
you are expecting an answer, would like it to pass with a brilliant flash
and crackle. . . . I long terribly, terribly for a steamer and for freedom.
This smooth pious life disgusts me." In one sentence he would praise
the charms of Melikhovo and in the next insist that he was deluding
himself, that all one could expect from life was evil: mistakes, losses,
illnesses, weakness, and all sorts of abomination. Melikhovo was all
right, he self-consciously assured Suvorin on another occasion, but it
would be a thousand times better to be off on a spree with him, on a
boat. "I want freedom and money. To sit on a deck, pop bottles of
champagne, talk about literature, and in the evenings — women." (*July
28, 1893*.) To some extent, perhaps, the endless struggle for money
contributed to these fits of moodiness. "My soul longs for breadth and
height," he declared to Suvorin on June 16, 1892, "yet I'm compelled
to live in a cramped condition pursuing scoundrelly roubles and kopecks. There is nothing more banal than bourgeois life with its two-
kopeck pieces, its absurd conversations, and its useless, conventional
virtue. My soul has withered from the consciousness that I work for
money and that money is the center of my activity. This gnawing feeling, together with my sense of justice, makes authorship a contemptible
pursuit in my eyes; I do not respect what I write, and am apathetic and
bored with it. . . ."

In these periods of depression, when — as Chekhov affirmed — an
impersonal and weak-willed state of mind, which explained the whole
structure of his life, gripped him, his immediate reaction was to get as
far away from his family as possible. One must have a purpose in life,
he said, and when you are traveling you have that purpose. In letter
after letter during 1892–1893, he announced his intention or desire to
set out for Sakhalin again, or South Africa, Japan, India, Constantinople, Madeira, France, Italy, and the Caucasus. With Leo, the son of
Tolstoy, he made definite plans to attend the opening of the World's
Fair at Chicago in April, 1893, a trip which he regretfully abandoned.
He repeatedly asked Suvorin to invite him to his place at Feodosiya.
When foreign travel seemed impossible, he planned to rent an apartment in Petersburg where he could live a few months every year. And
for this purpose, he set about obtaining, with Alexander's aid, an official

passport, which he lacked. This obliged him to enter government service as a medical official; when he received the necessary document, he promptly resigned his post.[4]

The discontents of man are not always easily discoverable. Beneath the characteristic surface optimism of Chekhov ran a deep underground stream of sadness. Its sources were his secret. At moments, however, almost against his will he reveals one source, especially in his correspondence. At this particular time, an agonizing awareness of the approaching consequences of his disease breaks through, as it did at the time of Nikolai's death from tuberculosis. And now, as then, his reaction was almost a frantic effort to run away from his thoughts, to forget them in the pleasures and experiences of travel.

However, another source of his unhappiness which also prompted him to escape from home was his family, although here his feelings are always veiled in allusions in his letters and can be interpreted only by reading between the lines. Statements of others, who knew the situation well, are also indicative. Despite his devotion to his parents, especially to his mother, it was now only a consuming sense of duty that kept him chained to the hearth he had made for them. The sophisticated world of mind and spirit which he claimed as his own was entirely incomprehensible to them. They regarded him as a kind of miracle, and had nothing to contribute to him, or he to them. When the house was full of company, this total disparity was less painful. But Chekhov plainly dreaded the long winter evenings at Melikhovo when there were often few or no visitors. Then the old-fashioned ways of his mother and her gentle nagging about his health, his excessive hours of work, and his bachelor state irritated him. And the dinner table conversation over the banalities of household tasks and family history became insufferably boring; or his father would persist in a long-winded argument with some hanger-on, such as Ivanenko, on whether it was better for man to be ignorant or educated.

The curtain was momentarily raised on this unhappy state of affairs by brother Alexander during a visit to Melikhovo in June, 1893. He departed hurriedly, obviously after a family quarrel, and while waiting for his train at the little station of Lopasnaya, scribbled the following

[4] Because of his lowly birth and the fact that he now lived in the provinces, Chekhov was not entitled to a permanent passport, which was necessary for traveling within Russia as well as abroad. His previous traveling had been done under a temporary permit, issued on the strength of his medical diploma.

note to Chekhov: "I left Melikhovo without saying good-by to Alya-trimantran [a made-up nickname of the brothers for their father]. He was asleep, and may God be with him. May he dream of salmon and olives. Mother said that I offended her by going, for she thought '*that you, Sasha* [Alexander] *would persuade Antosha.*' Sister grew sad when I got into the carriage. This is in the order of things. What is not in the order of things is my state of mind. Don't be angry because I fled in cowardly fashion. I'm very sorry for you. Indeed, I'm also a weak man, and cannot coldly look upon another's sorrow. I suffered all the time as I watched you and saw the frightful life you lead. This morning Mother, not realizing what she was doing, poured oil on the fire in the woods. In her opinion you are a sick man; day and night she worries about your welfare and peace of mind, and the chief reason is disorder. . . .

"In a word, all of them, without exception, wish you well, but the result is a complete misunderstanding. In order to allay all these misunderstandings and mutual offenses, the tears and unavoidable sufferings, the stifled sighs and bitter tears, only one course lies open to you, your recent resolution — to go away. Mother absolutely does not understand you, and will never understand you. . . . You are a good and excellent man. God has endowed you with a spark. With that spark, you are at home anywhere. Whatever it costs, you must keep your soul alive. Abandon everything; your dreams of a country life, your love for Melikhovo, and all the work and feeling you have poured into it. There is more than one Melikhovo in the world. What sense is there in letting the Alyatrimantrans devour your soul the way rats devour candles?! And it will not take long to devour it."

Here was Chekhov's own advice to the consumptive from Vologda. And how eagerly, in moments of depression, he yearned to accept it! In the depths of his consciousness, however, he probably realized its fallaciousness. For him the truth was inscribed on the pendant which he wore on his watch chain: "For the lonely man, the desert is everywhere."[5]

[5] One of Chekhov's friends asked where he got this inscribed pendant. He replied: "It was my father's. When my grandfather saw it on him, he said: 'Pavel must marry.' And they married him."

CHAPTER XIV

"Twice Rejected"

ON JANUARY 12, 1894, Chekhov wired his brother Ivan in Moscow to inform Lavrov, Nemirovich-Danchenko, and Potapenko that he would be in the city the next day to lunch with them. Lavrov, taking advantage of this visit, arranged a dinner several days hence in honor of the fiftieth anniversary of Grigorovich's literary career. Recently the Petersburg writers had celebrated the event and Lavrov, in whose *Russian Thought* the ancient Grigorovich had occasionally appeared, felt that the Moscow literary fraternity could do no less. Even if the Muscovites were unable to equal the splendor and distinction of the Petersburg dinner, Lavrov was comforted by the expectation that they would have as their chief speaker the distinguished Chekhov, whose talent Grigorovich had "discovered" eight years previously. Invitations were hurriedly sent out and space was reserved in the Hermitage Restaurant.

When he was informed of the plans, Chekhov became gloomy and remained silent all day. By evening, however, his customary humor had returned. Potapenko, who tells of this incident in his *"Several Years with A. P. Chekhov,"* relates that Chekhov would interrupt the conversation with what appeared to be phrases from a speech:

" 'Dear and worthy writer . . . We are gathered here in an intimate family . . .' Then, after a moment of silence, 'Our friendly literary group, in your presence, profoundly esteemed . . .'

" 'What is this?' I asked.

" 'Why, this is your speech which you'll deliver at the dinner in honor of Grigorovich.'

" 'Why is it mine? You'd do better to think up something for yourself.'

" 'Well, tomorrow I'm leaving.'

" 'Where to?'

" 'To Melikhovo.'

" 'But how can you? Grigorovich, his letter . . . Such relations . . . Finally, the disappointment of Lavrov and all the others . . .'

" 'To be sure, this is understandable. I was discovered by Grigorovich, and consequently I ought to make a speech. Not to say something simple, mind you, but precisely a speech. And in this speech to say, without fail, how he discovered me. Otherwise I'll be considered ungracious. My voice must tremble and my eyes fill with tears. In this situation I'll not be able to make such a speech however much they pester me, because I simply cannot do it. Then Lavrov will arise and tell how Grigorovich discovered me. And Grigorovich will heave himself up, come over to me, stretch out his arms and embrace me, and will weep from tenderness. Old writers love to weep. Well, that is his business, but the principal thing is that I ought to weep and I'm not able to do this.' "[1]

Chekhov was not joking, Potapenko observed. To play the part of a hero in any scene caused him acute suffering. The dinner took place without Chekhov. Potapenko lied nobly on his behalf, announcing that Chekhov had fallen ill and had had to return to the country. But old Grigorovich unwittingly saved him any further embarrassment by at once taking the floor and launching into a speech about Chekhov, how he had discovered his talent, their correspondence. . . . Shortly after the event Chekhov informed Suvorin that those who had attended were now saying to each other, "How much we lied at that dinner and how much *he* lied!" (*January 25, 1894.*)

At times, indeed, Chekhov's behavior puzzled the writers and artists he liked to dine with in Moscow restaurants on his trips from Melikhovo. Both Nemirovich-Danchenko and Potapenko wondered whether it was even possible to become a truly intimate friend of Chekhov. Many no doubt deeply loved him, and in turn he profoundly understood them. Perhaps it was his unusual capacity to see through people that kept him from revealing himself fully to his friends. Often a kind of impenetrableness surrounded his personality. Potapenko conjectures that Chekhov was nearly always in the posture of a person constantly creating, and Masha's testimony supports this notion. When free of the responsibilities of being a host, his usual attentive and friendly glance in conversation would become fixed, as though it had been turned inward, contemplating something mysterious and important that was taking place in his soul. The general conversation might be on

---

[1] The writer I. A. Bunin, a close friend of the family, once asked Chekhov's mother and sister if they ever saw him weep. "Never in his life," they both positively replied. Alexander observed that even at the death of their brother Nikolai, Chekhov never wept.

Marxism and he would suddenly ask: "Have you ever been to a stud farm? By all means you must visit one." One friend was talking to him about his recent trip to Italy, but eventually the conversation drifted into the field of literature. He noticed that Chekhov was clearly thinking of something else and the next moment he abruptly asserted, apropos of nothing: "One ought to go to Australia." Then, blushing slightly, he returned to the subject being discussed.

On the other hand, with his inexhaustible wit he would charm his Moscow literary friends, enter into lively disputes with Goltsev and Lavrov of *Russian Thought*, or play unexpected pranks on one of the editors of *Russian News*, "Granddaddy" Mikhail Sablin, who adored Chekhov.

« 2 »

One afternoon at Melikhovo, when all save Misha were enjoying their after-dinner naps, Chekhov dashed out of his bedroom, rubbing his eyes and forehead. Misha asked if he had had another attack of the "twitches." "No," Chekhov replied, "I've just had a terrible dream. A black monk appeared to me." The impression of the dream was so powerful, Misha recalled, that it took Chekhov some time to calm down. That summer he began his story, *The Black Monk*, which appeared in *Artist* in January 1894.

The tale is unlike anything Chekhov had written previously and he never returned to its supernatural subject matter. It was an attempt, he told Suvorin, to depict a young man suffering from the mania of greatness. *The Black Monk* is an absorbing study of mental disease, with perhaps shrewd moral implications. A spectral black monk appears to the mediocre philosopher Kovrin, whose nerves have been wrecked by overwork, and convinces him that he is among the chosen of God, the servant of eternal truth. Kovrin's fears about his sanity are neatly dismissed by the black monk, who explains that geniuses are above the common herd and are entitled to a modicum of instability. The clash between Kovrin's morbid state of exaltation and prosaic reality further unhinges his mind, and in the end his sanity, and his young bride and her father, both of whom worship him, are sacrificed to this illusion of greatness. Chekhov may well have been satirizing in Kovrin those members of the intelligentsia who elevated themselves above the common herd in the conviction that they possessed the secret of universal happiness.

Leontiev-Shcheglov quoted the editor of *Artist*, F. A. Kumanin, as saying that *The Black Monk* was "not an important thing, very watery and unnatural. . . . But you know, there is Chekhov's name. . . . It would be awkward not to print it." Readers were puzzled by the story, and Suvorin's suspicion that Chekhov had depicted his own spiritual malaise in Kovrin amused the author. Critics have also been sharply divided, some asserting that it was Chekhov's complete failure in his mature creative period, others that it was one of his best tales. A friend reported to Chekhov that Tolstoy, after reading it, had declared with unusual animation and tenderness: "This is charming! Ah, how charming it is!"

That same month *Russian Thought* published *A Woman's Kingdom*, another story which Chekhov had written in 1893. Its merchant milieu, factory scenes, and squalid proletarian tenements provide a striking contrast to the idyllic life of the gentry and the supernatural atmosphere in *The Black Monk*. The problem of the good-hearted but lonely heroine, Anna, whose inheritance of a large factory and much wealth has in no sense dimmed the memory of her working-class origin, is the conflict between her natural desire for marriage and the limitations thrust upon her by her recently acquired social position. A prisoner of but not a slave to her money, she considers marrying one of her attractive workmen, but in the end she has to admit to herself that this deviation from propriety would be out of place in her new world. The excellence of the story is to be found not only in the completely realized characterizations of Anna, of the lawyer Lysevich — an ingratiating gourmet — and of the sharp-featured, sly female pilgrim who urges the lonely heroine to sin in her youth, for there will be enough time left for forgiveness, but also in the realistic scenes in the factory, the workers' hovels, and in Anna's kitchen on Christmas Eve.

Chekhov's early manner of combining the grotesque and farcical with deft touches of the pathetic and somber is revived in the short story *Rothschild's Fiddle*, which appeared in the Moscow newspaper *Russian News* in February. The losses of old Yakov in his coffin-making sour his disposition and eventually dominate his whole existence. When he measures his sick wife for a coffin, he methodically enters this item as a loss in his account book. In his literal-mindedness, he finally decides that only in death are there absolutely no losses; there, all is gain. But in the end his wife's death stirs up in him a train of remorseful thinking. The hard-bitten old Yakov sorrowfully reflects that in their fifty-two years of life together he had never once spoken a kind word to this crushed woman, who with a quiet smile had welcomed her demise as a long-sought release. And just before his own death Yakov wonders why people, with hatred and malice in their hearts, hinder each other from living. As a last gesture of repentance for his harsh treatment of Rothschild, a fellow musician in a pick-up orchestra, he presents him with his precious fiddle. Like the best of Chekhov's early and similar tales, this piece is a perfect little study in the harmony of mood and tone.

« 3 »

Although Chekhov had a number of themes for stories in his head, and one for a comedy to be called *The Cigarette Case*, which he ultimately dropped, and although he had jotted down in his notebook observations and situations relating to several of these subjects, other matters now claimed his attention and time at Melikhovo. The commitment to civic duty which had led him into the cholera epidemic continued to involve him in community enterprises. Country doctors, especially P. I. Kurkin and I. G. Vitte, often sought his aid, and he found it difficult to deny the requests of these able members of the "rural intelligentsia" whom he so much admired. In January he attended a meeting of the Sanitary Council at Serpukhov, and in February participated in organizing a local charitable society whose purpose was to arrange for the care of convalescents and to build nurseries for the children of sick women. He also helped to organize a library for the Serpukhov hospital. Meanwhile, guests flowed in and out of Melikhovo with carefree abandonment — on February 25 Father Chekhov, whose humorless diary never seemed to distinguish between important and unimportant matters, entered the fact that eight guests had just left. Further, Chekhov's domestic and estate burdens were increased at this time by the departure of his faithful aid Misha, who had accepted a new post at Uglich.

And now the coughing, which had patently begun to worry Chekhov at the end of the previous year, grew worse. His "bronchitis," as he still described it, plagued him and wore him out. He kept threatening to go to the warmer climate of the Crimea; and suddenly, on March 2, he left for Yalta.

Spring was already well advanced at Yalta. The white summer houses with broad balconies and well-kept gardens dotted the many-tiered town and shone in the bright sunlight, reflected by the sea. Against the sky-line tall dark cypresses stood on guard.

Chekhov stayed at the Hotel Russia. He tried to improve the state of his health by giving up cigars and liquor and by keeping regular hours. Both friends and unknown admirers soon upset this regimen; and, as always, he found it hard to resist what he called his "bacchanalian mood." He helped to organize a concert at the hotel for the singer Viktor Mirolyubov, and many came simply because they knew that Chekhov would be in the audience. Later Mirolyubov, as the publisher and editor of the popular monthly *Journal for All*, became a close friend. With the aging and half-forgotten Moscow actress, Nadezhda Medvedeva, who was staying in his hotel, Chekhov talked daily about the theater — conversations, he said, which undermined his desire to write the play he had promised himself to do at Yalta. But when Vyacheslav Fausek, a young reporter, contrived to meet Chekhov, the reporter was promptly dragooned into running a piece in the local newspaper about the old actress, because Chekhov insisted "It will be pleasant for her to be convinced that people know and have not forgotten her."

Fausek managed to see a good deal of Chekhov and left an interesting account of this visit to Yalta. For the young reporter hailed from Taganrog and had attended school there, so they had much in common to talk over. To Fausek's anxious query, when he received an invitation to visit Chekhov at the hotel, whether this would interrupt work, Chekhov cheerfully replied: "I'm always busy. But I can always put aside my work. I love to take things easy and to chatter!" And he flashed his warm smile as he glanced inquiringly through his pince-nez. Fausek had some reason to be timorous, for he had observed how Chekhov was pursued by the curious at Yalta. People, aware that he was a physician, would come to him on the pretense of illness. A rich baron called to invite him to dinner one evening, and Chekhov refused on the score that he did not accept invitations to dine with people unknown to him. Later, he discovered that the baron had invited a group of Yalta high society to the dinner "to meet Chekhov." Fausek relates that once a young lady knocked on Chekhov's door and the author politely asked what he could do for her. Agitated and confused, she blurted out: "Pardon . . . Forgive me! I wanted . . . to look at you! I never . . . saw a writer!"

Chekhov also met the political exile I. M. Radetsky, who wished to give a lecture on the physical education of children. This subject interested Chekhov, and not only from the point of view of his medical practice. As his stories indicate, everything about children concerned him deeply, and he had definite opinions on their education, behavior, and psychology. Radetsky, who had to leave Yalta in a few days, despaired of obtaining the necessary official permission to give a public lecture in time. It occurred to Chekhov to obviate this difficulty by disguising the lecture as a "colloquy," but the next problem was to find a place to deliver the talk and to assemble an audience in a hurry. Fausek solved it by offering the use of his house and informing the people invited on such short notice that "Chekhov would be present."

Upon hearing from Fausek that the literary critic Leonid Obolensky had just arrived in Yalta and wished to meet him, Chekhov hastened to oblige. For Obolensky, in 1886, had been one of the very first critics to praise Chekhov's stories in a long article in which their author was compared with Korolenko, and Chekhov had never ceased to be grateful for this early recognition. They got together several times, and at their last meeting they discussed, strangely enough, the death penalty — particularly whether it was possible to demonstrate its harmfulness from a purely utilitarian point of view.

Fausek had ample opportunity to converse with Chekhov, for he persuaded him to sit for a bust executed by Fausek's wife, a sculptress of some ability. Their house was perched high upon a cliff, and as they sat on the veranda, with a wonderful view of Yalta and the sea, the insatiably curious reporter plied Chekhov with questions about his writing. Chekhov told him that he had published only half of what he had written and that he had a suitcase full of unprinted manuscripts in various stages of completion. He said that he loved success but that he also loved to see the success of others and to help them achieve it. When Fausek asked why the Russian life he portrayed in his latest stories was so gloomy, Chekhov replied: "My God! I've written enough of the cheerful sort of thing and much that was simply farcical. It is time for me to look on life more seriously." And in answer to a query on whether he drew his characters from nature or created them in a more complex way, he said: "I never draw directly from nature. However, this does not save me from certain difficulties as a writer. It occasionally happens that some of my acquaintances, with no basis whatever, recognize themselves as the heroes of my tales and get offended with me."

Early in his stay at Yalta Chekhov learned that Potapenko had gone to Italy, and not long after that he heard that Lika Mizinova also left for abroad to study voice. Shortly thereafter it did not come as any surprise to him to be informed that both of them were in Paris.

Lika's interest in improving her voice was no doubt genuine, but her presence now in Paris with Potapenko, a married man, must have signified to Chekhov something other than the pursuit of an operatic career. Did he care? If so, the record gives no evidence of it. In his reminiscences of Chekhov, Nemirovich-Danchenko remarks of him: "It seems that he had great success with women. I say 'it seems' because neither he nor I liked to chat on this theme. I offer this judgment on the basis of rumors that went the rounds."

While at Yalta, however, Chekhov received a letter from Lika from Berlin, the tone of which patently suggested that something had gone radically wrong in her affair. "I should like to reach my destination as soon as possible," she wrote, "and I also want to look around Berlin, for I'll soon die and will see nothing more." This from his beautiful Lika, who in her letter said that she had been "twice rejected" by him, and of whose deep feeling for him he could have no doubt.[2]

However, Chekhov could not have been aware of the seriousness of her plight at this point, and he preferred to answer her dark hint with one of his typical serio-comic letters which she knew so well: "Though you frighten me in your letter by saying that you are going to die soon, and you twit me with having thrown you over, thanks anyway. I know perfectly well that you are not going to die and that no one has thrown you over." He then launches into a light, amusing account of his doings at Yalta: helping the local aristocracy with their rehearsals of *Faust*; eating lamb fried in deep fat, onion fritters, and mutton chops in the company of the mistress of a girls' school, and writing endlessly. When she becomes a great singer and makes enormous sums, marry him, he begs her, so that he'll be able to live without working. And he concludes by urging her to take a quick trip back to Russia in June to visit him at Melikhovo. Following up a disarmingly casual comment in her letter, he writes: "You run into Potapenko occasionally. He'll also be returning to Russia this summer. If you make the trip with him, it will cost less. Let him buy your ticket and forget to pay him (you

[2] Besides the indications of her love for him in Lika's letters, Chekhov's sister, not long before her brother's death, told I. A. Bunin that Lika had been in love with Chekhov. See I. A. Bunin, *O Chekhove* (*Concerning Chekhov*), New York, 1955, pp. 66-67.

won't be the first). But if you won't make the trip, I'll go to Paris." (*March 27, 1894.*)

Actually Chekhov's health did not improve much at Yalta despite the sea air and lovely weather. After barely a month, the town seemed terribly dull to him. He could think of nothing but Melikhovo, and besides his money was running out. A few days before he left, on April 3, he wrote an interesting letter to Suvorin, in which he once again struck out against the Tolstoyan morality which had for so long shadowed his thoughts. "From childhood," he declared, "I have believed in progress and cannot help believing. . . . I liked intelligent people, sensibility, courtesy, wit, and was as indifferent to people's picking their corns, and having their leg wrappings emit a stench, as to young ladies who walk around in the morning with their hair done up in curl papers. But Tolstoyan philosophy had a powerful effect on me, governed my life for a period of six or seven years; it was not the basic premises, which had been known to me earlier, that acted on me, but the Tolstoyan manner of expression, its good sense, and probably a sort of hypnotic quality. Now something within me protests; prudence and justice tell me that in electricity and steam there is more love for man than in chastity and in abstinence from meat. War is evil and the court system is evil, but it does not therefore follow that I must go around in bast shoes and sleep on the stove along with the worker and his wife, etc., etc. This, however, is not the crux of the matter, not the 'for' and 'against'; it is that somehow or other Tolstoy has already passed out of my life, is no longer in my soul, and has left me, saying: 'I leave this your house empty.' I am free from this tenant." (*March 27, 1894.*)

« 4 »

For a time the familiar summer life at Melikhovo exercised its usual charm on Chekhov. He made new paths, planted flowers, chopped down dead trees, and chased the hens and dogs out of the garden. The fragrance of freshly cut hay intoxicated him. One had only to sit beside a haystack for a couple of hours, he wrote Leontiev-Shcheglov, "in order to imagine oneself in the embraces of a naked woman." (*July 5, 1894.*) Nearness to nature and idleness, he decided, were the necessary elements of happiness.

A new project absorbed him — building a small lodge in the berry bushes beyond his cherry orchard to take care of the overflow of guests.

He would have the men sleep there and the women in the main house. However, when it was finished he called it a "doll house." For with his slender means he could afford only two rooms and an attic and a porch, all adorned with a gingerbread design. The view from the porch of the flowering cherry and apple trees was lovely, but in the winter one had to dig a trench through the snow — often the height of a man — to approach the Lodge. Eventually he formed the habit of re-treating to it to escape his guests when he wanted to write. The Lodge became his "spiritual oven," and it was there that he wrote *The Sea Gull.*

That summer, in recognition of his civic activities, Chekhov was chosen a member of the Serpukhov Zemstvo (County Council) for three years, and he was also appointed to the executive committee of the local charitable society. And with a large group of rural doctors he participated in a tour of inspection at a district insane asylum. The place provided material for alienists rather than psychologists, he re-marked, in describing one of the inmates who assured him that Russia would come to ruin if it did not recognize the divinity of the Metro-politan of Kiev.

Sunburned from his work outdoors and with a few more pounds added to his frame, Chekhov enjoyed the illusion of returning health. But while strolling with a neighbor one day, something seemed to snap in his chest, and he experienced a feeling of suffocation and a ringing in the ears. He walked toward the porch, where visitors were sitting, and all he could think of was how awkward it would be to fall down be-fore these people and die. After drinking some water and taking a brief rest, he recovered. However, the significance of his "palpitations of the heart," which he had been mentioning to friends for some time, now stalked his mind.

Grim warnings such as this activated the discontent which seemed always to be a definite part of Chekhov's experience of happiness. He had hardly begun to enjoy the pleasures of Melikhovo that summer when he began pressing Suvorin to take a trip with him. First it was down the Volga to visit old monasteries and graveyards, which had a fascination for both of them. Then he suggested a trip down the Don — or the Dnieper — or, if he wished, to Feodosiya — or to Switzerland. In fact, he was willing to go almost anywhere if only Suvorin would agree. In justification he wrote him: "About ten years ago I was con-cerned with spiritualism, and Turgenev, whose spirit I evoked, said to me: 'Your life is nearing its decline.'[3] And in very fact I keenly want every sort of thing just as though it was the last meal before a fast. I seem to have tried everything. . . . But some inner force, like a presentiment, urges me on to make haste. Perhaps it is not a presentiment, but simply regret that life flows on so monotonously and tamely. A protest of the soul, one might say." (*July 11, 1894.*)

Suvorin failed him, however, and Chekhov seized upon Potapenko, who had returned from abroad, without Lika and quite uncommunicative about her. At the beginning they set out on a trip down the Volga. But they got only as far as Nizhny Novgorod when they met P. A. Sergeenko, Chekhov's old Taganrog schoolfellow and devoted admirer. In his memoirs Potapenko writes that the fear of having this chattering, boasting, and spiritually empty Tolstoyan on their hands caused Chekhov impulsively to change his plans. For, explains Potapenko, Chekhov was unable to be anything other than polite and friendly, for he felt that he must respond to whatever was good in people. Chekhov put it a bit differently in his explanation to Suvorin — the heat, the dry wind, the noise of the fair they were observing, and the conversation of Sergeenko suddenly made him feel so suffocated, so ill at ease, and so sick that he fled ignominiously to the railway station and returned to Moscow with Potapenko. Ashamed to go back to Melikhovo after such a brief time away, they decided to visit the Lintvarevs on the Psyol, where Chekhov's sister had spent a brief vacation earlier that summer. It turned out to be a happy choice.

Shortly after returning to Melikhovo, Chekhov received news that his Uncle Mitrofan, who had been ailing for some time, was now seriously ill and was asking Chekhov to come in his capacity as a physician. His affection for this uncle was strong, and so was his desire for a reason to leave Melikhovo again. He set out for Taganrog on August 24.

« 5 »

While Goltsev was delivering a public lecture on the literary characteristics of Chekhov,[4] the honored author was complaining to his brother Alexander that he found it difficult to combine a desire to live with a desire to write. Nothing was more irksome or less poetic, he felt, than the relentless pressure to write in the face of need; it took away

[3] Chekhov refers here to an actual experience while attending a spiritualist's séance as a youth. He then made use of it in his story, *A Terrible Night* (1884).
[4] Goltsev's lecture was published in the May 1894 issue of *Russian Thought*.

the joy of life and plunged one into apathy. Nor would he now stoop, like the bourgeois writer Barantsevich, to taking the easy way out by writing for the unsophisticated public that ate salt beef and horse-radish sauce with relish and did not care for artichokes and asparagus. Such bourgeois writers were false, he declared to Suvorin, because they could not help being false. "They are vulgar writers perfected. These vulgarians sin together with their public, and the bourgeoisie are hypocritical with them and flatter their narrow virtue." (*August* 15, 1894.)

This critical frame of mind is reflected in what little Chekhov did write over the summer of 1894. Once, in answer to the charge of critics that he was a pessimist, he told Bunin that *The Student*,[5] an optimistic tale which he had written at Yalta, was his favorite among all his stories. And his brother Ivan, when asked, replied that Chekhov regarded this brief tale as his most finished piece. Though the annals of literature have demonstrated repeatedly that authors are rarely the best judges of their own works, in this instance it is easy to understand Chekhov's preference. For in *The Student* he has achieved to perfection that exquisite harmony of form and content, of mood and substance which Tolstoy must have had in mind when he described Chekhov as the Russian Pushkin in prose. On the eve of Good Friday, a poor seminary student tells two simple people he encounters by a campfire the Biblical story of how Christ was bound and taken before the high priest, and of how Peter, fearful of his own life, denied Him thrice. The artless simplicity of the student's narration moves his hearers to tears. And as he goes on his way his soul is filled with joy, for he suddenly realizes that the past is linked with the present by an unbroken chain of events flowing one out of another. He had seen both ends of the chain. The truth and beauty which guided life there by the campfire and in the yard of the high priest had continued without interruption to this day. And the "inexpressible sweet expectation of happiness, of an unknown, mysterious happiness, took possession of him little by little, and life seemed to him rapturous, marvelous, and full of lofty meaning."

In *The Teacher of Literature*,[6] an entirely different note is struck,

[5] *The Student* was first published in *Russian News* (April 16, 1894) under the title *At Evening*. The title was changed in the collection *Stories and Tales*, 1894, and it remained *The Student* in subsequent collections.

[6] The first chapter, entitled *The Philistines*, was initially published in *New Times* (November 28, 1889), and the second chapter, with the title *The Teacher of Literature*, appeared in *Russian News* (July 10, 1894). Both chapters appeared together as one tale, *The Teacher of Literature*, in the collection *Stories and Tales*, 1894.

one of social satire. The life of the well-to-do provincial family, the Shelestovs, is depicted as a constant round of horseback parties through the city park, visits to their farm, stupid conversations at home, childish games, dances and lavish meals. And in the school where the hero Nikitin teaches, a low level of learning is patronized. A master does not dare to make the usual speech over the grave of a friend and colleague, because the headmaster had not liked the deceased. Young Nikitin, who has worked his way up from poverty to become a respected teacher, is at first flattered by the attention of the Shelestovs, who have two marriageable daughters. But the initial happiness he finds in marriage to the youngest is soon poisoned by the idleness and banality of his wife and her family. The story ends with Nikitin making an entry in his diary which foretells his approaching rebellion — and suggests perhaps Chekhov's own distaste for this way of life: "Where am I, my God? Vulgarity surrounds me everywhere. Boring, insignificant people, dishes of sour cream, pitchers of milk, cockroaches, stupid women. There is nothing more terrible, more offensive, more dull than vulgarity. To escape from here, to run away today, or else I'll go mad!"

More of this spirit of social satire, with perhaps a deeper personal note, rings out in *At a Country House*, which appeared in *Russian News* shortly after Chekhov left for Taganrog that August. The boringly loquacious Rashevich subjects his guest, Meier — an examining magistrate, and prospective suitor of one of his host's daughters — to a tiresome monologue on his favorite theme: the good things of life come from the well-born of society. All the finest qualities of mankind, he argues, and all the gifts of science and art belong exclusively to the aristocracy. All the great Russian writers, he declares — Pushkin, Gogol, Lermontov, Turgenev, Goncharov, and Tolstoy — were not the offspring of clerks. When Meier objects that Goncharov came from a merchant family, Rashevich counters by doubting Goncharov's artistic abilities. "In fact," he thunders, "as soon as your dirty-faced fellow gets above himself, he begins to sicken, to waste away, to lose his mind, and to degenerate; and you'll not find anywhere as many neurasthenics, mental cripples, consumptives, and starvelings of every kind as among these fine birds." The patient Meier can take no more, and to the dismay of both his host and his daughters, he explains that he himself comes from the working class. Meier leaves the house in a delightful scene of embarrassed small talk, which Chekhov, born of peasant stock, mercifully contrives in order to save the face of the blueblood Rashevich.

« 6 »

On August 31 the *Taganrog Herald* announced in its columns: "At present the famous writer Anton Pavlovich Chekhov, a native of Taganrog, is visiting here. He has been summoned in his capacity as a physician to his seriously ill relative, M. E. Chekhov, an elder of St. Mikhail's Church. From here the talented writer will proceed to the Crimea." Displeased by this local tribute, Chekhov called at the editorial office and scolded them for printing it. And he told one of the reporters that it would be more to the point if the press would frequently remind the people of how neglected their city was, that it lacked waterpipes and a decent public library.

Chekhov rendered what medical assistance he could to Uncle Mitrofan, but he saw that the old man had not long to live. With his usual kindness, he encouraged and even made arrangements for his uncle's daughter Sasha, then studying dressmaking, to go to Moscow to complete her training. He was so bored in Taganrog, he said, that he had learned to take snuff, and after a stay of only six days he escaped by rail to Feodosiya.

Not even the pleasures of Suvorin's company at Feodosiya could hold Chekhov for long. The weather had turned cold and windy, and there were no stoves in Suvorin's large summer house. Since his coughing had intensified, Chekhov had become extremely susceptible to weather conditions. He sought the warmth of the sun like a lazzarone, and in his letters, now, Egypt and Africa were countries that held a magic charm for him. After several days he left for Yalta, and there received the news of Uncle Mitrofan's passing. "I loved my deceased uncle with all my soul and I esteemed him," he wrote his cousin. (September 9, 1894.) Some of the pleasanter memories of his unhappy childhood were connected with this kindly, religious old man.

Chekhov soon left Yalta for Odessa, a gateway to Europe, — for he had a tentative arrangement with Suvorin to accompany him abroad. Something kept urging him on. Was it the half-joking promise he had made in March to see Lika if she failed to come to Melikhovo? On setting out for Taganrog he seems to have had no firm intention of continuing farther. In fact, he had writen Goltsev on September 4 that he would be back in Moscow in ten days. A feeling of opulence may have had something to do with his decision, for he had just received a fresh accounting from Suvorin's publishing firm that he owed in advances less than a thousand, with a large stock of his books on hand on which he had already paid his share of the printer's bill. "I'm rich," he jubilantly declared in a letter to Natalya Lintvareva. No doubt his search for the sun, as well as Suvorin's desire to go to Europe, helped him to overcome any wavering. In any event, on September 14 he left for abroad, his declared destination being Abbazia, a fashionable health resort on the Adriatic. At first, surprisingly enough, he did not inform his family, not even his closest confidant, sister Masha, who still imagined that he was at Feodosiya. And with a guilty conscience he confessed to himself that they would be hurt because his frequent journeys had caused them worry enough already.

Chekhov and Suvorin arrived at Vienna, by way of Lvov, on September 18 and he wrote Lika at once: "You stubbornly don't answer my letters,[7] dear Lika, but I'll continue to annoy you by inflicting more of them on you. . . . Potapenko told me that you and Varya Eberle[8] would be in Switzerland. If this is so, write me exactly where in Switzerland so I can look you up. Of course, I'd be delighted to see you. Address: Abbazia, *poste restante*. . . . I implore you, don't tell anyone in Russia that I'm abroad. I left secretly, like a thief. . . . I'm not at all well. I have an almost continuous cough. Evidently I've let my health slip just as I did you."

From Abbazia, three days later, he wrote Lika again, a brief note to tell her that he could not stand the gray, rainy weather and would leave for Nice, and he gave her an address there. On the way to Nice he made brief stops at Trieste, Venice, Milan, and Genoa. At last the weather turned warm and his spirits rose. From Milan he finally wrote Masha, for he had become worried about whether she had enough money on hand for the family expenses and the interest payment to the bank on his loan. Rather self-consciously he recapitulated his itinerary since he left Russia and the things he had seen and done and bought: three silk ties at Venice and a piece of glass painted in the colors of paradise. He praised the excellent beer abroad which, he said, threatened to turn him into a drunkard, the musical comedy of Milan, and a staging of Dostoevsky's *Crime and Punishment* in which he had found Italian acting superior to Russian. And he was looking forward, he

[7] Up to this point, in 1894, we have a record of only three letters of Chekhov to Lika. But others may have been lost.

[8] Varya Eberle was a close friend of Lika and of the Chekhov family, and had gone abroad, like Lika, to continue her operatic studies.

wrote, to visiting the superb cemetery at Genoa, having already inspected a crematorium at Milan. "It is regrettable that they don't burn the living here, for instance, heretics who eat meat on Wednesdays." (*September 22, 1894.*)

When Chekhov arrived in Nice on October 2, he found a number of Lika's letters from Switzerland which had been pursuing him through his various changes of address. At last he learned the details of her wretched situation. After reciting her fruitless pursuit of him, she confessed in one of her letters: "Then I . . . finally fell in love with Potapenko. What was there for me to do, Daddy? You always managed to escape and shove me off on someone else." The letters reflect her loneliness, and her fear for her future and that of her unborn child. "It is clear," she wrote on September 20, "that I'm condemned, that in the last analysis all whom I love will disdain me. That is why I want very much today to talk with you. I'm very, very unhappy. Don't laugh. Of the old Lika there remains not a trace, and whatever I may think, I can hardly say that it is all your fault!" Her one wish was to see him. "Hurry and let me know when you think of coming here, if you are thinking of it," she wrote him the next day. "I anticipate that you'll not be surprised by anything. If you don't fear to be disillusioned in your former Lika, then come. Of her, little remains. Yes, how these six months have overturned my whole life! . . . However, I don't think you will cast a stone at me. It seems to me that you were always indifferent to people, to their inadequacies and weaknesses."

Having read this sad parcel of news, Chekhov wrote his sister Masha that he was weary of traveling and that after a few days in Paris he would start for home. "I had counted on seeing Lika in Paris, but it now develops that she is in Switzerland. . . . Potapenko is a . . .[9] and a cad." (*October 2, 1894.*) Masha had some knowledge of the situation, for Lika had written her earlier from Paris to describe her unhappy existence — Potapenko stealing away daily from his wife and children there to hold secret meetings with her, and eventually abandoning his pregnant mistress to take his family to Italy.

Chekhov was plainly hurt by Lika's unjustifiable charge of his indifference to people; however "indifferent" he may have been to her ardent desire to win him for a husband, in any event he had been unwilling to play the part of a Potapenko in his relations with Lika.

[9] In the published letter in the Soviet edition, the dots indicate the deletion of an unprintable word.

But one detects in his answer to her letters, on October 2, a suggestion of coldness, or better perhaps a desire to avoid personal involvement in her unhappy circumstances: "Unfortunately, I cannot go to Switzerland, for I'm with Suvorin, who must leave for Paris. I'll be in Nice from five to seven days, in Paris for two to three, and then on to Melikhovo. In Paris I'll be staying at the Grand Hotel.

"You ought not to have written about my indifference to people. Don't languish — be cheerful, and take care of your health. I make you a low bow and firmly, firmly press your hand." He then adds a consoling postscript: "If I had only received your letter to Abbazia, I would have come to Nice by way of Switzerland and seen you, but now it would be inconvenient to drag Suvorin along."

His beautiful Lika remained abroad to have her baby alone, and Chekhov, after a few days in Paris, left for Moscow where he arrived on October 14. Did his conscience trouble him? There is some reason to suppose that it did. With a keen insight into his nature, Lika had pleaded in her letter of September 20: "Though all this is obscure, I think it is all clear to *you*. Not without reason are you a psychologist. At times it seemed that I would not be able to endure it any longer. But I have faith in *you*. . . ." Yet he failed to seek her out in her misery. Perhaps it was because he feared himself in such a confrontation, for he realized his weakness in the face of human suffering and loneliness. Besides, Lika had been less than dignified in her repeated charges that he was partly to blame for her misfortune. His ambivalent feelings on this occasion may well have been correctly diagnosed by his sister Masha, who wrote in her reminiscences: "I do not know what was in my brother's mind; but it seems to me that he strove to overcome his feeling for Lika. In her were certain traits alien to him: a lack of character and a fondness for a bohemian existence. And what he once wrote her in a joking spirit perhaps ought to be regarded in all seriousness in the light of later events: 'A huge crocodile lives in you, Lika, and as a matter of fact I'm doing the wise thing in obeying common sense and not my heart, which you've bitten into.'"

« 7 »

After his travels Chekhov willingly settled down at Melikhovo over the fall and winter months. During his absence the faithful Masha had redecorated the rooms and had new stoves put in, so that all was snug and warm against the cold. Only the mice annoyed him. The villians had eaten the wallpaper in the living room up to five feet from the floor, he wrote Masha in Moscow, and he pleaded with her to buy something to eliminate them. For the remainder of 1894 he made only one trip to Moscow.

Despite his worsening health, Chekhov continued his full energetic daily existence, which contrasts so sharply with the popular image of him as an inert, passive and melancholy singer of tender melodies in a minor key. Though he liked to joke about his laziness, and, when the pressures on him were great, to dwell upon the virtues of an idle life, in reality nervous energy and a dominating will drove him on to prodigies of labor. He resumed his medical practice when he returned to Melikhovo. In driving over the rutted roads to neighboring villages to visit the sick, all his innards, he told Masha, were turned inside out. When the Province School Council invited him to become a trustee of the Talezh village school, he gladly accepted this post, which ultimately involved him in extensive activities. That November, he also served on the Serpukhov jury. In the several cases he sat on he was made foreman, and the fact that nobles and peasants, the educated and the uneducated, could have such power of decision in vital matters impressed him. On the other hand, Chekhov was not impressed by the capabilities of the urban intelligentsia, in the face of the impending coronation of Nicholas II, to make known to the nation the need for reform. Their desires were extremely indefinite, he wrote Suvorin; they were naïve, superstitious, had little knowledge, and were afraid to voice their own opinions. When Suvorin countered by asking him what a Russian should desire, Chekhov responded: "Here is my answer: *To desire.* Most of all he must have some sort of desire, temperament. One gets weary of this sourness." (*December 12, 1894.*)

In addition to civic responsibilities, there were the ceaseless personal favors asked of Chekhov which he rarely refused. In the course of several weeks, for example, he urged Suvorin, at the request of the author Ertel, to send books to a library in Voronezh for peasants; provided a detailed bibliography on the Amur region which his friend Gorbunov-Posadov asked for, and at the same time requested him in return to aid an impoverished writer whose needs had been thrust upon Chekhov; agreed to help raise funds among his friends to erect a monument to Peter the Great in Taganrog; sent off a large parcel of books to the public library in that town; criticized the stories which budding authors sent him; and, with the aid of his sister, even undertook to teach two peasant servant girls how to read.

A mysterious form of personal aid at this time has left all commentators baffled. Chekhov wrote to Goltsev: "Obtain from somewhere *for me* two hundred roubles . . . and send them to the prodigal son. Hold this letter in confidence, and don't show it to anyone. I'll repay the two hundred roubles at the beginning of December." And in a postscript he wrote: "I'm ashamed to trouble you, but, in truth, I don't know how to act otherwise." (*November 25, 1894.*) It is known that the money was given to the "prodigal son," but who he was and what relation he bore to Chekhov are unknown.

Of course, in the midst of all these activities and of entertaining the usual guests, the major portion of Chekhov's time was spent on his writing. There were moments when he longed to conquer new worlds in fiction. "I'm tired of one and the same thing," he declared with some levity to Elena Shavrova, "I want to write about devils, terrible volcanic women, sorcerers — but alas! they demand well-intentioned novellas and tales out of the life of the Ivan Gavrilyches and their wives." (*December 4, 1894.*) To his growing volumes of collected stories was added another this winter: *Stories and Tales,* a careful reworking of his best pieces over the last two years, and this time published by the popular firm of I. D. Sytin, who offered a better financial arrangement than Suvorin had.

In December *The Tale of an Old Gardener* appeared in *Moscow News,* which he had been favoring as an outlet for his brief pieces since he deserted *New Times.* This slight story has the flavor of Tolstoy's moral tales, although it lacks their utter simplicity of language. The legend narrated by the old gardener is intended to illustrate the moral that it is better to let the guilty go unpunished rather than destroy absolute faith in the goodness of man. In the description of the doctor, whose murderer the judges refuse to convict because they simply cannot believe that anyone would kill such a good and universally revered man, Chekhov seemed unconsciously to draw upon his own traits: "He was a consumptive; he coughed; but when they summoned him to the sick, he forgot his own illness and did not spare himself. . . ."

But the literary effort that principally occupied Chekhov over the winter months of 1894 was the long story *Three Years,* which he had begun to think about much earlier according to various entries relating to it in his notebook. He finished this major undertaking in the middle of December and turned the manuscript over to the editors of *Russian Thought*, where it was published at the beginning of 1895.[10]

Three Years may be regarded as Chekhov's last attempt to write a novel (it runs to eighty-six pages in the Russian edition), but again he seemed incapable of making the necessary sustained effort; the ending clearly suggests the continuation — Yartsev's dawning love for Yuliya as the resolution of her unhappy marriage. The core of the story is the married life of Laptev, the younger son of a wealthy Moscow merchant, and his wife Yuliya, the daughter of a provincial doctor. *Three Years* is essentially a profound psychological study of character, but in it Chekhov is also intent upon revealing the deterioration of a merchant family portrayed against a brilliantly realistic backdrop of Moscow life. There are a few autobiographical touches that recall the miseries of Chekhov's childhood, and many details of the old merchant's business must have been drawn from Chekhov's knowledge of Gavrilov's enterprise, for which his father had worked. Laptev, whose will to live has been stunted by an upbringing spent in fear of his father, makes a furtive bid for independence after his university education. His marriage to Yuliya is another step in the process of emanicipation and of achieving a purpose in life; but the struggle ends after he discovers that she has married him to escape her father and live in Moscow. When she does experience a genuine affection for him after the death of their child, it is too late. Like Anna in *A Woman's Kingdom*, Laptev has become a captive of the very wealth he detests, but he realizes that in the end it will blunt his sensibilities and turn him into a philistine. On the whole, contemporary critics did not like *Three Years*, but in the richness of its detail, its rather leisurely pace, and the psychological density in the analysis of a considerable number of characters, it offers more of the flavor of a novel than does anything else Chekhov wrote.

A week after finishing *Three Years*, Chekhov informed Masha, who was spending Christmas with the Lintvarevs, that the house was full of guests. He also mentioned that he had received a letter from Lika, who wrote: "It will soon be two months since I've been in Paris and not a word from you. Is it possible that you've turned against me? . . . Without you I feel entirely forgotten and rejected! I'd give half my life to be at Melikhovo, to sit on your divan, to talk with you for ten minutes,

---

[10] The censor cut out some of the sentiments regarding religion in the story. "This kills every desire to write freely," Chekhov informed Suvorin. "As you write you feel as though a bone were sticking in your throat." (*January 19, 1895.*)

to dine, and in general to live as though this whole year had never existed, that I had never left Russia, and that all was as of old!"

The child that Lika had given birth to in Europe was her only comfort. But shortly after her return to Russia, this little girl died. It seemed to Lika that she had nothing left to live for. Her lover Potapenko thought it advisable to settle with his family in distant Petersburg. Chekhov saw him briefly in Moscow at the end of December, 1894, and somehow he found no difficulty in continuing his friendly relations with the "cad." In fact, together they bought and presented a silver cigarette case as a Christmas present to their mutual friend "Granddaddy" Sablin. But by now Chekhov had become conversant with all the sad details of the wretched Lika-Potapenko romance. Here was the stuff of drama, and Chekhov had a play on his mind.

CHAPTER XV

"Man Will Become Better Only When You Make Him See What He Is Like"

THE FAMILY HAD FINISHED SUPPER. It was a cold January night in 1895. Suddenly the dogs barked outside. A knock at the door. Masha went, followed by Chekhov. In the circle of light made by the open door stood Tatyana Shchepkina-Kupernik. Someone lurked hesitantly in the shadow — the artist Levitan. For more than two years he had refused to see Chekhov because of the belief that his friend had portrayed him in the character of the lecherous artist in *The Grasshopper*. For a moment the two now faced each other in silence, then warmly shook hands and began to talk about the trip to Melikhovo as though nothing had ever happened. What Levitan did not know was that after several futile attempts previously at a reconciliation, Chekhov had persuaded Tatyana to coax the artist into accompanying her on a visit to Melikhovo. For Chekhov, an old friend was always better than two new ones.

"I returned to what has been precious, to what in fact had never ceased to be precious," the temperamental Levitan wrote Chekhov after this renewal of their friendship. Again they began to see each other at regular intervals. Chekhov liked to visit Levitan's studio in Moscow to view his work in progress. The poetry of paint seemed to complement wonderfully the poetry of words in the Russian landscapes that both artists loved to portray. Although Chekhov regarded Levitan as easily the best Russian landscape painter, one who had the divine gift of hearing the mysterious voices of nature, he now began to detect the loss of something he had valued most highly in his canvases. "He is no longer painting youthfully, but with bravura," Chekhov wrote Suvorin. "I think women have exhausted him. The dear creatures give love and take from man just a trifle: his youth. It is impossible to paint a landscape without pathos, without ecstasy, and ecstasy is impossible when one has gorged oneself. If I were a landscape artist, I would lead almost an ascetic life; I would have intercourse once a year and eat once a day." (*January 19, 1895.*)

But Levitan was an epicurean whose excesses sometimes terminated in fits of melancholy and suicidal tendencies. Perhaps Chekhov was not inordinately surprised to receive a letter, in July of this year, from Levitan's latest conquest, a wealthy lady by the name of A. N. Turchaninova, informing him that the artist, then staying at her estate, had wounded himself in an attempt to commit suicide. She pleaded with Chekhov to come, as a close friend of Levitan rather than as a physician, to help him recover from his mood of deep depression. As it turned out, it was the rivalry between a mother and daughter for the artist's affections which had somewhat unhinged him. Chekhov set out for the estate in the Novgorod province. He found Levitan with a superficial scalp wound caused by a bullet and remained with him for five days in an effort to alleviate his low spirits. Apparently he succeeded, for not long after his departure Levitan wrote him: "I don't know why, but those few days which you spent with me were the most restful of the whole summer."

Fact and fiction bearing on *The Sea Gull,* which Chekhov would soon write, have emerged from this friendly mission. Misha traces the incident of the slain bird in the play to one which, he says, his brother told him in connection with this visit: after an altercation in the house, Levitan tore the bandage from his head, grabbed his gun, and left. When he returned, he threw at the feet of his lady a sea gull he had shot. Another version of this incident is that Levitan placed at the feet of Chekhov's sister a gull which he had needlessly destroyed and vowed never to do so again. Since there is no substantiation for these stories, it is also possible that the actual experience of Levitan's wounding a woodcock, when out hunting with Chekhov, inspired the scene in the play. Although Chekhov found the Turchaninova estate, situated on a large lake, sad, swampy, and unpleasant, there is good reason to suppose that this house and lake were in his mind when he created the famous setting for *The Sea Gull*.[1]

« 2 »

Though Chekhov had assured Fausek in Yalta that he did not draw his characters from life, many of them, like Levitan, have been identified as people among his numerous circle of friends and acquaintances, however much he transformed them by the alembic of his art. However, the popular contemporary belief that the able and attractive actress Lidiya Yavorskaya was the prototype for the heroine of *Ariadne*, a story which Chekhov wrote in the first half of 1895,[2] appears to be a rather far-fetched identification.

As one of the group of gay young ladies Chekhov made merry with on his trips to Moscow, Yavorskaya clearly attracted him, for a time at least. He made a point of attending the plays she acted in, and Shchepkina-Kupernik, another of the group, declares in her memoirs that Chekhov was interested in Yavorskaya and carried on a flirtation with her. And Leontiev-Shcheglov, in his diary, notes that Chekhov had a weakness for this actress. When Chekhov entered her drawing room, she would drop on her knee before him, and, mimicking the part she played in an Indian drama, would repeat her line: "My only one, my great one, my divine one . . ." Chekhov also mentions a letter in verse which she wrote him.

Moscow gossips were soon talking about a love affair. Lazarev-Gruzinsky, in his recollections of Chekhov, tells how he bumped into him one day as he was emerging from somewhere behind the scenes of the Korsh Theater, where Yavorskaya acted.

" 'Anton Pavlovich, what are you doing here?' I asked in surprise. 'I thought you were in Melikhovo. Ah, yes! I'd forgotten that you are courting Yavorskaya!'

" 'Where did you hear that?'

" 'Where? Why, all Moscow is talking about it.'

---

[1] For a discriminating analysis of the fact and fiction which grew out of Chekhov's visit to Levitan on this occasion, and which subsequently became connected with *The Sea Gull*, see David Magarshack, *Chekhov the Dramatist*, London, 1952, pp. 180-182.

[2] *Ariadne* appeared in the December issue of *Russian Thought*, 1895.

" '*Tout Moscow, tout Moscow!*'[3] Chekhov laughed, and in further conversation (we went off together) he denied the courting."

In fact, Chekhov gladly recommended Yavorskaya to Suvorin as an actress for the theater which Suvorin had taken over in Petersburg, remarking that she was intelligent, dressed well, and that if she could overcome her tendency to pose, she would be a fine actress. Suvorin employed her, and in answer to his suspicious inquiry as to whether she was living with Korsh, Chekhov denied this but added that Korsh was very jealous of her. In general, Chekhov told Suvorin, she was altogether too avid a publicity seeker.

When *Ariadne* appeared in print, however, rumormongers peddled the notion that the story was a pasquinade on Yavorskaya because she had jilted Chekhov. Ariadne in the story is certainly one of the most cruelly dissected Becky Sharp types in all of Chekhov's fiction. Extremely beautiful and desirable, she uses the men who pursue her, even the one who adores her with an entirely selfless love, with utter callousness. Whatever shred of conscience she has left she employs, not as a guide, but as a kind of accomplice in designing schemes of self-betterment. Affectation and pretense are the dress and loose ornament of her conversation and meetings; no scruple is allowed to stand in the way of being successful and fascinating.

Some of the surface features of Yavorskaya's personality may appear in Ariadne, who, however, is not an actress but the sister of a bankrupt owner of an estate. Otherwise this finished portrait of feminine sensuality and love of power bears little resemblance to that of the successful comedienne. Lazarev-Gruzinsky conjectures, and perhaps with some basis, that journalists hostile to Chekhov had helped to spread the gossip of a love affair, and that Yavorskaya, intent on publicity of any sort, willingly claimed that a famous author, disappointed in her affections, had spitefully portrayed her in this story.

In keeping with his harsh sentiment on Ariadne, Chekhov's letters to Suvorin over this year contain remarks on women and marriage that border on the cynical and yet reveal him in a state of worried indecision in relation to them. In commenting on a woman in his life, whose name Suvorin had obviously brought up but which is carefully omitted in Chekhov's reply, he wrote: "She is a talented girl but you will hardly

[3] That year Chekhov had informed Leikin that he had been studying French and had finally conquered the language to the extent that he would not make a fool of himself in Paris, could ask for help, and thank a waiter.

find her likable. I'm sorry for her because I'm vexed with myself; half the time she is with me I cannot stand her. She is as foxy as the devil, but her motives are so petty that she turns out to be a rat rather than a devil . . ." And further on he continues with the subject of women: "*Phui, phui!* Women deprive one of youth, only not in my case. In my lifetime I've been a clerk and not a proprietor, and fate has favored me very little. I've had few romances and am as much like Catherine[4] as a nut is like a battleship. Silk nightdresses mean to me only something comfortable, that is, soft to the touch. I'm well disposed to comfort, but debauchery does not attract me. . . ." (*January 21, 1895.*)

Suvorin had once again raised the question of marriage and Chekhov lightly answered: "I've probably not married up to now for the reason that wives are accustomed to give their husbands slippers. Yet I'm willing to marry, though not to a pockmarked widow. That would be dull." (*February 19, 1895.*) He faced the question in a more direct manner in a later letter: "Very well, I'll marry if you wish it. But here are my conditions: Everything must remain as before — that is, she must live in Moscow and I in the country, and I'll make visits to her. The kind of happiness which continues day in and day out, from one morning to the next, I cannot endure. When people tell me the same thing in the same tone of voice every day, I become furious. . . . I promise to be a splendid husband, but give me a wife who, like the moon, will not appear in my sky every day. Nor will I write better for being married." (*March 23, 1895.*) And still later that year he again reverted to the question: "I'm afraid of a wife and domestic routine, which would cramp me and in actuality would not be compatible with my untidiness; but it might be better than to drift about on the sea of life, tossing in the frail skiff of profligacy. I've already got over loving mistresses. . . ." (*November 10, 1895.*)

« 3 »

Suvorin was a wise and experienced older man and he must have at last realized that these lighthearted and even facetious rejoinders to his earnest advice to marry came from a Chekhov either committed to a bachelor existence because he preferred it or because of some overriding personal reason which he would divulge to no one. Certainly the two women, Lika Mizinova and Lidiya Avilova, with whom his name

[4] Catherine the Great, noted for her many love affairs.

has been seriously linked, continued to receive the same casual treatment. On January 21 Chekhov finally got around to answering the letter which Lika had sent him from abroad in the middle of December of the preceeding year. It was a kind, reassuring reply: "Dear Lika, I expect you in January or February; if I should be in Petersburg, then inform me of your arrival and I'll come to Moscow, to Melikhovo, or anywhere you say. I want to talk with you, not write you about things, for all remains as of old, nothing has changed." The chastened Lika, however, did not arrive until May.

Though Chekhov appears not to have written a single letter to Lidiya Avilova in 1894, at the end of that year he requested Alexander to find out her address at the editorial office of her brother-in-law. This seems to be another example of his forgetfulness, so strangely persistent in his relations with Avilova, and at the same time he apparently also forgot the mysterious arrangement (if it ever existed) which she mentions in her memoirs — that he was to send letters to her in Petersburg *poste restante*. The reason now for desiring her home address is not clear, unless it be the need to return some manuscript which she had sent to him for criticism.

At the beginning of February of 1895 Chekhov went to Petersburg, and on the twelfth Avilova tells in her memoirs (Chapter V) of meeting him, and some of his literary friends, at a dinner at Leikin's. Although she professed to guard her passion for Chekhov with great secrecy, at this point Mrs. Leikin, as well as Avilova's sister, appears to have been fully aware of her interest. She represents Chekhov as being in high spirits and amusing all with his remarks. At the end of the evening he offered to escort her home. She described his awkward and uncavalier behavior in seating her in the sleigh and then crowding her. When she complained good-naturedly he accused her, in mock seriousness, of constantly grumbling and being angry. When she asked if he were staying long in Petersburg, he answered:

" 'I want to remain another week. We ought to see each other more often, every day. Do you agree?'

" 'Come tomorrow evening,' I proposed before I had time to realize what I was doing.

" 'To your place?'

"For some reason we were both silent for a time.

" 'Will you have many guests?' Chekhov asked.

" 'On the contrary. Misha [her husband] is in the Caucasus, and with him away I expect no one.' "

Chekhov promised to come if he were not dragged off somewhere by the Suvorins, with whom he was staying.

In none of Chekhov's correspondence from Petersburg at this time is there any mention of the dinner at Leikin's, although he does indicate, in a letter to his sister on February 7: "Yesterday Leikin visited and asked me to come to his place for a family evening." Nor do Potapenko or Lazarev-Gruzinsky, whom Avilova mentions as among the writers present, say anything about this gathering in their memoirs of Chekhov. More surprising is the absence of any record of the evening in Leikin's extensive diary, of which the portion dealing with Chekhov has lately been made available in print. His other contacts with Chekhov over 1895 are meticulously entered.

The next day, however, we have positive evidence that Chekhov did visit Lidiya Avilova, and her absorbing account of it in her memoirs (Chapter VI) is like a clever scene from a comedy, but one with tragic overtones. She had carefully prepared everything for his arrival — first a visit to the nursery to make him jealous in watching the children being put to bed; next, tea in the dining room; then to the study, where it was cozy — and how much they would have to talk about! — finally, a supper with vodka, wine, beer, and fruit, all of which she had laid out. As she arranged it, the drawing room, with its large lamp dimmed, seemed to her to be pervaded by an appropriate atmosphere of gentle sadness.

Then the doorbell rang, but instead of Chekhov, friends of her husband, a married couple, bounced in. The wife was a roaring woman, aggressively opinionated, and she shouted with laughter at the slightest excuse. They pounced on the supper, devoured it, and stayed and stayed, until the anxious hostess gratefully concluded that it was at last too late for Chekhov to come. But to her mortification, he finally did. The roaring lady burst into laughter at the thought of meeting the famous author, and at once assailed him for wasting his time on silly little tales that proved nothing. Chekhov grew limp and silent. At a late hour, the husband at last dragged his argumentative wife away; Lidiya Avilova had only enough strength left to beg Chekhov, who also wished to leave, to remain a bit longer.

They talked about her writing, his criticism of it, and he reproved her for not following his directions about publishing her tales. Then she quotes Chekhov as saying: " 'You ought to be in bed; your visitors have worn you out. Today you're not the same as you were before. You seem indifferent and listless, and you'll be glad when I leave. Yes, before . . . Do you remember our first meetings? And do you know that I was seriously in love with you? It was serious. I loved you. It seemed that there was not another woman in the world whom I could love that way. You were beautiful and appealing, and there was such freshness and dazzling charm in your youthfulness! I loved you and thought only of you. And when I met you again after a long separation, it seemed to me that you had grown still more beautiful and that you were another, a new person, and that I must get to know you again and love you still more in a new way. And that it would be harder to part from you . . .' "

As he spoke his eyes seemed to her cold and remorseless, and she had the impression that he was somehow angry with her for having changed and for no longer being desirable. And she continues to quote him: " 'I loved you,' Chekhov went on now, quite wrathfully, and he bent over me, staring angrily into my face. 'But I knew that you were not like many women whom I left and who broke with me; that the love one has for you must be pure and sacred and last all one's life.' "

Then suddenly observing that it was one-thirty in the morning, Chekhov said that there was still time for him to have supper with Suvorin and discuss things with him. Taking up a packet of her manuscripts which she had prepared for him, he remarked: " 'I think I promised to see you again tomorrow, but I'll not be able to do so. For I shall be leaving for Moscow tomorrow.[5] That means that we shall not see each other again.' " And he left.

However accurately Lidiya Avilova may have recalled, over the years, what took place that evening, Chekhov's letter the next day, February 14, seems quite at variance with the passionate sentiments she attributed to him in her account and also with some of the facts she mentioned. Perhaps this is why she omitted the letter in her memoirs. Chekhov wrote: "You are wrong in saying that I was disgracefully bored at your place. I was not bored but somewhat depressed, because I could see from your face that your guests had tired you out. I wanted to have dinner with you, but yesterday you did not repeat the invitation and I again came to the conclusion that you were weary of visitors.

[5] Actually, Chekhov did not leave for Moscow until three days later.

"I did not see Burenin today and I shall probably not be seeing him, because I intend to leave for the country tomorrow. I'm sending you my book and a thousand sincere wishes and blessings."[6]

From this simple, matter-of-fact communication, it would appear that Chekhov had gone to Lidiya Avilova's in response to a dinner invitation and much earlier in the day than she represents; had found guests there, and left because he thought her weary and because, in the circumstances, she did not urge him to remain for dinner. In her memoirs she tells him that she had gone to Burenin to seek his aid in placing her stories in *New Times*. Then she describes his reaction: "Chekhov jumped up. Even the tails of his coat flew up. 'What idiot sent you to that scoundrel?' he asked sternly without raising his voice, but the frown on his face surprised me." She explains to him that she was aware of the risk of an indecent proposal from Burenin in return for the favor of publishing her fiction. Pleased that Chekhov displayed anger over the risk she had undergone, she adds for clarification to the reader: "This is what is known as coquetry." Chekhov's letter, on the other hand, appears to indicate an actual agreement between them that he would use his influence on Burenin to publish her tales in *New Times*. In fact, a letter from Burenin to Chekhov, dated February 15, reveals clearly that he did manage to see Burenin before he left Petersburg and secured' from him a promise to publish one of the stories which Avilova had sent to *New Times*.

A second letter which Chekhov sent Avilova the next day she did reproduce in her memoirs (Chapter VII), for it served the purpose of her narrative.[7] He had already read two of her stories, in manuscripts which he had taken away with him on the day of his visit. One he praised and the other he damned in forthright terms: ". . . It is not a story at all but a thing and a cumbrous thing at that." If by any chance she had been truthful about his expression of love for her that night, his passion in no sense assuaged the acerbity of his criticism of her as a

---

[6] This letter was published for the first time in *Polnoe sobranie sochinenii i pisem A. P. Chekhova* (*Complete Edition of the Works and Letters of A. P. Chekhov*), Moscow, 1949, XVI, 214. As previously mentioned, this is one of the two letters which Avilova asked Chekhov's sister not to publish in her edition. This edition of the letters very likely provided Avilova with much of the factual information in her memoirs and perhaps some of the inspiration for Chekhov's conversation. And the contrived aspect of an incident in the memoirs is revealed when a letter such as this one, not in the edition she used, turns up later in print.

[7] There are a few slight omissions, not indicated, in her version of the letter, but they do not significantly alter the meaning.

writer. "You are a talented person," he declared, "but you have grown heavy or, to put it vulgarly, you have become soggy and already belong to the category of stale writers. . . . You don't polish enough, indeed a woman writer ought not to write but to embroider on paper, for her work ought to be painstaking, slow." With the letter came her manuscripts, and a copy of his recent book, *Stories and Tales*, with the chilly inscription: "To L. A. Avilova from the author."

According to her memoirs, Chekhov's letter left her a prey to mixed emotions. She was convinced of her deep love for Chekhov and at the same time she was profoundly uncertain whether either of them was prepared, in the light of the circumstances conditioning their personal lives, to make the necessary sacrifices to consummate such a love. She tells how she finally came to a decision. Ordering a watch-chain pendant, in the form of a book, from a jeweler, she had it engraved on one side: "*Stories and Tales*. Works of An. Chekhov," and on the other: "Page 267, lines 6 and 7." The reference was to a sentence in his tale, *The Neighbors*: "If you ever want my life, come and take it." She sent the pendant to her brother in Moscow, with instructions to leave it at the editorial office of *Russian Thought* to be picked up by Chekhov. Lidiya Avilova then relates how she spent many days in Petersburg in a state of agitation and alarm, waiting for some reaction from Chekhov to her odd gift, and she concludes this section of her memoirs: "There could be no doubt that Anton Pavlovich received my pendant, but there was no response, and even our correspondence was broken off. I would have to live without him."

Other evidence, however, tends to disprove Avilova's assertion that at this juncture she waited impatiently in Petersburg for an answer and ceased to write Chekhov. For in the recently published diary of Leikin, already mentioned, there is an entry dated March 7, 1895: "This morning I arrived in Moscow. . . . The dilettante writer Lidiya Alekseevna Avilova is in Moscow. She left Petersburg last week. . . ." Clearly Avilova had left for Moscow less than two weeks after Chekhov had returned to that city from Petersburg, and only a few days after sending him the pendant.

On March 9 Leikin makes another entry in his diary: ". . . I drank tea with her [L. A. Avilova]. She is grieving: ten days ago she wrote from Moscow to Chekhov's estate and invited him to Moscow, but he has neither come nor answered her. She asked at *Russian Thought* whether he was at his estate, and they told her that he had gone to

Taganrog. But I reported to her that at *Russian Thought* they informed me he was at his estate, expected me, and I'm going to him tomorrow. How wretched she was. Chekhov is now in the country, he works, writes, and cannot waste time going to Moscow. That is why he asked the people at *Russian Thought* to tell all his female admirers (and Avilova among them) that he had gone to Taganrog."

This is the plain vanilla of "romance," the obtrusive reality that so unkindly denigrates the beautiful sentiment which Lidiya Avilova, in her memoirs, had Chekhov pronounce on her behalf less than a month previously: "But I knew that you were not like many women whom I left and who broke with me; that the love one has for you must be pure and sacred and last all one's life."

« 4 »

Leikin arrived at Melikhovo on March 10 in a fierce blizzard, bringing Yezhov and Lazarev-Gruzinsky with him. Icicles had formed on Leikin's beard and the visitors were covered with snow and half-frozen from the sleigh ride from Lopasnya station. Chekhov greeted them joyfully at the door and two servants, chunky girls with faces round as moons, took their bags. Vodka warmed the chilled bodies of the guests, and they and the family sat down to dinner in good spirits. Leikin was delighted to see the full-grown Bromine and Quinine, the dachshunds he had sent as puppies to Chekhov. That year they were mated; one of the puppies died, the other, which Chekhov named Saltpeter, he gave to a neighbor. After dinner, since the storm had ceased, the host showed the visitors around his property.

Chekhov's former protégés, Yezhov and Lazarev-Gruzinsky, struck him now as two young blockheads whose taciturnity spread a desperate boredom throughout the house. Leikin's chatter, however, made up for it, but if he said anything about Lidiya Avilova's languishing in Moscow it went unrecorded. Chekhov thought this tremendously prolific author and editor, who had given him his first real start in writing, had grown flabby but kinder and better-natured. He was amused at his mother's story of asking the local butcher for a good piece of meat for her guest Mr. Leikin. "Is that the one who writes books?" he asked, and he eagerly supplied a good cut. He wrote books, too, grumbled Chekhov, but the butcher sent him only gristle.

The account of this visit in Leikin's diary stresses his pleased amazement over Melikhovo, now a simple but attractively decorated house with bright rooms and comforts that could not be found even in Moscow apartments. And as a self-made man, it gave him obvious pleasure to compare the poverty of this family, when he first began to know them ten years before, to the relative well-being it now enjoyed.

They were indeed doing well. Though at times Chekhov got annoyed with Misha — who, he thought, suffered from tactlessness and a painful consciousness of his own mistakes — he did not hesitate to urge Suvorin to use his influence in government circles to secure a promotion for his brother. And that year Misha was transferred from Uglich to Yaroslavl as head of a division in the city government. At the same time Misha, in his ambitions to be a writer, was achieving some success in publishing children's stories. Masha, in her spare time, continued her painting and was taking a special medical course so that she might better help Chekhov in his practice. And Ivan's reputation as a pedagogue in the Moscow school system was growing and had won for him another official medal. Even the maverick Alexander had by now begun to reap some of the rewards of his unquestioned talents. His journalistic and editorial skills had won him respect on *New Times* and in other newspaper and magazine circles in Petersburg. He could now afford a *dacha* for his family in the summer, and he informed Chekhov that he had opened a savings account. However, he still mercilessly made a kind of accomplice of his brother in his pursuit of literary honors by continually asking him to criticize his stories and to use his influence in getting them placed in leading magazines. Chekhov pointedly informed him that he was arranging his papers and correspondence, and after debating with himself whether to place Alexander under "family" or "writer," had decided to compromise by putting him in the category of "petitioners." Alexander's tales, under the pseudonym of A. SEDOI, were beginning to attract some attention. When Chekhov, his severest critic, wrote him nearly unqualified praise of one of his stories, there was something almost pathetic in Alexander's rapture over this rare accolade from his famous brother. In 1895 appeared a new printing of Alexander's collection, *Christmas Tales*, which had been achieved, he innocently informed Chekhov, by binding up the nine hundred unsold copies and advertising them as a second edition. That year he was accorded the distinction of an invitation to one of the exclusive Petersburg literary dinners, which Chekhov had initiated several years before. Alexander pronounced the affair quite boring and then registered a complaint that Leikin, in his account of the dinner in the *Petersburg Gazette,* had eliminated his name in listing those who were present.

In his reflective moods Chekhov did not consider himself among those members of the family who were doing well. "I'm growing old," he wrote Bilibin, his friend from the days when he published in *Fragments.* "No money. No orders. No ranks. There are only debts." (*January 18, 1895.*) When he had money, he confessed to Suvorin, he felt a bit drunk and could not help spending it on all sorts of rubbish. He had squandered it heedlessly on a new bath house, Russian style, a large barn, Ukrainian style, a firehouse for the village of Melikhovo with a glorious bell; and now he planned to build a new schoolhouse for the village of Talezh, where his trustee duties compelled him occasionally to examine the students. If young cousin Volodya — a son of the late Uncle Mitrofan — would only go to a Medical School, Chekhov offered to guarantee him a small monthly stipend. Fortunately Volodya elected to go to a free seminary.[8]

When Chekhov finished tending Levitan that summer in the province of Novgorod, after the artist's suicide attempt, he made a hurried trip to Petersburg to see Suvorin and also visited Leikin, who noted in his diary Chekhov's changed appearance even in the short space of four months since he had last seen him. He seemed ill to Leikin — yellow and thin, and coughing constantly. Though Chekhov had once defended an artist somewhat given to vodka, whom he had recommended to paint Leikin's portait, by declaring that a man who did not drink was not entirely a man, he had to admit that he himself now preferred to sleep rather than drink. It annoyed him that his cough, which he still insisted was a mere habit, had finally given him the reputation of being an unhealthy man, and that people now greeted him by invariably observing how thin he had grown.

There were threats to go to Australia for eight or ten months or to the mouth of the Yenisei River, but actually Chekhov remained at Melikhovo during 1895. Visits to Moscow and two trips to Petersburg seemed to satisfy his persistent itch to travel. Among the many friends he saw in Moscow was Lika, shortly after she returned from Europe in May. Ashamed, perhaps, and consumed with her own sorrow, she made

[8] At this time, however, Chekhov was helping to put through school at Taganrog V. A. Yevtushevsky, the bright son of the brother of his aunt, the widow of Uncle Mitrofan. But so well did Chekhov conceal his aid that even the boy's parents were at first unaware of it.

only two brief visits that summer to Melikhovo to the family she so loved. It is possible that on one of his Petersburg trips Chekhov saw Potapenko, whose offense against Lika he seemed now to have forgiven or decided was none of his business. He liked Potapenko's cheerfulness and obligingness, and defended him against the criticism of Suvorin, although he made it clear that he placed no high value on his talents as a writer. Tikhonov remarked in his diary at this time that Chekhov always had to have an adjutant around him, and that Potapenko had obviously been selected.

In December, in Moscow, Chekhov met Ivan Bunin for the first time. They discussed the problems of the short story writer, Chekhov stressing his favorite theme of brevity and even suggesting the wisdom of deleting the beginning and end in one's first draft. A firm friendship began which was of importance to Chekhov in his later years.

Several of Chekhov's trips to Moscow were made on behalf of *The Annals of Surgery*, a professional journal that was in danger of suspending publication because of inability to make up an annual deficit of fifteen hundred roubles. Chekhov, as he expressed it, became "hot under the collar" at this news, and he plunged into the cause with incredible zeal. He threatened to go to Petersburg and bang on the door of every friend for the money, or even call on S. Witte, the Minister of Finance, rather than see this important professional journal, put out by eminent scientists, fail because of lack of funds. To Suvorin he said that if he had not committed himself to this sum to build the Talezh rural school, he would advance the fifteen hundred himself. Suvorin offered enough money to give the journal another year of life, but this was eventually rejected when the possibility arose, through Chekhov's efforts, of securing sustained publication by Sytin's firm. Though the journal did lapse in 1896, it was revived the following year when Chekhov again came to its aid.

Behind Chekhov's passionate interest in this cause was the reverence he had for medical sciences which had impelled him, shortly after he finished Medical School, to contemplate writing a dissertation in the field. And it was this same esteem which, in part, had driven him on to study the peoples and prisons of Sakhalin and to write a book about that island. Further, there is evidence about this time — the exact date is uncertain — that Chekhov contemplated submitting *The Island of Sakhalin* as a dissertation to help meet the requirements for a degree of Doctor of Medical Sciences which would have qualified him for the title of *privatdocent* and allowed him to lecture in the Medical School. Dr. G. I. Rossolimo, a fellow student of Chekhov at Moscow University and later a distinguished professor of neuropathology in its medical faculty, tells in his reminiscences of Chekhov, with whom he became very friendly after 1893, that he expressed a desire to teach in the University. " 'If I were a teacher,' Chekhov said to him, 'I would try to draw my audience as deeply as possible into the area of the subjective feelings of patients, for I think that this would really prove useful to the students.' " Dr. Rossolimo proposed to the Dean of the Medical School the possibility of a place on the staff, and conveyed Chekhov's suggestion that his *Island of Sakhalin* might be accepted in lieu of the required dissertation. The Dean scornfully walked out of his office, not even deigning to reply. When Dr. Rossolimo informed Chekhov of the results, he laughed and dropped the notion of an academic career.[9]

In more practical ways than teaching Chekhov relieved his medical conscience at this time by tending patients at Melikhovo, serving as a member of the auxiliary medical fund of the area, and inspecting the health conditions of factories in the district on behalf of the Serpukhov Sanitary Council. At the same time he was becoming more involved in educational problems. On September 25, 1895, the Serpukhov district rural council tendered him a vote of thanks for spending a hundred roubles of his own money to buy desks and other classroom appurtenances for the Talezh school, purchases that should have been made by the authorities themselves. But Chekhov was impatient with administrative red tape in general and especially in the sphere of national education. Ironically he praised an article of Suvorin on the need for physical games in the schools; games, he remarked, should be introduced only after Russian students have ceased to be starved. Describing how a decrepit peasant mother beat her drunken son with a stick because he had been bathing in the pond, and then chased him home barefoot through the snow, he declared to Suvorin: "What baseness it is to postpone the enlightenment of our dark masses." (*April 13, 1895.*)

Though Chekhov reacted sensitively and often with anguish to the misery, inequity, and cruelty of Russian life, he seemed to lack any deep concern for current questions of government or Russian inter-

[9] Some confirmation of Chekhov's desire for a position on the medical faculty of Moscow University may be found in the memoirs of another doctor friend, M. A. Chlenov: "A. P. Chekhov i meditsina," in *Russkie vedomosti* ("A. P. Chekhov and Medicine," in *Russian News*), 1906, No. 1.

national policy. There is very little in his voluminous correspondence concerning these questions. Perhaps because he knew of Suvorin's interest in such matters, for he often wrote about them in his newspaper, Chekhov would occasionally make pithy comments in his letters to him about the rejection of reforms by the new Tsar, Nicholas II, the wheat crisis, Witte's clever economic policy, the fear of war with Germany, or Russia's demands on Japan for ice-free ports which, he prophetically declared, would cost Russians more than if they set out then to conquer all of Japan. The human problems that confronted him daily, which he could touch and feel and do something about, appeared to dwarf these larger concerns of state.

« 5 »

Chekhov's faith in scientific progress as a major factor in human betterment had done much to undermine the early influence on him of Tolstoy's doctrine of moral perfectibility. The gray seer of Yasnaya Polyana, who was almost twice Chekhov's age, was concerned primarily with men's spiritual rather than with their bodily health, with their souls rather than with the material improvement of life which technological advances could bring to modern society. Yet Chekhov never lost his awe of Tolstoy, the great literary artist, the author of *War and Peace* and *Anna Karenina*, nor his deep conviction that this colossal figure represented the conscience of humanity, and that as long as he continued his public crusade against the moral failings of mankind, the world was somehow a better place in which to live.

Nearly every contemporary Russian writer of consequence, and many foreign ones, made the pilgrimage to Yasnaya Polyana or to Tolstoy's Moscow home. But after more than ten years of literary endeavor, at the conclusion of which Chekhov's name was being coupled with Tolstoy's by reviewers, the two writers had not yet met. Reports of Tolstoy's praise of his stories had been brought to Chekhov, and he had heard that the great man had once tried to see him in Moscow. On several occasions mutual friends had offered to introduce him to Tolstoy, but he had always refused, declaring that when the time came he would seek him out himself.

That time had arrived. Chekhov began inquiring where Tolstoy was spending the summer, for he wished to visit him. When I. I. Gorbunov-Posadov, a close friend of Tolstoy and a worker in his cause, was at Melikhovo at the beginning of August 1895, Chekhov learned that he was on his way to see Tolstoy at Yasnaya Polyana. Chekhov decided to accompany him and spent August 8-9 on Tolstoy's estate. Tolstoy made a wonderful impression on him. He felt as though he were in his own home and conversation flowed easily. They went for a walk on the Tula highway, for Tolstoy wanted to show his guests how the young people rode on bicycles, which were then coming into fashion in Russia, a technological advance which Tolstoy approved. In the evening Gorbunov-Posadov and V. G. Chertkov, Tolstoy's leading disciple, read to the visitors and members of the family parts of *Resurrection*, the first draft of which Tolstoy had just about finished at this time. Chekhov listened attentively, and after the reading he told Tolstoy that he thought the court scene had been especially well handled, but he pointed out that Katya Maslova's sentence of two years at hard labor was in error, for the courts did not stipulate penal servitude in such a short sentence. Tolstoy corrected this mistake.

In writing of the visit to Suvorin, who had some doubts about the sincerity of Tolstoy's moral views, Chekhov remarked that he found Tolstoy's daughters quite appealing: "They adore their father and believe in him fanatically. This shows for certain that Tolstoy is a mighty moral force, for if he were insincere and not above reproach, his daughters would be the first to regard him skeptically, for daughters are wise birds: you don't catch them with chaff. You can dupe a fiancée or a mistress as much as you please, and in the eyes of a loving woman even a donkey may pass for a philosopher, but daughters, well this is another matter." (*October 26, 1895.*)

The only recorded reaction of Tolstoy to Chekhov's visit is in a letter to his son Leo: "I liked him . . . he is very talented and he must have a kind heart, but up to now he has not revealed a definite point of view." However, the acquaintance between Russia's two foremost living writers had just begun. In questions of literature, the artist in Tolstoy always took precedence over the moralist. Later, in their friendship, he would find many hidden virtues in Chekhov.

« 6 »

Before their meeting, Tolstoy may well have read Chekhov's latest tale, *The Helpmate*,[10] which he extolled in the highest terms. For with his mounting misogamy at this time, because of his strained relations

10 Published in March 1895, *Beginning*, the Miscellany of the Society of Lovers of Russian Literature.

with his wife, Tolstoy no doubt discovered more truth than fiction in this revelation of feminine baseness. In an amazingly few words, *The Helpmate* pinpoints an emotional crisis in the husband's unhappy married life when he comes to the realization that the one thing left for him to do is to divorce his giddy wife so she can join her young lover abroad, only to learn that she wants this freedom while still remaining within the marriage bond. Misha asserts that the story was based on an actual situation, which he had related to his brother, in the married life of a government official.

The central situation of *Anna on the Neck*,[11] a general favorite with readers and a tale that has been put into the movies in Russia, is again marriage — but now treated with an element of humor in its exposure of the crass mores and morals of petty provincial officialdom. The scared, pretty young wife of a pompous bureaucrat three times her age turns the tables on him after her success at the governor's ball, which results in her husband's promotion and the Order of Saint Anna. But in the end Chekhov drives home the pathos of Russian life in this milieu. For the emancipated wife, now intent upon exploiting her social triumph, turns her back on the poverty of her young brothers and their father, a schoolteacher who has lost his wife and also his self-respect in his fondness for the bottle.

The longest story Chekhov wrote in 1895, *The Murder*,[12] one of the few tales connected with his Sakhalin experiences, offers a vein rather uncharacteristic and rarely mined by him. For it is a grim tale of pronounced narrative interest and not a little concrete action. The fanatical orthodoxy of the peasant Matvei leads him to interfere with the sectarian faith of his two cousins. This situation, aggravated by a quarrel over their common inheritance, ends in Matvei's murder by one of the cousins in a scene of violence described with superb realism. Chekhov offers only a glimpse, but a vivid one, of the horrors of penal servitude on Sakhalin, to which one of the cousins is condemned for his part in the crime and where, by suffering, he finds his way back to the true faith of the peasant.

Potapenko, in order to illustrate his account of how contemptuously editors treated their authors and how poorly they remunerated them, tells an anecdote connected with Chekhov which he asserts was true. D. I. Tikhomirov, the well-known editor of the journal *Reading for*

[11] *Russian News*, October 1895.
[12] *The Murder* first appeared in *Russian Thought*, November 1895.

Children and a good friend of Chekhov's, pursued him for a story for his publication. He even sent him a present of several bottles of wine from his vineyard (it was poor wine, says Potapenko), and Chekhov thanked him and eventually sent him a tale. Shortly after this both of them were at a large evening gathering. When Chekhov put on his overcoat to leave, Tikhomirov slipped a package in his pocket and mumbled something. Later, when Chekhov opened the package, he found twelve roubles and a bill which itemized the honorarium for the story, substracted the value of the bottles of wine, and indicated that the remainder was twelve roubles.

If there is any truth in this anecdote, it must have reference to the only story Chekhov published in *Readings for Children*, the altogether charming *Whitebrow* (1895), the tale of a hungry she-wolf that carried off a playful puppy, mistaking it in the dark for a baby lamb, and of the amusing adventures that subsequently befell Whitebrow, the puppy. Though Chekhov had already published several pieces that could be described as "children's stories," in general he condemned the practice of writing specifically for youngsters. It is more expedient and direct, he said, to select medicine and apply it than to try to invent some special concoction for a sick child simply because the patient is a child. Likewise, he reasoned, it is better to select for children something truly artistic that has been written for adults. And *Whitebrow*, like his wonderful *Kashtanka*, meets this specification.

As the artistic demands Chekhov made upon his own writing increased, he became more and more intolerant of current literature. Suvorin's weakness for popular contemporary novelists, especially foreign ones, particularly annoyed him. To his debunking of Suvorin's favorite Paul Bourget, he now added Sienkiewicz. His *Polaniecki Family*, he wrote Suvorin, was a devilish heap of scenes of family happiness in which the hero's wife is so extremely faithful to her husband, and by intuition understands God and life so thoroughly that the result is sickeningly cloying and clumsy — just as though one had received a wet, slobbery kiss. "The novel's aim is to lull the bourgeoisie by its golden dreams. Be faithful to your wife, pray beside her at the altar, make money, love sport — and your affairs are all set, both in this and in the next world. The bourgeoisie admire the so-called 'positive' types and novels with happy endings which calm their thoughts so that they can accumulate capital, maintain their innocence, behave like beasts, and be happy all at the same time." (*January 13, 1895.*)

What he particularly found lacking in popular bourgeois literature was a talent for humanity, that infinite compassion that made it possible to understand without condemning man's weaknesses, his diseases of body and soul. For Chekhov this often meant the difference between talent and art, as he told his disciple Elena Shavrova. He criticized her for allowing the women in one of her tales to regard syphilis as something unspeakable. "Syphilis is not a vice, not the result of wicked excesses, but an illness, and those afflicted with it require sympathetic and understanding treatment. It is not a good trait if your wife deserts her sick husband because he has an infection or loathsome disease. She, of course, may take what attitude she likes toward it, but the author must be humane to the tips of his fingers." (*February 28, 1895.*)

Though the poetic instinct in Chekhov was strong and he had positive likes and dislikes in verse, he reached a point at about this time when he refused to offer analytical judgments on the manuscripts that poets sent him. "Verse is not in my line," he informed A. V. Zhirkevich,[13] "I've never written it, my mind refuses to memorize it, and I react to it the way a peasant does, but I cannot say definitely why I'm pleased or bored by it. Formerly I tried to keep in touch with poets and to set my views before them, but nothing came of it and I soon gave the matter up, perhaps like a man who feels well but expresses his thoughts uninterestingly and indefinitely. Now I usually confine myself to writing 'I like this' or 'I don't like this.' Your poem I like." (*March 10, 1895.*)

« 7 »

Five years had passed since the failure of Chekhov's last full-length play, *The Wood Demon*, and though his disillusionment then had been painful, he once again began to turn his thoughts to the theater. In 1894 and over much of 1895 the notion of writing another play both repelled and attracted him, for the urge to experiment in dramatic writing, which had been reflected in *The Wood Demon*, still pursued him. In April, Suvorin suggested that he write for the theater which he had acquired in Petersburg. Chekhov answered that he might write a play in the autumn and that it would be a comedy. If he did do a play for Suvorin, he said, it would be something strange — that is, not the conventional type of play — another indication of his long dissatisfaction

---

[13] He wrote poetry under the pseudonym of A. Nivin.

when he took the children to a puppet show, Alexander was mightily pleased.

Besides his notebooks, which contain largely material bearing on Chekhov's stories and plays, in 1896 he began to keep a diary, the entries of which are extremely sparse and of little help as a record of his personal life. For example, the only entry on this visit runs: "In January I was in Petersburg, stayed at Suvorin's. Often with Potapenko. Saw Korolenko. Frequently attended the Maly Theater.[1] Once Alexander and I were coming down the stairs of the editorial office[2] at the same time as B. V. Gei,[3] and he indignantly said to me: 'Why do you take up arms against Burenin with the old man (i.e., Suvorin)?' However, I never spoke ill about the contributors of New Times to Suvorin, although I have no deep esteem for the majority of them."[4]

The diary also mentions that when Chekhov returned to Moscow, accompanied by Suvorin, both of them paid a visit to Tolstoy's house on February 15. On this occasion Chekhov found the great man in a dispute with another guest, testily denouncing the decadent writers and artists who were then coming into vogue in Russia. His wife, Sofya Andreevna, also seemed irritated as she criticized the painter of religious subjects, N. N. Ge, a devoted admirer of her husband. However, two of the daughters, Tatyana and Mariya, who played cards during the evening, struck him as being very considerate and touching in their relations with their father. Suvorin, in his diary, mentions only Tolstoy's regret that Chekhov had read the manuscript of Resurrection before its revision, and he promised to give it to him in its final form, to look over.[5]

« 2 »

In Chekhov's diary for this year, 1896, however, there is no mention of attending a masquerade in Suvorin's theater on January 27, an event

[1] Not to be confused with the famous Moscow Maly Theater. It was the old name of the Petersburg theater which Suvorin had taken over.

[2] Of New Times.

[3] B. V. Gei was head of the foreign news desk at New Times.

[4] Chekhov was not entirely candid here. His letters indicate that on a number of occasions he complained to Suvorin about the attitude and writings of leading contributors to New Times, and especially in the case of Burenin.

[5] There is no other evidence that Tolstoy gave Chekhov the manuscript of Resurrection to read, either before or after the revision. Suvorin may have had in mind that Chekhov heard parts of the novel read on his first visit to Tolstoy.

that figures prominently in Lidiya Avilova's memoirs. Since their last meeting and her gift of the engraved watch-chain pendant, almost a year had passed. Though he did not attempt to see her on his first visit to Petersburg, at the beginning of 1896, she knew he was in the city and sent him a copy of her book, *The Happy Man and Other Tales*, with the inscription: "To the proud master from an apprentice." When he was safely back at Melikhovo he wrote her: "I unexpectedly had to leave Petersburg — to my great regret. Learning from Nadezhda Alekseevna [her sister] that you had produced a book, I wanted to call on you to receive the offspring from your own hands, but fate resolved otherwise: I'm again in the country.

"I received the book on the day of my departure. I've not yet had time to read it, and therefore I can speak only about its external appearance: it has been very charmingly printed and looks fine.

"It seems that I'll be in Petersburg again after the 20th or the 25th, and will then see you; and in the meantime permit me to wish you everything good. Why did you call me a 'proud master'? Only turkeycocks are proud." (*January 17, 1896.*)

Perhaps the appellation mystified Chekhov because he was unaware of any manifestations of pride in his rather formal relations with her, but Avilova no doubt had in mind his imperviousness to her pursuit and, more precisely, his failure to react to the pendant's direction to come and take her life if he wanted it, or even to answer her request to meet her in Moscow. And now, despite the promise in his letter, he apparently had no intention of calling on her when he returned to Petersburg that January. But she found a way around this. Avilova's brother, visiting her from Moscow, proposed that they go to a masked ball at Suvorin's theater. Her memoirs give no indication that she knew Chekhov would be there, but her brother, upon spotting him in the throng, immediately drew her attention to Chekhov and said: " 'Now, of course, I'm released,' " and vanished. She went directly up to Chekhov and exclaimed: " 'How glad I am to see you!' "

In her memoirs (Chapter IX), Avilova describes the evening she and Chekhov spent together and quotes from their conversation. Though it is clear that he has recognized her in her mask and domino costume, for some undiscoverable reason she persists in her anonymity, terrified that he or anyone else will find out who she is. She even takes from her handbag two nuts, which had been left there after a game of lotto with the children, and puts them in her mouth to make sure that her voice will not reveal her identity! And she represents Chekhov as also being deeply concerned that no one in this crowd should recognize her. Presumably all this concealment was intended to heighten the element of romance in the account.

She asks: " 'But do you know who I am? Who am I? Tell me!' I snatched my arm from him and stopped. He smiled.

" 'You know my play will soon be produced,' he remarked, not answering my question.

" 'I know. *The Sea Gull.*'

" '*The Sea Gull.* Will you be at the opening performance?'

" 'I will. Unfailingly.'

" 'Then listen very carefully. I'll answer you from the stage. But you must listen closely. Don't forget.' "

At the time of this purported conversation, of course, Chekhov had not yet finished the revision of *The Sea Gull* and could not be certain that the play would be accepted for performance, to say nothing of where — actually, he first intended to submit it to the Maly Theater in Moscow. In fact, almost nine months were to pass before the opening night. However, the remainder of this ninth chapter of Avilova's memoirs describes the first performance of *The Sea Gull* as following hard upon the incident at the masked ball. Obviously she telescoped the two events chronologically in the interests of a more effective narrative.

In what immediately follows in her memoirs, she persists in being puzzled by Chekhov's reference to the answer which he promises to give to her in his play, and she wonders whether he has not mistaken her for someone else — possibly Yavorskaya. Then she presses her shoulder against his and utters a confession of love for him, which he evades by the simple expedient of telling her that he suspects she is Yavorskaya. Finally, her brother extricates Avilova from this situation by taking her home. In bed that night she could not refrain from thinking: "I — Yavorskaya? Will he answer Yavorskaya from the stage?"

« 3 »

In the early spring at Melikhovo Chekhov experienced several days of unusually severe coughing, accompanied by a discharge of blood, which brought on a mood of deep depression. Then later a weak right eye became infected, causing excruciating headaches, and he finally had to seek treatment from a Moscow eye doctor. Only now did he begin to adopt a less secretive attitude toward his illness. With growing frequency he frankly discussed the symptoms of his tuberculous condition in his correspondence, although he still continued to make light of it to his parents. When the architect Shekhtel, another of the good friends anxious about his unmarried state, urged a bride on him, Chekhov replied: ". . . I cannot marry at the present time, first because bacilli dwell in me, very dubious lodgers; secondly, I haven't a kopeck; and thirdly, it still seems to me that I'm very young. Let me roam around the world for another two or three years and we shall see — it may be that then I shall really marry." (*December 18, 1896.*) And he added by way of dispelling any alarm that, despite the bacilli and his cough, he did not feel badly and was constantly engaged in activities.

Indeed, Chekhov's activities, in defiance of all the laws of health, seemed to increase as his physical condition worsened. It was not merely an irrational challenge to the bacilli, the dubious lodgers within him, or the sense that time was running out, though there was something of this in his attitude, but rather his natural response to the demands made upon him as the first citizen in his community. His ambition was not simply to describe life in stories, but to reconstruct and transform it within the limited sphere of one man's activity. He had developed his small estate and beautified it with a growing forest and orchard and a wonderful garden of hyacinths, zinnias, asters, and rosebushes of every variety, in the growing of which he had become an expert. Now he turned his attention to the larger community around him. In 1896 he agitated for and secured the establishment of a postal and telegraph office at the nearby station of Lopasnya, and persuaded railway officials to have express trains stop there. Neighbors brought to his attention the dilapidated state of a bridge over the Lyutorka River, and he set about having it solidly rebuilt. At the request of Melikhovo peasants he collected funds for a church belfry for their village, supervised its construction, and for the cupola ordered a cross made of glass which was visible for miles around in the sun or moonlight. And he urged upon the County Board at Serpukhov, to which city he now made frequent trips on civic business, to lay a highway from Lopasnya to Melikhovo, a project that was finally voted.

Chekhov's major community effort in 1896, however, was the building of the new schoolhouse in Talezh. As a trustee, he had visited the old school often and was appalled at its wretched state and the shocking existence of the teacher and some of the students. He arranged hot meals for the poorer students and for those who came long distances. "The teacher," he had written Suvorin, "is paid twenty-three roubles a month, has a wife and four children, and is already gray though he is only thirty. He has been so beaten down by need that he can talk of nothing else except remuneration. In his opinion, poets and novelists ought to write only about increasing wages." (*November 27, 1894.*) This teacher provided the model for Medvedenko in *The Sea Gull.*

Since the school Chekhov wished to replace at Talezh was a parochial one, he met with unpleasant opposition from some of the village faithful. And the district authorities, who were in charge of educational matters, gave him only token support and very little financial aid. None of this discouraged him. He organized amateur concerts and plays to obtain funds, pleaded for contributions among the well-to-do in the neighborhood, and spent a considerable amount of his own money. Building anything fascinated him. He designed the schoolhouse with a functional skill rare at that time, aiming at a bright, airy building with a maximum of window exposure. All the materials he ordered himself, down to the tiles and doors for the Dutch ovens, and he supervised the work of bricklayers, plumbers, and carpenters. He seemed as much at home with lime and cement, foundations, beams and pilasters as a professional in the field.

Finally the school was finished and its formal opening was set for August 4. That distinguished pedagogue from Moscow, Ivan Chekhov, was the guest of honor at the ceremony. An ikon, two silver salt cellars, and loaves of bread, the traditional peasant symbols of greeting and hospitality, were presented to Chekhov. Three priests officiated at prayers, and an old peasant, on behalf of the village, spoke, "and he spoke very well," remarked Chekhov. The district board passed a vote of thanks for his efforts, but he derived much more satisfaction from the knowledge, in which all agreed, that the new Talezh schoolhouse was the finest in the area.

This experience served only to intensify Chekhov's interest in rural education, and encouraged him to plan the erection of additional schools. He even seriously contemplated writing a book, along the scholarly and scientific lines of his *Island of Sakhalin,* which would expose the economic lacks and the inadequate education of all sixty rural schools in the district, but this project was sacrificed to other activities that crowded in on him.

One of the most time-consuming in 1896 was his old project of aiding the Taganrog library, which now took on new life because of the enterprise of P. F. Iordanov, a member of the town council and later mayor of Taganrog. Under his zealous direction Chekhov's conception of the library's needs was significantly broadened. Instead of a special section of books inscribed by authors, which he continued to further, he now set out to make the library of his native town one of the best provincial libraries in Russia. At his request Iordanov sent him long lists of wanted books, and Chekhov combed the catalogues of publishers and bookstores for these items. Often he wrote authors for their works, asking at the same time that they inscribe them, but not informing them that they were destined for Taganrog. Some of the required books, he had to buy, and the money was refunded; but many of them he obtained gratis, and eventually some two thousand volumes from his own library were shipped. He offered discriminating advice on titles and translations, and also urged the establishment of an extensive information and reference division, for he believed this to be one of the most valuable adjuncts to a public library. When Iordanov approved the suggestion, Chekhov again busied himself writing to friends, publishers, and organizations for catalogues of important commercial firms, all the standing regulations and government enactments on current matters, various kinds of reference books — for anything, in fact, that might answer the questions of average citizens. Bales and boxes of books soon began to pour into the Taganrog library from Melikhovo, Moscow, and Petersburg. Chekhov also promoted the idea of a museum as a setting for the library, and encouraged Iordanov's dream of securing a bigger and better building for the collection. It was not glory he wanted but love, he said to one of his correspondents, and it must have been love for his fellow men that sustained a famous author, ill, busy, and hard-pressed, in all this activity, and in those long lists of books which he patiently copied out in his letters to Iordanov, carefully indicating whether he had paid for them or received them free. And the only thing he asked in return, since it had deeply annoyed him to have his name appear in the press in connection with his aid to the Talezh school, was that Iordanov strictly preserve his anonymity as a benefactor of the Taganrog library.

« 4 »

The rural activities of the schoolteacher Lidiya Volchaninova in the nostalgically poetic tale, *The House with the Attic*, which Chekhov completed in the first half of this year,[6] are in many respects faithful reflections of his own country experiences. In her concern for the peasants and in her practical endeavors on their behalf in education, dispensaries, and libraries, the coldly beautiful, well-born Lidiya represents the liberal-minded rural worker in contrast to the estate owners in the countryside who do nothing to aid the peasantry. The artist in the story, whom she scorns as a shiftless landscape painter utterly lacking in principles and social responsibility, condemns her activities: "In my opinion, medical stations, schools, libraries, apothecary shops, under existing conditions, serve only to enslave the people. They are fettered by a great chain, and you do not break that chain, you simply add new links to it — that is my conviction." And he goes on to develop a rather anarchistic line of thought in opposition to the gradualism of the liberals in achieving human betterment. He offers instead not schools but universities for the masses, in the hope they will realize that man's real vocation is spiritual activity — the continual search for truth and the meaning of life.

Critics have often identified the artist's views with those of his creator, as though Chekhov deplored individual practical efforts to improve the lot of the underprivileged as hopeless substitutes for a vast radical or revolutionary solution of all social and spiritual evils. Engaged in just such practical efforts himself, Chekhov could hardly take exception to Lidiya's warm defense of her similar efforts: "I'm telling you only one thing: It is impossible just to sit with your hands in your lap. True, we are not saving mankind, and perhaps we do make many mistakes, but we do what we can, and in that we are right. The highest and most sacred task of a civilized man is to serve his neighbor, and we are endeavoring to serve as best we can."

In fact, the views of the artist are entirely in keeping with his feckless, pessimistic nature — that of the defeatist segment of the intelligentsia, who sublimated their inactivity in sweeping verbal panaceas for social and moral improvement. Chekhov suspected this kind of pretentiousness, just as he suspected the pretentious messianism of Dostoevsky and the omniscient spirituality of Tolstoy's preaching.

[6] First published in *Russian Thought*, April 1896.

If Lidiya Volchaninova emerges as an unsympathetic character, despite her good deeds, it is because of her harsh and narrow crusading zeal, which Chekhov always deplored in people, and he points the moral of it in her wanton execution of her younger sister's love for the artist. For the ideological debate is only a motivational device in working out the destinies of two of Chekhov's most charmingly portrayed lovers. More than anything else *The House with the Attic* is a tale of vanished happiness suffused with all the poetry of the star-crossed fates of a Romeo and Juliet. There is an emotional wisp of Chekhov in the artist, which he himself suggested in a comment to Elena Shavrova when he began the story: "Now I'm writing a little tale: 'My Betrothed.' Once I had a betrothed. They called her 'Misyus.' "[7] (*November 20, 1895.*) Though the allusion is lost in the mist of Chekhov's secretive love life, he endowed Misyus, an enchanting wraith of feminine loveliness, with a background, appearance, and sentiments that belong to the heroines of fairy tales. But the moonlit recognition of love vanishes in the cold light of day when Lidiya, whose word is law for her younger sister, sends Misyus packing to a distant aunt. Time helps the artist to forget the house with the attic and the bewitching Misyus. Yet he often recalls the green light in the attic window, and a feeling of loneliness and sadness oppresses him. Then it seems to him that "I too am being remembered and waited for, and that we shall meet. . . . Misyus, where are you?"

« 5 »

Life at Melikhovo over the summer of 1896 was busier than ever, with more than the usual number of visitors, which included all three of Chekhov's brothers and their wives, the children of Alexander, the son of Ivan, and his aunt and her daughter from Taganrog. Because of guests, civic duties, care of the sick, and his writing, Chekhov regretfully had to put off a second visit to see Tolstoy at Yasnaya Polyana — two mysterious American visitors had brought him copies of certain works of Tolstoy printed abroad but banned in Russia, with the request to deliver them to the great man. But it occurred to Chekhov that in the summer Tolstoy had many more guests than he did, and that he would only be in the way there. He also had to abandon an idea

[7] The nickname of the younger sister Zhenya in the story, applied to her as a child because of her mispronunciation of "Mrs." in talking with her English governess.

of arranging for a hundred school children to visit the national Exhibition at Nizhny Novgorod.

However, Chekhov did manage to steal off to Moscow several times during the summer, and there, as he noted in his diary on June 1, he visited the graves of those who had been killed at Khodynka field. It is curious that this is Chekhov's only reference to the terrible catastrophe that summer at the coronation of Nicholas II, when over a thousand people were crushed to death, because of police incompetence, in a panic that occurred at the distribution of gifts in honor of the coronation.

Before the end of the summer neither his various activities, nor, as he said, the blooming beauty of his roses and masses of columbine could hold him any longer at Melikhovo. After a quick trip in July to a *dacha* not far from Rybinsk, which Suvorin had rented, and a brief visit, on the way back, to Misha and his wife at Yaroslavl, Chekhov set out again, on August 20, for the Caucasus. This lengthy journey was aided by a free railroad pass which Suvorin had obtained for him, and by a large advance from the magazine *Niva* for a long story, *My Life*.

Chekhov stopped briefly at Taganrog to visit the library and see his cousin Yegorushka,, and at Rostov he dined with his old schoolmate Volkenstein, who had become a lawyer. Then he pushed on to Kislovodsk, and there met acquaintances who, like himself, were vacationing at this resort. He listened to band concerts twice a day, ate his fill of Caucasian *shashlyk*, participtated in a hunting expedition, and bathed in the famous mineral springs. When the weather turned bad, he set out for Novorossiisk and there boarded a steamer for Feodosiya, to which he had been cordially invited by Suvorin. After a stay of ten days, during which they talked much about the theater and future plans for the production of *The Sea Gull*, Chekhov returned to Melikhovo on September 17.

Before and after his return Chekhov had considerable correspondence with *Niva* on censorship objections to *My Life*.[8] He was exasperated by the censor's demands that he change or delete a number of outspoken details of social existence in this searing exposé of provincial intelligentsia. There are various autobiographical echoes of Chekhov's youth in *My Life*, and his recent experience in building the Talezh school contributes to the account of the construction of the schoolhouse in the village of Kurilovka in the story. In essence, however,

[8] *My Life* first appeared in the "Monthly Literary Supplements" of *Niva*, 1896.

My Life tells of the revolt of a rigidly reared son and daughter against their unforgiving and hopelessly limited father, the local architect. More than this, their revolt is one against the whole social pattern of this provincial town, of which nearly all the characters are victims — against its vulgarity, meanness, social inequality, insincerity, filth, and cruelty. Up and down the social ladder the whole complex of daily existence is rooted in bribery, which has been virtually institutionalized in the town. And Chekhov's picture was no doubt intended as a representation of provincial town life in general in Russia.

The interesting fact, however, is that the revolt of Poleznev, the hero, is inspired by Tolstoyan principles. He rejects his position in the privileged class in order to become a common workman, a house painter. For, he argues, the strong and the weak, the rich and the poor, should share equally in the struggle for existence. And when Dr. Blagovo points out that such a doctrine would represent a menace to progress, Poleznev provides the stock Tolstoyan answer: "Progress consists in deeds of love, in fulfillment of the moral law."

Although *My Life* is commonly regarded as still another powerful indictment of Tolstoyan theory and practice, the evidence is not as clear-cut as that. Poleznev fails in his marriage, his father disowns him, and his sister dies, but he does not reject his Tolstoyan practices. He remains a common worker in the end, and his life seems to have more dignity and serenity than can be found among his old friends in the privileged class from which he came. If Tolstoyism, however, was not the answer to the gloomy provincial world that Chekhov described, he did not pretend that there was any other panacea. With his practical physician's mind, he knew there were no easy remedies or universal solvents. And with his artist's sense, he also knew that the activities and theories of human beings are not nearly so important as their sorrows. Steeled by their sorrows, the main characters of *My Life* move toward the Chekhovian conviction that progress and happiness are to be found, not in love, but in truth.

« 6 »

Throughout the earlier part of the year Chekhov had been revising the first draft of *The Sea Gull*. He must have finished the second version by the end of March, for at the beginning of April he sent a copy to Potapenko, no doubt to assure himself that the reworked characterization of Trigorin was no longer a close likeness of his friend. In fact, when the manuscript of *The Sea Gull* encountered difficulties with the censor — mostly over frank expressions of intimate relations between Arkadina and Trigorin — Chekhov entrusted Potapenko with the task of dealing with this official in Petersburg. And in order to meet last-minute objections by the censor, Potapenko, on his own authority, introduced a few slight changes and managed to obtain clearance for the play before the end of August.

An invitation from the Alexandrinsky Theater in Petersburg to stage *The Sea Gull* on October 17 as a benefit performance for the noted comic actress E. I. Levkeeva settled the matter of the opening with Chekhov. It was a fateful decision.

Although the official Theater and Literary Committee approved *The Sea Gull* for performance, its highly critical report might have forewarned Chekhov, if he had had the opportunity to read it, of difficulties ahead. The report stated that the play was a literary effort; that it contained a few characters drawn with refined humor, such as Medvedenko, Sorin, and Shamraev; and that in several scenes it achieved sincere dramatic quality. The report then went on to point out that the play "suffers from substantial defects." Its "symbolism, or more correctly its Ibsenism . . . running through the whole play like a red thread," was sharply condemned as ineffective and unnecessary. Faults were also found in the characterizations of Treplev, Trigorin, Arkadina, and Masha, and a looseness in the structure of the play was criticized.

Certainly the "tons of love," which Chekhov had mentioned to Suvorin, complicating the lives of four women and six men in four separate triangle situations, must have baffled the members of the committee, who were used to relatively simple, conventional plays. With a suicide at the end, they probably wondered why Chekhov described the work as a comedy, for the nontragic frustration that leads Treplev to take his life no doubt evaded them. They sought for the direct appeal and blatant theatricality of typical comedy, and found neither in *The Sea Gull*. Further, their report gives no indication that they perceived the subtleties and nuances of the play or the true significance of its symbolism. Nor is any mention made of the pervasive Hamlet motif, or the indirect appeal of the emotionally evocative dialogue. And the eloquent implications of the silences, the wonderfully effective mood of fused lyricism and wit, as well as the unanticipated truth that emerges from these characters variously disappointed by life, were dramatic innovations beyond the experience of this committee.

Chekhov himself sensed the artistic challenge which *The Sea Gull* would present to a contemporary audience, and at first he was impatient for the trial. One must not be hypnotized by the routine of life, he told Potapenko, who was in raptures over the freshness and originality of the play but worried by its flouting of dramatic conventions. Life was a jumble, Chekhov explained, in which the profound existed along with the trivial, the great with the insignificant, the tragic with the ridiculous, and that was the way it ought to be represented on the stage. And to do this, he declared, echoing Treplev in the play, new forms were needed. After some correspondence with E. M. Karpov, a mediocre dramatist and director of the Alexandrinsky Theater, who sought his approval on casting, Chekhov realized that he must go to Petersburg well in advance of the opening night to discuss these matters and attend rehearsals. "The thirst for fame" drew him to the northern capital, he wrote Leontiev-Shcheglov, and he left for Petersburg on October 7.

The next day Chekhov sat in the dark Alexandrinsky Theater and watched a rehearsal of *The Sea Gull*, the fourth that had taken place. He was mortified by what he saw. Nor did the fifth or sixth rehearsals show any improvement. And at this late point, only five days before the opening, the distinguished but temperamental actress, Mariya Savina, decided that she was unsuited to the role of Nina and rejected it — the very role on which Chekhov thought the whole play depended. In her place stepped the young, dedicated Vera Kommissarzhevskaya, who soon became one of Russia's most celebrated actresses. At that time she was slight of build, with large, luminous dark eyes, thin, tense but lovely features, and an extraordinary musical voice.

At the sixth rehearsal Chekhov observed with dismay that several of the cast were absent, a few still read their lines from scripts, and only an assistant director was present to guide the actors. *The Sea Gull* was just another play to them, and it was clear that the limited Karpov, in his staging and instructions to the actors, had failed to understand the structural innovations of the play, its poetic mood, and the tender and refined delineation of character. Shocked by the stilted, traditional intonation of the actors, their false emphasis in reading lines, and their lack of comprehension of the roles they were portraying, Chekhov frequently interrupted the rehearsal to explain the significance of a phrase or discuss the real essence of a characterization. "The chief thing, my dears, is that theatricality is unnecessary," he would repeat. "Really unnecessary. It is entirely simple. They are all simple, ordinary people." But, deeply discouraged as he left the theater, he said to Potapenko, who had accompanied him to the rehearsal: "Nothing will come of it. It is boring, uninteresting, and not needed by anyone. The actors are not interested, which means that the public will not be interested." Suvorin, with whom Chekhov was staying, noted in his diary that his guest had begun again to cough up blood.

Chekhov seriously contemplated withdrawing his play. He wrote Masha to say that it was going badly, and though he had urged her and Lika to make the trip from Moscow for the opening night, he now tried to discourage them. At the seventh rehearsal, however, things miraculously changed. Perhaps inspired by the superb acting of Kommissarzhevskaya, who with her fragile little figure and great eyes set in a tragic, childlike face seemed the very incarnation of Nina, the whole cast caught fire. People attending the rehearsal wept at the tender scenes. Chekhov was elated and dashed off a note to brother Misha filled with hope for his play. But the miracle failed to repeat itself at the last two rehearsals, including the dress one, which he attended. The cast had slipped back into its uninspired, hesitant performance of the earlier rehearsals. All was dull, flat and gray.

Suvorin noted in his diary on October 16: "Yesterday, after the dress rehearsal, he [Chekhov] was disturbed about the play and wanted to withdraw it. He was very unhappy over the performance. In truth, it was very mediocre." On the morning of the seventeenth, Chekhov met his sister at the railroad station. He looked ill, coughed constantly, and was in low spirits. She tried to cheer him up, but he persisted in complaining about the rehearsals and the fact that the actors did not know their parts.

That night, at the opening performance of The Sea Gull, Chekhov found the theater full. But this was not a typical Alexandrinsky audience for a première. Many of them were clerks, shopkeepers, merchants, and officers. They had come because the performance had been advertised as a benefit for their favorite, Levkeeva, a jolly, buxom actress who provoked laughter the moment she appeared on the stage in the homey, comic roles in which she specialized. Why she had selected for her benefit The Sea Gull, in which there was no suitable part for her, was a mystery. Ordinarily, actors and actresses so honored were at pains to choose a play which they knew in advance would delight their admirers. And no doubt Levkeeva's fans now anticipated a hilarious, conventional farce.[9] In any event, they were quite incapable of appreciating what they did see. Though a number of Chekhov's friends were present and, as it turned out, not a few of his envious literary rivals, the regular patrons of the Alexandrinsky, the intelligentsia, who might have been sympathetic to the innovations represented by *The Sea Gull*, did not attend in any number; they ordinarily kept away from benefit performances with their high-priced tickets, preferring to see the same play some other night.

Though the opening performance of *The Sea Gull* lacked inspired staging, and some of the cast, because they reacted negatively to its unconventional approach, played their roles unconvincingly, there was no wholesale attempt to undermine the performance. As the first scene unfolded, however, the audience sat in strained, silent incomprehension over this strange language spoken by the actors and these odd characters who seemed to move about like somnambulists. But when Nina (Kommissarzhevskaya) began the well-known monologue: "Men and beasts, lions, eagles, and partridges, antlered deer . . ." a sharp laugh was heard and loud talking broke out. At the end of the first act the slight, scattered applause was lost in the vociferous booing and whistling. And as the play wore on the noise became scandalous. Levkeeva's fans, ill-bred for the most part and feeling cheated by this incomprehensible play, roared with laughter at the most solemn moments and turned their backs on the stage to chat with friends. Leontiev-Shcheglov recalls the person next to him asking loudly, when Treplev placed the slain sea gull at the feet of Nina: "Why does this Apollonsky (Treplev) carry that dead duck around with him? Really, what nonsense this is!" The actors, bewildered by the uproar and inattention, fell into a semi-demoralized state. At intermission indignant comments were heard in the corridors and foyer: "Symbolic trash!" "Why doesn't he stick to his short stories?" Writers and journalists eagerly gathered in little knots to vent their venomous spite. All agreed that nothing quite like this failure had ever happened before in the Russian theater.

By the end of the second act Chekhov could stand no more. He left his box and took refuge backstage in Levkeeva's dressing room. What went through the mind of one of Russia's most popular and be-

---

[9] Levkeeva did have a role in a three-act comedy which immediately followed *The Sea Gull*. The staging of two plays in an evening was a familiar practice in the Russian theater of those days.

loved writers at this time is unknown. In his diary, after a bare entry that *The Sea Gull* had failed, he later added that while he sat in this dressing room, theater officials came and went, one of them a handsome young man from the police department. The actresses treated these officials with respect, he observed, and flattered them as old house-keepers flattered their masters when they visited. And he conjectured that just as men who attached themselves to something they knew noth-ing about — art, the theater, painting — and had no alternative other than to become officials, so did men become officials who knew nothing of life and were incapable of dealing with it. He must have wondered whether he, who thought he knew much about life and art, ought now to try and become an official.

When the performance ended — he later told Potapenko — he stole out of the theater with his coat collar up, like a thief in the night. He overheard one of the audience say: "That is the writer." And his friend added: "And a very poor one." A third asked: "Who is this Chekhov? Where did he spring from?" And he heard a short gentle-man exclaim indignantly: "I don't understand what the theater directors are about. It's insulting to put such a play on the stage." He wended his lonely way to Romanov's restaurant, had supper, and then walked the streets of Petersburg for hours.

Meanwhile, Masha and Lika, crushed by their experience at the theater, waited for Chekhov in their hotel room where he had promised to call after the performance and take them out to dine. Alexander arrived looking for him, and said that he had not turned up at the dinner in honor of Levkeeva, nor was he at Potapenko's. The ever loyal Alexander had scribbled his brother a note: "I learned about your *Sea Gull* only today at the theater — it is a wonderful, excellent play, full of profound psychology, thoughtful, and it grips the heart."

Finally, worried over Chekhov's failure to appear, Masha went to Suvorin's at one in the morning. His wife, with disheveled hair, over-whelmed her with trivialities, and Suvorin insisted upon telling her what needed to be done to *The Sea Gull* to improve it. He finally re-sponded to her plea to help find her brother by sending messengers to the theater, Potapenko, and Levkeeva. At two in the morning Chekhov entered his separate apartment at the Suvorins'. In his diary Suvorin recorded their brief conversation when he went in to say that Anton's sister wished to see him:

" 'Where have you been?'

" 'I walked the streets; sat. I couldn't just forget about the performance, could I? If I live to be seven hundred, I'll not give another play to the theater. In this field I'm a failure.' He then said he would leave on the morrow. 'And, please, don't try to stop me. I cannot stand listening to all their conversation.' "

Suvorin returned to tell Masha that her brother would see no one.

Callers began to arrive at nine on the morning of the eighteenth. Any moment Chekhov expected Davydov, who had played the part of Sorin, with advice and expressions of sympathy. The thought was unbearable. Potapenko, who had not been present at the performance, came at ten and found Chekhov writing letters, his open suitcase packed.

"It's good you've come. At least, I'll have company to the station. I can give you that pleasure since you were not among the witnesses of my triumph last night. Today I don't want to see the witnesses."

"Not even your sister?"

"We'll see each other at Melikhovo. Let's have a good time first. Here are the letters."

He wrote a brief, comforting note to Masha, telling her he was not upset, that he had been prepared for the outcome of the play by the rehearsals, and that he was leaving for Melikhovo.

Another note to Misha announced that the play fell with a crash. "Throughout the theater was a strained feeling of perplexity and disgrace. The actors played abominably, stupidly. The moral is: I must not write plays."

The last letter was to Suvorin, in which he ordered him to stop the publication of a volume of plays, including *The Sea Gull*, the manuscript of which Chekhov had turned over to him. "I'll never forget last evening, yet I slept well and am leaving now in quite a tolerable mood. . . . *Never* again will I write plays or have them staged."

He intended to take the first train he could get, and when Potapenko warned him it was a very slow one, he said: "All the better. I'll sleep and dream of glory. Tomorrow I'll be at Melikhovo. What bliss! No actors, no directors, no public, no newspapers. But a fine nose you have."

"Why so?"

"I ought to have said — 'a feeling of self-preservation'. Yesterday you didn't go to the theater. I also ought not to have gone. If you had only seen the faces of the actors! They looked at me as though I'd robbed them and kept as far as possible from me."

At the railroad station Chekhov joked at his own and Potapenko's expense. When a newsboy offered a paper, he replied: "I don't read!" And, turning to Potapenko, he said: "See what a kind face he has, yet his hands are full of poison. In every paper there's a review."

Despite Chekhov's efforts at witticisms and laughter, Potapenko observed, as the train pulled out, the deep distress in his gentle eyes.

« 7 »

"When you come to Melikhovo, bring Lika with you" — was it solace that he wanted when he added this in his letter to Masha on leaving Petersburg? They had eventually resumed their old relationship, on a more restrained level, after her dismal romance with Potapenko. Chekhov still enjoyed Lika's company and his urgent invitations to her to visit were renewed. Once again she began to come to Melikhovo often, and he resumed writing his serio-comic notes. He rarely missed an opportunity to see her on his trips to Moscow, writing in advance to suggest a meal together, but at the same time playfully warning that he would not permit her "to take liberties" with him; after all, he was still unmarried.

On the other hand, he may have wished to see Lika at this unhappy time because his conscience troubled him — the performance of *The Sea Gull* must have revived the anguished memories of her love affair and her dead child. Masha, in describing the opening night in her memoirs, wrote that Lika "only a short time before had had an unsuccessful romance with Ignati Nikolaevich Potapenko. In earlier readings of *The Sea Gull* to us, it had been clear that Anton Pavlovich had to some extent reflected this romance in his play. And, of course, the performance would agitate Lika." Another reason for concern was the possibility of an encounter in the theater between Lika and Potapenko and his wife. In Chekhov's letter to Masha on October 12, in which he tried to discourage her from coming to the play, he included a comment which he obviously intended should be passed on to Lika (both had planned to stay together in Petersburg) to discourage her also: "He [Potapenko] will be at *The Sea Gull* with all his family, and it may happen that his box will be next to ours — then Lika will be in a pickle." A mysterious note to Potapenko at this same time, in which Chekhov asked to see him — "I must speak with you confidentially" —

suggests that he also warned his friend of this possible encounter. In any event, Potapenko's decision not to appear at the opening night of *The Sea Gull*, a play with which he had closely associated himself, was no doubt taken in order to avoid meeting Lika.

However, as Lika watched the developing action of *The Sea Gull* in the Alexandrinsky Theater that evening, she must have been more amazed by how the witchery of art had transformed her rather sordid affair with Potapenko than hurt by the resemblance of anything in the play to the reality of her own experience. For Nina is not really the heroine of Trigorin's projected short story — the young girl free and happy as a bird until a man comes along, sees her, and from sheer idleness destroys her as Treplev had destroyed the sea gull. Rather, she is a poetic symbol of the indomitable quest of art that demands ultimate fulfillment in the face of all the slings and arrows of misfortune. Charmingly naïve when she first appears on the scene, and later rapturously in love with the writer Trigorin, Nina takes the bold decision to abandon her home in the country for Moscow to realize her consuming ambition to become a great actress. Trigorin betrays her, her baby dies, and she lives through a searing and vulgar theatrical experience in the provinces. However, when she returns two years later for a visit to the country, although she is still hopelessly in love with Trigorin, she is not a destroyed sea gull. "I'm now a real actress," she declares to Treplev in her moving monologue at the end of the play. "I act with delight, with rapture; I'm intoxicated when I'm on the stage and feel that I'm beautiful. And now, ever since I've been here, I walk about, I keep walking and thinking, thinking and feeling that my spiritual forces grow stronger every day. I now know, I understand, Kostya, that in our work, whether it is acting or writing, what matters is not fame, not glory, which I used to dream about, but the power to endure. Know how to bear your cross and to have faith. I have faith, and I no longer suffer so much, and when I think of my calling, I'm not afraid of life."

Here — Lika must have realized — was not the recalled bitterness of grief and shame, but fervent encouragement to accept one's suffering and have faith in work and life. Nor could Lika have discerned any marked similarity between Potapenko and Trigorin. Whatever image Trigorin may have had in the lost first draft of *The Sea Gull*, his resemblances to Potapenko in the revised version are superficial, such as his writing at a breakneck speed and his attitude toward women. In fact, the two writers in the play, Treplev and Trigorin, are occasionally the mouthpieces of Chekhov's own ideas, although he would have condemned the personalities and the artistic achievements of both. Treplev's attack on the conventional drama and stage and his demand for new art forms echo Chekhov's own position. And there is much in Trigorin's early experiences as an author that parallel those of Chekhov, even to Trigorin's confession to Arkadina that as a youth, always around some editorial office, fighting off starvation, he had missed the kind of love that's young and beautiful and is all poetry. Chekhov had once made a somewhat similar confession to Lika. Despite Trigorin's successes as a writer, art for him had become a matter of routine. Like the old professor of science in *A Dreary Story*, he has no ruling principle in his art which would enable him to transcend the obvious. And Treplev's trouble, in Chekhov's eyes, is that at the end, unlike Nina, he lacks faith in himself and in his art. Neither of these authors could rise to the prescriptions of Dorn in the play, which reflect Chekhov's own view — that there is no beauty without seriousness; that every writer must have a definite object in his work; and that in every work of art there must be a clear, definite idea.

If Lika could not clearly see herself in Nina, nor Potapenko in Trigorin, neither did the play effect a catharsis in her. Several weeks after the performance she wrote Chekhov: "Yes, everyone here says that *The Sea Gull* is also borrowed from my life, moreover, that you gave a good dressing-down to a certain person!"

That opening night another woman watched the performance of *The Sea Gull* just as eagerly as Lika — Lidiya Avilova. She tells in her memoirs (Chapter X) how she went alone to the theater — Leikin, in his diary, mentions that he saw her there with her sister. Her detailed account of the failure of the play is well written and in general accords with other authentic records. Of course, she followed the action breathlessly, intent upon discovering Chekhov's mysterious answer, promised at the masked ball almost nine months before, as to whether he had recognized her on that occasion. As the action wore on she began to think he had been joking or had mistaken her for someone else at the ball. Then, in the third act, Nina presents Trigorin with a medallion on which she had had his initials engraved, the title of one of his books, and the reference: "Page 121, lines 11 and 12," which, when Trigorin checked, read: "If you ever need my life, come and take it" — the sentence from Chekhov's own story and the one to which Avilova had referred on the engraved watch-chain pendant she had sent him. Avilova writes in her memoirs: "My head was in a whirl, my heart pounded madly. . . . The numbers were different, not those which I had had engraved on the watch-chain pendant. Undoubtedly this was his answer. He had really answered me from the stage, and me, only me, not Yavorskaya or anyone else."

At home, when her husband had gone to bed, she checked the reference from the stage in Chekhov's volume of stories, but the lines told her nothing: ". . . est phenomena. But why do you look at me with such rapture? Do you like me?" In bed, she could not sleep. Suddenly the thought flashed through her mind that the lines were chosen from her own book which she had sent to Chekhov. She jumped out of bed and ran to the study to check. Lines 11 and 12 on page 121 read: "It is not proper for young ladies to go to masked balls."

Lidiya Avilova could take cold comfort from the fact that she had contributed something to *The Sea Gull*. Chekhov had made very effective use in the play of her gift of the inscribed pendant. However, she professed to see something deep and personal in the way he employed the device. "This is his answer!" she exclaims ecstatically in her memoirs. "An answer to many things: to who had sent the pendant and the woman in the mask. He had guessed everything, he knew all." Did she think that he conveyed a moral to her in the fate of Nina, the aspiring artist, who made known her love to a celebrated author through the device of an inscribed medallion, and had then been betrayed? It is impossible to say, especially since Nina was a young, unmarried girl, and Avilova, the mother of three children, was living equably enough with her husband. But the plain truth of the matter would appear to be that Chekhov had played on her one of the practical jokes of which he was so fond. And in this instance, as so often in Lika's case, it was his way of transforming into a comic interlude the serious pretensions of a woman whom he wished to discourage. In the course of revising *The Sea Gull*, after the episode at the masked ball, he had searched through Avilova's volume of short stories, found a sentence that would serve his purpose, and placed the appropriate reference on Nina's medallion. But a sense of humor was not one of Avilova's strong points.

The levity with which Chekhov regarded Avilova's gift of the watch-chain pendant is suggested by an amusing letter he wrote, shortly after the performance of *The Sea Gull*, to Lika, who no doubt knew of the gift and perhaps also of the double use he had made of it in the play. After asking her to postpone for two or three years the bliss she plans for them, he adds: "With this I send you a design for a medal which I wish to offer you. If you like it, then write and I'll order one. . . ." And on the face of the medal which he drew, he placed the inscription: "Catalogue of the Plays of Members of the Society of Russian Dramatic Writers, 1890. Page 73, Line 1." When Lika checked the reference in the Catalogue, it turned out to be the title of the farce of a little-known writer: *Ignasha the Fool, or Unexpected Lunacy* — an obvious allusion to her affair with Ignati Potapenko.[10]

As a matter of fact, while Lidiya Avilova at the play was drawing her rapturous conclusions of the hallowed significance of her gift to Chekhov, she was unaware that he had already presented the watch-chain pendant to another woman — Vera Kommissarzhevskaya, the Nina who, on the stage, had given Trigorin a similar object, urging him to come and take her life if he wanted it! Perhaps it was a symbolic gesture on Chekhov's part, or just a thoughtless tribute to Kommissarzhevskaya's acting which had so thrilled him at that miraculous rehearsal. He had met her in the wings of the Alexandrinsky Theater and told her in his deep harmonious voice that his Nina, a role which she ultimately made famous all over Russia, had eyes like hers. And he presented her Avilova's watch-chain pendant. She was more than impressed, almost ready for sacrifice. But as events turned out, she too, like Lidiya Avilova and Lika, was unable to comprehend that all Chekhov desired from the women he liked was that they be beautiful, charming, and gay and not demand too much in return for the little bit of their hearts that he claimed. When Vera Kommissarzhevskaya returned after that night of terrible failure, she threw herself in her mother's arms, weeping for *The Sea Gull*, for herself, and for Chekhov.

« 8 »

Back at Melikhovo, after the disaster of *The Sea Gull*, Chekhov at first was extremely reluctant to talk with anyone about the play. He had been deeply hurt. This was no ordinary failure. He could not expunge from his mind the image of that audience with its derisive, roaring laughter ridiculing personal expressions of his faith in art and life. He frankly doubted the sincerity of admirers who sent him comfort-

---

[10] This letter, which appeared for the first time only in the recent Soviet edition of Chekhov's works, was unknown to Lidiya Avilova.

ing letters. Rather unfairly, he placed the blame on the actors, complained that he had no say in their selection, which was untrue, and even misrepresented the number of rehearsals, claiming that they were fewer than were actually held. He particularly offended by the practical-minded Suvorin, who called him "an old woman" and "a coward" for running away. It would have been cowardly of him, Chekhov replied, if he had remained behind, dashing from one editor to another, from one actor to another, begging their condescension and nervously introducing useless changes. "I acted just as reasonably and coolly as a man who has proposed, received a rejection, and has nothing left to do but to clear out. Yes, my vanity was wounded, but the thing was not a bolt from heaven; I expected failure and had prepared myself for it as I forewarned you in all sincerity." (*October 22, 1896.*)

The reviews, those which he saw, and those which were mentioned in letters to him, were devastating and increased his depression. The *News* dismissed the play as "entirely absurd" from every point of view — in ideas, as a piece of literature, and as a vehicle for the theater. In the *Bourse News*, Chekhov's fair-weather friend Yasinsky wrote that the general impression created by the performance was "confused and wild," and that the play was not "The Sea Gull but simply a wild fowl." The *Petersburg Leaflet* declared: "This play is badly conceived and unskillfully put together, and its contents are very improbable, or, it would be better to say, there are no contents. Every act reeks with despairing, dull, false, incomprehensible life and people. . . ."

Suvorin alone, in *New Times*, wrote a favorable review of *The Sea Gull*. Only a sincere dramatic talent, he said, could have written such an original play, one filled with the bitter truths of life, and he ascribed its failure to inadequate rehearsing, badly assigned roles, and poor staging. And a letter in defense of the play appeared in the *Petersburg Gazette*, signed by the initials of Lidiya Avilova.

The second and following performances of *The Sea Gull* in the Alexandrinsky Theater, which incorporated some production changes suggested by Suvorin, ought to have assuaged Chekhov's feelings, as well as brought home to him that the special character of the benefit audience on that first night had been the principal reason for the debacle.[11] Now the theater's customary audience paid close and curious attention to this new type of play and even the actors had begun to respond to its

[11] After the fifth performance, *The Sea Gull* was dropped from the repertory of the Alexandrinsky Theater.

peculiar values. Vera Kommissarzhevskaya wrote him after the second performance: "I've just returned from the theater. Anton Pavlovich, my dear, we've won! The success is complete, unanimous. . . . How I'd like to see you here now and still more to have you hear the shout of all: 'Author!' " Potapenko, who saw the second and third performances, wired: COLOSSAL SUCCESS. AFTER EVERY ACT CURTAIN CALLS, AFTER THE FOURTH — MANY AND A DEMONSTRATION. . . . THE ACTORS ASK ME TO CONVEY THEIR JOY. Bilibin and Leikin wrote letters of praise. Fresh reviews by Potapenko and Leikin hailed *The Sea Gull*. Further, news of highly successful performances in Kiev, Taganrog, Astrakhan, and other provincial cities began to come in, and amateur groups requested permission to stage the play. Then Goltsev pleaded with him to be allowed to publish the play in *Russian Thought*.

All this was balm. He began to write more cheerfully in his letters, gave his permission to Goltsev,[12] and rescinded his order to Suvorin not to publish his volume of plays.[13] However, perhaps nothing did more to sooth the profound artistic and moral hurt than a letter from A. F. Koni, the eminent lawyer, a man deep in the wisdom of life, a valued friend of great Russian authors, and himself a critic and writer of distinction. He thanked Chekhov for the pleasure he had derived from one of the later performances of *The Sea Gull*, "a work which stands out because of its design, the novelty of its ideas, and its thoughtful observations on lifelike situations. This is life itself on the stage, with its tragic alliances, eloquent abstractions, and silent sufferings — everyday life, accessible to all, and yet understood by almost no one in its cruel inner irony — life so accessible and close to us that at times you forget you are sitting in a theater and yourself are prepared to take part in the conversation you are hearing. And how wonderful is the conclusion! How faithful to reality that she, the Sea Gull, does not deprive herself of life. . . ."

Chekhov gratefully answered by recalling the nightmare of the opening performance and the way he had left Petersburg, ashamed and wondering whether he had lost his senses. "But your letter," he continued, "has acted upon me in a very positive way. I have known you for a long time, esteem you profoundly, and have more faith in you than in all the critics put together — you must have felt that when

[12] *The Sea Gull* appeared in the December issue of *Russian Thought*.
[13] This volume appeared in 1897. It contained, apart from *The Sea Gull*, *Uncle Vanya*, *The Swan Song*, *Ivanov*, *The Bear*, and *The Proposal*.

you wrote your letter, and that is why it is so fine and convincing. My mind is at rest now, and I can think of the play and the performance without loathing." (*November 11, 1896.*)

The critics of the first performance of *The Sea Gull*, Chekhov now began to discover, had not reached their almost unanimous verdict of condemnation without an element of conspiracy. Leikin wrote to tell him that he had observed how the reviewers congregated after the first act and did their best to provoke the offensive behavior of Levkeeva fans. And in November, *Theatergoer* published an article on the play in which it declared that *The Sea Gull* had been, in many respects, unique in the annals of the Alexandrinsky Theater. "There was a certain mockery of the author and the actors, and a kind of furious, malignant joy among certain parts of the audience. A good half of the theater was occupied by the worst enemies of Mr. Chekhov. . . . Especially malignant were those stern evaluators and judges of the 'scribbling' brotherhood. They were out to settle personal accounts."

All this once more left a bad taste in Chekhov's mouth. Again he felt nothing but loathing for *The Sea Gull* and found it extremely difficult to correct the proof of the volume of his plays. "You will repeat," he wrote Suvorin on December 14, "that this is unreasonable and stupid, that it is my conceit, pride, etc., etc. I know, but what am I to do? I would gladly rid myself of this stupid feeling, but I simply cannot do it. The reason is not that my play was a failure; indeed, the majority of my plays have failed, and every time it was like water off a duck's back so far as I was concerned. On October 17 it was I and not my play that failed. At the time of the first act I was struck by a particular circumstance, namely, that those with whom I had always been frank and friendly before October 17, with whom I had dined pleasantly, and on whose behalf I had broken lances (for example, Yasinsky) — all wore a strange expression, terribly strange. . . . I am quiet now, in my usual mood, yet I cannot forget what happened any more than I could forget a slap in the face."

« 9 »

Chekhov found an escape from his distressed feelings in the multitude of tasks that now customarily occupied him at Melikhovo. He visited schools, argued the cause of his project of a highway at Serpukhov, took care of the sick, and wrote numerous letters to friends to obtain reference books for the information division of the Taganrog library. And he took on the further obligation of a worker in the national census for the following year. A fire — in the wall by the stove in his mother's room — caused some excitement. The bell in the new firehouse he had built in the village clanged; the apparatus dashed up; a servant appeared with an ikon in her hands, and Father Chekhov ran about shouting nonsense. The damage, he informed Misha, would run to two hundred roubles.

To Tolstoy's daughter Tatyana he wrote to explain his failure to accept her earlier invitation to visit the family at Yasnaya Polyana to read them one of his new stories. His trip to Petersburg and the business of his play, he explained, had got in the way of the visit, and now, because of the snow, it was impossible to travel to them. He would like to have read them from the proof sheets of *My Life*, but now it had appeared in print, he said, and it had been so altered by the censor as to become unrecognizable and repulsive to him.

Literature in general seemed repulsive to him over the last months of 1896. When his *Sea Gull* appeared in print, he suspected that the the critics would lash out at him again. And in the course of correcting the proof of his plays for Suvorin, he wrote him: "Ah, why have I written plays and not stories! Subjects have been wasted, wasted to no purpose, scandalously and unproductively." (*December 7, 1896.*) And a project that he had recently, and enthusiastically, discussed with Goltsev — to start a newspaper in Moscow — he now began to discourage.

On one of his several trips to Moscow at this time, Chekhov visited Levitan, who was ill. He discovered that his friend had an enlargement of the heart and would probably not live long. In the face of this situation, he marveled at Levitan's passionate thirst for life and at the superb studies he continued to work on in his studio.

Though Chekhov ultimately tried to adopt a dispassionate attitude toward the cruel experience he had undergone in Petersburg, it is clear that it cankered his feelings and left a permanent scar. It was not so much the failure of his play, as he said himself, but the fact that this debacle could arouse such evil in many he had considered his friends. In the words of the critic of the *Week*, he must have wondered ". . . what evil could Chekhov have done to anyone, whom had he offended or obstructed, to deserve the evil which was suddenly heaped upon him?" The experience tended to deepen the natural distrust he had of the genuineness, loyalty, and capacities of the rank and file of his literary confrères and of the social milieu in which they functioned. When Nemirovich-Danchenko queried him on why men of letters seemed incapable of serious conversation, he replied — modestly including himself in his general censure — that writers are incapable of talking on general problems because they have no political interests, are isolated from the world, read few books, and seldom go places. And literary conversation, he insisted, inevitably ended in who wrote better, who worse. Conversation about personal life, he admitted, could sometimes be interesting, but in this area writers become shy, evasive, insincere, and the instinct for self-preservation restrains them. In this type of talk his friend Sergeenko, "shaking his finger in the air and loudly babbling in all the railroad cars and homes of the land, will reach a decision on why I live with N at a time when B is in love with me. I'm afraid of our morals and of our ladies." And Chekhov concluded: "To put it briefly, don't blame yourself or me for our silence or for the absence of seriousness or interest in our conversation, but blame what the critics call 'the times' or the climate, or the vast expanses of the country, or whatever you like . . ." (*November 26, 1896.*)

In December, upon hearing of the possibility of a conflict with England over the Near East, Chekhov wrote Suvorin and indicated the true state of his feelings at this time: "If there is a war in the spring, I'll go. During the last one and a half to two years so many events of all kinds have happened in my life . . . that, like Vronsky, there's nothing left for me to do but go to war, to heal, of course, not to fight. The only bright interval during this time was my stay with you at Feodosiya; all the rest was so rotten that I dismiss it." (*December 2, 1896.*)

But as the next New Year's celebration approached, Chekhov's customary resilience returned. Cheerfully he wrote Lika to come for the party and to bring some wine. "Only, I beg you, don't drink it up on the way."

CHAPTER XVII

"I'll Go with the Spring Freshets"

THE DISASTROUS FIRST-NIGHT FAILURE of *The Sea Gull* has often been credited with contributing to the crisis which five months later occurred in Chekhov's health. However, stubborn unwillingness to seek treatment for his disease and remorseless draining of his physical resources made the crisis inevitable.

As a worker in the national census, from January 10 to February 3, 1897, he went the rounds of peasant huts in the district, knocking his head against the low doorways which he could never get used to. During most of this period he ran a fever from an attack of influenza and his head ached constantly. He had the further responsibility of supervising a team of fifteen census-takers, lecturing them on the forms, checking the results, and turning in a final report. Officials of the County Council were supposed to aid him, but they knew little about the business and frequently pleaded sickness when they were wanted. The census had exhausted him, he wrote a medical friend, and never had he been so busy. By the time it was over he had become heartily sick of the effort, and without any comment he entered in his diary only the stark record of his reward: "I received a medal for the census."

Yet in the same letter in which Chekhov informed Suvorin of the conclusion of this task, he announced: "I'm building a school again. A deputation of peasants came and begged me and I did not have the courage to refuse. The County Council is giving a thousand roubles, the peasants have collected three hundred, and that is all, while the school will cost no less than three thousand. This means that once more I'll have to be thinking all summer about money and scraping it together here and there. In general, life in the country is full of work and care." (*February 8, 1897.*)

The school was to replace an old one in the village of Novoselki, halfway between Melikhovo and Lopasnya. As in the case of the Talezh school, this work absorbed him. Manuscripts of stories on his desk gave way to drawings of the new structure. Again he was both architect and contractor, as well as fund-raiser, not sparing his own money in the process. He promoted two amateur theatrical performances at Serpukhov in the interest of the project, one of which his literary disciple Elena Shavrova helped to arrange. And at about this same time he thought up an insurance program for teachers, agreed to supervise a plan to open public libraries in the area, and accepted the post of trustee of still another rural school. "The Moslem digs a well for the salvation of his soul," he jotted down in his notebook. "It would be good if each of us left after him a school, a well, or something of the kind, so that our life would not pass into eternity without leaving a trace." Here was a design for living perhaps more practical than a whole

Tolstoyan system for achieving the moral perfectibility of man. Chekhov took a positive joy in improving the well-being of his community. Jubilantly he wrote Alexander, when the Sanitary Council settled upon Melikhovo as the site of a new medical center: "They will build a hospital and apartments for physicians. And also an apothecary shop and a rest room. Melikhovo, as you can see, progresses, and you ought to wonder how this Shestakov[1] manages things!" (*March 2, 1897.*)

The project that now particularly excited Chekhov, however, was the erection of a "People's Palace" in Moscow. The previous year the idea had been broached to him in a vague form by some wealthy ladies who had in mind a kind of cultural center that would attract the city dwellers who now spent their leisure in vodka shops and in idle pastimes. The design called for a huge building that would contain a theater and library, a museum, and reading, lecture, and tea rooms. Chekhov at once asked his friend, the architect Shekhtel, to draw sketches for such a comprehensive structure. And on February 16 he attended a meeting of interested people, which he had called in Moscow, to hear Shekhtel describe the design of the proposed building and to discuss further plans. If government permission could be obtained, it was decided to form a corporation to raise a half million roubles by selling shares. Stanislavsky was present. The day before Chekhov had attended a literary evening to raise funds for needy Moscow University students and had heard Stanislavsky, who had already attracted some notice as an actor and theatrical director, read a scene from Pushkin's play, *The Covetous Knight*. Feeling that he had performed badly, the hypersensitive Stanislavsky was trying to leave the theater as inconspicuously as possible when he was confronted by Chekhov.

"They say you play my *Bear* splendidly," Chekhov bluntly began.[2] "See here, why not put it on again? I'll come and have a look at it and may even write a review."

The stiff and formal Stanislavsky remained silent, expecting that the next remark would be about his poor performance that evening.

"And I'll collect royalties, too," Chekhov added after a pause.

There was another silence.

"A rouble and twenty-five kopecks," joked Chekhov.

The offended Stanislavsky hurried off. He did not realize, as he

---

[1] Shestakov was a former mayor of Taganrog.

[2] In January, 1897, Stanislavsky had played the role of Smirnov in *The Bear* at the Korsh Theater.

pointed out in his reminiscences years later, that Chekhov's sallies were probably an effort to divert him from unpleasant thoughts over his performance that evening.

The next day at the meeting on the "People's Palace," Stanislavsky, still under the influence of his unfriendly reactions to Chekhov, complained of his walking about the room and making everybody laugh during his own efforts to comment on Shekhtel's design. He remembered Chekhov as being tall, ruddy, and unusually buoyant. "I did not understand then," he later wrote, "why he was so overjoyed. Now I know. He was rejoicing over a new and splendid project for Moscow. He was happy that a tiny ray of light would illumine the lives of ignorant people. Throughout his whole life anything that would adorn human existence delighted him. 'Look here! This is wonderful,' he would say on such occasions, and a bright, childlike smile would light up his face." Though the "People's Palace" did not materialize, one of its main features, a "People's Theater," may well have influenced Stanislavsky's conception of the Moscow Art Theater, which he established the following year under its initial title, "The People's Art Theater."

As usual when in Moscow, pleasure as well as business filled Chekhov's days and nights: dinner at the wealthy Madame Morozova's, pancakes with the publisher and art collector K. T. Soldatenkov, followed by a visit to the studio of the ailing Levitan, where Soldatenkov bought a picture and two sketches for eleven hundred roubles, an evening with the well-known doctor and professor of medicine A. A. Ostroumov, and gay dinners on two successive evenings at the Hermitage, with such literary friends as Ertel, Mamin-Sibiryak, Sytin, Tikhomirov, V. I. Sobolevsky, and Goltsev, which did not break up until four or five in the morning. At the Continental Hotel he also attended a large dinner in honor of the great reform (the emancipation of the serfs), on which he commented in his diary: "Boring and ridiculous. To eat, drink champagne, chatter, and make speeches about the people's self-awareness, national conscience, freedom, etc., at a time when slaves in dress coats, those very same serfs, wait on table, and coachmen wait on the street in the cold — this is to deny the Holy Ghost." The intelligentsia's callousness in the face of social inequities, as well as the government's repressions at a time when some alleviation had been anticipated under the new Tsar, troubled Chekhov more than ever. Only a few days before this event at the Continental, he had written Suvorin

about the police raid on the house of V. G. Chertkov, Tolstoy's principal follower, and on his harsh sentence of exile to England which
followed, a blow aimed as much at the master as at the disciple: "A
great many people are going to see him off, even Sytin. And I'm sorry
that I cannot do the same. I don't cherish tender feelings for Chertkov,
but the way they have treated him fills me with intense, intense indignation." (*February* 8, 1897.)

After sixteen days in Moscow Chekhov returned to Melikhovo in a
rather exhausted state. He was sick of jubilee dinners, he wrote Elena
Shavrova, and all he wanted was sleep. However, the pressing business
of the Novoselki school and the Taganrog library awaited him, as well
as a number of guests. And he was desperately trying to finish a long
story, *Peasants*. At this time, also, he had been requested to pose for a
portrait. The wealthy collector and art connoisseur, P. M. Tretyakov,
who for years had been assembling for his gallery portraits of Russia's
greatest writers, had commissioned an able young Petersburg artist,
I. E. Braz, to paint Chekhov.

Despite his various activities, increasing fatigue, and alarming spells
of coughing, Chekhov wrote Vera Kommissarzhevskaya on March 2,
in reply to a letter which contained her photograph and a warm invitation to visit, that he would soon be in Petersburg to pose for a portrait
and would call on the very day of his arrival. Having finished *Peasants*
and sent it off to *Russian Thought*, he set the date of his departure on
Friday, March 21, which would enable him to read the proof of his
story in Moscow and also meet Suvorin there, who promised to accompany him to Petersburg. Although he felt ill the night before and
coughed up blood, he left on Friday.

Chekhov put up at the Moscow Grand Hotel, and on Saturday, along
with Suvorin, attended a convention of theater workers, where the
distinguished actress Mariya Savina made an effective speech. That evening at the Hermitage, just as he was about to begin dinner with Suvorin, blood suddenly started pouring from Chekhov's mouth. Applica-
tions of ice were of little use and Suvorin had him removed to his own
hotel, the Slav Bazaar, where Dr. N. V. Obolensky was summoned.
Chekhov remained there that night. He was frightened by the flow of
blood and told Suvorin that he knew it came from his right lung.

The next morning, however, Chekhov insisted upon being taken to
his own hotel, because he had many letters to answer and a number of

people to see.[3] He wrote brother Ivan from there that he was a little unwell and to visit him if he had anything on his mind, and Goltsev he asked to send him Shekhtel's plans for the People's Palace, for he wished to show them to a wealthy man. But the hemorrhages continued, and on Tuesday Dr. Obolensky ordered him to the clinic of the specialist Dr. Ostroumov. Suvorin visited him twice that day and entered in his diary: "The patient was laughing and joking as usual in the midst of spitting blood into a large receptacle. But when I mentioned that I had seen the ice breaking up in the Moscow River, his face changed and he said: 'Really, is the river moving?' I regretted reminding him of this. Probably a connection between the thawing river and the flow of blood occurred to him. For, several days before, he had told me: When a peasant is being treated for consumption, he says: 'There's no help for it. I'll go with the spring freshets.' " It was in spring, Chekhov must have recalled, that brother Nikolai began his last illness.

« 2 »

Three days before Chekhov left for Moscow he had written Lidiya Avilova:

"I want very, very much to see you — in spite of your being angry with me and wishing me all the best 'in any case.' I'll be in Moscow before March 26, most probably on Monday at ten o'clock in the evening; I shall stay at the Moscow Grant Hotel opposite Iverskaya. I may possibly come earlier if my affairs permit — alas! I have very many. I'll remain in Moscow to the 28th of March and then, imagine it, I'm going to Petersburg.

"And so, good-by till then. Change your anger to mercy and agree to have supper or dinner with me. Really, it would be fine. I shall not fail you now whatever happens; only ill-health could keep me at home."

In her memoirs (Chapter XII, where this is quoted) she omits Chekhov's postscript: "The last phrase of your letter reads: 'Of course, I have understood.' What have you understood?" The phrase suggests that in Avilova's letter which he had answered she had at last come to understand his long silence and had decided to cease writing him — wishing him all the best "in any case." Though she asserts in her

---

[3] Suvorin, in his diary, says that Chekhov remained with him two nights. However, Chekhov wrote at least two letters on Sunday, the day after his hemorrhage, and both were sent from the Moscow Grand Hotel; their contents plainly indicate that he was there at that time.

memoirs that they had arranged to meet in Moscow in March, Chekhov's letter bears the tone of a response to a final ultimatum to see her — she had come to Moscow to visit her elder brother. Actually some fourteen months had passed since Chekhov's last letter to her, during which time, it may be assumed, she had written him more than once and he had failed to reply. In her memoirs (Chapter XI) there is a brief episode which seems to date, chronologically, shortly after the opening night of *The Sea Gull*. Here she describes how, alone at a theatrical performance, she saw him in a box with the Suvorins. He turned his back on her, but at the intermission asked to escort her home and she angrily refused. However, it is difficult to credit the reality of this incident, for Chekhov had not been in Petersburg since the day after the performance of *The Sea Gull*.

Avilova promptly answered his letter of March 18, but instead of agreeing to dine with Chekhov, as he had requested, she gave him her Moscow address and invited him to visit her there. Apparently this was a situation he wished to avoid. Elena Shavrova, another young and attractive authoress whose relations with Chekhov parallel to a certain extent those of Avilova — although she had no illusions about his emotional involvement with her — would also try to persuade him to call. Twice she made the attempt on his recent trips to Moscow, writing him on one occasion: "Won't you drop in tonight to see a poor, sick writer? By eight-thirty all will be out to a ball. . . ." He answered that he too had a cold and hoped she would get better quickly and visit him. In the same vein he now replied to Avilova's invitation of March 22: "I arrived in Moscow earlier than I expected. When shall we meet? The weather is misty and foul, and I'm a bit unwell and shall try to remain indoors! Will it be possible for you to come to me without waiting for my visit to you? Best wishes."[4]

Avilova hurried off a note to say that she would call at the Grand Hotel that evening, but when she arrived there was no Chekhov — at that time he was probably in Suvorin's rooms being treated by Dr. Obolensky. In the pile of letters awaiting him she found her note

[4] In her memoirs Avilova claims that she received this note by messenger on March 23. Quite clearly, it was written and delivered the day before. March 23, her birthday, was essential to her narrative. For on that day her younger brother Alexei, who was her confidant, had arranged a party at his house to celebrate the event, which was to be her excuse for getting away from her elder brother and his wife, who were not invited to the party, and thus find an opportunity to visit Chekhov in secrecy.

unopened, and she left very crestfallen. Chekhov wrote her a brief message on March 25 to tell her of his falling ill.[5] Then her brother Alexei discovered that Chekhov had been taken to Dr. Ostroumov's clinic,[6] and they both went there on the day he arrived. Over the formidable objections of the attending physician — that Chekhov was dangerously ill, ought not to see anyone but his sister, and under no circumstances should he be allowed to talk — Avilova secured admission to the sickroom, conveying the impression that she had come all the way to Moscow to hold a tryst with Chekhov. Three minutes were allowed her, and the doctor strictly warned that if the patient talked he might have another hemorrhage.

Avilova entered. " 'How kind you are,' he said softly," is the quotation in her memoirs.

" 'Oh, you mustn't talk!' I interrupted him, frightened. 'Do you suffer? Have you any pain?' "

So they carried on a conversation, according to her account, until the doctor came in at the end of the three minutes. Chekhov asked her to visit the next day, and when he wished to say something else the doctor raised an admonitory finger and insisted he write it. Chekhov wrote: "Get my proofs from Goltsev at *Russian Thought*.[7] And bring me something of yours to read and something else." Then he took the note from her hand and added: "I very much lo . . . Thanks." " 'Lo' he crossed out and smiled," she recalled. Avilova left, and all the way home, she wrote, "I was wiping away the tears which ran down my face." And she added: "Alexei was silent, breathed hard, and sighed. 'Alexei,' I said, 'don't feel sorry for me. My heart is joyously full, full.' "

Avilova visited the next day and brought him his proofs and some flowers. Although Chekhov's condition was reported as worse, the doctor, according to her memoirs, allowed her to visit. And now a lengthier conversation ensued — her husband had summoned her home (she showed Chekhov the three telegrams she had received) and she described the patient as pleading with her to remain at least one more

[5] In this note Chekhov says that he arrived in Moscow on March 22 and also that he had spent two nights at Suvorin's hotel. These were probably "white lies" to cover in each case his failure to get in touch with her sooner. The diary of Chekhov's father dates his departure for Moscow on Friday, March 21.

[6] In her memoirs she has Alexei ascertaining this information on March 24, which is consistent with her own garbled chronology, but Chekhov was not taken to the clinic until the day after.

[7] The reference here is to the proofs of *Peasants*.

day and come and see him again. She refused, fearful that such a decision would force a showdown with her husband and compel her to confess her love for Chekhov. Avilova left the hospital depressed, accusing and justifying herself for her decision.

On March 28 Chekhov scribbled Lidiya Avilova a thank-you note, very similar to the many he wrote people who sent or brought him gifts during his illness: "Your flowers don't fade but become better all the time. My colleagues allow me to keep them on the table. You are kind, very kind, and I don't know how to thank you. . . ."

On the day of Avilova's second visit to the clinic, Chekhov's sister also called. "Anton Pavlovich lay on his back," Masha recorded in her reminiscences. "He was forbidden to talk. After having greeted him, to conceal my agitation I moved over to the table, on which lay a drawing of his lungs. They were sketched with a blue pencil, but the upper parts were filled in with red. I understood then that they were already diseased."

More interesting, as a sidelight on Avilova's account of her visits, is an entry in Leikin's diary for April 16: "L. A. Avilova relates that during her stay in Moscow . . . she learned that Chekhov was in Professor Ostroumov's clinic. She went there to visit him, but the doctor, although he allowed her to see Chekhov, would not permit her to talk with him. Speaking to him was forbidden, and he lay on his back in bed, not stirring."

« 3 »

Chekhov's immediate concern, upon entering the Moscow clinic, was to keep the seriousness of his illness from his parents, and he warned his sister and brothers and intimate family friends on this score. The doctors diagnosed tuberculosis in the upper part of the lungs and prescribed a change in his way of life. "I understand their diagnosis," he wrote Suvorin, "but not their prescription, which is just about impossible. I have been definitely ordered to live in the country, but living permanently in the country involves continual trouble with peasants, animals, with elementary forces of all kinds, and to protect oneself from worries and anxieties in the country is as difficult as to escape burning in hell. Still I shall try to change my life as much as possible, and through Masha I have already announced that I shall give up medical practice in the country. For me this will be both a relief and a great deprivation. I shall drop all my district responsibilities, shall buy a dressing gown, warm my bones in the sun, and eat a lot. They tell me to eat six times a day and are indignant because I eat so very little. I'm forbidden to talk much, to swim, and so on and so on." (*April 1, 1897.*)

His behavior in the clinic, however, was a poor augury of his determination to abide by the prescriptions of the doctors. On his third day there, when Chekhov was still extremely weak, Tolstoy barged in, undoubtedly encountering no protests from the awestruck nurses and physicians. The modest patient was touched and impressed by this show of concern on the part of the great man. Unfortunately it was not in Tolstoy's nature to restrict himself to a brief stay or to the usual small talk of a hospital visit. He launched forth on a discussion of immortality, in which he maintained that humans and animals will continue to live on in a form of mind or love, the essence and purpose of which will remain a mystery to man. To Chekhov, who found it difficult to talk at all, this conception of immortality represented a kind of formless, jellylike mass with which he would be expected to fuse his individuality, his ego and consciousness. "Such immortality," he later wrote his friend Menshikov, in giving an account of the visit, "I don't need and I do not understand, and Tolstoy was surprised that I did not understand it." (*April 16, 1897.*)

Since the suffering and exhausted Chekhov offered little or no argument, Tolstoy, now possessed by one of his instructional moods, felt encouraged to introduce the subject of art. He had abandoned *Resurrection*, he declared, and had read sixty volumes to prepare himself to write a treatise on art, the substance of which he next proceeded to expound. "His thinking about it is not new," Chekhov wrote Ertel several weeks after this meeting; "all the wise men in every age have sung this song in a variety of tunes. Old men have always tended to see the end of the world and have said that morality has fallen to its *ne plus ultra*, that art has degenerated and grown tawdry, that people have become puny, and so on and so forth. In his book Tolstoy wants to prove that art has now entered its final phase and is in a blind alley from which there is no outlet except retreat." (*April 17, 1897.*) Tolstoy finally departed, leaving Chekhov in an agitated state. Late that night he suffered a relapse accompanied again by a hemorrhage.

As he regained strength, Chekhov's good spirits returned and he slipped easily into his customary activities. The author of *Ward No. 6*, he quipped, had been moved into Ward No. 14, a spacious room with lighting effects that reminded him of one of Potapenko's garish plays.

Cheerful notes were dispatched to Elena Shavrova for a roast turkey instead of the cold bouillon they were serving him, to Shekhtel to suggest a bottle of wine, and to Goltsev to thank him for the half-pound of caviar. "People come and go, bring flowers, candy, good things to eat. In a word, bliss," he wrote Suvorin. (*April 1, 1897.*)

Soon he was busying himself about his usual cares, such as arranging for a doctor to see his ailing friend Semashko and writing a letter to one of the village teachers to warn him that bricks for the new school would be delivered and to be sure someone was on hand to receive them. When Leontiev-Shcheglov visited he noticed Chekhov's sickroom table piled with manuscript. A Moscow young lady, studying to be a schoolteacher, had sent him her stories to read. He read them, and quite critically. She angrily sent a letter to the clinic, declaring that she had expected "more heart and greatness of soul" from him. Patiently he answered that if she wished to be an author she must learn how to write correctly, and he rather pathetically concluded by observing that it was difficult for him to write while lying in bed. Early in his illness he had written A. S. Yakovlev, the senator's son he had tutored years ago — they had recently renewed their acquaintance when, as one of a Moscow group of amateur actors, he had come to Serpukhov to stage a performance on behalf of the Novoselki school. Now Chekhov wanted him to visit the clinic so they could talk over a second performance to raise money, in which he himself would assume responsibility for the properties and stage design. Yakovlev came, but he was more interested in asking Chekhov to place a story for him in *New Times*. Chekhov recommended it to Suvorin, and also wrote the author a letter which contained criticism of the tale and a warning that a single good story, written over the course of a year, would not make an author of him any more than a single nail hammered into a wall would make a carpenter.[8]

As the news of Chekhov's illness got around, he received many touching testimonials of concern. Alexander, deeply worried over his brother, wrote: "Petersburg is talking with agitation and sympathy about you, for the news spread quickly and as always in such cases has somewhat exaggerated the situation. It shows that you are very popular and beloved by the public." But this popularity had unpleasant

---

[8] Yakovlev, apparently ashamed of troubling Chekhov on a matter of this sort while he was ill in the clinic, says in his published recollections that the story was not his but that of a friend.

consequences. In a cross mood Chekhov wrote Suvorin on April 7: "I ought to get married. Maybe a spiteful wife could cut down the number of my visitors by at least half. Yesterday they came all day long, it was simply awful. They came in pairs and each begged me not to speak and at the same time asked questions."

Eventually the doctors permitted him to exercise and he roamed unsteadily around the clinic and the grounds. He told Leontiev-Shcheglov on his visit that he had almost become used to the place and that it stimulated his thinking on a variety of subjects. "In the mornings I go for a walk to the Novodevichy Cloister, to the grave of Pleshcheev.[9] At other times I look in at the church, rest against the wall, and listen to the nuns singing. Then my soul becomes strangely quiet." If he could take no comfort in Tolstoy's vision of immortality, it was still less consoling to think that after death he would simply mingle with the sighs and torments of some universal life and that people would carry him off to the cemetery and then go home and drink tea.

But in the end Chekhov grew impatient to be at Melikhovo. He fully realized that an existence of semi-invalidism might be his future lot, and the question of how well he would be able to continue to support himself and his family troubled his mind. He had smiled bitterly when Leontiev-Shcheglov had expatiated on the plight of the writer, ill and surrounded by well-to-do adoring admirers, to no one of whom it occurred to offer a helping hand. Yes, he must work. If he enjoyed leisure, to anticipate an invalid's lifetime of it was abhorrent to him. "You write that my ideal is laziness," he replied to Suvorin, with whom he had been corresponding on his future course of action. "No, it is not laziness. I despise laziness as I despise weakness and a lack of mental and moral energy. I spoke to you not of laziness, but of leisure, and I did not say that it was an ideal, but only one of the essential conditions of personal happiness." (*April 7, 1897.*)

Chekhov left the clinic on April 10, and the next day, aided by his brother Ivan, he arrived at Melikhovo.

« 4 »

Chekhov had been home only a few days when *Russian Thought* appeared with his long story *Peasants*. Earlier, the printed sheets had

[9]Pleshcheev had died in 1893 and was buried in the celebrated graveyard of the Novodevichy Cloister, quite close to Dr. Ostroumov's clinic, which was also to be Chekhov's last resting place.

outraged an official of the Moscow censorship commission and he had demanded the story's exclusion from the issue unless certain changes were made. "The position of peasants living in the villages," he declared in his report, "is described in colors that are too gloomy." Quoting objectionable passages, he wrote: "The peasants are 'coarse, dishonest, filthy, and drunken, and do not live together in peace. . . . Who keeps the pothouse and makes drunkards of the people? The peasant. Who embezzles and drinks up the community money? The peasant. Who bears false witness in court for a bottle of vodka? The peasant.'" What particularly pained him was that Chekhov saw not improvement in the existence of the peasantry since the Emancipation Act, but rather retrogression. Under the threat of punishment, *Russian Thought* had to agree to cut out a whole page of Chekhov's story in the printed version and substitute another in which the most offensive lines were omitted.

The government had reason to be concerned by this stark revelation of rural life, nor could the wealthy, or those elements of the intelligentsia who tended to idealize the peasantry, remain undisturbed by the story. Chekhov, the keenest of observers, had packed into it the accumulated knowledge and impressions of his last five years of service among these people as a physician and district official.

Nikolai Chikildeev, who has long been a waiter in a Moscow hotel, is forced by illness to return to his native village with his wife Olga and their daughter. By this simple device the life of the numerous Chikildeev family, their neighbors, and of the whole village is seen, in all its agonizing barrenness, through the eyes of peasants who have achieved a smattering of education and some sense of human dignity in the city. Here in the country they live, ten or twelve in a family, in a one-room hovel, stinking, dirty, swarming with flies, and their food consists largely of black bread soaked in water, with a herring added on feast days. Whenever the old fall ill, the children tell them they have lived too long and that it is time to die. Drunkenness is the daily escape of the men. For the women, who are beaten as cruelly as the animals, there is no escape except death, which they often long for. And everywhere is depressing, grinding poverty, and bribery and peculation by the rural officials who stand over the peasants.

Despite the bestiality and harshness of this savage existence, Chekhov brings out the humanity of those whose gentle and resigned lives condemn them to suffer more than the rest. In church or on solemn feast days, emotionally stirred by the tolling bells or the religious procession with its marchers, banners, and singing, they have a vision of a different life:

"It was as though all suddenly understood," wrote Chekhov, "that there was no void between heaven and earth, that the wealthy and powerful had not yet seized everything for themselves, that there was still a defense against insult, bondage, terrible, unendurable poverty, and the horrors of vodka. . . . But the service came to an end, the ikon was removed, and everything went on as before; and again were heard coarse, drunken voices from the tavern."

In a series of striking genre pictures, Chekhov effectively illuminates the characters of Kiryak, Fyolka, Mariya, and Olga. The final scene of Olga, once her husband has died, leaving the Chikildeevs, who have no further use for her, to beg on the highway with her little girl, is executed with beautifully restrained pathos.

Throughout *Peasants* Chekhov seems to be asking only that some light be brought into the darkness of the lives of these people and that they receive relief from the crushing burden of their poverty. No tale of his up to this point had created such a public stir. Scores of reviews appeared, most of them ecstatically favorable. Their general tone is reflected in the comment of the *Northern Herald* which declared that the success of *Peasants* "revives for us that time when a new novel of Turgenev or Dostoevsky appeared." Violent polemics arose in the press over the meaning and significance of the story, and Chekhov received many highly laudatory letters from readers and literary friends whose judgment he valued. In effect they all wrote, as brother Alexander did: "A wonderful thing is *Peasants*.[10] There's talent for you!" All this was most heartening to Chekhov after the debacle of *The Sea Gull* and an illness which had brought him face to face with death.

[10] It appears that Chekhov planned to continue this work with the intention of revealing the often unhappy existence of those peasants who go to the city to seek their fortune. Drafts of two further chapters dealing with this theme have turned up in his papers and were printed in the Soviet edition of his complete works (IX, 480-484). And his notes for this continuation, mingled with entries bearing on the earlier part of *Peasants*, thus proving the connection between the two parts, have also been published in the Soviet edition (Vol. XII). These two additional chapters and the notes have been translated into English for the first time by Edmund Wilson and published in: Anton Chekhov, *Peasants and Other Stories*, selected and with a preface by Edmund Wilson, Doubleday Anchor Book, New York, 1956, 281-288.

« 5 »

During the spring and summer at Melikhovo, Chekhov tried to obey the orders of the "scoundrely doctors" who kept him "under surveillance" and forbade him liquor, smoking, and everything else, he said, except correspondence with friends. Though he had many fine themes for stories fermenting in his brain, he did little writing. He refused to treat the sick, but made every effort to secure the services of other physicians for them. Physically he was unable to work much in his garden and confined himself to pruning one rosebush a day and feeding the sparrows.

For the most part, however, Chekhov lived up to the reputation that good doctors have of being their own worst patients. The commitments he had undertaken before his illness he somehow could not abandon now, despite the protests of his sister who strove to take these burdens on herself. He continued to collect and dispatch books to the Taganrog library, mildly protesting the inefficiency of their cataloguing system that listed the works of other authors under his name and confused foreign books with Russian ones and their translators with the authors. Nor could he surrender his task as examiner in the district schools, which left him with taut nerves and utterly fatigued at the end of the day. Supervising the completion of the Novoselki school took most of his time and energy, and a brief entry in his diary reflects nothing of the relief he must have experienced upon the conclusion of the work: *"July 13:* At the dedication of the Novoselki school, which I constructed. The peasants presented me an ikon with an inscription. The County Council was not represented." Perhaps because no district official had graced the occasion, he made a brief speech to the peasants — a kind of public effort he always tried to avoid. And he apparently did it poorly. At least, Misha, who was present with his sister, thought the talk not very fluent.

These activities probably did not place as great a strain on his weakened condition as did his guests. Reports of his illness increased the number of visitors; but his boundless hospitality and natural fondness for having people around him, as well as his customary thoughtlessness in issuing invitations to all and sundry, contributed to creating a situation which was positively damaging to his health. Rather defiantly and irrationally he wrote Leikin: "I'm getting fat and have already improved so much that I regard myself as entirely well and do not make use of the opportunities of a sick man — that is, I no longer have the right to evade guests when I wish to, and I'm not forbidden now to converse a lot." (*July 4, 1897.*) Chekhov's father, in his patient record of Melikhovo comings and goings, would now add in his diary "Thank God" when a guest departed.

The married brothers with their wives and children were the chief offenders, though more distant relatives also visited, such as Cousin Volodya from Taganrog. "He stayed forty-three days" was Father Chekhov's remorseless indictment of Volodya in his diary when this cousin finally left. Repeated visits by close family friends, such as Lika, Levitan, and Ivanenko — to which must be added his old Taganrog tutee Alexandra Selivanova and his former Medical School comrades, Zembulatov and Korobov — were more than matched by priests, monks, teachers, estate owners, doctors, and officials in the district. However, total strangers would turn up, too, such as two students from the Medical School of Moscow University who discussed student agitation and literary endeavors, with Chekhov advising them to start a student newspaper. Another new guest was the able artist Alexandra Khotyaintseva, who soon became a favorite of the family and returned often. Five years younger than Chekhov, she endeared herself to him by her caricaturing pencil and brush (she executed several paintings and sketches of him), as well as by her clever writing and conversation.

Leontiev-Shcheglov, whom Chekhov urged in his most persuasive manner to come, perhaps because he was one of the few close friends who had not seen Melikhovo, finally arrived at the beginning of May. The visitor was appalled by a marked change in Chekhov's face from when he had last seen it — only six weeks before in the clinic. It seemed to him yellow, exhausted. And he noticed how often his friend coughed. As they sat on a bench near the house, the dachshund Bromine at their feet, admiring the bed of tulips in full bloom, Chekhov said with a note of suffering in his voice that what he needed most was a full year of complete rest. "Imagine," he complained, "in the last few days almost a dozen guests have come here from Moscow. It is as though I were running an inn. And one must feed them, give them liquor, and worry about where to put them up for the night." The noises from the house and the piano-playing bothered him in the garden. If he wanted to do any writing, he had to wait until all went to bed.

"Actually they did not give him a moment's peace!" Leontiev-Shcheglov wrote in his memoirs. "Early in the morning a certain landowner arrived and stayed a long time. Then a rural physician appeared, next the village priest, and after him someone in a military uniform, perhaps a Melikhovo police officer. . . . And in the small hallway outside Chekhov's study, peasants and their wives hardly ever ceased entering and leaving, some on business, some on trifles, some for medical aid. And to cap it all, at lunchtime, like a bolt from the blue, came a guest from Moscow — a fat, unknown German, young and foppish, perhaps a dentist by profession, whom Chekhov may have met by chance at the Moscow clinic, and, as a 'colleague' of a certain sort, had hospitably given him his Melikhovo address."

Leontiev-Shcheglov was correcting the proof of a play which he had to return to the publisher next day. Chekhov read part of it and, according to his friend, made some valuable suggestions (Chekhov later told Suvorin that the play seemed to have been written not by the humorist Leontiev-Shcheglov, but by a cat whose tail the author had stepped on). He had just finished persuading the willing Leontiev-Shcheglov to send the corrected proof by mail and remain an extra day, when his guest learned that the fat German, who was already beginning to get on Chekhov's nerves, liked it so much at Melikhovo that he had decided to stay a week or two since he had plenty of time on his hands. Dismayed, Leontiev-Shcheglov persuaded the German to leave by telling him of Chekhov's poor health and his need of complete seclusion to write. And to make the story good, to his own and Chekhov's chagrin, he announced that he would leave at once with the German — a decision that he regretted, for it was the last time he saw Chekhov alive.

Several brief trips to Moscow over the summer — against the doctors' advice — enabled Chekhov to escape the Melikhovo guests. There he saw Korolenko and Ertel, who thought he had altered a great deal in appearance since the winter, despite the apparent improvement in his health. On one of these visits he sought out Levitan on the nearby estate of the millionaire S. T. Morozov, a lavish establishment which reminded him of the Vatican. He quickly departed, disgusted by the army of liveried lackeys, the vulgar furnishings, and the expressionless face of his host. On such trips to the city he preferred to look up Lika for a meal and a chat, usually with the hope of trying to persuade her to return to Melikhovo with him.

Though Chekhov had cautioned Braz that Melikhovo was the dullest estate in Russia, the artist arrived on July 4 to paint his portrait and, taking advantage of his host's hospitality, brought along his two nieces. On the same day Misha and his wife came, and found Alexander's two boys already there. Chekhov took refuge in the Lodge. Braz worked for seventeen days amidst the hurly-burly of Melikhovo, with Chekhov posing twice a day, and he still had not finished the portrait. In the end, he destroyed the canvas, attributing his failure to the conditions under which he worked and to the traces of illness which he found in Chekhov's features.

Once Chekhov had got rid of Braz, he took the brash step of making the overnight journey to Petersburg, something he had been longing to do ever since he left the clinic. He wanted to disillusion his friends there, who would be expecting to see an exhausted consumptive, scarcely breathing, by showing them, "instead, a face as round as the moon." Certainly Leikin, whom he visited, thought that he looked well, and he noted in his diary that Chekhov had good color, ate well, and was cheerful. With Suvorin, who was now deep in theatrical enterprises, Chekhov discussed drama. Shortly before, he had written Suvorin that he was reading Maeterlinck's plays and found them strange and wonderful things. If he owned a theater, he said, he would stage *Les Aveugles*, though taking the precaution to avoid the play's failings by summarizing the contents on the programs for the semi-idiotic public. Suvorin noted the visit in his diary and also the fact that Chekhov, who now thought he knew enough French, wanted to translate the tales of Maupassant, whom he admired.

No doubt, Chekhov also discussed with Suvorin a project of Alexander's. His brother had sent him his published treatise on alcoholism, which Chekhov, in that ceaseless japery they maintained in their correspondence, promised to hang on a nail in the toilet so that visitors could tear out the pages. The work, however, had recommended its author to an able psychiatrist who associated Alexander with him in a plan to establish a clinic for the scientific treatment of alcoholics. Money was needed, and Alexander appealed to his brother, who had encouraged the idea, for ways on how to raise funds. Chekhov persuaded Suvorin to approach Witte, the minister of finance, and this important official agreed to find government support for the project.

Chekhov returned to Melikhovo apparently without making any attempt in Petersburg to see Lidiya Avilova, despite the touching scenes she had created out of her visits to him in the clinic some four months before (in her memoirs she says that he did not come to Petersburg at this time). The trip had clearly taken its toll on him, for shortly after it, abandoning the hopeful auguries of his improved health, he mentioned in a letter to Tikhonov: "Concerning my maladies, during the last week I've had a little trouble: I've been coughing and blowing my nose like hell; in a word, the same story. I ought to get away, but I've still not been able to arrange my financial affairs." (*August 6, 1897.*)

In fact, Chekhov's restless nature, now augmented by worry over his health, made it difficult for him to remain complacently at Melikhovo during the warm summer months, as the doctors advised. With the curbs which they had placed upon him, life was boring and stupid, and he had come to the conclusion that, except for a drunkard, it was impossible for a man to live permanently in the country. Sitting in one place, he frankly confessed, bored him. He passionately yearned to wander, and he told Suvorin, who had announced his intention of going abroad, that if he had the money he would accompany him anywhere. Actually Chekhov had originally planned to break the summer at Melikhovo by a trip first to the South, and then to an exhibition at Stockholm; but his determination to finish the Novoselki school, and then the obstacle of Braz and his portrait, and finally a lack of funds spoiled these plans.

The doctors, however, positively insisted that, once the cold winds arrived, Chekhov must seek a warm climate. He thought of going to Malta, Corfu, or Nice. A chance bit of news that his friend, Vasily Sobolevsky, editor of *Russian News*, was in Biarritz settled the issue. Chekhov at once wrote him for precise travel instructions and the best hotel to stay at, asserting that he was somewhat shy about traveling in Europe alone since he knew all languages except foreign ones, and when he spoke French or German abroad, the conductors usually laughed at him. As for transferring from one station to another in Paris, that was just like playing blindman's bluff. With the proceeds from the performances of *The Sea Gull* and advances which he took to finance his stay abroad, Chekhov set out for Biarritz on August 31.

CHAPTER XVIII

"To Be Doctored . . . Is a Form of the Most Repulsive Egoism"

FROM BERLIN TO COLOGNE the Germans on the train almost suffocated Chekhov with cigar smoke, but German beer — "not beer but bliss" — revived him. The Suvorins met him at Paris and insisted he remain for a few days to see the sights. And see them he did — the Moulin Rouge with its *danse des ventre* to tambourines and a piano; several popular cafés; then shopping with Suvorin's daughter and walking till he grew weary — yet he felt strangely well.

Chekhov was sorry to leave Paris, but he had already wired his new time of arrival at Biarritz to Sobolevsky and felt that he could not change it again. The editor and his wife greeted him at the station and offered him quarters at their *ménage*. He politely declined and took a room at the Victoria Hotel. This resort town by the sea delighted him — noise, glitter, laughter day and night, throngs of people constantly going and coming, striking Spanish types among them. And it all seemed so inexpensive: a lunch of six fat dishes and a bottle of white wine cost next to nothing. He bought a silk hat to promenade in, and when he tired sat on the *plage*, read the papers, or just watched the gay strollers — the ostentatiously wealthy, the lovely women flaunting their varicolored dresses and sunshades, the wandering minstrels with their guitars, and the open water and cliffs beyond. It all took him hundreds of versts from Melikhovo. "I don't want to go home," he wrote Suvorin. And for variation there was the Casino entertainment and a bull-fight at Bayonne.

Every Russian in Biarritz, Chekhov noted in his diary, regrets that there are so many Russians there. He appears to have seen little of them, apart from the Sobolevskys, whom he joined daily, and the eminent artist K. E. Makovsky, whose acquaintance he made. After Chekhov had been there almost two weeks, the Leikins arrived, and this old friend was surprised at his high spirits.

Whatever the distractions abroad, Chekhov was always eager to get letters from home. To one from Lika he replied in a spirit of fun not unmixed with sly criticism of her. "For whole days I sit in the sun and think about you and of why you love to speak and write about lop-sided things; and I've decided that you have a side which is not in order and you know this and like it." But if she would only come to Paris, he continued, "I'll meet you lovingly, will try not to notice your lopsidedness, and in order to give you sincere satisfaction, I'll speak to you only of dairy cheese." To annoy her, he added parenthetically that he was taking French lessons from a nineteen-year-old girl named Margot. "Your letters," he went on, "were a real joy," and he begged her to write longer ones. "Believe me, I value not only *Reinheit* in women, but also kindness. As far as I know, up to now you've been very kind: you have written my friends long, tender letters; extend this kindness to me." (*September 18, 1897.*)

Before Chekhov had been in Biarritz two weeks, the weather, now the capricious guardian of all his plans, turned cold, windy, and rainy. He had to leave. After writing Goltsev to send him a thousand roubles, and Lika to remind her to inform him if she came to Paris, he set out with Sobolevsky for Nice.

Since Chekhov anticipated remaining in Nice throughout the fall, winter, and early spring, it was necessary to find an inexpensive place to live. He followed Leikin's recommendation and rented a room in the Pension Russe — a large one on the second floor, with windows facing the south, carpeted floors, a bed like Cleopatra's, and a separate wash-room. The Russian cook, who had been there a long time, prepared excellent meals, both native and French. On awakening in the morning he was served two eggs, bread, and a large cup of coffee; for lunch at noon, omelet, beefsteak, sauce, cheese, and fruit; at two-thirty, a cup of cocoa; at six-thirty, dinner, usually consisting of soup or borsch, fish, cutlets, chicken, fruit, and cheese; and in the evenings, tea with biscuits. For all this, with the added privilege of entertaining guests in the salon, he paid only seventy francs a week! As he cheerfully wrote Masha, a bachelor could live well at Nice on between twenty-five hundred and three thousand roubles a year.[1] Only the mosquitoes, which he tried to drive away by burning candles, bothered him, and he also regretted that the Pension Russe was situated on a side street, the Rue Gounod, providing no view of either the sea or the mountains.

Nice struck him on arrival as a vacationer's paradise. Flowers and

---

[1] In short, Chekhov was paying about fourteen dollars a week for board and room, and the roubles his bachelor existence would require for a year would amount to about $1250-$1500.

greenery were everywhere — palms, eucalyptuses, oleanders — and from the crowded Promenade des Anglais stretched the lovely view of the caressing and tender sea. But most important was the precious sun that shone for days on end, so that into late fall Chekhov walked about without an overcoat and in a straw hat. This was the kind of life that warmed his soul. He loved the street noises and the vagabond musicians, who often performed under his window and for whom he always had coins ready — the tenor in one group, he wrote Alexander, was more talented than the best artist in Russian opera who received five hundred roubles a month. Then there were the cafés, and the bands marching in musical competition along the streets, which were full of excitement, dancing and merriment. In contrast to Russian social manners, the French sense of equality and their delicacy in conversation won his admiration. It amazed him to watch a group of schoolboys at play, their priest joining in with as much gusto as the youngsters. A servant at the pension, in performing tasks for him, would smile like a duchess on the stage, although he could see from her face that she was weary from hard work. And the polite form of address of clerks, gendarmes, even beggars, impressed him. "Culture here," he wrote Suvorin's wife, "oozes out of every shop window, every willow basket; every dog has the odor of civilization." If he remained alive, he promised, he would spend every winter abroad. His only chauvinistic strictures were that the sugar, matches, shoes and apothecary shops were incomparably better in Russia.

With some resistance at first, Chekhov eventually settled down to the narrowly circumscribed life of the pension dweller. There were about forty in the Pension Russe, mostly women, Russian provincials of small means, a few lawyers and academicians, and a titled lady with an old maid daughter. They came and went, and Chekhov regarded with a sinking feeling the departure of an occasional boarder he liked, whose place was taken by a dull guest. A number of them, like himself, were in various stages of illness. An irascible widow of a distinguished scholar, who sat next to him at the long pension table, seemed constantly angry; she believed that he deliberately took from the serving plate precisely the piece of meat or fish which she wanted. The fat old wife of a Moscow merchant was chronically dissatisfied, never went anywhere, and sat in lonely misery all day in the garden, dreaming of returning to Russia. Chekhov pitied her, for he found out that friends had abandoned her and she was afraid to travel home alone. The baroness and her daughter, long-nosed, severe, dressed fashionably but in poor taste, chattered constantly at the dinner table above the heads of their neighbors. Alexandra Khotyaintseva, whom Chekhov had persuaded to make a trip from Paris to visit him, drew an amusing set of imaginary caricatures which portrayed him pursuing and offering a proposal of marriage to the young baroness. Alexandra broke the pension rule by insisting on having tea with Chekhov in his room. She recalls in her memoirs that a Kiev couple, in the next room, were reading one of his tales aloud to each other and he put his ear to the wall to find out which one it was, a situation which the artist also caught in a deft caricature.

For the most part Chekhov found the pension ladies foolish, small-minded gossips, everlastingly speaking nonsense and banalities, and it was hard to restrain himself from answering their queries impertinently. "I regard these Russian ladies in the Pension Russe," he wrote Suvorin, "as ugly, dull, idle, selfishly idle, and I fear to become like them for it seems to me that to be doctored, as we here are doctored (that is, I and these ladies), is a form of the most repulsive egoism." (*December 14, 1897.*)

His defense was to develop a daily regimen of his own, consistent with the prescriptions of his doctors — indoors in inclement weather, no liquor, no spicy foods, and no fast walking. In the bright, sunny mornings he strolled along the Promenade des Anglais, and then sat in the shade to read. In the late afternoon and evening he remained in his room and read or tried to write. The study of French occupied him seriously and he took lessons. It was difficult, he remarked, for a man of his age to learn a foreign language, but his progress is indicated by several long letters to Masha, who was also studying French, in which he explained fine points of the language. He clearly learned to read French with some ease and wrote it after a fashion — a letter to the French governess in the Suvorin family elicited praise. But he spoke it haltingly and found it hard to understand Frenchmen when they carried on conversations among themselves.

Chekhov, however, soon sacrificed his daily regimen to the demands of the little band of loyal friends he made at Nice. Sobolevsky introduced him to Professor M. M. Kovalevsky, to whom he became quite attached. He had a villa at Beaulieu, a few miles from the city, and at this time was preparing a series of lectures to be delivered in Paris. A lawyer, historian, and sociologist, in 1887 Kovalevsky had been deprived of his professorship in Moscow University because of his political views and had emigrated to Paris, where he eventually founded the Russian Advanced School of Social Science. A story about him, which Chekhov fancied, was that he had once fallen in love with his namesake, Sofya Kovalevskaya, the eminent mathematician, who as a little girl had watched spellbound the courtship of her older sister by Dostoevsky. A huge, vital man, witty, vivacious, and fun-loving, he won Chekhov as much by these qualities as by his vast learning and incisive mind — more impressive, Chekhov told Suvorin, than the minds of the best intellectuals in Petersburg. Chekhov eagerly accepted Kovalevsky's invitation to accompany him on a trip to Algeria in January, after he finished his Paris lectures.

A sharp contrast to Kovalevsky was the well-known painter of historical scenes, V. I. Yakobi, whose splenetic temperament found an outlet in scolding everyone as swindlers and scoundrels, a foible which amused Chekhov. And the gentle, shy, but keen-minded old Russian vice consul, N. I. Yurasov, was a favorite of all three, and a friend frequently helpful to Chekhov in many ways. Chekhov took walks or played piquet with one of the other of these friends, and they would often dine together at the pension or at the Taverne Gotique, where he would permit himself oysters and beer.

Chekhov had other friends and acquaintances at Nice whom he saw from time to time, such as the bacteriologist, Dr. V. G. Valter, and he visited the officials at the Russian zoological station at Villefranche. On several occasions, despite his own illness, he performed medical services for distressed Russians, one of whom presented him with a traveling cooking kit as a remuneration. When the regular Nice "season" began, in late October — inaugurated by a visit of Queen Victoria — multitudes of people of all nationalities swarmed into the resort, including among the many Russians his old friends the Nemirovich-Danchenko brothers. The carnival spirit affected Chekhov and he wrote Sobolevsky for a correspondent's card in order to receive good seats at the various performances, such as those of Sarah Bernhardt and the famous soprano Adelina Patti.

« 2 »

While in Nice Chekhov maintained close contacts with home. It took five days for letters to travel to Russia, and though he asserted that he disliked writing them, he carried on a copious correspondence with various people. To Masha, his chief lieutenant at Melikhovo, he wrote very frequently, sending her instructions about renovating the Lodge, changes in the garden, the handling of poplar plants that he had ordered from Riga, or reminding her to give a rouble at Christmas to the worker who took care of the cattle, three roubles to the village priest, and small gifts to the children of the Talezh school.

He had hardly got settled at Nice, however, when he learned the distressing news from Masha, annoyingly supported by a letter from his father, that his financial arrangements for the household had broken down. The monthly two hundred roubles which she was supposed to receive from Suvorin's Moscow bookshop, income from the sales of his various works, had not been paid. Chekhov at once wrote to correct this situation, instructing Alexander to forward to Masha the royalty on *Ivanov*, which the Alexandrinsky Theater had reintroduced into its repertory, and he also advised Masha, in case of a financial crisis, to apply to *Russian Thought* for an advance against his future writings. To relieve his conscience immediately, he sent her more than three hundred roubles from the sum he had taken with him, but with the stipulation that this should be repaid from income she would receive.

Living seemed so deceptively inexpensive at Nice that he constantly sent presents home, as well as contraband French books which he asked returning Russians to deliver to Alexander. Though the slender margin of funds on which he existed sometimes reached the vanishing point, he firmly declined loans from people who feared that illness had lessened his earning capacity. In October, he kindly rejected an offer of money from Ya. L. Barskov, editor of a children's magazine, who had in the past unsuccessfully attempted to obtain a story from him. Chekhov delicately indicated that he had enough money to live on at Nice, and that even if this were stolen, he was still able to write. There is a rather cryptic reference to this matter in a letter to Lika on November 2. After informing her that Margot had come to Nice from Biarritz and then vanished from sight — Lika had jealously asked him about this young French teacher whom he had mentioned in a previous letter — he continues on a subject which, he writes, must remain confidential: "I received from Barskov a long registered letter which I had to go five versts to the post office to obtain. He writes that merchants don't give money and he scolds these merchants, tells me what a fine author I am, and promises, if I consent, to send me money every so often for my expenses. Lika, dear Lika, why did I yield to your urgings and write at that time to Kundasova? You have deprived me of my *Reinheit*; if it hadn't been for your persistent demands, I assure you I would not have written that letter which now lies like a yellow stain on my pride."

Olga Petrovna Kundasova, a mathematician by training, was familiarly known as "the Astronomer" in the Chekhov family, where she was a frequent visitor as an old friend of Masha's. Improvident and thoroughly eccentric, she was much admired for her intellectual ability and independence by Chekhov and Suvorin, both of whom covertly aided her financially. Though Chekhov's reference to her in connection with Barskov's offer is unclear, a possible explanation is that Lika had persuaded him, in the light of his illness and need for funds to go abroad, to write Kundasova of his inability to assist her further, and that she, in turn, alarmed over his financial situation, had conveyed this information to Barskov.

In this same letter to Lika, Chekhov added: "Principally because of Olga Petrovna, I have developed a persecution mania. I had hardly recovered from Barskov's letter when I received two thousand roubles from Levitan's Morozov. I did not ask for this money, don't want it, and I requested Levitan's permission to return it, of course, in a manner that would offend no one. Levitan doesn't desire this. All the same I shall send it back. I'll wait a month or so and return it with a letter of thanks." It seems that Levitan, who had a way with the wealthy, had asked his Maecenas S. T. Morozov to send this sum, while at the same time, for form's sake, he suggested to Chekhov that he should offer a promissory note for the two thousand. "My dear, amiable fellow," he had written Chekhov, "I most earnestly beg of you not to worry about money matters, everything will be arranged so that you can stay in the South for the sake of your health." Potapenko, in his memoirs, tells of a certain millionaire who came to Nice and, taking advantage of a loan he had made to Chekhov, unpleasantly thrust his company upon him. Annoyed by the millionaire's presumptuousness, Chekhov wired his publisher for the money and paid back the loan. Though the account does not correspond in all details with the facts mentioned in the letters of Chekhov and Levitan about Morozov's offer of money, it is possible that Potapenko has supplied the conclusion to this episode.

In his letters to Lika, Chekhov, though perhaps for different reasons, seemed as curious about who was courting her as she was about the women in his life — at this time he suspected that the dramatist and theatrical entrepreneur Sumbatov-Yuzhin was pursuing her. But Chekhov liked to get letters from Lika, not only to hear from her about the many friends they had in common, but also to learn of her own activities. In December she wrote to seek his reaction to her plan to open a millinery shop, from the income of which she hoped to pay for her continued musical studies. He began his reply on a light note — an excellent idea, he wrote, for it would enable her to eat and him to pursue the pretty models in the shop. "I shall not read you a moral lesson," he continues in a more serious vein, "I'll only say that work, however modest it may seem, whether it is a millinery shop or a grocery shop, will give you an independent position, peace of mind, and assurance for the future. With satisfaction I myself would also get into anything, in order, like all, to maintain the struggle for existence from day to day. In the last analysis, the privileged position of the idle is hellishly wearying and boring." In the end, however, he reverted to his flippant manner, wishing her a husband with mustaches and a good disposition. "The latter, in the light of your bad temper, is as necessary as air, otherwise the fur and feathers will fly in your millinery shop." (*December 27, 1897.*)

While in Nice, Chekhov was informed by the editor that the *Annals of Surgery* had once again got into financial difficulties. And again he sprang to its assistance. Eventually a wealthy benefactor was found, and with some satisfaction Chekhov wrote of this triumph to Suvorin, who had grown cold to the troubles of the *Annals,* referring to his comment that if this magazine failed, it meant that no one needed it: "But if some among us do not read books and magazines, that does not mean they are unnecessary." (*December 16, 1897.*)

Chekhov occasionally wrote his mother from Nice and ordered flowers to be sent to her on Christmas — he was much worried about her ailing legs, for she now suffered from varicose veins. Although his father wrote and tried to keep him supplied with odd copies of Russian newspapers and periodicals, and regularly sent his Melikhovo diary, Chekhov rarely replied, usually contenting himself with brief messages of thanks for his thoughtfulness in letters to Masha. But Chekhov kept his relatives in Taganrog informed of his health and activities abroad in letters to Cousin Yegorushka, in one of which he asked him to look out for the sister of Elena Shavrova, who had joined a theatrical company in the city.

Despite his desire for anonymity, Chekhov's efforts on behalf of the

Taganrog library and museum appear to have leaked out. Learning of his interest, some citizens persuaded his old teacher, Father Pokrovsky, who was head of the Council on Education, to invite Chekhov to become a trustee of the Taganrog parochial and rural schools. Though in his reply he made a show of being overburdened with educational duties, he was obviously pleased by this recognition, and accepted the honor. He was perhaps more pleased by a glowing letter he received at Nice from N. I. Zabavin, the teacher of the new Novoselki school. After writing of how wonderful the building was, and especially his own quarters, and how he and the students had already begun to plant trees to beautify the grounds, he concluded: "As I have said to you a thousand times, esteemed Anton Pavlovich, thanks for the school. Only now have I begun to live as a human being." This was all the reward Chekhov would ever want.

« 3 »

During Chekhov's lengthy stay at Nice nearly every day was warm, sunny, and with little or no wind, a blessed state of affairs which he tirelessly reiterated in his letters. In this salubrious climate his health for a time seemed to improve, an advance which fed the optimism that goes with his disease and gave him a feeling of buoyancy and well-being. Unfortunately, it encouraged him to take liberties with the strict regimen imposed on him and to ignore the warning tickling in his throat.

The first signs of a recurrence of hemorrhage he took rather lightly. "My health is so fine," he wrote Elena Shavrova on October 29, "that I'm not aware of it. There are times when I cough up blood, but this has no relation to the way I feel, and I frisk about like a calf they've not yet married. Oh, what a joy that I'm not married! What a comfort this is!"

Two days later, however, in a letter to Alexandra Khotyaintseva, he wrote a bit more frankly: "My health is so-so. . . . The day before yesterday an expectoration of blood, which had continued for three weeks, stopped — not a laughing matter! There was little blood but over a long time, yet I felt so splendidly that I ignored the blood and quite sincerely wrote home that I was entirely well. (Apropos, don't say anything there about my health.)"

The doctors, however, took the matter seriously. Besides insisting anew upon the usual dietary and physical regulations, they had him moved to the ground floor of the pension so he would not have to climb stairs, and they ordered that he be indoors by sundown. But throughout November and December, despite the continuing fine weather, there were periods when for days Chekhov coughed up blood, although there was no severe hemorrhage as in Moscow. "Because of blood," he wrote Suvorin on December 16, "I'm sitting at home, as though under arrest. . . . It is dull and sad for me to live all alone."

« 4 »

In her memoirs (Chapter XV) Lidiya Avilova states that in October Chekhov wrote her: " 'I shall probably spend the whole winter abroad.' He also wrote: 'I feel fairly well in the morning and splendid in the evening.' " She avoided quoting the whole of this particular letter, a very interesting one, perhaps because in it he indicated that it was really an answer to one of hers and one which she had sent to Melikhovo — that is, she had not even been informed that he had gone abroad. And once again, he had forgotten her address and told her that he was sending his reply by way of Potapenko. "You complain," he answers, "that my heroes are gloomy. Alas, I am not at fault in this! It happens involuntarily, and when I write, it doesn't seem to me that I'm being gloomy; at any rate, I'm always in a good mood when I work. It has been observed that gloomy, melancholy people always write gaily and the writings of cheerful people are always depressing. And I'm a cheerful man; at least, I have lived the first thirty years of my life, as they say, at my ease." (*October 6, 1897.*)

His next letter she quoted almost in full, for it offered praise, as well as criticism, of one of several stories she sent him: "Ah, Lidiya Alekseevna, with what pleasure I read your *Forgotten Letters*. It is a fine, clever, and elegant thing. It is a little, bobtailed thing, but in it there is such a depth of art and talent that I do not understand why you don't continue in this manner." (*November 3, 1897.*) But the other tales, he points out, betray the hand of a beginner. She cannot economize; one story disappears completely under the debris of landscape; and she does not eliminate the superfluous from her sentences or feel the roughness of her phrasing.

If Avilova did not appreciate his criticism at first — she confessed in her memoirs — it gave her a push in the right direction, and she blamed herself if nothing came of it. "I was convinced Chekhov realized this," she concludes in a moment of unusual illumination, "and that his attitude toward me was different from what it had been. When I wrote him, I felt that I was forcing myself on him, but I could not terminate our correspondence any more than I could commit suicide."

At the end of his October letter to Avilova, Chekhov wrote: "I'm doing nothing, I write nothing, and I have no desire to write" — a rather accurate description of his state of mind during the first few weeks at Nice as he enjoyed the novelty of his new abode and the glorious weather. He forgot literature, though that year the ninth and tenth printings of *Motley Tales* appeared, the tenth of *In the Twilight*, and the eleventh of *Tales*. Also Suvorin brought out another single volume consisting of the two long stories, *My Life* and *Peasants*. Controversy still raged in the reviews around *Peasants*, and that month, when he was elected to the Union to Aid Russian Writers and Scholars, some members at the open meeting tried to blackball him because of his radical views on the peasantry, an action which provoked an indignant entry in Suvorin's diary: "In truth, these gentlemen are asses, and they understand literature even less than swine understand oranges, yet these swine set themselves up as judges of a remarkable writer!" It is perhaps significant that at this time the government finally rejected Goltsev's request to publish a newspaper, with which he had associated Chekhov's name as editor, because of the dangerous revolutionary views of the applicant. *Peasants* and other tales were beginning to appear with increasing frequency, in translation, in French periodicals, and with elation he sent Masha the first remuneration he received in francs, to be preserved.

Somehow the fresh scenes and experiences of life abroad did not evoke a literary response from Chekhov. He viewed it all as in a movie, as something with which he could not identify himself. Later, when the Russian editor of *Cosmopolis*, a new magazine published in several languages, invited him to contribute a story on a theme of foreign life, he replied in terms very similar to those he had communicated to Fausek at Yalta several years previously: "In one of your letters you expressed a desire that I should send you an international tale, taking for my subject something from life here. Such a story I can write only in Russia, from memory. I am able to write only from memory and have never written directly from nature. I must let the subject filter through my memory until only what is important and typical in it remains in the filter." (*December* 15, 1897.)

Chekhov, however, eventually grew conscience-stricken over the idleness of his Nice existence, and felt that he would have to return to

Russia if he could not get down to work. On October 9 he wrote Masha that he was taking advantage of a day of poor weather to sit in his room and concentrate on a story. Many themes, he lamented, were rusting in his brain — in his notebook he jotted down several of them, which were used later — for he found it extremely difficult to write in an alien land, in a strange room, and on a table he was not accustomed to. It was like sewing on somebody else's sewing machine. The heavy repletion he felt after the large pension meals also bothered him — an author, he decided, should write on an empty stomach. And his weak health was an additional obstacle. Kovalevsky recalls in his memoirs how Chekhov would desert his little group of loyal friends for a week at a time when he was writing. "And then he appeared again in our company, and not without sadness we observed the change in his features. He was pale and seemed worse than before. And during our walks together, he often fell silent, as though preoccupied with his own thoughts. At such times, he was probably dwelling upon a story he had undertaken."

Chekhov informed Sobolevsky, for whose *Russian News* he was planning several tales, that he would not guarantee the quality of what he wrote, but the quantity would preserve him from poverty and the need of asking for loans. But he demanded from the reluctant editor that he send him proofs abroad: "I don't read proof in order to correct merely the surface features; I ordinarily complete the ending in proof, and correct the whole with its musicality in mind, as you might say." (*November 20, 1897.*)

In truth, the quantity was slender over October and November — three brief tales (*The Pecheneg, At Home, In the Cart*)[2] — and the quality was not always of the highest, but each has memorable characterizations and descriptive passages, and all reveal Chekhov's deep concern now for human problems that embody elements of social protest. For the locale of the first two stories Chekhov once again drew upon memories of his youth and his 1887 trip to southern Russia — the vast, silent expanse of the Donets steppe where man was dwarfed by the elemental, mysterious forces of nature. *The Pecheneg*[3] is a character study

---

[2] All three tales first appeared in *Russian News* in 1897: *The Pecheneg* (November 2), *At Home* (November 16), *In the Cart* (December 21).

[3] The Pechenegs, a word used to describe the central character Zhmukhin, were a tribe of fierce Mongolian nomads who fought the Russians in the tenth and eleventh centuries.

of a retired Cossack officer who has allowed his little estate in the steppe to run down, has brought up his two sons as young savages without any education — they throw chickens in the air and shoot them — and abuses his cowering, sad-eyed young wife: "I must own that I don't consider a woman a human being," he says. Utterly shiftless, he enjoys "philosophizing" endlessly with any stray visitor; in the story, he ruminates on the vegetarian convictions of a fellow traveler whom he brings home for the night. Chekhov extracts not a little humor from the Pecheneg's soliloquizing to his sleepless guest through most of the night on the golden age, when all will have become vegetarians and men and beast will live in brotherly love, although it is difficult for him to assign pigs a place in this picture. Between the lines Chekhov is pointing out in the story the national problem involved in the widespread deterioration of rural estates.

A similar problem exists in *At Home*, which concerns another steppe estate where the vicious customs of the past in master–peasant relations are only below the surface. But the story focuses on Vera, who, after her father's death and her years of education and travel abroad, returns to run the estate, filled with high ideals of serving the people. With keen psychological insight Chekhov details the struggle that goes on within Vera between her ideals and the crass reality of life in this rural community. Reality wins out as she finally decides to marry one of the products of this vulgarization of life whom she detests: "Evidently truth and happiness existed somewhere outside real life. . . . One must give up one's own life and merge oneself into the luxuriant steppe, boundless and indifferent as eternity, with its flowers, its ancient barrows, and its distant horizons, and then all will be well."

The beautiful euphoric moment of the rural schoolteacher in *On the Cart*, as she imagines what her life might have been if her father and mother had lived, only serves, by way of contrast, to underscore the pathos of the unhappy years she has spent in the damp village schoolhouse on a mere pittance of salary, insulted daily by menial officials, and harrassed by endless cares about firewood and how well her charges will do before the incompetent examiners. Insensibly she has begun to sink to the level of the peasants, bowing and scraping before every petty official. The tale is a crushing indictment of rural schools and the lot of their teachers, subjects close to Chekhov's heart. In fact, the heroine is modeled on a Talezh schoolteacher who more than once brought her troubles to him. *On the Cart* provides a concrete illustration of Chekhov's application of his method of filtering a subject through his memory. For what remained in his artistic filter, as indicated by the observations in his notebook drawn from the real life of his model, are the important and typical features which are then developed in the tale with the universality of art.

« 5 »

Chekhov made the comment that Nice was a place in which to read, not to write, and, in his inability at this time to concentrate on the latter, he read various authors, including Voltaire, but mostly the French periodical press; and he regularly scanned Russian newspapers and magazines that were sent to him. His reading provided him with new insights on France, a nation which, he had come to believe, was ahead of all the others and gave tone to European culture, with a people that knew how to make use of their mistakes. Of the French press, he liked especially *L'Aurore* and *La libre Parole*.

In November, on the basis of fresh evidence, the press once again began to pour forth news items and editorial opinions on the celebrated case of Captain Alfred Dreyfus, the French army officer who, in 1894, had been court-martialed and condemned to life imprisonment as a spy in the interests of Germany. Chekhov avidly ran down all the details, spending whole days in reading these accounts. And he was positively electrified when Zola, for whom he had no high opinion as a novelist, brought out his famous open letter, "*J'accuse*," in *L'Aurore* (January 1),[4] in which he denounced the efforts of the government and the War Office to stifle the truth in the case. In February Chekhov excitedly followed every scrap of the published stenographic reports of the proceedings of Zola's trial for libel in which he was convicted and sentenced to a year's imprisonment. Alexandra Khotyaintseva recalled that Chekhov could not talk about the case without agitation.

His careful study of the facts, as well as his liberal sympathies, so evident now in his activities and writing and in his association with such liberal publications as *Russian Thought* and *Russian News*, predisposed him to side with the growing number who believed Zola justified in his charges and Dreyfus innocent. It exasperated him to observe that a part of the Russian press, following the lead of con-

---

[4] This is Old Style Russian dating; Zola's open letter was published in France on January 13.

servative elements of the French press, condemned Zola and heaped slander on Dreyfus in a wave of anti-Semitism. In this respect, Suvorin's *New Times* was one of the worst offenders.

In October there had been an unpleasant episode in the relations of these two close friends. Because of his illness and the climate of Paris at that time of the year, Chekhov had refused to go there to meet Suvorin, then on a visit, and had cordially invited him to Nice instead. Suvorin declined, and wrote an angry letter which, as Chekhov noted in his reply, "disagreeably stunned" him. Their correspondence lapsed for several weeks and when it resumed the tone was less cordial on both sides.

Now it was Chekhov's turn to grow angry with Suvorin as he read the mounting invective in *New Times*, with its anti-Semitic innuendoes, against Dreyfus. "We talk of nothing here but Zola and Dreyfus," he wrote the Russian editor of *Cosmopolis*, F. D. Batyushkov. "The immense majority of educated people are on the side of Zola and believe Dreyfus innocent. . . . *New Times* is simply repulsive." (*January 23, 1898.*) And shortly after, to a query from Alexandra Khotyaintseva, he replied: "You ask whether I still think Zola is right. I ask you: do you think so ill of me that you can imagine for a moment that I'm not on Zola's side? I would not exchange one of his fingernails for all those who sit on the case at the court, all those generals and highborn witnesses." (*February 2, 1898.*)

Then, on February 6, in an effort to educate Suvorin on the facts of the case and perhaps influence him to alter the prejudiced stand of *New Times*, Chekhov wrote him a long, circumstantial letter, almost like a lawyer's brief, in which he condensed the mountain of evidence he had accumulated on the subject. He began: "You write that you are annoyed with Zola, but here all have a feeling that a new, better Zola has arisen. In his trial he has been cleansed, as though by turpentine, of all his outer grease spots, and now shines before the French in his true brilliance. He has a purity and moral elevation which no one had suspected." Then Chekhov provides a summary of the case from the beginning: the curious withholding of evidence, on the part of the War Office, from Dreyfus' attorney; the strange reluctance of the authorities to reopen the case when new facts became available; the current of anti-Semitism that developed; the failure to evaluate the evidence against Major Esterhazy, believed by many to be the real perpetrator of the espionage; and then the reasons behind Zola's courageous attempt to force the government into calling for a new trial in the face of what seemed like a terrible judicial error. The chief point, continued Chekhov, is that Zola is sincere, and bases his judgment, not on phantoms, but on what he sees. And though sincere people can be mistaken, such mistakes do less harm than calculated insincerity, prejudgments, or political considerations. "Suppose Dreyfus is guilty — Zola would still be right, for it is the business of a writer not to accuse, not to persecute, but to champion the guilty once they have been condemned and undergo punishment. But great writers and artists ought to engage in politics only to the extent necessary to defend themselves against politics."

Since Suvorin's letter to Chekhov has vanished, we have no conclusive information on whether his thinking on the Dreyfus case was influenced by this effort of his friend. However, the unpublished memoirs of Kovalevsky shed some light on the matter. Chekhov told him that Suvorin, after receiving his letter, replied: "You have convinced me." Then Chekhov added: "However, I never did. *New Times* did not retreat from its massive malice against the unhappy captain, which continued for weeks and months after this letter." Kovalevsky asked Chekhov how he explained this. "By nothing other than Suvorin's extreme lack of character. I've never known a man more irresolute, even in matters affecting his own family." And in Leontiev-Shcheglov's notes for an unpublished article on Chekhov, he quotes Chekhov as saying: "I like Suvorin very, very much, but do you know . . . people who lack character can behave like the most harmful rascals, and at times in the most serious moments of life."

Once again, correspondence with Suvorin lapsed, but Chekhov continued his criticism of the slanderous campaign which *New Times* kept up against two men he considered guiltless. He wrote Misha that the majority of Russian papers, although they were not for Zola, at least were not in favor of persecuting him as was *New Times*. And in a letter to Alexander he bluntly declared: "In the Zola affair *New Times* behaved simply abominably. The old man and I have exchanged letters on the subject (though in an extremely moderate tone), and now both of us have grown silent. I don't want to write and I don't want his letters, in which he justifies the tactlessness of his paper by saying that he loves the military — I don't want them because I have been thoroughly sick of it all for a long time." (*February 22, 1898.*)

Though over the years Chekhov had tried to disassociate Suvorin from the reactionary policies of his newspaper, he felt he could do so no longer. His sincere desire to construct an image of his friend at variance with all that he found repugnant in *New Times* did not lack support in Suvorin's actions, conversations, and even in some of his own journalism. About a year before this rupture Chekhov had commented, with almost pathetic eagerness, on two liberally directed pieces which Suvorin had written for his paper, one aimed against the black reactionary *Moscow News*, the other on student disorders, in which Suvorin had pleaded the cause of the new generation. "I endlessly love it," Chekhov wrote, "when you are liberal — that is, when you write what you want to." (*January 4, 1897.*) But more and more manifestations of Suvorin's opportunism and his lack of integrity had been undermining the strong affection Chekhov had for this older man. Perhaps it was only his profound sense of gratitude that prevented him, now, from ending a long and intimate friendship.

« 6 »

For months Chekhov had been eagerly looking forward to taking a trip to Algeria with Kovalevsky in January. Africa was a continent he had often dreamed of visiting, and, besides, pension living had long since begun to irritate him. Hence it was a keen disappointment when early that month Kovalevsky informed him of his inability to make the trip because of illness. Chekhov felt entirely at loose ends with nowhere to go. When his birthday arrived on January 17, he disconsolately declared that he felt like eighty-nine years old instead of thirty-eight, and that he had become a grumbler and a mere clinic patient.

The agitation of the Dreyfus case and the Zola trial during all of February fortunately occupied Chekhov's thoughts and much of his time, and then he was comforted by the news that Potapenko expected to pay him a visit at Nice — he arrived on March 2 and stayed at the Pension Russe. Another friend, Sumbatov-Yuzhin, had come, and March also saw the arrival of Sobolevsky and his wife, the novelist Boborykin, and "Levitan's Morozov," who struck Chekhov as a colossal bore. Chekhov's dull pension regimen quickly changed. Potapenko wanted to win a million at Monte Carlo so that he could write as he wished and never again have to think of advances from publishers, and Sumbatov-Yuzhin wanted only several hundred thousand francs in order to build a fine new theater. According to the account in Potapenko's memoirs, though gambling at Monte Carlo depressed Chekhov, he was not immune to its poison. With paper and pencil and a small roulette wheel which they bought, they spent feverish hours working out combinations that would realize the gambler's dream — the secret of always winning. They disputed and arrived at different systems which they tried out daily at Monte Carlo. Potapenko was more of a plunger; Chekhov, though excited at play, wagered cautiously.

In his memoirs Potapenko argues that the gambling instinct in Chekhov ought to correct, in some measure, the common conception that he stood apart from life, free of its weaknesses, passions, and errors. Though Chekhov's personality and the way he lived provide a complete refutation of this curious characterization, on this score the comments of Potapenko, who knew him intimately, have their interest. "No, Chekhov was not an angel," he writes, "not a self-righteous person, but a human being in the full sense of the word. And the even temper and sobriety with which he amazed all were achieved only with difficulty, after a painful inner struggle. The artist in him helped in this struggle, for art required all his time and energy, but life does not wish to submit to anything without a struggle. . . . And in Chekhov's life everything was experienced by him — the great and the insignificant."

Apparently it took experience some time to teach the two gamblers that they would never discover a magic secret for breaking the bank at Monte Carlo. In the end Potapenko had to borrow money from Chekhov to return to Petersburg. Chekhov gambled only very small sums, winning and losing, but he had the will power to stop, Potapenko admits, and once having taken his decision, he would not return to the gaming tables. A more logical explanation was one Chekhov himself gave — the realization that with his poor health gambling quickly exhausted him physically and he resolved to abandon it.

Meanwhile the artist Braz arrived in Nice to try a second portrait of Chekhov, for the wealthy collector Tretyakov had agreed to finance the painter's trip there for this purpose. For days again Chekhov posed for the painstaking Braz; though the results this time pleased the artist and Tretyakov, and ultimately became the writer's most popular portrait, Chekhov never liked it. While the painting was in progress, he wrote Alexandra Khotyaintseva that viewers agreed that his face and necktie were very lifelike, and that his expression, as in the first effort, suggested that he was sniffing horseradish. After Braz finished the portrait, Chekhov condemned it in more forthright terms for its photographic quality and its failure to embody anything of his own inner essence:

". . . if I have become a pessimist and write gloomy tales, the fault is in this portrait of me."

Despite the presence of friends, amusements, and the exhilarating early spring weather of Nice, Chekhov had begun to chafe as his stay there dragged on. As he had told Suvorin earlier: "I do nothing, only sleep, eat, and offer sacrifices to the Goddess of Love . . . but I've already grown weary of all this and want to go home." (*January 27, 1898.*) A major cause of his restlessness was an inability to work consistently; a Russian author, he now quixotically decided, needed bad weather to write. He had promised *Russian News* a short tale a month, had been dissatisfied with the three he wrote, and gave up any hope of fulfilling his agreement. Having taken an advance from *Cosmopolis*, he forced a story from himself, *Visiting with Friends*,[5] which he recognized as a limp performance and later excluded from the first collected edition of his works. Repeatedly he had to offer embarrassing excuses to *Russian Thought* for his failure to finish the long story he had agreed to send them. If only he were home in his little Lodge, he thought, how easily this writing would go.

By February he had begun to think of spring at Melikhovo. The problem was entirely one of weather. Anxiously he asked Masha to inform him as soon as the snow was out of the woods and the road from Lopasnya to Melikhovo was passable. His health had been fine, but toward the end of the month he informed Misha — in a letter sent to congratulate him and his wife on the birth of their first child, a girl — that a dentist had broken one of his teeth and that it had taken three sessions to extract it. Infection set in with high fever, which had him crawling up the wall in pain, and an operation had to be performed on his jaw.

In March Chekhov began hopefully bombarding his sister with instructions on spring needs for the pond, the garden, and on what supplies to lay in. He asked about Lika, wondering at her long silence — and perhaps worrying over whether Masha had passed on to her a comment in one of his earlier letters: "What about Lika and her shop? She'll sputter at her own workers, for she really has a frightful temper. Added to this, she has a weakness for green and yellow ribbons and enormous hats, and with such drawbacks in elegance, it is impossible to be a legislatress of fashion and taste." However, he thoughtfully

---

[5] Published in *Cosmopolis*, February 1898.

added a footnote to this: "But I'm not against her opening a millinery shop. Whatever it may be, it is work." (*January 9, 1898.*)

When Masha, who was perhaps more concerned about her brother's health than he himself, reported in early April that the weather was still unfavorable for his return, Chekhov, unwilling to remain in Nice any longer after a stay of almost eight months, decided to go to Paris and await there his sister's call home. He wrote Alexandra Khotyaintseva to meet him at the station and left for Paris on April 14. A few weeks before, he had broken his long silence with a brief note to Suvorin to ask for the annual accounting on the sale of his books. An answer informing him that he expected to be in Paris elicited a prompt and friendly response from Chekhov: "Wire me the day and hour of your arrival . . . and I'll meet you at the station. I've accumulated a mass of all sorts of things — both feelings and thoughts — to discuss with you. . . . We'll return to Russia from Paris together." (*April 6, 1898.*) And when Suvorin came Chekhov left his cheap hotel to stay with him at the expensive Vendôme. With his forgiving nature, Chekhov disliked quarrels and hard feelings, and though their falling-out over the Dreyfus case irreparably damaged their intimate relationship, neither wanted to be on unfriendly terms with the other.

In Suvorin's company Chekhov made the rounds of distinguished Russians in Paris. Suvorin noted in his diary that they dined with the well-known art collector Shchukin. One of the guests, A. F. Onegin, asked Chekhov to write in his album, which was arranged in the form of a calendar, with a printed epigraph at the head of each page. Under an epigraph taken from a poem of Lermontov . . .

> *Believe me — happiness is there only*
> *Where we are loved, where we are believed . . .*

he wrote, having underscored the second line of the epigraph: "*Where we are loved, where we are believed*, there it is dull for us; but we are happy there where we ourselves love and where we ourselves believe," and he signed his name.

Chekhov may have found it more interesting, as he indicated in his own diary, to be introduced by Kovalevsky, who had lived in Paris for years, to some of his French friends, including the brother of Dreyfus and Bernard Lazare, who presented him with a copy of his brochure that had been instrumental in reopening the case of Dreyfus. He also saw something of the bohemian group of artists among whom Alexandra

Khotyaintseva lived, and he visited the theater and exhibitions of sculpture and painting. However, much of his brief stay was devoted to the business of his native town. In Nice he had bought and made a gift to the Taganrog library of three hundred and nineteen volumes of the French classics, and now in Paris he gathered together for it an excellent collection of printed material on the Dreyfus case. Further, he persuaded the eminent Russian sculptor M. M. Antokolsky to present to Taganrog a statue of Peter the Great, which he had modeled, for the town's bicentennial celebration. And learning that the dream of his old Taganrog teacher Pokrovsky was to obtain a Bulgarian order, for his participation in the Russo-Turkish War, Chekhov sought the assistance of influential government friends to bring this about.

Eventually the lovely spring weather of Paris turned rainy and Chekhov was surprised that the dampness seemed to have no deleterious effect on his health. He was sitting there, he wrote Masha, waiting for her wire, for he wanted to leave and was weary of chattering to no purpose with so many people. Finally, word came that the weather was fine at Melikhovo. Loaded down with presents for friends and all the family, on May 2 he joyfully set out on the Nord Express for Petersburg. Before leaving he dashed off a note to Alexander: "Shine your shoes, dress up in your best, and come to meet me. Since I'm a rich relative, I suppose I'm right in requiring such etiquette. Tell no one about my arrival." He left Paris alone, without Suvorin.

Part V

THE YALTA PERIOD BEGINS
1898 – 1900

CHAPTER XIX

"As I Grow Older, the Pulse of Life in Me Beats Faster . . . "

NEITHER HE NOR LEVITAN had valued life when they were well, Chekhov told Alexandra Khotyaintseva; only since they had fallen ill had they discovered life's peculiar charm. And now, as though unwilling to forgo its slightest attraction, Chekhov tried to resume his former activities upon his return to Melikhovo in the summer of 1898. He courted the illusion of recovered health, and as he and Alexandra strolled about the estate, followed by Bromine and Quinine and a brown cow, it was difficult to believe that her companion, full of cheerful conversation, was a sick man. In the spirit of the occasion she drew an amusing cartoon of his hideout, the Lodge, with a flag raised to indicate that he was at home ready to receive visiting peasants and neighbors.

Indeed, after months of "idleness" abroad and the hated business of being doctored, Chekhov slipped into the familiar busy Melikhovo pattern with a sense of relief. He wrote an old family friend, Bishop Sergei, "now everything is fine, I feel well enough, at least I don't regard myself as ill, and I live as I have been living. As formerly, I'm busy with my medical practice and with literature; I heal peasants, write tales, and every year I build something." (*May 27, 1898.*) Nor did he allow the scores of visitors, eager to see him after his long absence, to prevent him from working in the garden or from collecting and packing off books to Taganrog. Though he finally gave up a contemplated trip to his native city to participate in the celebration of its two-hundredth anniversary, Chekhov felt equal to paying visits to Sobolevsky and Levitan in the country, and to Moscow, where he took Alexandra Khotyaintseva to the circus. But he resisted Sergeenko's invitation to appear at Yasnaya Polyana on the occasion of Tolstoy's seventieth birthday, for he divined correctly that the great man's life had become a continuous celebration which only annoyed him. Then there were the usual manuscripts of young authors to read and place, Alexander's oldest son to take care of at Melikhovo until he began his studies at Moscow in the fall, and school meetings at Serpukhov to attend.

In fact, Chekhov's interest in the district schools had in no sense flagged during his trip abroad. He now created a society for the aid of teachers in the area and discussed the establishment of a rural mobile school museum and library. And as though actually unwilling to let a single year pass without building something, as he had told Bishop Sergei, he began to lay plans that summer for a third model school, this time in his own village of Melikhovo, though in this project Masha took the lead in raising the money with a helpful gift of a thousand roubles from her brother. But with a substantial registration of children already anxious to attend in the fall, before money could be obtained to begin construction, he persuaded the local authorities to allow him to rent a hut in the village, renovate it, buy desks and other equipment, and hire a teacher. He offered the hospitality of his home to these rural teachers, gave them books, magazines, theater tickets, and often helped them out in their personal difficulties. One wrote of him in his recollections: "It is hard to say what was uppermost in Chekhov — the man or the artist. His warm personality represented an entirely harmonious whole, in which it was impossible to separate the human being from the artist or the artist from the man."

« 2 »

"My machine has already begun to work," Chekhov jubilantly reported to Goltsev soon after his return from abroad. The conviction that his writing, which had virtually ceased toward the end of his stay in Europe, would revive in the familiar setting of Melikhovo turned out to be correct. Sytin's proposal that he publish a volume of the early humorous tales in *Fragments* attracted Chekhov and he set about gathering these together. Misha, who was visiting, helped in searching through old issues. He read a story aloud: "Is that one of my tales?" Chekhov exclaimed, laughing with delight. "I don't remember it at all! But it is funny." Though Sytin had offered five thousand roubles for the volume, Chekhov soon abandoned the idea because, as he said, his heart was not in another book with a new title. A more practical reason perhaps was the idea that had occurred to him of getting out a collected edition of his writings, which he now proposed to Suvorin, who initially gave only a grudging assent.

Drawing upon outlines and observations which he had previously jotted down in his notebook, Chekhov wrote four short stories over the summer of 1898. Dr. Startsev in *Ionych*[1] belongs to that rather large group of rural physicians in Chekhov's writings who often begin their careers as idealists but in the end succumb in the unequal struggle with social injustice or ignorance or disease. After his rejection by the spoiled daughter of a pretentious provincial family, he turns his back on youthful ideals and merges his lot with the vulgarity of his surroundings in an orgy of grasping accumulation in his medical practice. Here Chekhov seems content, as in many of his tales, to reveal those forces that compel man's submission to a corrupting social order from which there appears to be no escape. But in other stories his heroes, like Nikitin in *The Teacher of Literature*, revolt.

And the sentiment of revolt, if not its action, rings out with startling clarity in the other tales he wrote this summer — *The Man in a Shell*, *Gooseberries*, and *About Love*.[2] These three stories are unique in Chekhov's fiction in being connected by a common framework that involves the same two characters. This fact has led some critics to suppose that they may have been contributions to the novel which Chekhov dreamed of writing one day. However, the idea of a series of short stories, connected by some loose framework, had occurred to him years before, and in the present instance he intended, but failed, to add more stories to this series of three. Besides the common characters, the teacher Burkin and the veterinary Ivan Ivanych, one may discern a common motif — the aspiration for freedom, freedom from all the stuffy conventions of life, from the regimentation of authority, the imbecility of functionaries, from everything that tyrannizes and debases the human spirit; that "most absolute freedom" which Chekhov had passionately claimed as his goal in life in his remarkable testimony to Pleshcheev ten years earlier. The poetic Melikhovo landscape also pervades all three stories, and its lyric presence somehow informs and illuminates the basic idea of freedom with its protest against the dead forms of life.

[1] First published in *Niva*, September 1898.
[2] *The Man in a Shell* appeared in *Russian Thought* for July 1898, and *Gooseberries* and *About Love* in its August issue that same year.

The story of the Greek teacher Belikov,[3] which Burkin tells to Ivan Ivanych in the barn when they are out hunting, etches to perfection the image of a petty man rendered arrogantly servile by the preposterous bureaucracy that enslaves him. Though Belikov is ridiculous, he is also sinister, for he demands that all other people, like himself, live in shells. To the thoroughly emancipated and philosophically-minded Ivan Ivanych, the Belikovs, all these men in shells, are the ghastly end-products of the Russian social system, and he draws the conclusion in words that clearly echo what Chekhov had come to believe: "To see and hear how they lie . . . and they call you a fool for putting up with these lies; to endure insult, humiliation, not dare to declare openly that you are on the side of honest, free people, and to lie and smile yourself, and all for a crust of bread, for the sake of a warm corner, for some lowly rank in the service that is not worth a farthing — no, one cannot go on living like this!"

In *Gooseberries*, rain overtakes the two friends, who are on another outing together, and they find refuge in the house of Alekhin, owner of an estate, where this time Ivan Ivanych narrates a story. It is about his brother, a kind of variant of the man in the shell, who slaves and half-starves himself in the city for years in order to buy a little estate in the country where he can be his own lord and master and eat his own gooseberries. This passion for self-sufficiency, for shutting himself up for the rest of his life on a bit of property, seems to Ivan Ivanych an illustration of Tolstoy's gloomy parable: How much land does a man need? The answer comes — only the six feet of earth that a corpse requires. But this is selfishness, declares Ivan Ivanych, a kind of monasticism without self-denial. "Man needs not six feet of earth, not a farm, but the whole globe, all nature, where he will have room for the full play of all the capacities and peculiarities of his free spirit." Here is expressed Chekhov's own unquenchable thirst for all of life, for everything accessible to man.

In the last tale, *About Love*, Alekhin tells his story to the two guests. Here the problem of freedom is related to a purely personal and emotional situation. Unlike Ivan Ivanych's brother, Alekhin is the kind of estate owner whom Chekhov would approve of — an educated man who

[3] A. F. Dyakonov, inspector of the Taganrog school when Chekhov was a student there, has sometimes been mentioned as the prototype of Belikov, but so have others, such as Chekhov's friend, the editor M. O. Menshikov. No doubt several people Chekhov observed in real life contributed to this brilliant characterization of a widely accepted social type at that time.

has dedicated himself to the hardest kind of labor in an effort to make a success of his estate. On his rare visits to town he becomes friendly with a court official, Luganovich, and his beautiful wife, Anna Alekseevna, who is much younger than her husband. Eventually, the bachelor Alekhin becomes an intimate of this family, "uncle" to the children, and a trusted participant in the joys and sorrows of his friends. This close relationship contributes to the inhibited nature of the love that soon develops between Alekhin and the young wife. He believes, as no doubt Chekhov did, that there is only one incontestable truth about love, namely that it is a great mystery, and that everything written or said about it is not a solution, but only a statement of questions that have remained unanswered. Yet Alekhin insists on posing these unanswerable questions. And he knows that the tormented Anna Alekseevna is also endlessly catechizing herself with very much the same questions.

In their unconfessed love, the sterile years pass and tender feelings shrivel and die in the furnace of doubt. To free themselves from the eternal questions dictated by convention is beyond the capacities of both lovers. Finally Luganovich is transferred to a post in a distant province. Alekhin goes to the railway station to bid farewell to the suffering and ill Anna Alekseevna. "When our eyes met there in the compartment, our spiritual strength deserted us. I embraced her, she pressed her face to my breast and wept. Kissing her face, shoulders, and hands wet with tears — oh, how miserable we were! — I confessed my love for her, and with a burning pain in my heart I understood how unnecessary, petty, and deceptive was everything that hindered us from loving each other. I realized that when you love you must, in your reasoning about love, start from what is higher and more important than happiness or unhappiness, sin or virtue, in their usual meaning, or you must not reason at all."

This was a lesson that must have come directly from Chekhov's heart. These stories, written during the summer of 1898, reveal a writer who had long since learned to compound the rich stuff of objective observation with the deep moral substance of the artist seeking for answers to the problems of life.

« 3 »

When Chekhov arrived home from Paris at the beginning of May, he found awaiting him a letter from Nemirovich-Danchenko. This old friend, dramatist and teacher of the theater arts, had joined forces with Stanislavsky — who had long been acting in and producing plays for the Society of Art and Literature — to establish the People's Art Theater, the name of which was soon changed to the Moscow Art Theater. It was a momentous partnership that soon revolutionized the Russian theater and eventually exercised a profound influence on the European and American theater. Most of the new company was made up of young amateurs in Stanislavsky's group, and the best students of Nemirovich-Danchenko's classes in a Moscow school of the theater. Since Nemirovich-Danchenko had assumed responsibility for selecting the repertoire, he now wrote Chekhov for permission to stage *The Sea Gull*. He expressed his profound admiration for the play and promised to give it the kind of production that would bring out the hidden beauty and essential dramatic conflicts of each of the characters, features that had been so utterly missed in the Alexandrinsky staging.

This letter reopened the deep wound which the initial failure of *The Sea Gull* had so recently inflicted on Chekhov. He had sworn to abandon playwriting and the theater. To be sure, the previous summer he had read *Uncle Vanya* to a Serpukhov amateur group which was preparing to perform it on behalf of the fund-raising for his Novoselki school project. Shortly after, however, he had refused Korsh permission to stage it professionally in Moscow. And although he was pleased with the revival of *Ivanov* at the Alexandrinsky, he had written Suvorin from Nice on March 13, 1898: "You are becoming more closely connected with the theater, but I obviously am getting further and further away from it — and I'm sorry, for the theater once gave me a great deal that is fine (and my earnings from it have not been bad; in the provinces this winter my plays have succeeded as never before, even *Uncle Vanya*). Formerly I had no greater satisfaction than in going to the theater, but now I go there with the feeling that someone in the gallery is going to shout 'Fire!' And I don't like actors. Writing plays has demoralized me."

Accordingly, Chekhov rejected the offer of the new theater to stage *The Sea Gull*. "He wrote," Nemirovich-Danchenko reports in his recollections,[4] "that he neither wished, nor did he have the strength, to undergo the great agitation of the theater which had occasioned him so much pain, and he repeated, not for the first time, that he was not a dramatist, that there were much better dramatists than he, etc."

[4] Chekhov's letter to Nemirovich-Danchenko has been lost.

Nemirovich-Danchenko, however, was not easily discouraged. At first he tried in vain to persuade Masha to use her influence on her brother, and on May 12 he wrote Chekhov again, praising him as the only contemporary playwright whose work represented any significant interest for the theater, and he promised, if permission were granted, that he would visit and discuss the whole production plan with him before rehearsals. This new request must have caught Chekhov in a good mood, or perhaps because of his unfailing hospitality he could not resist the prospect of a visit from Nemirovich-Danchenko, for he replied: "Come, do me the kindness! You cannot imagine how much I want to see you, and for the satisfaction of seeing and talking with you, I'm prepared to give you all my plays." (*May 16, 1898.*) Nemirovich-Danchenko regarded this as an expression of willingness to allow him to stage *The Sea Gull* and so informed Chekhov.

Debates and disagreements took place that summer between Stanislavsky and Nemirovich-Danchenko on the meaning of *The Sea Gull* and the most artistic way of staging it. The significance of its inner meaning evaded Nemirovich-Danchenko, who discovered its value in the fact that one felt the pulse of contemporary Russian life in the play. Stanislavsky frankly admitted that he could not understand *The Sea Gull*. And at first the young actors in the company, appalled at the thought that they were expected to succeed in a play which had failed dismally in Petersburg when performed by some of the most experienced actors in Russia, were entirely uncertain of how their roles should be played. Indeed, without the tireless and enthusiastic advocacy of Nemirovich-Danchenko, *The Sea Gull* might never have seen the boards of the Moscow Art Theater. Nevertheless, while Stanislavsky retired to his brother's estate near Kharkov to write his meticulous production notes for this play, the young actors, in their first exciting summer together, at a *dacha* outside Moscow, rehearsed it with others in the repertoire designed for their opening season. In September they came up to Moscow and were informed that Chekhov would be present at a rehearsal of his play.

Chekhov was the favorite contemporary author of most of these young actors, and Nemirovich-Danchenko had instilled in them a reverence for him. Though they had at first been puzzled by *The Sea Gull*, the more they worked over it the more they loved it, and they had come to believe that their future somehow depended on the performance of this play. When Chekhov appeared at their rehearsal on

September 9, a sense of agitated expectation swept through the company. But he quickly put them at ease by the charm of his personality and the simplicity of his behavior. With some embarrassment at first, he tugged at his beard and played with his pince-nez as he haltingly replied to their eager questions, and they could not be quite certain whether he intended his answers to be serious or funny. After he watched the first act and part of the second, however, there could be no mistaking the directness of his language as he spoke of his reactions. "They were very tense," Nemirovich-Danchenko wrote Stanislavsky, who was unable to be present. "He agreeably discovered at the rehearsal that we had a splendid company that worked excellently together." But Nemirovich-Danchenko took the precaution to introduce a number of changes that Chekhov had suggested. And when he attended a second rehearsal two days later, Chekhov expressed satisfaction over the improvements, although he severely criticized two of the actors, one of them playing the important role of Trigorin, and he suggested that Stanislavsky, who intended to portray Dorn, should take this part.

Although Nemirovich-Danchenko wrote Stanislavsky that the latter's elaborate mise-en-scène had impressed Chekhov, other sources indicate that some of the effects disturbed him.

Meierhold reports that one of the actors told Chekhov that Stanislavsky intended to have frogs croaking, the sound of dragonflies, and dogs barking on the stage.

" 'Why?' Chekhov asked with a note of dissatisfaction in his voice.

" 'It is realistic,' the actor replied.

" 'Realistic,' Chekhov repeated with a laugh, and after a slight pause he said: 'The stage is art. There is a canvas of Kramskoi[5] in which he wonderfully depicts human faces. Suppose he eliminated the nose of one of these faces and substituted a real one. The nose will be 'realistic,' but the picture will be spoiled.' "

Another actor proudly informed him that Stanislavsky expected to introduce a woman with a weeping child at the end of the third act.

"That's unnecessary," Chekhov said. "It is just like playing a *pianissimo* at the very moment the lid of the piano drops."

"But it often happens in life," one of the group of actors objected, "that a *forte*, entirely unexpectedly, becomes a *pianissimo*."

"True, but the stage," answered Chekhov, "is subject to *known conventions*. You have no fourth wall. Apart from this, the stage is art, the

---

[5] A celebrated Russian painter.

stage reflects in itself the quintessence of life, so one must not introduce on it anything that is superfluous."

At these early rehearsals of *The Sea Gull* Chekhov must have observed closely the actress who played the difficult role of Arkadina — Olga Leonardovna Knipper — a thin-lipped woman of twenty-eight with an expressive, intelligent face and a beautiful voice. She had only recently finished Nemirovich-Danchenko's dramatic school, and with the ardor and strong will that were part of her nature she had joyously dedicated her life to the theater. In a sense she had already fallen in love with Chekhov through her love for his play, and his first attendance at the rehearsal, as she remarks in her memoirs, was for her an unforgettable day.

It may have been a dawning interest in Olga Knipper rather than his growing curiosity about the artistic promise of the new theater that led Chekhov, two days later, to attend the rehearsal of A. K. Tolstoy's *Tsar Fyodor*, the historical tragedy with which the company planned to open its first season. He sat, muffled in an overcoat, in the damp, cold Hermitage Theater, not yet remodeled for the opening, its bare stage lacking a curtain and illuminated by candles stuck in bottles. "And it was a joy to feel," Olga rhapsodically recalled, "that a 'soul' beloved by all of us sat in that black, empty parterre and heard us." As he watched her in the role of Irina in *Fyodor* he obviously thought the discomforts worth it, for, not long after, he wrote Suvorin about the rehearsal: "Its cultured tone had an agreeable effect on me and the performance was a truly artistic one, although no great talents were acting. In my opinion Irina was splendid. Her voice, her nobility, her sincerity were so superb that I felt choked with emotion. Fyodor seemed to me not so good. . . . But best of all was Irina. If I had remained in Moscow I would have fallen in love with this Irina." (*October 8, 1898.*)

« 4 »

In fact, Chekhov left the next day for the Crimea, for with the approach of autumn he had begun to cough up blood again. The illusion of improving health had vanished. Now that travel had become a necessity, this enthusiastic devotee of it regarded his journey as a form of exile — he complained, toward the end of summer, that the very thought of having to leave Melikhovo for a warmer clime depressed his spirits and prevented him from writing or doing anything constructive.

Chekhov had written ahead to his friend Mirolyubov at Yalta for details on furnished rooms there, for he could not afford a lengthy stay in
a hotel. His selection of this resort town, the "pearl of the Crimea,"
was not dictated by any liking for it; his previous visits had left him
with a poor impression. Its climate, however, especially in the autumn
and early winter months, was regarded as excellent for consumptives.
He would have preferred to go abroad, but he lacked the money to do
this and continue his support of the family at Melikhovo, to say nothing
of fulfilling financial obligations he had assumed in building the new
school in his village. It is interesting to find the accomplished novelist
Ertel writing to a friend at this time that Chekhov — no less talented
than Maupassant or Turgenev, he declared — "must stoop to humiliating negotiations on loans in order to obtain money, because his writings,
which all of Russia reads, do not provide this sick man with an income
adequate for his needs, or for taking a period of rest or a journey to
the South, and especially so since he has on his hands the support of a
numerous family."

Chekhov arrived in Yalta on September 18 and rented two rooms in
a private *dacha* with an attractive garden and a pleasant outlook.
Sunny weather, beautiful views of the sea, and the surrounding greenery
and flowers still in full bloom delighted him. Life at Yalta flowed on
drowsily, zoologically. His daily walks along the shore usually took him
to the "intellectual center" of the town — I. A. Sinani's bookshop,
where the lively sale of tobacco, pipes, and cigarettes compensated for
the sluggish trade in belles lettres. Here gathered novelists, poets, and
artists on vacation in Yalta. Chekhov met at Sinani's and invited for
walks or meals Mirolyubov, S. Ya. Elpatievsky, distinguished physician
and writer, the singer Chaliapin, and the poet Konstantin Balmont. He
also encountered Rachmaninoff, who sent him one of his compositions,
Fantasy for an Orchestra, with an inscription which indicated that it
had been inspired by Chekhov's tale, *On the Road*.

As on his previous visits to Yalta, Chekhov, as a well-known figure,
was soon much pursued by the local gentry. Though he was as bored as
a sturgeon, he wrote Tatyana Shchepkina-Kupernik, wenches with or
without manuscripts were pestering him, and soon the familiar protest
was heard that too many visitors prevented him from working. He
took refuge, he paradoxically explained to Masha, in a girls' school,
where he often dined with the head, Varvara Kharkeevich, and her
teachers. In no time he found himself on the board of trustees, and he

enjoyed having the pretty little girls in their white pelerines curtseying to him as he roamed about the halls on his official duties.

Before long the irresistible urge to be useful in a community had overtaken him. He attended the Town Council to listen to the local Ciceros; joined the Red Cross chapter; accepted an invitation to a meeting of district physicians, started a campaign in the newspapers to raise money for starving peasant children in Samara, and he even indulged in a little medical practice. If he wished, he wrote Menshikov, he could build up a large practice — in this town of tuberculars!

One day, after he had been in Yalta almost a month, Chekhov dropped in at the bookshop and the proprietor handed him a telegram that had been sent by Masha to Sinani: HOW WOULD ANTON PAVLOVICH CHEKHOV RECEIVE THE NEWS OF HIS FATHER'S DEATH? This was on October 13, and Chekhov's father had died the day before. Masha, perhaps because she distrusted her brother's invariably optimistic reports on his health, had taken this precaution, which had served only to confuse Sinani so that he had delayed a day in conveying the telegram to Chekhov. News of the death was already going the rounds in Yalta. Chekhov hurried to the post office, but there he found only a letter from Ivan telling him of their father's operation. After sending a telegram to Masha, he also wrote her for details, adding: "However this may be, the news is sad, entirely unexpected, and has grieved and disturbed me profoundly. I'm sorry for Father, sorry for all of you; the realization that all of you in Moscow are experiencing such difficulties at a time when I'm at peaceful Yalta — this realization does not leave me and haunts me constantly." (*October 14, 1898.*) He concluded by making a number of inquiries about his mother, and urged that she come to join him at Yalta.

In lifting a heavy box of books at Melikhovo Chekhov's father had sustained a severe rupture. After a tortuous journey to a Moscow clinic, where he underwent a long and painful operation, he died. When Chekhov learned the details from his sister and brothers, he intensely regretted that he had not been home at this crucial time. If he had, he said more than once, things might have gone differently. It does seem that the operation had been bungled; but with the reputation of his profession in mind, Chekhov felt it necessary to write Masha to still rumors to this effect in the neighborhood. There had been no question of his going to the funeral. Because of the delay in his receiving the news, and the fact that at best it would have taken him three or four days to reach home, he could never have got there in time. Besides, his health and the weather in Moscow then made the trip unwise. It pleased Chekhov that his father was buried in the exclusive Novodevichy cemetery which he had visited when he was so near death himself as a patient in Dr. Ostroumov's clinic.

« 5 »

Father's death ended his diary, Chekhov wrote Masha, and also the course of Melikhovo life. He spoke frequently now of selling the estate and building a new nest for the family, for he believed that his mother would not wish to go on living at Melikhovo.

Even before his father's death Chekhov had begun to explore the notion of buying a place in or near Yalta, for by now he had come to realize, because of the state of his health, that at best he could live at Melikhovo only during the summer months. The delightful weather he had been experiencing at Yalta encouraged him. The climate was very healthy, he reasoned, and obviously agreed with him. He began to rationalize his former dislike of the town while at the same time confessing boredom as visiting friends and celebrities left with the onset of winter. His letters suggest almost a comic effort to balance drawbacks with virtues — there were no good books to be had in the library and the only theater was wretched, but after all Yalta was the most cultured spot in the Crimea. Though it took between two or three weeks for a parcel to arrive from Moscow, and the only way to reach Yalta was by boat from Sevastopol or overland in a carriage, still he had heard that a direct railroad would soon be built. Then there was the captivating scenery — the sea and the mountains — which compensated for the annoying provincialism of the natives. And to Masha he offered that last despairing justification of a sick man: "It is pertinent to point out that in Yalta there are neither noblemen nor bourgeoisie; all are equal before the bacilli, and this Yalta classlessness constitutes its true worth." (*December 2, 1898.*)

Sinani took him to see a house for sale near the Tatar village of Kuchukoi, eighteen miles from Yalta, located on the mountain road to Sevastopol. The little house, with four rooms and a red roof, perched on dizzying heights, with a magnificent view of the sea, entranced him. No one could have been more practical than Chekhov in outlining to his sister and brothers every defect and virtue of this house and location, totally impractical for him and his family. But the place was so charmingly touching, cozy, original, and artistic (he would conclude)! Under no circumstances would he buy it unless they agreed, but it was cheap — only two thousand roubles!

The family failed to respond to his enthusiasm for this mountain retreat. Meanwhile the advice of the local doctors that if he wished to remain any time in Yalta he should buy a house, he construed as a command for immediate action. The doctors had also told him that he should not spend a full winter at Yalta. But why buy a house if he could build one? He quickly found the ideal spot in the suburb of Autka, about twenty minutes' walk from Yalta — an advantage, he thought, for the remoteness would protect him from visitors. The elevation was quite high and provided the kind of striking view of the sea and mountains which he loved. Just fine for a little house, he wrote Masha on October 9, where you could turn the key in the lock and leave everything. But he promised to wait, on both the Kuchukoi and Autka possibilities, for he did not wish, he joked, to subscribe to the old caricature of himself — Chekhov pursuing two hares at once.

The news of his father's death settled the matter. Chekhov decided to buy the site in Autka. Besides, he was weary of wandering from one hotel or rented apartment to another (he had moved three times so far during his stay in Yalta), and of taking potluck on meals. The altered circumstances of his life seemed to demand that he make definite plans for the future. Of course, there was the question of money. He asked and received from Suvorin an advance of five thousand roubles against the income from the sale of his books, to be paid back at the rate of no more than a thousand a year. The land cost four thousand and the estimate for building a house was ten thousand, toward which the bank was willing to give him a mortgage of seven thousand.

Before going further with the plans, he waited for a promised visit from Masha, who would have to pass on everything relating to the building of the house. She arrived at Yalta for a week at the end of October. Chekhov was surprised to learn from her that their mother wished to keep on living at Melikhovo. This desire did not discourage him, although it seriously upset his financial calculation. However, he believed that he could persuade his mother to live with him most of the year at Yalta and they would occupy Melikhovo in the summer.

When he took Masha to inspect the site of the future house, she could not conceal her chagrin. It was too far from the sea, she thought. An old ragged vineyard overgrown with weeds . . . not a tree or a bush on the plot . . . and hard by a Tatar graveyard where, as though staged for their benefit, a funeral was taking place . . . Her unconcealed disappointment vexed Chekhov and she quickly tried to make amends. She praised the view — the sea in the distance, the breakwater with ships anchored in the port, and the background of mountains. Soon they were sitting down together with paper and pencil, happily blocking out the locations for the house, for the garden, grottoes, fountains. . . .

If he had any notion of playing the part of the architect for the new house, Masha apparently discouraged it, if for no other reason than the strain it would place upon him. While she was there Chekhov met, at Sinani's bookshop, L. N. Shapovalov, a young architect fresh from Moscow. This shy young man was overwhelmed by an introduction to the great writer, but after a brief acquaintance Chekhov invited him to be his architect. Shapovalov was overcome by doubts as to whether he could build a house where so famous an author could live and work. However, Chekhov calmed his fears and said that he had in mind only a simple, modest, comfortable structure. The eager architect promptly drew up preliminary plans, which Chekhov and Masha went over in detail, and a bargain was struck.

After Masha's departure, Chekhov's letters home were full of enthusiastic accounts of the house, the construction of which had begun: the view was unexampled and he had already been offered four times as much as he had paid for the land, which was large enough to support an orchard and a vegetable and flower garden. Friends were already showering him with gifts of trees and flowering bushes. But most of the virtues he stressed were clearly designed to convince his mother how desirable living would be in this new house at Yalta, a town which would remind her of Taganrog, he declared. Everything will be under one roof, he explained, and the coal and wood will be in the cellar. The kitchen will be splendid, with American conveniences and running water, and there will be a drying room, pushbells for servants, and a telephone. Hens there laid all the year round, coffee was inexpensive, and there were a bakery shop, a market, and a coachman nearby who could be hired cheaply. Further, the church in Autka had a ten-o'clock Mass — his mother's favorite time — and she could gather mushrooms all through the autumn in the Crown woods.

In the midst of these panegyrics on the advantages of Autka and the new house, Masha was no doubt quite shaken to hear from her brother, on December 8, that he was "the owner of one of the most beautiful and curious estates in the Crimea!" Chekhov could not resist the charm that had appealed so much to his artistic soul — he had bought the little house at Kuchukoi, and the land that went with it. But she must not tell anyone except the family, he self-consciously warned, for he was afraid it would get in the paper that he had squandered a hundred thousand on the place.

Apparently Masha did express some wonderment at her brother's extravagance — she had had to take a somewhat larger apartment in Moscow so that her grieving mother could stay with her for a time. Hurt, Chekhov at once replied: "If, as you say in your last, it is now necessary to sell Melikhovo, then it is not because I've been piling up debts at Yalta. My financial affairs are not exactly brilliant, true, but there is a way out." Then he gives a detailed accounting of his dealings on both houses. He had accumulated an indebtedness of some sixteen thousand roubles, but he reminds her that besides the five thousand advance he had taken from Suvorin and the seven thousand mortgage from the bank, he had already earned two thousand on stories and expected to earn two to three thousand more by April, not counting any income he received from his plays. He had even rejected a proffered loan again from Levitan's Maecenas, S. T. Morozov, because his friend had insisted that Chekhov deal directly with the millionaire. In any event, he declared, he expected to be free of all but bank debts by the beginning of 1900. And if he got stuck, he concluded, he could mortgage the new estate he'd bought, but, he added: "All are in raptures with my Kuchukoi." (*December 17, 1898.*)

« 6 »

Chekhov had not exaggerated his earnings on short stories over 1898, especially if he included in his estimate the income from the last two that he had written since he reached Yalta — *A Doctor's Visit*[6] and *The Darling*.[7] The first, no doubt based on Chekhov's experience in doctoring a member of a wealthy factory-owning family near Melikhovo, is penetrated by a fresh sense of the social inequities that poison human relations. The moment of illumination comes when the doctor, with his cool, scientific mind, which is not devoid of a certain emotional sensitivity, perceives that the young heiress he is treating for a nervous disorder is really suffering from a case of conscience. The

[6] *Russian Thought*, December 1898.
[7] *Family*, January 1899.

cause is her wealth wrung from the labor of factory workers living on the verge of starvation.

In Chekhov's stories love rarely succeeds in an ideal sense, but *The Darling*, one of his best-known tales, seems to be something of an exception in this respect. For here he is concerned with illustrating the contention that the object of a woman's love is of comparatively little importance, for it is the law of her being to love something or somebody. He tells us with delicate insistence throughout the story that Olenka was always fond of someone and could not exist without loving. One may be amused at the swift transfer of her affections as fate removes the objects of her love — first the theater manager, then the timber merchant, and next the veterinary — yet one never doubts the sincerity, self-abnegation, and devotion of her warm nature; at the end all these qualities are bestowed on a little boy — a supreme act of love for the one individual who can offer least in return.

Gorbunov-Posadov wrote Chekhov that Tolstoy was in raptures over *The Darling*. "He tells everyone that this is a pearl, that Chekhov is a great, great writer," and that he had read it four times to friends and the family with added attraction each time. Later Tolstoy included the story in his *Readings for Every Day in the Year* and wrote a critical foreward, in which he expressed the curious opinion that Chekhov's heroine was intended to be a satire on the "new woman," a seeker after equality with men. Though his purpose was to ridicule her, Tolstoy conjectures, in the end the poetry in his soul forbade this. What makes the story so excellent, Tolstoy concludes, is that the effect is unintentional.

If Chekhov had been able to read this comment — it was published only after his death — he would probably have been more amused than annoyed. At about the time he was working on *The Darling*, he received a letter from Gorbunov-Posadov, who informed him that Tolstoy had assigned all the profits from *Resurrection* to aid the emigration of the persecuted sect of Dukhobors to Canada: "In all my life," Chekhov responded, "I've never esteemed a man so profoundly, one might even say, so unquestioningly, as Leo Nikolaevich." (*November 9, 1898.*) The wonderful poetic effect which Tolstoy so much admired in *The Darling* is not unintentional but an achievement of Chekhov's conscious artistry. He is not mocking his pitiful heroine's need to love. With all his acute insight, Tolstoy never quite perceived the breadth and tolerance of Chekhov's judgment, his tenderness for those who suffered, or his charity in the face of forgivable weakness.

A writer who did perceive and appreciate these qualities was Gorky, whose star had just begun to rise in the literary firmament. In Nizhny Novgorod he and his wife at this time were reading Chekhov's stories aloud to each other, and Gorky sent him two volumes of his own tales with a covering letter in which, in characteristic fashion, he poured forth his admiration: "How many marvelous moments I've spent over your books, how many times have I wept and been vexed by them, like a wolf in a trap, and how sadly and long have I laughed!"

A first letter from Chekhov on November 16 begged forgiveness for not answering sooner, welcomed his friendship, and promised a longer reply once he had read his books. Before the promise could be fulfilled, however, another and quite remarkable letter came from the impetuous Gorky. He had seen a provincial performance of *Uncle Vanya*, wept like a girl, and had gone home "stunned, exhausted by your play. . . . You have an enormous talent." Gorky's further criticism of *Uncle Vanya*, which he clearly recognized as "an entirely new kind of dramatic art," is quite intuitive rather than reasoned, and this, as well as his personal comments on his own literary outlook as compared with that of Chekhov, reveal at once the sharp difference between his typical artistic visceral abandonment and Chekhov's artistic restraint. Will you write more plays? he eagerly asks at the end of his letter.

Chekhov replied in a long letter that set the tone for their future close relationship: "In general, I react coldly to my plays, have long since lost touch with the theater, and now I don't care to write for it any more." In answer to Gorky's request for an opinion on the tales he had sent him, Chekhov, with his customary generosity toward younger writers and literary rivals, praised his "genuine, immense talent," especially as reflected in Gorky's story *On the Steppe*, which he envied, he said. "You are an artist and a wise man. You feel superbly. You are plastic — that is, when you describe a thing, you see it and touch it with your hands. That is real art." It was not easy to speak about his defects, Chekhov continued. "To speak about the defects of talent is like speaking about the defects of a fine tree growing in an orchard; the chief consideration is certainly not a question of the tree itself but of the tastes of the person who is looking at it. . . . I'll begin by saying that in my opinion you have no restraint. You are like a spectator in a theater who expresses his rapture so unreservedly that he prevents himself and others from hearing. This lack of restraint is especially felt in descriptions of nature with which you interrupt your dialogues; when one reads these descriptions one would like them to be more compact, shorter, let us say two or three lines. The frequent reference to voluptuousness, whispering, velvet softness, and so forth, color these descriptions with a cerain rhetorical quality and monotony and they chill the reader, almost fatigue him. This lack of restraint is also felt in your descriptions of women. . . ." After more of this kind of sharp observation about Gorky's faults as a writer, Chekhov advised him to get out of the provinces and live for a time with literature and literary people, "not in order to learn, to crow like the rest of our cocks, or to become more skillfull, but rather to plunge headlong into literature and fall in love with it." (*December 3, 1898.*)

« 7 »

While in Yalta Chekhov had to shift most of the burden for the construction of the Melikhovo school, which was scheduled to start in the spring, to the capable shoulders of Masha. Amidst various demands to send him items of clothes he had forgotten were requests to see that the right kind of lumber for the school was delivered and to take care of the annoying complaints of the Talezh teacher about the lack of desks and firewood. For the time being he had assigned virtually all the income from his plays as a contribution to the fund he had to raise for the Melikhovo school, and when the peasants of Novoselki refused to pay their share for the school he had built in their village — a sum which he was counting on for the Melikhovo structure — he threatened to take them to court. In general, affairs back home worried him since his father's death, especially his mother's health and her grief over the loss of her husband. He sent her gifts and brief but tender notes, and to Masha he wrote: "Tell Mother . . . that after summer winter must come, after youth old age, after happiness unhappiness, or the contrary; man cannot be healthy and cheerful all his life, bereavements always await him, he cannot avoid death even though he were Alexander of Macedon — therefore, one must be prepared for anything and accept it as unavoidable and necessary, however sad it may be. According to one's strength, one must fulfill one's duty and nothing more." (*November 13, 1898.*)

From his brother Ivan, who visited him during the Christmas season, Chekhov learned more in detail about the state of things at home. No doubt they also talked about Ivan's hope to achieve the rank of Collegiate Registrar. One of the difficulties was the lack of official government rank in the family, with which went certain privileges. Ivan's years of service as a teacher did not entitle him to climb the hierarchical ladder. In this matter, Chekhov obtained the assistance of his old student, A. S. Yakovlev, whose father was a senator; but not even this degree of influence could succeed unless Ivan was willing to apply for a regular government post.

Chekhov's third move in Yalta to rented rooms was to the house of Kapitolina Ilovaiskaya — "Catherine the Great" he nicknamed her — the consumptive wife of a retired general. Her excellent cuisine compensated for her insistence on discussing with him her favorite subject, homeopathy. He was relatively comfortable in this combination of private home and pension, where many fine people called and conversed on interesting subjects. Here too he entertained his own friends, such as the Shavrovs, the tuberculous Dr. I. G. Vitte, who had come from Serpukhov for treatment, the former Moscow tenor D. A. Usatov, who either discoursed on borsch or gossiped like a wench, the Moscow lawyer A. I. Urusov, a special favorite of Chekhov and a great admirer of his plays, and from the Ukraine Natalya Lintvareva, whom Chekhov encouraged to buy a house in Yalta.

However, Varvara Kharkeevich, the headmistress of the local girls' school and a lover of literature, seemed to attract Chekhov most in a social way. He liked to visit her, introduced Masha to her, and there was some talk of his sister taking up a post as a teacher in the school should she decide to leave Moscow and join her brother at Yalta. Such a step would have pleased him, but it was one which he cautioned her to consider from every angle. In his notebook Chekhov gives an account of attending a large birthday party in honor of the headmistress, where there was much feasting and dancing: "I chattered happily with neighbors and drank wine. The atmosphere was lovely. Suddenly N. arose with a grave face, exactly like that of a public prosecutor, and announced a toast in my honor: 'Magician of words, ideals, in our time when ideals had become tarnished . . .' I had the feeling at first that a nightcap I had on had been removed, and that now they were all staring at me. After the toast there was a clinking of glasses, then silence. The merriment vanished. 'You must now say something,' a neighbor remarked. But what was I to say? I would willingly have let him have it with a bottle. So home to bed with a draft in my soul."

Chekhov was totally unequal to a situation of this sort. It was not merely his innate modesty or shyness in crowds, or his fear of being undressed, as it were, in public, but also an abiding sense of the futility and insincerity of such performances. A. N. Leskov, son of the famous writer, tells in his recollections of a similar siege of embarrassment that overtook Chekhov at a New Year's Eve party at the girls' school. Here there were many toasts in his honor. He silently bowed at the conclusion of each, appalled at their monotony, and at the first favorable opportunity withdrew from the crowd.

Catching him alone, young Leskov introduced himself. Chekhov asked about the relations of his distinguished father with Suvorin. The son replied that at times they were very hostile but that his father regarded Suvorin as essentially a good man who had been spoiled by his love of money and the low journalists who surrounded him. Chekhov agreed: "Suvorin is not an evil man. His money, of course, has corrupted him, but more so that shocking *New Times* camarilla! . . . He involuntarily submits himself to their influence. They corrupt him, the whole editorial staff, the newspaper, and its readers."

Indeed, shortly before this talk with Leskov, Chekhov, in a letter to Alexander, who still worked on *New Times*, denounced another attack in that paper against Dreyfus. He despised the reactionary political world in which Suvorin lived. Though it is difficult to credit the evidence, A. Ya. Bechinsky, editor of the Yalta newspaper *Crimean Courier*, reports Chekhov as telling him in conversation that Bechinsky, "together with other young political activists, ought to set up an extreme-left Yalta organization and struggle everywhere and in everything for social activity and fight against reactionary tendencies in society." However much Chekhov had come to desire social improvement in Russia, he was no revolutionist. Now, as in his youth, his profound skepticism about the sincerity of the efforts of political organizations to achieve human betterment kept him from giving his allegiance to any.

Despite the simple pleasures of Yalta and the life and friends he had already made for himself there, Chekhov could never lose sight of the fact that it was a provincial town. At times he had acute misgivings at the thought of having committed himself to building a house and living there through the fall and perhaps the winter. He would rather be bored in Moscow, for whose theaters and restaurants he languished. There were moments when even the snow of the north seemed attractive to him in this pleasant climate, and he gloomily declared that staggering around health resorts and his enforced idleness were worse than the depredations of bacilli.

But the bacilli gave him no peace of mind. A telegraphic report from an Odessa correspondent, published on the front page of the Petersburg *News* on October 25, announced: THE CONDITION OF THE WRITER CHEKHOV, LIVING AT YALTA, HAS WORSENED: CONSTANT COUGH, FLUCTUATION OF TEMPERATURE, PERIODIC BLOOD-SPITTING. Anxious queries soon began to arrive. He was furious, largely because of the anxiety this report would cause his family, whose members he had regularly been informing of the improved state of his health. He at once set about denying the newspaper account, sending a correction to the press. Rather defiantly he answered Suvorin's query: "I don't know who found it necessary to frighten my family by this cruel telegram, which is entirely false. All this time my temperature has been normal; I've not once taken my temperature, for there has been no occasion to do so. I have a cough, but it is no worse than always. My appetite is wolflike, I sleep well, drink vodka, wine, etc. The day before yesterday I had a cold, remained at home in the evening, but now I'm again feeling fine." (*October 27, 1898.*)

Though it was not in Chekhov's nature to be unfriendly to anyone, newspaper reporters were almost an exception, and this incident increased his dislike. Dr. Isaac Altschuler, a specialist in tuberculosis as well as a victim of the disease, who had decided to settle in Yalta at about the same time Chekhov did, tells in his valuable memoirs of the origin of the false report. Two ladies called early one morning, before Chekhov had arisen, to ask him to participate in a literary evening for charity. In order to get out of it, he explained to the visitors, through his barely opened bedroom door, that he must decline because he had recently been spitting blood. "There you have it," explained Chekhov, "one of the ladies told this to an acquaintance, adding the word 'frequent' blood-spitting; the acquaintance wired to the Odessa newspaper, which added 'cough'; the Petersburg *News* printed the telegram, adding 'fever'; the Moscow *Daily News* put in 'racking cough,' and so forth. . . . I've always told you that the Odessa reporters are awful people."

When Dr. Altschuler first saw Chekhov in October, he found him cheerful, but at times he noticed a weary look on his face, a shortness of breath when the author went up an incline, and the throaty efforts made to stifle a cough when talking. Like so many others, he quickly became an admirer of Chekhov on short acquaintance, and he observed how the various distinguished writers who came to Yalta soon fell under the spell of the charm of his personality, talent, and original and brilliant mind. "His kindness, his desire to be useful in anything, to help in trifles as well as in important matters, was most exceptional."

At the beginning of their acquaintance Dr. Altschuler sensed, as did other physician friends, that Chekhov under no circumstances wished to talk about his health. To the usual question how he was feeling, he invariably replied: "At the moment, fine, almost well, only there is this cough." Yet he would often call attention to Dr. Altschuler's cough, and seriously advise him to take care of himself. Doctors in particular, Altschuler explains, were inclined either to overestimate their own symptoms of illness and exaggerate the treatment, or underestimate them and rationalize little or no treatment by irrelevant medical conclusions. Chekhov belonged to this second category. And in addition, he had fallen a victim to the special psychology of the tubercular, largely an outgrowth of the uncertain and long development of the disease, which compelled him to reject what would appear to be clear and indisputable evidence of his affliction.

On November 27, however, Dr. Altschuler received a note from Chekhov asking him to come at once. The secret could no longer be concealed. The physician found him in bed in a state of slight hemorrhage from the lungs. The examination revealed his serious condition, and from that time on Chekhov became his patient. Yet Dr. Altschuler could not prevail upon him then to undertake a serious course of treatment. Chekhov firmly insisted that being doctored was repulsive to him, and he wanted no one to remind him of his illness or to pay attention to it. Dr. Altschuler noticed that Chekhov had trained himself to speak slowly, not raising his voice, and if he did cough he would try rather furtively to get rid of the sputum in a paper cone which he would later dispose of. Though he concealed this relapse from the family, he wrote Suvorin: "I've had five days of spitting blood and only today has it ceased. But this is confidential, don't tell anyone. I'm not coughing at all, my temperature is normal, and my blood frightens others more than me — therefore I try to keep this a secret from my family." (*November 29, 1898.*)

« 8 »

A knowledge of Chekhov's illness, however, did not discourage those who were anxious to see him married, and they obviously shared the common notion of those days that tuberculosis was not easily communicable. While Chekhov was still in Nice, Kovalevsky, though concerned about his friend's health, inquired whether he was thinking of marriage. "Alas, I'm not up to such a complex, intricate thing as marriage," Chekhov explained. "The very role of a husband terrifies me, for there is something grim in it, like the role of a captain. Lazy as I am, I'd prefer a much easier role." (*February 10, 1898.*)

His brother Misha more seriously prodded him, and not for the first time, and now Chekhov decided to give him a serious answer: "Concerning my marrying, on which you insist — how can I explain it to you? To marry is interesting only when one is in love; to marry a girl simply because she is attractive is like buying something unnecessary at a bazaar merely because it is nice. The most important thing in family life is love, sexual attraction, being of one flesh — all the rest is unreliable and dreary, no matter how cleverly we may have calculated. So it is not the question of an attractive girl but of her being loved; as you can see, my delaying the matter counts for little." (*October 26, 1898.*)

However attractive she may have been to him at one time, Lika had never really inspired this kind of love in Chekhov. Yet there was hardly any woman in his life whose company he appeared to enjoy more than hers, and perhaps just because the war of the sexes between them never ceased, and he had the satisfaction of knowing that the victory would always be his. Now, though he had apparently written Lika a number of times, he had heard nothing from her for months. She was again in Paris studying singing, and mutual friends there had reported to him fine things about the quality of her voice combined with criticism of her lack of musical taste. Then suddenly a letter to Yalta rejoiced him. She, too, twitted him about rumors of his forthcoming marriage, and he replied in that familiar, jocose tone he had invented especially for her: "That I'm going to marry is another fable you have thrust into the world. You know that I'll never marry without your permission. You are sure of this, yet you circulate these various rumors — probably by the logic of the old hunter, who does not use his gun, or lets others use it, and merely grumbles and groans while lying on the oven. No, my dear Lika, no! I'll not marry without your permission. . . ." Then after a few amusing details about mutual friends, his doings at Yalta, and the hope that he will see her if he goes to Moscow in January, he concludes: "I repeat once again that your letter made me very, very glad, but I'm afraid you won't believe it and will fail to answer soon. I swear, Lika, that I miss you." (*September 21, 1898.*)

In reply, Lika sent him her latest photograph and urged him to visit her in Paris. He answered promptly, but after a serious opening about the death of his father and the changes this might bring about at Melikhovo, he thanked Lika for her portrait: "You are even beautiful, which I somehow didn't expect." He expressed the strongest desire to see her, but he had no money to go to Paris, he said, and he ended: "Where did you get the idea that I had a bald spot? What impertinence! I know: You are revenging yourself on me because once in one of my letters I pointed out to you, in friendly fashion and not at all wishing to offend you, that you are lopsided; and that this is the reason why, unfortunately, you have not yet found a husband." (*October 24, 1898.*)

On the other hand, since Lidiya Avilova's visit to Chekhov in Dr. Ostroumov's clinic, her persistent assault upon his affections had been going from bad to worse. She grew progressively irritated by the fact that he never wrote her except to answer her letters, and because the imaginary relationship she had concocted seemed to be moving further and further away from any contact with reality. With his dread of hurting anyone's feelings, he was helpless in the face of her tendency now to nag and indulge in quite unprovoked recriminations. Occasionally, however, a note of annoyance would creep into his answers. This seems to have been the case in his reply to a letter she had written him in July 1898 — one which she, again understandably, did not quote in her memoirs. She had pleaded "for only three words" — it was some nine months since he had last written her — and, apparently in the hope of seeing him, she asked if he would be in the Skopin district where she was vacationing. "I've not been in the Skopin district and am hardly likely to go there," he rather brusquely answered. "I'm staying at home, doing some writing — that is, busy." To her resentment over the criticism of her stories which he had expressed in his letter of the previous November, he remarked that he was sorry. "If my letters are sometimes harsh or cold, this comes from my lack of seriousness and skill in writing them; I ask your indulgence and I assure you that the phrase with which you conclude your letter — 'if you are happy, then you will be kinder to me' — I definitely do not deserve." (*July 10, 1898.*)

Avilova must have answered this rather pleasantly, for less than two weeks later he replied in an amiable, chatty letter which she quoted in her memoirs. He tells her how busy he is at Melikhovo, how much he receives for his stories, but that he is getting fed up with writing: "Now when I write, or think that I have to write something, I have the same kind of repugnance I would feel in eating cabbage soup from which a cockroach had just been removed — forgive the comparison." Then, as a kind of afterthought, he ends: "I must send something for the August issue of *Russian Thought*; I've already written it, but I must polish it."

Avilova avidly seized upon this afterthought — she was certain that Chekhov was covertly drawing her attention to the August number of *Russian Thought*. As she explains in her memoirs, she had got used to reading between the lines of his letters. She obtained a copy of the magazine as soon as it appeared, and of course she found two tales there — *Gooseberries* and *About Love*. "The one title *About Love* threw me into violent agitation," she wrote in her memoirs (Chapter XV). "Making all sorts of surmises, I ran back home with the magazine in my hand."

With her incredible propensity for wishful thinking, Lidiya Avilova jumped to the conclusion that the love of Alekhin and Anna Alekseevna in the story was solidly based on her relations with Chekhov. As she read it and came to the passage where Alekhin gives the reasons why he did not declare his love, Avilova writes in her memoirs: "I was no longer crying but sobbed hysterically. . . . So he did not blame me. He did not blame, but justified, understood, and grieved with me." When she came to Alekhin's conclusion, that in love man must be guided by something higher than happiness or unhappiness, Avilova decided that she could not understand what that something "higher" was: "I knew and understood only one thing, that life had crushed me and that it was impossible to free myself from its vise. If my family prevented me from being happy with Anton Pavlovich, then Anton Pavlovich prevented me from being happy with my family."

There is an element of the preposterous in the correspondences that Lydiya Avilova professed to see in the tale. Many more differences than resemblances can be pointed out between the love story of Anna Alekseevna and Alekhin and Avilova's fancied relations with Chekhov. Actually, there is very little in common between the characterizations of the wife, husband, and lover in the tale and Lidiya Avilova, her husband, and Chekhov. Although it is conceivable that their strange relationship may have contributed something to this tale, it is even more conceivable, in the light of Chekhov's special interests and emphasis in his fiction, that he would have written such a story even if he had never known Lidiya Avilova. Even the outline of the central theme of *About Love* in Chekhov's notebook in no sense supports Avilova's contention.

Nevertheless, Avilova wrote Chekhov an angry letter, sarcastically thanking him for the honor of appearing as the heroine of one of his stories, and telling him of a writer she heard about who does all sorts of mean and disgusting things in order to describe them realistically in his fiction. How many themes, she asked, must an author discover in order to publish hundreds of short stories? "That is, the writer, like the bee, gathers his honey where he can find it. . . . He is bored and sick of writing . . . but he goes on coldly and indifferently describing feelings that his soul can no longer experience, because his talent has crowded out his soul. And the colder the writer, the more sensitive and touching are his stories. Let the readers weep over them. That is art."

This outburst probably worried Chekhov more than it exasperated him. His reply was cautious and temporizing, as though he were dealing with a neurotic person. He mentioned first his impending departure for the Crimea and how distasteful was this vagabond life forced upon him by his illness. In his only reference to the contents of her letter, he wrote: "Your judgment about the bee is incorrect. It must first see the bright, beautiful flowers, and only then does it gather the honey. And as for what followed — indifference, boredom, and that talented people live and love only in a world of their own images and fantasies — all I can say is: Another person's soul is darkness. . . . I press your hand. Keep well and happy." (*August 30, 1898.*)

It would appear that the very innocuousness of Chekhov's reply, his pointed evasion of her charge that he had exploited for literary gain what she regarded as their hallowed relationship, infuriated Lidiya Avilova. He refused to play her romantic game of make-believe or "Let's pretend." She was getting older, and the claims of marriage and now three children were binding her to a fate she resisted. In her prolonged pursuit, she might have been placated by just a bit of emotional sentiment or personal feeling for her; but this, too, Chekhov failed to give. In her next letter, if we may judge from Chekhov's answer,[8] she seized upon his polite "Keep well and happy" as a deliberate attempt on his

---

[8] This letter is entirely ignored in Avilova's memoirs. In fact, it was one she asked his sister to exclude from her collection, a request with which Masha complied.

part to end their correspondence. To this half-mad accusation, he answered: "I read your letter and could only throw up my hands in despair. If I wished you health and happiness in my last, it was not because I wished to break off our correspondence or, Heaven forbid, because I wished to avoid you, but simply because I have always wished you happiness and health, and I do so now. It is very simple. And if you see things in my letters that are not there, it is probably because I don't know how to express myself." Then, on a calmer note, he told a bit about his life at Yalta, the death of his father, and the fact that this would probably necessitate building a new nest for his family in the South. And with his dislike of giving offense, even if it were imaginary, he ended: "At any rate, do not be angry with me, and forgive me if there was anything cruel or disagreeable in my last letter." (*October 21, 1898.*)

Clearly Chekhov had not found in Lika, Lidiya Avilova, or in any other woman that special essence — "love, sexual attraction, being of one flesh" — which he had singled out in his letter to Misha as the *sine qua non* of happy married life. But then he gave no evidence of having been searching for it. Throughout his mature existence the emphasis he placed on getting married had been largely negative. Now, seriously ill and at the age of thirty-eight, had the desire to begin the search for such a love caught his imagination as one last experience he must enjoy or suffer before it was too late? It will be remembered that he had enthusiastically written Suvorin, after he had seen Olga Knipper as Irina in *Tsar Fyodor*, that he could have fallen in love with her if he had remained in Moscow. The feeling may have been mutual, for this was possibly the rumor Lika had referred to in her letter in September. Though he had passed off as a joke her guess that he was planning on marriage, he perhaps did betray the direction of his thoughts in a couple of sentences which repeat what he had told Suvorin: "Nemirovich-Danchenko and Stanislavsky have a very interesting theater. Beautiful actresses. If I were to remain there a little longer, I would lose my head. As I grow older, the pulse of life in me beats faster and stronger." And he dropped still another unconscious hint in a letter to Nemirovich-Danchenko. In congratulating him on the laudatory reviews of the Moscow Art Theater's performance of *Tsar Fyodor*, he remarked: "But why don't they write about Irina — Knipper? Is anything the matter? I didn't like your Fyodor, but Irina was extraordinarily good; yet Fyodor gets more mention than Irina." (*October 21, 1898.*)

Chekhov was hardly in love with Olga Knipper, but her image some-how had never left his thoughts since the night he first saw her.

« 9 »

Perhaps because of both Olga Knipper and the impending perform-ance of *The Sea Gull*, the Moscow Art Theater was very much in Che-khov's thoughts while he was in Yalta. He had admired the zeal and artistic sense of its directors and the enthusiasm and dedication of the young actors. In his own thinking, Chekhov had anticipated, in certain respects, Stanislavsky's revolution against the stultifying conventions of the Russian theater. He shared the new company's detestation of the old method of acting with its theatricality, false pathos, declamation, and he sympathized with the intention to achieve artistic staging and a higher level of repertoire. In writing Nemirovich-Danchenko on the success of *Tsar Fyodor*, with which the Moscow Art Theater had opened its first season on October 14, he had declared: "Judging from the news-papers, the start was a brilliant one — and I'm very, very glad; you can't imagine how glad I am. Your success is still another proof that the public as well as the actors need an intelligent theater." All this, he no doubt felt, augured well for *The Sea Gull* when its turn came.

Fortunately for his peace of mind, what Chekhov at Yalta did not know was that between the success of their opening night and the date set for the first performance of *The Sea Gull*, December 17, the new theater had suffered comparative failures in five other plays in their repertoire. Another failure threatened to ruin the new company, which had become an object of ridicule on the part of some of the critics because of its bold challenge to the conventional Russian stage. Though Stanislavsky had lavished all his brilliant talents in devising an exhaus-tive *mis-en-scène* that would highlight every external action and bring out what he believed to be the melancholy mood of Chekhov's play, he had very little faith in *The Sea Gull*, whose meaning was still unclear to him. It was a bad omen that late changes had to be made in the cast-ing; the dress rehearsal went off poorly; and a last-minute complication ensued when Chekhov's sister appeared at the theater and pleaded with tears in her eyes that the play be postponed because she was desperately worried over the effect a second failure would have on her brother's precarious health.[9] The directors wavered, but in the end they decided

---

[9] In her memoirs Chekhov's sister denies that she ever made such an appeal, but the evidence appears to support the allegation.

to go through with the performance; much money and twenty-six rehearsals had been expended on *The Sea Gull*. To withdraw the play meant to close the theater.

The evening of December 17 came. The audience was not large. In his *My Life in Art*, Stanislavsky relates that the actors were determined to create not success but a triumph, for they believed that if they failed the man and writer whom they loved would die, killed by their hands. Stanislavsky could not recall how the first act went off, only that all the actors smelled of valerian drops — a common Russian sedative. Playing the part of Trigorin, he also remembered how he tried to still the trembling of his leg while sitting with his back to the audience — one of the theater's breaks with convention in order to suggest a fourth wall to the stage.

When the final curtain fell, there was a tomblike silence throughout the auditorium. Olga Knipper fainted — she was ill, and had acted the role of Arkadina in a high fever. In deep despair the cast started to move to their dressing rooms. Suddenly there came an unearthly roar from the auditorium. The curtain went up and the surprised actors were caught in various odd postures, grim expressions of failure still on their faces. Pandemonium broke loose as the antics of the audience turned into a demonstration. The actors embraced each other, kissed, shouted, and wept. Stanislavsky did a wild dervish dance of triumph on the stage as the audience roared its demand that a telegram be sent to Chekhov.

The telegram arrived at Yalta: JUST PERFORMED THE SEA GULL, SUCCESS COLOSSAL. PLAY SO TOOK HOLD FROM FIRST ACT THAT SERIES OF TRIUMPHS FOLLOWED. CURTAIN CALLS ENDLESS. . . . WE ARE MAD WITH JOY. The next day another telegram came from Nemirovich-Danchenko: WITH WONDERFUL UNANIMITY ALL NEWSPAPERS ACCLAIM SUCCESS OF THE SEA GULL AS BRILLIANT, TUMULTUOUS, ENORMOUS. REVIEWS OF PLAY RAPTUROUS. FOR OUR THEATER SUCCESS OF THE SEA GULL SURPASSES SUCCESS OF FYODOR. In truth, the extraordinary performance of Chekhov's play saved the Moscow Art Theater and set it on its glorious course of future achievements and world influence. The Moscow Art Theater became Chekhov's theater, a fact symbolized by the emblem of the sea gull that henceforth appeared on its curtain.

Chekhov answered Nemirovich-Danchenko with a telegram: CONVEY TO ALL: INFINITE THANKS WITH ALL MY SOUL. I'M CONFINED TO YALTA, LIKE DREYFUS ON DEVIL'S ISLAND. I GRIEVE THAT I'M NOT WITH YOU. YOUR TELEGRAM MADE ME WELL AND HAPPY.

Olga Knipper's illness delayed repetition of *The Sea Gull* for some days and Chekhov dismally commented that he had such bad luck in the theater that if he were to marry an actress she would no doubt give birth to an orangutan or a porcupine. When it resumed, each performance had a full house. Tatyana Shchepkina-Kupernik tells how she often passed the theater in the early hours of the morning and saw the square filled with people, mostly young, some sitting on stools and reading books by lanterns, others dancing, but all waiting through the night to buy tickets for *The Sea Gull*, the lucky purchasers then rushing off to their various jobs.

Telegrams and letters from friends and family kept pouring into Yalta, most of them ecstatic in their praise of *The Sea Gull*. Even Gorky in Nizhny Novgorod, who had only read the play, hurried off a letter because a friend — an old, experienced hand in drama criticism — had told him, "with tears of agitation," that in forty years of going to the theater he had "never seen such a marvelous, *heretically talented* piece as *The Sea Gull*." And Gorky added: "So you don't want to write for the theater?! You must, by God! Forgive me that I write so boldly, but truly I feel terribly fine and merry and I love you."

For days Chekhov was busy answering these congratulatory communications — he felt it his duty. All his thoughts were in Moscow. When and where would he see his play? In replying to A. L. Vishnevsky, an old Taganrog school comrade who acted the part of Dorn, he pathetically exploded: "Ah, if you could only feel and understand how bitter it is for me that I cannot be at *The Sea Gull* and see all of you!" (*December 19, 1898.*) To have been present at that first terrible failure and now to have missed the superb triumph was a piece of ill-luck which he never ceased to regret. But to the depths of his being he felt that he had been morally and artistically resurrected.

CHAPTER XX

"I Have Become a 'Marxist'"

"IF I DID NOT HAVE TO LIVE IN YALTA," Chekhov wrote his admirer Urusov on February 1, 1899, "this winter would be the happiest of my life." Indeed, as reports continued to come in on successive performances of *The Sea Gull*, capped by greetings and thanks signed by three hundred spectators, Chekhov's happiness grew lyrical. The play was creating a furor — wrote Masha, who saw it a number of times — everybody was talking about him; she joyfully suggested that he call his new Yalta house "The Sea Gull." Chaliapin, among the many, sent a telegram of rapturous praise of his talent, and news of a successful staging of *The Sea Gull* in Prague reached him. In letters he urged friends to see the play and write him about it, and soon the first royalties of over thirteen hundred roubles added to his pleasure. "Who could have thought," Chekhov wrote Sergeenko about their Taganrog schoolfellow, "that this former dunce and starveling Vishnevsky would act in the Art Theater in a play written by another former dunce and starveling?" (*January* 1, 1899.)

But this letter to the Tolstoyan Sergeenko, whose loud laughter and comic demeanor always made Chekhov feel uncomfortable, concerned a proposal which Sergeenko had conveyed to him: the well-known publisher A. F. Marx had offered to buy all Chekhov's works and get out a complete edition. Chekhov had heard rumors of this interest earlier. Tolstoy, it appears, had urged Marx, who had published his *Resurrection*, to make such an offer, assuring him that Chekhov's writings were of more consequence than those of Turgenev or Goncharov. Even Masha in Moscow had heard from Sergeenko that he would be willing to negotiate with Marx and that Chekhov should demand at least a hundred thousand roubles.

An obstacle to such an arrangement was Chekhov's agreement to let Suvorin publish his complete works; in fact, at that very time Chekhov was correcting proof on the first volume. However, he had become involved in prolonged wrangling with Suvorin's editors. They lost his manuscripts and failed to answer his letters; in exasperation he remarked that at the rate they were going the edition would not appear until 1948. For several years now Chekhov had been expressing considerable dissatisfaction over the shoddy way in which his books were handled by Suvorin's minions. One of the chief reasons was Suvorin's failure to devote much attention to this aspect of his many enterprises. Delays in publishing, poor promotion and distribution, and execrable bookkeeping had resulted in substantial financial losses to Chekhov. He now averaged only about thirty-five hundred roubles annually on the various editions of some thirteen volumes in circulation, but the little book *Kashtanka*, he maintained, could alone earn him a thousand a year if properly pushed. During the past year his earnings had run up to eight thousand simply on the strength of the publication of *Peasants*. Besides, he had grown weary of fighting often losing battles over paper, type face, bindings, titles, and the size of an edition. He longed to be relieved of all these decisions, which Marx's firm promised to undertake, and in addition this publisher had the reputation of turning out attractive books and selling them well. Then, too, Marx sought to buy all his writings outright, whereas Chekhov's arrangement on the Suvorin edition was the old one — he would receive a percentage of the income from the sale of the books. The prospect of an immediate large sum of money was perhaps the conclusive argument in favor of Marx's proposal, for Chekhov urgently needed funds for his new house and to pay off his debts. Further, in the light of his precarious health, he now felt it essential to plan for the future of his mother and sister as well as of himself. So with almost impatient eagerness he assured Sergeenko that he was more than willing to have him negotiate a contract with Marx.

The news distressed Masha. He was popular, she wrote him, even famous, and she considered the sum of a hundred thousand roubles for his works cheap. She readily offered to publish his writings herself, as Tolstoy's wife was now doing in the case of her husband's works, in the conviction that her brother would make much more money. Chekhov tried to assuage her worries by representing himself as a sharp bargainer. Marx was stingy, he admitted, but he gave him a hard time. He had countered Marx's initial offer of fifty thousand roubles with a demand for seventy-five thousand, and he had insisted that the publisher have no control over the income from performances of his plays.

In reality, the astute publisher found Chekhov a rather easy mark, as the contract, which was signed on January 26, plainly indicated. For seventy-five thousand roubles, Chekhov sold Marx the rights to everything he had published or would publish in the future. Twenty thousand was payable upon Chekhov's formal agreement to all the terms, and the remainder, in varying sums, at four set dates over the course of the next two years. However, Chekhov retained first publishing rights to anything he wrote after signing the contract, but thereafter it became the property of Marx, who would reimburse him at the rate of two hundred and fifty roubles for a printer's signature (sixteen printed pages) during the first five years, this rate to increase by two hundred roubles for each of the next three five-year periods. Though Chekhov had the privilege of deciding on which of his writings would go into the proposed edition, Marx reserved the right to veto anything he regarded as unsuitable. Finally, Chekhov was required to turn over to Marx, within six months of signing the contract, a complete bibliography of all that he had published, as well as copies of these works. And if he held back an item or made arrangements with anyone else to publish his writings, for such breach of contract he was obligated to pay Marx at the rate of five thousand roubles for each printer's signature.

Marx had drawn up a shrewd contract. As the possessor of the total corpus of Chekhov's works, he had the sole right to print them in any number of editions without further remuneration to the author, except the initial payments for new stories. His shrewdness is attested by the large profits he reaped from the deal.

Chekhov, however, was not unaware of some of the drawbacks of the contract — he would be feeding Marx's heirs and widow, he told Serge-enko, while his own widow would get nothing. From a long-range point of view he realized that he risked losing much, despite the steeply rising rate of remuneration over the years for new works. In his telegram of acceptance, he jokingly promised Marx not to live more than eighty — a remark, said Sergeenko, which almost ruined the deal, for the publisher took it literally. Chekhov's agreement was clearly influenced by his own cool assumption that his years were numbered. He told Suvorin that the contract would be profitable if he lived less than five or ten years, and unprofitable if he lived longer. When his former student Yakovlev, who shared Masha's conviction that her brother ought to publish the works himself, protested about his excuse that he had not long to live, Chekhov replied: "My friend, you forget that I'm a doctor, however bad a one I may be. The medical experts do not at all deceive me; my case is a poor one, and the end is not far off."

To Masha, he wrote reassuringly that, whatever might be the disadvantages, there would at last be order in his publishing affairs; and so, glory be to God! The initial payment, he pointed out, would take care of all his debts and cover the expenses of building the Yalta house, and of a new piano and furniture; the remainder he would put in the bank at 4 per cent interest. And he optimistically estimated his future annual income from bank interest, the sale of new stories to magazines and then to Marx, and royalties from the performances of his plays as nine and a half thousand roubles. "I am now a 'Marxist,'" he cheerfully told his friends.

In all these negotiations Suvorin was very much on Chekhov's conscience. He wired him as soon as he received Marx's offer and also asked Sergeenko to inform him of the details, for Suvorin must cease publication of Chekhov's works after January 26. Although the contract was not explicit on the matter, it appears that the remaining copies of Suvorin's various editions could be sold or Marx had the option of buying them up. Suvorin sent Chekhov a long telegram in which he pointed out some of the obvious financial pitfalls in the proposal, urged him to delay his decision, and, if what he needed was ready money, offered to send him twenty thousand roubles at once. Brother Alexander, however, reported from Petersburg that Sergeenko represented the deal as already consummated when he called on Suvorin, although Sergeenko denied this to Chekhov. However, Suvorin accused Chekhov of unwarranted secrecy in the matter and of not wanting to sell to him. Alexander described a quarrel between Suvorin and his two older sons, who now played an important role in their father's business, over his desire to make a counter-offer to Chekhov; the sum involved, the sons protested, was too large an investment. In a letter to Misha months later, Chekhov confirmed some of these details. When he had put the question to Suvorin whether he wished to buy all his writings, Suvorin had replied that he did not have the money, that his sons would not agree to it, and that anyway no one could pay more than Marx. The advance of twenty thousand roubles which Suvorin offered, Chekhov pointed out, would have meant purchasing all his works for that sum and he would never be able to wrest himself free from debts. And he added that when the deal with Marx had been concluded, Suvorin had written that he was glad of it, because his conscience had always troubled him on account of the poor job he had done of publishing his writings.

Chekhov, who obviously felt badly about this severance of his publishing relations with Suvorin, tried whimsically to minimize its significance. His fiction was of no consequence, he declared; the important thing was the royalty from his plays, and this was out of Marx's hands. Only the need of securing a large sum at once had compelled him to take this step, he wrote Suvorin, and now he experienced the nasty feeling of having married a woman for her money. Repeatedly he suggested that they get together to celebrate, in some fitting manner, the termination of their close relations as author and publisher over the last thirteen years. "We part peacefully," he said, "but we also got along very peacefully together, and I seem to recall that we never had a single misunderstanding during all the time you printed my books." (*January 27, 1899.*)

« 2 »

Chekhov immediately undertook the formidable task of gathering together all his stories, listing the newspapers and magazines in which they had appeared, and preparing edited copy for the first two volumes of his collected works. He had been condemned to hard labor, he soon protested, and if he had foreseen the magnitude of the effort he would have insisted upon a hundred and seventy-five thousand roubles. Many early tales in the humorous newspapers and magazines had vanished entirely from his memory, to say nothing of the issues and dates when they had been published. To list all this material, he asserted, was like being asked to enumerate precisely every fish he had caught over the last twenty years. As the copy piled up he was overwhelmed by its bulk, and found himself wondering how all this could possibly have come from his pen. Much of it he was ashamed of, and excluded from the collected works; and every story he accepted he subjected to rigorous editing, sometimes amounting to rewriting it. In going over the old magazines he came across forgotten illustrations by Nikolai, and he was so impressed by their brilliance that he decided to collect them in a bound volume and send them to the Taganrog library as a memento to his dead brother.

Working at Yalta, far from the sources, Chekhov at times had to depend upon bibliographers to run down the publication data of his early tales. And in a number of cases he had to request old friends of his youth, such as Yezhov and Lazarev-Gruzinsky, and also Masha and Alexander, to locate stories and hire people to copy them when he did not possess the publications. Apparently after some thought, he decided to ask Lidiya Avilova to arrange for someone to list his stories in the *Petersburg Gazette* and to copy certain ones which he would designate. No doubt his choice in this instance was influenced by the fact that she lived in the capital and that her brother-in-law edited the *Petersburg Gazette*. His request was couched in friendly tones, and he stressed that he wished her merely to find some young miss to do the copying after Avilova had secured permission for her to use the file at the newspaper's office. This appears to have been the only instance when Chekhov assumed the initiative in writing her, and perhaps a bit embarrassed now to ask a favor after their quarrelsome correspondence of some four months ago, he interjected, in a spirit of reconciliation: "At least write that you are not angry, if in general you don't wish to write me." (*February 5, 1899.*)

This unsolicited letter filled Avilova with happiness. What a joy it meant for her, she exclaims in her memoirs, to do some work for Chekhov! His simple request seemed somehow to satisfy the inextinguishable and by now pathetic yearning in this woman for any degree of "closeness" to him. She performed the task he required with love and meticulous care, and his grateful response to her efforts effected a change in her demeanor. For in the brief correspondence that ensued over the details of the work, the strained hints and irritating demands on his affection seem to have vanished from her letters, if we may judge from his answers. Pleased with the change, and perhaps warning her away from a resumption of her former carping manner, he pointedly remarked in one of his replies: "I love letters which are not written in a preaching tone." And in another, after indulging in some critical comments on contemporary writers, among whom he included her, he suddenly caught himself up: "But I seem to have gone in for criticism; I'm afraid in reply that you'll write me something edifying." (*February 26, 1899.*)

In general, however, he repaid her altered mien with chatty, cheerful letters about mutual friends, how to behave to the peasants on the estate her husband had bought, his daily life, and the work she was doing for him. Once, in reaction to her flattering comments that he seemed to know how to make the best of life, he slipped into that familiar mood of disenchantment caused by the strictures which illness imposed upon his freedom of movement. Of what use is the knowledge of making the best of life, he asked, when he had to live away from everything as though he were in exile? "Why am I in Yalta? Why is it so dull here? . . . I dislike the thought of writing and I'm not writing anything." (*February 18, 1899.*) This note, now frequently expressed to various people, at once evoked an unaccountably personal response in Avilova. "Will I never, never bring him anything but grief?" she asks in her memoirs.

At the end of three months Avilova had completed her task. Learning that he was in Moscow then, she apparently suggested a meeting when she passed through the city on the way to her new estate.[1] This time Chekhov was happy to see her, for he wanted to thank her personally for her labors on his behalf. The description in her memoirs of their meeting in the compartment of the train, with her three children gamboling about, is probably a curious mixture of reality and fantasy. Its unconnected, cross-grained, and often angry dialogue is entirely inconsistent with his gratitude for a job well done and the anticipated pleasure he expressed in his letter over the thought of meeting her. The explanation may lie in the fact that her possessiveness always rubbed him the wrong way. The passage in her memoirs, as he arose to take his leave, suggests as much: "I recalled the parting of Alekhin with Anna in the compartment of the train just before it left the station: 'I embraced her and she pressed herself to my breast.'[2] I suddenly felt my heart beginning to pound as though I had received a blow on the head. 'But we are not saying good-by forever,' I tried to console myself. . . . The train began to move slowly. I saw the figure of Anton Pavlovich float past the window, but he failed to look back. I did not know then, nor could I have imagined, that I was seeing him for the last time. . . ."

Lidiya Avilova's work for Chekhov on the *Petersburg Gazette* having been finished, it was months before an occasion arose for them to correspond again.

« 3 »

He was no Vanderbilt, Chekhov joked, after receiving the first fifteen thousand roubles from Marx,[3] but with so much money, the most he had ever had in his hands at once, he could not resist the expansive tendencies of his nature. Nothing would now give him more pleasure, he declared, than to go to Monte Carlo and lose two thousand on a throw without worrying over it. In the course of building the Yalta house he contemplated buying another one in Moscow, and he rented an apartment in that city for a whole year, although he knew that he could spend only a few weeks in it. A patch of beach property near

---

[1] In her memoirs (Chapter XVI) she changes the chronology of his letters at this point, perhaps in an effort to suggest that the initiative for a meeting was Chekhov's.

[2] Quoted from Chekhov's story *About Love*.

[3] No explanation is offered of why the initial installment was fifteen thousand roubles instead of the twenty thousand specified by the contract.

Yalta struck him as an ideal bathing spot to purchase, even though the doctors had forbidden him to swim. And he also dreamed now of tearing down the little Tatar house at Kuchukoi and erecting in its place a modern European dwelling. He welcomed the idea, which Masha suggested, of investing some of his money in a factory, but fortunately he abandoned this notion.

Always partial to charitable requests, Chekhov now distributed largesse with a freer hand. Although he was devoting the income from his plays to the funds necessary to build the Melikhovo school, he unhesitatingly contributed five hundred roubles towards the construction of a new school in a village not far from Yalta. And he offered to pay school tuition for the daughter of Gavrilyushka, the former Ukrainian apprentice who had worked in his father's grocery shop and was then doing quite well in Kharkov, where he owned a house. In Moscow Chekhov supported the consumptive S. A. Epifanov, a journalist and third-rate poet whom he hardly knew. A plea to aid the starving people of Kazan was promptly answered by a gift of a hundred roubles and an offer to organize a newspaper campaign on behalf of the sufferers. Upon his election to the board of trustees of the Taganrog charity school — he had already been made a member of the library board of Taganrog — he sent a donation of a hundred roubles. And in a covering letter to Iordanov, he begged to be informed if there were any other ways in which he could aid his native town. Humorously he signed himself: L'HOMME RICHE and PHILANTHROPIST in his letters to Alexander, who seems to have taken him seriously, for he borrowed a thousand roubles to help build a little *dacha* outside Petersburg. Chekhov's money flew away from him like a wild fledgling; in two years, he conjectured, he would have to become a philosopher.

However, most of this first installment from Marx was spent on building the Yalta house. A rather substantial structure of two stories on the north side, rising to three on the south in a kind of tower effect, it was adorned with spacious verandas and a glassed-in porch. Yet he now described it as a "sardine can" and lamented that if he could only have anticipated the Marx windfall, he would have set out to build one much larger. As at Melikhovo, he spent lavishly to beautify the surroundings — a stone fence, paths, and landscaping. He ordered hundreds of flower pots from Taganrog, saplings from Odessa, and he gratefully accepted gifts of flowering shrubs from Yalta friends. With two Turks in their red fezzes to assist him, he supervised uprooting the old vineyard on the plot, preparing the soil, and laying out a garden design. Like an eager child he went from hole to hole, planting the saplings, shrubs and rosebushes. "Yesterday and today," he wrote Masha, "I set out trees on the plot, and really I was filled with bliss it was so wonderful, so warm and poetic. It was simply a prolonged rapture. I planted twelve cherry, four pyramidal mulberry, two almond, and others. The trees are fine and they will soon bear fruit. The old trees are blossoming, and the pear, almond, and also the rosebushes are flowering. The birds on their way north spend the night in the garden and sing in the morning, especially the thrushes. In general, it is very delightful, and if only Mamasha were here, she would not regret it." (*March* 14, 1899.) If Chekhov loved to build, plant gardens and ornament the earth, Gorky pointed out, it was because he felt the poetry of labor and was convinced of the importance of work as the foundation of all culture.

But this was early spring. The winter at Yalta had been an unusually harsh one and construction work on the house had been slowed almost to a standstill. The bad weather frequently compelled him to sit at home in his rented rooms and mope, as he said, although he had a mountain of work to do for the Marx edition. At such times his spirits yearned for Moscow. Chekhov could not get over his curious ambivalence about Yalta. To the ill he loyally defended it, insisting this resort town was to be preferred over Nice and that he knew many consumptives whose health had much improved at Yalta. For himself, however, he declared that he would much rather be destroyed by the rigorous climate of the North than by the provincial boredom of this town where the doctors had condemned him to live.

For a "bored" person, however, he kept surprisingly active over the winter months at Yalta. As a member of the town committee to plan the celebration of the hundredth anniversary of Pushkin's birth, he played a prominent part in organizing the staging of scenes from the poet's *Boris Godunov*. And he arranged two amateur performances on behalf of his current charity, the famine-ridden peasant children of Samara, for whom he collected a thousand roubles. For a time he attempted to hold "Thursdays" in his rooms for callers. But he complained that they sat too long, and when the literary-minded headmistress of the girls' school began to introduce her awed teachers of literature, who embarrassed him by their dogged silence, he abandoned his Thursdays.

Despite the off-season period, friends visited Yalta — Lavrov of *Russian Thought* and Dr. N. I. Korobov, his old Medical School comrade who had lived with the family in those dark, poverty-stricken Moscow days. Chekhov busied himself arranging for suitable accommodations for Korobov's wife, who had tuberculosis.

One day toward the end of winter, Nadezhda Golubeva, the sister of Mariya Kiseleva at Babkino, visited Yalta and decided to call on Chekhov. It took some courage, for it was six years since she had last seen him in her Petersburg home, when he had behaved rather strangely at dinner and discouraged her literary ambitions. Besides, she had already heard that many Yalta ladies pursued him, threw flowers in his window, and wrote him confessions of love.

After she had waited a considerable time, he appeared. She hardly recognized him; his face had changed and taken on the appearance of parchment. He explained that he had kept her waiting because he had hesitated to see her for fear that she would summon up the past. But he soon laughed and recalled the happy days at Babkino. He spoke enthusiastically of his new house and his hideaway at Kuchukoi. She knew this tiny and nearly inaccessible village and remarked that one must be queer to want to live in such a remote spot. He coughed, she recalls in her recollections of the meeting, and replied: "You involuntarily become a queer fellow when all is lost and life sputters like a candle going out."

Chekhov also renewed his acquaintance with Bunin, who visited Yalta in the early spring. As the two sat talking on a bench by the shore, Bunin asked if Chekhov liked the sea. Yes, he answered, and added after a pause: "It is very difficult to describe the sea. Do you know the description of it that I read in the copybook of a schoolboy not long ago? 'The sea was huge.' Only that. I think it is beautiful." Though this might appear to be a mannerism, Bunin ruminated, it reminded him that Chekhov always preferred naturalness in description. Hence, Bunin concluded, with his dislike for anything pretentious or strained, "The sea was huge" seemed to him precisely "beautiful."

The early spring also brought Gorky, who arrived in Yalta with Mirolyubov. For some time Chekhov had been urging Gorky to visit, for the two had never met. Though Gorky had incipient tuberculosis and had come to Yalta for treatment, to see Chekhov was perhaps the real reason for his decision to make the trip from Nizhny Novgorod.

Up to this point these two writers, whose personalities and artistic practices were so different in many ways, had got to know each other only through correspondence. Though full of admiration for some of his stories, Chekhov had not spared the younger author's faults of characterization and style. Early in January Chekhov had written him again of his lack of restraint and of what he called "grace." There was a feeling of excess in his lavish use of words, Chekhov insisted. "When a person expends the least possible movement on a certain act, that is grace." Recalling his comment to Bunin, he disapproved of Gorky's anthropomorphism in nature descriptions, "When you have the sea breathe, the heavens gaze down, the steppe caress, nature whisper, speak, or grow mournful, etc. — such usage makes your descriptions monotonous, occasionally saccharine, and sometimes unclear; picturesqueness and expressiveness in descriptions of nature are attained only through simplicity, by the use of such plain phrases as 'The sun came out,' 'It became dark,' 'It rained,' etc." And he warned Gorky of his fondness for portraying the unattractive aspects of local officialdom. He knew these people well, he assured Gorky, and they were altogether untypical and usually of no interest.

The repetitive and flamboyant effects in Gorky's stories sometimes annoyed him, and in a letter to Avilova he sharply commented: "I like Gorky, but lately he has begun to write nonsense, disgusting nonsense, so much so that I'll soon have to give up reading him." (*March 9, 1899.*) Nor did he hesitate to pass on to Gorky, because he thought it justifiable, Tolstoy's observation: " 'You can invent anything you please, but it is impossible to invent psychology, and psychological inventions abound in Gorky; he describes what he has not felt.' " (*April 25, 1899.*)

Chekhov criticized perhaps because he found so much promise and many right instincts in Gorky the writer. It was primarily a lack of artistic self-discipline that troubled him. He did not like Gorky's first novel, *Foma Gordeev*, and later that year he agreed to his request to dedicate it to him with diffidence and only if he restricted the dedication to a simple ascription. In his letter of acceptance he quite characteristically advised that in the proof of the novel Gorky delete as many superfluous words as possible. The reader's mind, he observed, finds it hard to concentrate on them and he soon grows tired. "You understand it at once when I write: 'The man sat on the grass.' You understand it because it is clear and makes no demand on the attention. On the other hand, it is not easily understood and it is difficult for the mind if I write: 'A tall, narrow-chested, middle-sized man, with a red beard, sat on the green grass trampled by passersby, sat silently, looking around him timidly and fearfully.' This is not immediately grasped by the mind, whereas good writing should be grasped at once, in a second." (*September 3, 1899.*)

Gorky was impressed by Chekhov's criticism and by the time they met at Yalta he had already formed an image which was compounded of awe of the artist and reverence for the man. Nor was he disappointed. He promptly wrote his wife: "Chekhov is a rare person. Kind, gentle, thoughtful. The public is frightfully in love with him and gives him no peace. He has no end of acquaintances here. To speak with him is pleasant in the highest degree, and I cannot remember when I've talked with anyone with so much satisfaction." They spent whole days together discussing and disputing, and on one occasion, according to Gorky, they continued right through the night until six in the morning. They also gave a charitable public reading together, along with Elpatievsky, on behalf of aid to the famine-ridden in Samara.

Gorky was a keen observer of men, and his characterization of Chekhov in his letters, reminiscences, and diary is often extraordinarily acute and understanding. He noticed that when Chekhov laughed his eyes were fine, tender, and caressing, and that his laugh, which was almost a silent one — he laughed in a "spiritual" way, Gorky said — suggested always an intense delight. But coarse anecdotes never provoked even a smile. Gorky also discovered the extent to which Chekhov's illness made him misanthropic and even capricious at times in his judgments, and morose in his attitude toward people. While lying on a couch one day, coughing and playing with a thermometer, Chekhov said to Gorky: "To live in order that we may die is not very pleasant; but to live knowing that we shall die before our time is up is profoundly stupid." Despite the worshipers who constantly surrounded Chekhov, according to Gorky, he was essentially a lonely man — one born too soon, a victim of the envy of the untalented. Gorky was talented enough to be a humble follower, and was almost inordinately proud of the attention Chekhov gave him. "His confidence in me touches me deeply," he wrote his wife, "and in general I'm tremendously glad that a man who has an enormous and original talent, the kind of writer out of whom epochs in the history of literature and in social thought are made, sees something in me which has to be reckoned with. It is not only flattering but extremely good for me, for it will compel me to be more stern and exacting with myself."

Chekhov's reactions to meeting Gorky at Yalta were naturally more subdued and peculiarly Chekhovian. He read Gorky's tale *The Peasant* at this time and told Mirolyubov that all the characters speak the same way and that it was time to get rid of this kind of writing. To Avilova he commented: "Gorky is in Yalta. In appearance he is a tramp,[4] but inside he is quite an elegant person — and he pleases me very much. I would like to introduce him to women, thinking it might be useful for him, but he bristles at this." (*March 23, 1899.*) And he also informed the distinguished writer, critic, and thinker, V. V. Rozanov, of Gorky's visit: "He is a simple man, a vagabond, and he first began to read when he was already an adult — and thus he was reborn, and now he reads eagerly everything that is printed, and he reads without prejudice, sincerely." (*March 30, 1899.*) Nevertheless, Chekhov advised many to whom he wrote at this time to be sure and read Gorky.

In his reminiscences Gorky tells of the trip they took to Chekhov's place at Kuchukoi. While showing him around the grounds Chekhov spoke with animation of his desire to build a sanatorium on this lovely spot for invalid rural teachers — a large, bright building, with a fine library, musical instruments, bees, a vegetable garden, and an orchard. He was quickly carried away by his favorite subject of the deplorable position of teachers and education in Russia. Without widespread education, he declared, Russia will collapse, and yet the teacher, who ought to be an artist, in love with his calling, was regarded as a mere journeyman who went from village to village to teach children as though he were going into exile. Then he suddenly stopped and jestingly dismissed the whole subject. "That was characteristic of him," Gorky wrote, "to speak so earnestly, with such warmth and sincerity, and then suddenly to laugh at himself and his words. In that sad and gentle smile one felt the subtle skepticism of a man who knows the value of words and dreams; and there also flashed in the smile a lovable modesty and delicate sensitiveness."

Spring in Yalta, however, only reminded Chekhov of Moscow; Masha's letters from there about her social life, her meetings with literary and theater groups, filled him with envy. Besides, there were questions to be settled — what to do with Melikhovo and whether to buy a house in Moscow. Though Masha's news about the weather in Moscow was anything but encouraging, he left Yalta on April 10.

---

[4] When Gorky first called on Tolstoy, the latter's wife, taking him for a tramp, invited him into the kitchen for a glass of tea and a roll.

« 4 »

Always an eager reader of newspapers and magazines, Chekhov now intently followed their accounts of student strikes which were disturbing the whole country. They began that winter while he was still at Yalta. In an effort to prevent excesses in the traditional revelry of Founder's Day, February 8, at Petersburg University, the Rector threatened the suspension of any students who participated in unseemly acts. Resentful students demonstrated against this order and were beaten with whips by mounted gendarmes. They declared a strike and cut all classes. Further demonstrations followed and more violent clashes. Nicholas II publicly commended the actions of the authorities. The strike quickly spread to other university centers throughout Russia and a serious situation developed which reactionary advisers, such as K. P. Pobedonostsev, represented to the Tsar as a deliberate insurrectionary movement. A government commission was appointed to investigate.

Chekhov received a number of letters on the situation and some suspended students visited to seek his advice. Modesty and perhaps an excessively restrictive view on the limitations of the literary artist always prevented him from taking public stands on political, social, and moral problems, although at times he seems to have admired those who did. In writing Lidiya Avilova about the prerogatives of literary artists in such matters, he declared: "Is it for us to judge in this business? Rather it is the business of gendarmes, of the police, or of officials especially destined by fate for this calling. Our business is to write and only to write. If we are to wage war, to become indignant, to judge, then we should do it only by the pen." (*April 27, 1899.*) He meant, of course, only in the sphere of one's literary activity, and over the last few years he had been doing just this in a number of his stories — waging war, growing indignant, and passing judgment on national moral, social, and even political problems.

Whatever his reluctance to speak out publicly on such matters, he had very definite views about them, as his letters and the memoirs of close friends testify. He did his own thinking on these problems; and by now it tended to be somewhat to the left of the average Russian progressive. When he discovered that *Life*, in which he later published and with which Gorky and V. A. Posse were associated, had Marxist leanings, it did not trouble him. Nor was he in any sense disturbed by the surprising request of the celebrated political and social thinker

Peter Struve, who invited him to contribute to *Nachalo*, the organ of the legal Marxists. Chekhov laughingly reported to Altschuler that Mariya Vodovozova, head of the literary division of *Nachalo*, declared that he had become a real Marxist but was unable to recognize the fact.

Chekhov's private views, however, would have discouraged the Marxists. As a gradualist with a pronounced sense of measure, he warned Leontiev-Shcheglov that one must be fair and objective in evaluating the abuses of the present. It was in this spirit that he approached the student disorders. Latent in his judgment was the conviction he had formed during the student troubles in Moscow University when he was there — the insincerity and misdirection of organized efforts on the part of the educated to bring about social and political change. Now, in a letter to his old friend Ivan Orlov — a Serpukhov rural physician who was having difficulties with the government in organizing medical assistance in the district — Chekhov wrote that "those very ones who make life difficult for you are the children of the times. It is not the tutor[5] but the entire intelligentsia that is at fault, all of it, my good sir. While the young men and women are still students, they are a good, honest set, our hope, the future of Russia; but no sooner do these university students enter upon independent life and become adults than our hope and the future of Russia vanish in smoke and in the filter all that is left are doctors, owners of *dachas*, greedy officials, thieving engineers. . . . I believe in individuals. I see salvation in individual personalities scattered over all of Russia — they may be intellectuals, or peasants — for although they may be few, they have strength." (*February 22, 1899.*)

Chekhov's opinions were further elaborated in his correspondence with Suvorin, who had become publicly involved in the controversy over the student strikes. At the beginning of the disorders, Suvorin published an article in *New Times* in which he condemned the actions of the students and praised the Tsar for appointing a committee to investigate the reasons for the spreading strikes. Students promptly demanded a boycott of the newspaper and Suvorin printed a second article in an effort to defend his position. This further enraged the students, who bombarded him with indignant letters and publicly called on people to cancel their subscriptions to *New Times*. Advertisers hesitated to patronize the paper, and organizations refused to admit its reporters

---

[5] Chekhov uses the word *guverner* (tutor) in place of *gubernator* (governor), no doubt as a precaution against the prying eyes of a censor.

to their meetings. The boycott was effective and it spread to various cities. Even in far-off Yalta a club of intellectuals published a scathing denunciation of Suvorin and requested subscribers to cease reading his paper. A rumor soon spread that Suvorin had received ten thousand roubles from the government for writing the articles. And finally the Russian Writers' Mutual Aid Society publicly summoned him before its Court of Honor to answer charges of behavior unbecoming one of its members, an action which carried with it the threat of suspension. Alexander, who was Chekhov's main source of information on the details of this whole situation, reported that the business of *New Times* had greatly fallen off, several of the staff had quit, and that Suvorin's health was cracking under the strain. He had heard, he said, that the students had sent a collective letter to Chekhov, asking him to judge between them and Suvorin.

Meanwhile, the harrassed Suvorin telegraphed and wrote Chekhov to explain his actions and to seek advice. He may well have been hoping that Chekhov would offer to support his stand in the Russian Writers' Mutual Aid Society. How could one give advice in such a predicament to a man like Suvorin? Chekhov asked. He was further embarrassed by Gorky's open letter in *Life* to Suvorin on the student disorders, quoting a passage from a minor journalist's attack on Suvorin's handling of the Dreyfus case in *New Times*. " '[Chekhov] was in France at the time of the Zola trial,' " Gorky quoted the journalist. " 'Ask him what he thinks about the culpability of Dreyfus, and the base tricks of the defenders of Esterhazy? Ask him what he thinks about your relations to this affair and to the Jewish question in general? Neither you nor *New Times* will rejoice over his opinion.' "

Chekhov hastened to write Suvorin, not to disavow the substance of the journalist's statement, but to condemn his motive in making it. At the same time he bluntly told Suvorin that he found his two articles on the student disorders quite unsatisfactory. He charged that Suvorin had airily written about this deplorable situation and about the government's rights and prerogatives when he knew full well that it would not permit the real truth of the disorders to appear in print, and that the government regarded its rights and justice as one and the same thing. "The conception of government," he argued, "ought to be based on concrete, lawful relations — otherwise it is a bugaboo, an empty sound and terrifying to the imagination." (*March 4, 1899.*)

In a letter a few weeks later Chekhov felt it necessary to drive home

an obvious point, in connection with a public demonstration at
Kharkov on behalf of the students, a point which Suvorin, publisher
of a leading newspaper, seemed unable to appreciate fully: "When
people do not enjoy the right to express their opinion freely, they
will express it heatedly, with exasperation, and often, from the point
of view of the government, in an ugly and shocking form. Grant
freedom of the press and freedom of conscience; then the calm which
all desire will come, and though it may not last long, it will suffice
for our lifetime." (*April 2, 1899.*)

Suvorin refused to appear before the Court of Honor, but he
privately printed his correspondence with its committee and sent
copies to friends, among them Chekhov, for their reactions. With
some misgivings Chekhov wrote him and opposed the whole procedure.
Such a court, he declared, might be all right in the army, but in an
Asiatic country where there was no freedom of expression or conscience, where life was so oppressive, and where the government and
nine tenths of society regarded journalists as enemies, these recriminations put writers in the ridiculous position of animals in a cage biting
each other's tails. And if such a court condemned you for writing what
you desired, he declared, then this in itself was a violation of freedom
of the press and could well compel other journalists to fear that sooner
or later they would also fall under the judgment of this same Court of
Honor.

Although Suvorin's articles on the student disorders might warrant
sharp attacks on him, Chekhov asserted, for the Court of Honor to
concentrate on them only evaded the chief reason for the whole
scandal. Then he frankly stated what he thought was the reason: "Over
the last few years society (not merely the intelligentsia, but Russian
society in general) has been hostile to *New Times*. The conviction
exists that *New Times* receives a subsidy from the government and
from the French General Staff. And *New Times* has done everything
possible to support this undeserved reputation. . . . The opinion also
exists that you are a person with powerful friends in the government,
and that you are harsh and implacable; and once again *New Times*
has done everything possible to support this prejudice in society."
(*April 24, 1899.*) Chekhov concluded by pointing out that people
and the Court of Honor were judging Suvorin on the basis of the
legend that had grown up about him, and this degree of insincerity
deeply troubled him.

Chekhov's honest attempt to clarify the unhappy situation that had overtaken Suvorin elicited only a brief comment in his diary: "I wrote Chekhov. Sent him my explanation of the Court of Honor. He found it of 'little significance.'"

Suvorin's wife, however, perhaps reflecting her husband's feelings, wrote Chekhov a letter of sharp reproof. "You reproach me for disloyalty," he replied, "in that Alexei Sergeevich is good, and disinterested, and that I do not respond to this. But as a seriously well-disposed person, what can I do for him now? What? The present situation has not come about all at once, it has been going on for many years, and what people say now they have been saying everywhere for a long time — and you and Alexei Sergeevich did not know the truth, as kings do not know it. I'm not philosophizing but stating what I know. *New Times* is experiencing difficult days, but certainly it is still a power and will remain one; after a little time has elapsed, everything will get back into its groove and nothing will change and all will be as before." (*March 29, 1899.*)

To a considerable extent Chekhov was right. He well understood the short memory of the public and its inertia in national affairs. But the dwindling relations between the two men were further eroded by this controversy. In this difficult period of personal misfortune for Suvorin, Chekhov tried to be friendly and repeatedly invited him, without any success, to visit or meet him in Europe. Chekhov was not a man to desert anyone in adversity. But the fissure in their friendship which had begun over the Dreyfus affair was widened by the sale of Chekhov's works to Marx and by Chekhov's unsympathetic attitude toward Suvorin's behavior in the student disorders. Though they did not entirely lose contact with each other, at the end of 1899 Chekhov wrote his brother Misha, who requested him to appeal to Suvorin for a favor on his behalf, "With Suvorin I have long since broken off correspondence . . ."

« 5 »

Masha's small Moscow apartment, where her mother also lived when not at Melikhovo, was suddenly transformed into a crowded salon when Chekhov arrived in April. What a joy to be back in the metropolis after Yalta, a cross that not everyone can bear, he had complained to Orlov, for it abounded in drabness, slander, intrigue, and the most shameful calumny.

From eight in the morning to ten at night the samovar was kept boiling as friends visited the improvised study, its table piled high with copies of the stories Chekhov was editing for the Marx edition. Often an unbidden guest — an unknown admirer, a writer from Siberia, a Melikhovo neighbor, or a school comrade whom he had entirely forgotten — would sit there in worshipful silence, making Chekhov and favored visitors feel uncomfortable. Yet he could not get himself to turn such a caller away or even hint that he was remaining too long. At times, according to Stanislavsky, he would lose patience with one of these long-sitting silent interlopers, call Masha to the door, and whisper: "Now listen, tell him that I don't know him and that I never studied with him at school. I know he has a manuscript in his pocket. He'll remain for dinner and read it. This is really impossible." Or the bell would ring and Masha would go to the door. The guests would retreat to the corners; Chekhov sat on the divan, trying not to cough, and a pained silence fell over the room. An unknown voice would be heard from the entrance: "Oh, so he's busy? . . . This will take only two minutes." . . . ("Good, I'll give it to him," came the firm tones of Masha.) "Only a little tale . . ." ("Good-by," Masha would say.) "The support of young talent . . . certainly an enlightened patron . . ." ("Good-by," firmly insisted Masha.) . . . "Humble, profound, full of . . . aesthetic moments . . . profound . . . full to the depths . . ." (The door finally would close, and Masha would enter the study and place on the table a bundle of rumpled manuscript tied with a string.) "You should have told him that I don't write any more, that there is no point in writing!" Chekhov would exclaim with a sigh, looking over the manuscript. Nevertheless, he would not only read all these manuscripts, remarked Stanislavsky, who witnessed this scene, but would answer the letters sent to him about them.

Masha's apartment soon proved inadequate to accommodate all these callers and provide Chekhov with a room to which he could retreat for work. He rented another on the same street, Malaya Dmitrovka, near the Strastnoi Monastery whose bells he loved to hear. Tolstoy was one of his first visitors, but two actors among those present insisted on talking so much about the theater — as though it were the greatest thing in the world, Chekhov remarked dryly — that he was prevented from holding any conversation with his famous guest. The next day he had dinner at the Tolstoys' Moscow house. The two writers talked much about Gorky, and Tolstoy praised him, compliments which Chekhov hastened to pass on to his new friend.

But the excitement of being in Moscow during the Easter season proved too much for Chekhov. He reported to his physician at Yalta, Altschuler: ". . . Crowds of visitors, endless conversations — on the second day of the festivities I could hardly move from weariness, and I felt as lifeless as a corpse. Yesterday I had supper at Fedotova's[6] which lasted till two in the morning. I do this to spite you." He was glad to retire to Melikhovo on May 7 for a rest. This month of pleasure at Moscow had cost him about three thousand roubles, at which rate, he reckoned, all the money from Marx would soon be an agreeable memory.

But there was not much rest at Melikhovo, for Chekhov was obsessed with the desire to finish the construction of the new village school in a hurry. He had angrily resigned trusteeships in two of the district schools because of the tiresome bickering between the teachers and the local authorities and their tendency to descend upon him for aid whenever any little thing went wrong. For months Chekhov had been perhaps unconsciously preparing himself to part with Melikhovo, this beloved estate, in which he had put so much of himself and which was associated with *The Sea Gull* and a number of his best stories. The sudden notion of buying a house in Moscow was vaguely connected in his mind with the idea that he would some day soon have to get rid of his estate. Although his mother and sister strongly approved of purchasing a Moscow house, on which he was extravagantly prepared to spend as much as thirty thousand roubles, ultimately nothing came of this, although Masha searched long and hard for a dwelling that would please him. Behind this plan was a far-fetched belief he entertained that within a couple of years his health would be sufficiently improved for him to spend his winters in Moscow.

The assertion of his mother and sister, now, that they found it difficult to continue to live at Melikhovo after the father's death, was something of a rationalization of the real reason for selling the estate, which he finally decided to do in June. Masha herself was getting tired of Melikhovo. She deplored the mounting costs of maintaining its expanded developments. Further, she had become increasingly annoyed over the unpleasant behavior of the peasants and their thieving

---

[6] Glikeriya Nikolaevna Fedotova, a well-known actress.

propensities. And if her brother could not live there most of the time, the estate lost all its attraction for her.

Chekhov perhaps gave the real reason for selling when he explained that Melikhovo had become a luxury once his health prevented him from living there regularly, and besides, he confessed, since the writing of *Peasants*, Melikhovo had lost its literary importance for him. With this new real estate mania that had come over him, he hardly knew where he would stay and at what time of the year — at Melikhovo, or Moscow, or at his new Yalta house, or at Kuchukoi. "Now I have four places to live," he whimsically wrote Varvara Kharkeevich, "and I ought to have a wife in each, so that after my death all of them could assemble on the shore at Yalta and tear each other's hair out. . . ." (*May 20, 1899.*)

Masha had to assume most of the burden of trying to find a Moscow house and of arranging for the sale of Melikhovo. Chekhov hoped to receive twenty-five thousand roubles for the estate and its furnishings, ten thousand of which he intended to give to Masha in return for her years of effort in taking care of the affairs of Melikhovo. But weeks passed and no house was found in Moscow, nor did a buyer of the estate turn up among the several interested parties, although advertisements were inserted in newspapers and an agent was employed. The delays increased Chekhov's restlessness. He was willing to lower his price for the estate, and, convinced that he would never live in Melikhovo after this summer, he busied himself in supervising the packing of personal belongings, books, and porch furniture to be sent to Yalta. Rather sadly he wrote Iordanov to excuse himself for not having fulfilled the latest requests to aid the Taganrog library and museum: he had lost the right to a settled life, he explained. "I don't know what to do with myself. I'm building a *dacha* at Yalta but I've come to Moscow, which I've suddenly grown to like despite the stink; there I rented an apartment for a whole year, and now I'm in the country; the apartment is locked, they are building the *dacha* without me — what an absurdity it all is." (*May 15, 1899.*)

On June 10 Chekhov made a hurried one-day trip to Petersburg to talk over with Marx various details of the edition of his works and returned to Moscow in the hope of interviewing prospective buyers of Melikhovo. The city was hot and stuffy. He visited his father's grave for the first time, and later ordered a simple stone with only the name and dates inscribed on it. To Gorky, to whom he had sent presents of a watch and his photograph, he wrote that he paraded along Tverskoi Boulevard, talked with prostitutes, and dined in the International Restaurant. Then suddenly, in a letter to Masha at Melikhovo, he announced that he was leaving for Taganrog on July 12 to inspect some factories there.

CHAPTER XXI

"Hello, Last Page of My Life, Great Actress of the Russian Land"

HOWEVER GENUINE HIS REASON for going to Taganrog, Chekhov's unexpected departure for the South was really to keep a rendezvous with Olga Knipper. When a telegraph operator in Moscow had noticed his signature on the blank and excitedly declared that he had treated her mother's illness fifteen years previously, he remarked about the incident to a friend: "But how old I've become! However, though I've been a doctor fifteen years, I still want to traipse after the young ladies." Indeed, shortly before he had left Yalta for Moscow, he had written to Lika in Paris, to urge her to visit him; he would take her for a trip along the Crimean shore, and then they could go on to Moscow together.

Lika had turned him down, yet curiously enough Chekhov now proposed to take this same trip with Olga Knipper. In fact, his eagerness to get to Moscow that April may well have been subconsciously connected with a desire to see again the charming actress who had so deeply impressed him the previous September in the role of Irina in *Tsar Fyodor*. Throughout that fall and winter Masha had been feeding his imagination about Olga with ecstatic comments in her letters. "Knipper, as formerly, is ravishing," Masha reported after seeing *The Sea Gull* for the second time. At the third performance, Vishnevsky took Masha backstage and introduced her to the cast: "Knipper began to cut capers, I gave her your regards," his sister wrote. "I advise you to pay some attention to Knipper. In my opinion she is very interesting." Soon Masha and Olga were exchanging social visits.

After his arrival in Moscow, Chekhov had lost little time in getting in touch with Olga and in being introduced to the "mad Knipper family," as Gorky later described them. The widowed mother, children, and two uncles lived together in a small Moscow flat. They were a noisy, talented lot — the mother's singing pupils bellowed in one room while Olga practiced her roles in another, and the uncles — especially Sasha, who liked the bottle — quarreled with each other or read Tolstoy or Chekhov aloud. On his first visit, however, Chekhov had eyes only for Olga and ignored the other guests. A few days later they visited an exhibition of Levitan's paintings.

Olga was his first visitor at Melikhovo that May, "three wonderful spring days," she recalls. She adored his mother, "a quiet Russian woman with a sense of humor." Chekhov, in the liveliest of spirits, showed her around his little estate — the pond, the orchard all in blossom, the vegetable and flower garden — and she observed how his face grew sad at the sight of cut or uprooted flowers. He presented her with a photograph of the Lodge, where he had written *The Sea Gull*. Everything about the atmosphere of Melikhovo, its pleasant, simple, happy, family life, attracted her. "The cordiality, affection, coziness, the conversation full of jokes and wit, captivated me. . . . These were three days filled with a beautiful presentiment, with joy, with the sun."

Long after this visit she wrote him: "How delighted I was with everything! I was a little afraid of you then. But that heavenly morning when we took a walk together!"

Olga's gay, ardent nature and love of life recommended her to the family, especially to Anton. He respected her dedication to her art and the hard work she devoted to it, but he liked also the fact that she enjoyed talking about the infinite commonplaces of life, far removed from the theater and literature. She knew how to make him laugh and how to fascinate him with her changeable moods, as though she were trying them all out in order to discover the one that would most please his fastidious taste. When she left Melikhovo they were both obviously filled with a consuming curiosity to learn more about each other.

Olga went to the Caucasus to spend her vacation at her brother's *dacha* near Mtskhet, but before she left it is clear that she and Chekhov had some understanding that they would meet in the South. On June 16 he wrote her his first letter, a brief note cast somewhat in the light, bantering tone of his correspondence with Lika — why had they not heard from her, had she married in the Caucasus? The author had been forgotten — and how terrible, how cruel and perfidious! At about the same time he added a postscript to one of Masha's letters to Olga: "Hello, last page of my life, great actress of the Russian land. I envy the Circassians who see you every day. . . . I wish you a wonderful disposition, captivating dreams."[1]

Olga wrote that they might meet after she left Mtskhet and he could accompany her to Yalta — a plan he had pretty certainly suggested himself. "Yes, you are right," he replied, "the author Chekhov has not forgotten the actress Knipper. Besides, your proposal to go together from Batum to Yalta seems to him charming." He set up the conditions of their meeting, and the third one was "that you don't turn my head. Vishnevsky regards me as a very serious person, and I would not want to reveal myself as weak as all the others." (July 1, 1899.) But he had to communicate to her a change of plans — he had to go to Taganrog and would meet her at Novorossiisk on July 18. After a few days at Taganrog, where he saw Iordanov and other friends, and actually did inspect factories — though the purpose is not clear unless it was to collect material for a story — he left for Novorossiisk on July 17. There he and Olga met and went by steamer on the two-day trip to Yalta.

Chekhov stayed at the Hotel Marino on the shore and Olga with the family of Dr. L. V. Sredin, friends of her own family and also of Chekhov, who had got to know them well at Yalta. Chekhov seems to have divided his time during the next ten days between taking Olga to see the sights in Yalta and its environs and making frequent trips to Autka to superintend the construction of his house, which was by now well underway. No doubt he took her out to Oreanda for the view, and perhaps they sat there on that same bench, not far from the church, where the two lovers sat in his tale, *The Lady with the Dog*, and looked down at the sea. From there Yalta was barely visible in the morning mist. White clouds rested on the mountaintops. And from below came the monotonous muffled sound of the sea. Perhaps he thought, as the lover in the story did in that peaceful spot, how really beautiful everything is in the world, everything except what we ourselves think or do when we forget the higher aims of life and our own human dignity.

Olga despaired of the irregularity of his life, of the way he would skip meals and avoid invitations to dinner to the homes of friends.

[1] *Literaturnoe Nasledstvo* (*Literary Heritage*), Moscow, 1960, LXVIII, 225.

"Knipper is in Yalta," he wrote Masha, who no doubt was quite surprised to receive this bit of news. "She is depressed. Yesterday she visited me, drank tea; she just sat and was silent." (*July 21, 1899.*) In a second letter, in answer to one from Masha, in which she expressed her uncertainties on reaching decisions without him with prospective purchasers of Melikhovo, he turned on her with unusual sharpness, as though annoyed that she should bother him with a commercial matter at a time like this. He had given her power of attorney, he declared, and would have nothing to do with selling the estate. "The price is entirely up to you. Sell it even for fifteen thousand, I won't quarrel with it. Knipper is here, she is very sweet, but is in the dumps. . . . Knipper likes your room very much. It isn't a room but a bit of magic." (*July 22, 1899.*)

On August 2 the couple set out for Moscow, taking a roundabout way — a carriage to Bakhchisarai over the Ai-Petri range. The setting was romantic, the weather lovely, the southern air soft and caressing. The hilly countryside had a wild beauty. They passed white villas among fields of roses edged with cypress trees, deserted Moslem cemeteries, and little Tatar villages clinging to the shore. As they drove by a rural hospital, people on the porch frantically beckoned to them; but they did not stop, thinking that the wavers were probably insane patients — actually it turned out that they were some of Chekhov's Yalta medical friends, who had recognized him, and the incident became the subject of much chaff. The picturesque Kokkoz valley had its own special enchantment, and Olga recalled the pleasure of driving along in the springy carriage, breathing air laden with the fragrance of pines, and chatting in the charming, amusing Chekhov style. And, when the sun reached its height, languid from the heat, they dozed. At Bakhchisarai they boarded a train for Moscow. This lovely excursion had brought them closer together, and the memory of it sustained them in the following months of separation.

Immediately upon their arrival, Olga had to plunge into rehearsals for the second season of the Moscow Art Theater and he saw very little of her. His mind was much relieved when he learned from Masha that a timber merchant, M. Konshin, had bought Melikhovo and wished to take possession of it as soon as possible. The man had a pleasant personality, Masha reported, but he appeared to have little money. The Chekhovs had to agree to an installment form of payment for the twenty-three-thousand-rouble purchase price, and it was some time before the first installment was paid. Eventually the whole agreement broke down, a fact that may have had something to do with Chekhov's dropping the idea of buying a Moscow house.[2] The village school had been completed in late June, the estate was now sold, and Chekhov, without any apparent regret, rolled down the curtain on the Melikhovo period of his life — perhaps his happiest.

He lingered on in Moscow for a few weeks, purchased books for the Taganrog library, completed the editing for the first volume of his collected works, and visited friends. Somewhat to his mortification, he found it necessary to ask Marx for an advance of five thousand roubles on the next payment, basing his request on the fact that he had completed copy for the first volume on time. He had already run through the initial payment of fifteen thousand roubles. The publisher advanced him only two thousand. As a favor for Sinani in Yalta, he saw the rector of Moscow University in an endeavor to persuade him to admit a Jewish student as a transfer from another institution; but he was very brusquely treated, the request was denied, and the experience almost made him feel unwell.

In fact, shortly thereafter he did fall ill. "I don't know whether the bacilli are in revolt," he wrote Suvorin on August 19, "or if the weather is making itself felt, but I seem to have reached the end of my endurance and my head inclines to the pillow." Yalta, he believed, was the answer, and he left for that town a week later.

« 2 »

Masha and her mother came to the new house at Autka on September 8 and the real Yalta period of Chekhov's family life began. It was not a very auspicious beginning. Workmen hammered, sawed, and drilled all day, and weeks passed before the house was finally finished. To complicate matters his old Serpukhov friend Dr. Kurkin came the day after his mother and sister, and remained for a month. The pounding prevented Chekhov from doing any consistent work, yet the pressure to write was great, for Marx's advance of two thousand had already vanished — bills for labor on the new house were endless and now he had to support two old servants who had been brought from Melikhovo and two men hired to do odd jobs. He contemplated a bank loan, but

[2] In fact, after living on the estate three years, Konshin defaulted on his payments and Melikhovo was resold to a certain Baron Styuart.

fortunately the delayed first payment of the purchaser of Melikhovo saved the situation for the time being. Eventually the noisy workmen finished, Chekhov could settle down to writing in his new study — a possibility he had been eagerly anticipating for months — and most important, his mother liked living in Yalta. Before Masha returned to her teaching position in Moscow, he took her and his mother to see his Kuchukoi hideaway and they grudgingly admitted to its charm — despite the dizzy climb, which terrified his mother.

He liked to receive letters, Chekhov said, but not to answer them. By now his volume of mail, which he handled entirely himself, had grown very large.[3] His study had become a post office, he grumbled, as he tried to keep down essential answers to five a day. One answer on October 11 throws some light on the influence of science on his literary practices. When in Moscow the past spring, he had begged off an invitation to attend a dinner of his Medical School class on its fifteenth reunion. The gathering sent him a flattering greeting; and now he was requested by his old classmate and friend, Dr. Rossolimo, to send his photograph for a class album, an autobiographical sketch, and dues for a class mutual aid society — decisions that had been taken at the reunion. Chekhov forwarded the picture and dues, but pleaded that he was afflicted by a disease called "autobiographophobia." It had always been a real torment, he explained, to prepare such sketches for publication, but he agreed to provide the bare facts, which he managed to telescope into half a page. However, he did add the following interesting comment:

"My work in medical sciences has undoubtedly had a serious influence on my literary development; it significantly extended the area of my observations, enriched my knowledge, and only one who is himself a physician could understand the true value of all this for me as a writer; this training has also been a guide, and probably because of my closeness to medicine, I have managed to avoid many mistakes. Familiarity with the natural sciences and scientific method has always kept me on my guard, and I have tried, whenever possible, to take scientific data into consideration, and where that was impossible, I've preferred not to write at all. I may note, however, that artistic considerations do not always permit one to be in complete agreement with scientific data; you cannot show death by poisoning on the stage

[3] Some 7000 letters to Chekhov have been preserved, and this was probably a fraction of the total he received.

as it actually occurs. But even in these circumstances one must feel one-self consistent with scientific data, that is, it must be clear to the reader or spectator that this is only a convention and that he is dealing with a writer who knows what he is talking about. I do not belong to those literary men who adopt a negative attitude toward science, and I would not want to belong to those who achieve everything by clever-ness."

If we may believe Leontiev-Shcheglov, however, Chekhov also sensed the inhibiting force of his scientific training in the act of literary creation. He quotes Chekhov as saying to him: "Now, for example, a simple person looks at the moon and is moved as before something terribly mysterious and unattainable. But an astronomer looks at it with entirely different eyes . . . with him there cannot be any fine illusions! With me, a physician, there are, also, few illusions. Of course, I'm sorry for this — and it somehow desiccates life."

It was both as a physician and as a famous figure at Yalta that an intolerable burden was thrust upon Chekhov at this time. Perhaps because of his offer to a Serpukhov school organization to provide for one of its tubercular teachers at Yalta, a garbled report appeared in a Moscow newspaper that he intended to establish a sanatorium on the Crimean shore for rural schoolteachers. This news item was copied in many provincial newspapers, and in no time he was harried by requests for admission to the sanatorium, and even by visits of unfortunate and often indigent people who sought his assistance.

Though Chekhov endeavored to have this news account repudiated, his compassion was aroused by the extent of the human need which it brought to his attention, and he undertook the task of organizing effective aid. He formed a number of his Yalta medical friends and wealthy people into a charitable society, and, drawing up an appeal for funds to construct a sanatorium at Yalta for the indigent sick, he used his influence to have it published in a number of newspapers. Many requests, such as this one to Gorky, went out to friends: "The consumptive poor are overwhelming here. . . . Just to see the faces of these sick when they beg for something, or to see their wretched blankets when they die — this is hard. We have decided to build a sanatorium and I've written an appeal: I've done this because I don't have any other means. If it is possible, get this appeal printed in the Nizhny Novgorod and Samara newspapers where you have acquaintances and connections. Perhaps they will send something. The day before yesterday Epifanov, the poet of *Diversion*, died in loneliness and neglect in a refuge for chronic consumptives; two days before his death, he asked for an apple tart, and when I brought it to him he suddenly brightened and his sick throat joyously wheezed: 'The very thing! Imagine!' " (*November 25, 1899*.)

Agitated and wringing his hands, Chekhov said to a physician's widow interested in charitable work, Sofya Bonnier, who had visited Epifanov at Chekhov's request and reported on his hopeless condition: "Ah, how terribly we need a sanatorium here! We must remove these unfortunates from the care of people who think only of their *dachas*. . . . The situation of the sick is frightful. . . . Let us arrange something. Only let us do it ourselves. Money will be available."

Money did begin to arrive, but so did the sick, and it seemed that all of them wished to discuss their misfortunes with Chekhov. It was impossible to become reconciled with this nightmare, he exploded to Masha, and he asserted repeatedly that if something constructive were not done about it, he would leave Yalta. Nothing so distressed him as that acquiescence of many progressive Russians to doing nothing because it was impossible to do all. He never preached love for mankind, but his compassion for the individual in distress was an all-consuming one. His efforts in this instance were eventually successful. At first a pension arrangement was established to care for tuberculars with little or no money, and later a sanatorium was provided.

Despite his varied activities and concerns that winter at Yalta, and the fact that he had once again secured for himself a settled existence in his own home, Chekhov experienced many lonely and unhappy moments. Shortly after Masha's return to Moscow, he answered one of her letters: "What you write about the theater, the group, and every conceivable allurement just provokes me; you really don't know how dull and stupid it is to go to bed at nine in the evening and lie there in a fury and with the consciousness that there is nowhere to go, no one to talk to, and nothing to work for because it makes no difference what you do if you don't see or hear your work. The piano and I are the two objects in the house existing mutely, wondering always why we have been placed here, since there is no one to play us." (*November 11, 1899*.) Was he missing Olga Knipper and perhaps envying the theater that absorbed her?

« 3 »

Chekhov had delayed little, after his arrival in Yalta bearing a potted cactus plant which Olga had presented to him, in replying to the questions she had posed in a letter. Beneath the customary bright, jesting surface of his epistolary prose, one now detects for the first time in his letters to a woman a different and deeper note. No, he answered, he was not eating regularly, not drinking Narzan water or taking walks, only sitting at home thinking of her. "But driving past Bakhchisarai I recalled you and our trip together. My sweet marvelous actress, wonderful woman, if you only knew how happy your letter has made me. I bow down before you, bow so low that my forehead touches the bottom of my well which by now has reached a depth of fifty-six feet. I have got used to you and am so lonely without you that I cannot reconcile myself to the thought that I won't see you until spring; I'm in a bad humor and, in short, if Nadenka[4] only knew what was going on in my soul, there would be quite a scandal." (*September 3, 1899.*)

One of Olga's letters was full of her concern over the role of Elena in *Uncle Vanya* which she was presently rehearsing. Though *Uncle Vanya*, which Chekhov regarded as an entirely new play, despite the fact that it is an adaptation of *The Wood Demon*,[5] had been staged with much success in the provinces, he hesitated a long time before permitting it to be performed by a major theater. Perhaps because he had always desired to have one of his full-length plays staged at the famous imperial Maly Theater, the oldest in Russia, he rather thoughtlessly agreed in February, at the director's request, to submit *Uncle Vanya* for consideration. The decision stunned Nemirovich-Danchenko. In the light of the glorious success of *The Sea Gull*, he had every reason to expect that *Uncle Vanya* would be given to the Moscow Art Theater.

Uncle Vanya was tentatively accepted, but the literary committee of the Maly Theater, on which sat several distinguished professors, had not yet passed on it. When they did, a number of changes were demanded, especially in the third act. It has been conjectured that the

[4] Nadenka was an imaginary lady Chekhov invented who played the part of a jealous bride or stern wife in their correspondence.

[5] Chekhov provides no information about the creative process he went through in turning *The Wood Demon* into *Uncle Vanya*. For speculation on the time of the actual writing of *Uncle Vanya*, see Chapter IX, Section 7, Note 4.

professors were offended by Chekhov's characterization of Professor Serebryakov as a pompous, giftless poseur, a kind of academic fraud. Stanislavsky represents Chekhov as laughing uproariously over the committee's contention that it was impossible for an enlightened man like Uncle Vanya to shoot at Professor Serebryakov, the former holder of a university chair. He might well have laughed at this, but he was angry enough to refuse these requests for changes and to withdraw *Uncle Vanya* from consideration by the Maly Theater — much to the dismay of some of its more practical-minded officials, for Chekhov's plays were then being eagerly sought by various theaters.

Taking advantage of this situation at once, the directors of the Moscow Art Theater pressed their claims on *Uncle Vanya* and promised to perform it exactly as Chekhov had written it. But he had never seen this company act one of his plays, he protested that spring when he was in Moscow. Their season was closed, the theater rented, and the scenery all stored until the fall. But his word was law, for they not only hoped to get *Uncle Vanya* but also to persuade him to write a new play for them. So on May 1, in a rented theater and without any scenery, the company put on a special performance of *The Sea Gull* for Chekhov and about ten other spectators.[6] Stanislavsky recalls that, because of the conditions under which the play was staged, the impression created was only a middling one. After every act Chekhov ran on the stage, but his face bore no signs of inner joy. Some of the actors he praised but others he criticized, especially M. L. Roksanova, who acted Nina — he adamantly insisted that she never be allowed to portray this role again. Stanislavsky, who still felt shy and awkward in Chekhov's presence, waited in his dressing room after the performance for the storm he was sure would break over his head. He finally had to search out Chekhov: "Scold me," he pleaded. "Wonderful! Listen, it was wonderful!" Chekhov replied. "Only you need torn shoes and checkered trousers." More than a year passed before Stanislavsky fathomed the import of this cryptic comment — he had played Trigorin as a handsome, talented and elegantly dressed writer, whereas Chekhov was indicating that the inexperienced, sentimental Nina would more likely be attracted by an untalented writer who dressed in old checkered pants and worn shoes.

[6] This date coincided with Lidiya Avilova's visit to Moscow when Chekhov met her at the railway station (See Chapter XX, p. 459). In her memoirs she tells that he tried to persuade her to stay over for the special performance of *The Sea Gull*, but she refused.

In a letter to Gorky, Chekhov expressed himself more frankly about the performance and the acting of Stanislavsky: "I cannot judge the play dispassionately, because the Sea Gull [Nina] played abominably and kept sobbing all the time, and Trigorin [the writer] walked about the stage and talked like a paralytic; his interpretation of the role was that of a man who has no 'will of his own,' and it sickened me to watch him. On the whole, however, the play was not bad and it gripped me. In places I could hardly believe that it was I who had written it." (*May 9, 1899*.) There was now no doubt in Chekhov's mind that the Moscow Art Theater should stage *Uncle Vanya*.

During that summer Chekhov attended a number of the rehearsals of *Uncle Vanya*, which he thought were going extremely well. Directors and cast sought his advice on the staging and interpretation of roles. Finding it difficult often to discuss his plays or to answer questions about the inner significance of a portrayal or an action, he would invariably fall back on the simple declaration: "Listen, I wrote it all down, it is there." But when he observed an actor doing something which he thought was incorrect, he could become sharply declarative in his protest. Or if one of these actors should write him on the interpretation of a role — as Vsevolod Meierhold and Olga Knipper did at this time — feeling more at home on paper, he became eloquently expansive. In answering Meierhold's question on how he should act Johannes in Gerhart Hauptmann's *Lonely Lives*, Chekhov pointed out that no matter how spiritually healthy the character was, Meierhold should try to bring out the social loneliness or social tragedy of the man and above all avoid naturalistic emphasis and stage conventions or any nonessential effects which might destroy the typicality of a portrayal.[7] Chekhov soon became closely attached to these brilliant young actors and their remarkable theater and they to him. And the fact that Olga Knipper was a prominent member of the troupe intensified his affection for them. Jokingly they had begun to call him "inspector of the actresses." That summer he posed for a photograph with the cast of *The Sea Gull*, pretending to read a copy of the play to them. When a false rumor got around that winter that he would come to Moscow, Meierhold wrote him: "Come quickly! Don't fear the cold. You must know that the love which your numerous admirers have for you

[7] Chekhov's letters to Meierhold were deliberately excluded from the Soviet edition. However, this letter was published in *Literaturnoe Nasledstvo* (*Literary Heritage*), Moscow, 1960, LXVIII, 227-228.

will warm you, not only in Moscow, but even the North Pole."

Back at Yalta in the fall Chekhov was anxious for any news about the preparations for the opening of *Uncle Vanya* and of Olga's part in it as the beautiful Elena. On September 29 he replied to Olga's "sensible letter with a kiss for my right temple," with congratulations in advance on the start of the second season. A few days later she urgently requested an explanation of her last scene. Stanislavsky had insisted that Astrov — the role he played — was passionately in love with Elena even at the very end. Nothing of the kind, Chekhov answered. Elena attracts Astrov by her beauty, and by the last act he knows that nothing will come of it and kisses her quite casually, to pass the time. And Chekhov adds: "Ah, sweet actress, how I would like to be in Moscow! However, your head is in a whirl, you have caught the poison, you are in a daze, and now you have no time for me."

Just before the opening of the season, the troupe, in the names of Stanislavsky and Nemirovich-Danchenko, wired Chekhov, "dear friend of our theater," their heartful greetings and expressed the hope that he would soon be among them again. On October 1 he sent his thanks in a telegram and, associating himself with the troupe, hoped that they would go on to further triumphs, so that "the life of their theater would become a bright page in the history of Russian art and in the life of each of us." Olga wrote: "Yesterday with delight we performed your beloved *The Sea Gull*. . . . Before the third act I read the telegram of 'the writer Chekhov,' pinned up on the bulletin board, and I was deeply moved."

After the first performance of A. K. Tolstoy's *Ivan the Terrible*, Olga wrote him, at four o'clock in the morning, a temperamental, self-lacerating letter, because she felt sure of a failure. Success had spoiled the whole troupe, he replied, and he urged her, after *Uncle Vanya* was played, to go to bed and sleep soundly if she thought it a failure. Then, forgetting his calm, he burst forth: "There are insufferably many visitors. Their idle provincial tongues wag. I'm bored and I rage and rage and I envy the rat that lives under the floor of your theater." (*October 4, 1899.*)

The first performance of *Uncle Vanya* took place on October 26. Olga had written that all the cast were tremendously excited and the house sold out. On the evening of the 27th, when Chekhov was in bed, the telegrams began to be telephoned in. "Each time I woke up," he wrote Olga, "and I ran to the telephone in the dark in my bare feet and got very much chilled; then I had scarcely dozed off when the bell rang again and again. It was the first time that my own fame has kept me awake." (*October 30, 1899*.) Though the telegrams announced a great success, he detected something subtle and elusive about them that led him to suppose that all was not well. The reviews, when he read them, confirmed this feeling. Though nearly all of them praised the performance highly, few failed to point out defects both in the play and the acting. In her letter to him the day after, Olga insisted that *Uncle Vanya* had been "a tremendous success" and "gripped the whole audience," but that she had not slept all night and kept crying because she had "acted inconceivably badly."

Chekhov tried to comfort her by demeaning his own art. Neither her role nor *Uncle Vanya* were "worth wasting so much feeling and nerves over. The play is an old one, already out of date, and there are all kinds of defects in it; if more than half the performers have not grasped the right tone, then it is really the fault of the play." And he warned her again that she and the company had been spoiled by too much success, that there would be more failures, and that they should be prepared to accept them with equanimity. It was more important that she not forget him, he wrote, not let their friendship die, and he hoped that they could go away somewhere together this coming summer. "Masha writes that the weather is not good in Moscow and that I must not come, yet I so want to get away from Yalta where my loneliness bores me. I am a Johannes without a wife, not a learned Johannes and not a virtuous one."[8] (*November 1, 1899*.)

The paeans of praise for *Uncle Vanya*, however, mounted as the staging and acting improved over successive performances and the public understood better its inner meaning and nuances of feeling. For spectators and critics began to perceive that realism is raised to the level of inspired symbolism in the striking contrast between the idleness and futility of the lives of Serebryakov and his parasitic wife Elena and the useful work performed by Uncle Vanya, Sonya, and Astrov. The terrible truth that they had been sacrificing themselves for years to sustain the false fame and very existence of Serebryakov is a tragic discovery for Uncle Vanya and Sonya, but it does not overwhelm them. Like Astrov, who loves life and has the courage and zeal to attempt to transform its ugliness, they too believe that everything about a human

---

[8] A reference to the hero of Hauptmann's *Lonely Lives*, which the Moscow Art Theater staged that season.

being should be beautiful. And Sonya's wonderful speech at the end to Uncle Vanya is filled with the courage born of defeat, a spiritual symphony of the undying hope that is to be found in lives dedicated to work and service to others.

Uncle Vanya, like *The Sea Gull*, became a permanent fixture in the Moscow Art Theater. More than ever now Chekhov felt his fortunes closely bound up with this organization and its charming actress Olga Knipper. Stanislavsky's outstanding performance as Astrov had even softened Chekhov's objections to this member of the company, whose plea, as well as that of Nemirovich-Danchenko, that he write another play for the theater was now favorably entertained. When Nemirovich-Danchenko informed him in the course of the winter that he was getting weary of his duties as one of the directors, Chekhov replied: "Oh, don't get weary, don't grow cold! The Art Theater will supply the best pages of the book that will one day be written about the contemporary Russian theater. This theater should be your pride, and it is the only theater I love, although I have not been in it once. If I lived in Moscow, I would try to get on the staff, if only in the capacity of a janitor, so that I could help out a little and, if possible, keep you from growing cold to this dear institution." (*November 19, 1899.*)

« 4 »

Early in 1899 two short stories, *The New Country House*[9] and *On Official Duty*,[10] which Chekhov had actually written at the end of the preceding year, appeared in print. Among the last of the tales that draw upon his experiences in the Melikhovo district, they are curiously contrasting pictures of the relations of the gentry to the peasantry. One suspects that some of the difficulties which the estate owner encountered with the peasants — who cut down his trees, picked the mushrooms on his land, and let their cattle roam over his planted terrain — were those which Chekhov had endured at Melikhovo. No kindness on the part of the owner of the estate and his wife could deter them, for such behavior had become an ingrown habit of the peasants, almost a way of life sanctioned by generations of hostility in master and serf relationships. They belonged to two different worlds, quite incapable of understanding each other's virtues.

The other side of the medal is revealed in *On Official Duty*, where

9 *Russian News*, January 1899.
10 *Books of the Week*, January 1899.

a young examining magistrate arrives at a village during a blizzard to conduct a post-mortem on an insurance agent, an impoverished gentleman who had committed suicide out of disillusionment with his lowly lot in life. There he hears the report of the village policeman, a garrulous old peasant, who also tells the story of his life, which serves as a brilliant characterization of this pathetic figure. For a mere pittance he delivers official government papers all over the district, and has been so constantly on his feet for thirty years that they ache even when he is not walking. The gentry are harsh with him and easily offended, and he is more likely to get a bite and a drink at a peasant's than at a gentleman's house. The magistrate, rather than spend the night on some hay in a wretched village hut, where the corpse of the suicide is laid out, accepts an invitation to stay at the estate of a local landowner. In bed that night, after enjoying his host's cheery hospitality in a warm and comfortable house while the storm roars outside, he dreams of the village policeman and the suicide. They are walking together through the open fields in the blizzard, chanting: "We go, we go, we go . . . You are where it is warm, bright, and cozy, but we tramp on in the storm, in the deep snow and bitter cold. . . . We know no rest, no joys. . . . We carry the whole burden of this life of yours and ours." The dream repeats itself throughout the night, and in the morning the conscience of the disturbed magistrate is troubled over the miseries of such people as the suicide and the peasants. And he thinks of how terrible it is to be reconciled to the fact that they, submitting to their fate, shoulder all that is darkest and most burdensome in life. Tolstoy deeply admired the warm, human sympathy of this story and especially the effective portrayal of the village policeman.

The pressure of preparing material for the collected edition of his works and his unsettled condition prevented Chekhov from undertaking much serious writing during the early part of 1899. The first volume of the complete edition appeared in December, and when Marx, who placed more emphasis on quantity than quality, complained that Chekhov had eliminated too many of his youthful stories, he commented: "Chekhonte could write much that Chekhov would never write." Nor did Marx appreciate Chekhov's self-effacing wish that no photograph or biographical statement appear in the volume. For a time Chekhov contemplated accepting Lavrov's invitation to become literary editor of *Russian Thought*, on the condition that all manuscripts be sent to wherever he happened to be living. However, he soon gave up the idea when he learned of the precarious financial situation of the magazine and that Lavrov appeared to have the notion that he might wish to invest some of the money he received from Marx.

In fact, the speed with which his first installment of money had disappeared drove Chekhov back to his writing desk as soon as some degree of quiet reigned that fall in the newly constructed Yalta house. *The Lady with the Dog*[11] he soon finished, and later a brief sketch of the simple annals of the poor, *At Christmas Time*,[12] for the holiday issue of that repository of so many of his youthful stories, the *Petersburg Gazette*. He also planned *The Bishop* and completed a long story, *The Ravine*, but too late to be published that year.

The Lady with the Dog is the first literary fruit of Chekhov's Yalta life and the beginning of the tale is penetrated with the atmosphere of this resort — its sights and sounds, its dusty roads, eating places off the esplanade, the stately cypresses, the soft, warm lilac color of the sea under the bright sunlight and the golden band of moonlight across it at night. Turgenev might have written a whole novel on this theme, in which case it would have lost the powerful, concentrated impact Chekhov's amazing compression imparts. There is a Maupassant flavor in this story of adultery, which begins on a note of casual philandering and mounts through a series of intensifying emotional experiences to a crescendo of profound but hopeless love. Though the conclusion may be anti-romantic, Chekhov's sympathy — as so often in his fiction — with these helpless, illicit lovers, whose star-crossed fate is not of their own making, is plainly apparent at the end. Gorky, with his characteristic ebullience, declared after reading the story that he wanted to change wives, and to suffer and swear in the same spirit. Everything else seemed written not with a pen but with a fencepost. "No one can write so simply about simple things as you can," he told Chekhov. "Your tales are exquisite phials filled with all the smells of life. . . ."

« 5 »

During November and December Chekhov was so busy with his writing, with editing copy for Marx, and with "bombarding the philanthropists of the capital and the provinces" for money for the projected sanatorium, that Olga complained he had deserted her. Certainly

[11] *Russian Thought*, December 1899.
[12] *Petersburg Gazette*, January 1900.

Masha did not let him forget Olga, who had sent him gifts of candy and scent. He had replied by shipping her a jewel box. For by now Masha and Olga had become quite intimate friends, often dined together, and on occasion Olga stayed the night with her. Everything Olga said about Chekhov, his sister reported to him. At an evening with the Knipper family she teasingly wrote of getting acquainted with his "mother-in-law," and archly mentioned the fondness of other men, like Nemivorich-Danchenko and Vishnevsky, for Olga. "But what a fine person she is," wrote Masha. "Of this I become more convinced every day. A great worker and, in my opinion, very talented." And, she pointedly continued, "Lika is bored. At least, I saw her looking bored in a group. She rarely visits me." In one of Masha's letters, Vishnevsky appended a postscript to tell Chekhov that Olga was sitting by with emptiness in her head and heart, and when he had said that he'd give twenty-five roubles to see Chekhov at that moment, she had added that she would give only three kopecks.

"I thank you," Chekhov retorted in a letter to Olga on November 19. "You are very lavish. But let a little time pass, say a month or two, and you will not give even two kopecks. How people change! Meanwhile, I'd give seventy-five roubles to see you." (*November 19, 1899.*) Not until December 8 did he send her another brief note: "Sweet actress, charming woman, I don't write because I'm deep in work and don't allow myself to be distracted," and he promised she would hear from him soon again.

Masha visited Yalta for the Christmas holiday season, and she must have been unpleasantly surprised to observe that her brother, now thoroughly settled in his new house, had reverted, in some measure, to the practice of medicine. For she notes in her recollections, "The poor people of Autka came to him at any hour of the day or night for medical aid." And the local journalist Beschinsky recalled: "I personally knew of the ways Chekhov sometimes helped the sick 'to arrange things for themselves cheaply.' Through me he paid for their quarters, or he assumed their total expenses in the shelters for chronic cases of the charitable society, and at his request I used to visit these sick people there." At this time Chekhov was also very anxious over the report, which turned out to be true, of the serious illness of Tolstoy — he told the minor writer B. L. Lazarevsky, whose manuscripts he was correcting, that Tolstoy's "moral influence is so great, that there are people who are ashamed to do evil things simply because Tolstoy lives."

Chekhov was particularly delighted by a visit from Levitan in December. This old friend was in the best of moods. After listening to Chekhov's complaints that he was bored with the scenery of Crimea and longed to see again the fields of his northern Russia, Levitan, in the course of half an hour, painted such a scene — a night in a hayfield — cocks of hay, a forest in the distance, and a moon reigning on high above it all. Grateful, Chekhov set the canvas in a niche over his fireplace. With his customary modesty he appears not to have informed Levitan that he had received, shortly before his arrival, the government's award of the Order of Saint Stanislav for his zeal on behalf of national education, a rather belated tribute to his extensive efforts in this field.

However, it was not only a nostalgia for northern scenes of nature that turned Chekhov's thoughts in that direction. To be sure, as he remarked more than once, the weather in Yalta that winter was again so bad that he might just as well be in Moscow. He was already in bed every evening, he wrote Nemirovich-Danchenko, at about the time the second act had begun in the Moscow Art Theater. His thoughts were there and on Olga. "Ask Olga to stay with us at Yalta all summer," he pressed Masha, "for it is dull without her. I'll pay her a salary." (*December 1, 1899.*) For some weeks, in fact, he had been suggesting and then virtually demanding that the whole Moscow Art Theater take a tour to the south in the spring and offer performances at Sevastopol and Yalta. To Nemirovich-Danchenko he promised to talk over with him the possibility of a new play he had in mind, to be called *The Three Sisters*, but it could be discussed only with him and the troupe at Yalta. An affirmative decision finally came, and he rejoiced. He would see Olga in the spring!

CHAPTER XXII

"My Dear Enchanting Actress"

CHEKHOV RECEIVED A TELEGRAM from Moscow dated January 17, 1900: GATHERED TOGETHER IN A FRIENDLY GROUP AT THE KIND INVITATION OF THE HOSTESS ON THE DAY OF ANTHONY THE GREAT, WE DRINK TO THE HEALTH OF A CHERISHED WRITER AND A PUSHKIN ACADEMICIAN. It was signed by Masha, Olga Knipper, the Lavrovs, Lika, Goltsev, Levitan, and Cousin Yegorushka from Taganrog. Earlier that evening Masha had taken Lika to a performance of *The Sea Gull*, the first she had seen since the failure of the opening at Petersburg. Lika wept as the play revived sad memories of her futile love for Chekhov and her unhappy affair with Potapenko.[1]

The party at Masha's apartment after the performance was a merry one for all except Lika; she had to be polite to Olga Knipper, who she knew was in love with Chekhov. The company were celebrating not only his fortieth birthday, but also his election to the exalted Academy of Sciences. In December of the previous year the government decreed that a Pushkin Section of Belles Lettres, in honor of the hundredth anniversary of the birth of the famous poet, should be set up in the Academy, and that distinguished writers as well as scholars could be appointed to it. When Chekhov heard of this move, he told his learned friend at Yalta, the archeologist N. P. Kondakov, who was already a member of the Academy, that such a special section was superfluous, for Russian literature would not gain in interest because of the second-rate authors the Academy would inevitably select.

When the news arrived of his election, very appropriately the day before his birthday, Chekhov could hardly have been less interested — he was in bed, ill. Unable to savor the new title, he remarked later, by the time he recovered he had got used to being an academician. Yet he was obviously pleased to be one of the first ten selected, in a list which included Tolstoy and Korolenko. Congratulatory telegrams poured in, and in honor of this "significant event" the Taganrog town council voted two scholarships in his name to be awarded to students in schools for boys and girls.

When he learned more about the details of the award, Chekhov took less satisfaction in it. Authors of belles lettres were only honorary members, for full membership and participation in the active work of the Academy were reserved for learned scholars, who were remunerated. He detected favoritism to celebrated professors and hostility to writers among the bigwigs of the Academy. Tolstoy, he suspected, had been elected only with a gnashing of teeth, for Chekhov was certain that he

---

[1] The experience prompted one of Lika's now rare letters to Chekhov, which he answered: he had heard that she had grown fat, but he had grown old, he wrote, and when he looked at a pretty woman he now smiled in an aged way. But he did give her the cold comfort of saying: "In your letters, just as in your life, you are a very interesting woman." (*January 29, 1900.*)

was regarded as a nihilist by these conservative academicians. But he liked the privileges, for even honorary membership entitled him to the right of inviolability — he could not be arrested — and to a special passport for foreign travel which relieved him of the supervision of customs officials. And at the first opportunity he exercised his right to nominate for membership, recommending such writers as Boborykin, Ertel, and Mikhailovsky — the latter choice of his one-time critic testifies to the objectivity of his judgment. Curiously enough, it gave him some pleasure to learn that his fellow physicians were happy that one of their number had been elevated.

As time wore on, however, Chekhov tended to treat his new honor rather lightly. He jokingly signed his letters to intimates "Academicus" or "Hereditary Honorary Academician," and he delightedly wrote Masha that the old family servant had warned a new caller that her master was now a "general,"[2] so the man constantly addressed Chekhov as "Your Excellency." More prophetically, he informed Menshikov that as a writer he was pleased with the title of academician. "But I shall be still more happy when I lose this title after some misunderstanding. And there will most certainly be misunderstandings, for the learned academicians very much fear that we shall shock them." (*January 28, 1900.*)

« 2 »

In the Ravine, the long story Chekhov had finished at the end of the previous year, most auspiciously inaugurated the new magazine *Life* in January. He wrote Suvorin that Russian society "is weary, hatred is making it as rank and sour as grain in a bog, and it has a longing for something fresh, free, and light — a desperate longing." (*January 8, 1900.*) Chekhov describes a slice of this society in his memorable tale, but it is written out of Russian life rather than being a direct criticism of it. "I depict life here as it is found in the central provinces," he told his protégé S. N. Shchukin. "In reality the merchants Khrymin actually exist but are in fact still worse. Their children begin to drink vodka from the age of eight and are depraved even in their childhood; they infect the neighborhood with syphilis. I do not mention this in my story, because I would regard it as inartistic to do so."

In this work Chekhov introduces more characters than usual in his

[2] In the traditional table of ranks, the title of academician was equated with that of general.

tales, but each possesses a distinctive personality — the old village shop-keeper Tsybukin who will deal in anything, legally or illegally, to ac-cumulate money; his second wife Varvara, who tries by small acts of charity to compensate for the greed of her husband; the rapacious daughter-in-law Aksinya who is faithless to her weakling of a husband and finally usurps the position of Tsybukin and drives him out of his home; and the ugly son Anisim whose crime helps to ruin his father. The desperate longing for something fresh, free, and light, which Che-khov had mentioned to Suvorin, is beautifully embodied in the lovely Lipa, the peasant girl wantonly sacrificed in marriage to Anisim. Lipa's long walk home from the hospital that night, cradling in her arms her dead infant, horribly scalded by the jealous Aksinya in a fit of rage, is described as an elegiac pilgrimage of human suffering. In the moon-light the grief-stricken Lipa carries on a dialogue with the mysterious noises of the night, seeking an answer to why her baby, who has no sins, should be so painfully tormented before its death. The old peasant carter, who gives her a lift, provides a simple answer: "Yours is not the worst of sorrows. Life is long, there will be more good and there will be more bad, there is everything yet to come. Great is Mother Russia!"

Like the earlier *Peasants*, *In the Ravine* caught the public eye be-cause it mercilessly revealed ugly commonplaces of Russian life which had been swept under the national rug. The majority of the many reviews stressed that Chekhov invented nothing in his searing realism yet treated even his sinning men and women with a compassion born out of his love of life. Mirolyubov wrote him that he was thrice over-come by tears while reading *In the Ravine*; Gorbunov-Posadov that he powerfully felt "not only your talent but your heart, the love for man-kind in your heart, a tender, profound love for all who suffer . . ."; and Koni, who had also been made an academician, wrote: "It seems to me that it is the best of all you have written, that this is one of the profoundest productions of Russian literature." Gorky's outstanding review of the story, Chekhov told him, was balsam to his soul, and later Gorky informed him of how he read *In the Ravine* to a group of peasants and they wept over parts of it and he with them.

Gorky also reported that he had heard from Tolstoy how deeply he had been affected by *In the Ravine*. On the other hand, Tolstoy made it amply clear that Chekhov's plays did not similarly affect him. On one of his rare visits to the theater at this time, to see *Uncle Vanya*,

Tolstoy occupied the governor's box and received an ovation from the audience. Like *The Sea Gull*, which he had only read, he condemned *Uncle Vanya*. "Where is the drama? In what does it consist?" he stormed at the actor A. A. Sanin. The action never moved from one place, he declared, and Uncle Vanya and Astrov were simply good-for-nothing idlers escaping from real life into the country as a place of salvation. Nemirovich-Danchenko tried to soften the blow by reporting to Chekhov that Tolstoy just did not understand the play, and when he tried to explain its focus, Tolstoy objected that there was no tragic situation, and anyway there was no point in trying to discover it in guitars and crickets.

Far from being offended, Chekhov was vastly amused. P. P. Gnedich quotes a conversation he had with Chekhov at this time about Tolstoy:

" 'You know, he does not like my plays — he swears that I'm not a dramatist! There is only one thing that comforts me,' he added.

" 'What's that?'

" 'He said to me: "You know, I cannot abide Shakespeare, but your plays are even worse." '

"And the restrained, calm Anton Pavlovich threw back his head and roared so that his pince-nez fell from his nose."

Tolstoy's foibles and extreme opinions did not lessen Chekhov's reverence for the all-pervasive humanity of this colossus of a genius. In the letter to Menshikov previously mentioned, Chekhov praised the recently published *Resurrection* as a remarkable work of art. With unerring critical insight he singled out a section dealing with the secondary characters as the novel's highest achievement — "my heart beat furiously, it was so good," he wrote. But the relations of the hero and heroine he dismissed as uninteresting, and the theological device of the conclusion as a contrived one. And in this same letter he tells of his anxious efforts to ascertain the nature of Tolstoy's recent illness. "His illness frightened me and kept me in a state of tension. I dread Tolstoy's death. If he should die, there would be a big empty place in my life. To begin with, I have never loved any man as I do him; I am an unbeliever, but of all the faiths I consider his the closest to my heart and the one most suited to me. In the second place, as long as there is a Tolstoy in literature, then it is easy and agreeable to be a writer; even the realization that one has done nothing and will do nothing is not so dreadful, since Tolstoy will do enough for all. His accomplishment is a justification of the hopes and expectations built upon literature. In the third place, Tolstoy takes a firm stand, he has immense authority, and as long as he remains alive, bad taste in literature, any vulgarity — whether it be insolent or tearful — all coarse, irritating vanities will be kept at a distance, deep in the shadows. His moral authority alone is capable of maintaining the so-called literary moods and trends at a certain high level. Without him writers would be a shepherdless flock or a hopeless mess, of which one could make neither head nor tail." (*January 28, 1900.*)

Despite various promises to editors, Chekhov wrote no fiction in 1900. The desire was not dormant but he seemed to lack the energy to apply himself. Much of his working time was expended on the Marx edition, the second volume of which appeared this year; and he saw the third through the proofreading stage. The humor in these early tales Tolstoy compared favorably with that of Gogol. But in general he tended to compare Chekhov to Maupassant. He preferred Maupassant, because the French writer distilled greater joy out of life; but Chekhov, he told A. B. Goldenveizer, "is cleaner than Maupassant . . . The illusion of truth in Chekhov is complete, his pieces produce the impression of a stereoscope. It seems as though he is flinging words around in any fashion, but like an impressionist artist he achieves wonderful results with the strokes of his brush."

Though Chekhov had formerly been excited over translations of his stories, he now seemed pleased with a French version of *Peasants* only because his friend, the famous artist Repin, illustrated it. But to Olga Vasilieva, who wished to translate a selection of his best stories for British periodicals, he wrote in a discouraging tone: "It seems to me that I would have such little interest for the English that it is a matter of indifference to me whether or not I'm published in an English magazine." (*August 9, 1900.*)

Although he could find little time to concentrate on his own writing, he continued his practice of devoting plenty of it to the efforts of beginners. The writer and editor M. K. Pervukhin relates that he witnessed a conference which Chekhov had with a young hopeful at Yalta. Chekhov offered a complete review of all twenty stories in the manuscript, citing separate passages and dwelling on single phrases. It must have taken him several full working days, Pervukhin estimated, to prepare himself for this review, yet he knew that not one of the tales was worth publishing. When Pervukhin later remonstrated over the many hours expended on this effort, Chekhov retorted: "You ought to be ashamed of yourself! Is it possible to behave otherwise toward the work of beginners? Do you want me to throw the manuscript in the young man's face? Maybe he is stupid, unsuccessful, ridiculous, but has he not put his heart into this work? Would you regard it proper to snub him?" This attitude, countered Pervukhin, seemed hopeless. "And it also seems so to me," replied Chekhov. "But what if you and I are mistaken? No, your way out is impossible! He turns to us for the truth, and it would be disgraceful to ignore him."

Indeed, the young writers then, as the brilliant novice A. I. Kuprin expressed it, were beginning to be drawn to Chekhov as to a magnet. The young people who clustered around the old liberal Goltsev at *Russian Thought* dedicated two weeks to a special study of *The Sea Gull* and *Uncle Vanya*, for they found in these plays an intellectual content and the hope at least of discovering a way out of the impasse of Russian life. That winter, when it was proposed to set up a village library in honor of Goltsev on the occasion of the twentieth anniversary of *Russian Thought*, Chekhov characteristically suggested that instead a scholarship be offered in Goltsev's name to provide for the complete education of any "cook's son" who evinced a hatred for the liberal editor's opponents. Masha was present at the celebration banquet in Moscow, which was attended by many distinguished guests. She thought it boring and was annoyed that champagne was spilled on her new dress. But when Lavrov proposed a toast to the absent Chekhov, and the whole company arose, extending their glasses to her, and shouted a request that their greetings be transmitted to her brother, Masha forgot her displeasure and, amidst applause and cries of bravo, offered thanks in Chekhov's name.

« 3 »

Though the final touches on the new Yalta house seemed endless, it took on a finished appearance during the winter of 1900 when Chekhov's mother settled there. The efforts of the efficient Masha during her long visit that winter also helped to put things in order. The simply furnished study had an air of refinement about it. Its huge window — the rounded top was set with stained glass — provided a view of the garden, the valley of the Uchan-Su River, a circle of Yalta houses, and the sea beyond. Over the plain fireplace was Levitan's landscape, and the walls were adorned with portraits of Tolstoy, Turgenev, and Grigorovich. Above the large table desk, covered with many tiny carved figures in wood and stone, hung a printed sign: "Please do not smoke," although it never occurred to Chekhov to draw it to the attention of unseeing offenders no matter how much their smoking provoked his coughing. Off the study was his bedroom, girlish-looking in its whiteness and neatness.

Chekhov's main concern, however, was to transform this patch of wasteland that he had bought into a thing of beauty. Despite the clouds of thick dust that arose from the road beyond the fence he had built and the constant lack of water in the well which had been dug, the grounds and garden in the rather small enclosure had begun to take on an attractive appearance. Apart from the many fruit trees he planted, he experimented, with varying success, on a mixture of northern and semitropical trees — birch, poplar, cypress, eucalyptus, and palm. His avenue of acacias grew up incredibly fast. And he accounted it a triumph that of the seventy rose bushes he had planted the previous autumn, only three had failed to take root, and that he had successfully introduced camellias to Yalta. He had placed wooden seats, which he intended to paint, all about the garden and had supervised the erection of three tiny bridges over the brook than ran through the property. "It seems to me," he happily wrote Menshikov, "that if I had not been a writer, then I could have been a gardener." (*February 20, 1900.*)

Two gray cranes with clipped wings had made their home in the garden. They would follow Chekhov as he pruned his rosebushes, but never allowed themselves to be touched. The cranes were particularly devoted to the servant Arseny, the indispensable jack-of-all-trades. When Arseny returned from a trip to town all were amused by the raucous shrieks of greeting from the birds and by the odd antic dance these long-legged creatures would perform around him. Chekhov had also taken in two stray mongrel dogs, Little Ace and Chestnut — his Melikhovo dachshunds had died. The fat, clumsy, submissive Chestnut would follow the more aggressive Little Ace all day, barking whenever Little Ace barked at anything that moved. But Chekhov had only to beckon to Chestnut and the dog would run to him and roll over on its back while he stroked it lightly with his cane, watching the play of insects on its belly. "Get on with you, get on with you, fool," he would say with mock severity. Then, turning to a guest, he would add with pretended exasperation: "Don't you want this dog as a present? You won't believe how stupid it is." With the exception of cats, for which he had a repulsion, Chekhov loved animals. As at Melikhovo, he continued to catch mice alive and take them through the garden to the Tatar cemetery, where he released them.

Firmness in matters of principle, fits of temper which he usually controlled, and occasional capriciousness born of his illness contrasted with the invariable kindness and even tenderness of Chekhov to all who were weak, lowly, or unprotected — to animals, children, old people, servants. This delicacy and refinement, so apparent in his fiction and plays, became more noticeable in his own human relations as he grew older, and was largely the source of the widespread affection in which he was held by those who knew him and even by those who only read him. Kuprin relates an incident, told to him by an eyewitness, that took place once when Chekhov was disembarking from the Sevastopol steamer at Yalta. A Tatar, who usually served him, dashed on the deck ahead of the other porters to carry his luggage. An officious subordinate of the ship's captain struck the Tatar in the face for getting out of line. "What?" the enraged porter shouted, beating his chest. "You hit me? Do you think it is *me* you hit? There's the man you've hit," and he pointed at Chekhov. Chekhov, his face white and his lips trembling, went up to the subordinate and said quietly: "Are you not ashamed?"

Before he had time to get used to the pleasures of a well-run household once again, Chekhov gave in to the urge to buy the piece of beach property which he had had his eye on. It was on the shore of an inlet, hard by the pier at Gurzuf, about twelve miles from Yalta, and it consisted of a three-room hut and a bathhouse, one tree, and a fine view. His intention was to use the place for vacations in the summer with his mother and sister. He wrote to Masha about the purchase, carefully adding that he was now willing to sell his enchanting Kuchukoi, which none of the family seemed too enthusiastic about anyway because of the difficulty of reaching it and its distance from the water. This time Masha approved and slyly inserted in her reply that so did Olga Knipper.

For the time being he had little worry about finances. In January, Marx had paid another installment and the income from his plays was steadily rising. He felt far enough ahead to place five thousand roubles in the bank for Masha, to fulfill the promise he had made her of a part of the money from the sale of Melikhovo, although the delinquent purchaser had not yet paid in that much.

The influx of consumptives that winter gave Chekhov little rest. Contributions to the Board of Guardians for Visiting the Sick which he had organized to promote the building of a sanatorium were lagging, and he fulminated against owners of lodgings and hotels who refused to accept seriously ill patients and against doctors who sent hopeless cases to Yalta. They were dying from exhaustion and neglect, he complained, and in some despair he wrote Masha of the incessant stream of callers, ". . . doctors keep sending people from Moscow and the provinces with letters asking me to find lodgings, to 'make arrangements,' as though I were a renting agent!" (*March 26, 1900.*)

In a sense nothing could have been so tragically ironic as this man, wasting away from tuberculosis, expending his last meager strength to save others afflicted with the disease. In fact, he suffered a severe relapse himself in January. Dr. Altschuler examined him and found that his right lung had improved somewhat but that the left one had grown worse. Whatever may have been the doctor's orders, Chekhov could hardly have followed them very faithfully, for his mother fell ill at this time and he gives a picture in one of his letters of tending her through the night while he coughed up blood.

When his spirits were lowest that winter Chekhov declared that it seemed as though he had lived in Yalta a million years. He was as sick of this charming town, he said, as he would be of a disagreeable wife. The word "wife," indeed, was very much on his mind, for tongues were wagging again in Petersburg and Moscow. Brother Alexander had jokingly written that he had heard he was going to marry two actresses. Gorky wrote at the beginning of January: "They say you are getting married to an actress with a foreign name. I don't believe it. But if it is true, then I'm glad." And Gorky's other letters at this time contain pointed praise of Olga Knipper, "a divine actress and a charming and highly intelligent woman" whom he had been seeing at the Moscow Art Theater. Even the cautious Masha, on her birthday congratulations, added "and I wish you'd marry soon; take an intelligent, reasonable girl, even though she lacks a dowry." Whether she intended the implication, Chekhov could hardly fail to jump to the conclusion that Olga Knipper was the "intelligent and reasonable girl" in his sister's mind. For now nearly every letter of Masha to her brother was full of Olga: Olga took care of her when she was ill; sat beside her when she wrote to Chekhov and added her greetings; they were constantly going to each other's houses and to parties and social events together. In the summer, wrote Masha, the family ought to remain quietly at Gurzuf and refuse to see any visitors, except Olga. When living at Yalta seemed to Chekhov as drawn out as the siege of Sevastopol and he threatened to sell his new house and go off to Europe for the summer, Masha pleaded with him not to do this, and added, in a broad hint, "some people are distressed that you wish to go away." To Masha, however, this was only another of his passing infatuations. Her own starved emotions were nourished in playing the part of surrogate in a promising romance. But she was sure of her famous brother — he would now never marry.

If the promised spring visit of Olga and the Moscow Art Theater was the only ray of hope in Chekhov's deep discontent, there were times that winter when he doubted its realization. Though he grew querulous to Masha over the few letters from Moscow, meaning from Olga, he himself wrote her quite infrequently, which was perhaps some measure of his low spirits. But rarely did he omit mentioning that he was looking forward to the visit. "I still dream that you will all come to Yalta," he interpolated in a letter on January 2, which was concerned with his conviction that suffering on the stage ought to be expressed as it is expressed in life, not by gesticulation, but by grace. And in his next, almost three weeks later, he interlarded among chatty comments: "I'm told that in May you'll be in Yalta."

When Olga learned from Masha of his dark speculation about going abroad for the summer, she promptly wrote to implore him to abandon the idea. In his reply he explained that he had contemplated it because it was so dull in Yalta. Unlike her full existence, he wrote, his was a different matter: "I'm torn up by the roots, I'm not living a full life, I don't drink although I like to drink; I love excitement and have none of it, in brief, I'm now in the state of a transplanted tree, uncertain whether to take root or begin to wither." (*February 10, 1900.*) Then he assured her that at most he would go to Europe only at the end of the summer, to attend the International Exhibition at Paris, and he gave her the best of news, which he had just learned from Nemirovich-Danchenko: that the Moscow Art Theater would definitely perform at Sevastopol and Yalta that spring.

Shortly thereafter, however, Chekhov received a shattering telegram from Nemirovich-Danchenko to inform him that the troupe, instead of going to Yalta in the spring, would remain in Moscow to play a special engagement in the Korsh Theater. But subsequently wiser coun-

sel on the proposed tour must have prevailed. The Moscow Art Theater
had run up a large deficit. Chekhov's two plays were the only ones in
the repertoire that consistently packed the house. Stanislavsky frankly
admitted that the purpose of the Yalta tour was to show Chekhov the
full productions of the Moscow Art Theater at their best, with all the
refinements of staging which he had never seen, in the hope of prevail-
ing upon him to do a new play. As Stanislavsky put it, if Mohammed
could not come to the mountain, the mountain must go to Mohammed.
And the grateful Chekhov was delighted. "I rejoice, rejoice," he wrote
Vishnevsky, "primarily for myself, for to see all of you, and especially
in a finished production . . . I confess this is a dream the realization
of which I had not believed in until recently; and now I tremble with
every ring of the telephone at the thought that it is a telegram from
Moscow to announce cancellation of the plans." (*March 17, 1900.*)

Playbills went up in Yalta. Tickets at Sinani's bookstore were soon
sold out. It would cause a scandal now, Chekhov reassured himself, if
the theater failed to turn up. To make doubly sure, and at a financial
loss to himself, he informed Nemirovich-Danchenko that he had told
Petersburg's Alexandrinsky Theater, which was pressing him for permission to produce *Uncle Vanya,* that it could do so only by agreement with the Moscow Art Theater. Every letter now joyfully alerted
his friends of the projected visit, and urged them to make the trip to
Yalta to see the performances of this remarkable theater. Masha was
instructed to ship from Moscow quantities of special dainties for the
large amount of entertainment he expected to do.

Olga sent him presents of candy, and a pocketbook so that a man
who intended to buy up the whole south coast of the Crimea, she wrote,
would have a place to put his money; and she complained of her dull
life. She, too, was impatient to meet him, and had decided to come a
few days in advance of the troupe with Masha, who had her spring
vacation. "It is splendid that you are coming with Masha before the
others," Chekhov wrote her, "for we shall at least have time to talk, to
stroll, to see things, and to drink and eat a bit. Only please don't bring
Vishnevsky with you, because he'll follow us about and will not allow
us to say a word to each other. . . ." (*March 26, 1900.*)

« 4 »

Masha and Olga arrived at the beginning of April. Olga found the
new house, which she had seen only in the process of construction the

still a third group, and some of the young actors in the garden competed to see who could throw stones the farthest. Chekhov's face was transformed. He acted as though he had been reborn. Here were the gaiety and movement he loved. Stanislavsky recalled how their happy host, his hands behind his back, or constantly removing and replacing his pince-nez, moved from group to group, talking with everyone. With a kind of childish naïveté, he spoke to all of the thing that attracted him most at the moment. And, during the ten days the Moscow Art Theater was at Yalta, this gay company of actors and writers made a daily pilgrimage to Chekhov's for lunch or tea, creating their own atmosphere of mingled jollity and seriousness, of art and poetry until, like one happy family, they ended by idealistically planning to make an annual event of this gathering and to build a house to accommodate all these kindred spirits.

Uncle Vanya was the opening play on April 16. Overdressed ladies and cavaliers of Moscow and Petersburg, teachers, civil servants from neighboring provincial towns, local citizens and consumptives made up the audience. Chekhov's mother, digging out of her trunk an ancient silk dress, insisted on attending. The picture of her sitting in a box in her frayed gown, seeing her son's play for the first time, struck Chekhov as agonizingly sentimental and upset his nerves. Though the town park band always seemed to come in with a march or polka at just the most tragic moments of the play, the performance was hailed as a great success and Chekhov was accorded an ovation.

He appears not to have attended most of the other plays, but he was present at a special performance of dramatic readings which he persuaded the company to offer on behalf of his Board of Guardians for Visiting the Sick. However, he felt obliged to come to an extra and final performance of The Sea Gull presented in his honor. This was turned into a personal triumph with a prolonged ovation and the presentation of a scroll signed by almost two hundred local citizens and many distinguished visitors. A Yalta female Maecenas tendered a farewell luncheon to the whole company on the roof of her palatial home, and the Moscow Art Theater, as a parting gift, gave Chekhov for his garden the bench and swing that had been used in Uncle Vanya. Either then or a little later Chekhov presented gold medallions to the casts of The Sea Gull and Uncle Vanya. The medallions were made up in the form of books, the front inscribed with the titles of the plays and the author's name. On the reverse side the name of the actor was engraved. The book opened up and on the left the role or roles of the actor appeared, and on the right was set a miniature copy of the photograph which had been taken of Chekhov and the cast of *The Sea Gull.* On the back of Nemirovich-Danchenko's medallion was engraved: "You gave my *Sea Gull* life. Thanks!" The company left Yalta with the pleasantest memories, more devoted than ever to Chekhov, and Stanislavsky left with the precious promise from him that he would definitely have another play for their next season.

« 5 »

Chekhov confessed to the need of rest after two weeks of going to bed at three or four in the morning and the strain of dining constantly in the company of large groups. But Yalta now seemed more dull and empty than ever. By the beginning of May the momentum of the recent excitement carried him on, in an act of truancy, to its source — to Moscow and Olga. She had had to return with the company to do some rehearsing before the regular summer vacation set in, but her letters to him were filled with nostalgic yearning for the happiness she had left behind. He could have seen very little of her at Moscow, however, for the delayed illness caught up with him, and in less than two weeks he was back in Yalta, leaving a record of having talked with reporters at a championship wrestling match on the virtues of physical prowess, and of having visited the seriously ill Levitan. "My dear, enchanting actress," he wrote Olga on his return, "I was very unwell on the way back to Yalta. In Moscow I had a bad headache and a fever, and it was sinful to conceal this from you, but I feel pretty well now." (*May 20, 1900.*)

Chekhov soon felt well enough to succumb to the blandishments of Gorky about the beauties of the Caucasus. For at the beginning of June, along with Gorky, a physician friend A. N. Aleksin, the celebrated artist V. M. Vasnetsov, and Dr. L. V. Sredin, who joined the group later, he took a tour of two weeks through parts of this picturesque region. (There is some evidence that Chekhov and Olga had a plan to meet at Batum on this trip.) The group traveled into Vladikavkaz along the Georgian Military Road to Tiflis. After visiting monasteries in the area, they left for the return trip. On the train from Tiflis to Batum, by one of those inexplicable coincidences, they met Olga and her mother on the way to a short vacation in the Caucasus, and they traveled together for six hours before she had to change trains. (The hard, four hundred times." When she skipped a day in writing him, he complained that he had not had a line from her "in ages." Olga tried to soothe him. Don't rage, don't fret, she comforted, for when they saw each other they would forget it all. But when would they get together again? She kept asking him in nearly every other letter.

Olga had much reason to feel depressed, for in the course of some ten weeks after her departure from Yalta Chekhov again and again advanced the date of his rejoining her in Moscow. The principal reason for the delay was *The Three Sisters,* which he had begun to work on seriously after Olga left. Much pressure was being placed upon him to finish the play in time for the current season of the Moscow Art Theater, and over this period Stanislavsky visited him twice to urge him on. As he told Masha, however, *The Three Sisters* turned out to be more difficult for him than any of his other plays. He kept Olga fully informed of his progress, for she was as eager as her theater directors that he write the play, and Chekhov wished to create for her one of its richest and most important roles.

Chekhov wrote her, at the beginning of his efforts, that he had got into a sort of tangle, that there were too many characters and he might have to give it up. Then he had a spurt and felt that he had started well, but he soon cooled off, he declared, and it had all grown cheap to him. "I don't write you," he informed Olga on August 30, "because you must wait a bit, for I'm writing my play. Although it is rather tedious, yet it seems to me all right, it is intellectual. I write slowly — that I did not expect." Some days, he told Olga, he would just sit and sit at his desk and think and think about the play, and then pick up a newspaper. Or, he reported sadly, he had done nothing on it for a whole week and the play looked at him dejectedly as it lay on the table and he thought of it dejectedly. Then one of his heroines had gone a bit lame, he said, and he could do nothing for her.

Chekhov asserted that a play ought to be written without taking a breath, and he actually contemplated finishing a first draft of *The Three Sisters* in a month. But there was no hope of a month of free, uninterrupted time. "Oh how they break in on me, if you only knew!!! I cannot refuse to see people," he confessed to Olga. "I'm just not equal to it." The poet V. N. Ladyzhensky, visiting Yalta, called on him for ten straight days running, Sofya Malkiel from Moscow spent the night, Sergeenko arrived from Petersburg, the headmistress of the school and Mme. Bonnier came on problems of the sick, and other local citizens were daily visitors. Chekhov's almost hysterical bitterness now over what had long been a commonplace in his life was no doubt caused by his impatience to finish his play and get to Olga at Moscow. Both she and Masha grew alarmed at the expressions of intense dejection in his letters over these endless interruptions. Masha wrote him not to place too much significance on such matters and it would be easier for him to get along. Olga was more aggressively practical over "these visitors who keep hindering you from working." Day after day, she exclaimed, spent in empty gossip while the play was clamoring to take shape and he became indignant over the delays. Darling, dear one, she demanded, do something to get rid of them so you can work quietly and unhindered.

By the end of August Chekhov began to doubt that he would be able to finish the play at Yalta, and he hinted to Olga that he might come to Moscow and work on it. His mother, however, declared her unwillingness to remain alone. Sympathetic to her wishes, he asked Masha in Moscow to take her in. Masha objected at first; she had sent all her kitchenware to Yalta, was living almost in dormitory style in a tiny new apartment, and she pleaded that Mother would be most uncomfortable there. It was not until the end of September that this difficulty was straightened out and their mother left for Moscow. Meanwhile Chekhov had an attack of influenza and both the play and his trip had to be put off.

Olga tried to understand the reasons behind all these delays in his coming, but her letters now began to reflect despair. If her fears were momentarily assuaged when he told her that he would love her like an Arab, or declared "My sweet Olga, my angel, I'm very very lonely without you," they were again revived when he postponed his arrival week after week. "Why don't you come, Anton?" she burst out in her letter of September 24. "I cannot understand it. I don't write because I'm expecting you all the time, because I want terribly to see you. What's holding you back? What's troubling you? I don't know what to think and I feel dreadfully uneasy. . . . Every day I want to cry."

Olga, with her impetuous, optimistic nature, could not penetrate, at least at this stage in their relations, the terrible secret he bore within him — that circumstances compelled him to dwell more on death than on marriage. With his natural reticence about expressing his inmost thoughts and feelings, the most he could do was to hint, as though he expected her to divine the rest. He did not want to write her, he declared, but to talk and talk on, even be silent with her, only with her. Yet to go to Moscow for that, he added, defied his understanding. "What for?" he asked. "To see you and go away again? How interesting that is. To arrive, look at the theatrical crowd, and once more depart." (*September 22, 1900.*)

But in her emotional state Olga was incapable of divination. She did not hesitate to write him of the way people were talking about them, or to throw out broad hints of their future life together. But these passages he ignored and perhaps disliked. The daily doings at Yalta were the substance of his letters and only occasionally did he dwell on intellectual or creative things. It soon occurred to Olga that he was holding something back and she pleaded with him to write her all, to be clear and open. We are not children, she insisted, and she wanted to hear everything that was in his heart. Patiently but realistically, he responded: "You write: 'You have a loving, tender heart, then why do you harden it?' But when have I become hard-hearted? And in what, precisely, have I shown this flintiness? My heart has always loved you and been tender to you, and I've never concealed it from you, never, never, and you accuse me of hard-heartedness simply for no reason at all. If I may judge from your letters in general, you wish and expect some explanation, some sort of long conversation — with grave faces and consequences; and I don't know what to say to you except one thing which I have told you ten thousand times already and shall probably go on telling you for a long, long time, that is, that I love you — and nothing more. If we are not together now, it is neither your fault nor mine, but that of the devil who put bacilli in me and the love of art in you." (*September 27, 1900.*)

With obvious elation Chekhov wrote Gorky on October 16 that he had at last finished *The Three Sisters*, and he added that it had been terribly hard work. The principal reason for his remaining at Yalta no longer existed. The next day a wire went off to Olga that he was leaving for Moscow, "without fail," on October 21.

« 7 »

Five days to two weeks was Chekhov's estimate of the length of time he could risk in Moscow. It would all depend on the weather. Actually he remained seven weeks. He knew that he ought not to be there at that time of the year, and it is ironic to find him just then answering a query of Lidiya Avilova about the best treatment for her

tubercular brother by advising that he should at once go to Yalta because consumptives improve there very quickly.

Though Chekhov stayed at the Dresden Hotel, he appears to have
made the Moscow Art Theater his headquarters. There were the excitement and art that he loved; there also was Olga, frantically busy with
rehearsals in the daytime and performances at night. Like some stage-
door Johnny, he waited for Olga after working hours so he could "talk
and talk on or even be silent with her." Like him, she loved nature, and
on her rare free days they perhaps strolled in one of the city's parks —
a desire he had expressed in his letters — when she would not have to
be worrying constantly about getting back to rehearsals. He frequently
attended these rehearsals and saw regular performances, sometimes
more than once, of all the plays in the repertoire that season: his own
Uncle Vanya and *The Sea Gull*, Hauptmann's *Lonely Lives*, and Ibsen's
Dr. Stockman[4] and *When We Dead Awaken*, although he continued
to regard Ibsen's work as too involved, artificial, and intellectualized.
Gorky, who was then in Moscow, often accompanied him, and the
audiences, recognizing the two authors, accorded them ovations. At
the end of the third act, in one of the performances of *The Sea Gull*,
Nemirovich-Danchenko presented Chekhov with a laurel wreath bearing the inscription: "To a highly talented friend of the management
and actors of the Art Theater."

Soon after Chekhov's arrival, Stanislavsky arranged for a reading of
the first draft of *The Three Sisters*.[5] Chekhov and the directors sat at
the center of a large table set up in the foyer of the theater. All the
company was present, including the ushers, stagehands, and even a
tailor or two. Stanislavsky recalled that Chekhov was excited and felt
out of place in the chairman's seat, and that the atmosphere of the
gathering was a triumphant and uplifted one. During the reading Chekhov would occasionally jump up and walk about the room, especially
when the lines seemed to him to ring falsely.

According to Olga, a puzzled silence reigned at the conclusion of the
reading. Chekhov, concealing his embarrassment by smiling and coughing nervously, circulated among the troupe. Soon she heard snippets of
conversation: "This is really not a play, it is only a prospectus . . ."

---

[4] The Moscow Art Theater's title for Ibsen's play, *An Enemy of the People*.

[5] In Olga Knipper's account, she asserts that Chekhov himself read the manuscript. However, it is most unlikely that he would have elected to read the whole
play before a group of experienced actors.

"Impossible to act it, there are no roles, only some hints or other . . ."
Some argued whether it was a drama or a tragedy, and one speaker
began in a loud voice: "Although I don't agree with the author in
principle, still . . ." Chekhov, so Stanislavsky remembered, could not
survive this "in principle." When no one was looking, he disappeared.
Afraid that illness might have compelled him to leave, Stanislavsky
hurried to his hotel. He found Chekhov in a mood of black anger: "It
is impossible. Listen — 'in principle'!" he exclaimed. The real reason
for his anger, Stanislavsky concluded, was that Chekhov had believed
he had written a happy comedy, and now felt the play was already a
failure.[6]

In an earlier letter to Olga, Chekhov had indicated that one of the
reasons he wished to go to Moscow was to be present at the rehearsals
of *The Three Sisters*. "Four responsible female roles, four young women
of the educated class, I cannot leave in the hands of Alekseev [Stani-
slavsky] despite all my respect for his gifts and understanding." (*September 15, 1900.*) At this point, however, he did not consider the play
as finished. While he was in Moscow he revised two acts and hence it
seems that very little was done by way of formal rehearsals. The initial
reaction, however, had discouraged him. On November 13 he wrote
Vera Kommissarzhevskaya, who requested *The Three Sisters* for her
benefit performance in Petersburg, that it was dreary, long, and more
gloomy than gloom, and that people were saying that its spirit was
suicidal. But Chekhov had certainly misjudged the reaction of Stanislavsky, whom he saw a great deal of in discussing the staging of the
play, for this co-director wrote L. V. Sredin that he regarded *The Three
Sisters* as "wonderful and most successful."

A tragedy occurred while Chekhov was in the city — the Moscow
student son of I. A. Sinani, that genial and helpful bookseller friend
of all the Yalta celebrities, committed suicide. Chekhov met the grief-
stricken father at the station to comfort him, and he and Olga attended
the funeral.

While in Moscow Chekhov received a letter from Suvorin, which
was now a rather rare event. At the beginning of 1900 Suvorin had
sent him a copy of his new play and had also wired congratulations on
Chekhov's birthday and election to the Academy of Sciences. Chekhov

[6] Stanislavsky may well have been incorrect in this conclusion. Chekhov was
rather precise in the description of his plays, and he nowhere refers to *The Three
Sisters* as a "comedy." His own description of it in the printed volume of his plays
is: "A Drama in Four Acts."

wrote him a favorable appreciation of the play and added a suggestion on how to improve the fourth act. But in another letter he sharply criticized an article of Suvorin in *New Times* which attacked the jury system.

In the meantime, Brother Misha, seeking Suvorin's aid in obtaining a position, had called upon him in Petersburg and Suvorin and his wife had presented a kind of bill of particulars on why their long friendship with Chekhov had been soured. In what he imagined was an effort to reconcile the two friends, Misha conveyed the substance of the Suvorins' complaints in a letter which has unfortunately been lost. Obviously annoyed with Misha's good intentions, Chekhov wrote his brother to clarify his own position on all these old scores and ended: "Of course, I ought not to be writing this to you, for it is all too personal and dull, but once they had bewitched you and presented the affair to you in that light, I had to tell you all this. . . . There can be no talk about a reconciliation, because Suvorin and I did not quarrel and we are again corresponding as though nothing had happened." (*January 29, 1900.*)

Now, after a silence of some eight months, Chekhov answered Suvorin's letter in a pleasant, unstrained manner. He congratulated him on the marriage of his daughter, and from the bottom of his heart wished happiness to the whole family "to which I am joined almost as to my own." After bringing him up to date on his doings, he took the occasion once again to criticize *New Times*, which had published an account about him and Gorky. It appears that during the intermission of a performance of *The Sea Gull*, admirers of Gorky cheered him in the foyer of the theater. Annoyed, Gorky berated them: ". . . it is offensive to me as a professional writer that while you are attending a play of Chekhov, one filled with such enormous significance, you occupy yourself with such trifles in the intermission." Chekhov protested in his letter: "What was written in *New Times* about Gorky and me is incorrect, even though reported by eyewitnesses. They say that Gorky turned on the public with certain words; nothing like this was said in front of me." (*November 16, 1900.*) However, Chekhov urged Suvorin to come to Moscow, for he wanted very much to see him. According to Suvorin's diary, he went, and he reported Chekhov as saying that he was going to Algeria and inviting Suvorin to visit him there.

Chekhov brought with him to Moscow something of the passion for gaiety that he had evinced during the visit of the Moscow Art Theater to Yalta. A part of this mood was no doubt the natural reaction to weeks of work on *The Three Sisters*, another perhaps was his persistent feeling that time was running out on him. How he enjoyed being in Moscow! (he told Suvorin). The Dresden Hotel was only a place to sleep in; daily he was off from morning to the early hours of the next with Olga, with Gorky, with Chaliapin or the painter Vasnetsov. Old friends, like Korobov, could never find him in, and in answer to their despairing notes, he made appointments with them for a half-hour at the Moscow Art Theater or at his sister's, where he was entertaining. The distinguished Dr. M. A. Chlenov ran him down finally, to discuss a project for establishing in Moscow an institute for medical specialists in skin diseases and syphilis. After several vain efforts, the well-known artist V. A. Serov persuaded him to squeeze out some time to pose for a portrait.

Weeks of this hectic existence, in addition to bad weather, took their usual toll — extreme headaches, temperature, and prolonged fits of coughing. He knew that he must leave Moscow, but he could not abide the thought of returning to Yalta for another winter. Once again he settled upon Nice. Masha agreed to keep their mother with her until his return, and Marx, pleased that the corrected proof of the third volume was already in, willingly paid part of the next installment in advance.

What Olga's thoughts were on their parting on December 11 are unknown; they are discreetly omitted from any of the records. She wrote him later that she cried bitterly after he left. It would have pained her to read a sentence in Chekhov's last letter to Suvorin, even if he had meant it jokingly: "You have heard that I am marrying? It is not true." For shortly after her return from that unofficial honeymoon at Yalta, Nemirovich-Danchenko wrote to Stanislavsky that Olga Knipper had informed him that her marriage to Chekhov had definitely been decided upon!

Part VI

MARRIAGE AND DEATH
1901 – 1904

CHAPTER XXIII

"What Do You Know, I'm Going to Get Married"

"AH, YOU LIMP Slav jelly," scolded Olga — Chekhov's letter from Vienna led her to believe that he had not budged from his hotel during an overnight stop. But she had no reaction to his observation: ". . . I keep looking with ardent longing at the two beds in my room; I'll sleep, I'll think! Only it is a shame that I'm here alone, without you, my naughty child, my darling, an awful shame." (*December 12, 1900.*)

At Nice the next day Chekhov took rooms at the Pension Russe. Nothing had changed about this old lodging of his. The Russian women there were the same "horrible frights," nor had the gay town with its lovely weather changed. And his old friends gathered around — the vice consul Yurasov, the irascible artist Yakobi, and the brilliant scholar Kovalevsky, who took away from his conversations the conviction that Chekhov anticipated the equality of the peasantry and the eventual disappearance of the landed gentry from the Russian countryside.

At Nice Chekhov also resumed acquaintance with Olga Vasilieva, a young Russian lady who had corresponded with him on the translation of his tales into English. Now his interest in her deepened. She sought his advice on the charitable use to which she might put a large sum of money she expected to inherit soon from the sale of extensive Odessa properties of a deceased relative. He at once recalled his recent talk with Dr. Chlenov in Moscow, about the need for an institute for skin diseases. Though one has reason to suspect the motives of the young heiress in turning to Chekhov, he involved himself in an extensive correspondence, various interviews, and even an investigation of the Odessa holdings in a vain effort to realize this project. He was more successful with his own charitable enterprise, for he learned that the funds he had set out to collect were now adequate, along with a contribution of five thousand roubles of his own money, to set up a small sanatorium for consumptives in Yalta.

However, Chekhov's primary concern upon arriving at Nice was to revise and recopy the last two acts of *The Three Sisters* while rehearsal of the first two he had revised was taking place in Moscow. Olga Knipper wrote him on December 12 that Tolstoy, at a "Chekhov Evening" arranged by the Society of Arts and Literature, had laughed uproariously during the performance of those old one-acters, *The Wedding* and *The Bear*, and had told L. A. Sulerzhitsky that he regretted not having seen Chekhov before his departure. The next day she informed him in another letter that the cast had had a splendid rehearsal of *The Three Sisters*, in which she had found the right walk in her part of Masha. He must not fear, Olga added, that she would overdo the rough manner of the character. But Stanislavsky, she complained a bit later, was introducing his usual effects, such as the sound of a mouse scratching in Masha's scene with Vershinin.

Chekhov soon finished his revisions, making a number of changes, especially in the fourth act.[1] Through the rest of December and much of January he was in correspondence with individual actors who asked for interpretations on this or that aspect of their roles. Meanwhile he kept forwarding to the theater additional alterations, deletions, or suggestions on the handling of a piece of stage business. "These little diamonds that he sent to us," declared Stanislavsky, "when studied in the rehearsals, put life into the action in an unusual degree and brought the actors close to the truth of what they were experiencing." And in a letter to Chekhov, he said that with every rehearsal he fell more and more in love with *The Three Sisters*. "We often talk of you and we marvel at your sensitiveness and knowledge of the stage, the stage of which we dream."

Information had come to Chekhov that Moscow military authorities,

---

[1] Only recently has the original "Yalta manuscript" of *The Three Sisters* been discovered in Russia. A comparison between this version and the printed edition that appeared in Chekhov's lifetime reveals the extensive revisions he made in the drama. The play was first printed in the February issue of *Russian Thought*, 1901, without his being able to correct the proof, and next in Volume VII of the collected edition of his works, 1902. For a study of the changes, see A. R. Vladimirskaya, "Dve rannie redaktsii pesy *Tri Sestry*," in *Literaturnoe Nasledstvo* ("Two Early Versions of *The Three Sisters*," in *Literary Heritage*), Moscow, 1960, LXVIII, 1-86.

hearing that he had written a play about army officers, were fearful that he intended to satirize them. Actually, he had specifically instructed Stanislavsky that the officers must be played realistically and not as the typical stage caricatures of the time, for he regarded them as enlightened bearers of culture in the provincial town that was the setting of *The Three Sisters*. And he had insisted that his friend, Colonel Viktor Petrov, should attend rehearsals and check on all aspects of military dress and deportment. The colonel, it appears, took his assignment too literally, for he objected, in a letter to Chekhov, that to permit the married officer Vershinin to seduce another man's wife was an act of immorality outside the military code.

In nearly every letter to Olga now, Chekhov begged for news about the progress of rehearsals. He had given her many more words in his revision of her role, he chided, begrudged her nothing, so why did she not report to him? His play would be a failure, he gloomily confided to her, and now he wondered why he had ever written it. This mood of uncertainty was partly a reflection of his mounting discontent with Nice after he had been there only a few weeks. Exquisite summer weather, yes. Flowers, ladies, bicycles — but it was only an oleograph. And he knew more people at Nice than at Yalta; it was impossible to hide from them. He even deplored the amount of Russian money wasted at Monte Carlo, some of it his own. Only her "dear," "clever," and "poetic" letters sustained him. You need a husband, he told her, a spouse with side-whiskers and a cockade. And what am I? he asked dolefully, and answered: No great shakes. "However that may be, I kiss you affectionately, hug you furiously, and once more thank you for your letter, and bless you, my joy. Write to me, write. I beg you!!" (*January 2, 1901*.)

In the meantime, his sister, who had been spending the Christmas vacation at Yalta with her mother, wrote: "Without you, the Yalta house is empty and boring. If you would only come home for Easter, it would be wonderful! The sun pours into your study and makes it cozy and cheerful. I'm very sad at leaving! I kiss you affectionately." She could see little point in his being away from the Yalta house, which she had grown to love, at that time of the year. Back in Moscow she heard from him after a lapse of some time, and on January 22 she replied in a hurt tone: "I imagined that you had been ill but I was afraid to send you a telegram. Knipper has done this and I'm satisfied." The implication was that Olga, unlike his sister, did not have to worry over his annoyance at being asked about the state of his health. Masha suspected or was aware that her brother and Olga were now lovers and she was concerned; both she and her mother had observed their conduct together that previous summer with some disapproval.

Since he had anxiously asked Masha for a report on the rehearsals of his play, she hastened to reply on January 28: "The first dress rehearsal of *The Three Sisters* took place yesterday. I sat in the theater and wept, especially during the third act. They staged and acted it splendidly." She continued with criticism of several of the actors, told of her difficulty in persuading Olga to dispense with a red wig which made her head too large, but she assured him that the play would enjoy a big success.

However, Chekhov did not receive this letter until after the première of *The Three Sisters*, which took place on January 31. In fact, he was unaware that the play had been performed. Unable to stand Nice any longer, he had set out for Pisa on January 26 — he wanted to see the Sahara, and his original intention was to go to Algeria, but Kovalevsky and the Villefranche zoologist A. A. Korotnev, who went along, persuaded him to give up the sea voyage because of a bad storm. His change of plans temporarily broke his connections with Moscow, and telegrams about the success of *The Three Sisters* from Olga and Nemirovich-Danchenko went astray.

It was just as well, for his informants stretched a point in their praise, perhaps out of consideration for Chekhov's health. As Stanislavsky asserted later, *The Three Sisters* had only a middling success on its first performance. Nemirovich-Danchenko and Gorky at once singled it out as the profoundest and most effective of Chekhov's plays, but it took the general public and the critics several years to recognize this fact. No doubt a subjective note is heard in the "to Moscow, to Moscow" theme of the three sisters, reflecting Chekhov's own yearning to leave his "warm Siberia" of Yalta for the life and love that Moscow represented. And one suspects that he created the character of Masha with the acting abilities of Olga Knipper very much in mind. Masha, with her earthy, blunt, yet sensitive nature, stands in striking contrast to her duty-loving sister Olga and to Irina with her passion for work. Certainly Masha is one of Chekhov's finest stage creations.

The subtle interaction of symbol and reality creates an atmosphere of unusual psychological density in *The Three Sisters* and contributes to the difficulty of understanding the play. And the inner action, so characteristic of Chekhov's last four plays, is made more meaningful through the medium of the seemingly disconnected dialogue. For beneath the surface features of the dull, commonplace existence of the people of this provincial town Chekhov reveals the ultimate values of life which stir and yet so often evade these characters. Tuzenbach, in his love for Irina, ironically identifies himself with her doctrine of work. In a kind of revolutionary fervor he declares that something formidable will soon sweep the world clean of laziness, indifference, and prejudice against work. Vershinin, in love with Masha, associates himself with what he imagines is her mission to spread culture in her backward town, and he eloquently dreams of the beautiful and glorious life two or three hundred years hence when society will be led by cultured people. But the down-to-earth Masha sums it all up in a Chekhovian sense: "Life is all right if you don't waste it!"

However, the illusion of happiness is perhaps the main theme of the play. In the end the three sisters fail to make their way to the imaginary paradise of Moscow. Irina's hopes are dashed by the death of her lover Tuzenbach in a duel, and Masha's lover Vershinin marches off with his wife and children to a new military assignment. As in the conclusion of *Uncle Vanya*, however, Chekhov distills from frustration and failure a renewed faith in life and its purpose. Though this ending may be interpreted as another illusion of happiness, given the natures and values of the three gallant sisters, one suspects that this was not Chekhov's intention. As the band plays and the troops march off, Masha declares that she and her sisters must start their life anew; they must live. Irina agrees and adds that she will dedicate herself to work in service to those who need her. Olga embraces them both in affirmation: "Oh, my dear sisters, our life is not yet at an end. Let us live! The music plays so gaily and joyfully, and it seems that in a little while we shall know why we live and why we suffer. If only we knew! If only we knew!"

Chekhov was sending letters to Olga from Pisa, Florence, and Rome, asking whether *The Three Sisters* would go on that season, while the first and second performances of the play were taking place in Moscow. Happy as always in traveling, he assured her of his old conviction that one has not lived who has not seen Italy, but in a reflective mood in Rome he said to Kovalevsky, "As a physician, I know my life will be short." Only in Rome did Nemirovich-Danchenko's telegram of success catch up with him. Chekhov's casual mention of it in a letter to Olga made *The Three Sisters* seem like ancient history. Then the weather suddenly turned cold. It snowed. He gave up a projected trip to Naples and sailed for Yalta by way of Odessa.

Chekhov stopped off at Odessa to make inquiries about the estate of Olga Vasilieva. His information, he wrote her, indicated that real estate values in the city were then low, and he advised her to postpone the sale of her property until more could be realized from it toward the establishment of the proposed institute for skin diseases. In Odessa he also met the two young writers A. I. Kuprin and A. M. Fyodorov. In his hotel room they sat at his feet in admiration as he talked about literary matters, coughing frequently and spitting into little paper bags which he threw in the stove. Fyodorov recalled that Chekhov twitted him about being married to an actress. Both young authors agreed that his conversation, his tone, bearing, the expression of his eyes, and his sad smile marked him as a most unusual man. The next day, February 14, Kuprin and Fyodorov and his wife and child insisted on accompanying Chekhov on the remainder of his boat trip to Yalta.

« 2 »

Of the numerous friends who promptly called to pay their respects when Chekhov returned to Yalta, Bunin was no doubt the most welcome. When Chekhov was in Nice, Bunin had turned up at Yalta and Masha invited him to stay with her and her mother. His talents, genial nature, kindness, and profound devotion to Chekhov quickly made him a favorite. He and Masha became very friendly, took excursions together, and it is possible that her attachment went deeper than simple friendship for this future winner of the Nobel Prize in literature. When she had to return to her teaching in Moscow, Bunin was pressed to remain with her mother, who also enjoyed his company. Chekhov, when informed at Nice of this arrangement, was pleased and grateful, for he knew that his mother disliked remaining alone.

When Chekhov returned in February, Bunin moved to a Yalta hotel, but for a time the two friends saw each other almost daily. To a certain extent Bunin was a disciple of Chekhov, and in literature they had much in common. Both shared a reverence for Tolstoy the man and literary artist, and disliked the new decadent school — they were like healthy peasants, Chekhov told Bunin, who ought to be assigned to disciplinary battalions. Bunin, whom Chekhov nicknamed "Monsieur Bukishon," because he resembled the picture of a French marquis he had seen in a newspaper, amused him endlessly with his anecdotes narrated with much histrionic ability.

On his frequent visits Bunin observed closely Chekhov's pedantic love of order in the house, his morbid fear of appearing before anyone unless fully dressed, his dislike of portmanteau words in conversation, and his effort to behave with equal attention and politeness to all his guests whatever their rank. His sense of fun and the irresistible urge to play practical jokes, Bunin recalled, was ever-present no matter how poorly he felt. As they were coming home from a walk one night, Bunin noticed that Chekhov seemed weary, silent, his eyes half-closed. A light silhouetted a woman's form behind the canvas covering of a balcony they passed. Suddenly Chekhov opened his eyes and said in a very loud voice: "Have you heard the news? It's terrible! Bunin's been murdered! In Autka by some Tatars!" And to his dumbfounded companion he whispered: "Not a word! Tomorrow all Yalta will be talking about the murder of Bunin."

On another night in the early spring, as they were taking a carriage drive, Chekhov said to him:

"Do you know how many more years they'll read me? Seven."

"Why seven?" Bunin asked.

"Well, seven and a half."

"No," Bunin replied. "Poesy lives long and the longer it lives the more powerful it becomes."

They left the carriage and sat on a bench in full view of the sea, brightly illumined by the moon.

"My dear sir," Chekhov continued, "you regard as poets only those who use such words as 'silvered distance,' 'accord,' or 'To battle, to battle in the struggle with darkness!' "

"You are sad tonight," Bunin said, looking at his face, which was somewhat pale in the moonlight.

He replied, laughing slightly: "It is you who are sad. You're sad because you've wasted money on a cabby." And then turning serious again, he continued: "Even though they may read me only seven more years, I have less than that to live: six."

Kuprin, who also saw much of Chekhov at this time, spending hours with him in discussing manuscripts of his stories, writes in his reminiscences: "About midday and later his house began to fill up with visitors. And at the same time gawking girls in broad-brimmed straw hats hung for hours on the iron fence separating the grounds from the road. The most varied people called on Chekhov: scholars, writers, rural officials, doctors, army men, artists, male and female devotees, professors, society people, senators, priests, actors, and God knows who else." Kuprin gives a dismal picture of the plaguing petitioners against whom Chekhov seemed absolutely defenseless. Some came to persuade him to political action, as though, Kuprin protests, he was indifferent to social problems and the burning questions of the day. "Who, knowing him well," asserted Kuprin, "does not remember the favorite phrases which he so often pronounced suddenly in his firm tone, even when they were out of keeping with the conversation: 'Listen, do you know what? In the next ten years there will be a Constitution in Russia.'"

In his desire to correct a common misconception, Kuprin no doubt exaggerated the ardor of Chekhov's political convictions. Gorky, a political activist himself, more correctly evaluated Chekhov's position when he wrote him, after their initial meeting: "You are, I believe, the first free man I've ever met, one who does not worship anything. How fine it is that you can regard literature as your first and primary business in life." Nevertheless, over the early spring of 1901 Chekhov was concerned with reports that reached him at Yalta of political disturbances in various parts of the country. The government's "Provisional Rules," under which demonstrating students were punished by expulsion from universities and by enforced military service, only worsened the disorders which had continued from the previous year. Bloodier riots broke out, universities were closed, an unsuccessful attempt was made to assassinate Pobedonostsev, the magazine *Life* was banned, and Tolstoy was excommunicated by the Church.

One of the ugliest incidents took place on March 4 before the Kazan Cathedral in Petersburg. A huge demonstration was broken up by mounted Cossacks. Several students were killed, and many people were hurt on both sides. Members of the Russian Writers' Mutual Aid Society signed a petition deploring the actions of the government, and in retaliation the organization was padlocked by the police. Gorky, who was an eyewitness and was later arrested, along with other figures in the literary world, wrote a long account of the affair to Chekhov. Also young Meierhold, who worshiped Chekhov, wrote to him: "I'm frankly indignant over what I saw the police do in Petersburg on March 4, and I cannot quietly devote myself to creative work when my blood boils and everything challenges me to enter the struggle."

Since the Moscow Art Theater, in a guest role, was performing in

Petersburg at this time, Chekhov was particularly anxious. In fact, the revolutionary fervor did seem to spill over into the performances, especially into that of *Dr. Stockman* (Ibsen's *An Enemy of the People*). Although the hero despised the masses and believed in individual action, when Stanislavsky, who played the part of Stockman, said his line: "One must never put on a new coat when one goes to fight for freedom and truth," pandemonium broke loose in the audience, many of whom had been present at the riot that day in front of the Kazan Cathedral.

Back in Yalta Chekhov wrote Olga: "I receive letters from Petersburg and Moscow, quite ominous ones, and I read the press with aversion." (*March 18, 1901.*) He had in mind not only political disturbances, but also the Petersburg reviews of the performances. Though Olga and Nemirovich-Danchenko had informed him of the success of *Uncle Vanya* and *The Three Sisters*, the newspapers did not bear them out. Olga was in tears over the abuse of the actors. In some exasperation Chekhov reminded her of his prediction of failure in Petersburg and angrily declared that he would give up writing for the stage, since in Russia dramatists were kicked and not forgiven either their successes or failures.

Actually, the audience reception of his plays in Petersburg, especially *The Three Sisters*, had been wonderful. But the critics of the conservative press, influenced by the ancient rivalry between the old and new capital, and also by the progressive trends of the Moscow Art Theater, which they somehow associated with the tense political situation, could find nothing good in the performances. As was to be expected, *New Times* was the most offensive — Suvorin's house had been spattered with ink by the student demonstrators. Although at the end of the previous year Chekhov had received as a peace offering a gift of a silver goblet from Suvorin, he now wrote his brother Misha in a last effort to persuade him not to take a position on *New Times*: "Of course, in your place I would prefer service in the printing establishment, disdaining the newspaper. *New Times* now has a very bad reputation, smug and satisfied people work there exclusively (if you don't count Alexander, who sees nothing), and Suvorin is given to lying, to terrible lying, especially in his so-called moments of 'frankness' — that is, he speaks sincerely, perhaps, but it is impossible to say that in the course of the next half-hour he will not do exactly the contrary." (*February*

27, 1901.) Nevertheless, Misha accepted a position with Suvorin on *New Times*.

« 3 »

One of the first things Chekhov did when he arrived in Yalta from abroad was to wire Olga: AWAIT DETAILED TELEGRAM. WELL, IN LOVE, BORED WITHOUT DOG. AM SENDING LETTERS. HOW ARE THINGS, HEALTH, SPIRITS? (*February 19, 1901.*) "Dog" was one of his pet names for her and it had its uses in telegrams. He followed this up the next day with a letter: "My precious, my divine treasure, I embrace and kiss you ardently . . ." and he explained that one reason for his return was wretchedness over not hearing from her during his travels. "You ask when shall we see each other?" he continued. "At Easter. Where?"

During the remainder of February, Chekhov pressed Olga to spend her Easter vacation at Yalta after the Petersburg tour. He was feeling quite unwell, and a trip to Moscow, which she had expected, seemed difficult. His insistence moved Olga to a revolt that had been building up in her for some time: mutual friends were now talking freely about their marriage. Would he never declare himself, never set a date? Did he expect her to go on being his mistress, seeing him only in secret? Olga wrote him on March 3, indignantly refusing to come to Yalta at Easter. "Think a little," she declared, "and you will understand why." With all his delicate perception, she asked, did he want her to submit again to his mother's suffering, which she had observed when they were together at Yalta the previous summer, and to his sister's bewildered looks? Why should they have to go on hiding their affections? "It seems," she concluded rather unfairly, "that you no longer love me as you used to, and that all you really want is for me to come and hang about you. . . ."

Chekhov had anticipated just such an outburst. Mentally he had been prepared for marriage with Olga for some time. She had discussed it in her letters and he even called her his "spouse" in his. He had found the essential love he had described to brother Misha three years before, and he had experienced with joy its "sexual attraction, being of one flesh." But the ceremony of sanctifying it by marriage seemed now entirely inconsequential in the harsh circumstances that limited his life. Like his hero Alekhin, in *About Love*, he knew how needless, petty, and deceptive was everything that hindered man and woman from loving each other. It was not that his marriage now would uproot the lives of his mother and sister who so depended on him, nor the fact that Olga must have her own life in art. And perhaps he did not worry much now about the sacrifice of that free element of his personality which he had stubbornly clung to for so long. For in his heart he knew that Olga, much as she desired, would never really possess that element. "Just as I'll be alone in my grave," he had jotted down in his notebook, "so in essence shall I live alone." The terrible, overriding obstacle was to consign his diseased, wasting body to a healthy young woman! He had given himself six years. Perhaps he was optimistic. In his evasive way he had tried to tell her this, but it made no difference. Some people go through their whole lives without receiving one drop of happiness, he had written her once. No doubt, that was the way it had to be. But he had found this drop of happiness, and how simple it would be now to drift along, enjoying it to the end. But life was not like that; it had its accursed formalities.

One evening, during that February, while Bunin was still at Yalta, they sat in Chekhov's study. Bunin read *Gusev* aloud. As he came to the end of the tale, with its gorgeous description of the massed clouds under the setting sun tinting the water with varied colors, Bunin wondered out loud whether he would ever see the Indian Ocean, which had attracted him since childhood. Chekhov's deep subdued voice interrupted him: "What do you know, I'm going to get married." And at once, Bunin recalled, he began to say jokingly that it would be better to marry a German than a Russian; she would be more efficient and her child would not crawl around the house and beat a copper pot with a spoon.

"I of course knew of his romance with Olga Leonardovna Knipper," Bunin commented at this point in his memoirs, "but I was not convinced that it would end in marriage. I was already on friendly terms with Olga Leonardovna and I realized that her background was entirely different from that of the Chekhovs. I realized also that when she became the head of the household, it would not be easy for Masha. In truth, Olga Leonardovna was an actress and would hardly abandon the stage, but nevertheless, much would have to change. Between sister and wife difficult problems would arise and all this would have its effect on Chekhov's health, for as always in such situations he would suffer because of one and then the other and for both together. And I thought: Yes, this is really suicide — worse than Sakhalin! But of course I kept silent."

Chekhov had made up his mind, but with his horror of ceremonies and sentimentality, he treated their forthcoming marriage in a light vein, as though to warn off any notion she might have of making a solemn event of it. He agreed to come to Moscow at Easter, even though he was awfully disinclined to leave Yalta, he said. On March 16 he wrote: "I'm so weary of racing about, and my health has so obviously become that of an old man, that you'll acquire in my person a grandfather, so to speak, instead of a husband. . . . I've quite given up literature, and when I marry you, I'll order you to quit the stage; and we'll live together like planters. You don't want to? Well, so be it, act another five years and then we'll see." But he hastened to add that he was working on his story, *The Bishop*, a subject which had been haunting him for fifteen years. Indeed, he was also working hard on the proofs of the Marx edition.[2]

Just as Chekhov was about to take off for Moscow, Olga relented and came to Yalta for her Easter vacation. She was obviously determined to settle the question of marriage once and for all. Her first few letters after her return on April 14, however, indicate that she was still somewhat uncertain about Chekhov's intentions. She had left, she wrote him, with a sour taste in her mouth, with an impression that the whole thing had still been left hanging in the air. Come to Moscow, she pleaded in forthright terms, and let us get married.

This time Chekhov definitely promised. He wrote to Olga that he would come to Moscow early in May, marry, and they would take a trip on the Volga and he would live the whole or the greater part of the winter with her in a flat in the city. "If only I keep well and don't get seedy," he added cautiously. "My cough takes away all my energy. I think apathetically of the future and write quite without zeal. You must think about the future, you manage for me and I'll do as you tell me, otherwise we shall never live, but go on sipping life a tablespoonful once an hour." (*April 22, 1901.*)

Olga was in no sense deterred by the state of his health, which in fact took a turn for the worse at this time. Her concerns were only that he would delay his coming or forget the necessary papers for marriage. On April 26 he repeated reassuringly, "Dog Olka! I'm coming early in May. . . . If you will give me your word that not a single soul in Moscow will know of our marriage until it is over, then I'll

[2] By the end of 1901, with the exception of *The Island of Sakhalin*, Chekhov saw the remainder of the ten volumes of this edition through the press.

marry you on the very day of my arrival if you like. For some reason I have a terrible dread of a wedding and congratulations and champagne which one has to hold in one's hand while smiling vaguely."

When Olga informed him that Vishnevsky had jestingly said he himself would soon be marrying her, Chekhov retorted with macabre humor: "Obviously he's counting on your soon becoming a widow, but tell him that to spite him I'm going to leave a will forbidding you to marry again." (*May 2, 1901.*) Three days before he left, Chekhov wrote to his good friend Koni, whose aid he was seeking to support Bunin's candidacy for the Pushkin Prize, and he closed his letter: "I'm sick and I've decided that I'll not soon get well. Nevertheless, on Tuesday I'm going to Moscow." (*May 6, 1901.*)

« 4 »

Having registered in the Dresden Hotel, Chekhov maintained a curious façade of intense activity and correspondence over the next two weeks which seemed designed to convince his family and Moscow friends that marriage had never entered his head. He busied himself arranging a meeting between Olga Vasilieva and Dr. Chlenov, on the project of a clinic for skin diseases; pushed the publication of Beschinsky's guide to the Crimea with Goltsev; concerned himself with a plan to secure a medical affidavit that would bring about Gorky's release from prison; saw the actress Olga Sadovskaya and promised to write a play for her benefit performance; and wrote letters to Iordanov on additions to the Taganrog museum. He also attended a rehearsal of Ibsen's *Wild Duck* and entertained the poets Balmont and Baltrushaitis.

Though Masha and Ivan were in Moscow then, Chekhov appears to have seen little of them and told them nothing of his plans. To his mother in Yalta he wrote simply that his health was all right, and enclosed instructions to Arseny about the garden. However, on May 17 he had his all-important physical check-up by the specialist Dr. V. A. Shchurovsky. Three days later Chekhov wrote Masha, who by then had gone to Yalta for the summer: "Well, at last I've been to Dr. Shchurovsky's. He found a deterioration in both the left and right lungs, in the right a large lump beneath the shoulder blade, and he ordered me to go immediately to Ufa Province for a kumiss[3] treatment, and if kumiss does not agree with me, then to Switzerland. To have to

---

[3] A fermented liquor made by the Tartars from mare's or camel's milk.

spend two months drinking kumiss is most tiresome and inconvenient. I really don't know what to do. To go there alone is dull, to live on kumiss is dull, but to take someone along for company would be egotistic and unpleasant. I would get married, but I don't have the necessary documents; they are all at Yalta in the desk."

This lighthearted, almost flippant, reference to marriage seems intentionally misleading, as well as the comment on the documents, a matter which had already been taken care of by Olga. Masha, no doubt, had her own premonitions, for, before she could receive this letter, she wrote him, on May 21, that it was wonderful in Yalta, the garden was splendid, the roses all in bloom, and the house clean, dry, and cool. And she added: "All day Mother and I wander around the whole house, and we both feel how empty it is without you, it seems as though it is not home. If you would only come back soon or at least write more often!"

According to an account by Stanislavsky, Chekhov requested Vishnevsky, in his name, to arrange a large dinner on May 25 for the relatives and close friends of Olga Knipper and himself. The guests all assembled and waited patiently for their host and hostess to appear. Meanwhile, in a Moscow church Chekhov and Olga were being married. The only people present were the four necessary witnesses — Olga's brother and uncle, and two university students. The bride and groom went directly to the home of Olga's mother to say their farewells and departed shortly thereafter for Ufa Province. Before he left Chekhov sent a telegram to Yalta: DEAR MAMA, YOUR BLESSINGS, I'M MARRIED. EVERYTHING WILL REMAIN AS BEFORE. I'M OFF TO TAKE A KUMISS TREATMENT. He also announced the marriage by telegram to Vishnevsky. The bewildered guests disbanded. Chekhov had had his way — a marriage minus congratulations and champagne.

After a day's visit at Nizhny Novgorod with Gorky, who was now only under house arrest, the couple continued the long journey on the Volga, the Kama, and the White River to the little station of Aksenovo in Ufa Province, where they took rooms in a sanatorium. Though a telegram from his mother, conveying her blessings, greeted Chekhov upon his arrival, he was disturbed not to hear anything from Masha. The next day he wrote her: "That I'm married, you already know.[4] I don't think the fact will in any way change my life or the conditions

[4] Masha, at Yalta, would have learned this fact from the telegram that Chekhov sent his mother on May 25.

under which I have lived up to now. Mother is no doubt saying God knows what, but tell her that there will be absolutely no changes, that everything will go on as before. I will live as I have hitherto, and Mother as well; my relations with you will remain as unalterably warm and good as they have always been." After a few comments about the kumiss treatment he had begun and arrangements for Masha to receive money if her funds were low, he rather gratuitously concluded: "At the end of July I'll be in Yalta, where I shall live until October, then in Moscow until December, and then back again to Yalta. That is, my wife and I will live apart — a situation, by the way, to which I'm already accustomed." (*June 2, 1901.*)

There is almost something naïve in Chekhov's insistence that his marriage would change nothing in the kind of life he had been living for so many years, a determination that could hardly have pleased his wife. But he anxiously wished to assure his sister that her lovely house of cards had not tumbled down. However, the next day he realized that it had already tumbled, when he received Masha's answer of May 24 — much delayed in reaching him because of his traveling — to his letter of May 20, in which he had lightly mentioned the possibility of his marrying. "Now let me express my opinion on the score of your marriage," she wrote with obvious feeling. "For me personally this course of action is shocking! And in your case these emotions are superfluous. If people love you, they will not abandon you, and there is no question of sacrifice on that side nor of egoism on yours, not in the slightest. How could that have entered your mind? What egoism?! You will always be able to get married. Pass that on to your Knipshits.[5] To begin with, you need to think about the state of your health. For God's sake don't imagine that selfishness directs me. For me you have always been the nearest and dearest person and your happiness is my only concern. I need nothing more than for you to be well and happy. In any case, act according to your own judgment, for perhaps I am showing partiality in this situation. And it is you who have taught me to be without prejudices!

"My God, how hard it will be to live without you for two whole months, even in Yalta! If you would only permit me to visit you while you are taking the kumiss treatment, even if it were only for a week. Write more often, please." And Masha appended an anxious

[5] Another of Chekhov's pet names for Olga Knipper.

postscript: "If you don't answer this letter right away, then I'll be ill. Greetings to 'her.'"

In short, Masha saw no reason why Olga should not remain her famous brother's mistress and be grateful for the privilege. Her reaction deeply troubled him and the emotional implications behind it even more so. On June 4 Chekhov answered her in a letter which Masha saw fit to conceal from the world after his death:[6] "Dear Masha, your letter, in which you advise me not to marry, reached me here yesterday from Moscow. I don't know whether or not I'm mistaken, but the principal reasons I married are: in the first place, I'm now more than forty years old; secondly, Olga's family is a good one; thirdly, if I have to part with her, I will part without any let or hindrance, just as if I had not married; she is an independent person and lives on her own means. So an important consideration is that this marriage has in no sense changed either my form of life or that of those who have lived and still live with me. Everything will positively remain as it was, and as formerly I will continue to live in Yalta alone." The rest of the letter seizes eagerly upon her request to join him, and after explaining the necessary travel and financial details, he slipped in a peacemaking comment: "When I told Knipshits that you were coming, she rejoiced." At the same time, in order to save Masha any further anxious waiting for his reply to her disturbed letter, he sent a telegram: I'M SENDING A LETTER IN WHICH I PROPOSE A TRIP TOGETHER ON THE VOLGA. WELL. YOU ARE AGITATED TO NO PURPOSE, ALL REMAINS AS OF OLD. GREETINGS TO MOTHER. WRITE.

These commonplace and pedantically itemized reasons for his marriage were in Chekhov's characteristic, half-humorous manner of deflecting queries that concerned his inner life. No doubt they were also calculated to lessen the tension in the family circle. But the tension had mounted higher. Conscience-stricken over her letter of May 24 once she had learned of his marriage, but still not having heard from

---

[6] It did not appear in her six-volume edition of Chekhov's letters, 1912–1916. In 1951, however, she turned the letter over to the Manuscript Division of the Lenin Library with the notation: "I request that it not be published." Accordingly, it was not included in *Polnoe sobranie sochinenii i pisem A. P. Chekhova* (*Complete Works and Letters of A. P. Chekhov*), 1944–1951. However, in 1954, when Masha published her own *Pisma k bratu A. P. Chekhova* (*Letters to Brother A. P. Chekhov*), she included her letter of May 24 and, in a note, part of Chekhov's answer of June 4. Hence, it was recently found possible to publish the whole of Chekov's letter for the first time in *Literaturnoe Nasledstvo* (*Literary Heritage*), Moscow, 1960, LXVIII, 236-237. Masha died in 1957.

him, Masha wrote on May 28: "I go about thinking, thinking without end. My thoughts crowd one another. How terrible I felt when I learned that you had suddenly married! Of course, I realized that sooner or later Olya would manage to get close to you, but the fact that you got married somehow at once disturbed my whole existence and compelled me to think about you and myself and about our future relations with Olya. And they suddenly change for the worse and how I fear this. I feel more alone than ever. Don't think there is malice in me or anything of that sort, no, I love you more than before, and with all my soul I desire every happiness for you, and for Olya also, although I don't know how she will regard us and I cannot now give an account of my own feeling toward her. I'm a little angry with her because she said absolutely nothing to me of a marriage, and it could hardly have happened impromptu. You realize Antosha that I'm very sad and low in spirits, I am good for nothing and everything sickens me. I want only to see you and no one else. . . ."

After receiving Chekhov's telegram and letter of June 4, Masha confined her reply of June 6 to grateful acknowledgments and to some comments on the furor his marriage had caused in the press. But she could not resist a spiteful dig at Olga over their pictures in the *Daily News:* "Which is the celebrated one, you or Knipshits? They portrayed her in her costume in *Uncle Vanya,* but you in your pince-nez."

Masha, however, had sense enough to reject her brother's strange request to come and join him and his bride on their honeymoon. But a letter from Olga, perhaps intended to be friendly, aroused her bitterness all over again. Masha wrote Chekhov on June 16: "Dear Antosha, Olya writes that you were very distressed by my letter. Forgive me for being unable to restrain my disturbed state of mind. I'm sure that you will understand and forgive me. This is the first time that I've indulged in such frankness and I regret that it has distressed you and Olya. If you had married someone other than Knipshits, then I would probably never have written you a thing, for I would have hated your wife. But the present situation is quite different: your wife was my friend to whom I had grown attached and we had experienced much together. That is why I was filled with various doubts and fears, perhaps exaggerated and to no purpose, but I sincerely wrote what I thought. Olya once told me how difficult it was for her to live through the marriage of her oldest brother, so it seems to me that she should all the more readily understand my situation and not scold me. In any case, it makes me unhappy to have distressed you and I'll never, never do it again. . . . So don't be angry with me and remember that I love you and Olya more than anything in the world."

Poor Masha! She had dedicated the best years of her life to Chekhov. Hardly any practical endeavor was undertaken without her assistance — the renting of apartments in Moscow and of summer houses in various places, the buying and selling of Melikhovo, the building of his house at Autka; and she had been his principal assistant in all his social endeavors and in his medical practice. The porridge wouldn't boil without her, he had rightly said. Even her own opportunities to marry she had probably sacrificed out of love for her brother. And would her best friend now take her place in this hallowed attachment which Masha had built up over the years? The anguish would not leave her. She poured it out to Bunin, the one writer among Chekhov's friends with whom she felt on intimate terms and now regarded as almost a member of the family: "I'm in a murderous mood and constantly feel the wretchedness of my existence. The reason for this partly is Brother's marriage. It happened so suddenly. . . . I've long been emotionally upset and keep asking myself: Why did Olechka have to allow a sick man to take such a beating, and even more so in Moscow? But it seems that the affair has ended all right. . . . I've begun to think about my own marriage, and so I ask you, Bukishonchik, find me a bridegroom, and may he be rich and generous! I've no desire to write but would talk with you with great satisfaction. Write me some more. I'm very broken up over Antosha and Olechka."

True, an intangible bond between brother and sister had been severed. Despite Chekhov's firm determination that nothing would change in their relations, the change had already begun, and both Masha and Olga were fully aware of it. Though they tried to avoid the inevitable offenses when the hostess of a household is displaced by another, the offenses multiplied whenever they and Chekhov occupied the same house together. This may have been in the back of Chekhov's mind in his odd assertion that he would continue to live apart from Olga as much as he did before their marriage. But Masha was wrong. In gaining a wife Chekhov had not lost a beloved sister. Never for a moment did their years together fail to invoke a warm glow of remembered associations or allow him to forget the gratitude that he owed Masha.

CHAPTER XXIV

"A Wife Who, Like the Moon, Will Not Appear in My Sky Every Day"

THE KUMISS TREATMENT added weight to Chekhov's thin body but boredom to his soul. How he loathed this business of doctoring himself! Though the sanatorium was situated in a lovely oak forest, its accommodations were primitive in the extreme. He liked the wild flowers in the steppes and the sound of snorting from the large droves of horses, but the Bashkirs and local inhabitants in general were inexpressibly dull and he thirsted for books and newspapers — the only newspapers he could find were a year old. He went fishing with Olga, who chattered and laughed merrily on her honeymoon. But nothing compensated for the lack of gay, sophisticated friends who now had become a necessity when he was unable to work. The quips in letters from Aksenovo are the humor of discontent: "Well, sir, I suddenly up and got married," he wrote to Sobolevsky. "I've already grown accustomed, or almost so, to my new state, that is, to the deprivation of certain rights and privileges, and I feel fine. My wife is a very decent person, not at all stupid, and a good soul." (*June 9, 1901.*) After informing Koni that Dr. Shchurovsky had discovered a definite worsening in his condition, Chekhov continued: "This disturbed me a bit and I hastened to get married and go off for a kumiss cure. Now I'm fine, have added eight pounds, only I don't know from what — the kumiss or marriage." (*June 12, 1901.*) However, he did know that he had had enough of the cure — after one month, instead of the two that had been prescribed, and he and Olga set off for Yalta.

For the first time Olga took her place in the Chekhov household as his wife. A stream of Yalta friends called to greet the newly married couple and Bunin came from Odessa to see them. Though Olga tried to avoid interfering in the household chain of command, she naturally insisted upon assuming the sole care of her husband. With some reason, she believed that he had been spoiled by doting females who catered to his fixed bachelor habits, and, with the efficiency and practicality of her German background, she tried to introduce order into his daily existence. He must change his tie frequently, have his clothes and shoes brushed regularly, wash his head and have his hair cut and his beard trimmed more often.

Olga was particularly concerned about his health. Shortly after his return from the kumiss treatment, Chekhov began to feel unwell again and to cough up blood. One of the factors contributing to his steady decline, as Dr. Altschuler recognized, was Chekhov's insistence on travel and his refusal to subject himself to a strict regimen of continued and quiet living at Yalta. When the doctor had explained the seriousness of his condition to Masha, she had expressed her willingness to give up teaching at Moscow, live permanently at Yalta, and nurse her brother. Even if he had been willing to accept this sacrifice, which might well have prolonged his life, his marriage and the fact that his wife spent most of her year in Moscow made it impossible. Olga concentrated on his frequent complaints of stomach trouble and ordered a changed diet and prescribed purgatives. She could not know that the tubercular bacilli had already invaded his intestines, a fact, which, if guessed by Chekhov, he failed to reveal even to his doctors. Olga surrounded him with care that summer, urged him to go on with his writing, and was very helpful, as he told Gorky, in assisting him in the endless job of proofreading.

Though Olga tried to be considerate to Chekhov's mother, and had quickly re-established her old friendship with Masha, her efforts to "dress him up" and to order special dishes for him, as well as her prescribing of medical nostrums, caused friction in the household. Masha and her mother, who had devotedly looked out for his every want for years, resented her interference. Exasperated, Olga confided to Chekhov that she would like to carry him off and keep him all for herself. Patiently he explained to her that his mother and the old servant Marfusha were anxious to do all they could, but that one was seventy and the other eighty and they could not be expected to understand about newfangled diets. When Olga wrote him of her jealousy of his mother and sister, shortly after she left for Moscow, he kindly assured her that her jealousy was not without grounds but it did not suit her character. Then he added: "You write that Masha will never get used to you, and so forth and so forth. What nonsense this all is! You exaggerate it all, think of silly things, and I'm afraid that before we know it you will be quarreling with Masha. Let me say this: Have patience and keep silent for only one year, then everything will become clear to you. No matter what they say to you, whatever you imagine, remain silent. For all newly married wives and husbands, all the pleasant things of life depend upon this nonresistance in the early days. Do as I say, darling, be a clever girl!" (*September 3, 1901.*)

Certainly Chekhov left Olga under no illusions about the permanence of his affection for Masha and the extent of his gratitude to her. For that summer he gave his wife a letter addressed to Masha, to be turned over to her at the time of his death. It was his will. "Dear Masha," he wrote, "I bequeath to you my Yalta house for possession during your lifetime, and the money and income from my dramatic productions; and to my wife Olga Leonardovna my *dacha* at Gurzuf and five thousand roubles. If you wish, you may sell the real estate. Give brother Alexander three thousand and Ivan five thousand, and Mikhail three thousand. To Alexei Dolzhenko[1] one thousand, and one thousand roubles to Elena Chekhova (Lyolya)[2] upon her marriage. After your death and the death of Mother, all that remains, except for the income from the plays, is to go to the Taganrog city administration for public education, and the income from the plays to brother Ivan; but after his, Ivan's death, to the Taganrog city administration for public education. I promised the peasants of Melikhovo village one hundred roubles to pay for the highway; I also promised Gavrila Alexeevich Kharchenko[3] (his home is in Kharkov, Moskalevka Street) to pay for his older daughter's school education if she is not released from tuition payments. Help the poor. Take care of Mother. Live peacefully." (*August 3, 1901.*)

By this will Masha was to receive by far the lion's share of his estate, although he probably took into consideration his wife's income from her acting. Nothing was left to his mother because he could be certain that Masha would take care of her, as well as fulfill the several promises of donations he mentions in his will.

Chekhov's letters to Olga after the first separation from his wife — she left for rehearsals at Moscow on August 20 — are filled with details of the local callers who annoyed him and the outside visitors whose company he enjoyed: the amusing Bunin, the clever newspaper writer V. M. Doroshevich whom he so much admired, the psychiatrist N. N. Reformatsky, and the wandering, loose-living actor P. N. Orlenev

---

[1] His cousin, son of his aunt, Fedosiya.

[2] Another cousin, daughter of his favorite uncle, Mitrofan.

[3] The former apprentice in the grocery store of Chekhov's father.

whose anecdotes on theatrical life delighted him. Orlenev assisted Chekhov in organizing a theatrical performance to aid the consumptives of Yalta, but he also shamelessly used his acquaintance to introduce his cronies to him, one of whom sought his influence in securing the admission of a Jewish youngster to the local school.[4]

With almost comic iteration, in the light of his recently forsaken bachelor existence, Chekhov dutifully itemizes his performance, or lack of it, of the commands Olga had left behind concerning scrubbing his teeth, bathing, changes of linen, keeping his clothes in order, and taking laxatives. He rarely mentioned financial matters to her, in which she was much more practical than he was — Masha bore the brunt of his concerns in this respect — but on August 23 he asked her to take care of the transfer of eight hundred roubles to his cousin, Alexei Dolzhenko, who worked in Moscow. It was obviously a loan, one of the many which he never expected to be paid back. Hence Olga must have been surprised to receive an outburst from him very shortly thereafter: "It is entirely incomprehensible how my money disappears daily, incomprehensible! I must get away from here, my darling. Yesterday one person got a hundred roubles, today another came to say good-by and took ten from me. I gave a hundred to still a third, promised a hundred to another and fifty to someone else, and all this must be handed over when the bank opens tomorrow." (*September 9, 1901.*) Despite his need, Chekhov rejected the proposal of Gorky, who only recently had learned of the disadvantageous terms of Marx's contract, to obtain funds to buy out the publisher's rights and to accept Chekhov in his own firm, Znanie, which would guarantee him a much larger income from the publication of his works. He had neither desire nor energy nor faith to undertake this business, Chekhov wrote Gorky. Besides, Marx was ill, he said, and even if he were well, to break his contract with this man would reflect badly on the publisher's business.

Aware of the monotony of the contents of his letters, Chekhov once asked Olga to forgive her "old husband" for writing so often about castor oil. The sameness was not entirely caused by the fact that they exchanged letters at the rate of one a day or every other day. Olga's letters, though limited largely to her Moscow social and theatrical world, are often lively and highly informative. But he seems to have erected a barrier between them on the higher things of the mind and

---

[4] In Tsarist times only a small percentage of the Jews in a given community were allowed to attend the local schools.

spirit which were part of his world, and he rarely vaulted it in his letters to his wife, a fact which the intelligent Olga sensed and resented. The lack is all the more surprising in the light of the intellectual brilliance and literary charm of so much of Chekhov's epistolary prose.

There was nothing lacking, however, in Chekhov's expression of love and tenderness for Olga in his letters. He had grown used to her like a little child and felt cold and comfortless without her, he wrote after her departure, and he had ordered her easy chair brought into his room. It was horribly dull sleeping alone, he assured her, and he was turning into a regular bourgeois husband who could not live without his wife. An almost feminine softness and submissiveness characterize his devotion which he playfully conceals by a pretense of severity. When she proposes to take in a cat in her new apartment, he protests, for he cannot abide cats. He suggests a dog instead — and then adds: "However, my love, you know best, keep a crocodile if you like; I permit everything and give you my leave and am ready to sleep even with a cat." (*August 30, 1901.*) In procuring the new passport of a married couple for her, he wrote: "At first I wanted to describe you as the wife of an 'honorary academician,' but then I decided that it was much more agreeable to be the wife of a doctor. . . . Write every day or I'll take away the passport. On the whole, I'm going to keep a stern hand over you in order to make you fear and obey me. I'll give it to you!" (*September 4, 1901.*)

So lonely was her "severe husband" without her that after a separation of only three weeks Chekhov abandoned the salutary Yalta climate in the fall and set off to join Olga in cold, blustery Moscow.

« 2 »

In Moscow Olga and Masha had taken a large apartment together. It was a money-saving device and would also provide a study for Chekhov on his visits. Olga had worked hard to have it all renovated, clean, and furnished by the time of his arrival. Masha, thinking of their new Yalta house, was displeased with this old building, but Chekhov informed his mother at once that the apartment was fine and had a room available for her — he now wrote her frequently when away, for he did not want her to feel deserted because of his marriage.

An event Chekhov had eagerly anticipated in the city was his first view of a performance of *The Three Sisters* by the Moscow Art Theater. Reviews and reports the previous season had left him dissatisfied and now he made a point of attending rehearsals and offering a number of observations on the staging. V. V. Luzhsky's acting as Andrei displeased him and he spent considerable time with him on the interpretation of the role. The portrait on the wall of General Prozorov, father of the three sisters, he banished because it resembled a Japanese general. Chekhov also thought that the cooing of doves as the curtain went up, simulated by a group of actors under the direction of Stanislavsky, was simply inane. "Listen," he declared to Luzhsky, "you coo marvelously, only it is like an Egyptian dove!" And somewhat to Stanislavsky's annoyance, Chekhov insisted upon staging the fire scene in the third act.

Stanislavsky indicated in his recollections that Chekhov's efforts on this occasion to usurp the prerogatives of the director adversely affected the September 21 opening performance of *The Three Sisters* in the 1901 season. The reviews, however, give quite the contrary impression. The *Daily News*, in describing the success of the performance, stressed the "whole series of rapturous ovations" tendered the author and the veritable demonstration by the audience when Chekhov appeared alone on the stage at the end of the play. And the critic of *Russian Word* wrote: "The presence of the author obviously electrified the actors and the play went off better than ever. Something in the performance had changed, and one might agree that this was because of the direction given to it by the author. It was especially noticeable in the role of Andrei, acted by Mr. Luzhsky."

There can be no question that this performance delighted Chekhov. For he wrote Sredin in Yalta: "*The Wild Duck* did not do well on the stage of the Art Theater. It was sluggish, uninteresting, and weak. However, *The Three Sisters* went magnificently, with brilliance, a great deal better than I have written the play. I did a bit of staging, made some author's suggestions, and they say that the play goes off better than it did last season." (*September 24, 1901.*)

Here Chekhov's statement that the performance had improved upon the quality of his play was not only his modesty but also indicated some measure of his esteem for the unusual abilities of the Art Theater. Stanislavsky tells in a letter of how Chekhov at this time attended a rehearsal of Hauptmann's *Michael Kramer* and "danced about and leaped with joy" over the performance of the second act. Chekhov's criticism of the theater during the first years of their association centered mostly in Stanislavsky's inability at times to perceive the artistic focus of his plays and in some of the director's more extreme devices in staging. A failure of communication existed between the two men, and

Stanislavsky frankly admits that it was largely his fault. Blind to the essential simplicity of Chekhov's nature, Stanislavsky could not behave in a simple way in his presence. He always felt that before him stood a celebrity and hence he tried to seem cleverer than he was. This unnaturalness served to restrain Chekhov in his relations and no doubt contributed to the difficulties that later arose between the two men.

Chekhov had to share Olga with the theater during the height of its season. The directors were perfectionists and demanded a great deal from their actors. Rehearsals could last for six hours, and sometimes Olga did not get back to the new apartment till one in the morning. Then there were the performances. Her devotion to her work never flagged, for she was determined to become, and eventually did become, the first actress of the Moscow Art Theater. But Olga seemed to have inexhaustible energy, loved late parties, sang well, played the piano, and handled fluently several foreign languages. Though she had few free hours, their life together seems to have been a full and intense one during his stay. She passionately loved her "Russian Maupassant," her "great talent," as she called him, and he endeavored to return her love to the extent that his frail health permitted. His delicacy, refinement of feelings, and tender human qualities delighted Olga, although she imperfectly understood the emotional wellsprings that fed these qualities.

While she rehearsed, Chekhov renewed his contacts with Moscow friends, worked away at proofs, and answered correspondence. He read the first three acts of Gorky's manuscript play, *The Petty Bourgeois*, and wrote him a perfectly balanced critique of its virtues and failings — he had been pushing Gorky hard to offer a play to the Art Theater. Chekhov had also planned to go to Petersburg for a few days to see his brothers Alexander and Misha. However, Alexander happened to come to Moscow in the middle of October and his warning about the unpleasant Petersburg weather convinced Chekhov that he should give up the projected trip. His appearance dismayed Alexander (who had not seen him for some time, and he wrote Misha: "I was with Anton in Moscow. He looks badly."

Indeed, the Moscow pace wore Chekhov down very quickly. On October 23 he felt unwell enough to visit Dr. Shchurovsky. The advice apparently was to return to Yalta and he left Moscow three days later. Shortly before departing, however, he wrote Mirolyubov, for whose magazine he had long since promised his story, *The Bishop*: "Now I'm going home. I shall start again at the beginning and will send it to you, so don't worry! . . . My wife, to whom I've become accustomed, and very attached, remains alone in Moscow, and I am going away a lonely person. She weeps, but I will not ask her to give up the theater. In short, it is a muddle." (*October 19, 1901.*)

« 3 »

Though Chekhov wrote Olga, after the first rush of callers upon his return to Yalta, that he had dropped back up to his ears in the old rut which was so empty and boring, actually he took much pleasure in some of the visitors. He was happy to renew his acquaintance with the poet Konstantin Balmont, who was then attracting notice, and he wrote appreciatively of him to Olga. That winter he also met for the first time Leonid Andreev, whose widely acclaimed early tales had already begun to excite Olga. "Yes, he is a good writer," Chekhov replied to her request for a reaction, "and if he would only write more, he would be more popular. There is a lack of sincerity in him and little simplicity, and hence it is hard to get used to him. Sooner or later, however, the public will become accustomed to him and he will make a great name." (*December 7, 1901.*) Chekhov urged Balmont and Andreev, along with Teleshov and Fyodorov, to write plays for the Art Theater, and he jokingly added, in reporting the effort to Olga, that he ought to be paid a commission of at least one rouble per man.

The news that Gorky intended to settle in the area for some time excited Chekhov. Still under police surveillance after his release from imprisonment, Gorky, forbidden to go to Moscow or Petersburg, was allowed to live in the Crimea because of his health, but not in Yalta. Nevertheless, he stayed with Chekhov for about a week when he arrived on November 12, a permissible circumvention of the restrictions — he could stop at a private house as a visitor but no hotel could have registered him. A policeman stood on guard outside, and if Gorky left the house the captain in the local station would telephone Chekhov to learn of the suspect's whereabouts. Chekhov detested these prohibitions and spying, which had increased during this year of political tensions. Later that winter he criticized his good friend Mirolyubov in Petersburg for joining the recently formed Religious-Philosophical Society which was supported by reactionary clergy, "that policeman

Rozanov,"[5] and the "hyper-satisfied Merezhkovsky."[6] He would like to write him at great length on the subject of the Society, Chekhov told Mirolyubov, "but I had better restrain myself, all the more so since letters nowadays are read chiefly by those to whom they are not addressed. I'll only mention that in the problems which concern you, the important things are not the forgotten words, not the idealism, but the consciousness of your own decency. . . . One should believe in God, but if one does not have faith, then its place should not be taken by any hue and cry, but by seeking, seeking, and seeking, alone and face to face with one's conscience." (*December 17, 1901.*)

Chekhov and Gorky got to know each other still better on this visit and their friendship deepened. The same nice fellow, Chekhov described him to Olga, and a very simple-hearted man — if only he did not wear those peasant blouses which he affected. And during this stay in Chekhov's home, with visitors constantly coming and going, Gorky accumulated much of the material that he made such effective use of in his reminiscences of Chekhov. He observed that in Chekhov's presence everyone involuntarily felt in himself a desire to be simpler, more truthful. Gorky remembered the three well-dressed ladies who called and desperately struggled through a halting conversation which they had initiated on war and the Turks and the Greeks, until Chekhov could turn them to a discussion on candied fruits, where the talk went so much more happily and smoothly. Everyone, he told Gorky, when the ladies had left, should speak his own language. Again there was the case of the young, pompous crown prosecutor whose conversation Gorky also overheard. As he rattled on indefatigably about his fierce zeal in protecting the state's property against criminals, Chekhov suddenly broke in to ask if he liked gramophones. Of course, he did, an amazing invention, declared the young man. But Chekhov declared that he loathed the gramophone because it spoke and sang without feeling. However, the young zealot of the law missed the point, and when he departed Chekhov remarked to Gorky that the crown prosecutor, so thoughtlessly disposing of the fate of people, was like a pimple on the seat of justice.

During these early winter months Chekhov alone, or sometimes

5 V. V. Rozanov's connection with *New Times* aroused Chekhov's animosity.

6 Chekhov's disapproval of Merezhkovsky's views and the political company he kept did not prevent him that year from recommending this distinguished poet and critic for election to the Academy of Sciences.

accompanied by Gorky, paid several visits to the seventy-three-year-old Tolstoy. His doctors had ordered him to South Russia, where he occupied the estate of Countess S. V. Panina at Gaspra, only some seven miles from Yalta. In fact, when Gorky left Chekhov's house, he rented a *dacha* for himself and family at Oleiz, which was only a long walk from Gaspra. Chekhov would collect Gorky on the way and they would proceed to Gaspra to attend the "court" of the ailing Tolstoy, perhaps the most celebrated man in the world at that time.

Tolstoy seemed to be pleased with his coming, Chekhov wrote Olga of one of his visits, was friendly and kind, listened with pleasure, and conversed readily. With Gorky there, the three foremost Russian men of letters at that time had come together. Tolstoy matched Chekhov's reverence for him with a profound admiration for the personality and art of this man who was more than thirty years his junior. "He loved Chekhov," Gorky noted in his reminiscences, "and always when he looked at him his eyes, tender at that moment, seemed to caress Chekhov's face. Once, when Chekhov was walking along a garden path with Alexandra Lvovna,[7] Tolstoy, still ill at the time, was sitting in an armchair on the terrace, and he seemed to stretch toward them, saying in a whisper: 'Ah, what a dear, beautiful man; he is modest and quiet, just like a girl! And he walks like a girl. He's simply wonderful!' " However, Tolstoy suspected him of being an atheist, a fault that he commented on unfavorably to his disciple Chertkov.

Perhaps amused by Chekhov's shyness in a discussion about women, Tolstoy confronted him with a question, phrased in the coarse peasant language which he sometimes used on his guests: "Did you whore a great deal in your youth?" And while Chekhov tugged at his beard and mumbled something inaudible, Tolstoy went on to tell how indefatigable he had been in that pursuit as a young man.

But mostly their discussions on these visits were about literature. It delighted Chekhov to hear Tolstoy rail against contemporary writers, and especially the Russian ones. He regarded them all as children, Chekhov told Bunin, and their works as child's play. "But Shakespeare is another matter," Chekhov perceptively observed. "He was an adult, exasperating him because he didn't write à la Tolstoy." The trouble with modern writers, Tolstoy complained, was that they were not at all Russian in their thought and wrote in a language incomprehensible

[7] Tolstoy's youngest daughter.

to him. "Now you," he said, turning to Chekhov, "you are Russian. Yes, very, very Russian."

One day, Gorky recalls, the company listened as Tolstoy spoke with rapture about *The Darling*. " 'It is like lace,' he said, 'made by a chaste young girl; there were such lacemakers in olden times who used to depict all their lives, all their dreams of happiness in the pattern. They dreamed in designs of all that was dear to them, wove all their pure, uncertain love into their lace.' Tolstoy spoke with emotion, with tears in his eyes. That day Chekhov was running a temperature, and he sat there with a deep flush on his cheeks, his head bowed, carefully wiping his spectacles. For a long time he remained silent, and then, sighing deeply, he said in a low, bashful voice: 'There are many misprints in it . . .' "

Bunin insists that a hemorrhage suffered by Chekhov late that winter was due in part to the agitation caused by the sudden news of the serious illness of Tolstoy who had come to Yalta to visit his daughter.

« 4 »

Chekhov's marriage affected Lika and Lidiya Avilova in different ways. Masha occasionally saw Lika in Moscow and the reports she sent to Chekhov suggest that her old friend was now neither happy nor above reproach. She had failed as an opera singer, abandoned her idea of opening a millinery shop, and lasted only one season as a worker in the Art Theater. Several months after Chekhov's marriage, Masha wrote him a note upon arriving in Moscow from her vacation at Yalta. "I had to spend the night with the Knippers," she informed him. "My apartment was occupied and smelled to heaven of tobacco smoke and liquor. I pity Lika."

Later that year, in December, Lika was at a rousing party of the Art Theater troupe which was celebrating the première of Nemirovich-Danchenko's *In Dreams*. Olga, in describing the affair to Chekhov, interpolated: "Lika was drunk and constantly pestered me to drink *Brüderschaft*, but I wiggled out of it for I don't like this sort of thing. I don't know her, find her utterly strange, and feel no particular attraction to her." Chekhov, however, understood the inebriated Lika's misplaced gesture toward his wife. The next year, when Olga announced to him, with something of a snicker, that Lika was marrying A. A. Sanin, then an assistant director of the Moscow Art Theater, Chekhov replied: "I've known Lika a long time, and whatever may have happened, she is a good girl, clever and decent. She'll not get along with Sanin, will not love him . . . probably within a year she'll have a bouncing baby, and in a year and a half she'll begin to be unfaithful to her husband. Well, it is all a question of fate." (*March 12, 1902.*)[8] Perhaps at that moment he recalled the inscription on Lika's photograph which she had sent to him several years before: "To dear Anton Pavlovich, a grateful token of remembrances of precious relations. Lika." And she quoted several lines from the popular contemporary poet, A. N. Apukhtin:

> Whether my days be bright or sad,
> Whether I vanish soon, my life spent,
> One thing I know — to the very end
> My thoughts, feelings, songs, and efforts —
> All are for thee!

And she added: "If this inscription compromises you, I'll be glad. . . . I could have written it eight years ago, but I write it now, and I'll write it ten years hence." No, his beautiful Lika would never forget him.

Some two months before Chekhov's marriage, when Olga was in Petersburg with the Art Theater, she received a note from Lidiya Avilova, who asked to see her.[9] The meeting never took place, for Olga, assuming that her correspondent, like so many others, merely wanted free tickets for *The Three Sisters*, answered with a polite note of regrets. However, Olga mentioned the matter to Chekhov, for she guessed that he must know the lady. Shortly after, on March 16, he jokingly queried: "Are you seeing Avilova? . . . No doubt you have already begun writing tales and novels on the sly. If I find out that you have, then good-by, I shall get a divorce." The tone of the query suggests the unimportance which he had always attached to Avilova's baffling pursuit of him, an incident in his life about which he had apparently said

---

[8] During that summer Lika with her husband visited Yalta when Chekhov was away. Masha saw much of them and, contrary to her brother's prognostication, found them a rather congenial married couple.

[9] Though neither here nor elsewhere does Olga give any indication of having previously known her, Avilova, in her memoirs, claims that as young girls in Moscow they acted together in amateur theatricals. Avilova writes that Olga was "an inconspicuous, shy, silent young girl." On the other hand, the director predicted that Avilova, according to her account, would have a great career as an actress if she went on the stage. This passage appears only in the 1960 edition of Avilova's "A. P. Chekhov in My Life" in *A. P. Chekhov v vospominaniyakh sovremennikov* (*A. P. Chekhov in the Remembrances of Contemporaries*), Moscow, 1960, p. 229.

nothing to Olga. It is a curious coincidence that when the writer Lazarevsky asked him that winter if he read the works of contemporary authoresses, he replied: "No, indeed, and I prefer to read something on physics or electrical engineering rather than female writing."

When Lidiya Avilova's sister in Petersburg suddenly announced to her one day that Chekhov had married, she "felt terribly limp," she writes in her memoirs, "cold perspiration appeared on my brow, and I dropped into the first chair." The sister chattered on, retailing the current gossip. Everybody thought it was a strange marriage, having nothing to do with either love or passion. "No, this is not a marriage," the sister declared. "It is some kind of incomprehensible escapade. Do you really think that Knipper was swept off her feet by him? It was calculation on her side. And do you think he does not understand this?" Avilova replied: "Well, so what then? Often calculations turn out successfully. On the whole, it is very fine that he married. I'm sorry that it was so late."

Shortly after, returning from a meeting of writers, Avilova talked with an author who had just been in Moscow. She could not remember his name but she had no difficulty recalling his words. He had seen Chekhov, who had spoken to him about her: "He even said that he knows you well. And for years. He asked about you. And he left me with the impression that he very . . . well, he referred to you very warmly." Yes, he replied to her query, he had seen Knipper, and Avilova quotes him as describing her in terms that involved those unpleasant innuendoes sometimes reserved for actresses: "In everything, you know, that special stamp. She strikes one strangely alongside of Anton Pavlovich. He is almost an old man, hollow-cheeked, an invalid. Hardly suitable for a young wife. Wherever she goes, Nemirovich traipses after her." Apparently feeling that she has made her point, Avilova, after several pages of such gossip, piously draws the curtain on it with the comment: "Afraid of gossip, I quickly turned the conversation on to another theme."

After some debate with herself, Avilova finally decided that she must congratulate Chekhov on his marriage, and she did it in a manner quite in keeping with her romanticized version of their relationship.[10] Still convinced that Chekhov's story *About Love* was inspired by their rela-

[10] This final chapter of Avilova's memoirs, "A. P. Chekhov in My Life," appears only in the 4th edition of *A. P. Chekhov v vospominaniyakh sovremennikov* (*A. P. Chekhov in the Remembrances of Contemporaries*), Moscow, 1960, pp. 287-293. See also herein, Chapter XI, Section 6, text and notes 6 and 10.

tions, she represents Anna Alekseevna Luganovich in the tale as writing a letter to her lover, P. K. Alekhin, to congratulate him on his marriage. She describes the device: "I wrote a note [to Chekhov], in which I conveyed the request of our mutual acquaintance, A. A. Luganovich, to send her letter to P. K. Alekhin, whose address was certainly known to Anton Pavlovich. I placed Luganovich's letter in a separate envelope. Luganovich wrote Alekhin that she had learned of his marriage, and warmly, from the bottom of her heart, wished him happiness. She wrote that she herself was calm, and although she recalled him often, she recalled him with love and not with grief, for there was much joy and satisfaction in her life. She was happy and would very much like to know if he also was happy. Then she thanked him for everything he had given her. 'Was our love a real love? But whatever it was, real or imaginary, how grateful I am to you for it! It suffused my whole youth with sparkling, fragrant dew. If I were able to pray, I would pray for you. I would pray thus: Lord, let him understand how good, lofty, necessary, and beloved he is. If he understands, then he will not fail to be happy.' "

Nearly anyone who has faithfully followed the long trail of make-believe in this strange affair will probably opt for the "imaginary" love in the easy choice which Lidiya Avilova, alias Anna Alekseevna Luganovich, offers to her readers at the end: ". . . whatever it was, real or imaginary . . ."

According to Avilova, Chekhov replied to Luganovich's letter, signing it "Alekhin":

"I bow low, low, and thank you for your letter. You wish to know if I'm happy? To begin with, I'm ill. And now I know that I'm very ill. There you have it. Judge as you wish. I repeat, I'm very grateful for the letter. Very.

"You write of fragrant dew, but let me say that it is fragrant and sparkling only on fragrant, beautiful flowers.

"I always desired your happiness, and if I could do anything for it, I would do it with joy. However, I cannot.

"But what, indeed, is happiness? Who knows? At least, recalling my own life, I'm now vividly aware that I was happy during those moments when it seemed to me I was most unhappy. In my youth I was joyous — but that is something else again."[11]

---

[11] When Avilova turned over copies of Chekhov's letters to his sister for her edition, this letter seems to have been one she held back, apparently because she

A suitable epitaph to this whole confused and confusing episode was provided by Chekhov's sister in the last recollections of her brother to come from her pen. A few days after Chekhov's death, Lidiya Avilova wrote Masha her condolences, mentioned that she had many letters of his, and asked to be allowed to call her "Beloved sister." However, she did say frankly in this letter: "I do not at all wish to insinuate that I knew him well, that I was for him anything special. . . . But I don't know how he referred to me. This to me is very sad." Masha, in printing this letter, merely remarks that one part of *A. P. Chekhov in My Life* contains many facts, but that the other part is sheer fantasy. "Out of this latter part of the memoirs," Masha writes, "comes the notion that Anton Pavlovich loved her, that their relations stood on the edge of a romance, and that he himself spoke to her about this. There was nothing to it."[12]

« 5 »

It may be remembered that Chekhov, on the eve of his return to Yalta in October, had written Mirolyubov to say that his wife wept and the situation was a muddle. The situation was indeed a muddle. While every thought and desire expressed the yearning of the recently married couple to be together, health condemned Chekhov to remain in Yalta until the spring, and Olga's career tied her to Moscow. He had hardly arrived home when he wrote: "My sweet, angel, my dog, darling, I beg you to believe that I love you, deeply love you; don't forget me, write and think about me more often. . . . I kiss you hard, hard, embrace you and kiss you again. My bed seems so lonely, as though I were a miserly bachelor, ill-natured and old." (*October 29, 1901.*)[13] He had become so used to her care, he wrote the next day, that he now felt that he was on a desert island in Yalta. It was as though he had been married twenty years and that this was the first year they had ever been

---

thought it too intimate for publication, although it is not any more intimate than others he wrote to her. Since she asserted that the originals of all his letters to her were later stolen, she obviously had to reproduce the contents of this one from memory. It is impossible to date the letter precisely.

[12] M. P. Chekhova, *Iz dalyokovo proshlovo* (*From the Distant Past*), Moscow, 1960, pp. 167-68.

[13] The last sentence is omitted in the Soviet edition of his complete works and letters. The omitted sentence is to be found in *Perepiska A. P. Chekhova i O. L. Knipper* (*Correspondence of A. P. Chekhov and O. L. Knipper*), ed. A. B. Derman, Moscow, 1934, II, 19. It should perhaps be added that similar intimate expressions have also been deleted from this collection.

separated. "I passionately want to see my wife," he wrote Olga on November 15, "and I miss her and Moscow, but there is no help for it." And two weeks later he told her: "What pleasure it would give me now to talk with my wife, to touch her brow and shoulder, to laugh with her. Ah, darling, darling."

If anything the separation and ache of unfulfilled desires tormented the younger and healthier Olga more than they did her husband. She could not get herself to make up the bed after his departure, she told him, for then it was easier to imagine her and him together in it. "I kiss you, my Antonka. I kiss you lovingly, softly, tenderly. . . . How I want to snuggle up to you." Two days later she wrote: "Weary, I've not wanted to get up in the mornings. Every time I turn around I want to see your dear blond-bearded face, but with sadness I see only the undisturbed part of the bed. I recall how it used to be — wonderful, warm . . ." She asked him if he caressed her in his thoughts, and she longed to have him beside her, fondling her, and calling her his dog. The image still persisted a month later when she wrote: "I terribly love to remember you as you sat on the bed in the morning after you'd washed, without your jacket, and with your back to me. You see what sinful thoughts I have, and there are still much more sinful ones about which I'll be silent. Forgive your wife for her wickedness."

He was glad that she was well and in good spirits, Chekhov told her in one letter, for it made his heart lighter. "And I have a terrible desire now that you should give birth to a little half-German who would amuse you and make your life fuller. You ought to, my darling! What do you think?" (*November 2, 1901.*) And when she informed him that her old nurse had asked for the job of taking care of her children, he replied that he favored it. "It seems to me that you would be very fond of a little half-German and would perhaps love him more than anything in the world, and that is just what is needed." (*November 22, 1901.*)

But she had to report to him, at the end of almost six months of marriage, "Once again, Anton, we shall not have a little half-German. I'm sorry. Yet why do you think this little half-German will make my life more full? Truly, do you not make it full enough for me?"

They tried to assuage mutual discontent by recounting the cheerful trivialities of their life apart from each other. Chekhov urged her to be merry, for when she was depressed, he said, she became old and faded, and when gay, she was an angel. And she regaled him with accounts of the politics of the Art Theater, rehearsals, performances, her great success in Nemirovich-Danchenko's play *In Dreams,* the many callers at her apartment, including Kuprin and Bunin, and the merry parties she and the actors had which sometimes lasted till the reviews appeared in the morning. In the gloom and sadness of his "exile," he told her that he loved such parties: "You write that on the evening of December eighth you were half drunk. Ah, darling, how I envy you, if you only knew! I envy your spirit, freshness, your health, temperament, I envy you because no hindrances such as hemorrhages and so forth prevent you from drinking. In the old days I could drink, as they say, with the best." (*December 13, 1901.*) Then, suddenly ashamed of the contrast she had forced between their respective capacities for pleasure, she dismissed these gay gatherings as sheer "madness." And by way of compensation she reminded him that he was a famous author whose very next work she anticipated with awe and trembling. "Do you know," she wrote: "that every time I go or drive past Opitts,[14] I always look at your portrait, and I smile and say to myself, 'Hello, Anton,' and I'm happy that you look at me. Am I a silly?"

At times in her letters Olga drifts into what she calls "philosophizing," passages in which she deprecates her lack of culture, her failure to read enough, or she complains of her loss of faith in herself and of her inadequacy as an actress. They seemed designed, in part, to provoke an outpouring of profound thoughts and weighty moral aphorisms which Olga apparently imagined were constantly at the beck and call of a great writer. Her husband, however, rarely reacted, perhaps because he felt that these attempts were not entirely sincere, and this failure annoyed her. Crossly she arraigned him: "You never want to tell me anything and you write as though from habit. Only *you* interest me. I wish to know your soul, all your spiritual world, what is being created there — or is this said too boldly and is entrance there forbidden?" And she accused him of being distant with her. His only reply to this sort of approach was: "You ask why I keep you at a distance from me. How silly, child!" (*December 12, 1901.*)

However, the question "When shall we get together?" appeared with agonizing iteration in their daily correspondence. Early in November Chekhov began planning to return to Moscow in January instead of in spring. He tried to justify the move by his work. "I'm writing, working," he told Olga, "but, my darling, I cannot work in Yalta, I can't, just can't. It is far from the world, uninteresting, and above all it is

[14] The owner of a photographer's shop on Petrovka Street in Moscow.

cold." (*November 17, 1901.*) She eagerly encouraged the plan if it only did not harm his health. How could she get through the winter without him? she asked. Besides, the new apartment she and Masha had taken — they had moved again — was warm. He could remain indoors and work in the study she had fixed up for him. Though he tried to find doctors who would support the idea, he had to admit finally that they firmly discouraged it.

Then Olga excitedly proposed that she come to Yalta for Christmas. For days they lived on this hope. It would be a heaven-sent blessing for him, he declared. "Do me this favor, my darling, I entreat you!" He even threatened to break with the Art Theater if the directors did not give her permission. But permission was not granted, she had sadly to inform him. The holiday season was the theater's "bread-and-butter period" and her services were absolutely required.

The unspoken cause of their separation constantly shadowed Olga's thoughts — her career as an actress which kept her in Moscow for the greater part of the year. Yet the social mores of the time demanded that she be at her husband's side. Chekhov's frequent expressions of loneliness in his letters, and his declarations that life was passing so stupidly, she could not fail to regard as accusations against her and her career, although he apparently did not intend them as such.

On November 6 she decided to bring the question out into the open by writing to him: "I want to be with you, I abuse myself for not giving up the stage. I really don't know what is happening to me and this vexes me. It is unclear to me. It makes me ill to think that you are alone, distressed and lonely, while I'm concerned here with some ephemeral business instead of surrendering to the feeling that is in me. What prevents me?! How I would like to have that little half-German, Antonka!"

More than three weeks later, however, detecting in his correspondence what she imagined was a personal criticism against the Art Theater, she firmly wrote him: "You are dispirited, in a foul mood, and hate the theater because of me. Yet it was the theater that brought us together. Darling, banish your dejection, it is not worth it."

Then, Chekhov's very reticence on the subject drew from her, on December 4, a frank expression of what appears to have been her real views on the tormenting problem of whether or not she should give up her profession: "It would be better to scold me, to say that you are dissatisfied with life, that instead of being such a ridiculous wife I ought to be living with you. I agree. Of course I've behaved thought-lessly. I had always hoped that your health would permit you to live in Moscow at least part of the winter. But it is not working out this way, my Antonchik! Tell me what I ought to do. Without my work I would utterly bore you. I would pace the room from corner to corner and nag at everything. I've now become completely unaccustomed to an idle life, and to destroy what I've achieved with so much difficulty is not wise at my age. I feel any number of reproachful eyes on me: Why don't I abandon the stage, how can I permit you to languish there all alone, etc. . . . . All this I know, all, my dear, and therefore I've been silent in much, particularly with you. And I don't know why I reveal this now."

If Chekhov in his love for Olga and because of his loneliness and growing dependence had wanted her to give up her career for him, he would have been the last to tell her so. He had too much respect for the dignity of work and the independence of the individual. In fact, his present distress was rooted precisely in the absence of those conditions for himself. He was not a free man; his poor health pre-vented him from working and from being with his wife when he so desired. When she first mentioned her concern, he replied, perhaps with a gleam of hope, but nevertheless with caution: "You want to give up the theater? So it seemed to me when I read your letter. Do you want it? You must think it over thoroughly, darling, thoroughly, and only then decide. All next winter I'll spend in Moscow — keep that in mind." (*November 7, 1901.*) Then four days later he warned her: "There is no sense in your quitting the stage for the kind of dreariness that we now have in Yalta."[15]

When in the first week of December Chekhov suffered a severe at-tack, accompanied by hemorrhages, this whole terrible question of her career was poignantly revived for Olga. He wrote her of his condition and then rather plaintively added: "I'm not expecting you for the holidays, indeed you must not come here, my darling. Do your work and one of these days we'll be able to be together. I bless you, my little girl. Be calm and keep well." (*December 11, 1901.*) Frightened, she wrote him: "Anton, I beg you, don't think of a trip to Moscow, watch

---

[15] This attitude is supported by a statement which Chekhov's brother Ivan made to L. Ya. Gurevich: "Olga Leonardovna wanted to leave the stage but Anton Pavlovich would not permit it, saying that to live without activity, without work, is impossible."

out for your health. I'm hellishly low in spirits. Be patient until the spring, and I'll be there with you all the time and in the winter we'll go to some warm region and I'll be all yours, yours, and I'll look after you and you will be well and calm. And we'll have that tiny being whom we'll adore — that is for certain, I want it." Two days later she wrote to announce her intention of taking him abroad for a whole year. "It is necessary to make arrangements and to change my life. In a year I'll leave the theater."

Chekhov kept her posted on his improvement. Occasionally he dropped a note of regret that she was not in Yalta: "There is no more blood-spitting, I have more strength, almost no cough, and the only trouble is a huge compress on my right side. And if you only knew how I think of you, how I regret that you are not with me when I have to put on this enormous thing and when I seem to myself so alone and helpless. But this, of course, is not for long; as soon as the compress is on, then I'm all right again. . . . I love you, my puppy, I love you very much, and I miss you terribly. It even seems to me improbable that we'll ever see each other again. Without you, I'm good for nothing. My darling, I kiss you hard, I embrace you a hundred times. I sleep excellently, but I don't reckon it as sleep when my sweet wife is not beside me." (*December 18, 1901.*)[16]

But Olga was swamped at the theater. She wrote him only that she now felt more calm because Masha had arrived at Yalta for the holidays and would be with him, "Although I'm jealous," she added. "Do you understand this?" Then suddenly, two days before Christmas, she was overwhelmed by an attack of guilt. How she regretted now not being there to change the compresses, to feed him, and nurse him! "I can imagine how you have suffered! I give you my word that this is the last year, my dear, that it will be so! I'll do everything to make your life pleasant, cozy, and not lonely, and you'll see how fine it will be with me, and you'll write, work. In your heart you probably blame me for a lack of love for you. Is it so? You blame me that I don't give up the theater, because I'm not a wife to you. I can imagine what your mother thinks of me! And she is right, right! Anton, my own, forgive me, giddy fool that I am, and don't think too badly about me. You, perhaps,

---

[16] The last sentence is omitted in the Soviet edition of his complete works and letters, but is included in *Perepiska A. P. Chekhova i O. L. Knipper*, Moscow, 1934, II, 159.

d that as soon as he obtained the money he would purchase

of their esteem for Chekhov the Art Theater, on January 11,
a special performance of *Uncle Vanya* for a huge congress of
ns meeting in Moscow. The cast outdid itself. Some of the
octors present wept as they identified their gloomy, harsh exist-
th that of Dr. Astrov in the play. A demonstration took place
nd. Two telegrams of gratitude were sent to their fellow physi-
ck at Yalta, and a reproduction of the Braz portrait of Chekhov,
ed in a heavy gilt frame, was presented by the doctors to the
eater. Olga wrote him all the details, how many of the audience
me backstage in raptures to shake her hand and to ask her to
im greetings. If only he could have been there! she lamented.
he performance she went on to a merry dinner with some of the
who joked much about their marriage, and from there to a variety
vhere they enjoyed oysters, champagne, and gypsy songs. Che-
had to content himself with thanking two of his close medical
who had participated in the congress: Dr. Chlenov, to whom he
ed regrets over the selection of the reproduction of the hated
ortrait; and Dr. Kurkin, to whom he wrote: "Such honor I did
d could not anticipate, but I accept the reward with joy, although
ess that it was not deserved." (*January 13, 1902.*)

as a time for honors. That January Chekhov was presented the
edov Prize[1] for his *Three Sisters.* How awkward, he wrote Olga.
will not bring me anything other than a scolding from Burenin,
esides I'm already too old for such encouragement." (*January 29,*
And the irresistible attraction that fame has for organizations
im honorary memberships in the Petersburg Society of Don Cos-
and in the Society of Russian Students of Dorpat University.
e small change of Chekhov's letters that winter, and it predomi-
in them, annoyed Olga. She wanted to know everything that took
between him and those famous figures, Tolstoy and Gorky, who
still in the neighborhood of Yalta, but he would mention only
ional visits: that Gorky was writing a new play, or that Tolstoy's
nued illness deeply worried him. His real concern over the mount-
olitical disturbances in the country was only hinted at to Olga,

___

[1] he prize was presented by the Society of Dramatic Writers and Opera Com-
. A. S. Griboedov was the author of the celebrated comedy *Woe from Wit,*
n in 1822–1823.

regret that you married me; tell me, don't be afraid to tell me frankly.
I feel myself terribly cruel. Tell me what to do?"

But he had nothing to offer as emotional as she perhaps hoped by
way of answering her outburst. Quite characteristically, he replied: "You
are silly, darling. In the whole time that I've been married, I've never
once reproached you about the theater, but on the contrary I'm glad
that you've been busy, that you have an object in life, and that you
don't aimlessly knock about like your husband. . . . Well, you sloven,
good-by, take care of yourself! Don't you dare be depressed and take on
meek airs. Laugh. I embrace you and I'm sorry that's all." (*December
29, 1901.*) And the next day he wrote: "I'm dull without you. Tomorrow I shall go to bed at nine o'clock in the evening in order not
to see in the New Year. I haven't you, which means that I have nothing
and so I need nothing." Perhaps he recalled wryly now what he had
told Suvorin six years ago: that he would be a splendid husband if he
could find "a wife who, like the moon, will not appear in my sky every
day."

CHAPTER XXV

"We Are Both Incomplete People"

WITHOUT HIS EFFULGENT MOON, the Yalta sky now held no further attraction for Chekhov. The town had become his prison and Dr. Altschuler his jailer. The good physician, whose sole concern was his
patient's health, was caught in the crossfire of a loving couple whom he
seemed to be keeping apart. In their yearning for each other, both at
times made a whipping boy of him. On January 9, 1902, Olga wrote
Altschuler and requested him to tell her confidentially and frankly
about Chekhov's condition. "I've somehow been thinking," she declared, "that Anton Pavlovich's health is in a better state than it really
is, and I've been imagining that it would be possible for him to spend
at least three winter months in Moscow. Indeed, January and February
are bad in Yalta. But now, of course, I don't mention the subject in my
letters."

Altschuler complied and gave Olga a clear account of her husband's
illness, although he probably did not say anything of his suspicion that

the disease had gone too far to be stopped. At this very time, however, Olga was excitedly writing Chekhov about the advice she was obtaining from Moscow doctors, all of whom agreed with her that Chekhov could live in or near the city in the winter provided he submitted to this or that form of treatment. Though Chekhov's own complaints about Yalta were somewhat responsible for Olga's zeal in this respect, he explained to her: "You never cease pressing me to come to Moscow. My dear, I would have come long ago, but they won't permit it. Altschuler won't even let me go out in bad weather, though I did go out today as I was sick to death of being cooped up inside." (*January 13, 1902.*)

Through Olga's lengthy letters to him at Yalta, Chekhov lived vicariously, as it were, her absorbing Moscow life of theater, concerts, art exhibitions, endless rounds of parties, and visits from mutual friends. At times she displayed a certain insensitivity to the restraints which illness placed upon him, in her detailed descriptions of the rich meals, dancing, and tippling she indulged in. She basked in the reflected glory of his name while making a name for herself, and distinguished people sought her out and extended courtesies because she was Chekhov's wife. Though he wanted her to be gay and happy, and encouraged her to live a full life, he sometimes worried over what he regarded as excesses. Yet his criticism, as usual, was cast in the form of light reflections: "My prodigal wife, do sit at home for even one short week and go to bed in good time! Staying up every night to from three to six o'clock in the morning — well, if you go on like that you'll soon grow old, withered, and bad-tempered." (*January 7, 1902.*) Olga explained that she could not sit at home when he was not there with her.

Masha looked with a more critical eye on the way Olga combined her exacting work in the theater with parties that lasted into the early hours of the morning. Continuing to live with Olga in Moscow was not an unmixed blessing for Masha, though she apparently obtained some emotional satisfaction out of being so close a part of the life of Chekhov's wife. In serving her — Masha was constantly at Olga's beck and call in the apartment — she believed she was serving her beloved brother. But it must have saddened Masha to be on the receiving end of outbursts of weeping when Chekhov occasionally failed to maintain his pace of almost a daily letter to Olga; Masha herself now felt fortunate if she got a postcard from him once a month. On the other hand, it angered Olga when she learned by chance that her sister-in-law was privy to confidences from Chekhov of which she knew nothing.

Masha wrote him on February 3, shortly after she [...] tion a[...] winter vacation at Yalta: "It has become dull for me [...] shares. cially since I'm unwell and am always sitting alone, g[...] Out home, for I almost never see Olga. Yesterday we n[...] staged tried to keep her from going to Morozov's ball, but s[...] physic[...] less and got back only by morning. Today, of course, [...] rural [...] out when she went to rehearsal, and tonight she has a[...] ence w[...] at the

Chekhov continued to enter fully into Olga's the[...] sponding with both her and Stanislavsky on the casti[...] cian b[...] Gorky's first play, *The Petty Bourgeois*. That winter [...] embos[...] undertook a substantial reorganization, largely in an e[...] Art T[...] firmer financial basis for the institution. Their "ang[...] had c[...] industrialist and patron of the theater arts, Savva M[...] send [...] and renovated a new auditorium for the company and [...] After subsidy for its operation. Then a selected group of [...] actors[...] administrative personnel were asked to buy shares and [...] show selves the board of managers. Chekhov, whom all regard[...] khov of the organization, was also invited to become a share[...] friend ingly agreed if he could obtain the rest of the money [...] expres chaser of Melikhovo still owed him, and on the conditi[...] Braz stipulated to Morozov, that any profits from the ventu[...] not a to him and the losses to his wife. However, he proteste[...] I con nation involved in singling out a special group for this [...] It the principle of the thing, he argued, and he suggest[...] Grib[...] ought not to be stressed, but that all who served three o[...] "This received a salary not below a certain figure ought to be [...] and [...] come shareholders. His fears were soon realized when se[...] 1902. who were not invited, including the highly talented Mei[...] won Art Theater, although in some cases differences with th[...] sacks artistic theories may have influenced the exodus. T[...]

At first Olga had qualms about taking up her option [...] nate for she realized that such action would bind her more [...] place theater and to her acting career. Once having decided, [...] were was more than anxious that her husband also invest. He [...] occa that though she, as an actress in the company, could r[...] cont shares on credit, he could not do that. Stanislavsky like[...] ing mayed over Chekhov's delay, for he imagined that this fa[...] a break with the Art Theater by their great dramatist, fr[...] 1 expected more plays. Chekhov had to reassure him of his u[...] pose[...] writt[...]

who took an interest in such matters. Although he was corresponding with the leader of an organization to aid imprisoned students and was writing to the recent political exiles A. V. Amfiteatrov and L. A. Suler-zhitsky to offer them any assistance within his power, he preferred to stick to chronicling the weather, to laconic and weary answers to her persistent queries on his health and daily regimen, or to telling her that he was in a vile humor on his birthday because he was unwell and the telephone kept ringing with congratulations, all of which reminded him to ask Olga the date of her birthday! "Masha says," Olga sharply declared, "that you don't know what to write to me. Is the correspondence difficult for you?" And in a moment of exasperation she protested: "You write of the weather, about which I can read in the newspapers. . . ." It was a thoughtless jibe, for she knew the weather determined his daily existence. But he meekly replied: "My darling, if I have written you often about the weather, it was because I imagined it would interest you. Forgive me, I won't do it again." (*January 19, 1902.*) Overwhelmed by remorse, she begged him to go on writing about the weather.

The long separation was fraying their nerves. It set her on fire, Olga wrote, even when he caressed her with words in his letters. Masha, aware of Chekhov's need, pleaded with the directors of the Art Theater to give Olga a brief vacation to go to Yalta. The possibility electrified both husband and wife. The visit would take place for a few days at the end of February, just before the troupe paid their second visit to Petersburg for a series of performances. Chekhov urgently pressed her to demand an extra day or two from her "master," Nemirovich-Danchenko, for he would have time only to kiss her and could not dare think of anything else. If the visit were only for two days, he pointed out, how hard it would be for them to part again! Finally Olga informed him that she could come for "four days and five nights." Now, he replied, everything is glorious. "Are you really coming soon? I'm hoping, hoping, hoping." Olga arrived at Yalta on February 22.

« 2 »

"Come back, darling, as soon as possible. I can't exist without my wife," Chekhov wrote Olga the day after she left for Petersburg. "My room and my bed are now like a summer cottage forsaken by its occupants." As he feared, their interlude had been one of intense but all-too-brief delight.

Just before her departure, Chekhov received a telegram, on February 26, informing him of Gorky's election to the Academy of Sciences. Chekhov was probably somewhat surprised. He himself had not recommended his friend, for he no doubt regarded him as too young and unproved for such a high honor. Though some thought, as Olga reported to him from Petersburg, that Gorky would reject the distinction because of his hostility to the government, Chekhov assured her that Gorky was very pleased.

Less than two weeks after the announcement, however, the official government gazette published a statement that the honor had been rescinded, because the nominating committee had been unaware of the incumbent's prison record — an allusion to Gorky's recent arrest for illegal political activities. Actually, Nicholas II, upon receiving an unfavorable report on Gorky's election from the Minister of Internal Affairs, personally recommended that it be annulled. His action in going over the heads of the distingugished members of the Academy caused something of a national scandal.

Chekhov was much disturbed by the turn of events. Friends urged him to resign from the Academy. He consulted an eminent lawyer in an effort to learn whether legal charges could be brought against the government for usurping the rights of the Academy to elect whomever they saw fit, but he was told that there was no appeal from an act of the Tsar. When he spoke to Tolstoy about the matter, the old man, although a duly elected member, sternly announced that he did not regard himself as an academician — he had never acknowledged the letter of appointment — and he ended the conversation by burying his head in a book.

Chekhov delayed taking any final decision until he had ascertained all the facts in the case, which he sought from close friends among members of the Academy, such as Kondakov and Korolenko. There was also a possibility that a meeting of the Academy in May would protest the government's annulment and reaffirm Gorky's election. Korolenko, however, after exploring the situation in Petersburg, informed Chekhov of the futility of expecting anything but supine submission from the learned academicians. Since he shared Chekhov's indignation in the matter and was also motivated by the same high principles, Korolenko made a special trip to Yalta at the end of May to discuss what action they would take. Both decided upon resignation from the Academy.

Accordingly, Chekhov wrote A. N. Veselovsky, head of the Division of Russian Language and Literature of the Academy of Sciences: "In December of the past year,[2] I received notification of the election of A. M. Peshkov[3] as an honorary academician. A. M. Peshkov was then living in the Crimea, and hence I did not delay in getting in touch with him and was the first to bring the news of his election and the first to congratulate him; shortly thereafter the newspapers announced that in view of an investigation of Peshkov under Article 1035, his election was considered invalid. Since it was definitely indicated that this announcement came from the Academy of Sciences, and since I am an honorary academician, then the announcement in part came from me also. In short, I was warmly congratulating and at the same time was declaring that the election was invalid — such a contradiction I can hardly accept, nor can I reconcile it with my conscience. A knowledge of Article 1035 explains nothing. After lengthy deliberation I was able to come to but one decision, extremely painful and regrettable to me, namely, most respectfully to ask you to relieve me of the title of honorary academician." (*August 25, 1902.*)

Characteristically Chekhov made no effort to publicize his resignation from the Academy. But the news spread rapidly, his letter appeared in the illegal Russian press abroad, and most intellectual circles acclaimed him and Korolenko for their courageous decision.

Gorky and the Academy's action were the main subjects of discussion among writers who arrived at Yalta that spring to enjoy the lovely weather and, hopefully, to talk with Tolstoy, Chekhov, and Gorky. Leonid Andreev came with his recent bride — very uninteresting, Chekhov described her to the curious Olga, and he assured her that he would desert such a wife. As usual, Chekhov's house was the favorite gathering place for these writers, and several of them have left interesting accounts of their visits and discussions on literature, publishers, new plays, and the political situation.[4] Batyushkov quoted him as say-

[2] Gorky was elected at a meeting of the Academy on February 21, 1902. Chekhov's mention of December, 1901, could only mean that he had confused the dates or that he had advance notice from friends in the Academy that Gorky's nomination would be proposed.

[3] A. M. Peshkov was Gorky's real name.

[4] For example, Batyushkov, Bunin, "Skitalets" (S. G. Petrov, popular in progressive circles and a friend of Chekhov's), and N. D. Teleshov have all left accounts. Apart from these writers and Gorky and Andreev, other literary visitors to Chekhov that spring were his old friend, the poet A. A. Belousov, S. Ya. Elpatievsky, V. N.

ing that a Constitution would soon be proposed in Russia, and another put him on record as opposing the central principle of Tolstoy's teaching — nonresistance to evil. At one of the gatherings Chekhov enthusiastically advocated a new kind of co-operative periodical free from the dictation of publishers and editors. Several of the visitors observed that his health and spirits seemed improved, though on one occasion he quietly disappeared and the company were informed that he had gone to bed.

Certainly, he must have felt unusually well, for, at Bunin's request, Chekhov agreed to sit for a portrait by the artist P. A. Nilus, a request which he had previously rejected. But the sittings were abruptly suspended, for early in April Chekhov received news of the serious illness of his wife in Petersburg.

« 3 »

Olga's letters to Chekhov on her long trip from Yalta to Petersburg were filled with joyful memories of their fleeting "second honeymoon," mingled with the despondency of parting. Thoughts haunt me, she wrote, "that you suffocate there day after day as in a prison, thirsting for another life, and being patient, patient without end." She also informed him of a strange pain in her stomach and a feeling of nausea. A woman passenger to whom she confided her indisposition wondered if she were not in an "interesting condition." "I also thought that, but it can hardly be," Olga wrote him, perhaps mindful of the "Pamfil" — so the "little half-German" was now called — they had dreamt about out loud in Yalta.

Soon, however, the performances of the Art Theater were in full swing, one of them a command affair before the Tsar and his entourage, and their success was unparalleled, greater than on the previous season. Even the conservative Petersburg press was on this occasion largely won over. *The Three Sisters* was acclaimed, nor did the company fail in the première of Gorky's weak play, *The Petty Bourgeois*, which was tampered with by the censor and much altered by Stanislavsky. And the fact that many secret police were in the audience, which the actors knew, made them intensely nervous.

Olga had never enjoyed such triumph. Her performances were singled out by the reviewers, she was showered with flowers, unknown

---

Ladyzhensky, V. M. Lavrov, V. A. Lazarevsky, and the dramatist S. A. Naidenov, some of whose plays Chekhov admired.

admirers sought to meet her, and Nemirovich-Danchenko informed her that Suvorin was prepared to offer her a thousand roubles a month to join his theater. Chekhov's brother Misha paid Olga the dubious compliment of praising only her in a review for *New Times*. She remonstrated with him over this awkward favoritism and complained to Chekhov. He advised her to pay no attention to it, saying a bit contemptuously that if Suvorin praised Misha that meant more to him than anything, but he urged her to see his brother and his family, which she did, for this would please his mother.

As always, in the midst of her triumph, Olga's elation was tinctured with remorse as she thought of herself out in the world of light and her husband sitting back in Yalta, alone. She wrote him: "At times I violently hate the theater, at others I madly love it. It has given me life, much grief, much joy, and it gave me you and made me into a person. Perhaps you think this is a false life, something imaginary. Perhaps. But all the same, it is life. Before the theater I vegetated, life was alien to me, and people and their feelings were strange."

Olga need not have worried. Chekhov gloried in her success, avidly read the reviews, and pressed her constantly to give him full reports of her performances. So she would soon become a famous actress, he wrote, a Sarah Bernhardt. Would she dismiss him, he jokingly asked, or take him about with her to keep her accounts? Then, with the wisdom of one who had enjoyed and perhaps was weary of fame, he gently reminded her: "My darling, there is nothing better in the world than to sit on a green bank and fish or stroll about the fields." And to this comment he added a footnote at the bottom of his letter: "I have nothing against your becoming famous and earning twenty-five to forty thousand a year, only first do your best for little Pamfil." (*March 17, 1902.*)

Olga was sought out by a number of Chekhov's old Petersburg friends. Though she liked to listen to their stories of the gay doings of his youth, she admitted to being jealous of his former life, which she surmised must have been much pleasanter than his present existence. "Why did we not meet when we were young?" she futilely asked him. But now it was her turn to be gay. Though from the very beginning of her Petersburg tour Olga complained of feeling badly and often depressed, as at Moscow she could not resist invitations to dinners and parties despite her intensive work schedule.

Chekhov anxiously warned "his tippler" not to wear herself out, and jestingly threatened that he would divorce her if she did not get enough rest. As an antidote to her despondency, his letters glowed with plans for the summer when her tour was over. They would rent a *dacha* near Moscow where he could fish, or better a little place on the Volga where they could be all alone and she could play at housekeeping. Or perhaps it would be nicer to go to Finland. Olga responded joyfully. She would go anywhere only to be with him — the Volga, Finland, even to Yalta where she now imagined him sitting in the garden, looking at the mountains and the sea, feeling the sun warming him, and thinking, thinking.

Then the blow fell. Chekhov received a letter from Olga, dated March 31: "I haven't written you for two days, my Antonchik! Here is what has happened to me: when I left Yalta it was with the hope of presenting Pamfil to you, but I was not aware of this. All the time that I felt unwell I thought it was a stomach upset, although I wanted to be but did not realize that I was pregnant. . . . They sent for doctors. Then for the first time I began to guess what it was and I cried bitterly — I was so heartbroken over my miscarriage with Pamfil." Olga next described how she was taken to the hospital and operated on, how all her friends in the Art Theater had rallied around, and her only thought now was to get back to him at Yalta. And she signed the letter: "Your unsuccessful dog."

For the next ten days, as she lay recuperating, Olga wrote her husband often, and the anguished burden of her letters was her sense of failure: "How I would have taken care of myself if I had only known I was pregnant!" "Will you receive your disgraced wife? She has disgraced herself! And how sorry I am for Pamfil!" ". . . Wire me, don't forget me, don't scorn me for my failure."

On April 14 Olga arrived at the Yalta house on a stretcher, pale and very weak.

« 4 »

A little more than two weeks after Olga reached Yalta, she was well enough to write Stanislavsky about herself and Chekhov: "During all this time he has been ill and only today has he had an appetite and shown signs of improvement. He has been much upset over my illness and this has been really bad for him." Very likely the gloomy atmosphere in the household contributed to Chekhov's condition. Though there is no evidence that he ever blamed his wife's "failure" on her way of life, apparently his mother and sister were not so charitable. Masha already had had words with Olga about burning the candle at both ends, and now here were the sorry consequences. At any rate, it is significant that on May 25, while Olga was still weak and ailing, she and Chekhov left for Moscow, although Yalta, in ordinary circumstances, would appear to have been the best place for her to convalesce fully. Masha's first letter to him three days after their departure was a terse little note which included a single chilly reference to Olga: "Greetings to your spouse and be well."[5]

Indeed, the doctor ordered Olga to bed when she arrived in Moscow, a fact which at first did not prevent numerous theatrical folk from dropping in at the new apartment on Neglinny Lane. Rather petulantly Chekhov wrote Masha that at the moment Olga was lying down in the living room listening to Nemirovich-Danchenko and Vishnevsky read a play which bored him so that he had to retreat to the dining room. Olga's condition fluctuated. On June 1 Chekhov was up all night with her as she screamed from an acute pain in her stomach; he hurriedly scribbled notes to her mother and Vishnevsky to find a doctor — most of them appeared to have left town during this holiday period. The pain eased. But ten days later the symptoms appeared in a more severe form, and this time the doctors, diagnosing peritonitis, advised an operation.

Chekhov, with his own wretched health, was worn out physically and spiritually by this ordeal. Olga suffers and all around her suffer, he wrote Gorky in some despair. Fortunately her mother and Stanislavsky and Vishnevsky stood by to aid. "She was near death," Stanislavsky recalled in his memoirs, "and we even thought the situation hopeless. Anton Pavlovich did not leave the bedside of his sick wife day or night and he made poultices for her, and so forth." In fact, Stanislavsky was worried as much about Chekhov's health as about Olga's. His endless care for her when she had fallen ill in Petersburg had claimed Chekhov's gratitude, and it was in the course of his patient attentiveness now in the sickroom that the two men discovered a community of interests and simplicity in intercourse which had previously been lacking in their relations. They became close enough for Chekhov to ask him one day to perform a rather intimate service, an injection of

[5] Masha appears to have been at Yalta when Olga arrived on April 14, but after ten days she had to return to Moscow. However, she came back to Yalta for her summer vacation about May 13.

arsenic which he required — Stanislavsky had assured him that he was proficient in this operation. As it turned out he could not get through the skin on Chekhov's back — in his account of the episode Stanislavsky claimed that the needle was dull. Then, losing his nerve when Chekhov coughed, this consummate actor faked the injection. Chekhov thanked him warmly, for, if he was aware of the deception, which was probably the case, delicacy would have prevented him from calling into question this assumed *expertise* of the morbidly proud Stanislavsky.

In this crisis of Olga's illness, the faithful Masha once again became Chekhov's confidante. "If you only knew, Antosha, how your letter saddened me!" she wrote on June 6. "Would it not be better, if only Olga improves, to bring her to Yalta? We will look after her and Altschuler will tend her. . . . And it will be better for you in Yalta. Should I not come to Moscow? Write more often, darling, about the course of Olga's illness, for we are very worried and every day we wait for news." Perhaps a bit self-conscious over having contributed to their sudden departure for Moscow, she added that she had bought Olga a large basin, pitcher, and pail in order that she might wash in comfort at Yalta. Chekhov, however, made it very clear that neither of them would return to Yalta that summer, and that he himself might not get there during the remainder of the year. Obviously their recent experience of trying to live together had been too much for him, and probably Olga's feelings had been deeply hurt over the attitude of Masha and her mother to her miscarriage. He was uncertain about his plans, he informed Masha, but when Olga recovered he would seek a rest at the estate of Savva Morozov in Perm, and upon his return would accept the invitation of Stanislavsky to stay at the estate of his mother near Moscow with Olga, or alone if she decided to go abroad as the doctor had suggested.

Before an operation could be undertaken after her last seizure, Olga's condition suddenly began to improve and within a few days the doctors pronounced her out of danger. Always partial to his own skill as a diagnostician, Chekhov proudly told Nemirovich-Danchenko that once the physicians agreed with his prescription of no food except milk or cream, Olga began to get better. By June 17 he felt that she had made sufficient progress to be left in the care of her mother. Greatly fatigued and badly in need of a change, Chekhov set out for distant Perm in the company of the wealthy Savva Morozov.

« 5 »

Chekhov believed that travel on the Volga and up the Kama at this time of the year was just what he needed after two exhausting and anxious months at the bedside of his sick wife. By telegram and letter he and Olga kept in constant touch. She rejoiced at his getting away for this brief period, and three days after his departure she wired that the doctor had pronounced her better. He wrote her affectionate letters, saying that he was terribly jealous of her. The Kama, which he had thought the dullest of rivers years before on his way to Sakhalin, was so wonderful, he declared, that some summer they ought to hire a steamer for the whole family and chug along in a leisurely fashion.

It took almost a week of journeying, by way of Perm and beyond to Usolye, to reach the estate of Morozov at Vsevolodo-Vilva. The steward, "Uncle Kostya," was on hand outside the huge sprawling manor house, looking like Mr. Pickwick — surrounded by servants and wreathed in gracious smiles as he prepared to greet the master. For days they had been polishing things in anticipation of the arrival. A troika dashed up and the heavily-bearded Morozov stepped out, his crafty eyes screwed up as he surveyed them all. He had a guest, he declared, and the tall Chekhov, stooped with fatigue and his face gray with the dust of the road, got out of the vehicle and at once had a fit of coughing. When it ceased, he looked at the river nearby and muttered that there must be a lot of pike in it.

After a light lunch, Chekhov had to submit to an inspection of this little Ural empire of the millionaire Morozov. The dark, smelly chemical works and the noise of the machines revolted him, but according to one witness he talked to some of the workers and asked them how much they earned and how many hours a day they labored; and he was credited later with persuading Morozov to reduce the working day from twelve hours to eight for experienced help and ten for common laborers. The schoolhouse Morozov was building for the villagers seemed of little interest to the weary Chekhov, but he did enjoy walking through the extensive park of birch trees. "It is fine here with these birches. We don't have them at Yalta," he remarked to A. N. Tikhonov, a young mining student with literary ambitions, who assisted Morozov and later left an account of Chekhov's visit. (Chekhov would soon receive the sad news from Masha that the birch tree he had been trying so hard to grow at Yalta had been uprooted by a storm.)

That evening Morozov staged a sumptuous dinner in Chekhov's honor, with the local intellectuals, officials, and superior officers of the plant present. They came dressed up as though attending a wedding. Chekhov sat silent at the end of the table, resisting all Morozov's attempts to draw him into the conversation. Of the seven courses, he ate only the soup and drank a little mineral water. To be sure, the guests were all creatures of Morozov and imitated his words and actions. Most of them did not know who Chekhov was except that he was a "writer," which meant that he was some sort of a clerk for their master. When he was in the city of Perm, Chekhov cut a news item out of the local paper and sent it to Gorky for his amusement. It announced the arrival in their midst of "our most popular author, Maxim Gorky," dressed "in a white peasant blouse, high boots, and a pince-nez."

Although to a certain extent Chekhov appreciated Morozov's friendliness, kindness, and even his ambition to be a philanthropist in the theatrical arts, in his presence he could not overcome an inherent distaste for the symbol of wealth and the servility that money bought. When it seemed that Chekhov would be unable to afford shares in the reorganized Moscow Art Theater, Morozov had rather crassly written him not to let money stand in his way. He informed Morozov politely but firmly that he did not do business in that manner. And when Olga told him of attending a huge Moscow dinner and ball given by Morozov, with many aristocrats present — Olga had a weakness for this kind of luxury — he replied: "Why, oh why, does Savva Morozov admit these aristocrats to see him? For they just stuff themselves with his food and then laugh at him behind his back as they would at a Yakut. I'd drive these animals away with a stick." (*February 13, 1902.*)

Now it was not a question of aristocrats, but of all the local gentry and officialdom in this remote spot in Russia fawning before the wealthy Morozov. Although Morozov tried to make his famous guest the center of these groups, here Chekhov was a nonentity and it obviously annoyed him. After returning from an inspection of the clinic facilities in a reception center serving Morozov's factory, Chekhov declared gloomily to young Tikhonov: "A rich merchant . . . he builds theaters . . . plays around with revolution[6] . . . but in his apothecary shop there's no iodine; the medical assistant is drunk — he has consumed all

---

[6] Morozov has been credited with substantial financial aid to the Russian revolutionary movement at this time.

the alcohol from the jar and cures rheumatism with castor oil . . . They are all the same . . . these are our Russian Rockefellers."

Toward the end of his stay, Chekhov felt unwell and refused to attend the dedication ceremonies for the new school, which was to be named in his honor. He gave as his reason the religious services that were to be part of the ceremony. However, after the official dedication, many of the participants crowded into the living room of the manor house, and the embarrassed, red-faced Uncle Kostya read the brief declaration on the naming of the school, which had been prepared by young Tikhonov. Chekhov was lying down. At the conclusion, he slowly rose to his feet, took the proffered scroll from Uncle Kostya's trembling hand, and, looking him over attentively, loudly declared: "Your pants are unbuttoned again!" The horrified Uncle Kostya threw his arms in front of him and sank down in a chair while all roared, the local police chief louder than the rest. The joke immensely amused Morozov, who later explained to Tikhonov that it was inspired by Chekhov's detestation of all forms of pomposity.

Morozov, busy with the affairs of his large holdings in the area, perhaps wisely left Chekhov in Tikhonov's charge. At first the young man found him uncommunicative, somewhat testy, anxiously asking a servant every hour whether a telegram had arrived from Moscow. Chekhov's natural friendliness, however, soon asserted itself, aided somewhat by fishing expeditions which the two of them undertook. He then talked much about literature, and the student movement, and told funny anecdotes about Morozov. Soon he had a devoted admirer in the young student.

One night, Tikhonov, who occupied the room next to Chekhov's, heard his prolonged and violent coughing through the wall, followed by a low moan. Frightened that he might be dying, Tikhonov, in his bare feet and nightshirt, dashed into Chekhov's room. In the light of a guttering candle, the young man saw him lying in the bed, his head over the edge and his whole body wracked with coughing. With each spasm blood poured out of his open mouth into an enameled receptacle he held. The terrified Tikhonov called his name. Chekhov fell back on the pillow and slowly turned his gaze toward him. His eyes, which the student saw for the first time without glasses, were large, helpless, like the eyes of a child, and were wet with tears. Softly, and with difficulty, Chekhov murmured: "I disturbed your sleep . . . forgive . . . my dear . . ."

In a few days Chekhov recovered enough to depart for Perm on the journey back to Moscow. According to one account, the laborers of Morozov's factory, perhaps because they had learned of his effort to shorten their working day, gathered at the station to give him a warm send-off.

« 6 »

Three days after Chekhov's return to Moscow, he and Olga, along with Vishnevsky, went to Lyubimovka, the estate of Stanislavsky's mother — the son had kindly offered them his wing of the estate while he and his wife were abroad. The village was almost a suburb of Moscow — Chekhov often went into the city to pick up mail — but the picturesque country setting, the large shade trees, and the river only a few yards from the door charmed him. Though Stanislavsky's mother and several other relatives were summering at or near Lyubimovka, it was possible for Olga and Chekhov to be quite isolated in their wing. In short, the place seemed like an ideal retreat for the convalescing Olga and her weary husband after weeks of illness and anxieties.

Though the couple were rarely without visitors — Vishnevsky and Nemirovich-Danchenko in particular stayed there frequently — Chekhov and Olga enjoyed a serene and almost idyllic existence at Lyubimovka. When he heard the village churchbells one day while fishing with Vishnevsky, he remarked: "Love for that sound is all that remains to me of my faith." His delight with the place was reflected in typical fashion by his desire to buy a piece of land in the area and build a *dacha* for summer use.[7] Olga wrote Stanislavsky abroad that her husband was in the best of spirits, joked, had an excellent appetite, gained weight, and soon hoped to start writing a play. Chekhov also wrote, thanked him warmly for the invitation, and said that they ate and slept like bishops. "It is long since I've enjoyed such a summer. I go fishing every day, five times a day, and the fishing isn't bad (yesterday we had perch chowder), and sitting on the bank is so agreeable that I cannot express it. In a word, everything is very fine. Only one thing is bad — I'm lazy and do nothing. I've still not begun the play, I'm only thinking about it. I'll probably not start to write earlier than the end of August." (*July 18, 1902.*) In the same strain he wrote to Gorky, the manuscript of whose new play, *The Lower Depths*, he had just finished

[7] Olga searched for a piece of land, but the prices were so high that Chekhov abandoned this project.

reading. His cheerful mood seemed to be reflected in his criticism: "It is new and undoubtedly fine. The second act is very good, the very best, the most powerful, and when I read it, especially the end, I almost leaped with joy." (*July 29, 1902*.)

In his letter to Stanislavsky Chekhov reported that Olga's doctor had found everything in order and had permitted her to take part in rehearsals as early as August 10. The only things forbidden were driving over bad highways and long trips, such as travel to Yalta. And he announced that he himself would go alone to Yalta in August. Chekhov repeated this information in other letters, including those to his sister. Despite these prior plans, which Olga may or may not have known, when he decided to leave their pleasant, restful, bucolic Lyubimovka existence for Yalta on August 14 she was deeply hurt. At that time he apparently offered no reasons for going, though later he gave several which were somewhat conflicting: he wanted to write, and his failure to do so at Lyubimovka turned him to Yalta; the damp weather had been causing him to spit blood, and he believed the dry Yalta climate would remedy this condition. Olga suspected other motives and could not understand why he did not invite her to go with him, although she knew of her doctor's prohibition against long journeys. This was his excuse for not asking her; but later he offered another which sounds suspiciously like the real reason for his departure: "You were already involved in your own interests — the theater, the Actors' Congress, lively conversations, and by then you were in no mood for Yalta." (*September 14, 1902*.) In any event, they had harsh words before he left and their first serious quarrel ensued.

Olga was still not entirely well, and perhaps this fact somewhat blurred her judgment. Besides, against the traumatic experience of her miscarriage she no doubt tended to exaggerate the significance of the critical attitude of her husband's mother and sister — she believed that during her illness they had tried selfishly to lure him back to Yalta alone. And it is possible that while he was at Lyubimovka Chekhov did receive letters from his sister pressing him to come — with or without Olga is not definitely known, for Masha, with one exception, strangely omitted all her letters to Chekhov during this period in her published correspondence with him.[8] When he left for Yalta over her protests, Olga asked him to carry a letter from her to Masha.

[8] That Masha wrote him more than once during Chekhov's stay at Lyubimovka is plainly indicated in his own letters to her and to Olga.

They were delighted to see him, Chekhov wrote Olga on August 17, but scolded him for not bringing her with him. However, when Masha read Olga's letter to her, he continued, she fell silent, and his mother was grieving. (In one communication he indicated that Masha had shown him Olga's letter; in another, that he had come across it on a table in his mother's room and mechanically read it.)[9] "Your letter is very, very unjust," he declared, "but what has been written with the pen can never be effaced; there's no help for it. I say again, and assure you on my word of honor, that Mother and Masha invited both of us, and not me alone, and that they have always felt warmly and cordially toward you." The incident, he indicated, had spoiled his homecoming. Grumpily he wrote that he would go to Moscow, although it was nice at Yalta, and that he would not write the play which she had been persistently urging him to do. Then, as a kind of comic concession at the end, he informed Olga that he was washing the back of his head, his ears, and his chest just as she had ordered.

In the face of this reproof, Olga's letters now bristled with recriminations. Masha had no right to show him her letter, she wrote; she had not said that Masha had invited only him to Yalta, but she knew they did not want him to remain with her when she was sick. Don't hurry to Moscow, Olga self-pityingly advised, for she could get along somehow, and anyway it was clear he did not love her.

Though deeply disturbed over these charges, Chekhov repeated to Olga that her letter to Masha had been terribly rude and, worst of all, unjust: "This won't do, it won't do, darling, one must avoid injustice. One must be above reproach in the matter of justice, entirely above reproach, and the more so since you are kind, very kind and understanding. Forgive me, darling, for these rebukes. I won't do it again, I fear this." And he ended on a sad note: "Don't part with me so soon, without having lived together as we should, without having borne me a little boy or girl. And once you have a baby, then you can behave as it pleases you. I kiss you again." (*August 27, 1902.*)

His mood frightened Olga. She had written Chekhov on August 28 to scold him for not telling her that he had left Lyubimovka because he had been coughing up blood — a reason that he now gave. This lack of frankness, she declared, could mean only one thing, "that we have lived together long enough. Is it time to part? Fine." Then, softening a bit, she alluded to the problem of her career which, she suspected, was

[9] The actual contents of Olga's letter to Masha are unknown.

at the bottom of all this contention. "In general, we are making a mess out of our life. My God, if I only knew that you needed me, that I could help you live, that you would feel happy if I were always near you! If you could only give me that assurance! However, you are able to live with me and never utter a word. Sometimes I've felt myself superfluous. I think that you need me only as an agreeable woman, and that as a human being I am lonely and a stranger to you."

The quarrel revealed that Olga's insight into her husband's enigmatic nature was at times extremely perceptive. With some truth she discerned that he really experienced no need to share himself and was inclined to look upon the daily lives of others quite indifferently. And she was aware of his fundamental discontent with whatever happened to be his situation at any given time, but her failure to understand the reasons for these baffling moods troubled her. "Sometimes," she told him, "it seems to me that it is entirely all the same to you where you live," and in this she was largely correct. No doubt Olga's belief that continuous living with Chekhov would make her insufferable to him was one of the factors that led her to hesitate to give up the stage. She could not escape the implication of his remark — a kind of casual justification for leaving Lyubimovka — that after all he had been with her constantly since early spring. "You, indeed, are an eminently fidgety person," she wrote him. "You are constantly bored. It seems to me that if I were together with you all the time, you would grow cold to me, or you would become as accustomed to me as to a table or a chair. Am I right? We are both somehow incomplete people." She would have realized how right she was if she had been aware of that statement to Suvorin that he wanted a wife who, like the moon, would not appear in his sky every day. And whether or not she would have complied, it obviously hurt Olga that he did not insist on her giving up the stage.

In certain respects, they were singularly different — Olga, like her family, temperamental, outgoing, fun-loving, at one moment soaring, at the next in the depths; Chekhov, though he admired some of these qualities, and had early revolted against the reserve and caution of his shopkeeper family, was nevertheless inherently withdrawn, self-contained, and disliked demonstrativeness, a behavior pattern now intensified by the state of his health. It is clear from her letters that Olga was a bit irritated by his failure to react positively to her frequent comments about the way Stanislavsky, Morozov, Nemirovich-Danchenko, and Vishnevsky flirted with her. In fact, he could see for himself that Nemirovich-Danchenko and particularly Vishnevsky were constantly dancing attendance upon her. If he experienced a twinge, he passed it all off in jokes about her pursuers, or he would plaintively say for effect in his letters ". . . Don't drift away from me." Nor could she understand his endless complaints about having too many callers, a situation that ordinarily seemed desirable to Olga with her highly sociable nature. In a palpable hit she twitted him about his visitors: "I've come to the conclusion that you like them and are merely showing off when you say that they vex you." He rather crossly answered: "I don't know whether I'm showing off or not, only I can't work and am sometimes much fatigued by conversation, especially with people I don't know." (*August 29, 1902.*) Olga would hardly have any sympathy with that trait of his personality which made it peculiarly difficult for him to turn people away.

In some respects their marriage represented a curious reversal of the conventional situation. Olga bantered him about it once in a letter. "You know, Antonka, I am really the husband and you are my wife. I am working, I come to pay visits to my wife, I watch out for her behavior — really, are you not my wife?" She was actually the stronger and more active, and in some aspects of their relations he played a submissive, almost feminine role. In a sense, too, there was a reversal of roles in the familiar situation of sacrifice in marriage. Here the male sacrificed instead of the female. It comes as something of a shock to learn that after almost a year of marriage, he had made no financial arrangement with Olga as her husband. For she was compelled to ask him, with much reluctance, for the sum of five hundred roubles to help pay off a long-standing debt. Rather charmingly, she reminded him, since she proposed to take the money out of his accumulated royalties in the Art Theater, that she had helped to earn it for him. Plainly embarrassed, he told her to draw on the account any time she desired without troubling to ask him.

In the matter of their quarrel, however, Chekhov was every inch the husband. He replied to Olga's acrimonious and rather morbid letter of August 28, pointing out in each case how utterly unfounded were her charges. Someone else had been talking to her, he guessed, and was to blame for all this muddle. "Distrust of my words and actions has been thrust into your head and everything seems suspicious to you, and if that is the case I can do nothing, nothing, nothing at all. Further, I'm not going to try to disabuse or convince you, for it is useless. . . .

My sweet, good darling, you are my wife, understand this once and for all! You are the person nearest and dearest to me. I have loved you infinitely and I still love you, but you go on writing about an 'agreeable' woman, lonely and a stranger to me. Well, God be with you, have it your own way." (*September 1, 1902.*)

Olga melted under this onslaught. The fact that by now she had returned to Moscow and got into the swing of her theatrical work no doubt contributed to her cheerier frame of mind. They were real people and not bloodless essences, she reminded him, and hence it was natural that they should suffer small heartaches. But she had not been influenced by anyone, she asserted. No man could encourage distrust for him in her. At the time she had simply been unable to reconcile herself to his departure from Lyubimovka. And as a kind of ultimate peace offering, for Olga realized where she had hurt him most, she informed him that she was placing flowers in Masha's room for her homecoming from Yalta. "What a wicked, wicked person I am. . . . When I think of you I always imagine myself on my knees before you, begging forgiveness." Their quarrel could hardly have ended otherwise — they loved each other profoundly. Has her doctor given her leave to have children? — he anxiously queries — "Ah, darling, darling, time is passing!" In a spirit of reconciliation she happily responds that the doctor has told her she has made a complete recovery and can do anything. "Are you satisfied? I'll give you a fine son next year."

« 7 »

A constant irritant in Olga's daily letter to Chekhov was her badgering him on getting ahead with his literary work. She prodded him to create plays and stories in very much the same language that she used to urge him to take castor oil and frequent baths. A clear understanding of the effort involved or the ideal human circumstances essential to the creative process were beyond Olga. Occasionally she tried to evince an empathy with his art by expressing provocative critical judgments on literature. The mood of Bunin's story *In Autumn*, she wrote Chekhov, struck her as well sustained, but Kuprin's tale *In the Circus* she found boring. And when Anatoly Lunacharsky[10] read her his verse drama *Temptation*, she ecstatically pronounced it original, bold, and beautifully written. Noting her enthusiasm for this play in his reply, Che-

---

[10] A minor writer and critic who later became the first Commissar of Education in the Soviet government.

khov dismissed it as a dilettante performance, "Written in a solemn classical style, because the author was unable to write simply, out of Russian life." And her other judgments he also disparaged: "Bunin's *In Autumn* has been executed by a stiff, constrained hand, and in any case Kuprin's *In the Circus* is far superior. It is a free, naïve, talented piece, and written by a man who undoubtedly knows what he is about. Well, God be with them! But why are we discussing literature?" (*January 31, 1902.*)

Chekhov's concluding query well represents his attitude — there was little point in discussing literature with his wife. Besides, they had much more interesting matters which they really held in common. At times he would inform her of his reading — theological journals and periodicals in general; Turgenev, about whose works he now offered the surprising judgment: "One eighth or one tenth of what this author has written will survive, all the rest will be consigned to the archives in the course of the next twenty-five or thirty years." (*February 13, 1902.*) On the other hand, to his literary friends, such as Gorky, he would write incisive comments on contemporary authors: "*Reflection* of Leonid Andreev is a pretentious thing, unintelligible and obviously unnecessary, but done with talent. There is no simplicity in Andreev and his talent reminds one of the singing of an artificial nightingale. Now Skitalets[11] may be a sparrow, but he is a real, living sparrow." (*July 29, 1902.*)

Olga's zeal in urging her husband to write was naturally encouraged by Stanislavsky and Nemirovich-Danchenko. They eagerly hoped for another Chekhov play to inaugurate the 1902–1903 season in their new theater, a structure which had revolving stage, advanced lighting effects, commodious quarters for actors, and simple, tasteful décor — unique in Russia at that time. Chekhov had every intention of complying. For more than a year now he had had a comedy in mind, a fact which he had several times mentioned to Olga. No doubt this was a reference to the original design of *The Cherry Orchard.* In January, when Olga took him to task for hinting to Masha but not informing her that he was thinking of beginning to write this play, he replied: "You silly! I didn't write you about my future play, not because I have no faith in you, as you say, but because I have no faith yet in the play. It has hardly dawned in my brain, like the first glow of sunrise, and I don't

---

[11] See Note 4 this chapter.

know myself what it is to be, what will come of it, and it changes every day." (*January 20, 1902.*)

During the whole of that year Olga kept reminding him of the proposed play and he himself spoke of his intentions to the directors of the Art Theater and even told Stanislavsky of the plot. Finally, as though annoyed by his wife's nagging on the subject, he tried to silence her in March: "I'm not writing my play; and I don't want to write it, because there are so many playwrights nowadays and it is becoming a boring, commonplace pursuit." (*March 16, 1902.*) And he advised that the Art Theater ought to put on things like Gogol's *The Inspector General* and Tolstoy's *Fruits of Enlightenment*. Though illness and domestic upsets were certainly factors that prevented him from writing, he also required, now, lengthy contemplation of a prospective work, a process characteristic of his last literary period. And the writing itself, in contrast to his earlier practice, had now become a prolonged, fastidious effort.

On several occasions, at Lyubimovka and later at Yalta, Chekhov tried to begin *The Cherry Orchard*, but each time he broke off. Though Nemirovich-Danchenko had told Stanislavsky that Chekhov would finish the play by August 1, Chekhov, in a letter to Olga on August 29, flatly announced: "Nemirovich-Danchenko is asking for the play, but I'm not going to write it this year, though, by the way, its subject is splendid." An additional inhibiting factor was an almost irresistible desire to return to the light, humorous one-act vaudeville type of his early period, perhaps the expression of a psychological need to compensate for the inner gloom which a knowledge of his fatal illness must have induced. The original comic design of *The Cherry Orchard* may also be regarded in this light.

Chekhov did not write a one-act play at this time, but his failure was somewhat redeemed by the thorough revision which he accorded an early piece in this genre. *On the Harmfulness of Tobacco*, "a stage monologue in one act," had first appeared in 1886,[12] and in several subsequent reprintings he altered it considerably. Although he initially ruled it out of the Marx edition, he now informed the publisher that he had completely rewritten the piece and wished to include it in the edition.[13] The changes between the first and last version of this slight

[12] It was published in the *Petersburg Gazette*, February 17, 1886.
[13] In this final form it was published, in 1903, in Volume VII of the Marx edition.

sketch admirably illustrates the transformation that had taken place in Chekhov's approach to the revelation of character on the stage. In the first version Nyukhin's monologue before the club audience on the harmfulness of tobacco, which his tyrant of a wife compels him to deliver for the purpose of advertising the girls' school she runs, is designed solely to amuse the audience by external comic effects which derive from the oddities, vagaries, and rambling speech of this pathetic old man who is lecturing on a subject he knows nothing about. In the final version the emphasis has entirely changed. Most of the external comic effects have vanished. Here, Nyukhin's monologue amounts to a subtle psychological analysis of the inner man. He reveals himself, not as he appears in real life, which had been the emphasis in the first version, but as he really is — a man whose fine qualities have been distorted and wantonly destroyed over the years by an insensitive, selfish, and dominating wife.[14]

In informing Olga again in September that he could not get on with his play, Chekhov explained that he was drawn just then "to the most commonplace prose" — that is, the short story. In the course of 1902 a number of editors importuned him for tales, and he invariably promised to submit something, though nearly always conditioning his promises by the state of his health. And illness usually did interfere with his concentration on this favorite genre. His vital forces were failing. He now averaged about a tale a year, and the manuscripts reveal the care with which he wrote them. In 1902 he finished *The Bishop*[15] — probably the reworking of an old draft; began *The Betrothed*; and he seems to have started two other stories which he never finished.[16]

It is not Chekhov the religious skeptic but Chekhov the superb literary artist who so beautifully and movingly evokes the faith of the old bishop in what is surely a concentrated masterpiece of the short-story form. In a series of exquisitely narrated impressions, subtly selected and arranged with the purpose of achieving a total final effect, Chekhov tells of the life and death of the bishop and at the same time creates

---

[14] Vishnevsky relates that Chekhov, at Lyumbimovka in July 1902, told him of a plan he had for a play without a hero. During the first three acts the characters discuss the life of the hero and await his coming with great expectation. But in the last act they receive a telegram announcing the hero's death. However, Chekhov never wrote such a play.

[15] *The Bishop* was published in the April issue of *Journal for All*, 1902.

[16] The unfinished stories are *Decompensation* and *The Letter*.

the vital atmosphere of the Church that gives meaning to his faith.

At times now, and especially in moments of irritation, Chekhov could take a destructively critical attitude toward contemporary Russian writers. One such moment was reported by the young student Tikhonov when Chekhov visited the estate of Savva Morozov in the summer of 1902. Though there could be no question of Chekhov's high regard for Gorky's talent, he severely castigated him on this occasion for the politically tendentious quality in some of his writings. And for good measure, he damned the students of the day, thus offending Tikhonov, for glorifying themselves as revolutionary heroes. One of their idols, Leonid Andreev, he set down as a "mere advocate's assistant," and the popular Decadents he described as knaves dealing in spoiled goods.

In this instance Chekhov was perhaps being deliberatively provocative, but the memory of the harsh criticism leveled at him in his youth may have contributed to this example of literary spleen. On another occasion at Morozov's, when he was conversing with Tikhonov on the terrace, he remarked: "Most of all, my friend, one must not lie. In this respect art is especially precious, for it is impossible to lie in it. One may lie in love, and in politics, and in medicine; one may deceive people and the good Lord Himself — there have been such cases — but it is impossible to deceive in art."

Then after a pause he continued: "I've often been blamed, even by Tolstoy, for writing about trifles, for not having any positive heroes — revolutionists, Alexanders of Macedon — or none even like those of Leskov, honest district police officers. But where am I to get them? I would be happy to have them! Our life is provincial, the cities are unpaved, the villages poor, the masses abused. In our youth we all chirp rapturously like sparrows on a dung heap, but when we are forty, we are already old and begin to think of death. Fine heroes we are!"

Chekhov fell silent, stared at young Tikhonov, the would-be writer, and resumed: "You say that you have wept over my plays. Yes, and not only you alone. But I did not write them for this purpose, it is Alekseev[17] who has made such crybabies of them. I desired something other. I only wished to tell people honestly: 'Look at yourselves, see how badly and boringly you live!' The principal thing is that people should understand this, and when they do, they will surely create for themselves another and a better life. I will not see it, but I know it will be entirely different, not like what we have now. And as long as it does

[17] Stanislavsky's real name.

not exist, I'll continue to tell people: 'See how badly and boringly you live!' Is it that which they weep over?"

When Tikhonov asked him what about those who already understood these conditions of Russian life, Chekhov answered simply: "Well, they will find the road without me."

« 8 »

A troubled conscience at having left behind an angry wife at Lyubimovka had clouded Chekhov's reunion with his family at Yalta in the middle of August. But Masha was there and in her quiet, efficient way she surrounded him with the care and comforts which he always missed when away from home. She and her mother, who kept remarkably well for her age except for ailing legs, had learned from long experience not to irritate him with daily queries about his health. Chekhov now had little contact with the rest of the family. The steady, plodding, and quite successful Ivan was a welcome guest at Yalta on the infrequent occasions when he elected to visit, and in Moscow he and his family were friendly with Olga. The talented Alexander, who continued in his odd way to do well enough in Petersburg, now rarely wrote to Chekhov. In one of only three letters published during 1902, he complained of growing old and assured his brother that, despite his failure to correspond, he loved him as much as ever. Misha, still sulking over Chekhov's opposition to his working for *New Times,* found his brother enthusiastic when he informed him that Suvorin had put him in charge of the network of railroad-station kiosks selling the firm's publications. Chekhov suggested some excellent innovations in developing this business, and expressed the opinion that the new job would compel Misha to bestir himself and cease sitting by the stove with his wife.

As usual, Masha was of great assistance in protecting Chekhov from the more offensive callers, but one visitor, at the beginning of September, whom they were both pleased to see was Suvorin. They had neither met nor corresponded for many months. The past winter Olga had seen Suvorin in Moscow, where he had attended a performance of *The Three Sisters* and lauded her acting, but she was not at all attracted by his munificent offer to join his Petersburg theater. In informing Olga of Suvorin's visit, Chekhov merely mentioned that they saw each other for two days running and talked about all sorts of things and much that was new. But the Yalta writer and editor of the *Crimean Courier,* M. K. Pervukhin, provides a more interesting account of the meeting. Chekhov, aware that the visit of so eminent a publisher and author would be written up in the local newspaper, took the precaution to see Pervukhin in advance and plead with him not to abuse Suvorin for the reactionary reputation he had acquired all over Russia. Later, after the visit, Chekhov discussed Suvorin at length with Pervukhin. While admitting his faults and condemning the policies of *New Times,* Chekhov declared: "Over the last few years there has been little in common between me and Suvorin. Nevertheless, there are the remembrances of my youth. I feel very much indebted to Suvorin." Then Chekhov defended him on the score of his achievements. Suvorin, he said, had been the first to increase the salaries and improve the working conditions of the newspaper profession; he had befriended many poor writers and had carried them along with sums of money which he realized he would never recover; and he had brought to the publishing business an instinct for developing Russian culture as well as making profits. "When history finally judges him," concluded Chekhov, "let us not forget these aspects of Suvorin's life."

A few weeks later Suvorin, who was in Moscow to see a performance of his play, *The Question,* at the Maly Theater, visited Olga. She wrote Chekhov that "old Suvorin talked a great deal and said that he loves you very much and had shed a few tears when he saw you."

Though Chekhov's move to the hot climate of Yalta at that time of the year had apparently remedied the blood-spitting which had afflicted him at Lyubimovka, he was soon complaining that the extreme dryness and dust in the atmosphere induced fiendish coughing and loss of what little appetite he had. As his letters indicate, he had intended to rejoin Olga after only a brief stay in Yalta, but now he had to confess that he did not feel well enough to travel, to write, or to do anything. She had some understanding of the inroads tuberculosis had made on him, as well as a sympathetic appreciation of his constant need to take every precaution; but his understatement of his condition, his periods of optimism, and his willful violation of every sane principle of treatment encouraged her at times to entertain false hopes and to imagine him capable of leading a more normal existence than she had any right to expect. At this point, for example, it was very hard for Olga to believe that even the short trip to Sevastopol would be physically difficult for him, to say nothing of the long train journey from there to Moscow. When Chekhov informed her, shortly after arriving at Yalta, that Dr. Altschuler had called, wanted to sound him, and insisted upon his being absolutely obedient to his orders, Olga, sulking at Lyubimovka, responded petulantly: "Go ahead and stay at Yalta all fall, it will be very good for you and Altschuler will be satisfied."

Again and again Chekhov had to postpone his departure. The "brutal coughing," as he described it to Olga, left him extremely weak, and he did not dare leave the house to go into town. At the end of August he assured his impatient wife that he was really not happy at Yalta, and in an effort to cheer her up he told her of the visit of his brilliant journalist friend, Doroshevich, who had said some handsome things about the Art Theater, and especially about her acting: "I take my dog by the tail," he whimsically concluded, "swing her around several times, and then stroke and pet her." (*August 29, 1902.*)

By the middle of September cooler weather came to Yalta, some rain fell, and the dust settled. Chekhov began to cough less, to eat more. In his letters to Olga he now grew definite about the time of his arrival in Moscow — early in October. In a happy mood he answered her conjecture that they were incomplete people and that he would be bored if he lived with her constantly: "I don't know, darling, whether I'm incomplete or not, I'm only certain that the longer I lived with you the deeper and broader my love would become. So, my actress, just realize that. And if it were not for my illness, it would be difficult to find a more settled man than I am." (*September 20, 1902.*)

Once Chekhov had made it quite clear that he would come, Olga began to exercise a surprising degree of caution. She warned him of the inhospitable Moscow weather in the autumn, the cold and slush. Why did he not remain in Yalta until the spring, she asked, and she would do her best to obtain a vacation that winter and visit him. Yet each letter of concern about his health and the risks of his taking the trip contained an expression of how wonderful it would be if they could only get together.

Finally, Chekhov submitted to the medical examination by Dr. Altschuler which he had refused during this whole stay in Yalta. And on September 22 he reported the results to Olga: "He found that my health has considerably improved and, if one may judge by the change that has taken place since the spring, that the disease is on the way to being cured; he even sanctioned my going to Moscow — it was so splendid! He says that I must not go now, but wait for the first frost. There, you see! He says that creosote helped me and the fact that I spent the winter in Yalta, and I replied that it was the holiday at Lyubimovka that did it. I don't know which of us is right. Altschuler demands that I leave Moscow almost as soon as I get there. I replied: 'I'll leave in December when my wife lets me.' "

How faithfully Chekhov reported Altschuler's diagnosis on this and other occasions is unknown. In his memoirs, Altschuler writes: "Olga Leonardovna, in her letters, often summoned him to Moscow. I tried in every way to oppose this. Hence she did everything possible to undermine my influence. And Anton Pavlovich tried in his letters to placate her in this situation and thus frequently sacrificed the truth."

In any event Olga's reaction to Chekhov's report was ecstatic: "Antoshka, my sweet golden boy, we shall see each other soon!!! Hurrah!!! Once again one may live with hope, be gay, and now it will not always be so black! How I'll kiss you, how I'll gaze on you, examine every bit of my wonderful man." She imagined their meeting at the station. Of course, she wrote, he would show the greatest indifference and ask about irrelevant matters, but, she assured him, she would know what was going on inside him at that moment.

Chekhov packed his mother off to Petersburg to visit Misha — he was again worried about her being alone at Yalta. And Masha also left for a short stay in Petersburg; she apparently did not relish being in the Moscow apartment when their reunion, after a quarrel in which she was involved, took place. Against Olga's warnings to come prepared for the weather, he replied that he would travel with his autumn overcoat, galoshes, and laprobe, and that she should meet him with his fur coat if it were very cold. In her letter to him on October 10, just before he left for Moscow, Olga promised to have on hand the cod-liver oil and creosote he asked for; and there will be beer and a bath, she added. "How I wish to live with you!" she wrote. "I wish to feel myself close to you, always, always."

CHAPTER XXVI

"To Moscow, to Moscow!"

THE REUNION OF CHEKHOV AND OLGA after their quarrel was a continuous delight. He not only had his wife again, but all the attractions of Moscow which so fascinated him. He admired the new Art Theater, the comfortable quarters of the actors, the simplicity of the decorations, and with pleasure he saw its production of Tolstoy's *Power of Darkness*. Chekhov enthusiastically wrote to Sulerzhitsky that V. I. Kachalov had taken Meierhold's place in *The Three Sisters* and did brilliantly, and that *Uncle Vanya*, as usual, was performed marvelously.

Many visitors left husband and wife little time to themselves. Gorky, who had been permitted to reside in Moscow again, was there for the rehearsal of his play, *The Lower Depths*. And among the other callers were such celebrities as Bunin, Chaliapin, Diaghilev, Menshikov, Rossolimo, and Suvorin. Very cold weather frequently confined Chekhov to the apartment, so there was often no evading the callers either day or night. He had hoped to do some writing; he soon informed Batyushkov, however, that sickness had prevented him from working at Yalta, but in Moscow it was visitors. Chekhov had expected to remain until well into December, and then leave for Italy with his friend Mirolyubov. As usual, however, the excitement and swift pace of Moscow life soon told on him. He began to cough and feel unwell, and after a stay of only five weeks, he was compelled, with many regrets, to return to his "dull Yalta home."

The ebb and flow of Chekhov's life had taken on a disheartening sameness. That December the depressing routine of Yalta existence was varied by very few interesting or cheerful happenings. The town was electrified by the presence of Nicholas II at the dedication of a new church. Extraordinary and often annoying precautions were taken to protect the Tsar. Chekhov, who did not attend, derived some satisfaction from the delight of his aged mother who saw the whole ceremony, to which she was admitted by special ticket. It amused Chekhov to learn at this time that the archbishop, in a visit to the local school, had disparaged his writings but praised Gorky's. In Moscow Gorky had involved Olga in his personal crusade, which he still continued, to break Chekhov's publishing contract with Marx. Olga, convinced that her husband stood to gain a great deal financially, used her best efforts to persuade him. But he wrote her: "I don't relish bothering about that agreement. Nothing will come of it. Once you have signed a contract, you must abide by it honestly no matter what the cost." (*December 4, 1902.*)

Later that month, when Chekhov received a telegram from Stanislavsky that the opening performance of Gorky's *The Lower Depths* had been an astounding success, he sincerely rejoiced, both for his friend and for the Art Theater, which at this point, lacking a new play by Chekhov in its repertoire, desperately needed a fresh triumph. Olga, who once again had been singled out by the critics for her acting, gave Chekhov a full account of the large expensive party which the enraptured Gorky had tendered the troupe and various friends after the première, an affair that ended in a brawl caused by a huge drunken actor. Chekhov commented rather humorously that if he had been present he would have exchanged blows with the brawny culprit.

Chekhov's own failure to get on with the writing of *The Cherry Orchard* was perhaps somewhat assuaged by the news that *The Sea Gull* had finally triumphed in the Petersburg Alexandrinsky Theater. Mindful of its catastrophic failure there six years earlier, he had discouraged every effort to revive it in that theater. But he had finally drifted into compliance, perhaps somewhat persuaded by a need for money — because of lack of funds, he had just been obliged to turn down a request of brother Misha for a loan. The Alexandrinsky had offered him an increased royalty rate. In any event, he now took particular satisfaction in the success of *The Sea Gull* in that theater.

One of the most interesting reviews of the performance, published in the fastidious *World of Art*, declared, among much laudatory comment: "The success of *The Sea Gull* on the imperial stage is very notable. It testifies to the fact that Chekhov's period of struggle is past. As a dramatist Chekhov has become a classic and a traditional government theater has officially recognized him." To be sure, *World of Art* had been assiduously pursuing Chekhov. Its editor, Sergei Diaghilev, who eventually became so celebrated in theatrical arts and ballet production, had been trying hard to persuade Chekhov to contribute an article on the deceased artist Levitan, and later Diaghilev invited him, without success, to assume the editorship of the literary section of the magazine. In his recent visit to Moscow, Chekhov had met Diaghilev, whose esthetic and ideological views, as well as those of his collaborators on the *World of Art*, were alien to him. On that occasion the two men had begun a discussion on whether a serious religious movement was then possible in Russia. But they had been interrupted, and Diaghilev now wrote to express the hope that they could renew their exchange of ideas on this theme.

Chekhov replied that the religious movement they had been discussing existed not in Russia as a whole, but only among the intelligentsia. "I'll not say anything about Russia, but the intelligentsia is only playing at religion and largely from a lack of anything else to do. The cultured part of our society has moved away from religion and is getting further and further from it no matter what people may say and however many religious-philosophical societies may be formed. Whether this is good or bad, I shall not undertake to decide; I'll only venture that the religious movement of which you write is one thing and the whole course of modern culture is another and one cannot place the second in any causal relation to the first. Modern culture is only the beginning of an effort in the name of a great future, an effort that will continue perhaps for tens of thousands of years, in order that humanity, if only in the remote future, may come to know the truth of the real God, that is, not guess at it or seek it in Dostoevsky, but know it just as clearly as we know that twice two makes four." (*December 30, 1902.*)

Earlier, in his diary, Chekhov had more pointedly summed up this eternal Russian questing for faith: "Between 'There is a God' and 'There is no God' lies a great expanse which the sincere sage traverses with much difficulty. The Russian knows only one of these two extremes, for the middle ground between them does not interest him. Hence, he usually knows nothing or very little."

Now, however, all Chekhov's intellectual and literary interests had to be subordinated to the inexorable logic of a wasting disease. His frail body, like a thermometer, responded to every fluctuation in temperature. Stormy December weather kept him indoors for days at a time, and coldness in the house prevented him from concentrating on his story *The Betrothed* or *The Cherry Orchard*. In his loneliness and despair his thoughts dwelt constantly on Olga and Moscow. "During this last visit," he wrote her after his arrival in Yalta, "you have become more precious to me. I love you more dearly than ever. Without you, going to bed and getting up is very boring, somewhat absurd. You have spoiled me terribly." (*November 30, 1902.*)

Perhaps unconsciously Chekhov began to stress in his letters the little undone domestic chores which she ordinarily performed for him: his coat needed brushing, a button had fallen off it, the lining of his waistcoat was torn, his nails were uncut. What a pity, he lamented, that they had married late. For he found not a single defect in her, except that she occasionally had a bad temper, at which times, he said, it was dangerous to come near her. "If you only knew, darling, how clever you are!" he wrote her on Christmas Day. "Among other things, this is clear from your letters. It seems to me that if I could lie only half a

night with my nose buried in your shoulder, I would cease to feel unwell. Whatever you say, I cannot live without you."

Olga's replies to his endearments were a mixture of despair over their
separation and anticipated joy in their next meeting. Since the last
time they had lived together the fear also beset Olga that the doctors
had concealed something after her operation and that she could not
have children. Patiently he kept reassuring her that he had talked the
matter over fully with them and that all she needed was to wait a bit
until she had recovered her strength fully after her illness. And when he
could live with her the year round, he declared, "then you will have a
little son who will break the crockery, pull your dachshund by the tail,
and you will watch him and be comforted." (*December 14, 1902.*)

« 2 »

Friends that winter were appalled at the change which had taken
place in Chekhov's appearance. He had grown still thinner, his face
had an ashen color, his lips were bloodless, and his hair was turning
gray. His heart action had weakened and the slightest physical activity
was accompanied by shortness of breath. During January and February
there were very few days when he felt really well, and for a time he was
confined to bed with a severe attack of pleurisy. Olga became panicky
over his cryptic and conflicting reports on his health, and she wanted
him to be examined by her own physician. She had lost faith in Dr.
Altschuler, who had written her that Chekhov's poor condition must
again be attributed in part to his recent trip to Moscow. Chekhov
assured Olga that Altschuler was only following the advice of the
distinguished Moscow physician Shchurovsky, and he wrote that he had
lectured Altschuler for upsetting her: "In the first place I fell ill in
Yalta, not in Moscow, which is clearer to me than to him; and in the
second place, I'll go to Moscow when I choose." (*February 3, 1903.*)

Chekhov's assurances, however, could not prevent Olga from again
castigating herself for not being by the side of her husband during his
illness, and as usual she blamed it all on her career. He tried hard to
exorcise this ghost once for all. They were a model couple, he pointed
out, for they did not interfere with each other's work. If she did not
love the stage, it would be a different question. "You keep writing,
my own, that your conscience torments you because you are in Moscow
and not living with me in Yalta. But my dear, what are we to do? Just
think of it sensibly: If you lived with me in Yalta all winter, your

life would be ruined and I would be conscience-stricken, which would hardly be an improvement. I knew that I was marrying an actress — that is, when I married you I fully realized that you would spend the winters in Moscow. I don't regard myself as injured or cheated one millionth bit; on the contrary, it seems to me that all is going well or as it must be, so darling don't worry me with your troubled conscience." (*January 20, 1903.*)

If he could only stroll about outside or work as hard as she did, Chekhov told his wife, he would feel infinitely happy. Not even the arrival of his literary friends among the usual spring visitors to Yalta could shake him from his lethargy. The news of Gorky's coming only reminded him that he would have to talk to his rather dull wife and the family governess and listen to their young son's yelling. "I've grown old!" he thought. Yet he entertained them — Gorky, Bunin, Kuprin, Mirolyubov, Fyodorov. Mirolyubov recalls his talking rather bitterly about the hardships he endured as a young writer, uttering sharp opinions on contemporary authors, and saying defensively when his marriage with an actress was discussed: "Everything depended on me, and I demanded that she not give up the stage. What could she do here in Yalta?" And V. V. Veresaev, a physician and writer like himself, whom Gorky introduced, remembered that Chekhov took an interest in social and political problems and grew indignant over recent brutal actions of the government and the stupidities of Nicholas II.

When the fine Yalta early spring weather came, Dr. Altschuler allowed Chekhov to go into town and walk by the seashore. His spirits rose somewhat. But he was more contented when working around his garden. Sadly he observed how the slightest effort tired him. For the most part he had to be satisfied with superintending Arseny in planting the German and Japanese iris bulbs he had ordered. More often he just sat by the hour on his favorite bench, gazing into the distance at the sea.

Chekhov now unreasonably hated Yalta, perhaps because it was associated with the one thing he wanted most to forget — his disease. Ceaselessly he planned for the future when he knew that he had no future. The feeling that some experience, some pleasure was escaping him through enforced inaction gnawed at him. He kept writing to Olga repeatedly: "We have not much life before us together . . . we must hurry, we must do our utmost to get something out of it"; "Don't forget me, you know we have only a little life left"; "You know it is wearing, it is fiendishly dreary! I want to live!"

Olga mentioned that she envied his even disposition and he replied that he was naturally hot-tempered but that over the years he had learned to control himself as he believed every decent man ought to do. Shortly after making this observation, he flew into a temper over Olga's failure to communicate promptly her new address — she and Masha had once again moved, taking a larger apartment that had a sunny, airy room where Chekhov could write undisturbed when he came to Moscow. The exacerbation with which he returned again and again to this minor matter betrayed the explosive tension induced by his long and hopeless struggle with tuberculosis. The offended Olga's protest that she had told him the address resulted in the angry threat that he would bring all her letters to Moscow and prove that she had never once given him the information.

But Olga was all he had left, the one tangible symbol of his future, and he concentrated on her with pathetic avidity, as though he must cheat time and drain the last drop from this remaining experience with life. When she feared that she was becoming old and ugly, he assured her that if she grew a nose like a crane's he would still love her and hug her until her ribs cracked. In answer to her teasing charge that he seemed to prefer Yalta and his friends there to her and Moscow, he replied that he wanted to be only with his wife and would live with her any place, even in Archangel, and would worry about nothing if only she were a mother.

In fact, Chekhov had begun planning their next meeting as soon as he returned to Yalta. He would come in March. They would rent a *dacha* near Moscow, and in June they would travel abroad to Switzerland, Italy, France. His imagination soared at the prospects. Then Dr. Altschuler informed him that his pleurisy was not thoroughly healed and forbade Moscow in March. Could she not obtain a vacation and come to Yalta for Easter? — Chekhov pleaded — If her entreaties were in vain, he promised to use his own influence on the directors of the Art Theater. "Think of what is best and most convenient for you," he wrote. "But I'm so dreary, I so yearn to see you that I have no patience left. I beg and beg you to come." (*March 5, 6, 1903.*)

Olga, however, had to go to Petersburg again on tour with the Art Theater. It would be quite impossible to get away before they left. His glorious bubble of enthusiasm deflated, he guiltily asserted that she was a busy, hard-working person while he loafed about like any whipper-snapper. Therefore, he would come himself, without any more talk, no matter what the doctor said.

« 3 »

The agonizing process of dissolution had also begun to affect Chekhov's writing habits and he could not reconcile himself to this fact. "Oh, what a mass of subjects there are in my head!" he exclaimed to Olga. "And how I long to write! But I feel that something is lacking — either in my surroundings or in the state of my health." (*January 23, 1903.*) Yet less than a month later he confessed to her: "Ah, my darling, let me tell you sincerely of the satisfaction it would now give me to cease being a writer!" (*February 16, 1903.*) Despite his physical incapacity, pride and will power drove him on to overcome insuperable obstacles. He continued to peck away slowly at *The Bethrothed*, a tablespoonful each hour, he told his wife. "I write six or seven lines a day, I can't do more even if my life depended on it. I have diarrhea daily. . . ." (*February 5, 1903.*) Repeatedly he had to offer excuses to the editor for not sending the tale in when agreed, because he could not find the strength to make a fair copy of it.

Chekhov had worked intermittently on *The Betrothed*, a short story of less than twenty printed pages, for some five months. And after he turned it in to the editor on February 27, it took him another four months to correct the three sets of proof he demanded, in the course of which he accumulated more pages of revision than were in the original draft.[1] This last tale that Chekhov wrote is another of his little masterpieces, a study in the formation of the character of Nadya, a charming Russian girl. Like her meek, widowed mother, Nadya never questions the way of life of her stuffy provincial home, which is dominated by her grandmother. Her comfortable existence, the daily routine of pleasures, visitors, and entertainment, the servants who wait on her and sleep on the floor of a vermin-infested kitchen — all is accepted by Nadya as a matter of course. Eventually, however, the persistent prodding of Sasha, a distant relative from the city who has turned his back on middle-class values, begins to arouse in Nadya a spirit of rebellion against the crassness and fecklessness of her life. Finally she abandons her impending marriage to a shallow nonentity and runs away to Petersburg to study, filled now with the desire to be

[1] The story did not appear in print until December, 1903, in *The Journal for All.*

of some use to herself and to society. One can discern no lineaments of Olga Knipper in Nadya, but Sasha, like Chekhov, burgeoning with hope for the future, makes light of his illness, goes to the Volga to take a kumiss cure, and dies of tuberculosis.

As though seeking an advance reaction to a new emphasis in his fiction, Chekhov took the unusual step for him of asking Gorky, Veresaev, and Elpatievsky to read the proof sheets of *The Betrothed*. Years later Veresaev recalled that in this form Chekhov had his heroine seeking a change in her life by entering the revolutionary movement. Veresaev must have been mistaken, for now all the variants of the story are available and they contain no such development of the plot. The version he did read, however, has expressions of revolutionary sentiments, especially in Sasha's talks with Nadya, which Chekhov omitted in the final draft, no doubt because of concern over censorship. Perhaps such sentiments, and the fact that in those days the revolutionary movement was the accepted outlet for young people who sought a change in their life, account for Veresaev's faulty memory of the tale.

Certainly Chekhov seemed to be trying in *The Betrothed* to avoid the note of gloom and futility with which he so often concluded the tales of his middle period. While he was working on it he told his wife: "You write, read it through, and see that this has already been done, that it is old, old. There ought to be something new, a little pleasantly acid." (*February 23, 1903*.) The direction he tried to give his story was not exactly revolutionary, but more in keeping with that in *The Three Sisters* and later in *The Cherry Orchard*. It was the gradualism that he espoused in his later years, the conviction that society was slowly and surely moving toward an order of things that would deliver men from want, injustice, and fear. When the emancipated Nadya returns from the university to visit her provincial town, it seems to her that everything in it has grown old and out of date and is only waiting for something young and fresh. "Oh if that new, brighter life would only come quickly," she exclaims, "then one would be able to look one's fate boldly in the face, to know that one was right, and to be happy and free! And sooner or later such a life will come!"

About the time Chekhov finished *The Betrothed*, he was surprised and pleased to receive a letter from his old friend Potapenko, inviting him to join in the editing and promotion of a new magazine. He replied affectionately, recalling pleasant memories of Potapenko, and assuring him that he had not changed over the years. "However," he added,

"I've got married. But at my age this is no more worth mentioning than growing bald." (*February 26, 1903.*) For a variety of reasons he refused Potapenko's offer, but certainly a major consideration was his desire to return once more to the oft-promised play. On March 1, having informed Olga of the completion of *The Betrothed*, he continued: ". . . But the play — well, I've laid out the paper on the table and written the title." Several weeks earlier, in thanking Stanislavsky for the "Order of the Sea Gull" which he had sent — a gold medallion with the bird engraved on it — Chekhov told him the title of the new play, *The Cherry Orchard*, and promised to have it written by about March 20.

Though the design for *The Cherry Orchard* had been in Chekhov's mind for some time, now, as at Lyubimovka, he could not seem to begin the writing. And it irritated him when the Art Theater, in a broad hint, asked him to suggest plays for their repertoire for the next season: he argued against those of contemporary authors, urging instead old standbys of Gogol and Turgenev. And when Olga, now once too often, blamed the lack of progress on his laziness, he snapped back: "My laziness has nothing to do with it. Why, I'm not an enemy of myself, and if I had the strength I would write not one but twenty-five plays." (*March 4, 1903.*)

But only two weeks after this Olga received the happy news that he was getting along well with the play except that one of the leading characters was causing him some difficulty. And three days later he jubilantly announced to her: "*The Cherry Orchard* will come off; I'm trying to have as few characters as possible; this will make it more intimate." Then on April 9 he informed her: "I'll write the play in Moscow for it is impossible to write here. They don't even give me a chance to correct proof." Not only the visitors, but the excitement and anticipation of his long-delayed meeting with his wife had cluttered his thoughts and slowed his pen.

« 4 »

Momentarily at least, Chekhov always seemed to gain strength upon touching Moscow earth. To his mother he wrote that he liked everything about the new apartment on Petrovka, but to negotiate three flights of stairs was an act of martyrdom. In considering the apartment, Olga and Masha had warned him of this disadvantage, but he had then offered no serious objection, although they perhaps should have realized how difficult it would be for him with his weak lungs. It took him almost half an hour to make the ascent. Although he had lost no time in informing his mother of his arrival, Chekhov was not particularly worried about leaving her on this trip. Besides the servants, his cousin Yegorushka had been transferred to a Yalta maritime concern, and Elena, Yegorushka's sister, was then on a lengthy visit to the Chekhovs; both had offered to look out for their old aunt.

Chekhov at first found the Moscow weather too cold to go out, but instead of using this opportunity to continue his work on *The Cherry Orchard*, in his expansive frame of mind he wrote letters to various friends to invite them to call. Even Suvorin in Petersburg was urged to come to Moscow and visit him, and he did. Learning of this fact the small fry descended upon Chekhov for favors — a poet to ask him to persuade Suvorin to publish his translation of Robert Burns, a novelist to have his stories published — and as usual Chekhov obliged. Then an impoverished former editor requested his assistance in obtaining a pension from the Literary Fund, and Iordanov at Taganrog asked for more books for the library and Chekhov collected a large packing case full and shipped them. Goltsev invited him to take charge of the literary department of *Russian Thought*, which he agreed to consider, and the Moscow court summoned him to answer a complaint, from which he was eventually exonerated, against Olga's dog Snap. Tolstoy, who presented Chekhov with an inscribed photograph of himself at this time, also sent him, through his son Ilya, a list of what he considered Chekhov's best tales. He singled out thirty stories and divided them equally into two groups, one of "first quality" and the other of "second quality."[2] It is an interesting list, revealing Tolstoy's critical insight as well as his personal bias in favor of Chekhov's early, brief, and quite objective stories where a simple theme is simply treated with a strong emphasis on moral feeling. This was a manner rather similar to Tolstoy's in the tales of his later years. In fact, Tolstoy told Lazarevsky that he had bound these tales of Chekhov together in a book and repeatedly read them with great satisfaction. "Just as one

[2] Tales of first quality: *Children, The Chorus Girl, A Play, Home, Misery, The Runaway, In Court, Vanka, Ladies, The Malefactors, The Boys, Darkness, Sleepy, The Helpmate, The Darling.*

Tales of second quality: *A Transgression, Sorrow, The Witch, Verochka, In a Strange Land, The Cook's Wedding, A Tedious Business, An Upheaval, Oh! The Public!, The Mask, A Woman's Luck, Nerves, The Wedding, A Defenseless Creature, Peasant Wives.*

may find in Pushkin's verses an echo of one's own personal experiences," Tolstoy remarked, "so this is true of Chekhov's tales. Certain of his things are positively remarkable."

Despite Chekhov's lack of co-operation, Gorky, and now some of his friends, were continuing to explore ways and means of evading the terms of the contract with Marx. They informed Chekhov that the publisher had already realized some two hundred thousand roubles on the sale of his works, which Marx had now begun to republish as book supplements to *Niva*, the magazine he controlled. The crusaders had interested a lawyer, who took a position more palatable to Chekhov. That is, there should be no question of breaking the contract by refunding Marx's payment of seventy-five thousand roubles. Rather Marx should be requested to reconsider the original terms in the light of his large profits, and be asked to pay Chekhov a third of all income from the sale of his works. In fact, if it were not for the markedly increased earnings from his plays, Chekhov would once again have been hard-pushed. But such income was an uncertain factor. By now he had also bought shares in the Art Theater and it pleased him immensely to be able to report to Masha that he had realized a thousand roubles from its profits this past season.

Reflecting on these circumstances, he reluctantly agreed to request Marx to reopen the terms of the contract on the basis suggested by the lawyer. Apparently early in May he gave Mirolyubov in Petersburg permission to approach Marx on the subject. The publisher responded quite stiffly, demanded that Mirolyubov present a written authorization to carry on such discussions, and indicated that he preferred to talk with Chekhov himself about the matter. In Chekhov's condition the trip was sheer folly, but he went to Petersburg for a couple of days in the middle of May. "I talked with Marx," he wrote Masha, "but nothing of consequence came of it. He gave me very many books (about 250 pounds) in rich bindings, and offered me five thousand roubles for 'medical expenses,' which I of course did not accept." (*June 7, 1903.*)

Shortly after his return from Petersburg, Chekhov and Olga spent a few days near Voskresensk, the little town he had got to know so well in his early Moscow life, on an estate belonging to V. A. Maklakov, the well-known lawyer and later celebrated orator of the Duma, whose acquaintance Chekhov had made in Yalta. They were planning to leave soon for Europe, a suggestion that Olga had enthusiastically accepted when he had mentioned it away back in February. For his medical checkup before so extensive a trip, Chekhov selected the eminent Professor Ostroumov, the doctor who had treated him several years before when he had his severe hemorrhage. The results were depressing, but the advice that followed was not entirely unwelcome to Chekhov. That very day he wrote to Masha that Ostroumov had found "that my right lung is not at all good, that I have a dilation of the lungs (emphysema) and catarrh of the intestines, and so forth and so forth. He gave me five prescriptions, and, above all, forbade me to live in Yalta in the winter, declaring that the winter there is generally bad; he ordered me to spend it in a *dacha* somewhere in the vicinity of Moscow. Now, make head or tail of all that! However that may be, I must now look for a refuge for the winter. Mme. Yakunchikova invites me, Teleshov offers to build a house, Sytin invites me. I'll not go abroad and will remain near Moscow and live at Mme. Yakunchikova's at Nara, where I go tomorrow. . . . Olga has been there already and she liked it. . . . Let Mother and Granny [the old servant] get ready at the end of October, for I'll take them to my *dacha* near Moscow. . . . Gurzuf and Kuchukoi must be sold." (*May 24, 1903.*)

Masha could not make head or tail of it. But Chekhov had at last found sanction for what he had wanted to do all along — live in or near Moscow in the winter. His wife was delighted. Back in Yalta, Dr. Altschuler regarded the decision as little short of a death warrant.

« 5 »

Chekhov had been less than candid with his sister. He wrote more frankly to old friends about the medical examination. Ostroumov had roundly scolded him, he said; had declared his condition to be "very poor," his right lung "badly damaged," and that additional complications had set in. When Chekhov raised the question of going abroad, the doctor not only forbade it but strongly reminded him, "You are a cripple." Medical nostrums, and especially in the case of tuberculosis, were not immune to the skepticism with which Chekhov regarded most of the so-called sure remedies for the ills of the human condition in general. Yet even as a doctor, he now expressed some bewilderment at the conflicting advice he had received from his professional brethren. Though he was pleased at being told to live near Moscow in the winter, he confessed that he did not know whom to believe or what to do. If Ostroumov was right, he told his friend Dr. Sredin, then why had he lived four winters in Yalta? To Lavrov he wrote: "And when I settle down near Moscow and begin to get used to it, the doctors will once again send me to the Crimea or to Cairo." (*July 1, 1903*.)

Strangely enough, however, the new radical advice he had received did not seem to discourage him. Rather he regarded it as a challenge, something that would lift him out of the physical and emotional doldrums he had been wallowing in. It meant change and change always excited him. He began to think of different places to live, of a new house, of fresh experiences that would bring him new friends and literary material. When Masha reacted with worriment and even grief over his report on the medical examination and the impending changes, he lightly replied that he did not understand how she could write with sadness in her heart and such gloomy thoughts.

Mariya Fyodorovna Yakunchikova's estate was only a short distance from Moscow and less than a mile from the tiny station of Naro-Fominsk on the Bryansk railroad. Connected with the wealthy Mamontov family, she owned factories in her own right and espoused the cause of arts and handicrafts among workers. She had cultivated Olga as an actress, and it was probably Olga, since Chekhov knew the lady only slightly, who made the decision in favor of her estate that summer. There they had a separate establishment spacious enough, Chekhov remarked, to accommodate ten persons. His first impressions were good — fine walks, lovely gardens and a park where birds sang all day, and a deep river nearby which, however, yielded no fish to this expert angler. He could do some work and Olga could rest; he wrote Vishnevsky that she was well, jolly, and did not think about the theater.

From this summer retreat Chekhov and his wife explored the surrounding countryside for an ideal spot and house which they could rent or buy for occupancy during the winter months. Since those old haunts of his youth, which he much admired — Zvenigorod, New Jerusalem, and Voskresensk — were not far away, they spent a few days roaming in these localities, occasionally coming across old friends of his student years. The business of house-hunting, however, discouraged and fatigued him. The very few attractive places he saw were too expensive. He and Olga rested up for a couple of days at the estate of Savva Morozov, whose wife remembered Chekhov's telling her that he was deeply troubled by the fear that he had nothing more to say in literature.

Actually, however, Chekhov was saying some important things in *The Cherry Orchard*, to which he again returned that summer. The rich industrialist and well-known benefactor of the first private opera company in Russia, Savva Mamontov, who was visiting at Naro-Fominsk, recalled an incident connected with the play. In a sudden thunderstorm the wind blew several pages of the manuscript through the open window of Chekhov's study and they were so smudged by the rain as to be undecipherable. When asked by one of the guests whether he could recall the passages, he smilingly replied that he would have to write the scenes afresh.

Chekhov also read much, mostly the fiction of new authors, the celebrated *Family Chronicle* of the old writer Aksakov, and as always quantities of newspapers and magazines. It is interesting to find him turning again to Suvorin, so widely regarded now as an arch conservative, for copies of the illegal political journal *Liberation*, which had to be smuggled from abroad. In conspiratorial fashion, they referred to the publication as "Yezhov's Works," and Chekhov took the precaution to return the precious bound volumes through Suvorin's bookstore in Moscow. Though Chekhov faithfully read these social and political tracts aimed against the government, he wrote Suvorin that he found them as monotonous and dull as an encyclopedia. Only a section of belles lettres, he declared, could rescue this periodical. On one article in *Liberation* he did comment — Gorky's open letter on the terrible massacre of Jews at Kishinev, a crime perpetrated by government inspired reactionaries.[3] "Gorky's letter about Kishinev," he wrote, "has one's sympathy, as everything he writes, but it is contrived rather than written, has none of Tolstoy's youthfulness and assurance, and it is also too long." (*June 29, 1903.*)

There can be no question of where Chekhov's sympathies lay in the Kishinev pogrom which appalled the Western world. When the eminent Jewish author Sholem Aleichem asked him to contribute a new story or one of his old tales in translation to a collection to be published in Warsaw to aid the victims, he promptly replied that he would write one if his health permitted. As for using his published stories, "they are at your entire disposal, and Yiddish translations of them published in your collection for the benefit of the Kishinev Jewish victims would afford me heartfelt pleasure."[4] (*June 19, 1903.*)

During this unusual summer spurt of energy Chekhov also worked

[3] This open letter appeared in *Liberation*, June 2, 1903. Though the piece circulated illegally in lithograph copies in Russia, it could be printed only abroad at that time.

[4] A translation of Chekhov's tale, *Difficult People*, appeared in the collection.

on the second set of proofs of *The Betrothed*, and he may have done some correcting on an additional eleventh and final volume of the Marx edition which contained his most recent stories. For in his letter to Suvorin on June 29 he pointed out that this volume would soon appear and would contain some tales which his friend had probably never read. When Marx had bought his writings, Chekhov now confessed to Suvorin — with perhaps a twinge of regret over the sum he had received — the publisher had imagined that they would print up to only three or four volumes!

Perhaps influenced by the belief that he would hereafter be living near Moscow for a good part of the year, Chekhov, who had always refused formal editorial connections with magazines, now accepted Goltsev's invitation to take charge of the literary department of *Russian Thought*. Financial considerations no doubt had a bearing on his decision, but it was a surprising one in the light of his wretched health. This move, however, seemed a part of his desire for a radical change in his life after Dr. Ostroumov's diagnosis. Though he did not plan to assume his new duties immediately, Chekhov read some manuscripts of stories for *Russian Thought* that summer. And he zealously pursued an idea suggested by the Tolstoyan Sergeenko: that he begin his editorship with a grand flourish by bringing to the magazine the manuscript of Tolstoy's remarkable tale *Hadji Murad* — a possibility which he lost through no fault of his own.[5]

Though Olga seems to have enjoyed the luxury of Mariya Yakunchikova's estate, living there soon palled on Chekhov. Rather unenthusiastically he wrote to Masha about his hostess, saying she was neither a bad nor a stupid woman. Several months later, provoked by Olga's weakness for this kind of society, he frankly declared to her: "For some reason I keep thinking of every day of life at Yakunchikova's. It would be difficult to find again such a hideously idle, absurd, and tasteless existence as that in her white house. The people lived exclusively for the pleasure of seeing General Gadon[6] or of going out with the deputy minister, Prince Obolensky. And how can Vishnevsky, who reveres these people as though they were gods, fail to understand it? There were only two good persons worthy of respect in the place,

---

[5] Tolstoy decided not to publish *Hadji Murad* during his lifetime because of the controversy with his wife over the sale of his works.

[6] Actually, Colonel V. S. Gadon, adjutant of the Governor-General of Moscow.

Natalya Yakovlevna[7] and Maxim.[8] The others were . . . Well, let us drop the subject." (*October 21, 1903*.)

It is not surprising, then, that shortly after he arrived at the estate, Chekhov informed Masha that he expected to return to Yalta in August. In fact, he had come to a decision, which probably did not entirely square with Dr. Ostroumov's orders, to spend the winter months, November, December, and January, and then May, June, July, and August in or near Moscow, and the rest of the time at Yalta. A series of letters from Masha, ecstatic about the wonderful weather at Yalta, neither hot nor dry and with frequent showers which turned the garden there into a paradise of bloom, convinced him that he was wasting his time at Yakunchikova's. Never had he heard of Yalta's weather being so attractive in the summer, he wrote Masha, whose poetic bulletins were no doubt also inspired by the desire to see her brother. And they were successful, for he and Olga left for Yalta at the beginning of July instead of in August.

« 6 »

Masha had not exaggerated. The frequent gentle rains had neutralized the customary summer heat and dust of Yalta, and all growing things flourished. Chekhov found the garden a riot of color and the interior of the house freshly redecorated by his industrious sister. Olga took advantage of the Gurzuf bungalow to rest, swim, and stroll on the beach. She grew plumper and healthier, Chekhov observed approvingly, showing no traces of her recent illness. And as usual she fussed over him, over his clothes and diet, even assisting in the daily sponge bath which she decreed. But again Olga fell afoul of the jealous guardianship which his mother and sister exercised over these details of his existence. Shortly after she left, Olga wrote him: "Why is it that when I'm there it is always difficult? Why do you torment me and never do anything? . . . But as soon as I go away, or as soon as you leave me, then remedies are prescribed and you begin feeding up, and Masha can do anything for you."

The family was not much disturbed by visitors while Olga was at Yalta. On August 14 Chekhov wrote to his medical school comrade, D. T. Saveliev, whom he had regretted not seeing when he was nearby at Naro-Fominsk, that another of their classmates, "Makar" Zembula-

---

[7] Natalya Yakovlevna Davydova, an artist.
[8] A worker on the estate.

tov, had called on him at Yalta. He has grown horribly fat, said Chekhov, but Korobov, the fourth of the group of roommates of those old student days, has grown gray. "In short," he remarked, "little by little all of us subside into a state of venerableness." Chekhov also made the acquaintance that summer of N. G. Garin-Mikhailovsky, a railway engineer by profession but also a minor fiction writer of some charm and popularity. He was then engaged in surveying the possibilities of a Crimean railroad, and assisting him was Olga's amiable brother, Konstantin Knipper, who frequently visited the Chekhovs.

Garin-Mikhailovsky introduced the artist N. Z. Panov, who did a black-and-white portrait study of Chekhov. In the course of the sittings they discussed Levitan and the eminent scientist Ilya Mechnikov, whose theories on the problems of old age much interested Chekhov. When the artist brought up the subject of Mechnikov's belief in the possibilities of prolonging human life, Chekhov sharply answered: "It is unnecessary! We need another kind of Mechnikov who could make ordinary life healthy and beautiful. And I think that this will come about."

The news that Chekhov intended to accept the editorship of the literary section of *Russian Thought* had already been publicized, for no sooner did he arrive at Yalta than manuscripts began to pour in. Goltsev also started to turn over to him now the magazine's current file in belles lettres. Chekhov needed all that strange fund of energy he had summoned up — a last miraculous expenditure of vital forces at the end of the race — to cope with this task. Yet he tackled it uncomplainingly, although he had been under the impression that his new duties would not really begin until the start of the next year. Successive batches of manuscript were returned to Goltsev with his selections and editorial annotations. Even Alexander, always on the lookout for a sure literary market, tried to make use of his brother's new connection, but Chekhov deftly put him off by replying that the remuneration of *Russian Thought* was unworthy of him. It was unworthy of Chekhov also, for when Goltsev, in the fall, offered him two hundred roubles for all the editorial labor he had expended up to that point, Chekhov ironically replied that it was not worth a rouble and promised to get in touch with him about the matter when he was next in Moscow.

That fall Chekhov was elected provisional president of the well-known Society of the Lovers of Russian Literature. Flattered by the honor, he requested that the post be held in abeyance for a year, when improved health would enable him to attend meetings, but in the meantime he offered to participate in the society's publishing program as an editor. He was not so pleased with Taganrog's unexpected announcement that it would celebrate that year the twenty-fifth anniversary of his literary activity. The date was premature, he told his wife, and besides, he objected, this customary form of glorifying writers would inevitably result in the telling of a lot of lies about him.

« 7 »

Upon his return to Yalta that summer, however, the main task that Chekhov set for himself was to complete *The Cherry Orchard*. All his plays had been written in a continuous flow of inspiration and in a remarkably short time, whatever polishing he might do on them later. He seemed convinced that an initial swift effort was an essential concomitant of dramatic writing, enabling one to avoid prolix development of theme and action. Though he had lately become accustomed to a slower, more careful and thoughtful approach to writing, illness largely accounted for the delay in completing *The Cherry Orchard*. And now only a magnificent triumph of will over bodily weakness made it possible for him to finish this last play.

The pressures on Chekhov to complete the work were considerable. Having already missed the previous season of the Art Theater, he now set as his target date the season of 1903–1904, which meant that he must have a manuscript ready by the late fall or early winter. Stanislavsky, Nemirovich-Danchenko, Olga, and Masha urged him on. Over July and August they wrote to him, and to each other, about progress of the play. All were aware, though perhaps not fully enough, of the obstacle of Chekhov's health, and the driving spirit of their concerted endeavor was reflected in Stanislavsky's letter to Olga in July: "Most of all it distresses us that Anton Pavlovich does not feel entirely well and is sometimes in low spirits. Often we have recalled the fateful words of Ostroumov. He made a mistake and spoiled the fine mood of Anton Pavlovich, for it is clear that his health depends on an inner calm. Do not think badly of us. We grieve for Anton Pavlovich and those around him, we think of the play only in those moments when we are agitated about the fate of our theater. However you regard it, our theater is Chekhov's, and without him, it will go badly for us."

To this lament Olga replied: "He now works every day; however, yesterday and today he was unwell and did not write. . . . Now there are few people around, and if his health permitted it he would work more assiduously. Don't worry — now he has just sat down to write."

Chekhov's immediate goal was to have the play ready for Olga to take to Moscow on September 19 when she left Yalta to resume her theatrical work. By September 2, he felt able to inform Nemirovich-Danchenko that, if he could maintain the pace he had struck, *The Cherry Orchard* would soon be finished. "I call the play a comedy," he wrote, and he added that the second act had caused him much difficulty, that Olga ought to play the part of the mother, Ranevskaya, but that he had no notion of who should take the role of her daughter Anya. Several days later, however, illness brought the pace to a standstill, and on September 15 he had to write Stanislavsky's wife, who acted under the name of Lilina, that Olga would not arrive in Moscow with a manuscript after all, but that he hoped to send all four acts soon. Once again he emphasized the fact that "Not a drama but a comedy has emerged from me, in places even a farce," and he worried over the effect this might have on Nemirovich-Danchenko.

Now, in almost daily letters to Olga in Moscow, Chekhov kept her posted — and, through her, the directors of the Art Theater — on his tortuous progress. It is a record of heroic struggle against the disintegrating forces of nature in a supreme effort to achieve a work of artistic beauty. Added to extreme debility, loss of appetite, and endless coughing was a protracted bowel disturbance, one of the complications of his disease. The incommunicable sadness of his hopes as he worked away in the wretched light of the candle-illuminated study at Yalta is somehow conveyed in one of his reports to Olga: "The last act will be merry, and indeed the whole play will be merry and giddy." (*September 21, 1903.*)

On September 26 Chekhov wired his wife that he had at last finished the first draft of *The Cherry Orchard*. But he still had to recopy and revise it. Always more inclined to disparage than to praise his artistic efforts, he now could not resist the temptation to claim that he had contributed something new in his play. "My people have turned out alive, that is true," he wrote Olga, "but what the play amounts to, I don't know." (*September 27, 1903.*) As the days slipped by and his wife failed to receive the promised manuscript, she charged him with deceiving her about having finished the play. Her impatience was no doubt intensified by the anxieties of the directors of the Art Theater. Repeatedly he pleaded with Olga to realize that in recopying it he had to think over many points, to change much, and that this process made for a better play and more clearly delineated characters. "There is still weakness and coughing," he informed her on October 2. "I write every day; though only a little, still I write. When you read the play after I send it, you will see what might have been done with this subject under favorable circumstances — that is, with good health. But now it is a shame, I write a couple of lines a day, get used to what I've written, and so on and so on." And the next day he besought her not to be cross, for he could not write any faster: "Darling, forgive me about the play! Forgive me! On my honor I've finished it, and am only recopying it." Then in five more days he exclaimed: "I tell you the holy truth, darling: if my play is not a success, it can be blamed on my bowels." Actually, Chekhov was involved in not only a second but also a third draft of *The Cherry Orchard*.

Finally, on October 12, he informed his wife: "And so, pony, hurrah for my long-suffering and yours! The play is finished, finished at last; and tomorrow evening, or at the latest on the morning of the fourteenth, it will be sent to Moscow!" And he added, with a degree of feeling which Olga could perhaps never appreciate: "Darling, how hard it was for me to write the play!"

Chekhov waited impatiently at Yalta for reactions to *The Cherry Orchard*. Perhaps he had a premonition that this play, created with so much effort and pain, was to be his last, for he seemed hypersensitive about its success and everything connected with it. For some time he had been wondering whether his powers had failed. After he received telegrams from Olga and Nemirovich-Danchenko, he wrote his wife on October 19 that all day he had waited for news with a flutter at his heart and in a state of funk, for he was terrified. Nemirovich-Danchenko's telegram of a hundred and eighty words described the play as Chekhov's finest, the characters as new, interesting, and rich in substance, and the social content as not new but freshly apprehended, original, and poetic. But he had some reservations, which concerned' mostly a heaviness in the second act and a superfluity of tears among the characters.

Stanislavsky's telegram, which arrived two days later, was lyrical by comparison: I WAS OVERCOME, CANNOT COLLECT MYSELF, I FELL INTO UNPRECEDENTED RAPTURE. I REGARD YOUR PLAY AS THE BEST OF ALL THE BEAUTIFUL THINGS WRITTEN BY YOU. MY HEARTFELT CONGRATULATIONS TO AN AUTHOR OF GENIUS. And soon thereafter both directors sent telegrams of the reaction of the troupe when Nemirovich-Danchenko read *The Cherry Orchard* to them: ENORMOUS IMPRESSION . . . ; GREAT AND REMARKABLE EXCITEMENT . . . ; EXCEPTIONALLY BRILLIANT SUCCESS . . . ; THEY WEPT AT THE LAST ACT. And Stanislavsky then informed him, revealing that he had somewhat missed the point: "This is not a comedy or a farce, as you wrote, it is a tragedy whatever the solution you may have found for the better life in the last act." Further, Chekhov promptly received an offer from Gorky to publish the play in the annual of his firm Znanie, at a remuneration of fifteen hundred roubles a signature, the highest Chekhov had ever received. Because of his contract with Marx, which restricted publication of new works to newspapers and magazines, or to books that appeared for charitable purposes, it seemed at first that Chekhov would have to reject this alluring proposal. Violation of the contract carried a penalty at the rate of five thousand roubles for every printed signature. However, a way out was found. Both Chekhov and Gorky were interested in an appeal to aid indigent women medical students in Petersburg, and the Znanie Annual, including *The Cherry Orchard*, was published on behalf of this charitable purpose.[9]

Chekhov had reason to feel elated by all these encomiums, but he was also a bit dismayed. He had been conscious of weaknesses in the second act and was prepared to alter it, as well as other things, for he did not regard the manuscript he sent in as the final form of the play. But he had no notion that he had written a tragedy, and he resented the imputation that his characters constantly gave way to tears. He wrote Olga: "Today I received a telegram from Alekseev (Stanislavsky) in which he calls my play a work of genius; this amounts to overpraising the play and robbing it of a good half of the success it might have under favorable circumstances." (*October 21, 1903.*)

In fact, at this point several disagreeable happenings occurred which soured Chekhov's initial enthusiasm for *The Cherry Orchard* and caused him to wonder why he had ever written it. In what appeared to be a misguided effort at promotion, Nemirovich-Danchenko had given an account of the contents of the play to N. E. Efros of the *Daily News*. When the story appeared it was garbled. In Act III, instead of the

[9] With certain changes and corrections, *The Cherry Orchard* was first published in the Znanie Annual in Petersburg in 1904, and a second edition appeared the following year. The play was also brought out in a separate edition by Marx (Petersburg, 1904).

action taking place in a drawing room, a hotel was indicated, the name of a leading character was distorted, and other details were wrong. Worse, it was plainly announced in this premature notice that the author's wife would act the lead (the casting had not yet been done). Olga at once wrote her husband to deplore this mess, and Chekhov sent an indignant telegram to Nemirovich-Danchenko, for the news item was picked up by the press in general and widely reprinted. The incident grew in complexity — with Chekhov inserting a denunciation in the *Crimean Courier*, and this in turn answered by the *Daily News*. He ultimately accepted Nemirovich-Danchenko's apologies, but the whole affair left him with the eerie feeling that either the play had been misread in Moscow or that there were things in this manuscript which he did not remember and which ought to be eliminated.

An additional annoyance was the failure of the co-directors, after the first flush of excitement about *The Cherry Orchard*, to inform Chekhov promptly whether the play would be produced that season and, if so, what the casting would be. Here his impatience, no doubt aggravated by his illness, was somewhat unreasonable. The Art Theater's season was under way, and, among their many problems of repertoire, the directors were struggling with a new production of *Julius Caesar*. Further, latent differences between the co-directors were cropping up, rumors of which reached Chekhov. When he eventually received a letter from Stanislavsky on October 29 about the details of the casting, he replied the next day and curtly pointed out that he was all alone at Yalta, that letters were precious to him, and that if it had not been for his wife, he would have remained entirely in the dark about the play ever since he had submitted the manuscript. Indeed, Olga had become the butt of his irritation and he inflicted on her his complaints over the delays as well as much interesting information on casting, the interpretaton of roles, and staging which he was really anxious to impart to the directors.

One thing that particularly disturbed Chekhov was his fear that Nemirovich-Danchenko would assign roles out of diplomatic considerations. In order to anticipate this possibility, Chekhov wrote him a long letter on November 2, in which he provided brief sketches of the salient features of most of the characters and then suggested actors in the company to fill each of the roles. He also commented firmly on the growing estrangements of the co-directors, a development which Nemirovich-Danchenko himself had mentioned. Chekhov tended to side with him in the dispute, and rejected his pious characterization of the company as "Stanislavsky's theater." If Nemirovich-Danchenko left, Chekhov asserted, so would he. And in reacting to the news that Gorky intended, in imitation of the Moscow Art Theater, to set up a "people's theater" in Nizhny Novgorod, Chekhov declared: "Let me say in this connection that people's theaters and people's literature are just foolishness, something to sweeten up the people. Gogol should not be lowered to the level of the people, but the people should be raised to Gogol's level."

Not until November 7 did Nemirovich-Danchenko wire Chekhov the names of the actors in the cast, with the exception of Anya, Varya, and Charlotta, where he offered several suggestions and asked Chekhov to make the final choice. On the whole, the total selection pleased him. Shortly thereafter, Stanislavsky announced that rehearsals would begin on November 10. Though Chekhov's main questions had now been answered, he still felt uneasy about the play. When he learned that a scheduled public reading by Nemirovich-Danchenko of an act of *The Cherry Orchard* had been canceled because students, convinced that they had been discriminated against in the assignment of tickets, stormed the auditorium, Chekhov wryly commented in a letter to Olga: "So Nemirovich-Danchenko did not read my play to the Society of Lovers of Russian Literature? We began with misunderstandings and we shall end with them — such, it seems, is the fate of my play." (*November 25, 1903.*)

« 8 »

In replying to the letter of an old acquaintance, the writer V. L. Kign-Dedlov, from whom he had not heard for some time, Chekhov mentioned in bringing him up to date: "Two or three years ago I married and I'm very glad of it; it seems to me that my life has changed for the better. What they ordinarily write about married life is the utterest fibbing." (*November 10, 1903.*) Indeed he never wearied now of telling his pony — his new nickname for Olga — that he could not live without her. In fact, when she left for Moscow on September 19, he had every intention of rejoining her there at the end of that month and spending the rest of the autumn and winter with her.

The worsening of his health at that point, rather than any desire to remain at Yalta to finish his play, resulted in a series of agonizing postponements. And in his weakened state Chekhov seemed inclined to accept, for the time being, the wise advice of Dr. Altschuler against any form of travel. The physician, Chekhov reported to Olga, had thrown up his hands in horror when he told him of the sponge baths which she had favored. He forbade them. The cold water and exertion were too much. With his shortness of breath, even to dress himself now was a difficult task. A week later Chekhov wrote to Olga that "your enemy" Altschuler had visited again to prescribe pills to remedy his protracted diarrhea. And he added that "Altschuler had a long talk with me about my illness and spoke most disapprovingly of Ostroumov for allowing me to live in Moscow in the winter. He implored me not to go to Moscow, not to live there. He said that Ostroumov had probably been drunk." (*October 2, 1903.*)

Chekhov's helplessness in his illness elicited from Olga the usual flow of self-denunciations which, however sincere, now annoyed and even angered him. She knew that he was ill, she wrote, and that she must seem to him like a nonentity who came, stayed with him, and then left. There was such horrible falsity in her life — and she concluded that under no circumstance should he come to Moscow. Stop writing such dismal letters, he warned her. He would come anyway, even if he had to live in a hotel, he quipped, for he felt the urge to be immoral. And when she relented and glorified him as her superman, he capped it: "Your superman who runs so often to a super watercloset."

Though the clinical tone now of so many of Chekhov's letters to his wife was an understandable outgrowth of his sickroom existence, much of it must be attributed to his conscientious effort to respond to her incessant catechizing him on his condition and on his daily routine. Often he tried to treat the matter lightly or whimsically. Ferns and fungi were growing all over him, he assured Olga in answer to her obsession on cleanliness. Yet he was painfully conscious of the lack of gaiety in his letters, and more than once deplored their concentration on medical details.

The truth of the matter was that their prolonged daily correspondence, as a kind of surrogate for a normal life together, had reached the point of diminishing returns. This was particularly so in Chekhov's case, where sickness compelled a narrower and narrower daily routine that left nothing to be said that was not repetitious. And the obvious compensation of his intellectual and spiritual world he somehow could not share with Olga.

After Chekhov finished *The Cherry Orchard*, which had been such an active theme in their correspondence throughout the fall, he felt desperately lonely at Yalta. If illness and Altschuler's advice had not prevented it, he would have left at once for Moscow and Olga. Besides, he very much wanted to be present at the rehearsals of his play. With the greatest impatience he waited for an improvement in his condition, as well as word from Olga that he should come — for they had agreed that she would set the time, depending on the weather in Moscow. Though he admitted that the weather then at Yalta left nothing to be desired, he was stubbornly determined to reject Dr. Altschuler's entreaties and follow Dr. Ostroumov's counsel to stay in Moscow for the winter. Somehow cold did not seem to matter to him any longer.

But the days dragged on into November with little improvement in his health. Besides, reports of both Olga and Masha on Moscow weather were anything but encouraging. Chekhov's exasperation mounted, and he quite humanly took it out on his wife. Why had she not sent him the repertoire of the Art Theater, which he had repeatedly asked for? Or the boots for one of the servants, and the toilet paper? Did she think he was going to wear a fur coat or collar of imitation sealskin? he fumed — over her desire to save money on a fur coat which he had asked her to have made for him in Moscow; surely there was nothing wrong, he expostulated, in his having a fur coat that cost three or four hundred roubles! She was a miser, he charged; and then he wired her to cancel the whole thing.

Chekhov's mother added to his problems at this time, for she fretted over the prospect of remaining at Yalta when he left. Though he thought her behavior arbitrary, he managed with some difficulty to send her to Ivan for a stay in Moscow, convinced that she would soon want to return to Yalta. And now he had to protest guiltily to Masha and Olga that he had not really quarreled with his mother.

With a slight improvement of his condition in the second half of November, Chekhov began irrationally pleading with Olga to tell him to come, as though she were the legislatress of Moscow weather. He threatened to cease writing to her, to go abroad. Did she not know that it was revolting to live at Yalta, and that thanks to its water and excellent air he had to be on the trot all day? He would live on nothing but lentils, he wrote, and get up respectfully whenever Nemirovich-Danchenko and Vishnevsky came into the room, if only she would summon him. "I'm impatiently waiting for the day and hour when my wife will finally permit me to come to Moscow," he wrote Stanislavsky on November 23. "I now begin to suspect that she is up to some trick or other. The weather here is calm, warm, remarkable; but when one re-calls Moscow and the Sandunov baths,[10] all this delight seems stale and useless to anyone. I sit in my study and keep looking at the tele-phone. I receive my telegrams by telephone and am expecting every minute to be summoned at last to Moscow."

Two days before, he had written to Olga: "There's no news. I'm writing nothing, for I keep waiting for you to order me to pack and travel to Moscow. To Moscow, to Moscow! That is not said by THREE SISTERS but by ONE HUSBAND. I embrace my little turkey."

In a few days his little turkey finally gave him the signal. Chekhov set out joyously, entirely unconcerned about the consequences, as though convinced that the living go on dying and the dead are forever dead. How passionately he wanted to live as long as he could enjoy life!

CHAPTER XXVII

"Ich Sterbe"

CHEKHOV told a friend that he found every subject interesting except sickness, and he seemed determined now not to allow it to prevent him from participating in staging the first performance of *The Cherry Orchard*. From some mysterious inner resources he summoned reserves of strength to carry him through this last adventure in the theater which he had both loved and hated throughout his life. A good part of the first six weeks after his arrival in Moscow on December 4, 1903, he spent at the Art Theater, attending rehearsals of his play in the daytime and in see-ing performances of other plays in the evenings.

What the censor might do to *The Cherry Orchard* had worried Chekhov, but the play was quickly certified with the deletion of only two brief passages — in Act II from the remarks of that "eternal student" Trofimov, where he speaks of most Russians living like savages in filth and stuffiness, and where he tells Anya that the old bark on the cherry trees seems to be tormented by painful visions of what happened years ago. Indeed, Chekhov had more reason to be con-cerned with what Stanislavsky would do to his play. "It is not blooming now," Stanislavsky wrote of the rehearsals of *The Cherry Orchard* to

[10] Chekhov's favorite public baths in Moscow.

an actress friend on December 26. "The blossoms had only just begun to appear when the author arrived and messed up everything for us. The blossoms vanished and only now are new buds starting to show themselves."

Chekhov admired Stanislavsky's extraordinary inventiveness in his mise-en-scènes, but he also deplored his naturalistic excesses in these respects, especially in the use of sounds. He mimicked a character in *The Cherry Orchard*, speaking loud enough for the director to over-hear: "What fine quiet. How wonderful! We hear no birds, no dogs, no cuckoos, no owls, no clocks, no sleigh bells, no crickets." Though Stanislavsky described Chekhov as growing pale when he suggested that the whole end of the second act be shortened, he did not hesitate to revise it, for he had been dissatisfied with it all along.[1]

Such minor differences, however, were not those that prompted Stanislavsky to declare later that "The production of *The Cherry Orchard* was accomplished with great hardships," or Chekhov's wife to admit: "The directors and author could not understand each other, could not agree." Their fundamental disagreement was that Chekhov regarded his play as a happy comedy and Stanislavsky planned to stage it — and in this he had convinced his actors — as the poetically tragic drama of the vanishing life of the gentry, crushed by economic de-mands of vulgar commercialism. "I do not remember," Stanislavsky wrote in his recollections, "that Chekhov ever defended any opinion of his with such vigor as he did this one when he first heard these reactions to his play at a meeting." No doubt Stanislavsky's aesthetic preferences, the ethos of the time, and the popular identification of Chekhov as the sad and pessimistic chronicler of the fading beauty of an irrecoverable age — all contrived to force an emphasis upon his play which he never intended. He told his former student Yakovlev, who visited him in Moscow: "I can't figure it out; either the play is no good or the actors don't understand me. . . . As it is now being done, *The Cherry Orchard* is impossible to put on." And four days before its

[1] Stanislavsky gives the impression that Chekhov made changes in Act II only after the première of *The Cherry Orchard*. However, recent evidence proves that he introduced changes before the opening of the play. Further, he did not delete Charlotta's monologue, as Stanislavsky claims, but transferred it to the beginning of the act and also rewrote the end of the act. See "Avtograf dobavlenii ko vtoromu aktu *Vishnevogo sada*," in *Literaturnoe Nasledstvo* ("Manuscript Additions to the Second Act of *The Cherry Orchard*," in *Literary Heritage*), Moscow, 1960, LXVIII, 141.

première, he gloomily wrote to his old friend the headmistress of the Yalta school: "I expect no particular success, the thing is going poorly."

Apparently neither did Stanislavsky expect *The Cherry Orchard* to achieve any particular success on the opening night, for he points out, in *My Life in Art*, that the date of the première, January 17, 1904, Chekhov's forty-fourth birthday, could also be used to celebrate the twenty-fifth anniversary of his literary activity: "Our reckoning was simple. If the actors were not able to put the play over, its lack of great success could be blamed on the unusual conditions of the jubilee evening, which would not fail to draw the spectators' attention to the author and away from the actors." In various quarters plans to celebrate this literary anniversary had been going on for some time despite Chekhov's efforts to discourage them. In April of the previous year he had responded with some agitation to Mirolyubov, who brought up the subject of a jubilee: "What is there to be festive about? To celebrate? No, it won't take place. There would be too much that would be burdensome." And when Iordanov, his beneficiary of many years, wrote him of plans for a big celebration in Taganrog in 1904 — a small one had been held there in 1903 — Chekhov deliberately put him off with such excuses as lack of interest, illness, and uncertainty about the actual date of the beginning of his literary career.[2]

In anticipation of the jubilee a final effort was made by Gorky and his friends to compel a renegotiation of Chekhov's contract with Marx. Gorky and Leonid Andreev drafted a letter to the publisher and were busily collecting the signatures of some of the most distinguished authors, artists, and scholars. In the letter they pointed out that all of Russia would soon be celebrating Chekhov's literary jubilee; that he was ill and in poor material circumstances despite the great artistic service he had rendered to his country; and after analyzing the terms of the contract and indicating how profitable they were to the publisher, and disadvantageous to Chekhov, the letter concluded with a plea to Marx to reconsider the whole matter as a kind of patriotic and cultural duty. The initiators were confident of success and planned to announce the results at the jubilee celebration. However, when the move came to Chekhov's attention, he asked the leaders to desist and he was reported

[2] Chekhov's first known published story was in 1880, but some trifles of his, which his brother Alexander submitted to the humor magazine *Alarm Clock*, may have appeared as early as 1877. However, this earlier date has never been established.

by Teleshov as saying: "I signed the agreement with Marx and for me to repudiate it would be distasteful. If I sold my works cheaply, it is my fault. I committed a stupidity. Marx ought not to have to answer for another's mistake. On another occasion I'll be more careful."

Perhaps a bit more realistically, Chekhov told Yakovlev at this time: "I ought soon to go abroad, but I have no money at all. Only a disagreeable memory remains of the seventy-five thousand roubles from Marx. Yes, you were right formerly; I ought to have published the works myself. But how could I have supposed, then, that I would go on for five more years? And at that time seventy-five thousand seemed to me inexhaustible wealth. Now, if it were not for the income from my plays, I would have nothing! But you know, they regard me as a very wealthy man. Even today I received two letters; one asked for a loan of five hundred roubles, the other for seven hundred and fifty. Really, isn't this bitter irony? I've never failed to answer a single letter, but I'll not answer these, not because I'm ashamed to confess my poverty; but I'm convinced they will not believe it!"

Although Chekhov was aware that the jubilee plans were underway, it is not clear whether he knew that the celebration would take place during the première of *The Cherry Orchard*.[3] His refusal to attend the opening of the play may well have been caused by suspicion that some attempt would be made to honor him publicly. At the end of the second act, Nemirovich-Danchenko sent him a note to say that the audience had called for him and the actors wished to see him. Chekhov arrived before the last act. He was ushered on the stage before the whole troupe of the Art Theater, led by Stanislavsky and Nemirovich-Danchenko, and representatives of Moscow's leading theatrical and literary societies. The packed house, apparently as much surprised as Chekhov, roared their approval in a prolonged and noisy demonstration. Flowers, wreaths, and various gifts were showered on him. He stood there blinking in the bright lights, thin, deathly pale, weak, struggling to restrain fits of coughing. Then the speeches began — greetings by A. N. Veselovsky from the Society of Lovers of Russian Literature, by Goltsev on behalf of a series of Moscow publications, and from S. A. Ivantsev for the Literary-Artistic Circle. As they droned

---

[3] Stanislavsky asserts that Chekhov knew that the jubilee would take place at the première of the play, and protested; Nemirovich-Danchenko and one of the actors, L. M. Leonidov, insist that he did not know. Chekhov's sister also claimed that he was unaware that the celebration would take place at the opening performance of *The Cherry Orchard*.

on, someone in the audience shouted "Be seated!" to the plainly weary
Chekhov, but there were no chairs on the stage. He frowned, looked
confused, did not know what to do with his hands, and remained
patiently standing. Next came the praise of representatives of a series
of leading newspapers followed by greetings from the Maly Theater,
represented by the eminent actress G. N. Fedotova. Telegrams were
read from magazines, organizations, and well-known personages from
all over Russia. Perhaps the most stirring speech was that of Nemirovich-Danchenko on behalf of the Art Theater. "Our salutations may
have wearied you," he concluded in a voice full of emotion, "but you
ought to take comfort from this: that you observe here only a part
of the limitless devotion which all Russian educated society has for
you. To such an extent is our theater indebted to your talent, to your
tender heart, to your pure soul, that you in all justice may say: 'This is
my theater. . . .' "

How often had Chekhov laughed at this Russian passion for jubilees
and satirized it in his writings! Had he not refused to attend the
jubilee for old Grigorovich? He knew they told lies at such affairs, and
perhaps this was in his thoughts as he stood there listening, a faint
smile occasionally appearing on his face, as though he were not really a
part of all this fuss and bother. But if he joyfully scented the odor of
triumph, he also scented the odor of death. The triumph, Stanislavsky
prophetically remarked, with the pale, sickly Chekhov in mind,
"smelled of a funeral. Our souls were heavy within us." Two days
later, Chekhov wrote to his friend Batyushkov: ". . . They honored
me so expansively, joyously, and so unexpectedly that I've not yet
recovered from it."

At the same time, however, Chekhov informed Leontiev-Shcheglov
that his play had been performed and that he was not in a good mood.
The noisy jubilee had not distracted the audience from the inadequacies
of the performance, as Stanislavsky had hoped. He himself admitted
that the première had enjoyed only a mediocre success, and to his
credit he accepted the blame. The reviews, on the whole, while in no
sense damning either the play or the performance, criticized much of
the acting, and interpreted *The Cherry Orchard* from the point of view
of the emphasis which Stanislavsky had imparted to it — namely, the
social tragedy of the passing of the old order symbolized by the sale of
the cherry orchard.

Nearly all the characters, however, have pronounced comic aspects, and some of the situations designedly verge on the farcical. Though drawn with wonderful sympathy, Ranevskaya and her brother Gaev are not very serious people, nor is their predicament in any sense tragic. In the end, they quickly become reconciled to the loss of their estate and the cherry orchard. She is more intent on getting back to her shiftless lover in Paris, and Gaev is quite excited by his first real job in the bank — which he will certainly not hold for long. And the young couple, Anya and Trofimov, gaily welcome the loss of the cherry orchard, for it opens the door to a new life filled with exciting possibilities. "All Russia is our orchard," Trofimov had declared to Anya. "Our land is vast, and beautiful; there are many wonderful places in it." In these words of Trofimov, who also has his comic aspects, lies the real symbolism of the loss of the cherry orchard — Chekhov's favorite theme of the destruction of beauty by those who are blind to it. Trofimov expresses another favorite theme of Chekhov, that of hard work as a solution for the ills of Russia. Even the merchant Lopakhin, whom Varya in a farcical scene cracks on the head with a stick, is a lover of beauty. But Lopakhin, whom Chekhov regarded as the central character, also destroys beauty if it gets in the way of his accumulation of wealth.

In short, Chekhov was concerned in *The Cherry Orchard* with the portrayal of a group of characters whose faults are ludicrous but who nevertheless gain the sympathy of the audience because of the magic of their creator's art. As always in the plays of his last period, and much more so in *The Cherry Orchard*, he combines the comic with the serious, for he had come to think of comedy as not only accusatory but also as life-affirming. He saw no contradiction between the development of serious themes through comic expression, situations, and action. Nor did he feel it necessary to indulge in polemics with his characters in exposing their faults. He saw no reason for disputing with people who are drones, eating and drinking too much, spending other people's money, deceiving themselves, pretending to sympathy for the misfortunes of the lowly while posing as idealists, liberals, lovers of beauty, and victims of fate. Chekhov regarded such people as truly comic; he felt that they should be allowed to ridicule themselves through their words and action while at the same time arousing the compassion of the audience because of their failure to see themselves as others see them. This is the situation of most of the characters in *The Cherry Orchard*.

It is little wonder then that Chekhov argued so vigorously with the Art Theater over its interpretation of his play. If it had not been for his illness, which no doubt reduced his capacity to struggle, he might well have withdrawn *The Cherry Orchard*. Months after the première, still annoyed by the Art Theater's rejection of his description of the work as a comedy, he wrote Olga on April 10: "Why is it that my play is persistently called a drama in posters and newspaper advertisements? Nemirovich-Danchenko and Stanislavsky see in my play something absolutely different from what I have written, and I'm willing to stake my word on it that neither of them has once read my play through attentively. Forgive me, but I assure you it is so." Ironically enough, despite Chekhov's conviction of the Art Theater's misinterpretation of *The Cherry Orchard*, it became the most successful of all his plays and was retained in their repertoire for years.

« 2 »

Shortly before the première of *The Cherry Orchard*, Chekhov had attended the Art Theater's New Year's party — which, according to Stanislavsky, had been arranged especially for his amusement. At the Punch and Judy show he refused to occupy the seat of honor reserved for him and merged with the crowd somewhere in the back rows. Among the more or less impromptu skits on the theater stage was an uproariously fake wrestling match, a sport that Chekhov liked to watch, between the huge Chaliapin, dressed as an Oriental, and the tiny, short-legged Sulerzhitsky, at the conclusion of which both sang Ukrainian songs. Then four actors, disguised as Vienna grisettes, sang a nonsensical quartette and danced a cascade jig. At the conclusion of the show, a supper of every imaginable delicacy was served in the foyer, accompanied by much laughter, drinking, merry toasts, and the reading of telegrams. After the meal, chairs and tables were pushed back and the dancing began. Soon the foyer with its bright decorations was transformed into a varicolored carousel of whirling ribbon, lace, stylish coiffures, flying tails of dresscoats and military epaulets. But in a far corner at a table by a window sat Chekhov and Gorky, trying to maintain a conversation above the hubbub, each periodically falling into coughing spells. "It could be said of you and me," remarked Chekhov, "that two authors have spent a fine evening together having an interesting cough with one another."

Bunin was a welcome visitor on those evenings when Olga was acting and Chekhov felt too weary to go to the theater. This cheerful companion would stay until she returned. Bunin recalls one evening when Olga, with a night off, elected to go to a charity concert with Nemirovich-Danchenko. Her escort, handsome in his tails and smelling of cigar smoke and eau de cologne, arrived, and Olga, young, fresh, and especially lovely in her evening dress, said to her husband: "Don't be bored without me, darling, but I know you're always happy with Bukishonchik. *Au revoir*, sweet" — and departed. Bunin was delighted to be allowed to remain and chat with his friend. Chekhov washed his head while he reminisced about his past, his family, or discussed mutual literary acquaintances. Bunin also remembered on this occasion that Chekhov dreamed out loud, as he had done several times recently, of wanting to go off as a wanderer to holy places and then settle down in some monastery near a forest and lake where he could sit on a bench outside the gates on the long summer evenings. When Bunin informed him that he and the playwright Naidenov were planning soon to leave for Nice, Chekhov at once offered to put him in touch with his friends there. Earnestly he gave Bunin advice about his health, and urged him to take a more professional attitude toward literature, give up dilettantism, and do some writing every day. At about four in the morning Olga returned, reeking of wine. "What, you are not yet asleep darling? That's bad. And you are still here, Bukishonchik, but of course he's not bored with you!" Bunin arose and quickly left.

After the excitement of attending rehearsals, the party and jubilee and the opening of his play, Chekhov seemed content to remain at home. Besides, real Moscow cold had set in. Occasionally he would venture out with Olga, on her free days, for he loved to walk along Petrovka or Kuznetsky Most, looking at the shops and crowds, pleased as a child with his new fur coat and beaver cap which she had finally had the furrier make for him. Later he was to thank her for being so nice and for the wonderful time they spent together during those winter months.

Indeed, because of his painful difficulty in managing the three flights to his apartment, only what Chekhov considered important events persuaded him to make the effort, such as attending the opera benefit performance at the Grand Theater of his friend Chaliapin or going to the funeral of Dr. N. V. Altukhov, a teacher and medical classmate.[4] At the university church he joined in the singing with his deep voice, and

[4] The burial of Dr. Altukhov took place on December 17, 1903.

there he met another classmate, Dr. Rossolimo. Before proceeding to the cemetery, Chekhov requested that they go to Rossolimo's house and rest a bit. There the hostess asked to take a picture. As they posed, Chekhov, in the spirit of the occasion, joked about which of them would be the first to follow their dead classmate to the grave. At the entrance to the cemetery youths bore the casket over the heads of the funeral procession, and others, with proud faces, carried a huge wreath of fresh flowers, bearing the inscription: FROM HIS STUDENTS. Chekhov whispered to Rossolimo: "Here are those who bury the old and bring fresh flowers and the hopes of youth together with him into the kingdom of death."

Chekhov made another exception to attend a meeting of the Wednesday Club, an informal group of Moscow literary people got together by N. D. Teleshov and ordinarily gathering at his home to read and discuss works in progress. His sister and Olga accompanied him. The fare of the day was a rather heavy paper on the philosophy of Nietzsche read by Goltsev. Little debate followed on this subject and at the end some of the members, including a few of the foremost authors of the time, gathered around Chekhov. One young writer, S. T. Semenov, observed that his face was that of a sufferer, his chest seemed to have fallen in, and his clothes hung on him as on a peg. Yet he was kindly, smiling, sociable; and while they listened, often laughing, he talked amusingly about his early failures in literature. Yet all of them, related Semenov, felt that he was not long for this world and they grew thoughtfully sad after he left.

On the whole, however, Chekhov's health remained surprisingly good that winter, and he seemed to enjoy keeping himself busy correcting the proof of *The Cherry Orchard* and with his editorial work for *Russian Thought*. By preference he concentrated on the manuscripts of new authors, leaving those of established writers to the judgment of Goltsev. And hopefully he continued to promise tales of his own to pleading publishers. But the usual visitors and the commissions he undertook for friends and strangers — not the least of which was trying vainly to have repaired the battered watch of the Yalta headmistress, and finally buying her a new one — ate into his time. As early in his stay as January 20, he wrote to Sredin: "There is such a terrible press of people here that I have not one free moment, for I'm constantly receiving or seeing visitors off, talking endlessly, so that in those rare times when I am free I begin to dream about returning to my Yalta penates, and I must say that I dream of it with satisfaction."

One much discussed subject that greatly disturbed Chekhov at this time was the outbreak of the Russo-Japanese war. Though he believed there was a lot of lying about the issues in the press, he expressed normal patriotic sentiments, was sure his countrymen would triumph, and even vaguely contemplated going to the front as a physician, in which post he was convinced he would learn more about the fighting than the journalists. But when someone approached him to write a patriotic play about the war, he objected, said Stanislavsky, and declared: "Listen, it is necessary that twenty years should pass. It is impossible to speak of it now. The soul must first be in repose. Only then can an author be unprejudiced." And when Lidiya Avilova, like some strange voice arising out of the depths of the national crisis, wrote to ask him to contribute a story for a volume she was preparing to aid Russian war victims, he firmly discouraged the project. There were some fifteen such collections in the making, he replied, and they wasted time and made little or no money. If she must persist, he advised an anthology of the best sayings on wounded soldiers, on compassion and aid for them, drawn from the world's foremost writers. That would be quick and easy to do, he said, and might even be interesting.

What turned Chekhov's thoughts toward hated Yalta again after he had been in Moscow less than two months? It would be hard to say. As we have seen, first he contemplated going abroad, but a lack of money seems to have prevented this. For some time now travel had become a habit, a way of life. After a short time in one place, he longed to leave it, even if it meant leaving his wife, and his reasons for leaving often seem like mere rationalizations.

Chekhov did not offer the reason of ill health for wishing now to leave Moscow, and "too many visitors" he knew from long experience would be a nuisance duplicated at Yalta. Further, he was once again disobeying the doctor's orders. Ostroumov's advice to live in or near Moscow through the winter months and to avoid trips abroad was possibly motivated, like Altschuler's advice, by the realization that travel only worsened Chekhov's condition. At best, the search up to this point for a house on the outskirts of the city, which was suitable and within his means, had been half hearted, although at first he had so enthusiastically accepted this prospect. Perhaps the knowledge that Olga would again be going to Petersburg on tour influenced his decision to leave, yet he left considerably before her departure.

As though to appease his conscience, he and Olga, on February 14, went to Tsaritsyno, about twenty miles from Moscow, to look at a house there for sale. He regarded it as a good possibility but he could come to no decision. Unable to get a train, they had to drive all the way back in an open sleigh in freezing weather. But according to Olga, he enjoyed watching the white fields sparkling in the sun and listening to the scrunch of the runners in the hard snow. Some years later, in recalling this episode, she wrote: "It was as though fate had been gracious and had resolved to bestow upon him during the last year of his life the joys he prized most: Moscow, winter, the production of *The Cherry Orchard*, and the people he loved."

However, that very day, shortly after he got back from Tsaritsyno, Chekhov prepared to desert these joys, and also Olga, for Yalta. Among the last-minute matters to attend to was an answer to another letter of Lidiya Avilova, who now seemed disposed to reopen their correspondence again with more of her emotional self-laceration. After agreeing in her letter on the unwisdom of publishing a volume of tales to aid Russian victims of the war with Japan, she suddenly plunged into a curiously cryptic apologia for the whole course of her behavior toward him. "I would very much like to see you," she wrote, "to speak to you in order to relieve my mind of much that is so hateful to me. It is all the more ludicrous and sad, especially at my age when life has passed, to carry on so painfully! Truly, it is shameful. In all conscience, however, I do not feel that I have deserved it. Forgive this unsolicited frankness, Anton Pavlovich. Although I did not seek it, I've seized this opportunity. I feared I would die without succeeding in saying that I have always profoundly esteemed you and regarded you as the best of men. And what of it if I have lowered myself in your opinion? So it had to be. It has been the greatest sorrow of my life. Now it is time to say it. . . . I don't want you to forgive me, but I do want you to understand."[5]

There was perhaps more evasion than understanding in his reply, which he apparently scribbled off with the ease of one of the many prescriptions he used to write for the common cold: "Forgive me. I'm frozen, for I've just returned from Tsaritsyno . . . my hands can

[5] This letter, dated February 9, 1904, is not quoted in Lidiya Avilova's memoirs. It is one of three of her letters to Chekhov which by chance survived in his archives, and it was recently published, in part, in A. P. *Chekhov v vospominaniyakh sovremennikov* (A. P. *Chekhov in the Remembrances of Contemporaries*), 4th ed., Moscow, 1960, p. 726.

hardly write and I must pack. All the best to you, keep cheerful, take a less complicated view of life, for it is probably much simpler in reality. And whether life, of which we know nothing, deserves all the tormenting thoughts on which our Russian minds wear themselves out — this is still a question." And it remained one, for this was the last she heard from Chekhov.

« 3 »

Chekhov's birthday and jubilee presents arrived at Yalta shortly after he did, and they were unpacked and many were put on display in the study. Some were costly antiques, such as ancient chests, fabrics, and an eighteenth-century silver inkstand and pen. An artist friend had presented him with an exquisite, hand-carved miniature of an old Russian village. Stanislavsky had searched long for a mediaeval gift of richly embroidered cloth which he used to decorate the jubilee wreath. Chekhov had mercilessly commented that it ought to be in a museum, and when the hurt director asked what they should have given him, he replied, with pretended seriousness, a mousetrap, for mice had to be destroyed, or socks, for if his big toe stuck out of his right sock his wife would suggest that he wear it on his left foot. Actually, he declared to Stanislavsky, he regarded the fishing poles of his artist friend Korovin as his most beautiful present. As he displayed the gifts to Altschuler, he comically complained that someone had spread a rumor that he was a lover of antiques when in reality he could not abide them. The physician particularly admired the old silver inkstand. Chekhov remarked: "Well, we don't blot with sand nowadays but with blotting paper, and goose quills have also gone out." Then he added with his charming smile: "However, if you like the inkstand, I'll order that it be turned over to you as a punishment after my death." Little did Altschuler realize then that in a very short time the inkstand would be delivered to him, for he thought that Chekhov looked uncommonly well upon his return from Moscow.

Chekhov was surprised and a little apprehensive to find his vacationing brother Alexander, his wife, one son, a servant and a dog all ensconced in a cottage near him when he arrived at Yalta. They remained for over a month, and Chekhov was soon writing to Olga and Masha that his brother was leading a sober life, was kind and interesting, and in his conduct altogether a comfort to him. There was some hope, he explained to Olga, that Alexander would not take to drink again, although his case, he reminded her, was somewhat like that of her Uncle Sasha's, another extremely amiable and talented alcoholic. After Alexander's departure, the brothers resumed for a short time their amusing correspondence. Alexander agreed, on Chekhov's urging, to visit Olga and see her act, and he promised, exercising the rights of a firstborn, to pass stern judgment on his younger brother's wife. "One must understand everything, Antosha!" he humorously admonished, while at the same time plagiarizing him. "Even that flies purify the air." And Chekhov retorted in his last words to the brother who, he once said, was too gifted in many things to be able to devote himself to any one thing: "Don't preen yourself on being the firstborn, for the principal thing is not to be the firstborn, but to have a mind." (*April 19, 1904.*)

Much encouraging information reached Chekhov about the great success of *The Cherry Orchard* in provincial towns where performances were frequent, often unauthorized, and on the basis of dubious copies of the play, for the corrected version had not yet appeared in print. If only some of the actors in Moscow had been better, he lamented to Olga in conveying this good news. In March her brother and his wife reported to him that they had seen a Moscow performance and they said that Stanislavsky had done abominably in the last act and had dragged it out interminably. "How awful this is!" he wrote Olga. "An act that ought to take no more than twelve minutes lasts forty with you people. I can say one thing: Stanislavsky has ruined my play. But there, bless the man." (*March 29, 1904.*)

Chekhov's enthusiasm for provincial actors, however, was somewhat dampened when in April a Sevastopol group staged *The Cherry Orchard* in Yalta. Posters all over the town advertised that the performance would follow the mise-en-scène of the Art Theater, under the supervision of the author. These vile actors had murdered his play, he told Olga. The telephone kept ringing, friends kept sighing, while he, a sick man, so to speak, there for the good of his health, was bound to dream of how to escape — a subject fit for a comic article, he said. His Petersburg acquaintance E. P. Karpov, now a director of Suvorin's theater and a "dramatist of no talent but of boundlessly grandiose pretensions," as Chekhov described him, saw the Yalta performance and called on him to discuss it. He reported Chekhov's comments, which were directed toward a criticism of the pattern the Art Theater had already established for staging his play. "Is this really my *Cherry Orchard?* Are these my types? With the exception of two or three roles, none of this is mine.

I describe life. It is a dull, philistine life. But it is not a tedious, whimpering life. First they turn me into a weeper and then into a simply boring writer. However, I've written several volumes of merry tales. But criticism has tricked me out in the guise of some kind of mourner or other."

Chekhov's faith in the Art Theater was revived by Stanislavsky's telegram on the occasion of the Petersburg opening of his play on April 2, that "the success of *The Cherry Orchard* with the audience was very great, incomparably greater than in Moscow," a judgment confirmed by the telegram of Nemirovich-Danchenko, who declared that never in all his long experience with the theater had he observed an audience that reacted so positively to every slightest nuance of a psychological drama. Chekhov had long ago committed himself to this remarkable theater which had revolutionized the whole course of theatrical developments in Russia. And whatever may have been his quarrels with its directors over the interpretation of his plays, his final conviction, as he expressed it to his wife in urging her not to worry over stupid Petersburg reviews, was: ". . . No one can tear you to pieces, do what they will. For as artists you have already accomplished what you set out to do and you can regard the present and the future almost dispassionately." (*March 31, 1904.*)

Although the weather was quite good at Yalta and his health rather tolerable, at least during the early part of his stay, Chekhov rarely went into town. One venture was to see P. N. Orlenev in Ibsen's *Ghosts*, which Chekhov described to Olga as "a rotten play and the acting not up to much. . . ." This amiable, wandering actor, whose talent and tales of the road so fascinated Chekhov — he advised the Art Theater to engage him — had turned up in the middle of March. He had sworn off liquor and offered to pay back a loan of a hundred roubles — one of the few loans that Chekhov ever recovered. When Orlenev declared his intention soon of taking his troupe abroad, much to his surprise Chekhov offered to write a play for him, a fact that he confirmed in a letter to his sister. Orlenev thought he was joking, but Chekhov insisted that it would be very easy to write a three-act play for performance abroad, without the worry of censorship, and apparently he intended to base it on Orlenev's life. He assured the actor that the work would be ready for him in September when he left for Europe, one of a number of Chekhov's future plans which fate prevented him from realizing.

Much of the time Chekhov spent in his study working away at the heaps of manuscripts that Goltsev sent him. He did this work carefully, sometimes writing criticism directly to the contributors, but more often he returned the manuscripts to *Russian Thought* with his reports. Of the many stories he read, he found extremely few that were acceptable to him.

Though Chekhov had promised to write tales for a number of editors and informed Olga in several letters that he was making progress, probably on the unfinished stories *The Letter* and *Decompensation*, nearly always he ended with the usual excuse that the parade of visitors prevented him from working. He told Garin-Mikhailovsky at this time that he had just finished copying in ink ten years of jottings in his notebook which concerned literary themes because the original penciled entries had begun to fade. "There are five hundred printed signatures of unused material here," he declared. "Enough for five years of work. If I'm able to write it all, the family will remain secure."

Ironically enough, only now, when the possibility of sustained creative work had ended, did Chekhov begin to receive the kind of fee which would long since have provided adequate security for him and his family if he had been paid at this rate since he had first achieved fame. For in February Marx, apparently worried by information of the national protest in the making over his profitable contract, at the time of Chekhov's jubilee, paid him a thousand roubles for the reprint rights of the short story, *The Betrothed* — four times the contract rate and actually seven hundred roubles more than Chekhov had received for its original publication. And less than a month later Marx gave Chekhov the handsome sum of twenty-five hundred roubles for the reprint rights to *The Cherry Orchard*.

Chekhov used the excuse with Olga that the war also hindered his writing. He kept fancying, he said, that because of the fighting no one would read what he wrote. Actually, as Altschuler pointed out, he was much agitated by the war, followed it closely in the press, and shared the national gloom over every Russian defeat. And when Olga's uncles, Sasha and Karl, went to the front, he anxiously followed their fortunes, wrote letters to his favorite Uncle Sasha, and sent him tobacco. By way of comforting his literary disciple Lazarevsky, who was with the forces in the Far East, he drew an alluring picture of the area from memories of his Sakhalin journey. In this letter of a restless dying man to a homesick soldier breathes an acute nostalgia for remembered beauties which he yearned to see again.

In fact, visitors at this time found Chekhov quite willing to drop any work at hand and talk about his future plans and about the many themes for stories that were fermenting in his mind. Or, as Altschuler noted, he would complain of feeling very weary and of needing a complete rest. Sometimes a caller would discover him sitting in his large armchair in the study without a manuscript, newspaper or book in his hands, just staring into space.

« 4 »

When Chekhov left Moscow for Yalta in the middle of February, he had already decided upon a schedule for the following months. He intended to remain in Yalta during Olga's tour with the Art Theater in Petersburg and rejoin her in Moscow about May 1 when she returned. By then, or shortly thereafter, he hoped that the bothersome question of renting or buying a house near Moscow would be settled. During the summer, however, he expected to take the tour which he and Olga had been promising themselves for some time — either to a remote section of Russia or, preferably, abroad. Then, when Olga resumed her theatrical duties at the end of August, he would probably remain at Yalta in the autumn months and return to their newly acquired house to spend the whole winter near Moscow.

This definite schedule, however, and his rather full days at Yalta again did nothing to assuage his chronic impatience with life there, and he had to restrain himself from taking off for Moscow earlier than he anticipated. At one trying point he even contemplated a dash to Olga at Petersburg. He had hardly been in Yalta a week when he wrote his wife: "Life is dull and uninteresting; the people around here are vexatiously uninteresting, they have no interest in anything and are indifferent to everything." (*February 27, 1904.*)

This kind of harsh judgment, patently an offhand generalization because of some boring, long-staying local visitor, had by now become symptomatic of Chekhov's rebellion against the destiny allotted him. Olga tried to cheer him up in her letters. In one she wrote that she and Masha had found a fine new apartment on Leontievsky Lane which had an elevator — they were determined to end the misery of his climbing stairs. This pleased him, but he grumbled that elevators always seemed to break down when he wanted to use them. When she casually mentioned in a postcard that she had been ill with bronchitis, he flared up: How dreadful and stupid! Why had she not telegraphed? She spent money on telegrams to her relatives, so why did she begrudge spending it on him? And rather unfairly he then blamed his wife for not telling her sister-in-law, as he had urged, to bring her sick child to Yalta for treatment. He was convinced, he declared, that Olga had a low opinion of him as a doctor and that her sister-in-law eschewed Yalta because she did not wish to be near relatives, none of which was true.

One of the major causes of friction in their correspondence during this period was the old problem of finding a house. He now strongly favored the place they had seen together at Tsaritsyno, although he felt the price too high, and he kept pressing his wife to check up on various details and to see if she could not get the cost lowered. Olga did not particularly favor this location, partly because she had heard that there was much fever in the area. And later she was quite offended when he made the mistake of asking her to take Masha's advice on the matter. In her annoyance Olga skipped a couple of days in her letters to him and he exploded: "You rail against Tsaritsyno, that is, you write about fever there, but I still stick up for Tsaritsyno. If the owner of the house affirms that there is no fever in her district, then we must believe her. . . . I write this not knowing where you are, how you are, or what I'm to think of your silence. . . . Why, oh why have you not once telegraphed me about your health? Why? Obviously for you I count for nothing, I am simply superfluous. In short, it is beastly." And then, as though to frighten her, although he had several times made the same statement to others, he declared: "If at the end of June or in July I'm feeling well, I shall go to the front; I'll ask your permission. I'll go as a doctor." (*March 12, 1904.*)

Olga had become used to these outbursts, which were by no means frequent, and perhaps she had some idea of the ominous factors that caused them. Then, too, it was easy for her to overlook them, for Chekhov's letters were still abundantly expressive of his unwavering love for her. When she was low, he urged her to think of what their summer together would be or he told her what a great actress she was. And he may have drawn a smile when he wrote that the only thing he did not like about her was her habit of dawdling over the washstand. She worried too much about the eternal verities, he told her. "You ask: What is life? That is just the same as asking: What is a carrot? A carrot is a carrot, and nothing more is known about it." (*April 20, 1904.*)

Even the knotty problem of finding a house seemed on the way to solution, for Sobolevsky knew of one in the same village of Tsaritsyno and offered to use his influence to obtain it for them for a moderate price. Chekhov excitedly wrote about it to Olga at Petersburg: it was absolutely dry, well-built, suitable for living in all year round, and best of all a sturgeon, weighing more than a hundred pounds, had been caught in the pond nearby. He pleaded with her to attend the boat exhibition in Petersburg and pick out for him a light, pretty, and inexpensive craft to use for fishing. "I'm dreaming of the summer!" he wrote Olga. "I'm longing so to be alone, to write, to think!" (*April 18, 1904.*) A few weeks earlier, when she had informed him that their mutual friend, the actor Moskvin, had just become a father, he rather touchingly responded: "Tell Moskvin I envy him; I would give ten thousand for a baby now. I'm very dreary without a living creature to comfort me. But there, you will do your best, I rely upon you." (*March 20, 1904.*)[6]

Shortly before Chekhov set out for Moscow, the slight degree of good health he had been enjoying at Yalta vanished again. Yet his spirits remained high at the thought of their being together and the things they would do. Incorrigible stalker of the future that he was, did he sense the futility of it all? In an earlier letter to Olga, after an imaginative flight of planning for their summer and autumn, he had suddenly stopped short and declared: "But that is all dreams, dreams!" (*March 3, 1904.*)

« 5 »

Chekhov fell ill during the journey, ate nothing, and upon his arrival in Moscow on May 3 was at once put to bed, in the new apartment with the elevator, on Leontievsky Lane. Olga called in her own family physician, Yu. R. Taube, a German and a general practitioner. The diagnosis was "catarrh of the intestines," for some time now a chronic condition with Chekhov and no doubt a warning that the tubercle bacilli had spread through his stomach, and this affliction was complicated by an attack of pleurisy. Breathing grew extremely difficult, severe pains in the arms and legs kept him awake at night, and his temperature ran high. Dr. Taube gave him morphine injections, put him on a rigid diet, insisted that he remain in bed, and ordered that as soon as he regained sufficient strength he should travel to Germany for treatment by a

---

[6] This quotation is entirely omitted, without any indication, in the Soviet edition of Chekhov's *Complete Works and Letters*. The quotation may be found in *Pisma A. P. Chekhova* (*Letters of A. P. Chekhov*), ed. M. P. Chekhova, Moscow, 1916, Vol. VI.

specialist in tuberculosis. Chekhov, in reporting this new medical situation to Dr. Altschuler back in Yalta, concluded with rather grim humor: "Now I lie on a divan the whole day, and from lack of anything to do I constantly scold Ostroumov and Shchurovsky. It gives me great pleasure."[7]

On the other hand, just before he had left for Moscow Chekhov had jestingly urged Altschuler to come there soon, to "save him from the Germans." In short, he anticipated that if he fell ill his wife would insist upon his being treated by German physicians or one of German origin, to whom her family were naturally quite partial. Later Altschuler indignantly pointed out that Dr. Taube had not taken the trouble to consult any of the Russian doctors who had attended Chekhov, and that his ordering him abroad for treatment was contrary to Dr. Ostroumov's advice. In the end, Altschuler blamed the German doctors for what he considered to be Chekhov's premature death.

Chekhov's strict regimen soon prompted him to write Masha, who had left for Yalta on May 14 for her regular summer vacation and also to be with their mother, that he felt like roaring from boredom. As a doctor, curiously enough, he could not submit to the "rest and quiet" he had so often prescribed for his own patients. His nature required activity, and his sense of duty compelled him to continue the struggle with life's demands no matter what the adverse circumstances might be. The day after he took to bed he wrote Goltsev to forgive his inability to call at the office of *Russian Thought* and he requested that manuscripts be sent to him for editing, and they were. To a young writer who had solicited his opinion on a lengthy poem, Chekhov replied with rather detailed criticism. He concluded: "In general, there is often an absence of logic in the actions of your hero, whereas in art, just as in life, nothing happens by chance." (*May 28, 1904.*) From his sickroom he also tried to take care of his various petitioners — a Moscow teacher, whom he hardly knew, begged him to use his influence to have her son transferred from a distant institution to the Moscow School of Medicine, where the student could live at home and thus save money. Think, the father is a fine man and is poor, Chekhov wrote to Goltsev in an effort to persuade him to assist in the matter. And in informing the father of the steps he had taken, Chekhov assured him that when he returned from Europe, he would continue to do everything in his power to fulfill his request. Then another teacher, this one

[7] *Literaturnoe Nasledstvo (Literary Heritage)*, Moscow, 1960, LXVIII, 258.

from Yalta, sought help in securing permission to marry the sister of his dead wife. Chekhov consulted a lawyer and wrote the petitioner a lengthy statement which amusingly reveals the subtle legal chicanery that was practiced in that shadowy region between church and civil law in Russia.

Nor did Chekhov allow his illness, or the fact that at best he could appear only in dressing gown and slippers, to interfere with his desire for visitors. Not infrequently he summoned them by letter; often they were friends who heard that he was sick and felt they must call. Gilyarovsky, that swashbuckling, strongman reporter and poet of Chekhov's youthful days of struggle in Moscow, was readily received by Olga, according to his account. Chekhov, stretched out on a Turkish divan, greeted him with his charming smile and the visitor observed the wax-like appearance of the skin of his hollow cheeks. Gilyarovsky spoke of his recent trip to the steppes and of his experiences among the drovers of huge herds of horses. "Ah, the steppes, the steppes!" exclaimed Chekhov. "What a lucky man you are. There you find poetry and strength. Everything is bronzed, not the way we are. Only remember: Drink vodka till you are fifty but don't dare to after that; change to beer." They talked of former times, of happy memories — and Chekhov laughed, pleased to avoid serious subjects, the visitor recalled. At one point Chekhov, a blissful smile on his face, closed his eyes and dropped his head on the pillow. "I imagined," remarked Gilyarovsky, "that he was seeing the steppe."

One day, probably at the end of May, Rossolimo received a few lines from Chekhov asking him to call. Though evening was coming on and it was a warm and humid day, he went at once. The air in Chekhov's study, where he lay, was close. By a lamp with a green shade Olga sat with her elbows on the table, turning the pages of *Russian Thought*. Chekhov's hand seemed hot and dry to his visitor, his cheeks flushed, and though he spoke with some difficulty, he talked cheerfully. To Dr. Rossolimo's queries about his condition, he described the severe stomach pains he had been having but mentioned appreciatively Dr. Taube's inventiveness in devising tasty dishes that caused him no discomfort. About his tuberculosis, the visitor recalled, Chekhov spoke with the optimism customary among those so afflicted. These two old classmates also chatted warmly about their student days and the many medical friends they had in common. When Chekhov asked what he had been doing, the visitor gave him an interesting account of his recent trip to

Greece. Chekhov listened with rapt attention. "It seemed to me," Rossolimo wrote later, "that I relieved his depression and drove away the phantom of the 'Black Monk' by directing his thoughts to this enchanted region, far from his immediate situation."

Toward the end of May, surprisingly enough, Chekhov's temperature went down to normal and the doctor gave in to his entreaties to be allowed to take a drive on the first good day. Masha had been informing him of the lush season at Yalta, but at the same time expressing her fears over his condition: "Please write more often about your health, for I'm terribly anxious when I don't know. I'm especially anxious in the evenings. When you are feeling up to it, darling, write, please. If I only knew that you enjoyed my letters, I'd write more often." He had kept her and his mother only vaguely informed of his condition; and he tried to urge Ivan to join them at Yalta, but Ivan, worried about his brother, insisted upon remaining in Moscow. However, once he had good news, Chekhov wrote it to Masha on May 31: "Dear Masha: Just imagine, today for the first time I dressed in my best boots and frock coat . . . and for the first time also I went out for a drive." With Olga by his side he felt proud of his accomplishment. She had tended him faithfully over these weeks of confining illness. In his correspondence with others, Chekhov hardly ever mentions his wife except in passing. He seemed to regard their life together as their own intimate secret of the heart. But in writing of his illness to their mutual friend Dr. Sredin, he added: "My wife waits on her sick husband — this is pure gold. I've never seen such a nurse. It means that it is fine, very fine that I married, otherwise I don't know what I would do now." (*May 22, 1904.*)

It is possible that on this drive, or earlier at his apartment, Chekhov saw Stanislavsky and some of the actors of the Art Theater, for as Stanislavsky mentions in his memoirs, Chekhov was intensely interested at just this time in their preparations to produce the plays of Maeterlinck, an idea that he had long favored, and he wanted to be shown the designs for the staging and to have the mise-en-scène explained. And both Olga and Stanislavsky mention that Chekhov outlined roughly to them the theme of a new play he had in mind. The hero was to be a scientific man. He goes off to the far north because of his disillusion over a woman who either does not love him or is unfaithful to him. The last act was to present an ice-bound steamer. The hero stands alone on the deck amid the complete stillness and grandeur of the

Arctic night. And against the background of the northern lights, he sees floating the shadow of the woman he loves.

By the end of May it seemed to Dr. Taube that his patient had gained enough strength to be permitted to travel to Badenweiler on June 3. Adequate funds for the journey worried Chekhov, and he was also concerned with taking care of the household expenses at Yalta. Mirolyubov fortunately paid him the three hundred roubles for *The Betrothed*, and Chekhov made bold to ask K. P. Pyatnitsky, managing the Znanie publishing firm, to send his honorarium for *The Cherry Orchard*. He promptly received the generous sum of forty-five hundred roubles. His pleasure at such munificence, however, was somewhat spoiled by the controversy that arose at this point over the timing of the publication of his play in the Znanie Annual and the separate reprint edition of Marx. Largely because of the censorship, the Znanie volume was delayed, and Marx, despite Chekhov's protestations, insisted upon bringing out his edition very close to that of the Znanie Annual. In a sense, Marx, by this action, violated the spirit if not the letter of his contract with Chekhov, who promptly broke off relations with him. Later Chekhov wrote to Pyatnitsky that he felt himself somewhat responsible for the situation, insisted on refunding his honorarium and on assuming part of any losses which the firm may have suffered, and urged a suit against Marx to recover damages. In Chekhov's weakened state and on the eve of his departure for Europe, no misfortune could have been more ill-timed.

Shortly before leaving, Chekhov apparently had another upset. What he described as severe rheumatic pains troubled him so much that he dispatched a note to Vishnevsky to send a *masseur* to him. He curiously asked that this be done in secret, with no hint to Dr. Taube — perhaps Chekhov wished to avoid alarming his physician and thus delaying the trip to Europe. On July 2 his old friend Olga Kundasova, "the Astronomer," came to say farewell. She later wrote Suvorin: "I saw Anton on the eve of his departure and had with him one of the most distressing meetings, the kind which fall to the lot of only those on the threshold of death, but I cannot write about it."

Teleshov also came that day, leaving simply a farewell note, for he did not wish to trouble him with a visit at such a time. But Chekhov sent the servant to call him back. Teleshov was appalled at the transformation in Chekhov's appearance as he saw him propped up on the divan with pillows — a withered, narrow-shouldered little man with a small, bloodless face. After their greeting Chekhov said, with eyes that no longer smiled: "Tomorrow I leave. Good-by. I'm going away to die."

Chekhov employed a harsher word than "to die," Teleshov remarked, but he did not wish to repeat it in his account.

"Convey my greetings to your comrades in the Wednesday Club. You have brought together a fine group of people. Tell them that I remember them, and some of them I love. Wish them for me happiness and success."

A quiet, conscious submissiveness, Teleshov observed, was reflected in his eyes.

"Tell Bunin that he must write and write. A great author will emerge from him. Yes, tell him that for me. Don't forget."

And Teleshov concludes his recollections of this meeting: "It did not occur to me to doubt that we were seeing each other for the last time. It was so clear. I was afraid to begin speaking out loud again at that moment and I feared to make a sound with my shoes. Some tender stillness was essential, those few words had to be taken in with an open heart, because for me, without question, they were the last that would come from the pure and beautiful heart of Chekhov."

« 6 »

This sad, foreboding frame of mind in which Teleshov found Chekhov the day before he left Moscow was quickly forgotten in the joy of the journey to Berlin. As always, traveling was his elixir of life. He and Olga took a comfortable room in the fashionable Savoy Hotel, and from the comments and impressions in his letters to Masha one would imagine that a miracle had taken place. They were thoroughly enjoying themselves, he wrote; it was long since he had eaten so well and with so much appetite, and he was already beginning to fill out. The pains in his legs had disappeared and so had the diarrhea. He was on his feet all day, "dashing around Berlin," to the Tiergarten, to the shops. Nor did he fail to be jauntily critical of what appeared to him foreign deficiencies — he had not seen a single handsome German woman, they all dressed abominably, and he now could understand why taste was grafted so slowly and painfully upon the Moscow Germans. An indication of his irrational hopefulness was the comment in his first letter to Masha on June 6 that he expected to be back in Yalta in August if not earlier.

Learning that Gorky's wife, on her way to Karlsbad, had stopped over in Berlin with her children, one of whom had come down with measles, Chekhov asked Olga to look her up. Both women returned to the hotel room and Gorky's wife found Chekhov pale and thin — "But he was lively," she recalled, "and his eyes shone with a kindly irony." Aware of her deep concern over the method which a German doctor had employed in treating her sick child, he quizzed her about it, remarking: "Of course, I'm also a physician and this is interesting to me." Then he assured her in a comforting manner that the remedy employed was a good one. In their subsequent conversation he informed her that once his condition improved at Badenweiler, he expected to spend some time in the Italian lake region before returning home.

One of Chekhov's reasons for pausing in Berlin was to submit to an examination by a certain Professor Karl-Anton Ewald, a distinguished German specialist in intestinal ailments, to whom Dr. Taube had written about the case. Professor Ewald thoroughly examined Chekhov, silently indicated his astonishment, and left without saying a word. "This, of course, was cruel," Altschuler commented, "but no doubt his astonishment arose from bewilderment over why they had allowed so sick a man to travel such a distance."

The image of returning health which Chekhov conveyed to his family was apparently convincing. "Today I received your letter from Berlin," Masha wrote at Yalta, where she, Ivan and their mother had been anxiously waiting for news. "We all rejoiced and at once grew merry." To be sure, he had always shielded them from the worst in his sickness, and this trip abroad may have been a conscious effort to save them the final agony of witnessing his end. Though there can be no question of his improved spirits at the outset of the trip, the reality of improved health did not impress those he met. The Berlin correspondent of *Russian News*, G. B. Iollos, who won Chekhov's warm devotion by his innumerable kindnesses, reported to his editor Sobolevsky: "In Berlin I've already personally got the impression that Chekhov's days are numbered — he appears to me gravely ill, terribly emaciated, coughing and gasping for breath at the slightest movement, and always with a high temperature." And describing Chekhov's departure for Badenweiler, Iollos wrote: "In Berlin it was difficult for him to mount the slight stairway of the Potsdam Station; for several minutes he sat, helpless, and breathing heavily. I recall that when the train started, despite my request that he remain quietly in his seat, he hung out the window and long nodded his head as the train pulled away."[8]

The picturesque little watering place of Badenweiler, situated at the western edge of the Black Forest, sheltered by the Blauen, and less than thirty miles from Basel, cheered Chekhov after the unpleasant train trip from Berlin. They stayed temporarily in a pension until they could get their bearings. As usual the charm of a new lovely spot buoyed his spirits and set him to chatting about future plans, which now took the form of a journey home to Yalta by way of Constantinople.

In a few days they discovered the private Villa Friederike, which took paying guests, and they moved in. The setting seemed ideal. The villa, situated in a large garden with flowers beautifully tended, looked out on the mountains. The sun did not burn, he wrote his sister, but caressed one. Life in the little town oozed by slowly and quietly as he sat or reclined in the sun in his comfortable armchair from morning until seven in the evening. And he described the local doctor, Schwöhrer, who attended him, as pleasant and proficient. Perhaps for the first time in the long course of his illness, Chekhov now received and submitted to effective treatment for tuberculosis — to rest and quiet in a salutary locale and climate. The German doctors had turned his life upside down, he admitted to Masha in describing the rigid daily schedule and diet. Though he grumbled that there was a lot of quackery about the various dishes he had to eat, which Olga supervised on orders from Dr. Schwöhrer, yet he confessed that for the first time in his life he had learned how to keep himself well fed.

His letters home and to friends now exuded extraordinary confidence. He was gaining health here by "leaps and bounds," he told Masha, and when he walked around he no longer felt aware of his illness. He slept and ate splendidly, he informed Kurkin; his doctor was a wise and knowledgeable man, he told Sobolevsky; and he good-naturedly wrote Rossolimo that the only thing incurable about him was his laziness. With pathetic optimism he declared in a letter to his mother on June 13: "My health is improving so that I must say that I'll be entirely well in the course of a week." Olga felt confident enough to leave him occasionally to take trips to Basel to have her teeth fixed, and to request the Art Theater to send her for study the script of a new play they intended to perform during the next season.

By the end of a quiet week of treatment at Villa Friederike, how-

---

[8] This report and others of Iollus to Sobolevsky, on Chekhov in Berlin and Badenweiler, were later published in *Russian News*, July 1904.

ever, Chekhov's incessant craving for motion, action, change reasserted itself. That forces outside himself should be the arbiters of his destiny seemed intolerable. His mounting dissatisfaction began to manifest itself in the sick man's carping criticism of his surroundings. On July 16 he wrote Masha that he just could not get used to German peace and quiet. "There is not a sound in the house or outside it, except that at seven in the morning and at noon a band plays in the garden, expensive, but very untalented. You don't sense a single drop of talent in anything here, nor a single drop of taste; yet there is order and honesty, and to spare. Our Russian life is much more talented, and as for the Italian and the French, there is really no point in comparing them." Five days later he struck a more ominous note in another letter to Masha: "Dr. Schwöhrer, who treats me — that is, makes visits, puts in an appearance — is Taube's idol; what he prescribes Taube also prescribes, so that my treatment differs very little from that in Moscow. The same stupid cocoa, the same oatmeal." That day they left the lovely Villa Friederike — it had become "too common," he explained to his sister — and rented a room in the excellent Sommer Hotel.

While Chekhov's own medical knowledge may have told him that all this doctoring, which he despised anyway, was too late, his optimism and intense love of life kept his thoughts focused on future plans. Hardly a letter back home now failed to contain some mention of his eagerness to be off. He had not yet had his fill of traveling, he told Masha. The Italian lakes were celebrated for their beauty, and it was pleasant and inexpensive to live there. After that he would surely come to Yalta and see them all in August. His cousin in the shipping business at Yalta was asked to provide the sailing schedule from Trieste to Odessa. Rossolimo was importuned to tell him whether it was possible to take a steamer from Marseilles to Odessa, and whether the ships provided comfortable quarters. "What a despairing heap of boredom is this German resort Badenweiler!" he declared in this letter to Rossolimo.

Chekhov and Olga liked their room in the Sommer Hotel. He enjoyed sitting on the balcony and watching the street scenes below, especially the movement of people in and out of the post office. But his move coincided with a change for the worse in his condition. In a letter to Masha on June 28 he complained of the heat, and for the first time since he came to Germany he struck a discouraging note on his health: "I'm eating really delicious food, but it is of no use, for my stomach gets out of order. Clearly my stomach is hopelessly ruined and it is hardly possible to set it to rights except by fasting, that is, to eat nothing — and that's that. As for the shortness of breath, there is only one cure — not to move." That same day Masha, convinced from all his previous reports that he was on the way to recovery, wrote to tell him that she and Ivan were planning a trip together to the Caucasus. "So, keep well, dear Antosha, try not to cough and eat more, gather your strength and come home." These were the last letters Chekhov and his beloved sister exchanged.

« 7 »

On the next day, June 29, correspondents of *Russian News* and the *Daily News*, who had been closely following the course of Chekhov's illness, telegraphed their newspapers: . . . AFTER A SEVERE ATTACK ON TUESDAY, THE CONDITION OF THE HEART DID NOT APPEAR TO BE VERY DANGEROUS, FOR AFTER AN INJECTION OF MORPHINE AND INHALING OXYGEN THE PULSE BECAME FINE AND THE PATIENT SLEPT QUIETLY. The following day another sinking spell took place, and when Chekhov recovered he took the precaution to send a request to a Berlin bank that funds should be forwarded in his wife's name. When Olga asked why he did this, he replied: "Well, you know, just in case. . . ."

On Friday, July 1, Chekhov seemed to feel better. The correspondents sent encouraging wires to the effect that he had spent the day relatively well and that his heart action had become stronger. Toward evening he insisted that Olga, who had not left his side for three anxious days, take a stroll in the park. When she returned he was worried that she had not gone down to the dining room for supper, but she answered that the gong had not yet sounded, though it actually had and they had failed to hear it.

To pass the time Chekhov began to improvise a story. He described a fashionable health resort which catered to well-fed bankers and red-cheeked English and American tourists who doted on rich and abundant food. They had been out all day on various sight-seeing expeditions and returned in the evening, weary, famished, dreaming of an elaborate meal. But at that moment they learn that the cook had vanished and that there would be no wonderful dinner. Chekhov then went on to describe, with humorous touches, how each of these gourmands reacted to this terrible blow to their stomachs. And Olga, curled up on the sofa, laughed heartily over his narration, which served to release the tensions she had been under.

Soon Chekhov slipped into sleep. But after several hours he suddenly awoke at half-past midnight, and asked for a doctor. The request surprised Olga. She tells in her reminiscences that she had never remembered his voluntarily asking for a doctor. For a moment she was overwhelmed by a feeling of helplessness and loneliness in this large hotel, surrounded by people on all sides who were fast asleep. But the sense of something awesome about to happen lent decision and direction to her thoughts and actions. She recalled two Russian students in the hotel with whom they were acquainted, and she aroused one of them and asked him to fetch a doctor. "I can hear now," she later wrote, "the sound of retreating footsteps on the crunching gravel in the stillness of that unbearably sultry July night."

Then Olga went to get some ice. In his fevered condition Chekhov began to rave; to speak of some sailor or other, to ask about the Japanese. But when his wife tried to place a bag of cracked ice on his heart, he suddenly came to himself and said with a sad smile: "Don't put ice on an empty heart."

It was two o'clock in the morning when Schwöhrer arrived. As he approached him Chekhov raised his head and said clearly: *"Ich sterbe!"* The doctor gave him an injection of camphor. Chekhov gasped for breath, but when the doctor ordered that oxygen be administered, he objected: "Now nothing more is needed. Before they bring it, I'll be a corpse."

The doctor, who later remarked how stoically calm Chekhov remained in the face of death, asked that champagne be brought in. Chekhov took the proffered glass, and turning to Olga with a radiant smile said, "It is some time since I have drunk champagne," and slowly drained the glass. Then he quietly lay down on his left side and in a few moments was silent forever.

The doctor departed. Olga was left in the solemn stillness of the dead, broken only by the sound of a large black moth which had flown in the open window, beating its wings against the glowing electric lamp. Suddenly there was the shattering explosion of the cork shooting out of the unfinished champagne bottle. It slowly grew light outside as she watched his serene face, lit up by a smile that seemed to suggest an awareness of some secret of life beyond human comprehension. As nature awakened, the tender, lovely singing of birds seemed like the first requiem. "No sound of human voice was heard, there was none of the bustle of daily life, nothing but peace, beauty, and the grandeur of death."

Bibliographical Survey

THE BIBLIOGRAPHY of Chekhov's writings and of works about him is very extensive. The present survey is highly selective, including largely the books and articles that are quoted or were used in the preparation of this biography. A few other titles, which may prove to be of help to students of the field, are added.

1. ARCHIVE MATERIAL

Chekhov usually destroyed manuscript drafts of his works after they were published, and with minor exceptions copies sent to editors disappeared after publication. Since his death, however, all archival remains have been carefully collected, consisting of some manuscripts of published and unpublished material, vast quantities of his letters and of letters to him, copybooks and diaries, memoirs, and a variety of other material bearing on his life and works. Though some of this archive material still exists in private hands, the major portion of it by far has been brought together in three main collections: The Manuscript Division of the Lenin Library, Moscow; The Institute of Russian Literature (Pushkin House), Academy of Sciences, Moscow; and The Central Government Archives of Literature and Art, Moscow. Additional archive material may be found in The Manuscript Division of the Saltykov-Shchedrin Public Library, Leningrad; The Gorky Museum of the Moscow Artistic Academy of the Theater; the A. A. Bakhrushin Central Theater Museum; the Taganrog Museum; the Yalta House Museum of A. P. Chekhov.

Published descriptions of much of this material may be found in:

Rukopisi A. P. Chekhova — Opisanie. Sost. E. Ye. Leitnekker. Moscow, 1938. A catalogue of the collection of manuscripts and letters of Chekhov in the Lenin Library, Moscow.

Arkhiv A. P. Chekhova: Annotirovannoe opisanie pisem k A. P. Chekhovu. Vyp. 1. Sost. E. Ye. Leitnekker. Moscow, 1939. A description of letters to Chekhov in the Lenin Library, Moscow.

MALOVA, M. M.: *Rukopisi Chekhova v sobranii Instituta literatury (Pushkinskogo doma).* Moscow-Leningrad, 1947. A description of the Chekhov manuscript material in the Institute of Russian Literature (Pushkin House).

A. P. Chekhov — Rukopisi, pisma, biograficheskie dokumenty, vospominaniya, teatralnye postanovki, risunki, fotografii. Opisanie materialov Tsentralnogo Gosudarstvennogo Arkhiva literatury i iskusstva. Moscow, 1960. A listing and description of the archive material on Chekhov in The Central Government Archives of Literature and Art.

II. BIBLIOGRAPHIES

No single definitive bibliography of Chekhov's writings and the works about him has been published. But the following specialized items are helpful:

KLENSKII, M. P.: "Bibliograficheskoe spisok sochinenii Chekhova," in A. P. Chekhov. Zateryannye proizvedeniya. Neizdannye pisma. Vospominaniya. Bibliografiya. Editors, M. D. Belyaev and A. S. Dolinin. Leningrad, 1925, pp. 253-301. A bibliography of the works of Chekhov, 1880–1904.

MASANOV, I. F.: Chekhoviana — Vyp. I: Sistematicheskii ukazatel literatury o Chekhove i ego tvorchestve. Ed. A. B. Derman. Moscow, 1929. A descriptive bibliography of the literature about Chekhov up to 1929.

FRIDKES, L. M.: Opisanie memuarov o Chekhove. Moscow-Leningrad, 1930. A descriptive bibliography of memoir material on Chekhov in books and periodicals from 1904–1929.

SAKHAROVA, E. M.: Anton Pavlovich Chekhov, 1860–1904 — Pamyatka chitatelyu i materialy v pomoshch bibliotekaryu. Moscow, 1954. Among other things, contains a selective annotated bibliography of basic editions and material about the life and literary activities of Chekhov.

POLOTSKAYA, E. A.: Anton Pavlovich Chekhov — Rekomendatelnyi ukazatel literatury. Moscow, 1955. One of the best selective listings of material on all phases of Chekhov's works and life.

GITOVICH, N. I.: Letopis zhizni i tvorchestva A. P. Chekhova. Moscow, 1955. Though in no sense a formal bibliography, a great many titles are listed. This is the most indispensable reference work for all aspects of Chekhov's life and writings.

POLOTSKAYA, E. A.: "Bibliografiya vospominanii o Chekhove," in Literaturnoe Nasledstvo, Moscow, 1960, LXVIII, 881-928. Continues the descriptive bibliography of memoir material in the L. M. Fridkes' compilation from 1930 to 1960, and also adds a number of titles missed by Fridkes in the earlier period.

For bibliographical aids on English translations of Chekhov, and works about him,[1] see:

---

[1] Reviews of the interest in Chekhov's works in the United States and England, containing much bibliographical data, have recently been published in Russian: Thomas G. Winner, "Chekhov v Soedinenykh Shtatakh Ameriki," and M. A. Shere-

HEIFETZ, ANNA: *Chekhov in English*. Edited and with a foreword by Avrahm Yarmolinsky. New York, 1949. A list of works by and about Chekhov.

MAGARSHACK, DAVID: *Chekhov: A Life*. London, 1952. See pp. 393-423 for a valuable index of all Chekhov's writings: the English title, followed by the Russian title and its date of publication, and the English translations and their publication dates. Works that had not been translated up to the time of the publication of this book are also indicated.

III. EDITIONS OF CHEKHOV'S WORKS

A number of collected editions of Chekhov's works have appeared since the ten-volume one which he edited in his own lifetime and which was published between 1899 and 1901. However, there is little point in mentioning any of these (data on them may be obtained in the bibliographies mentioned above), since they have all been superseded by:

Polnoe sobranie sochinenii i pisem A. P. Chekhova. Under the general editorship of S. D. Balukhatyi, V. P. Potemkin, and N. S. Tikhonov. Twenty vols., Moscow, 1944–1951.

This unusually fine scholarly edition, which has been the indispensable major source of the present study of Chekhov, leaves little to be desired in the matter of final texts, variant readings, commentaries, indices, and bibliographical aids which, in important ways, supplement the published bibliographies listed above. However, since the completion of this edition in 1951, new manuscript material has been discovered, especially of early stories, drafts of plays, and hitherto unknown letters.

Much of this fresh material has recently been brought together and published in:

Literaturnoe Nasledstvo: Chekhov. Various editors. Vol. LXVIII, Moscow, 1960.

The editors promise that additional fresh material on Chekhov's life and works will appear in subsequent issues of *Literaturnoe Nasledstvo*. And apparently a new complete edition of Chekhov's works and letters is being planned, which will include all the material that has appeared since the edition of 1944–1951.

IV. CHEKHOV'S LETTERS

The great importance of Chekhov's letters for an understanding of the man and his works, as well as of the cultural, ideological, and social life of

---

shevskaya, "Angliiskie pisateli i kritiki o Chekhove," in *Literaturnoe Nasledstvo*, Moscow, 1960, LXVIII, 777-800, 801-832.

the 1880's and 1890's, was early recognized and publication of them in periodicals and in book form began to take place not long after his death in 1904. But the first attempt at a systematic collection and publication of Chekhov's letters was undertaken by his sister, in:

Pisma A. P. Chekhova. Ed. M. P. Chekhova. Vols. I-VI. Moscow, 1912–1916.

However, this edition, containing 1898 letters, was far from complete, and over the years additional letters began to appear in periodicals and occasionally in books.

Perhaps the major contribution of the twenty-volume edition of Chekhov's works (1944–1951) was the publication, in Volumes XIII-XX, of as exhaustive a collection of Chekhov's letters as was possible at that time — 4200 of them. This magnificent service, however, was marred by the omission of a few letters, and by deletions — sometimes indicated and sometimes not — of passages in other letters for ideological reasons.[2] Further, words, phrases, and even sentences, dealing with intimate matters, are occasionally dropped without much cause. (These omissions can often be ascertained by referring back to earlier publications of the letters, especially the six-volume edition of Chekhov's sister.)

A number of the deletions in earlier editions, and the omission of a letter to Meierhold, have been corrected in a twelve-volume edition of Chekhov's collected works, including many of the letters, which has appeared since the edition of 1944–1951:

A. P. Chekhov, *Sobranie sochinenii v dvenadtsati tomakh.* Moscow, 1954–1957.

Since the appearance of the complete edition, 147 new letters have been discovered, and these have been published in "Novonaidennye i nesobrannye pisma Chekhova," in *Literaturnoe Nasledstvo,* Moscow, 1960, LXVIII, 149-261. Incidentally, in this same publication, a number of mistakes and omissions in the letters in the twenty-volume complete edition are corrected on the basis of the discovery of the originals of ninety-nine letters which were not available to the editors of the complete edition. (See pp. 261-263.)

Chekhov's Letters in English Translation:

A number, unfortunately too few, of Chekhov's letters have been translated into English. The principal collections are:

[2] For a treatment of this matter, see Gleb Struve's "Chekhov and Soviet Double-think," *The New Leader,* November 22, 1954, pp. 22-24, and "Chekhov in Communist Censorship," in *The Slavonic and East European Review,* XXXIII, No. 81, June 1955, pp. 327-341.

Letters of Anton Chekhov to His Family and Friends: With a Biographical Sketch. Translated by Constance Garnett. New York, 1920.

Letters on the Short Story, the Drama, and Other Literary Topics, by Anton Chekhov. Selected and Edited by Louis S. Friedland. London, 1924.

The Letters of Anton Pavlovitch Tchekhov to Olga Leonardovna Knipper. Translated from the Russian by Constance Garnett. New York, n. d. (This is a translation of *Pisma A. P. Chekhova k O. L. Knipper-Chekhov.* Berlin, 1924.)

The Life and Letters of Anton Tchekhov. Translated and Edited by S. S. Koteliansky and Philip Tomlinson. New York, 1925.

The Personal Papers of Anton Chekhov. Introduction by Matthew Joseph-son. New York, 1948. Along with translations of the Notebooks and Diary of Chekhov are translations of a selection of letters dealing with the writer, writing, and the theater, 1882–1904.

The Selected Letters of Anton Chekhov. Edited by Lillian Hellman and translated by Sidonie Lederer. New York, 1955.

V. LETTERS TO CHEKHOV

In the archives are some 7000 letters to Chekhov, many from leading literary and artistic personalities of his time. There are a great many letters also from his wife, Olga Knipper. Chekhov made a practice of saving and filing letters to him, and he considered it a duty to answer them. The great disproportion between the extant letters to him and his own suggests that very many of his letters have been lost. These letters to Chekhov often contain extremely valuable material that has a bearing on his personal life, activities, views, and his literary labors. Only a fraction of this huge corres-pondence has been published, but it is perhaps the most significant part. Many of these letters to Chekhov may be found in the following works:

Slovo: sbornik 2. Moscow, 1914. Contains letters of D. V. Grigorovich, N. K. Mikhailovskii, P. I. Tschaikovsky, Ya. P. Polonskii, A. N. Pleshcheev.

Perepiska A. P. Chekhova i O. L. Knipper. Ed. A. B. Derman. Vols. I-II. Moscow, 1934, 1936. A promised final volume has not appeared, but some of the correspondence of Chekhov and his wife over 1903 to 1904, which was to be published in the third volume, has been printed in the magazines *Novyi mir,* 1938, Nos. 10-12; *Oktyabr,* 1938, No. 7; *Teatr,* 1960, No. 1.

Pisma A. P. Chekhovu ego brata Aleksandra Chekhova. Ed. I. S. Yezhov. Moscow, 1939.

Zapiski Otdela rukopisi. Vyp. 8: A. P. Chekhov. Ed. N. L. Meshcheryakov. Moscow, 1941. Contains letters to Chekhov of K. S. Barantsevich, P. I.

Kurkin, V. M. Lavrov, B. Lazarevskii, M. O. Menshikov, V. A. Posse, I. N. Potapenko, M. I. Tschaikovsky, and others.

M. Gorkii i A. Chekhov. Perepiska. Stati. Vyskazyvaniya. Sbornik materialov. Ed. N. I. Gitovich. Moscow, 1951.

KONSHINA, E. N.: *Iz perepiski Antona Pavlovicha Chekhova.* Moscow, 1954. Contains especially the letters of the actor P. M. Svobodin to Chekhov, 1889–1892.

CHEKHOVA, M. P.: *Pisma k bratu A. P. Chekhovu.* Ed. N. A. Sysoev. Moscow, 1954.

TEPLINSKII, M. V.: "Novye materialy o sakhalinskom puteshestvii A. P. Chekhova," in *Anton Pavlovich Chekhov, sbornik statei.* Yuzhno-Sakhalinsk, 1959. Contains an interesting group of letters to Chekhov from acquaintances on the Island of Sakhalin.

"Neizdannye pisma k Chekhovu," in *Literaturnoe Nasledstvo,* Moscow, 1960, LXVIII, 293-448. Letters to Chekhov from A. N. Pleshcheev, A. I. Kuprin, I. A. Bunin, V. Ye. Meierhold.

Iz arkhiva A. P. Chekhova. Moscow, 1960. Letters to Chekhov from N. V. Altukhov, V. V. Bureiko, V. G. Valter, D. P. Golitsyn, S. S. Golushev, I. Ya. Gurlyand, S. P. Dyagilev, and others.

VI. BIOGRAPHY

Before the 1917 Revolution the Russians were never partial to formal full-length biographies of their great literary figures, and since then they have been even less so. At best, specialized treatments of a single period of a subject's life, or brief sketches of a famous author's life and works, seem to be preferred. On the whole, biographies of Chekhov in the West, although few in number, tend to be more comprehensive than the Russian. The following are the best-known biographical treatments — arranged, for the sake of convenience, in alphabetical order:

BRISSON, P.: *Tchékhov et sa vie.* Paris, 1955.

CHUKOVSKII, KORNEI:"Podvig," in *Ogonyok,* No. 28, 1954. (Translated by Pauline Rose as *Chekhov the Man.* London, n. d.)

DERMAN, A. B.: *Anton Pavlovich Chekhov: Kritiko — biograficheskii ocherk.* Moscow, 1939. A short sketch in which Chekhov's life shares almost equal space with his writings.

———— : *Moskva v zhizni i tvorchestve A. P. Chekhova.* Moscow, 1948. A specialized study of the relation of Chekhov's life and works to his years of residence in Moscow.

GERHARDI, W.: *Anton Chekhov, a Critical Study.* New York, 1923.

HINGLEY, RONALD: *Chekhov: A Biographical and Critical Study.* London, 1950.

IZMAILOV, A. A.: *Chekhov 1860–1904: Biograficheskii nabrosok.* Moscow, 1916.

MAGARSHACK, DAVID: *Chekhov: A Life.* London, 1952.

NÉMIROVSKY, IRENE: *La vie de Tchékhov.* Paris, 1946. (Translated by Erik de Mauny as *A Life of Chekhov.* London, 1950.)

ROSKIN, A. I.: *Antosha Chekhonte.* Moscow, 1940. The author employs the Western technique of fictionized biography, telling the story of Chekhov's youth up to 1887. However, he sticks very close to the facts, and introduces fresh archive material on the early life of Chekhov.

———— : *Chekhov: Biograficheskaya povest.* Moscow, 1959. A new edition of a 1939 book, again offering an attractive fictionized biographical sketch — this time of the whole of Chekhov's life — but always being faithful to the facts.

TOUMANOVA, N. N.: *Anton Chekhov. The Voice of Twilight Russia.* New York, 1937.

TRIOLET, ELSA: *L'histoire d'Anton Tchékhov: Sa vie — son oeuvre.* Paris, 1954.

YERMILOV, VLADIMIR: *A. P. Chekhov.* Moscow, 1954. This originally appeared in 1946, and the present edition is somewhat augmented. (One of the earlier editions was translated into English by Ivy Litvinov and published in Russia as *Anton Pavlovich Chekhov,* Moscow, n. d.) Perhaps the most extensive Russian attempt at formal biography of Chekhov, but a good half of the book is devoted to critical analyses of a number of stories and plays, and these and the life are interpreted from the point of view of Soviet ideology.

VII. MEMOIR LITERATURE

However lacking the Russians may have been in contributing formal full-length biographical studies of Chekhov, they have published without stint the preparatory materials for such studies. This memoir literature is very extensive. Chekhov knew a large number of people, and it seems as though most of them felt the urge to tell, in print, of their acquaintance with him and their impressions of his life. Many of the contributors were individuals of distinction in the world of literature, art, and learning. Significant items have been written by Chekhov's sister and brothers. On the other hand, much of this material, especially scores of magazine articles, is of unequal value, and a good deal of it is buried in miscellanies devoted to various aspects of Chekhov's life and works. Fortunately, perhaps the most important articles have been collected in book form and hence made more accessible. With some few exceptions, only those titles in this memoir literature which have been drawn upon in the preparation of the present work are listed. For easy reference they have been arranged alphabetically.

ALTSCHULER, I. N.: "O Chekhove," in *Sovremennye zapiski*. Paris, 1930, pp. 470-485.

A. P. *Chekhov — Sbornik statei*. Moscow, 1910.

A. P. *Chekhov — Literaturny byt i tvorchestvo po memuarnym materialam*. Ed. V. Feider. Leningrad, 1928.

A. P. *Chekhov — Sbornik dokumentov i materialov*. Moscow, 1947.

A. P. *Chekhov — Sbornik statei i materialov*. Rostov, 1959.

A. P. *Chekhov v vospominaniyakh sovremennikov*. Eds. N. I. Gitovich and I. V. Fedorova. Fourth ed., Moscow, 1960. There are a number of variations in the table of contents of the four editions. However, this item includes some of the most important memoir literature on Chekhov, written by such figures as Alexander P. Chekhov, Mikhail P. Chekhov, Mariya P. Chekhova, V. A. Simov, V. A. Gilyarovsky, I. L. Leontiev-Shcheglov, V. Fausek, I. E. Repin, A. S. Lazarev-Gruzinsky, L. A. Avilova, I. N. Potapenko, T. L. Shchepkina-Kupernik, K. S. Stanislavsky, V. I. Nemirovich-Danchenko, V. V. Luzhsky, V. I. Kachalov, P. N. Orlenev, L. N. Shapovalov, A. M. Gorky, A. I. Kuprin, N. D. Teleshov, I. A. Bunin, V. V. Veresaev, S. Ya. Elpatievsky, S. N. Shchukin, I. A. Novikov, M. A. Chlenov, A. Serebrov (A. N. Tikhonov), E. P. Karpov, N. Garin (Mikhailovsky), R. I. Rossolimo, O. L. Knipper.

A. P. *Chekhov — Zateryannye proizvedeniya. Neizdannye pisma. Vospominaniya*. Eds. M. D. Belyaev and A. S. Dolinin. Leningrad, 1925.

AVILOV, LYDIA: *Chekhov in My Life*. Translated with an Introduction by David Magarshack. New York, 1950. Apparently this is a translation of Avilova's memoirs as first published in A. P. *Chekhov v vospominaniyakh sovremennikov* (Moscow, 1947). The fourth edition of this work, 1960, provides a corrected and fuller version of Avilova's memoirs.

BELOUSOV, I. A: *Literaturnaya sreda. Vospominaniya 1880–1928*. Moscow, 1928.

BUNIN, I. A.: *O Chekhove. Nezakonchennaya rukopis*. New York, 1955.

Chekhov, A. P.: *Sbornik dokumentov i materialov*. Ed. A. B. Derman. Moscow, 1947.

CHEKHOV, ALEKSANDR P.: "Paskhalnaya zautrenya vo dvortse imperatora Aleksandra I v Taganroge." In *Istoricheskii vestnik*, 1901, No. 8, pp. 567-581.

——— : "A. P. Chekhov v grecheskoi shkole." In *Vestnik Evropy*, 1907, No. 4, pp. 545-571.

——— : "Anton Pavlovich-lavochnik." In *Vestnik Evropy*, 1908, No. 11, pp. 192-224.

——— : *V gostyakh y dedushki i babushki. Stranitsy iz detstva*. Petersburg, 1912.

CHEKHOV, M. P.: *Anton Chekhov i ego syuzhety*. Moscow, 1923.

────── : *Vokrug Chekhova.* Moscow, 1959. (Originally published in 1933.)

CHEKHOVA, M .P.: *Dom-Muzei A. P. Chekhova v Yalte.* Moscow, 1954.

────── : *Iz dalyokogo proshlogo.* Zapis N. A. Sysoeva. Moscow, 1960.

Chekhov i teatr — Pisma, feletony, sovremenniki o Chekhove dramaturge. Moscow, 1961.

"Chekhov v neizdannykh dnevnikakh sovremennikov." In *Literaturnoe Nasledstvo,* Moscow, 1960, LXVIII, 479-528. Chekhov in the diary entries of I. L. Leontiev-Shcheglov, V. A. Tikhonov, N. A. Leikin, V. A. Telyakovskii, V. S. Mirolyubov, V. G. Korolenko.

Chekhovskii sbornik — Naidennye stati i pisma. Vospominaniya. Kritika. Bibliografiya. Moscow, 1929.

Chekhovskii yubileinyi sbornik. Moscow, 1910.

DROZDOVA, M. T.: "Vospominanie Chekhova." In *Sovetskaya kultura,* 1960, No. 8, 10.

Ezhegodnik Moskovskogo Khudozhestvennogo Teatra. See Vol. I. 1944; Vol. I and II, 1948; and years 1949–1950.

GEIZER, I.: *Chekhov i meditsina.* Moscow, 1954.

GILYAROVSKII, V. A.: *Moskva i moskvichi.* Moscow, 1959, pp. 347-373.

GOLDENVEIZER, A. B.: *Vblizi Tolstogo.* Moscow, 1959, pp. 392-394.

KONI, A. F.: *Izbrannye proizvedeniya.* Moscow, 1959, II, 340-348.

LEVITAN, I. I.: *Vospominaniya i pisma.* Moscow, 1950. (See especially pp. 52, 55-56, 64-67, 80-87, 88-89, 90-91, 95-114.)

NEMIROVICH-DANCHENKO, V. I.: *Iz proshlogo.* Moscow, 1938. (See chapter on Chekhov.)

────── : *Teatralnoe nasledie.* Vol. I. Moscow, 1952. (See especially pp. 79-109, 148-150, 161-162, 183, 190-193, 218-219, 221-222, 317-322.)

O Chekhove — Vospominaniya i stati. Moscow, 1910.

Pamyati A. P. Chekhova. Moscow, 1906.

PLESHCHEEV, A. A.: "U An. Chekhova." In *Peterburgskii dnevnik teatrala,* 1904, No. I.

Slovo. Sbornik vtoroi — K desyatiletiyu smerti Chekhova. Moscow, 1914.

STANISLAVSKII, K. S.: *Moya zhizn v iskusstve.* Moscow, 1954. (Translated into English by J. J. Robbins as *My Life in Art.* New York, 1956.)

────── : *Sobranie sochinenii.* Moscow, 1958, V, 329-360.

SUVORIN, A. S.: *Dnevnik.* Ed. M. Krichevskii. Moscow, 1923.

SYSOEV, N. A.: *Chekhov v Krymu.* Fourth ed., Simferopol, 1960.

TOLSTOY, L. N.: *Polnoe sobranie sochinenii.* (See *Dnevniki,* Vols. LIII-LVII.)

TURKIN-ANDREEV, M. M.: "Chekhov v Taganroge." In *A. P. Chekhov i nash krai.* Rostov, 1935, pp. 25-45. Recollections of parents, relatives, and classmates of Chekhov's childhood and youth.

VINOGRADOVA, K. M.: *Chekhov v Melikhove.* Moscow, 1956.

"Vospominaniya o Chekhove." In *Literaturnoe Nasledstvo*. Moscow, 1960, LXVIII, 531-702. Recollections of M. D. Drossi-Steiger, Z. E. Pichugin, K. A. Korovin, N. V. Golubeva, K. A. Karatygina, M. K. Zankovetskaya, A. S. Feldman, A. S. Yakovlev, A. A. Khotyaintseva, E. P. Peshkova, A. P. Sergeenko, L. K. Fedorova, I. A. Bunin, I. N. Altschuler.

ZAITSEV, BORIS: *Chekhov — Literaturnaya biografiya*. New York, 1954.

VIII. LITERARY STUDIES AND CRITICISM

There exists a very large bibliography, articles and books, of scholarly investigations and critical appreciations on all aspects of Chekhov's creative art in fiction and drama. Often a single story or play has been repeatedly studied from different points of view. This material has necessarily played a minor part in the preparation of the present biography, but the listing of a few titles that have been helpful seems desirable.

ALEKSANDROV, B. I.: *Seminarii po Chekhova*. Moscow, 1957.
Anton Chekhov, 1860–1960. Ed. T. Eekman. Leiden, 1960.
BALUKHATYI, S. D.: *Chekhov-dramaturg*. Leningrad, 1936.
BERDNIKOV, G. P.: *Chekhov-dramaturg — traditsii i novatorstvo v dramaturgii Chekhova*. Leningrad, 1957.
BRUFORD, W. H.: *Chekhov and His Russia. A Sociological Study*. London, 1948.
BULGAKOV, S. N.: *Chekhov kak myslitel*. Kiev, 1905.
Chekhov i ego sreda. Ed. N. F. Belchikov. Leningrad, 1930.
ELIZAROVA, M. E.: *Tvorchestvo Chekhova i voprosy realizma kontsa XIX veka*. Moscow, 1958.
ERENBURG, ILYA: *Perechityvaya Chekhova*. Moscow, 1960.
GARNETT, EDWARD: *Chekhov and His Art*. London, 1929.
GUSHCHIN, M.: *Tvorchestvo A. P. Chekhova, ocherki*. Kharkov, 1954.
MAGARSHACK, DAVID: *Chekhov the Dramatist*. London, 1952.
MYSHKOVSKAYA, L.: *Chekhov i yumoristicheskie zhurnaly 80-kh godov*. Moscow, 1929.
PANERNYI, Z.: *A. P. Chekhov — Ocherk tvorchestva*. Moscow, 1954.
SHKLOVSKII, VIKTOR: *Zametki o proze russkikh klassikov*. Moscow, 1953. (See pp. 289-322.)
SOBOLEV, YURII: *Chekhov — Stati, materialy*. Moscow, 1930.
STROEVA, M. N.: *Chekhov i Khudozhestvennyi Teatr*. Moscow, 1955.
Tvorchestva A. P.: Chekhova — Sbornik statei. Moscow, 1956.
YERMILOV, VLADIMIR: *Dramaturgiya A. P. Chekhova*. Moscow, 1954.

INDEX

Index

297-298, 301-302, 305, 314, 317, 321-322, 344, 349-350, 351, 361, 364, 366, 372-373, 375, 377, 389, 408, 409, 410, 412, 416, 417, 425, 427, 430-431, 438-439, 448, 450, 463, 466, 469, 480, 482, 488, 493, 497, 499, 504, 509, 513, 520, 522-523, 545, 577-578, 579-580, 581-582, 588, 592-593, 598-599, 603, 604-605, 612, 615-616, 623-624, 625, 631-632

CHARACTERISTICS, MOODS, PERSON-ALITY, 18, 20-21, 26-27, 32-33, 36, 46, 50, 53, 59, 75, 80, 89, 95-99, 103-104, 106, 110-112, 113, 130, 140, 163-164, 181, 188, 190, 191, 201, 203-204, 212, 232, 234, 269, 271, 274-275, 282, 307-310, 312-313, 317, 321, 329, 343, 352, 362, 376, 378-380, 383, 401, 406, 409, 410, 415, 416-417, 424, 426, 430, 440, 441-442, 444, 448, 449, 452, 458, 465, 467, 470-471, 476, 481, 484, 488, 499, 505, 508, 511, 512, 514-515, 523, 525, 540, 545, 553-554, 555, 557, 560, 570, 571, 574-576, 579, 591, 598, 602, 603, 613, 616, 622, 623, 626, 628, 629, 631, 634, 636, 638

CIVIC ACTIVITIES, 235-236, 255, 261-262, 275, 290-292, 315, 320, 328, 344-345, 354, 358-360, 378-379, 381-382, 384, 394, 397, 407, 419, 424, 432-433, 440, 460, 461, 472, 480-481, 489, 491, 500, 505, 519-520, 539, 595

DEBTS AND FINANCIAL AFFAIRS, 23-25, 28, 31, 37, 44, 51-52, 58, 59, 62-63, 66, 70, 76, 77, 78-79, 87, 88-89, 91, 108, 115, 116, 119, 123, 128, 135, 139, 146, 148-149, 150, 156, 163, 177, 178, 187, 190, 213-214, 216-217, 224, 225, 237, 240, 241, 242, 245, 248, 262-263, 265-266, 272-273, 296-297, 304, 308, 324-325, 329, 343, 349, 381, 391, 398, 400, 404, 405, 406, 409, 424, 432, 435, 437, 440, 453-456, 459-460, 472, 473, 477-479, 489, 499, 515, 540, 559, 570, 576, 586, 587, 596, 600, 602, 606, 613-614, 625, 632, 637

DRAMATIC INTEREST, ACTIVITY, AND WRITING, 20-21, 43-44, 49, 80, 134-138, 146-147, 171-172, 173-174, 174-176, 177, 180, 189, 195-200, 208, 239, 254, 316, 331, 350-353, 364-365, 366-371, 377, 382-383, 397, 428-431, 439, 449-452, 453, 474, 482-487, 491, 501-502, 503-506, 509-510, 512, 513, 520-522, 541-543, 552-553, 554, 559, 564-565, 578-579, 585-586, 587, 594, 603-604, 607-608, 611-612, 623-624, 631

EDUCATION, 11-15, 26, 32-33, 34, 37-39, 42, 50-51, 55-56, 60, 61

FAMILY AFFAIRS AND RELATION-SHIPS, 3-17, 18, 20, 22, 25, 28-31, 34-37, 46-47, 53-54, 55, 56-57, 59, 66, 67, 76-78, 79, 82-83, 87, 90, 104, 107, 108, 109-113, 114, 118-119, 119-120, 139, 150, 154, 159-160, 161, 162, 178-179, 185-186, 187, 188, 190, 196, 217, 224-225, 233-234, 241-242, 244, 247, 254, 265-266, 270, 271-272, 275-276, 278, 279, 282-284, 306, 309-310, 315, 321, 324, 328, 341-343, 354, 362, 388, 395, 397, 404, 406, 417, 423-424, 433-436, 437, 440-441, 449, 454, 460, 465, 470-471, 472-473, 475, 477, 478-479, 490, 497-498, 499, 500-501, 507, 510, 515, 521-522, 524, 528-529, 531, 532-536, 537, 538-539, 541, 543, 547, 556, 558-559, 565, 568, 573-574, 577, 582, 585, 586, 591, 594-595, 597, 601, 610, 622-623, 626, 631, 634-637

FRIENDS AND ACQUAINTANCES, 27, 38-39, 44-45, 51-52, 57, 59, 60, 67, 79-80, 83-87, 89-90, 104-105, 106, 114, 119, 120-121, 139-140, 142, 147-148, 149, 151, 152-154, 155-156, 159, 161-163, 172, 175-176, 177, 179, 180-181, 187, 188-189, 190, 213, 217, 227, 236, 238, 241, 242, 243, 244-245, 254, 256, 263, 270, 274, 275, 277, 278-282, 293-294, 295-296, 311, 313, 316-317, 321, 324, 328, 330, 331-332, 341, 343, 344, 346-347, 353-354, 363, 379, 383, 384, 389-391, 394-395, 396-397, 399, 401-403, 405, 413-415, 418-419, 423, 429, 432, 434, 436, 439, 441, 442, 444, 453, 457, 460,